# GREEN ARROW

VOLUME 5

## BLACK ARROW

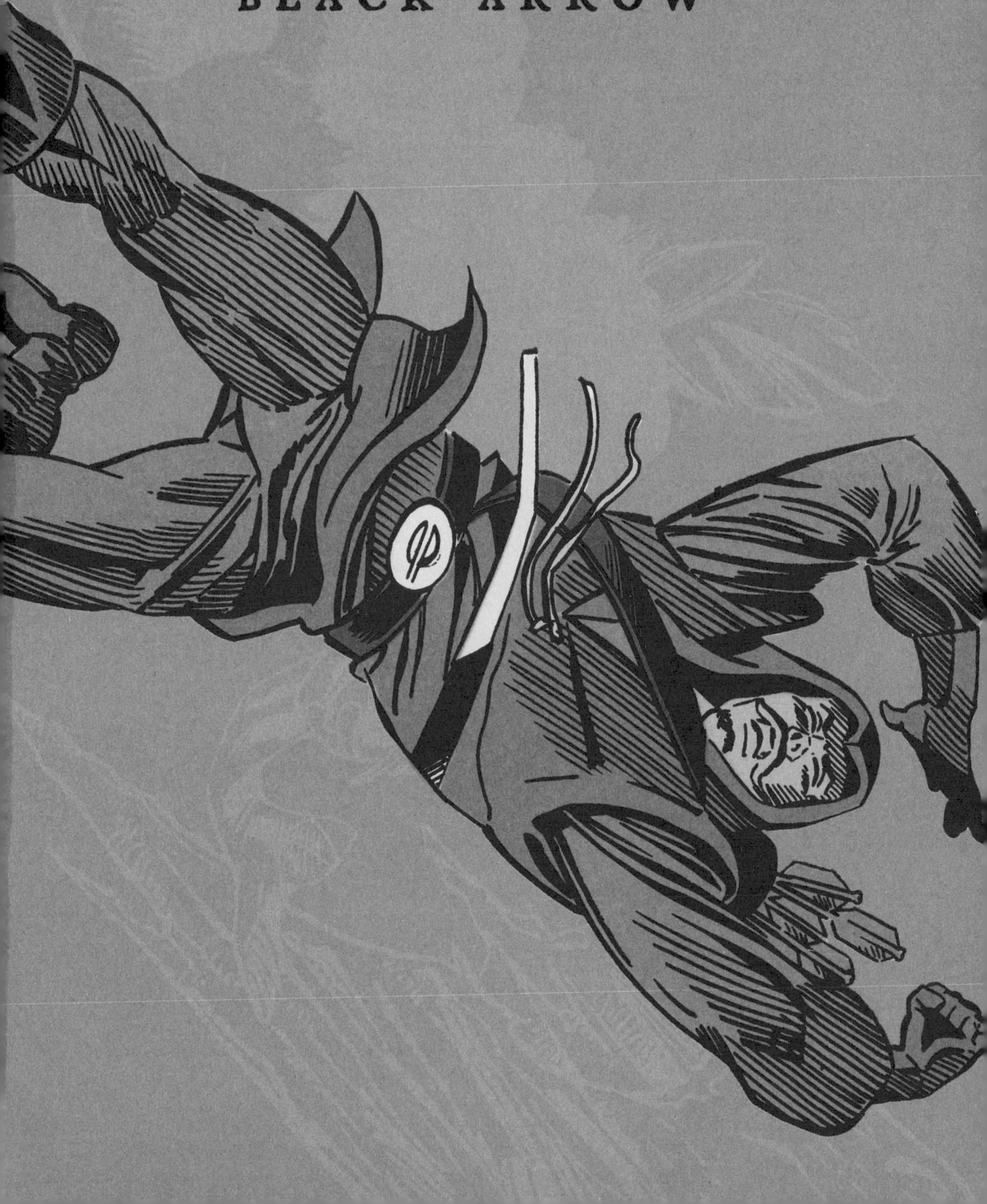

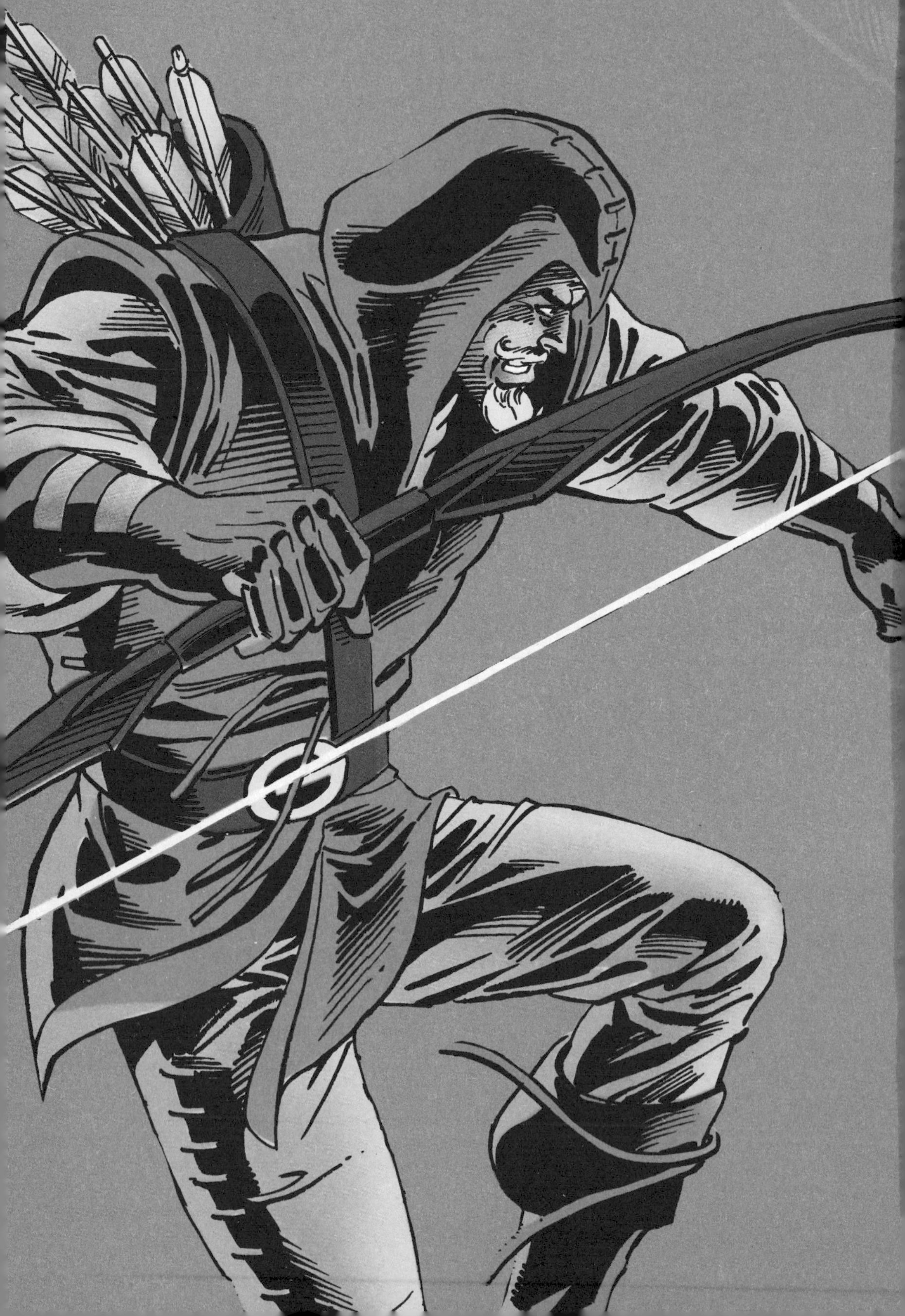

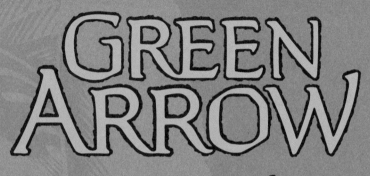

# GREEN ARROW

## VOLUME 5
## BLACK ARROW

**MIKE GRELL**
Writer

**DAN JURGENS**
**GRANT MIEHM**
**MARK JONES**
**RICK HOBERG**
Pencillers

**DICK GIORDANO**
**FRANK MCLAUGHLIN**
**BILL WRAY**
Inkers

**JULIA LACQUEMENT**
Colorist

**JOHN COSTANZA**
**STEVE HAYNIE**
Letterers

**ED HANNIGAN**
**DICK GIORDANO**
Cover Art

**DAN JURGENS**
**GRANT MIEHM**
**ED HANNIGAN**
**DICK GIORDANO**
Original Series Covers

Mike Gold Editor – Original Series
Katie Main Associate Editor – Original Series
Jeb Woodard Group Editor – Collected Editions
Liz Erickson Editor – Collected Edition
Steve Cook Design Director – Books

Bob Harras Senior VP – Editor-in-Chief, DC Comics

Diane Nelson President
Dan DiDio and Jim Lee Co-Publishers
Geoff Johns Chief Creative Officer
Amit Desai Senior VP – Marketing & Global Franchise Management
Nairi Gardiner Senior VP – Finance
Sam Ades VP – Digital Marketing
Bobbie Chase VP – Talent Development
Mark Chiarello Senior VP – Art, Design & Collected Editions
John Cunningham VP – Content Strategy
Anne DePies VP – Strategy Planning & Reporting
Don Falletti VP – Manufacturing Operations
Lawrence Ganem VP – Editorial Administration & Talent Relations
Alison Gill Senior VP – Manufacturing & Operations
Hank Kanalz Senior VP – Editorial Strategy & Administration
Jay Kogan VP – Legal Affairs
Derek Maddalena Senior VP – Sales & Business Development
Jack Mahan VP – Business Affairs
Dan Miron VP – Sales Planning & Trade Development
Nick Napolitano VP – Manufacturing Administration
Carol Roeder VP – Marketing
Eddie Scannell VP – Mass Account & Digital Sales
Courtney Simmons Senior VP – Publicity & Communications
Jim (Ski) Sokolowski VP – Comic Book Specialty & Newsstand Sales
Sandy Yi Senior VP – Global Franchise Management

GREEN ARROW VOLUME 5: BLACK ARROW



DC Comics, 2900 West Alameda Avenue, Burbank, CA 91505
Printed by Transcontinental Interglobe, Beauceville, QC, Canada. 4/1/16. First Printing.
ISBN: 978-1-4012-6079-8

Library of Congress Cataloging-in-Publication Data is Available.

PEFC Certified
Printed on paper from sustainably managed forests and controlled sources
PEFC
PEFC/01-31-106
www.pefc.org

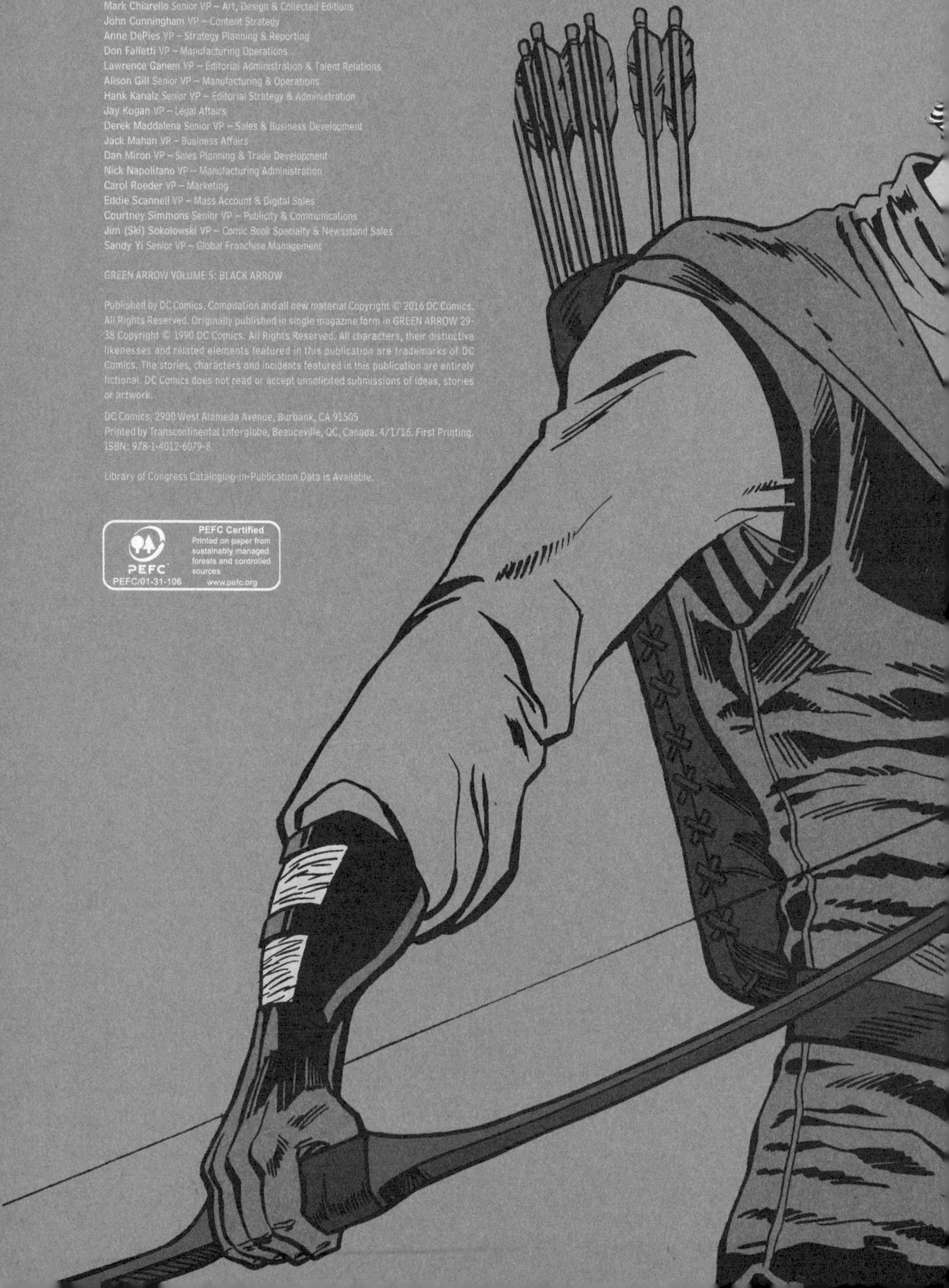

# TABLE OF CONTENTS

\*THIS STORY WAS ORIGINALLY UNTITLED AND IS TITLED
HERE FOR READER CONVENIENCE.

# GREEN ARROW

## BLACK ARROW

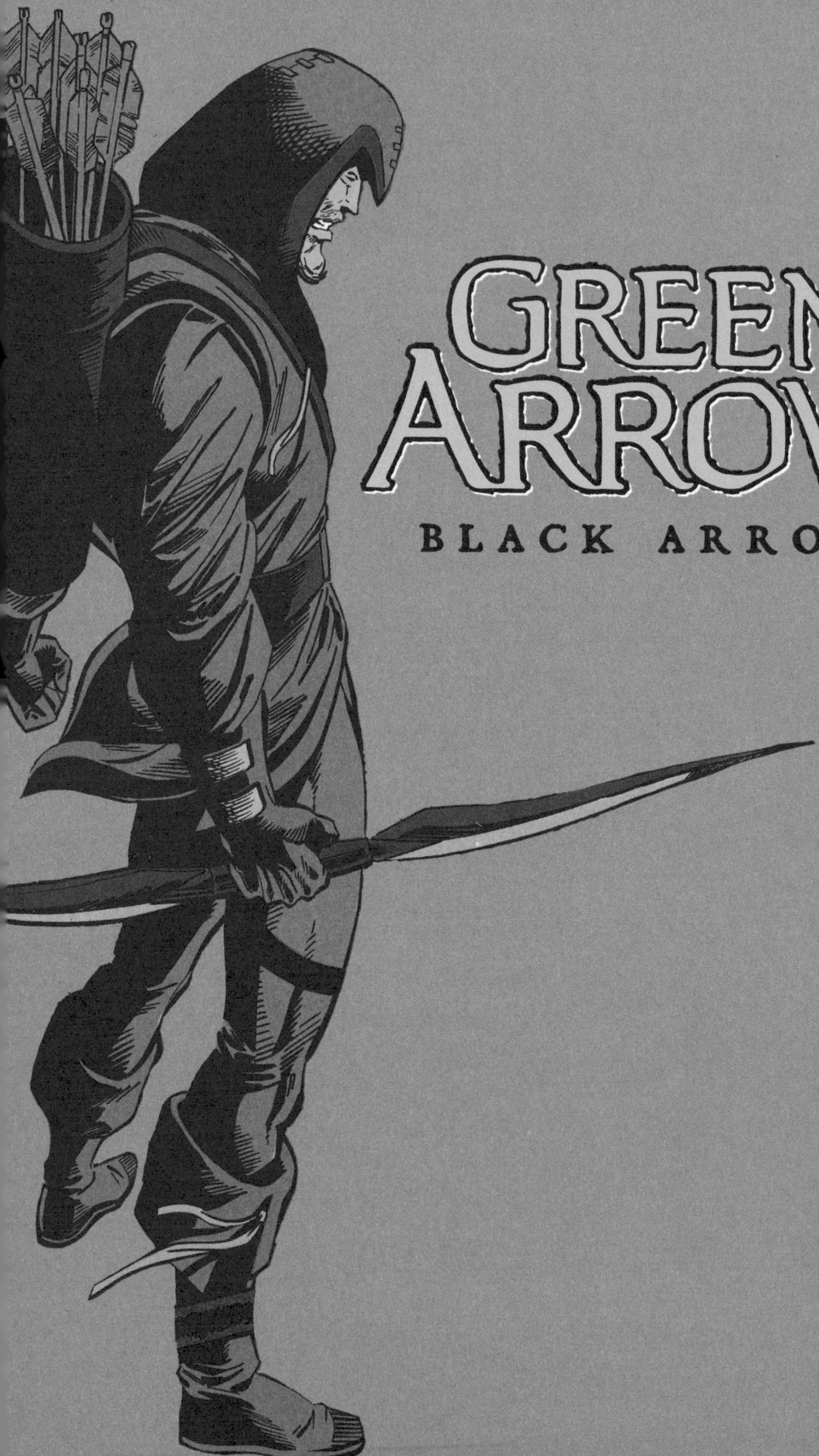

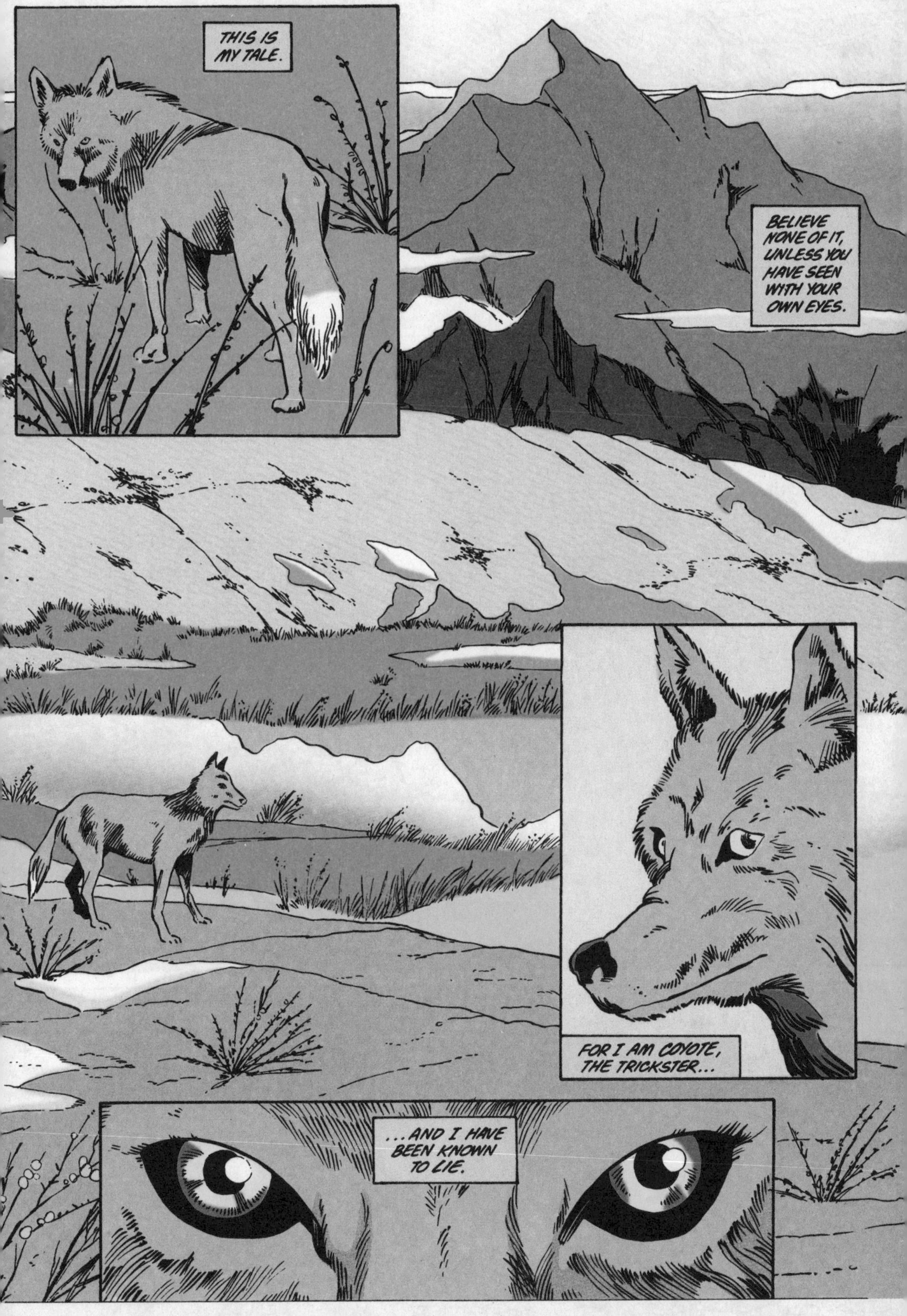
THIS IS MY TALE.
BELIEVE NONE OF IT, UNLESS YOU HAVE SEEN WITH YOUR OWN EYES.
FOR I AM COYOTE, THE TRICKSTER...
...AND I HAVE BEEN KNOWN TO LIE.

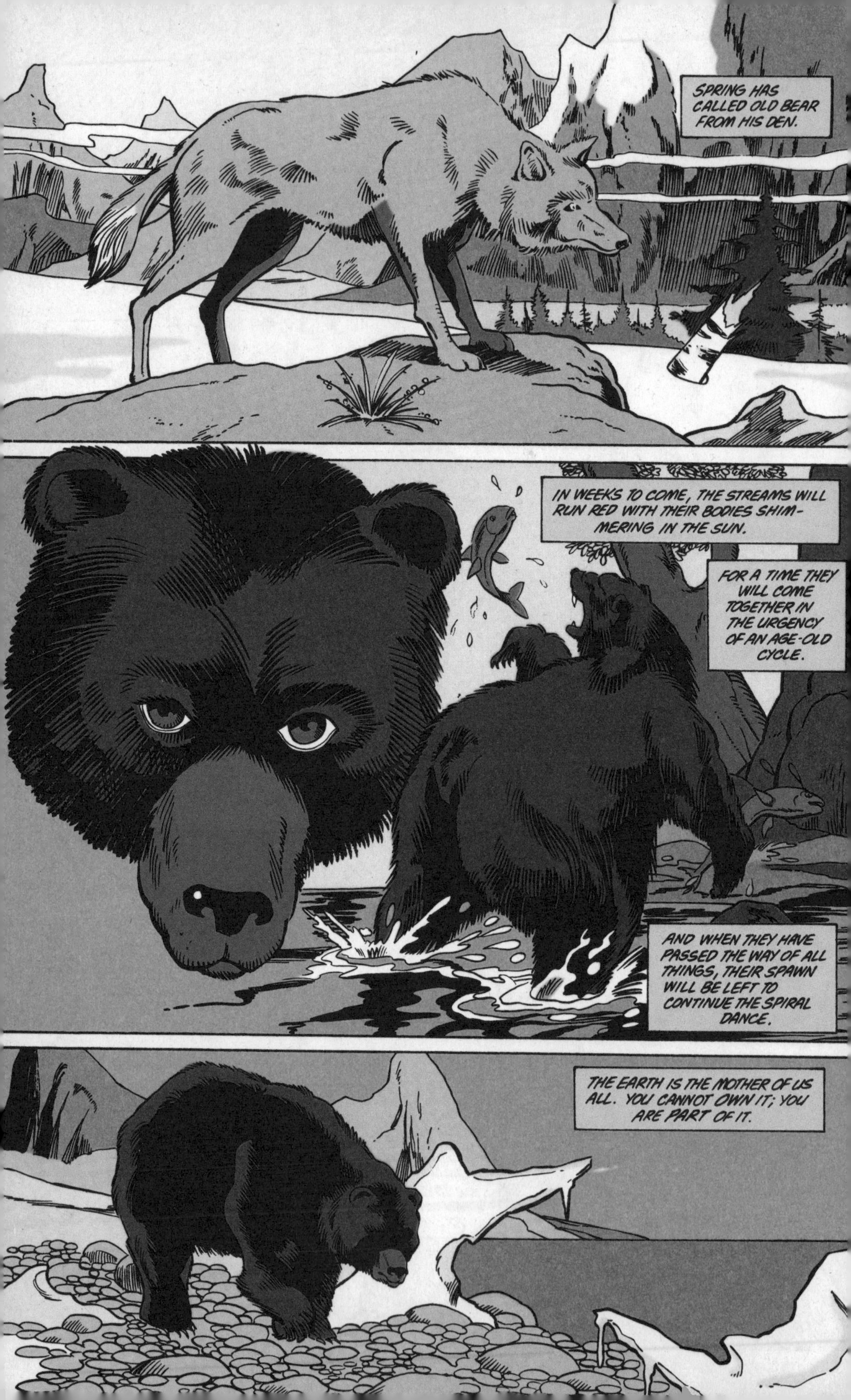
SPRING HAS CALLED OLD BEAR FROM HIS DEN.
IN WEEKS TO COME, THE STREAMS WILL RUN RED WITH THEIR BODIES SHIM-MERING IN THE SUN.
FOR A TIME THEY WILL COME TOGETHER IN THE URGENCY OF AN AGE-OLD CYCLE.
AND WHEN THEY HAVE PASSED THE WAY OF ALL THINGS, THEIR SPAWN WILL BE LEFT TO CONTINUE THE SPIRAL DANCE.
THE EARTH IS THE MOTHER OF US ALL. YOU CANNOT OWN IT; YOU ARE PART OF IT.

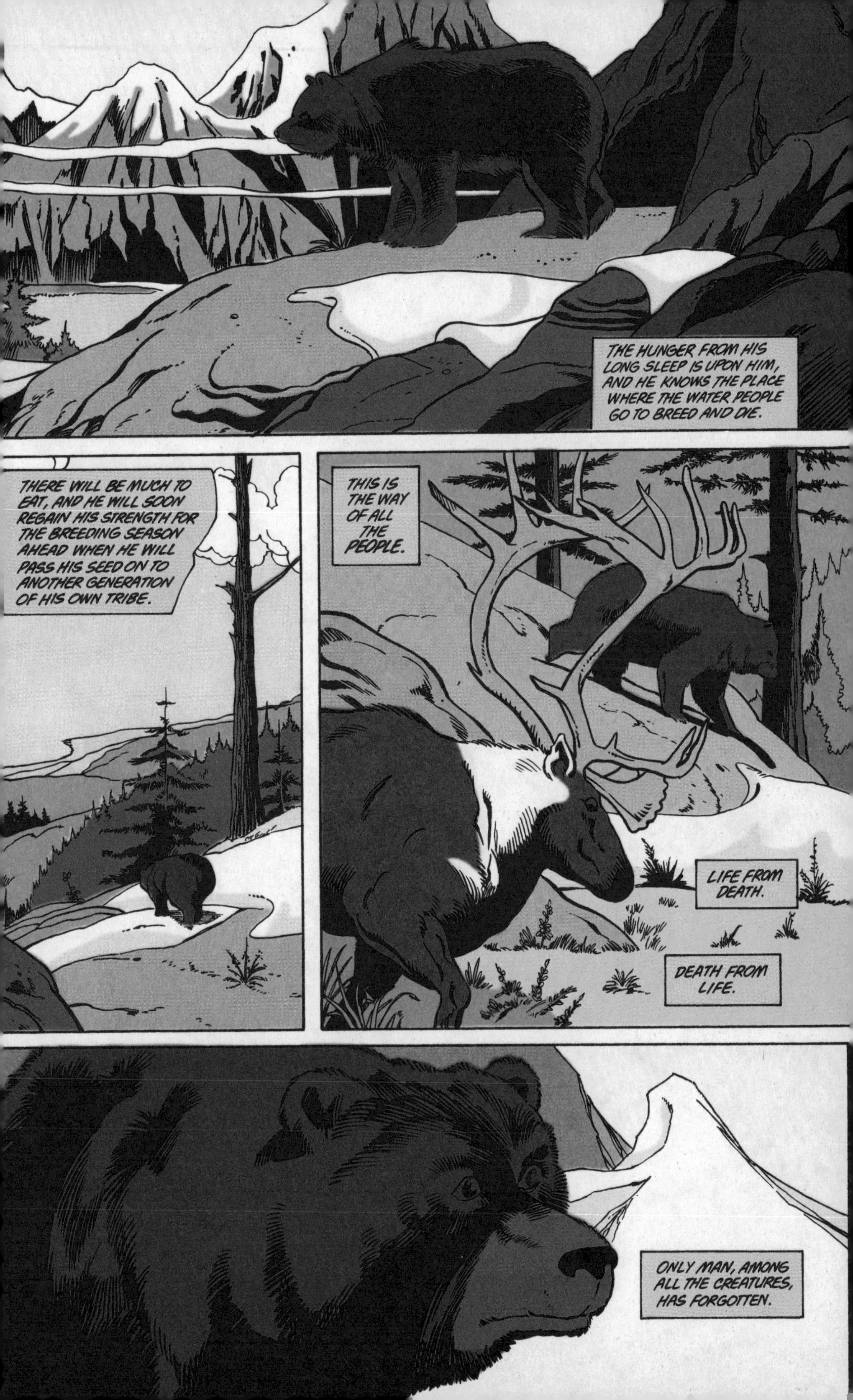

THE HUNGER FROM HIS LONG SLEEP IS UPON HIM, AND HE KNOWS THE PLACE WHERE THE WATER PEOPLE GO TO BREED AND DIE.
THERE WILL BE MUCH TO EAT, AND HE WILL SOON REGAIN HIS STRENGTH FOR THE BREEDING SEASON AHEAD WHEN HE WILL PASS HIS SEED ON TO ANOTHER GENERATION OF HIS OWN TRIBE.
THIS IS THE WAY OF ALL THE PEOPLE.
LIFE FROM DEATH.
DEATH FROM LIFE.
ONLY MAN, AMONG ALL THE CREATURES, HAS FORGOTTEN.

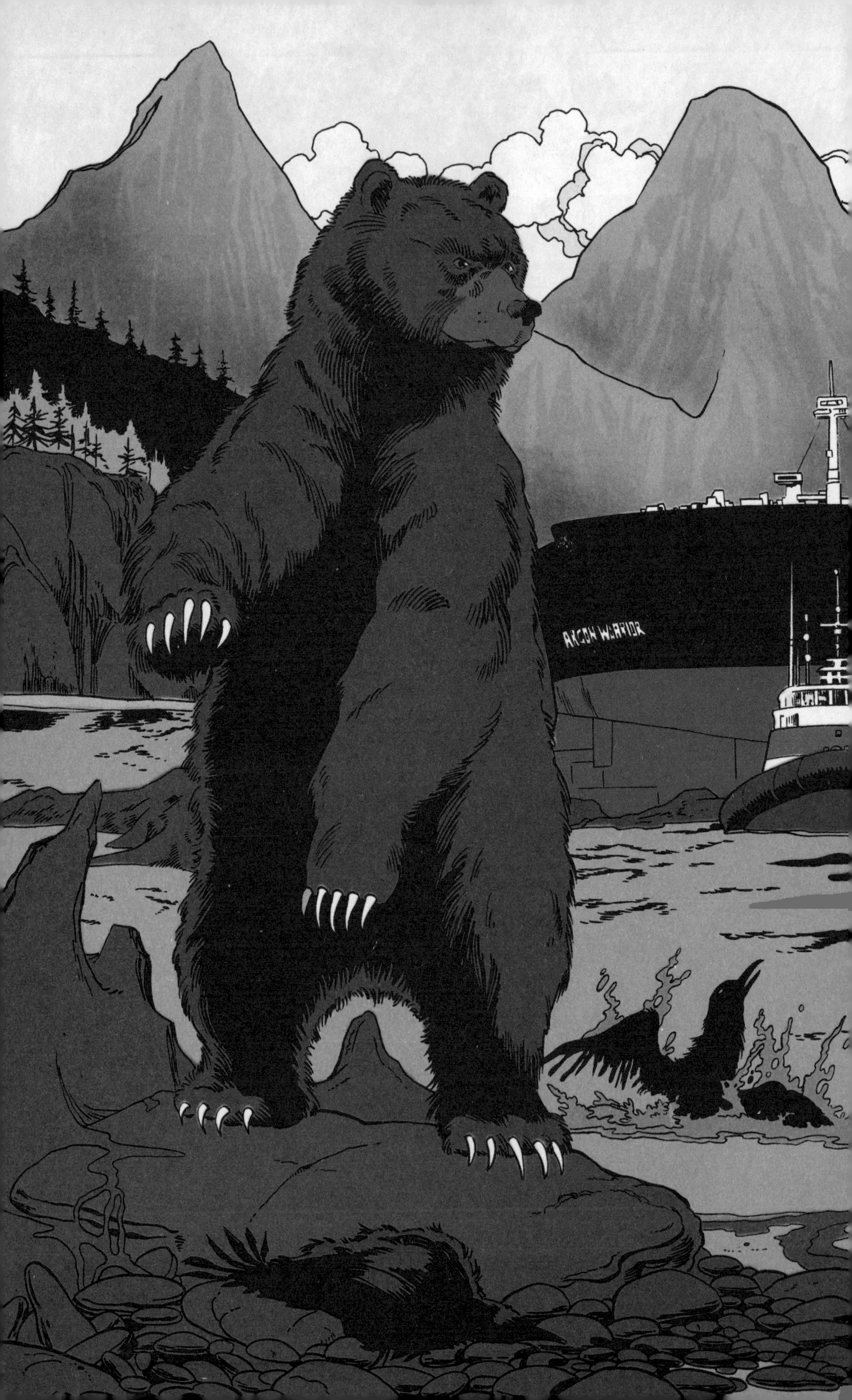
ARGON WARRIOR

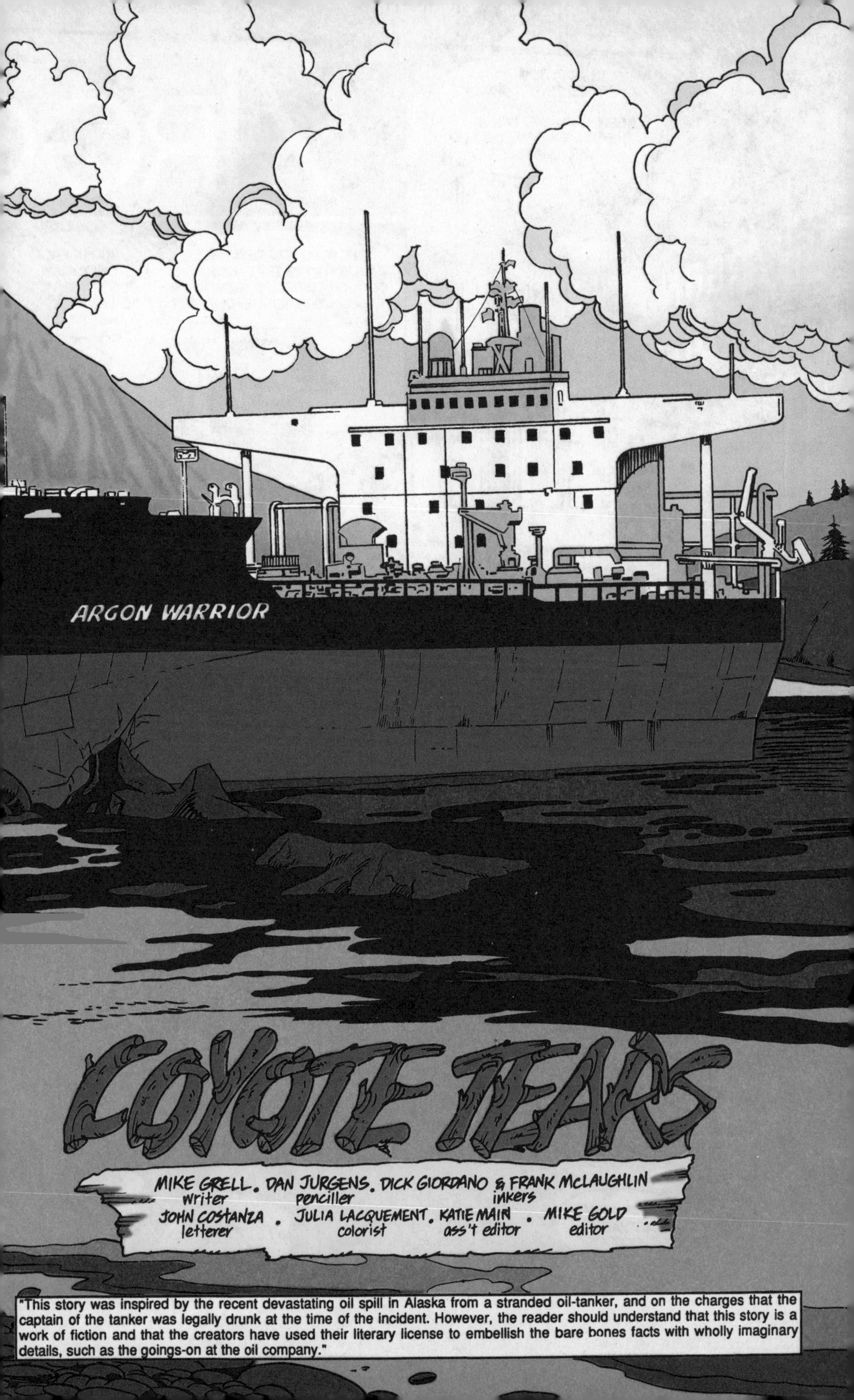
ARGON WARRIOR
COYOTE TEARS
MIKE GRELL . DAN JURGENS . DICK GIORDANO & FRANK McLAUGHLIN
writer penciller inkers
JOHN COSTANZA . JULIA LACQUEMENT . KATIE MAIN . MIKE GOLD
letterer colorist ass't editor editor
"This story was inspired by the recent devastating oil spill in Alaska from a stranded oil-tanker, and on the charges that the captain of the tanker was legally drunk at the time of the incident. However, the reader should understand that this story is a work of fiction and that the creators have used their literary license to embellish the bare bones facts with wholly imaginary details, such as the goings-on at the oil company."

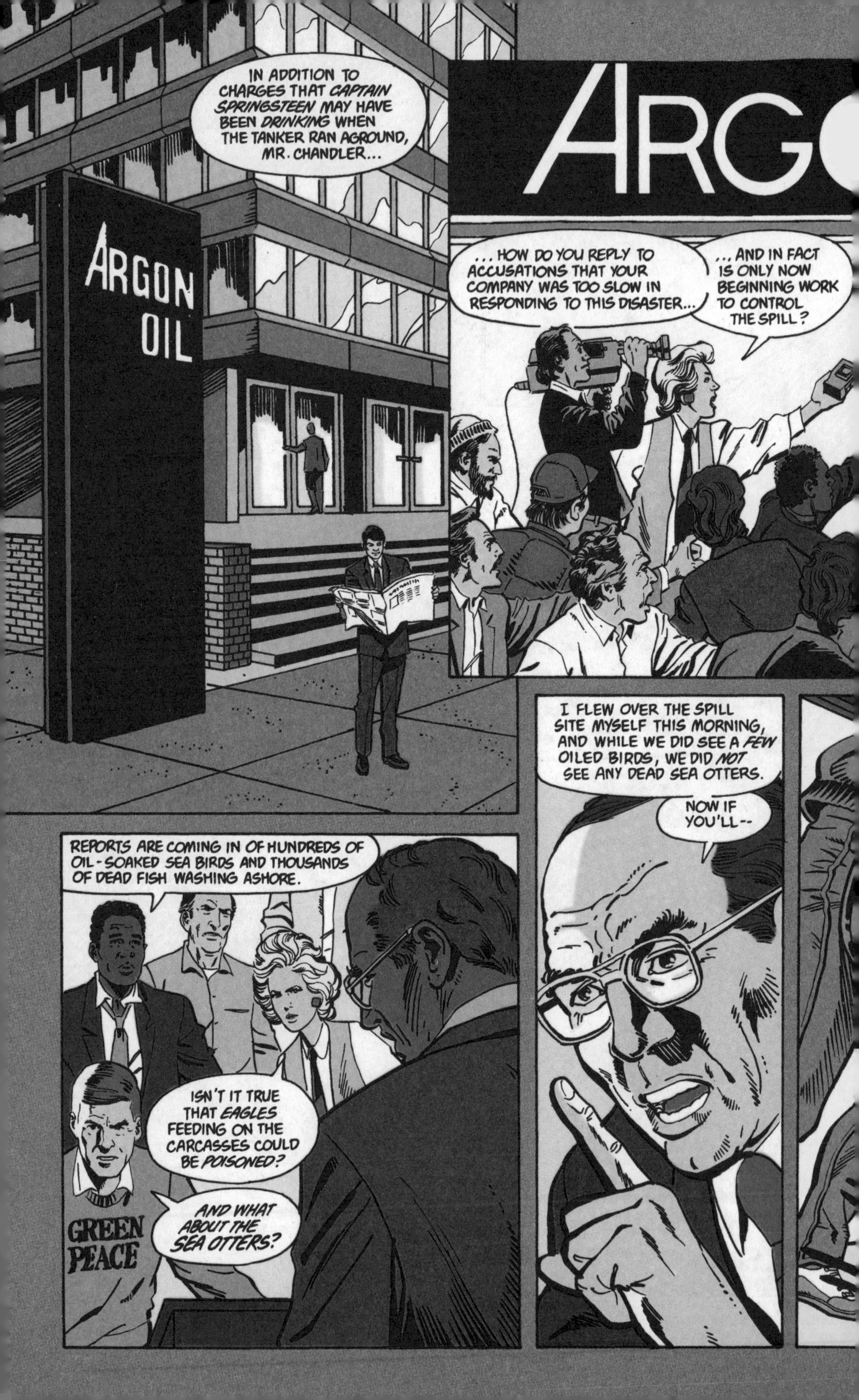
IN ADDITION TO CHARGES THAT CAPTAIN SPRINGSTEEN MAY HAVE BEEN DRINKING WHEN THE TANKER RAN AGROUND, MR. CHANDLER...
ARGON OIL
ARG
... HOW DO YOU REPLY TO ACCUSATIONS THAT YOUR COMPANY WAS TOO SLOW IN RESPONDING TO THIS DISASTER...
..., AND IN FACT IS ONLY NOW BEGINNING WORK TO CONTROL THE SPILL?
I FLEW OVER THE SPILL SITE MYSELF THIS MORNING, AND WHILE WE DID SEE A FEW OILED BIRDS, WE DID NOT SEE ANY DEAD SEA OTTERS.
NOW IF YOU'LL--
REPORTS ARE COMING IN OF HUNDREDS OF OIL-SOAKED SEA BIRDS AND THOUSANDS OF DEAD FISH WASHING ASHORE.
ISN'T IT TRUE THAT EAGLES FEEDING ON THE CARCASSES COULD BE POISONED?
GREEN PEACE
AND WHAT ABOUT THE SEA OTTERS?

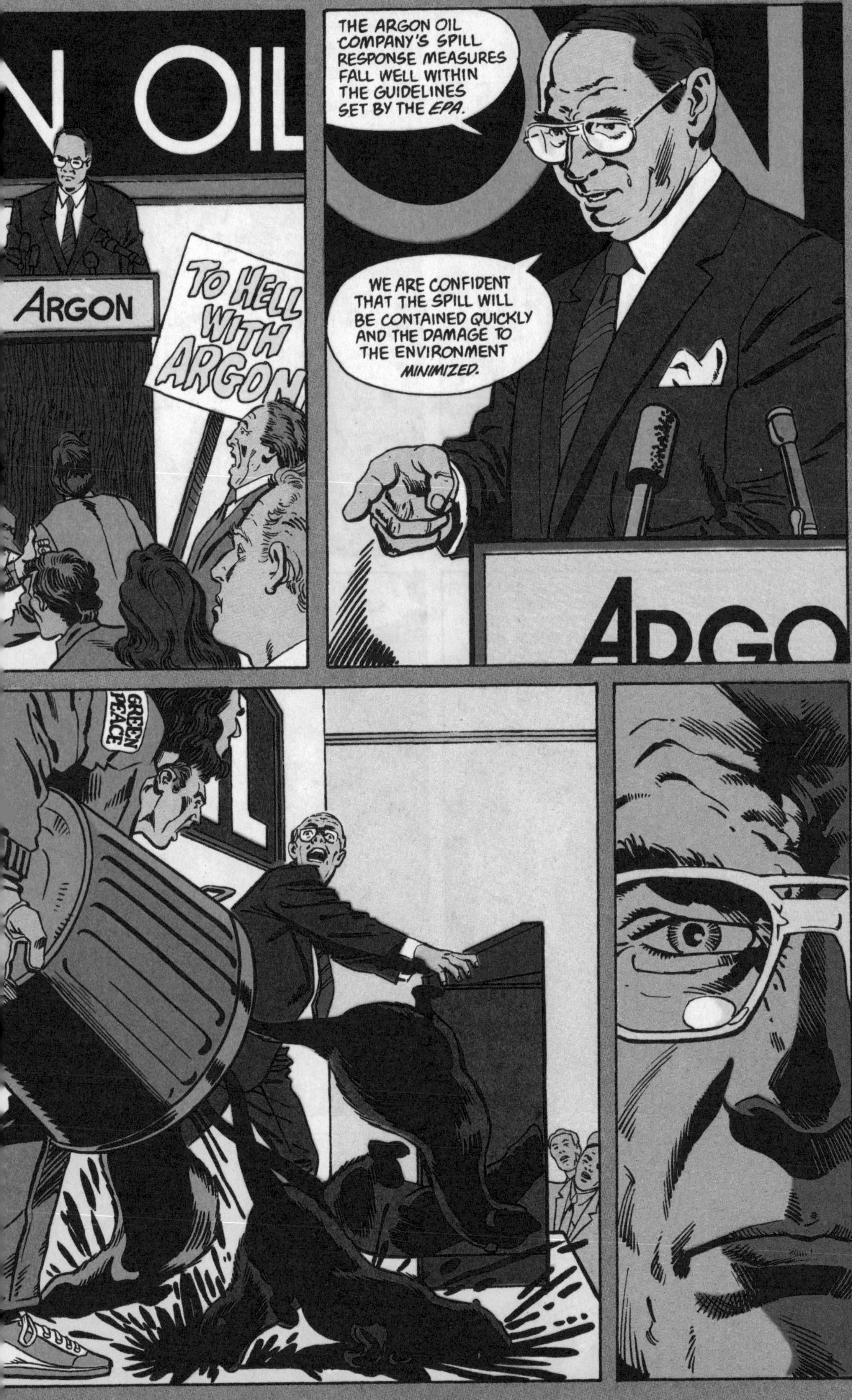

N OIL
ARGON
TO HELL WITH ARGON!
THE ARGON OIL COMPANY'S SPILL RESPONSE MEASURES FALL WELL WITHIN THE GUIDELINES SET BY THE *EPA*.
WE ARE CONFIDENT THAT THE SPILL WILL BE CONTAINED QUICKLY AND THE DAMAGE TO THE ENVIRONMENT *MINIMIZED*.
ARGO
GREEN PEACE

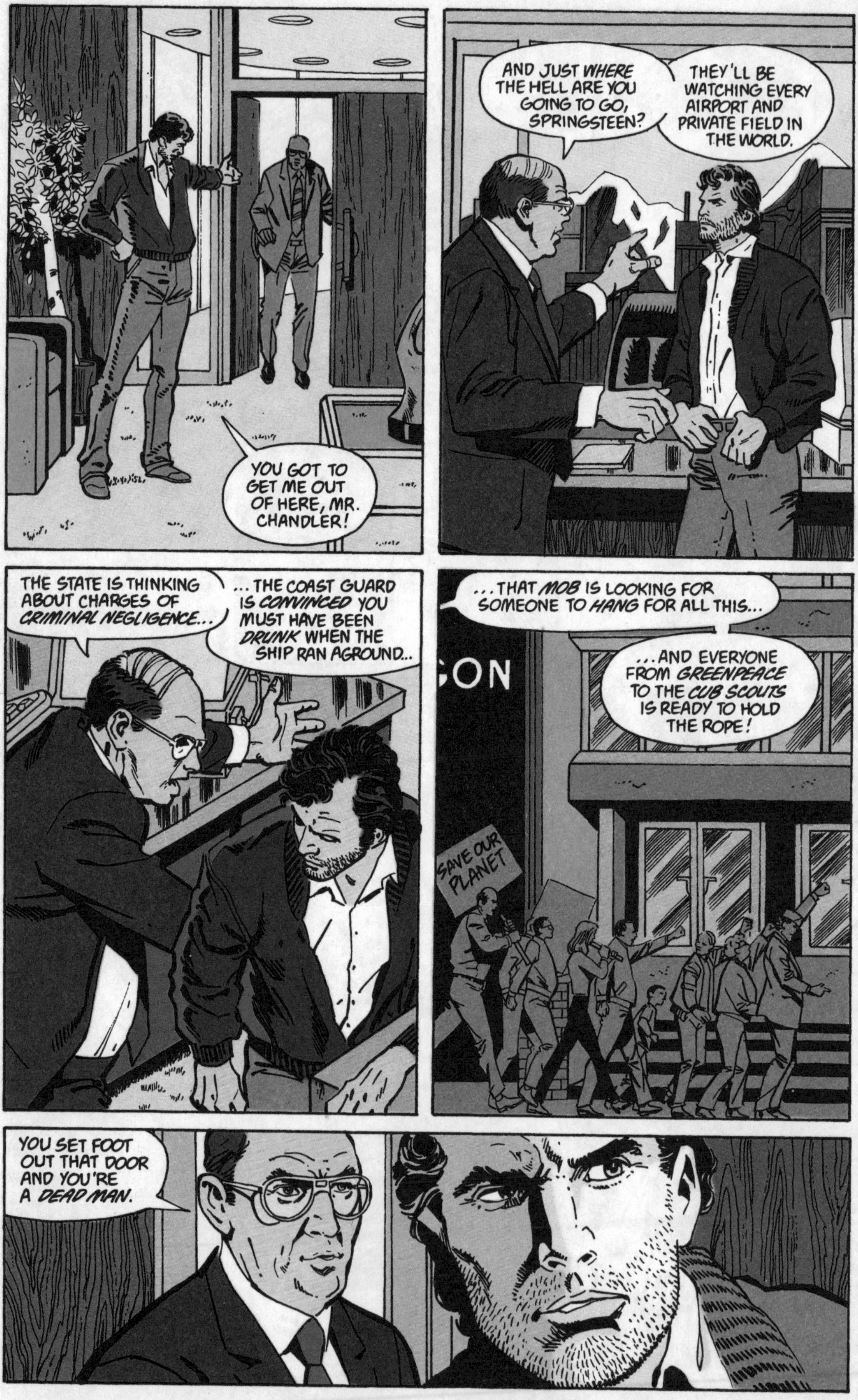
YOU GOT TO GET ME OUT OF HERE, MR. CHANDLER!
AND JUST WHERE THE HELL ARE YOU GOING TO GO, SPRINGSTEEN?
THEY'LL BE WATCHING EVERY AIRPORT AND PRIVATE FIELD IN THE WORLD.
THE STATE IS THINKING ABOUT CHARGES OF CRIMINAL NEGLIGENCE...
...THE COAST GUARD IS CONVINCED YOU MUST HAVE BEEN DRUNK WHEN THE SHIP RAN AGROUND...
...THAT MOB IS LOOKING FOR SOMEONE TO HANG FOR ALL THIS...
...AND EVERYONE FROM GREENPEACE TO THE CUB SCOUTS IS READY TO HOLD THE ROPE!
GON
SAVE OUR PLANET
YOU SET FOOT OUT THAT DOOR AND YOU'RE A DEAD MAN.

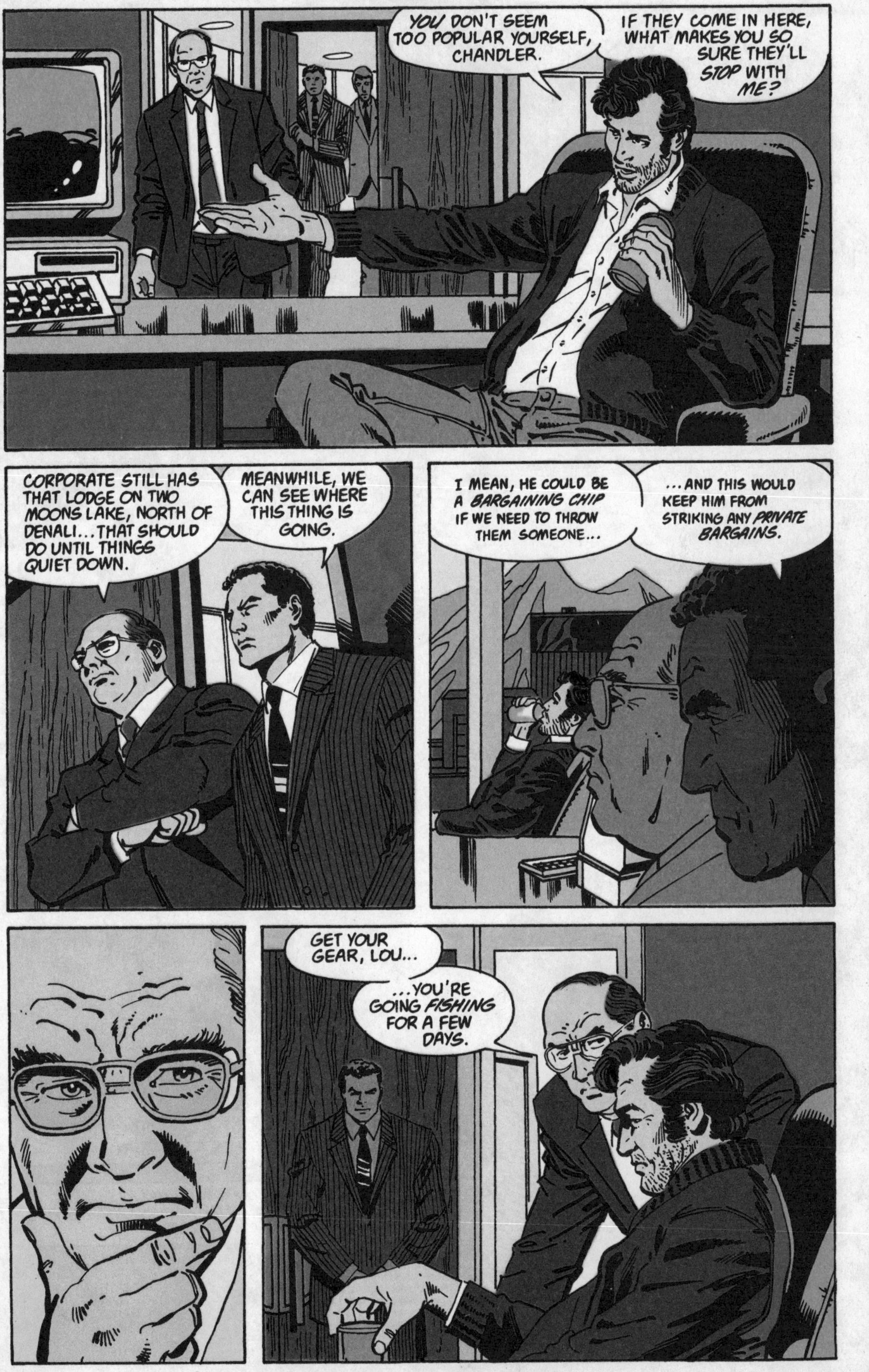
YOU DON'T SEEM TOO POPULAR YOURSELF, CHANDLER.
IF THEY COME IN HERE, WHAT MAKES YOU SO SURE THEY'LL STOP WITH ME?
CORPORATE STILL HAS THAT LODGE ON TWO MOONS LAKE, NORTH OF DENALI... THAT SHOULD DO UNTIL THINGS QUIET DOWN.
MEANWHILE, WE CAN SEE WHERE THIS THING IS GOING.
I MEAN, HE COULD BE A BARGAINING CHIP IF WE NEED TO THROW THEM SOMEONE...
...AND THIS WOULD KEEP HIM FROM STRIKING ANY PRIVATE BARGAINS.
GET YOUR GEAR, LOU...
...YOU'RE GOING FISHING FOR A FEW DAYS.

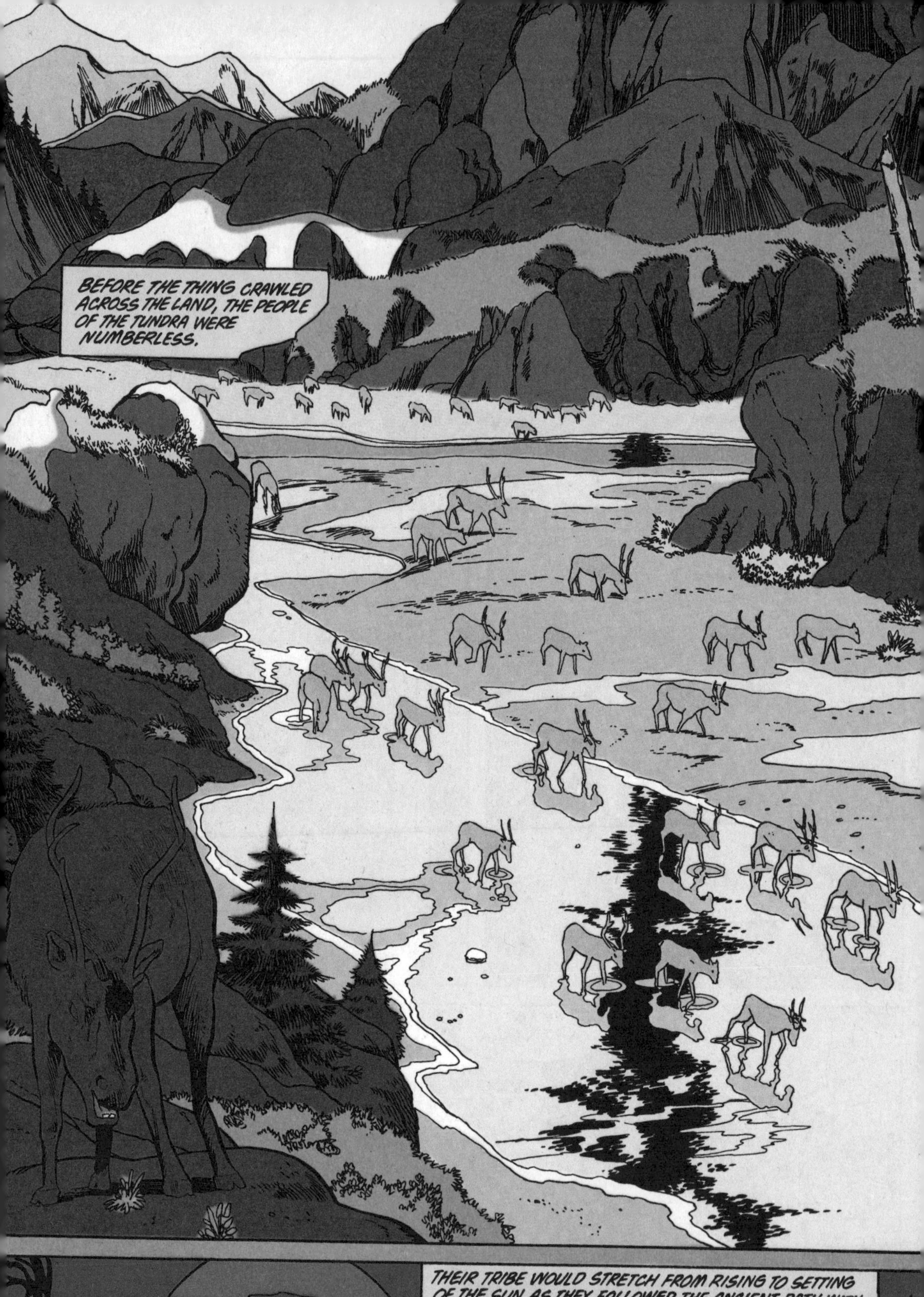
BEFORE THE THING CRAWLED ACROSS THE LAND, THE PEOPLE OF THE TUNDRA WERE NUMBERLESS.

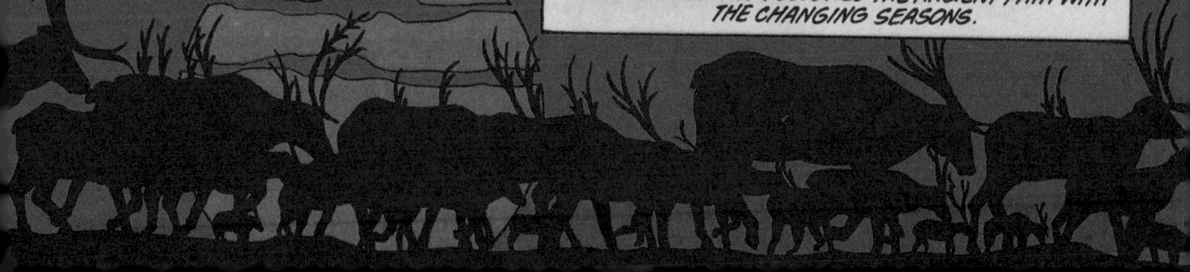
THEIR TRIBE WOULD STRETCH FROM RISING TO SETTING OF THE SUN AS THEY FOLLOWED THE ANCIENT PATH WITH THE CHANGING SEASONS.

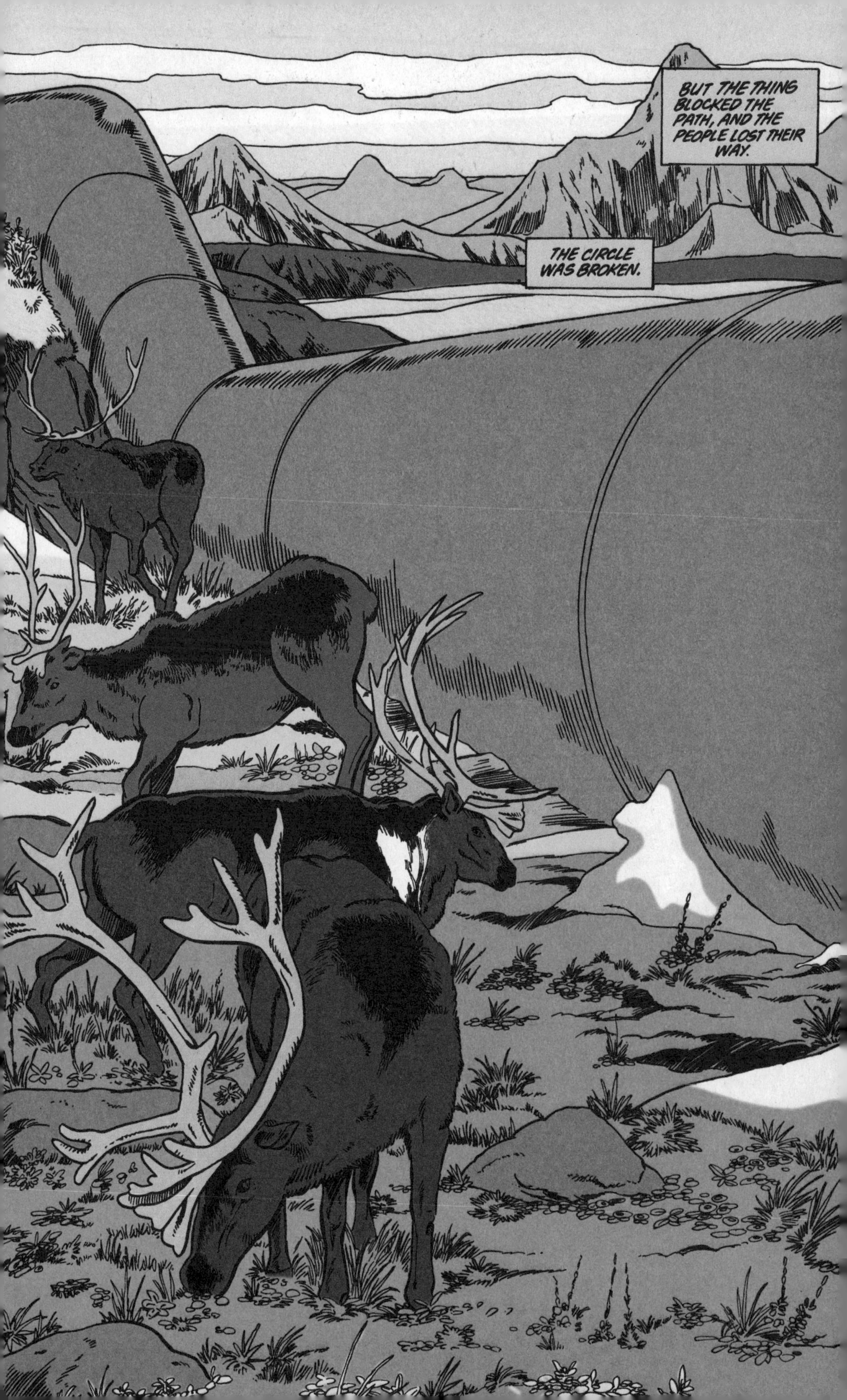
BUT THE THING BLOCKED THE PATH, AND THE PEOPLE LOST THEIR WAY.
THE CIRCLE WAS BROKEN.

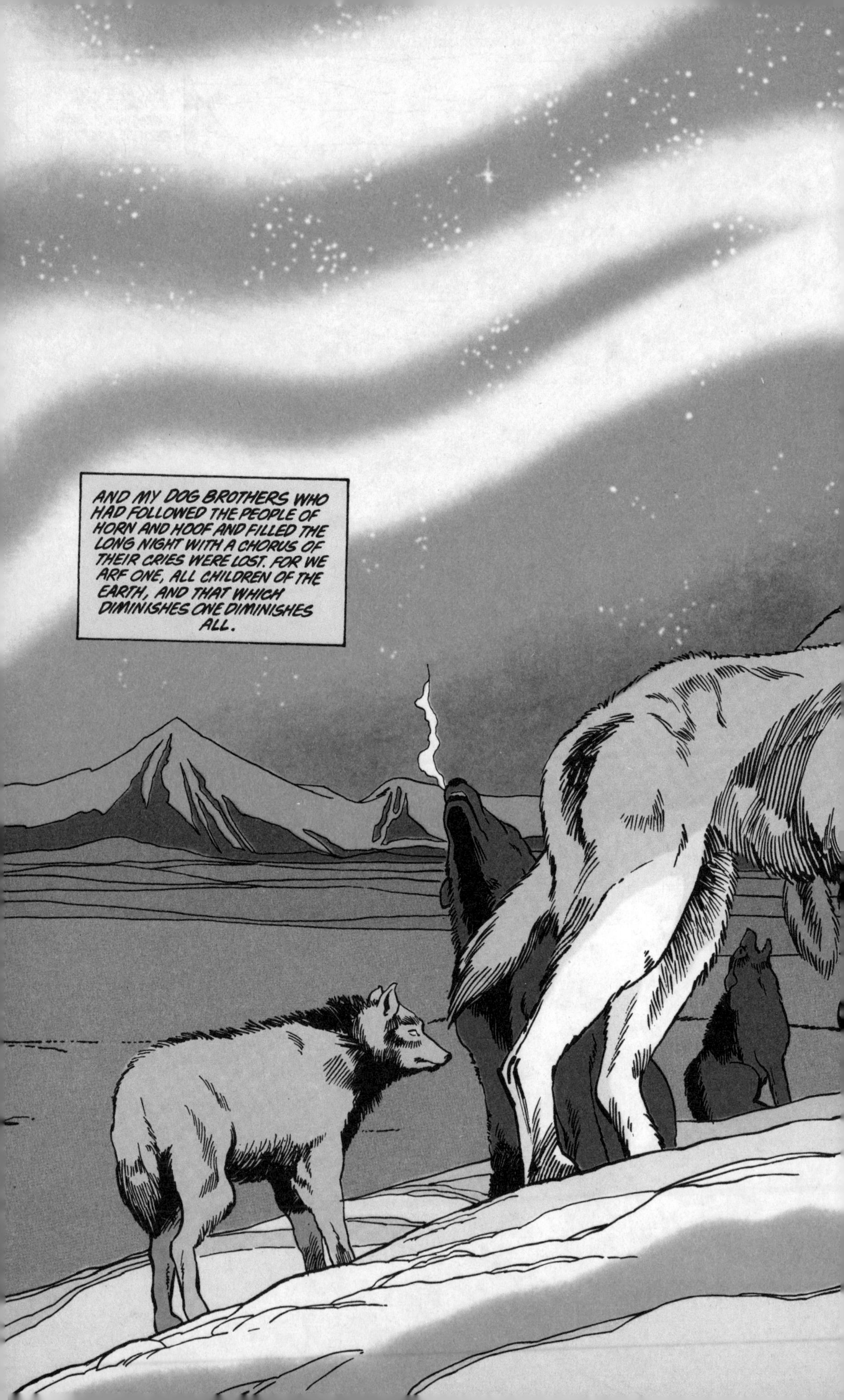
AND MY DOG BROTHERS WHO HAD FOLLOWED THE PEOPLE OF HORN AND HOOF AND FILLED THE LONG NIGHT WITH A CHORUS OF THEIR CRIES WERE LOST. FOR WE ARF ONE, ALL CHILDREN OF THE EARTH, AND THAT WHICH DIMINISHES ONE DIMINISHES ALL.

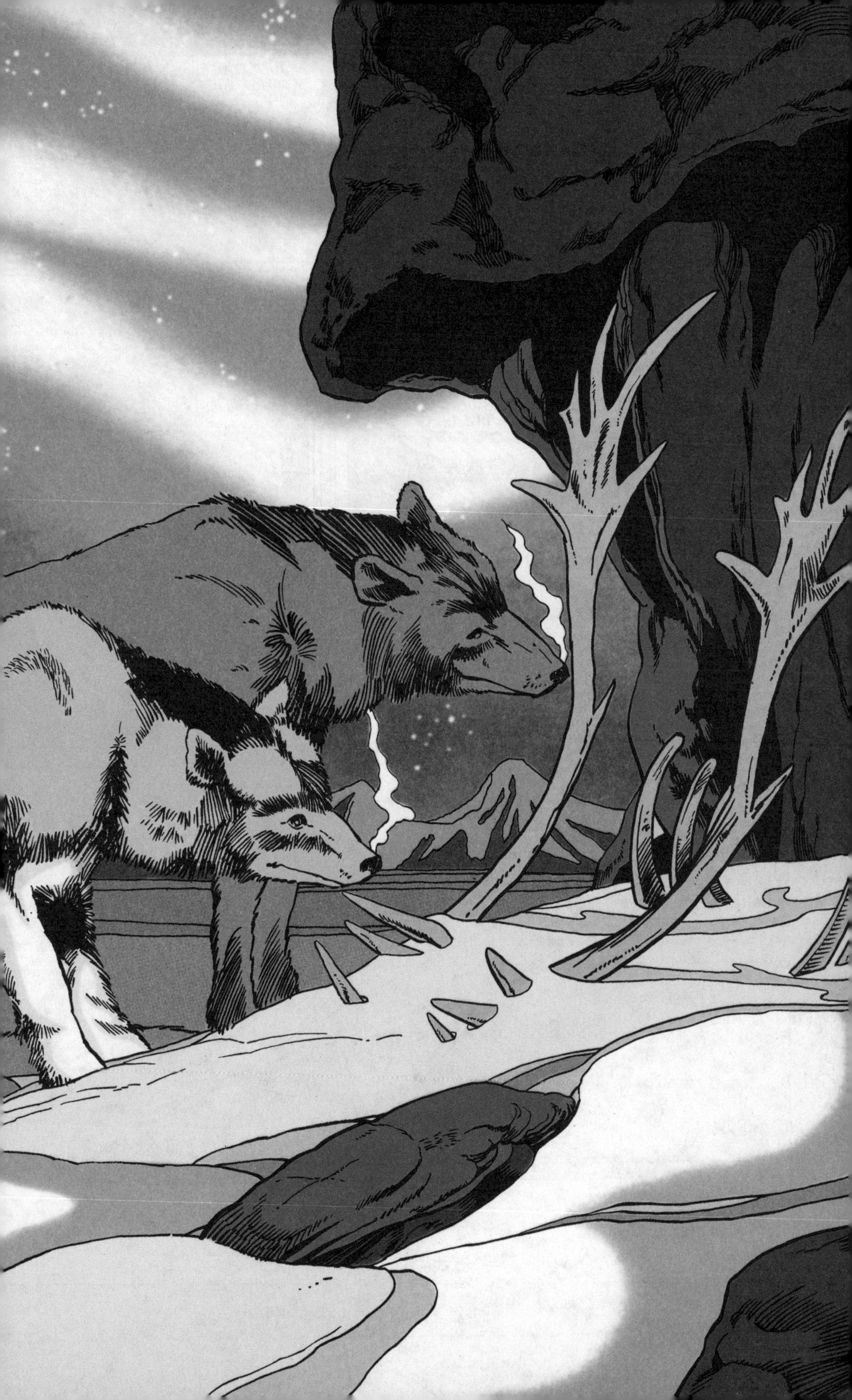

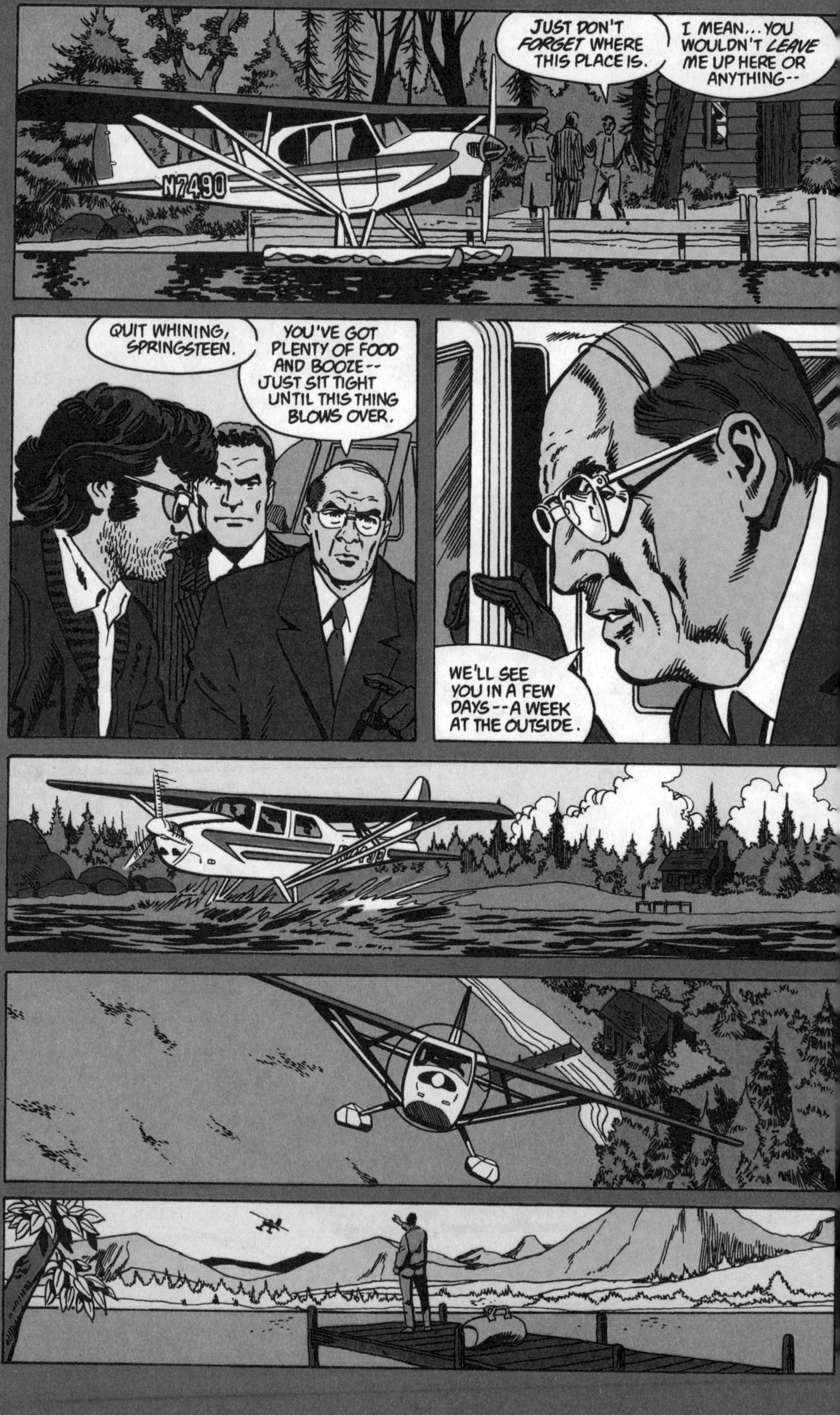
JUST DON'T FORGET WHERE THIS PLACE IS.
I MEAN... YOU WOULDN'T LEAVE ME UP HERE OR ANYTHING--
N7490
QUIT WHINING, SPRINGSTEEN.
YOU'VE GOT PLENTY OF FOOD AND BOOZE-- JUST SIT TIGHT UNTIL THIS THING BLOWS OVER.
WE'LL SEE YOU IN A FEW DAYS--A WEEK AT THE OUTSIDE.

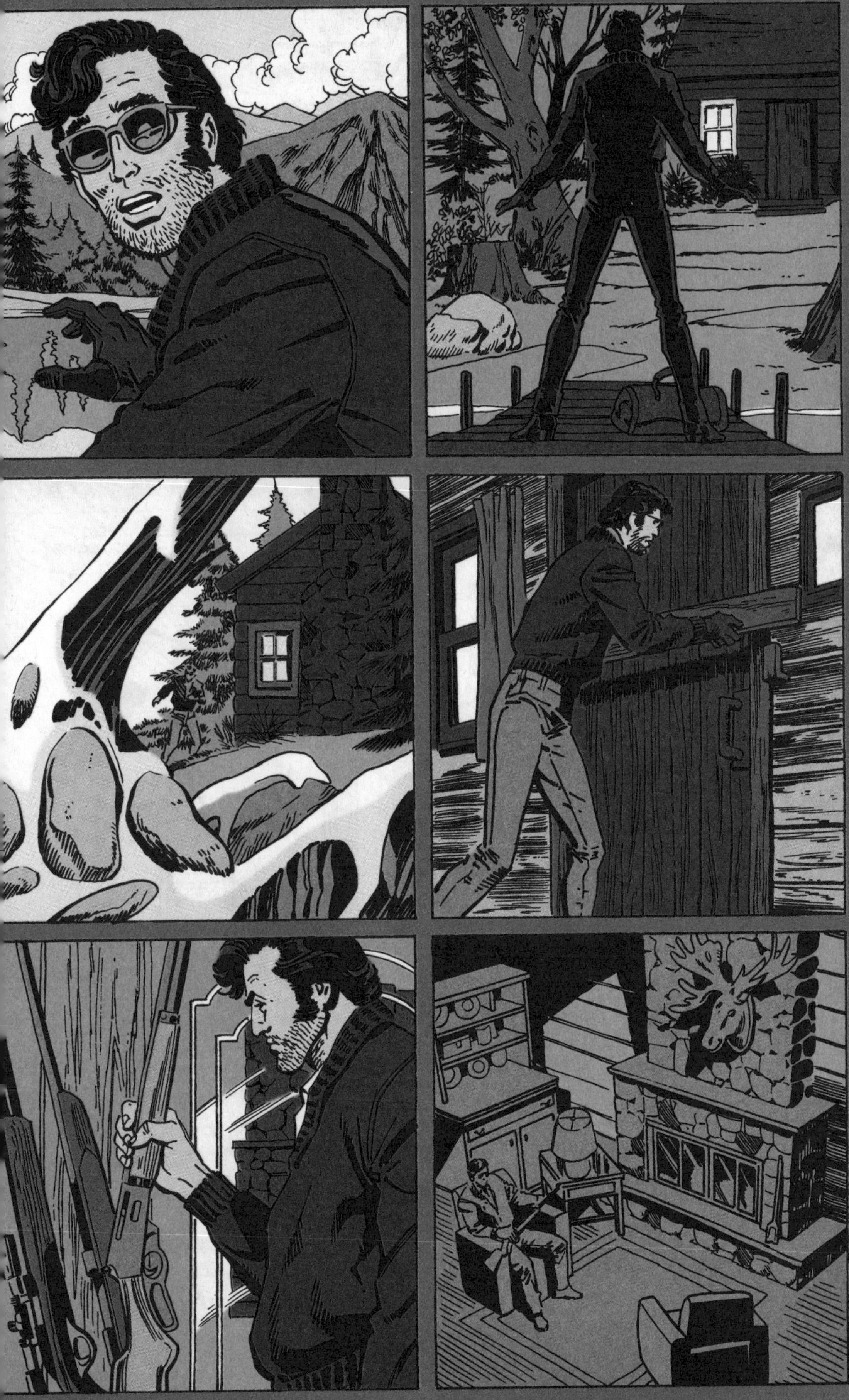

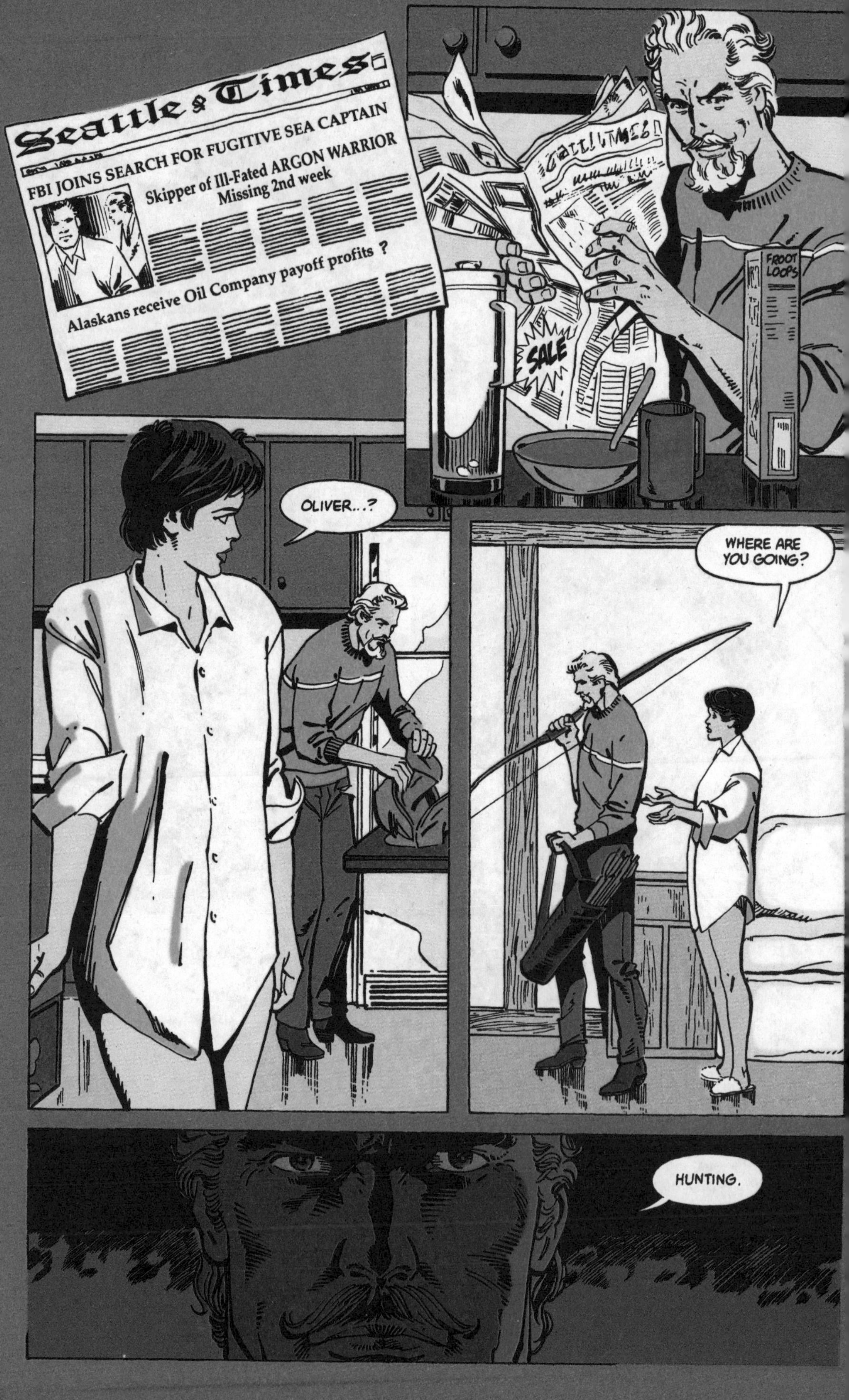
Seattle Times
FBI JOINS SEARCH FOR FUGITIVE SEA CAPTAIN
Skipper of Ill-Fated ARGON WARRIOR
Missing 2nd week
Alaskans receive Oil Company payoff profits ?
SALE
FROOT LOOPS
OLIVER...?
WHERE ARE YOU GOING?
HUNTING.

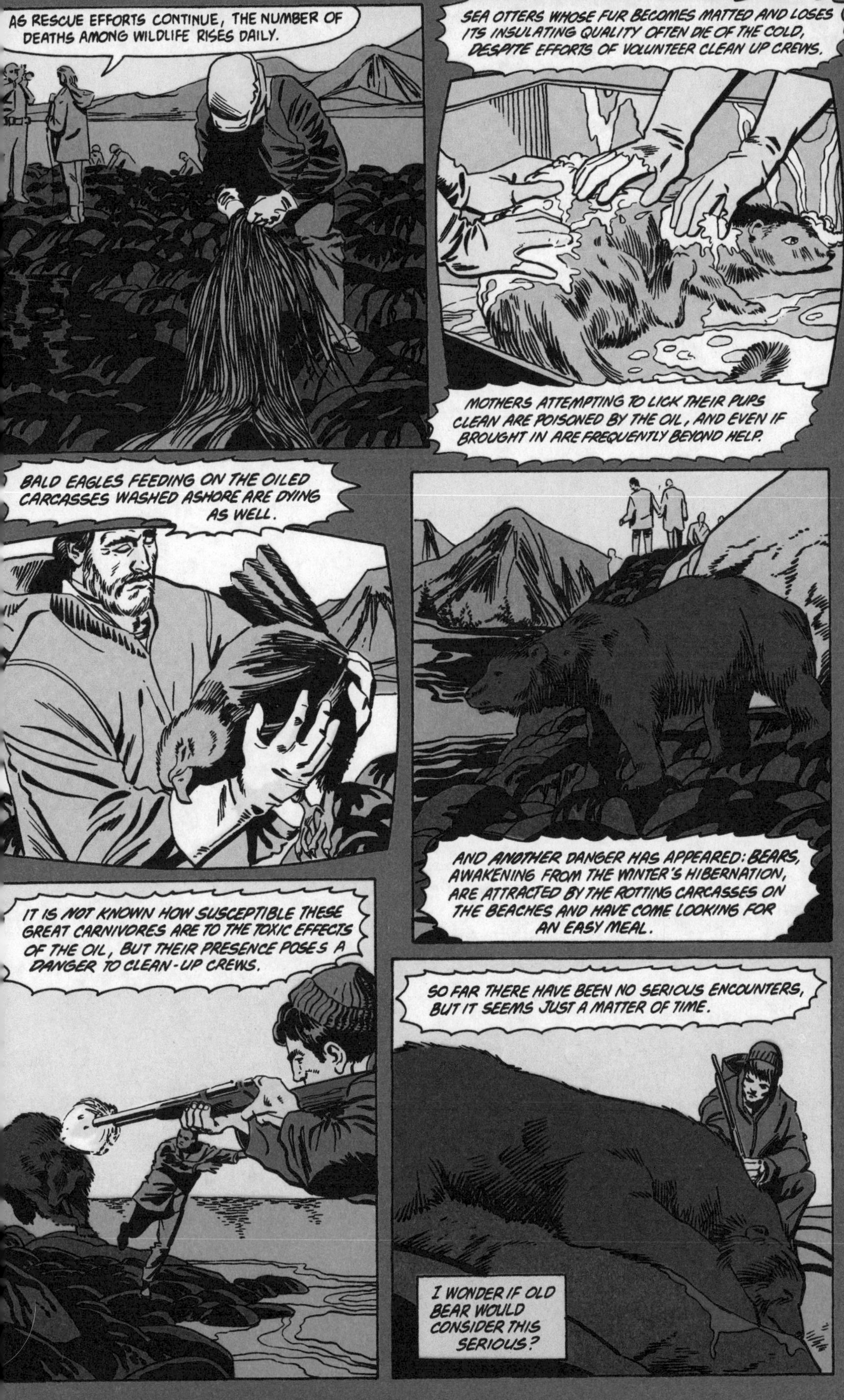
AS RESCUE EFFORTS CONTINUE, THE NUMBER OF DEATHS AMONG WILDLIFE RISES DAILY.
SEA OTTERS WHOSE FUR BECOMES MATTED AND LOSES ITS INSULATING QUALITY OFTEN DIE OF THE COLD, DESPITE EFFORTS OF VOLUNTEER CLEAN UP CREWS.
MOTHERS ATTEMPTING TO LICK THEIR PUPS CLEAN ARE POISONED BY THE OIL, AND EVEN IF BROUGHT IN ARE FREQUENTLY BEYOND HELP.
BALD EAGLES FEEDING ON THE OILED CARCASSES WASHED ASHORE ARE DYING AS WELL.
AND ANOTHER DANGER HAS APPEARED: BEARS, AWAKENING FROM THE WINTER'S HIBERNATION, ARE ATTRACTED BY THE ROTTING CARCASSES ON THE BEACHES AND HAVE COME LOOKING FOR AN EASY MEAL.
IT IS NOT KNOWN HOW SUSCEPTIBLE THESE GREAT CARNIVORES ARE TO THE TOXIC EFFECTS OF THE OIL, BUT THEIR PRESENCE POSES A DANGER TO CLEAN-UP CREWS.
SO FAR THERE HAVE BEEN NO SERIOUS ENCOUNTERS, BUT IT SEEMS JUST A MATTER OF TIME.
I WONDER IF OLD BEAR WOULD CONSIDER THIS SERIOUS?

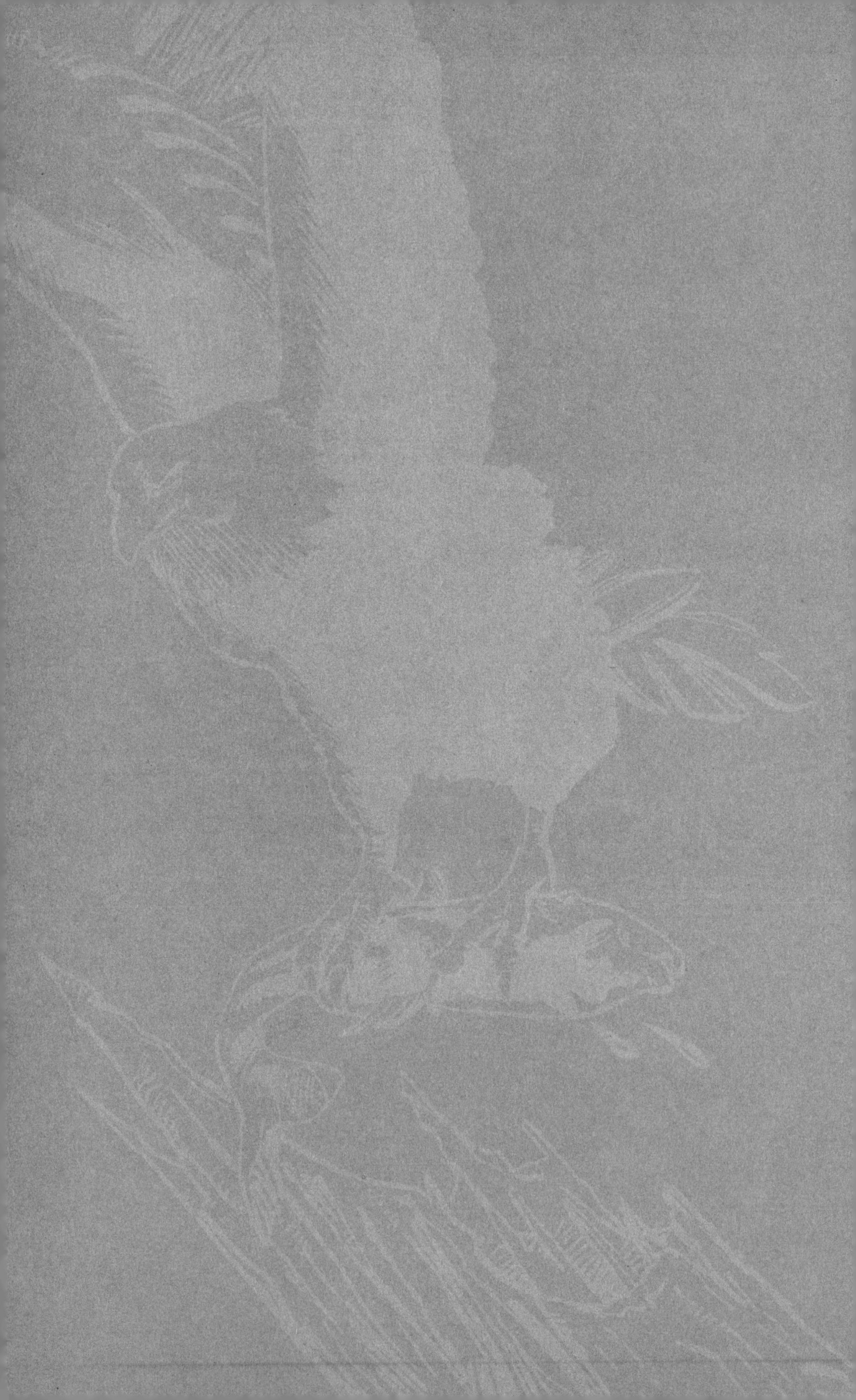

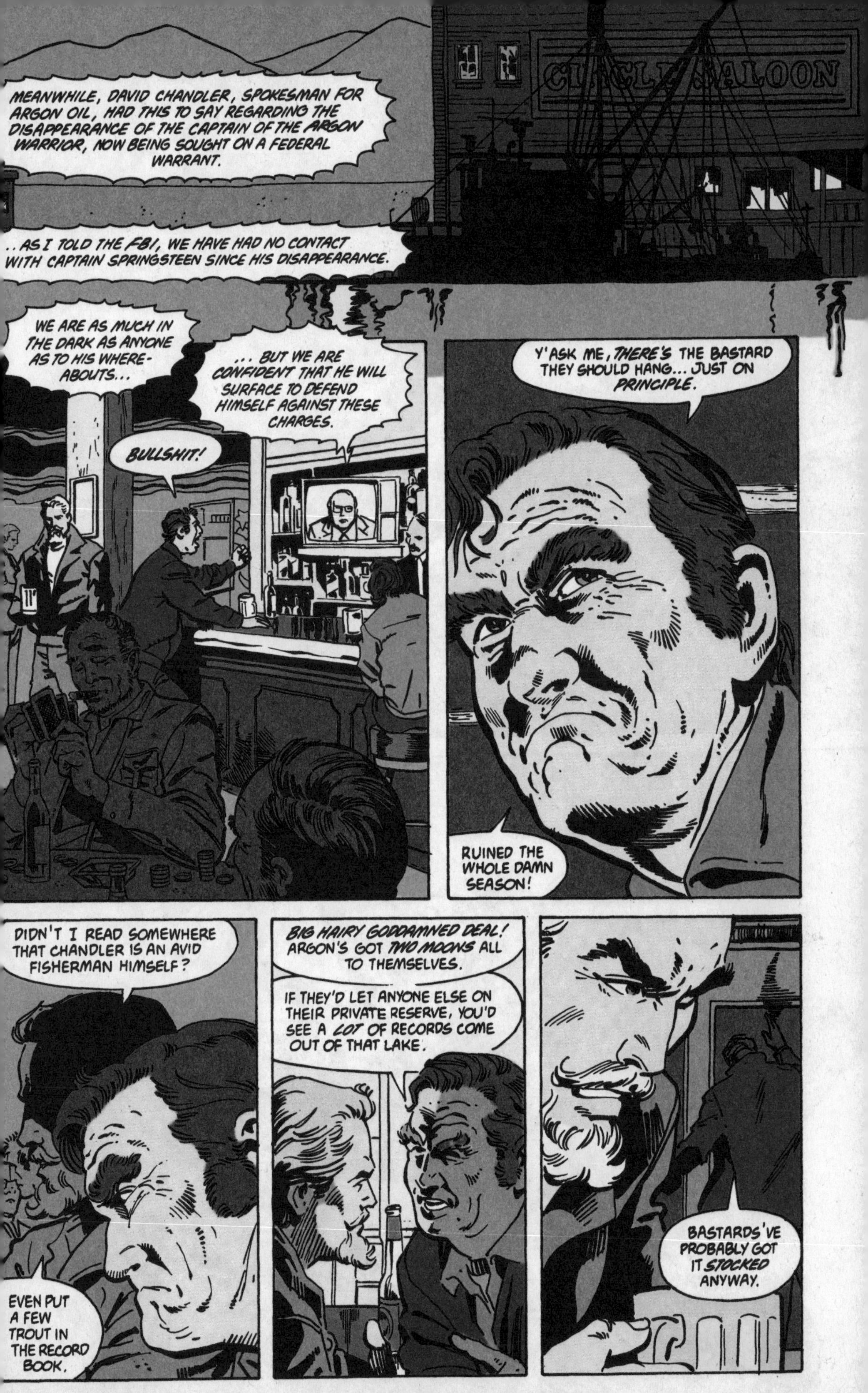

MEANWHILE, DAVID CHANDLER, SPOKESMAN FOR ARGON OIL, HAD THIS TO SAY REGARDING THE DISAPPEARANCE OF THE CAPTAIN OF THE ARGON WARRIOR, NOW BEING SOUGHT ON A FEDERAL WARRANT.
..AS I TOLD THE FBI, WE HAVE HAD NO CONTACT WITH CAPTAIN SPRINGSTEEN SINCE HIS DISAPPEARANCE.
WE ARE AS MUCH IN THE DARK AS ANYONE AS TO HIS WHEREABOUTS...
... BUT WE ARE CONFIDENT THAT HE WILL SURFACE TO DEFEND HIMSELF AGAINST THESE CHARGES.
BULLSHIT!
Y'ASK ME, THERE'S THE BASTARD THEY SHOULD HANG... JUST ON PRINCIPLE.
RUINED THE WHOLE DAMN SEASON!
DIDN'T I READ SOMEWHERE THAT CHANDLER IS AN AVID FISHERMAN HIMSELF?
EVEN PUT A FEW TROUT IN THE RECORD BOOK.
BIG HAIRY GODDAMNED DEAL! ARGON'S GOT TWO MOONS ALL TO THEMSELVES.
IF THEY'D LET ANYONE ELSE ON THEIR PRIVATE RESERVE, YOU'D SEE A LOT OF RECORDS COME OUT OF THAT LAKE.
BASTARDS'VE PROBABLY GOT IT STOCKED ANYWAY.

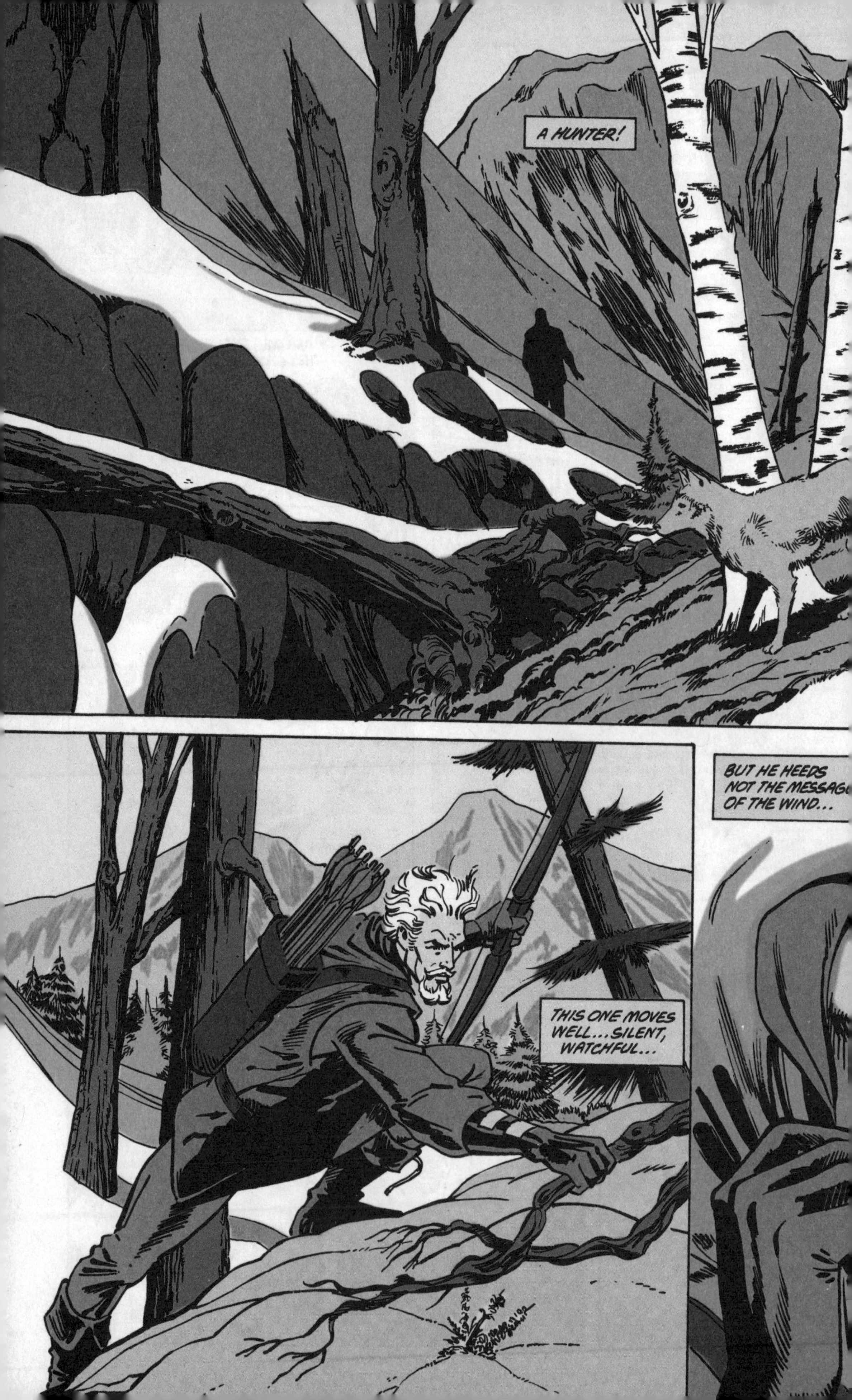
A HUNTER!
THIS ONE MOVES WELL... SILENT, WATCHFUL...
BUT HE HEEDS NOT THE MESSAGE OF THE WIND...

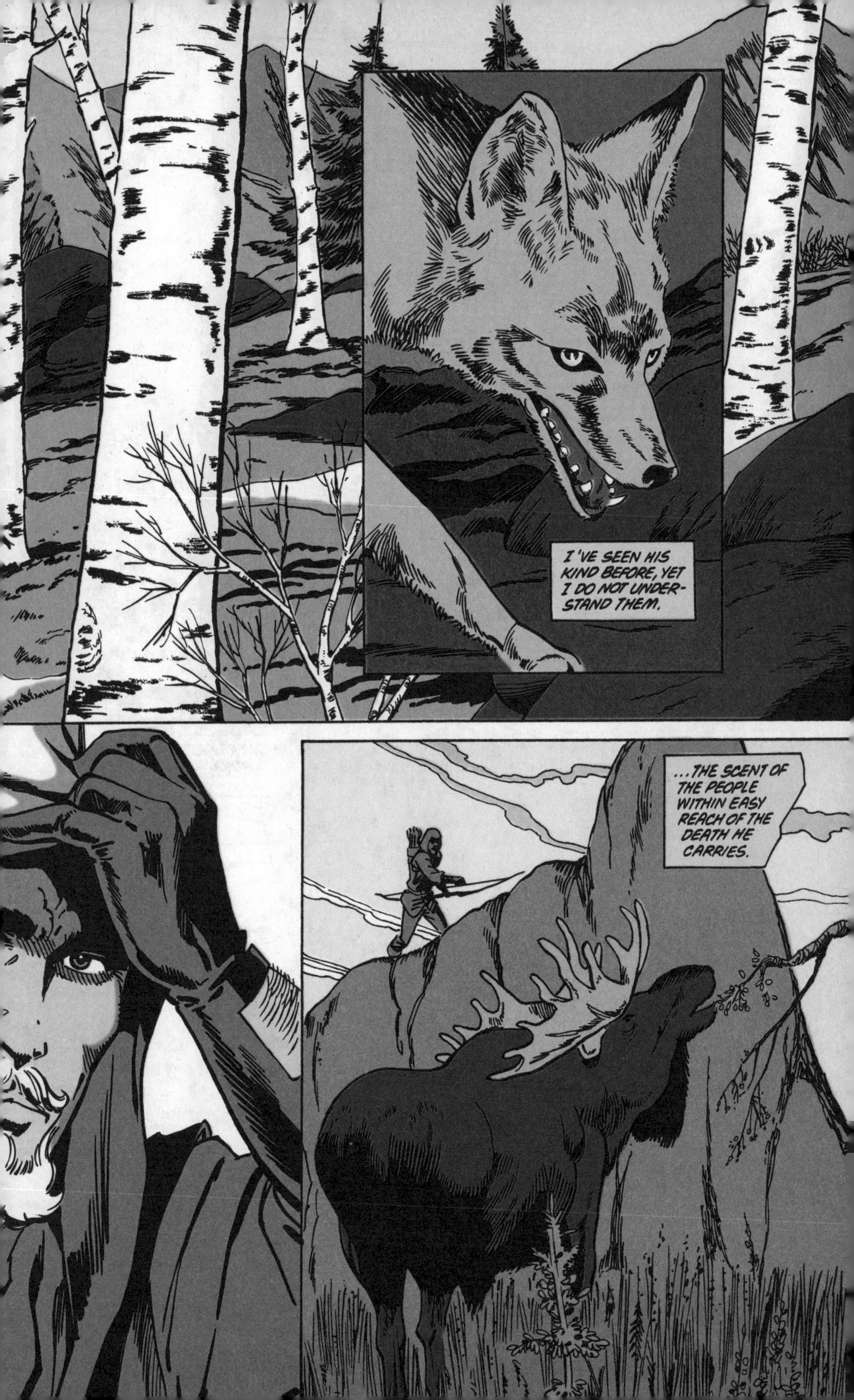
I'VE SEEN HIS KIND BEFORE, YET I DO NOT UNDERSTAND THEM.
...THE SCENT OF THE PEOPLE WITHIN EASY REACH OF THE DEATH HE CARRIES.

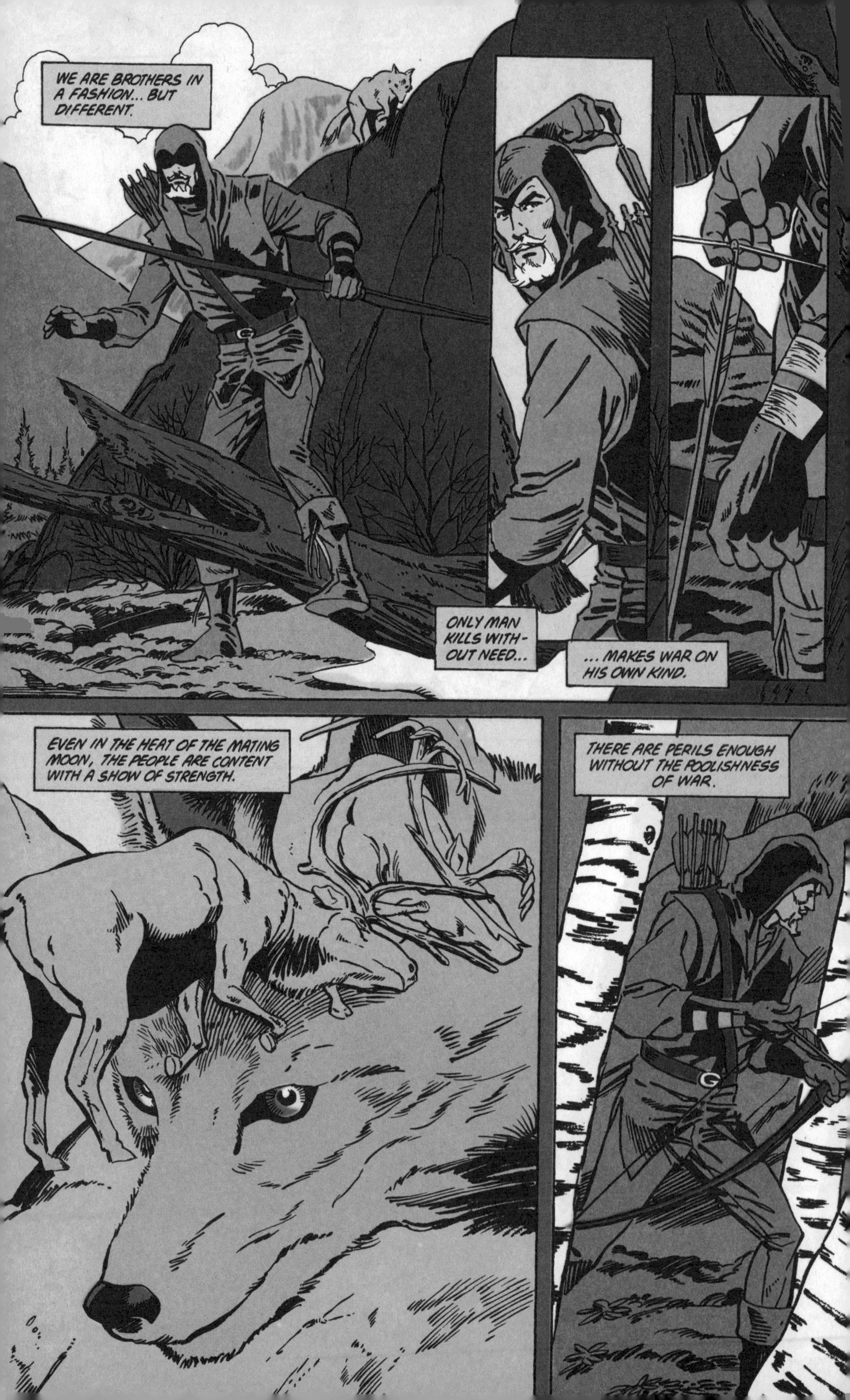
WE ARE BROTHERS IN A FASHION... BUT DIFFERENT.
ONLY MAN KILLS WITH-OUT NEED...
... MAKES WAR ON HIS OWN KIND.
EVEN IN THE HEAT OF THE MATING MOON, THE PEOPLE ARE CONTENT WITH A SHOW OF STRENGTH.
THERE ARE PERILS ENOUGH WITHOUT THE FOOLISHNESS OF WAR.

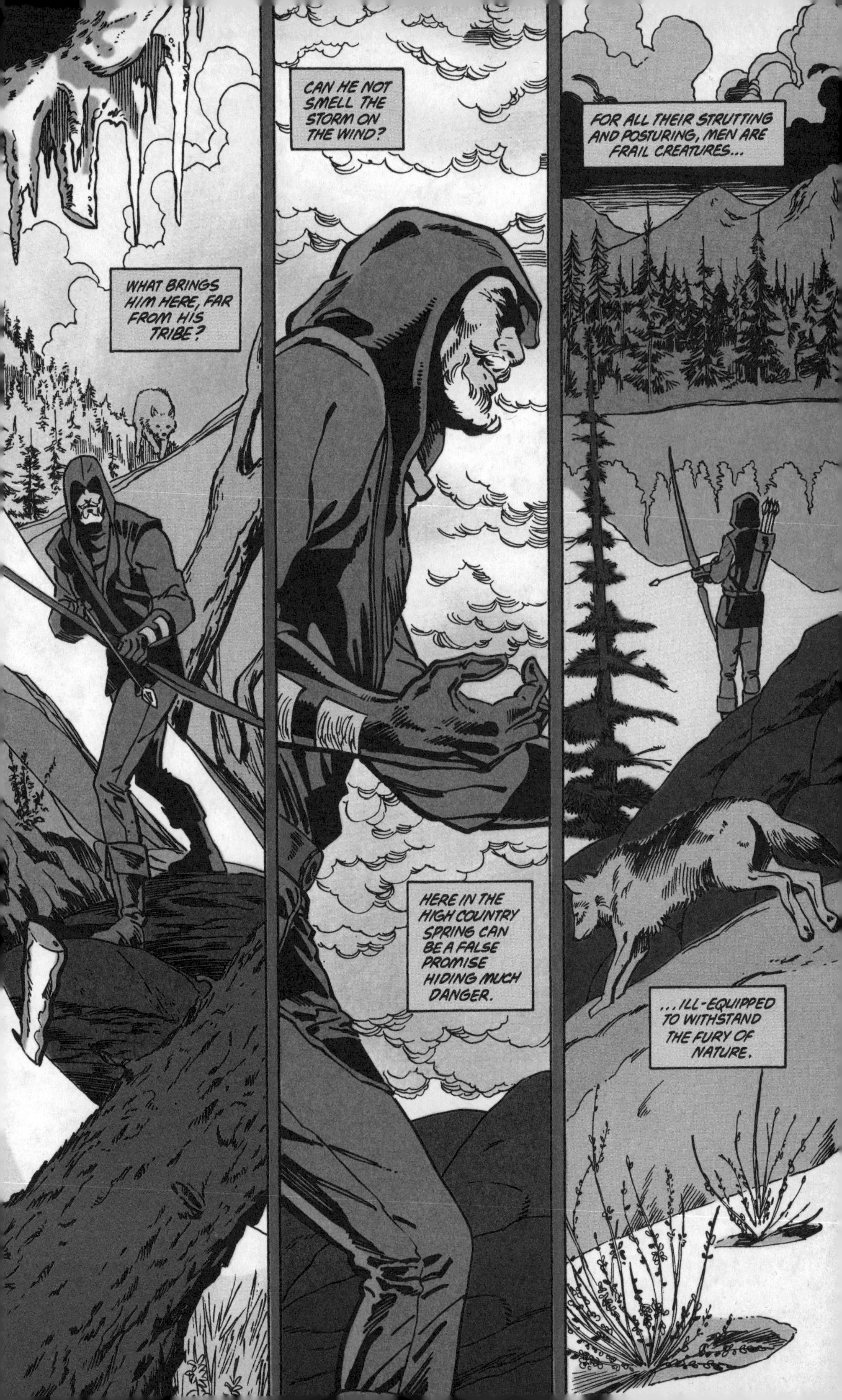
WHAT BRINGS HIM HERE, FAR FROM HIS TRIBE?
CAN HE NOT SMELL THE STORM ON THE WIND?
HERE IN THE HIGH COUNTRY SPRING CAN BE A FALSE PROMISE HIDING MUCH DANGER.
FOR ALL THEIR STRUTTING AND POSTURING, MEN ARE FRAIL CREATURES...
...ILL-EQUIPPED TO WITHSTAND THE FURY OF NATURE.

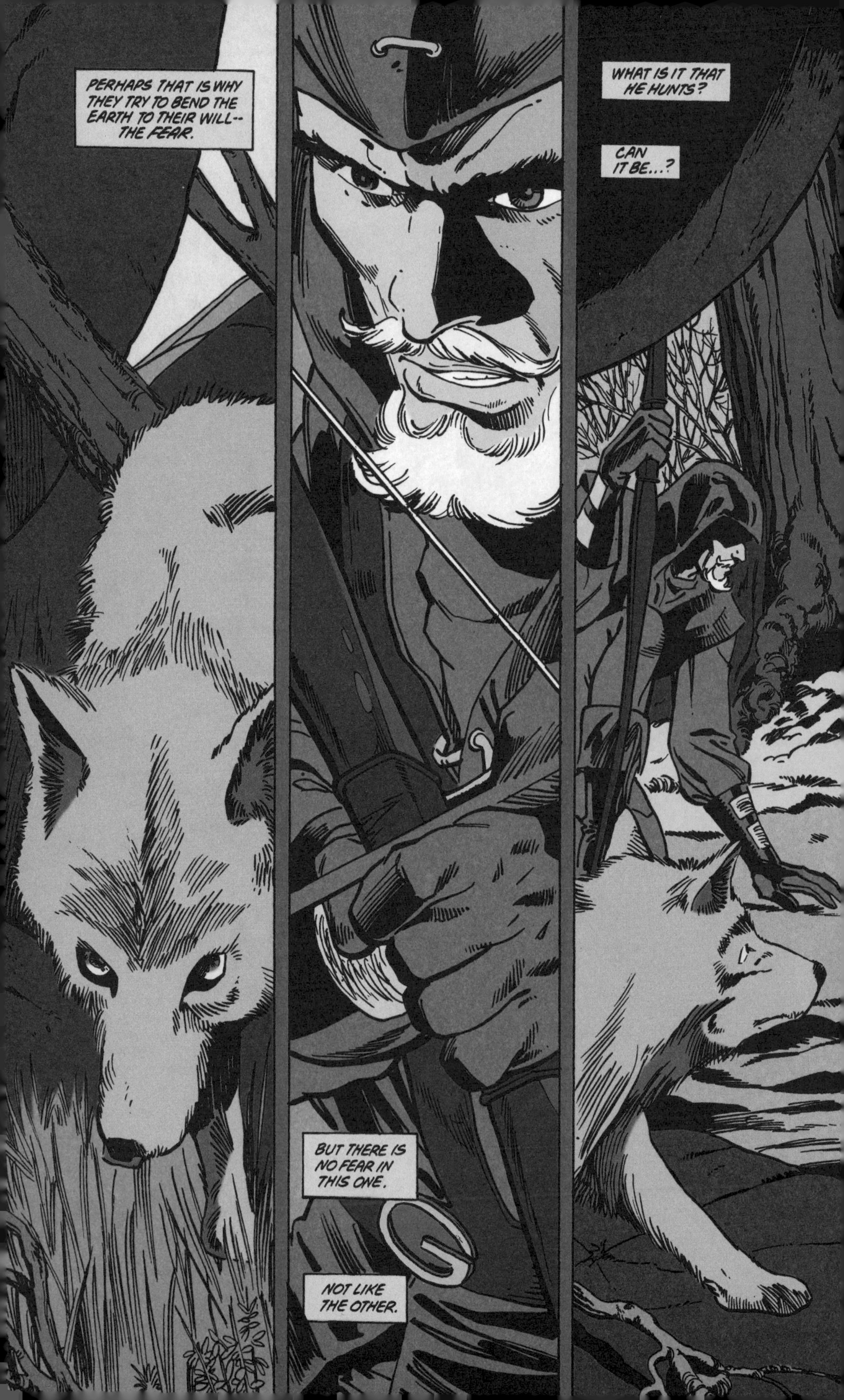
PERHAPS THAT IS WHY THEY TRY TO BEND THE EARTH TO THEIR WILL-- THE FEAR.
WHAT IS IT THAT HE HUNTS?
CAN IT BE...?
BUT THERE IS NO FEAR IN THIS ONE.
NOT LIKE THE OTHER.

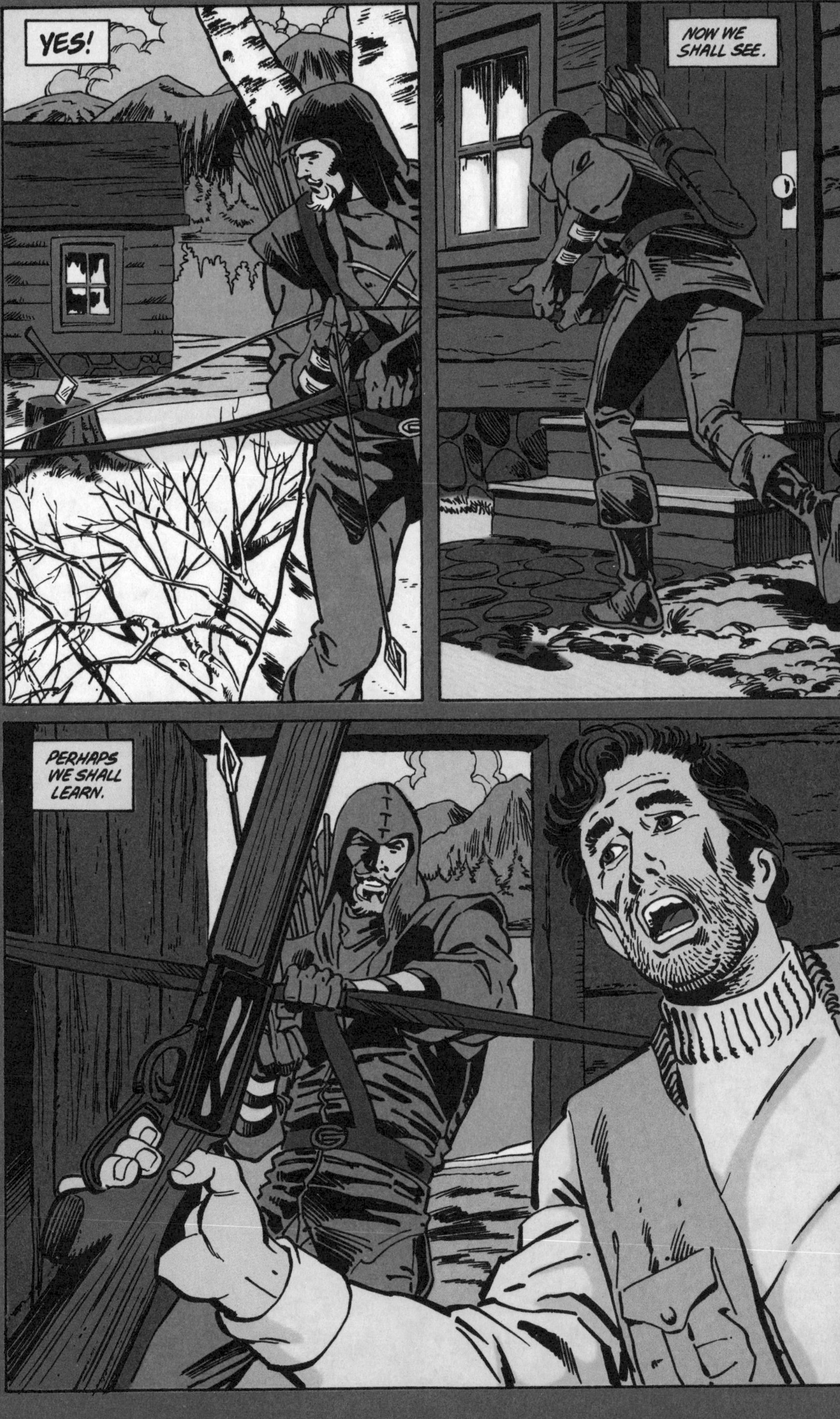
YES!
NOW WE SHALL SEE.
PERHAPS WE SHALL LEARN.

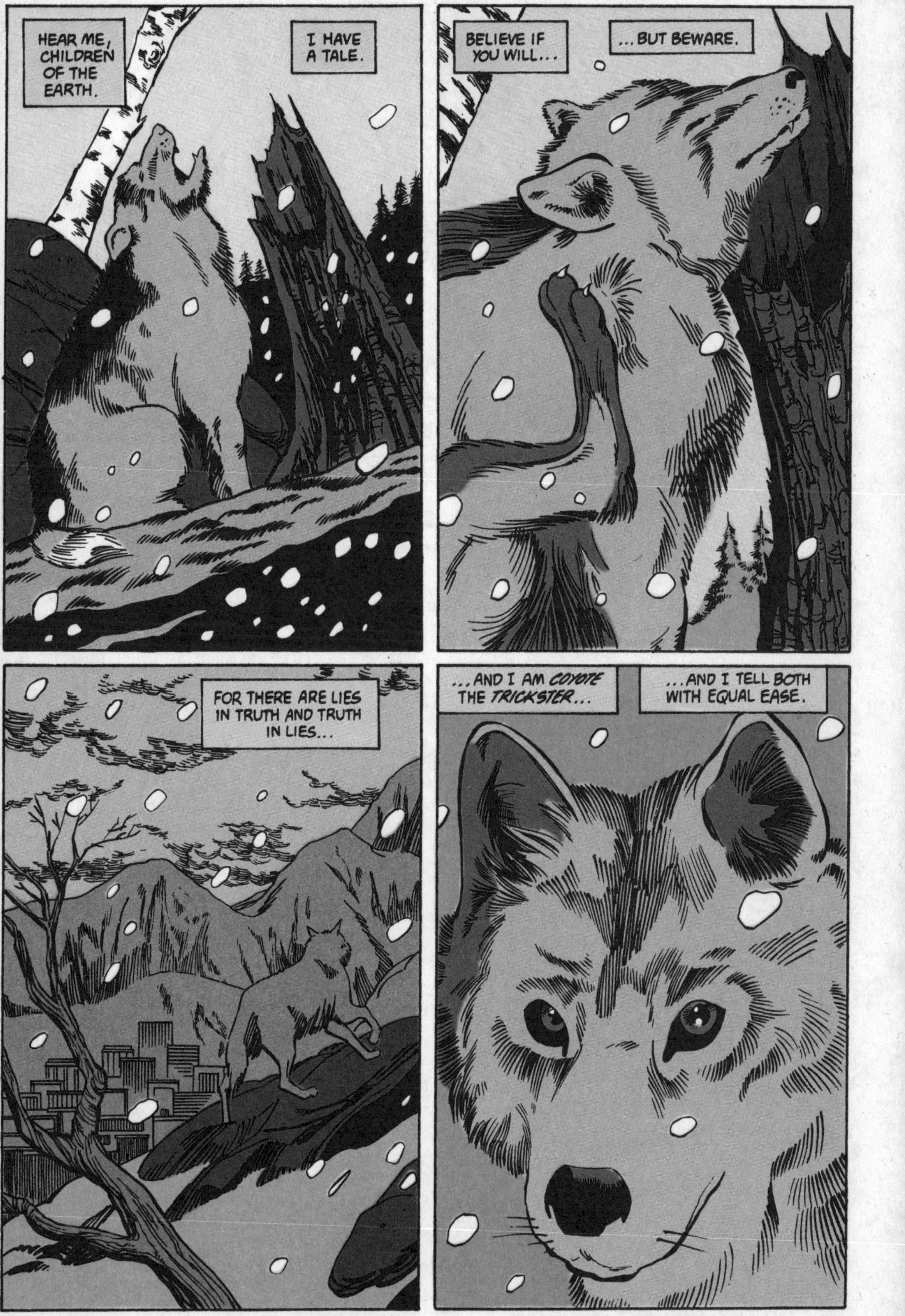
HEAR ME, CHILDREN OF THE EARTH.
I HAVE A TALE.
BELIEVE IF YOU WILL...
...BUT BEWARE.
FOR THERE ARE LIES IN TRUTH AND TRUTH IN LIES...
...AND I AM COYOTE THE TRICKSTER...
...AND I TELL BOTH WITH EQUAL EASE.

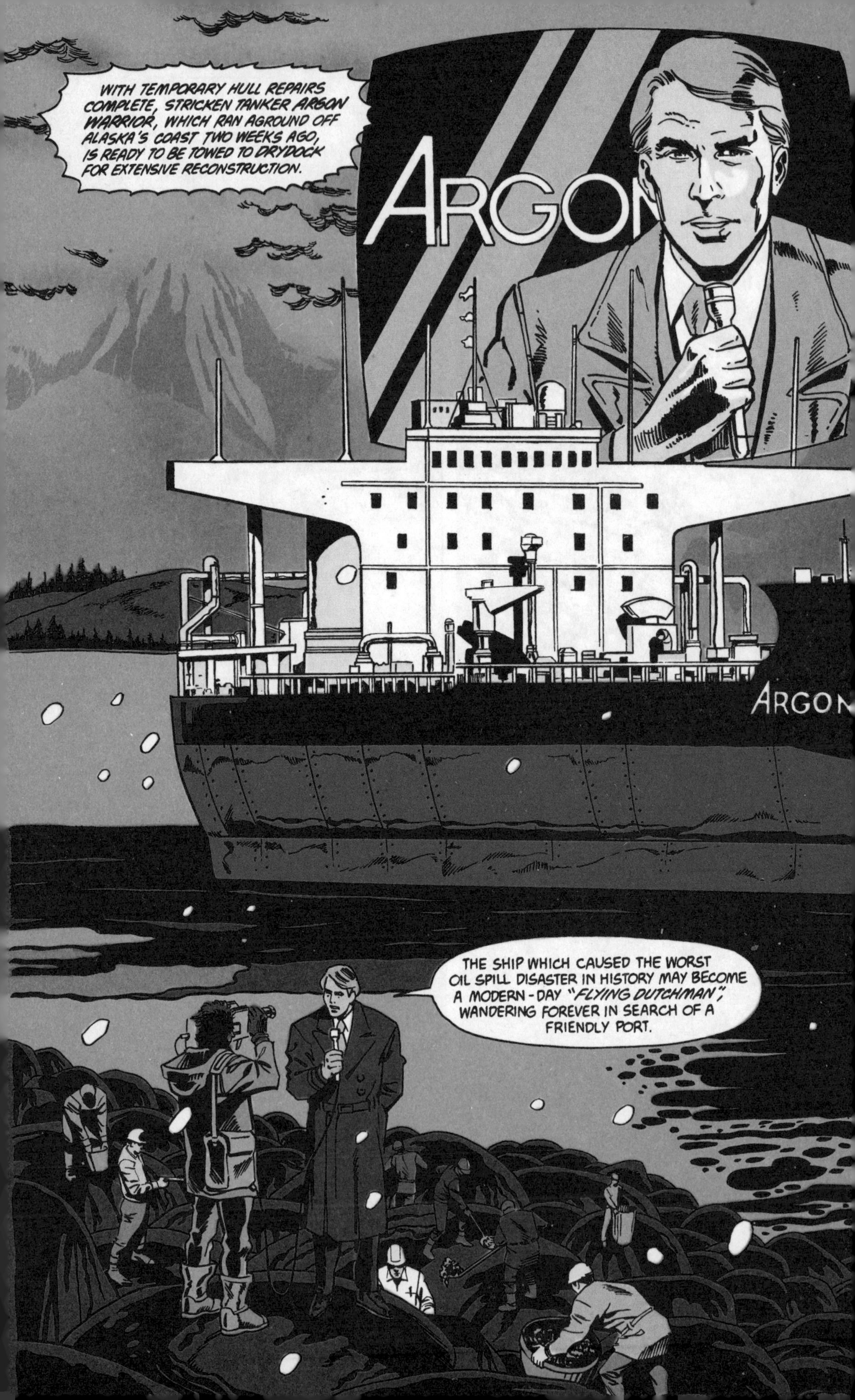

WITH TEMPORARY HULL REPAIRS COMPLETE, STRICKEN TANKER ARGON WARRIOR, WHICH RAN AGROUND OFF ALASKA'S COAST TWO WEEKS AGO, IS READY TO BE TOWED TO DRYDOCK FOR EXTENSIVE RECONSTRUCTION.
ARGON
ARGON
THE SHIP WHICH CAUSED THE WORST OIL SPILL DISASTER IN HISTORY MAY BECOME A MODERN-DAY "FLYING DUTCHMAN," WANDERING FOREVER IN SEARCH OF A FRIENDLY PORT.

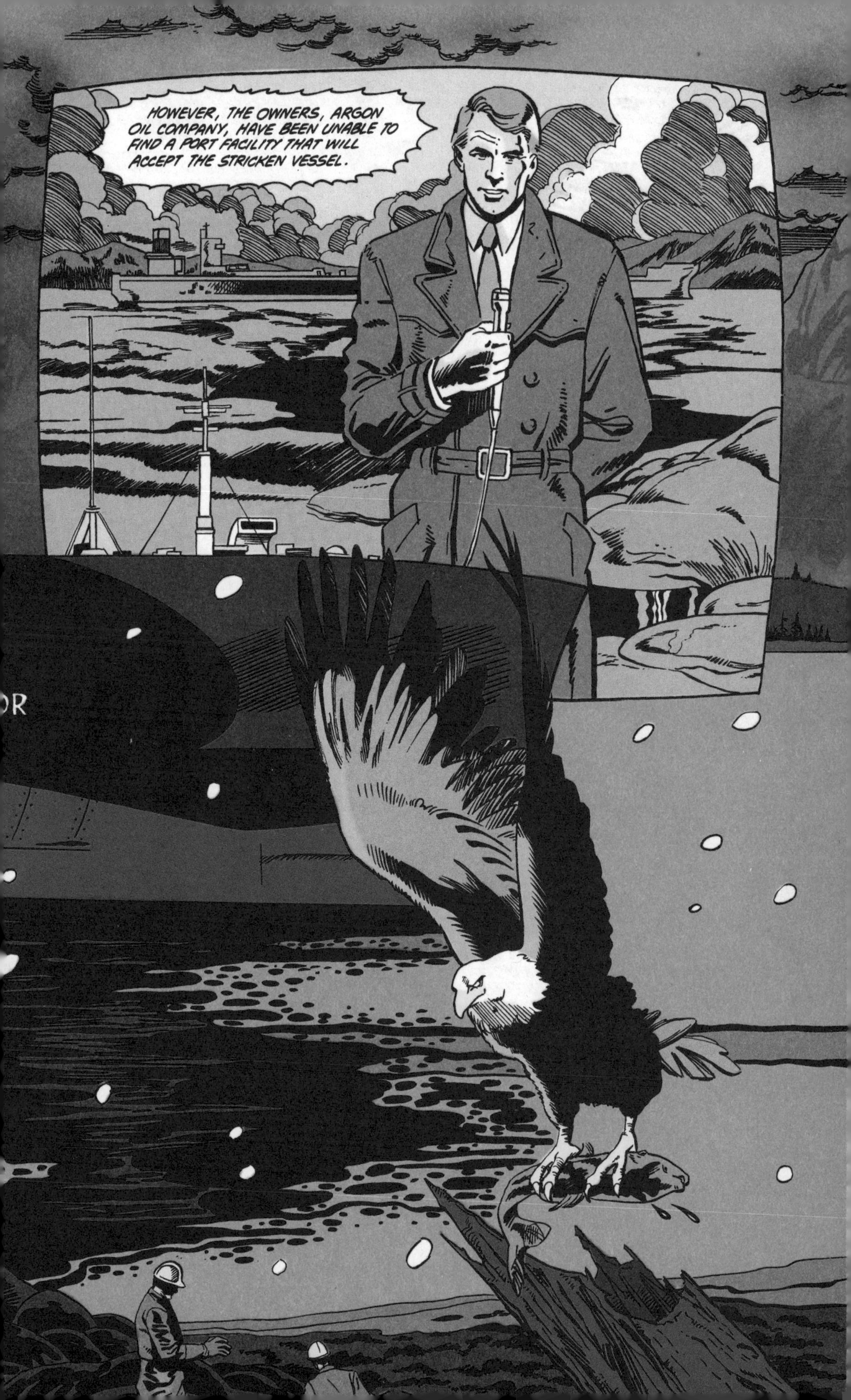
HOWEVER, THE OWNERS, ARGON OIL COMPANY, HAVE BEEN UNABLE TO FIND A PORT FACILITY THAT WILL ACCEPT THE STRICKEN VESSEL.

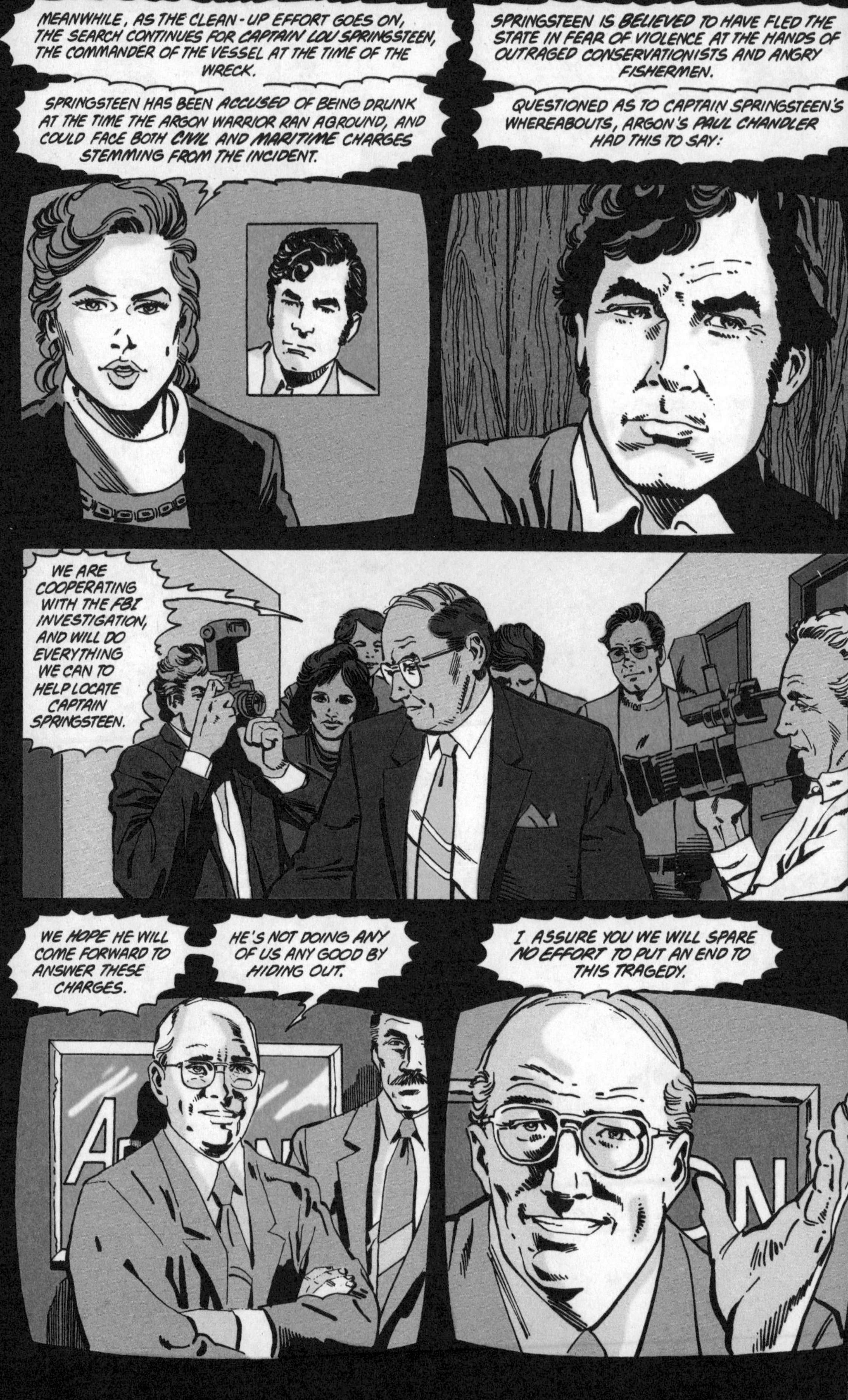
MEANWHILE, AS THE CLEAN-UP EFFORT GOES ON, THE SEARCH CONTINUES FOR CAPTAIN LOU SPRINGSTEEN, THE COMMANDER OF THE VESSEL AT THE TIME OF THE WRECK.
SPRINGSTEEN HAS BEEN ACCUSED OF BEING DRUNK AT THE TIME THE ARGON WARRIOR RAN AGROUND, AND COULD FACE BOTH CIVIL AND MARITIME CHARGES STEMMING FROM THE INCIDENT.
SPRINGSTEEN IS BELIEVED TO HAVE FLED THE STATE IN FEAR OF VIOLENCE AT THE HANDS OF OUTRAGED CONSERVATIONISTS AND ANGRY FISHERMEN.
QUESTIONED AS TO CAPTAIN SPRINGSTEEN'S WHEREABOUTS, ARGON'S PAUL CHANDLER HAD THIS TO SAY:
WE ARE COOPERATING WITH THE FBI INVESTIGATION, AND WILL DO EVERYTHING WE CAN TO HELP LOCATE CAPTAIN SPRINGSTEEN.
WE HOPE HE WILL COME FORWARD TO ANSWER THESE CHARGES.
HE'S NOT DOING ANY OF US ANY GOOD BY HIDING OUT.
I ASSURE YOU WE WILL SPARE NO EFFORT TO PUT AN END TO THIS TRAGEDY.

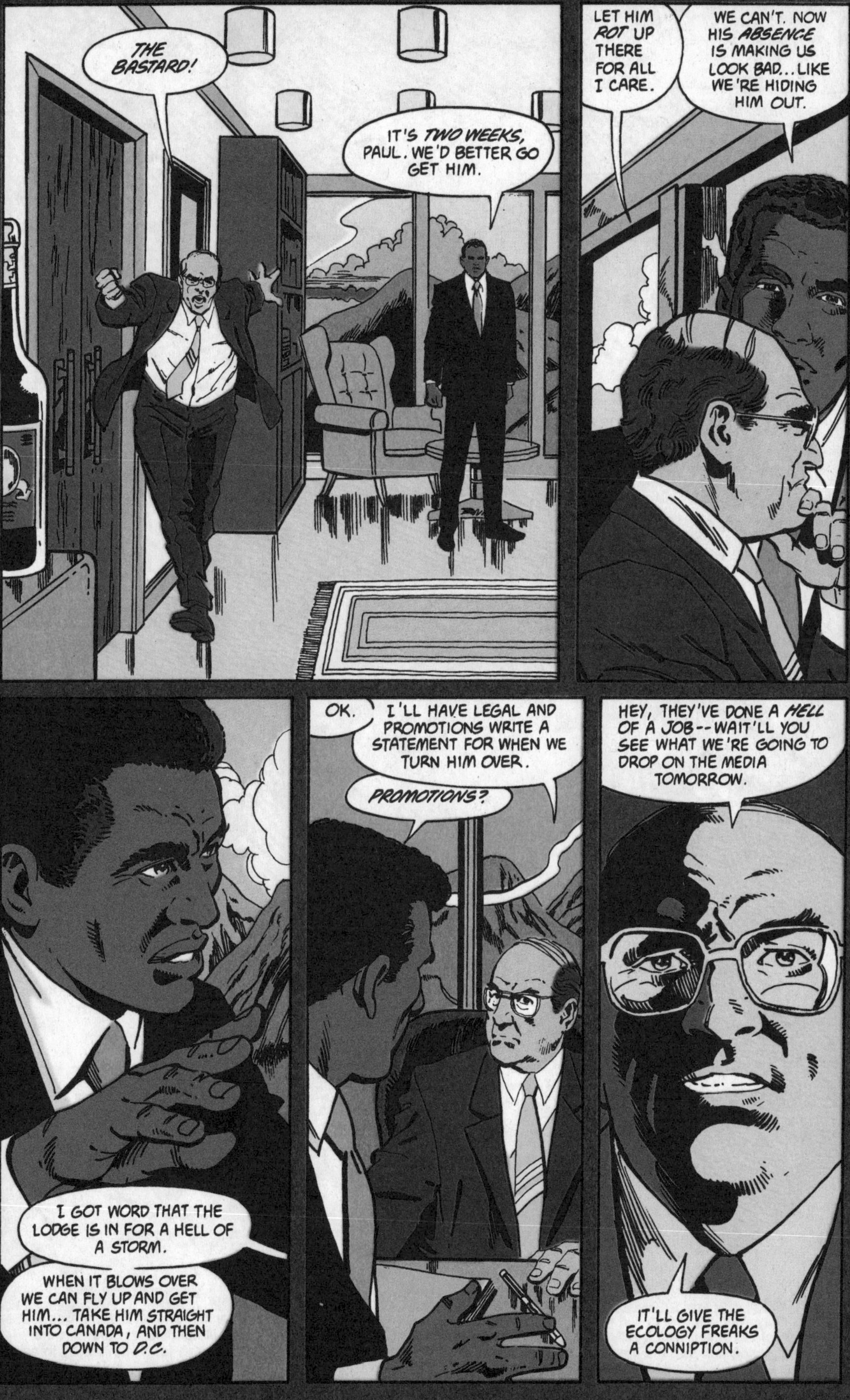
THE BASTARD!
IT'S TWO WEEKS, PAUL. WE'D BETTER GO GET HIM.
LET HIM ROT UP THERE FOR ALL I CARE.
WE CAN'T. NOW HIS ABSENCE IS MAKING US LOOK BAD... LIKE WE'RE HIDING HIM OUT.
I GOT WORD THAT THE LODGE IS IN FOR A HELL OF A STORM.
WHEN IT BLOWS OVER WE CAN FLY UP AND GET HIM... TAKE HIM STRAIGHT INTO CANADA, AND THEN DOWN TO D.C.
OK.
I'LL HAVE LEGAL AND PROMOTIONS WRITE A STATEMENT FOR WHEN WE TURN HIM OVER.
PROMOTIONS?
HEY, THEY'VE DONE A HELL OF A JOB--WAIT'LL YOU SEE WHAT WE'RE GOING TO DROP ON THE MEDIA TOMORROW.
IT'LL GIVE THE ECOLOGY FREAKS A CONNIPTION.

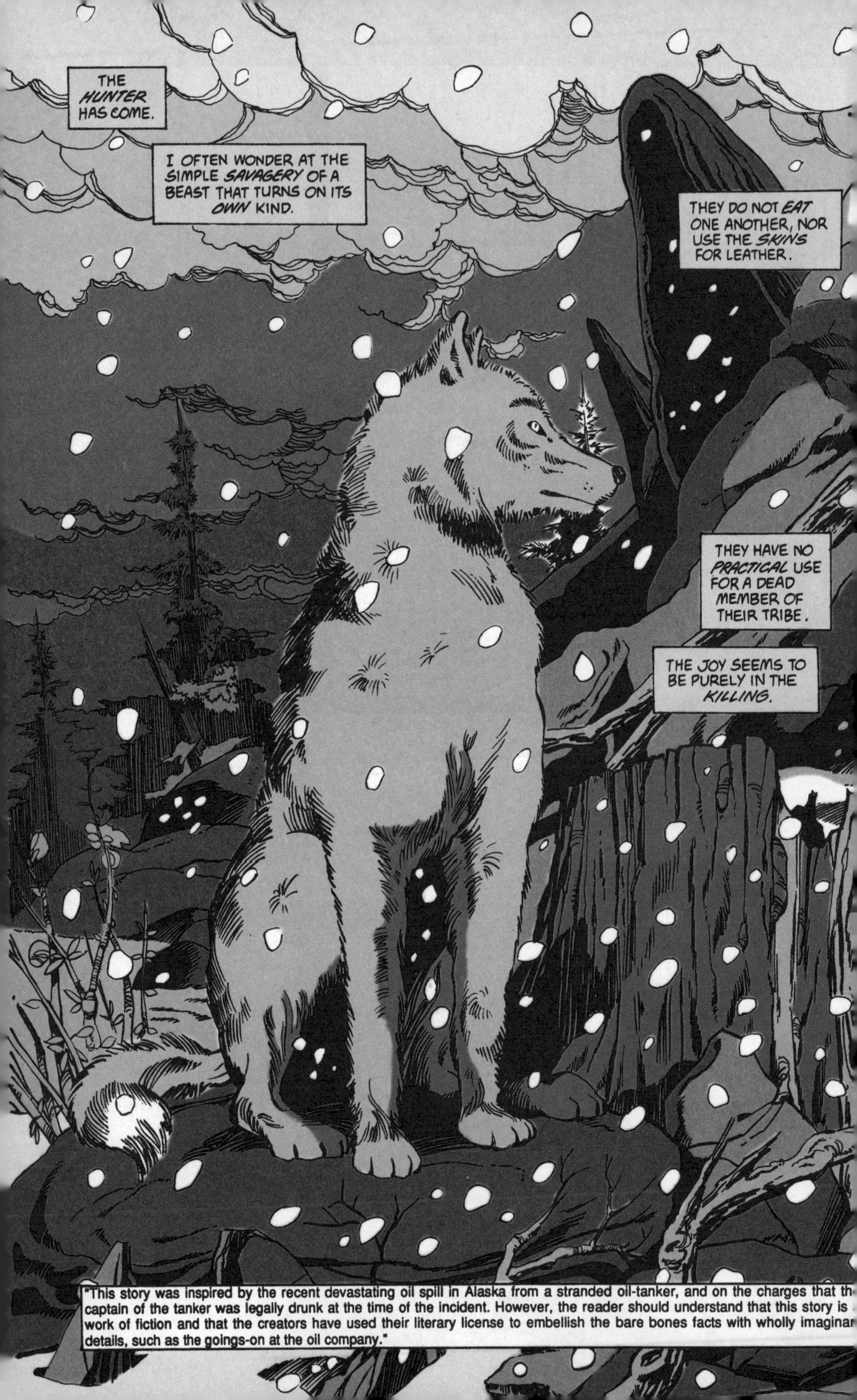
THE *HUNTER* HAS COME.
I OFTEN WONDER AT THE SIMPLE *SAVAGERY* OF A BEAST THAT TURNS ON ITS *OWN* KIND.
THEY DO NOT *EAT* ONE ANOTHER, NOR USE THE *SKINS* FOR LEATHER.
THEY HAVE NO *PRACTICAL* USE FOR A DEAD MEMBER OF THEIR TRIBE.
THE JOY SEEMS TO BE PURELY IN THE *KILLING*.
"This story was inspired by the recent devastating oil spill in Alaska from a stranded oil-tanker, and on the charges that th captain of the tanker was legally drunk at the time of the incident. However, the reader should understand that this story is work of fiction and that the creators have used their literary license to embellish the bare bones facts with wholly imaginar details, such as the goings-on at the oil company."

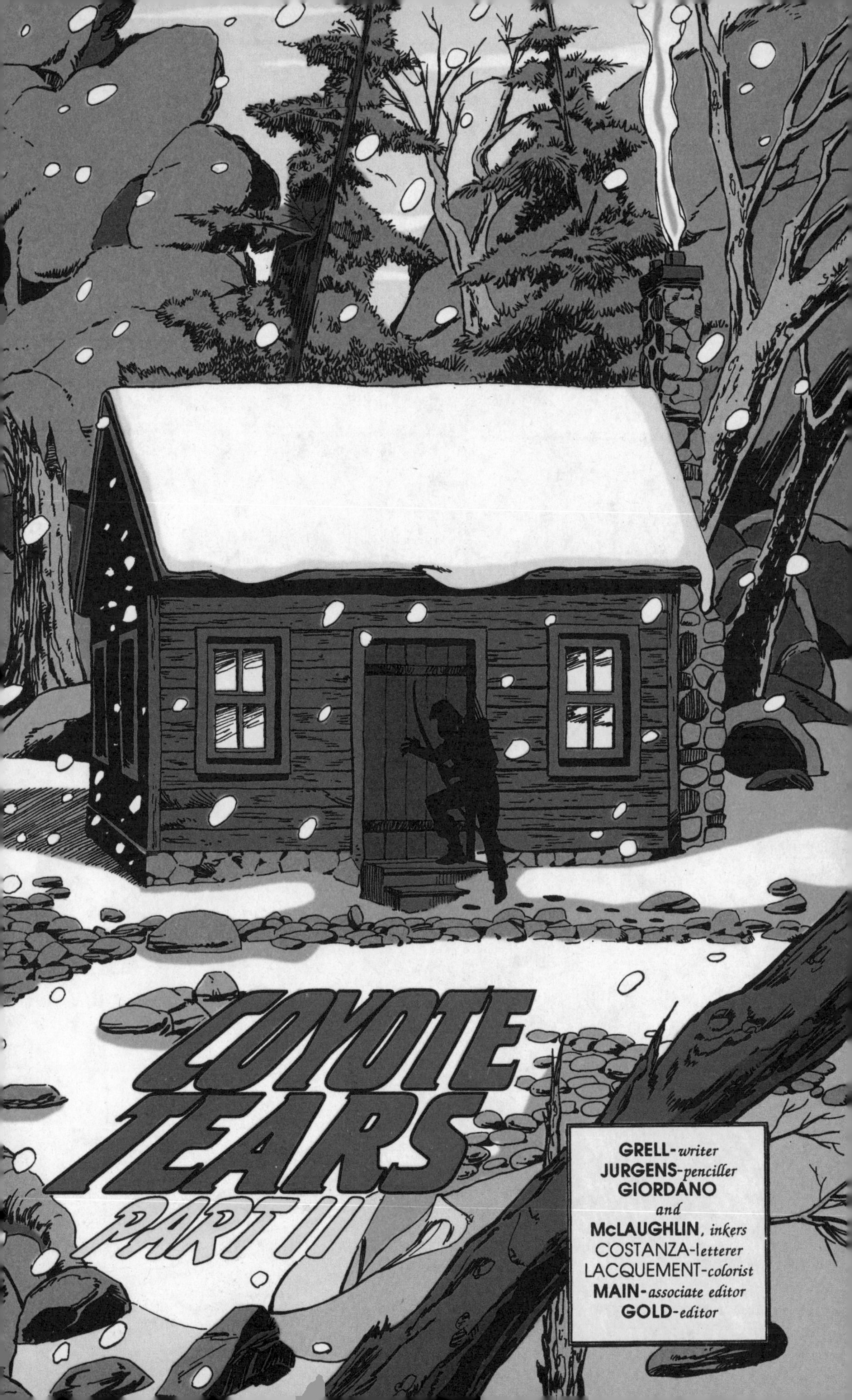
COYOTE TEARS
PART II
GRELL-writer
JURGENS-penciller
GIORDANO
and
McLAUGHLIN, inkers
COSTANZA-letterer
LACQUEMENT-colorist
MAIN-associate editor
GOLD-editor

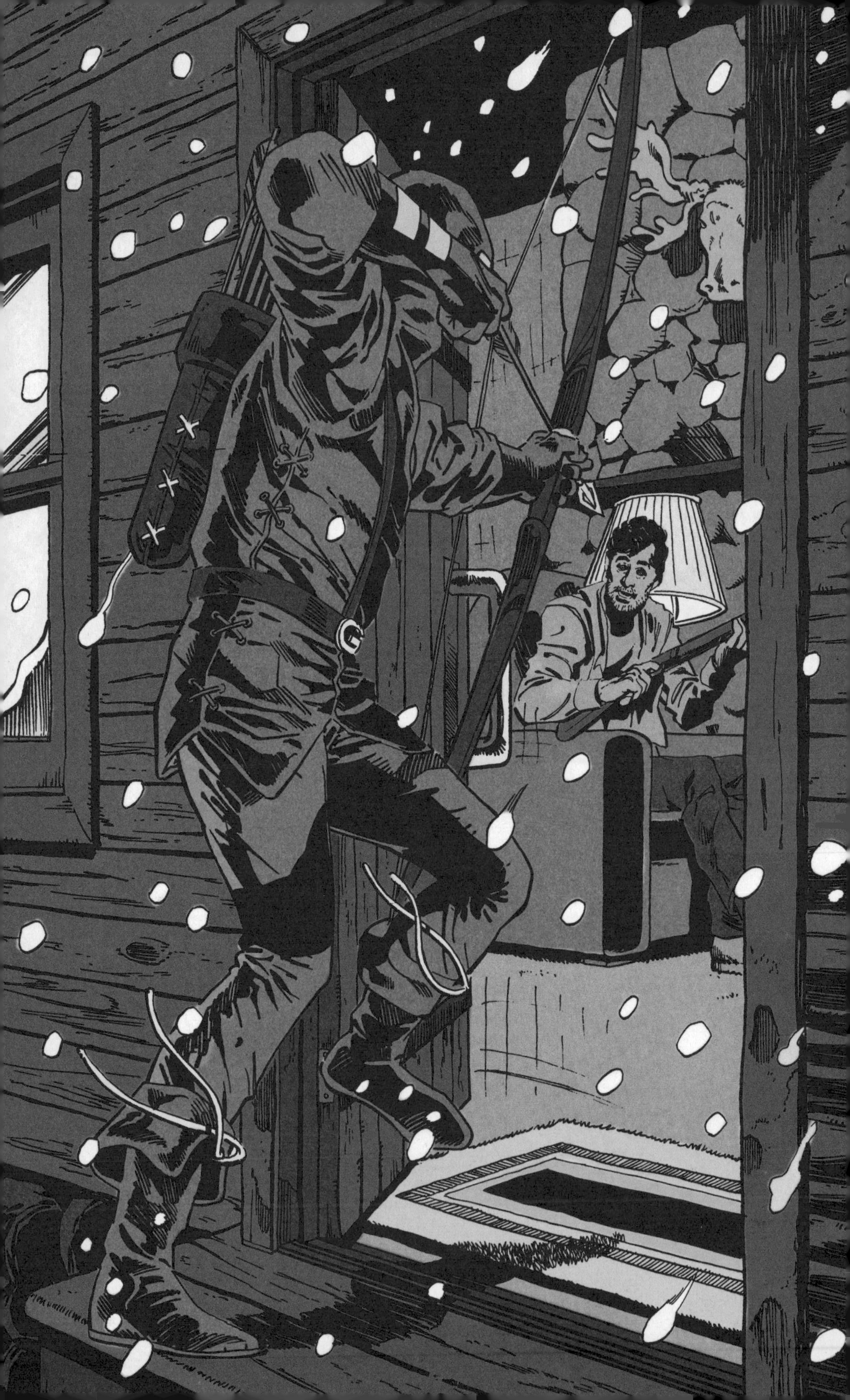

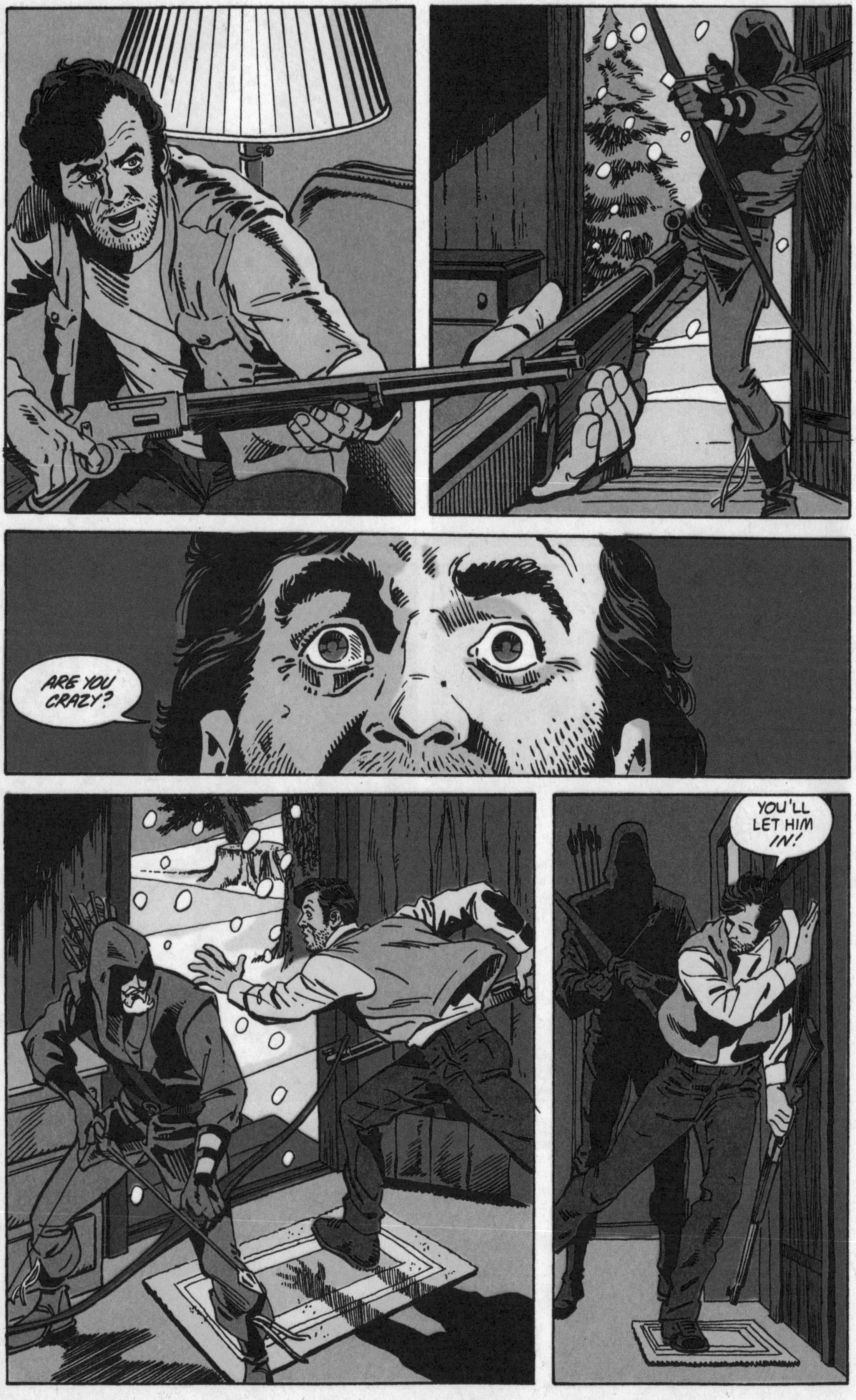
ARE YOU CRAZY?
YOU'LL LET HIM IN!

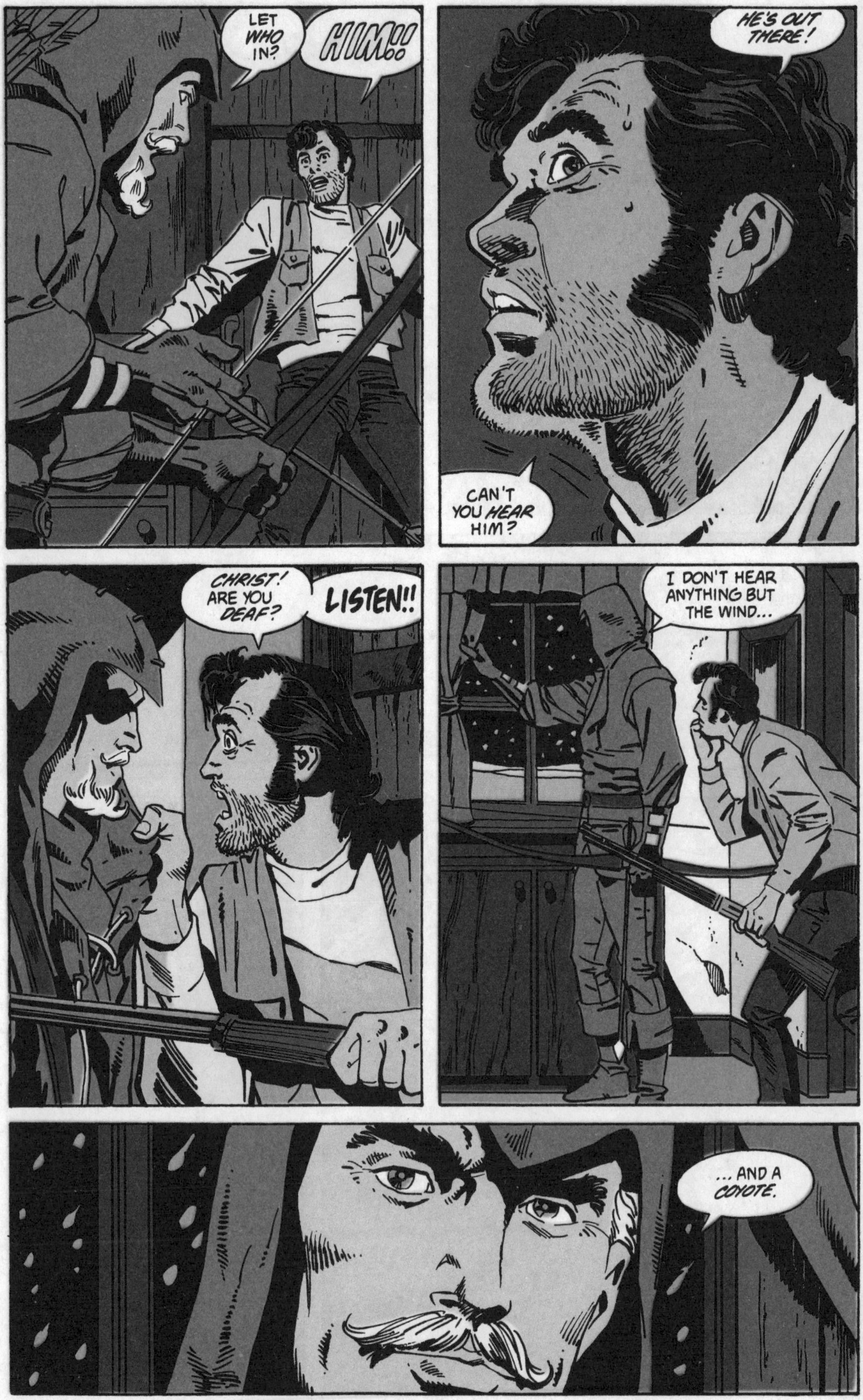
LET WHO IN?
HIM!!
HE'S OUT THERE!
CAN'T YOU HEAR HIM?
CHRIST! ARE YOU DEAF?
LISTEN!!
I DON'T HEAR ANYTHING BUT THE WIND...
...AND A COYOTE.

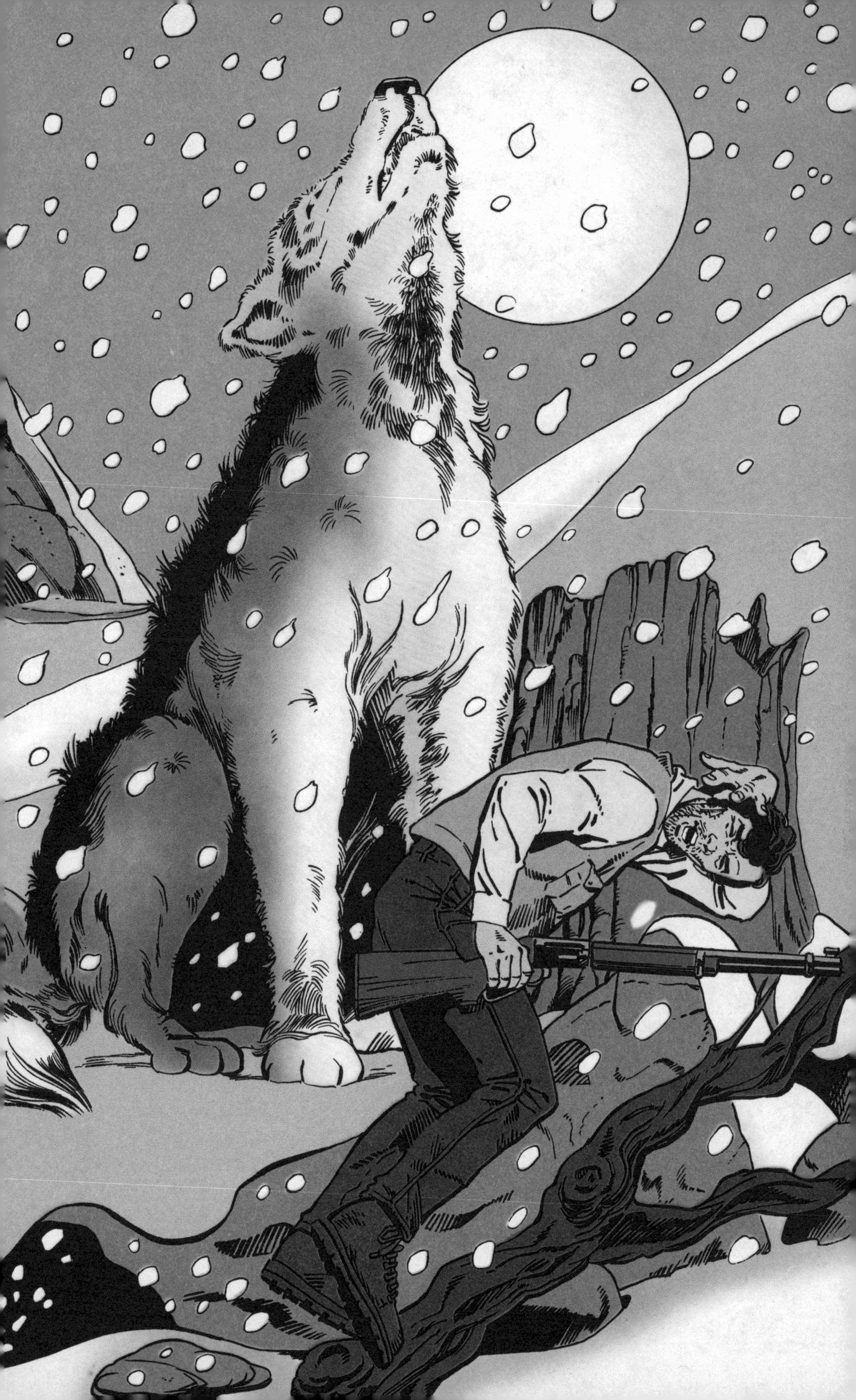

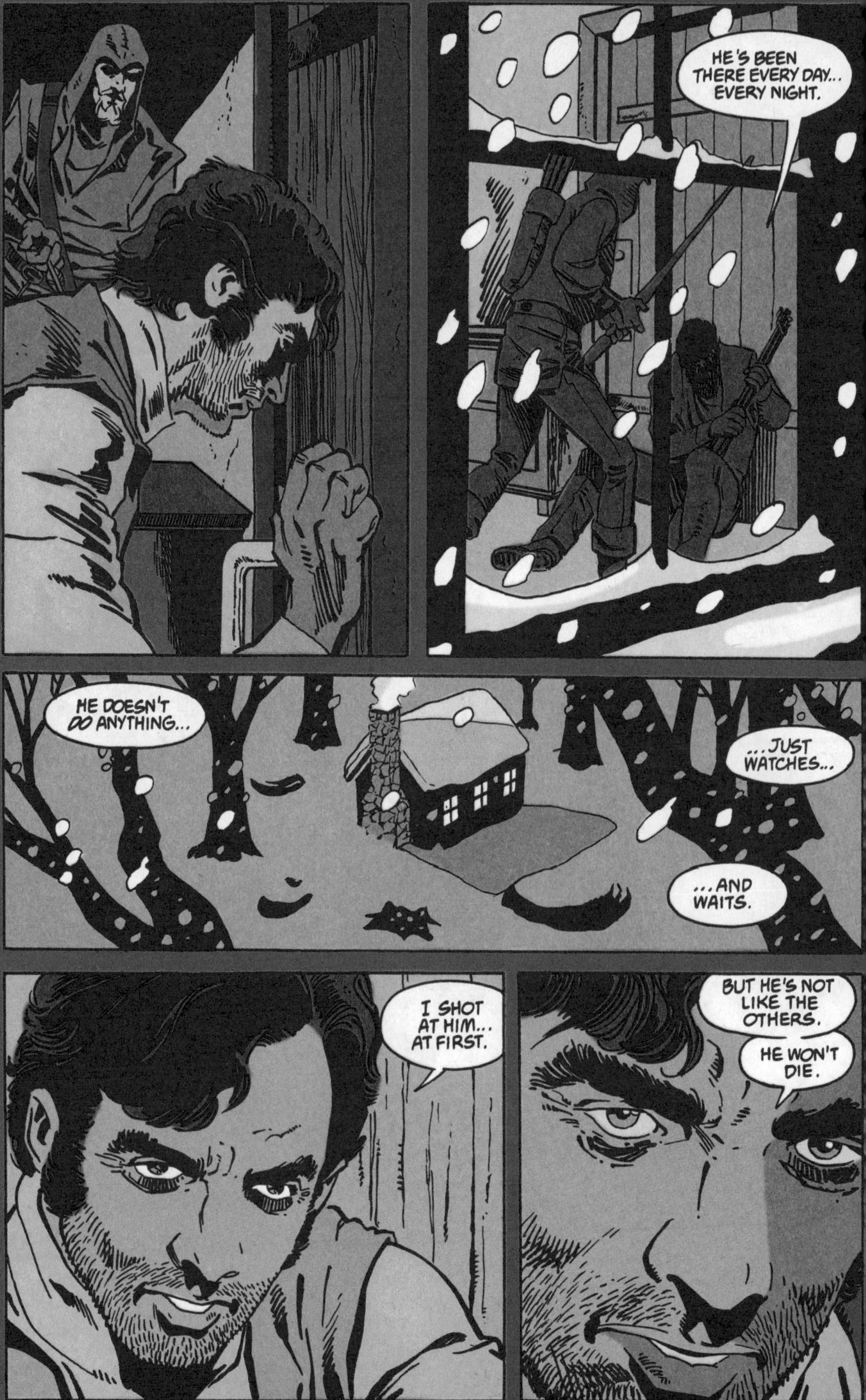
HE'S BEEN THERE EVERY DAY... EVERY NIGHT.
HE DOESN'T DO ANYTHING...
...JUST WATCHES...
...AND WAITS.
I SHOT AT HIM... AT FIRST.
BUT HE'S NOT LIKE THE OTHERS.
HE WON'T DIE.

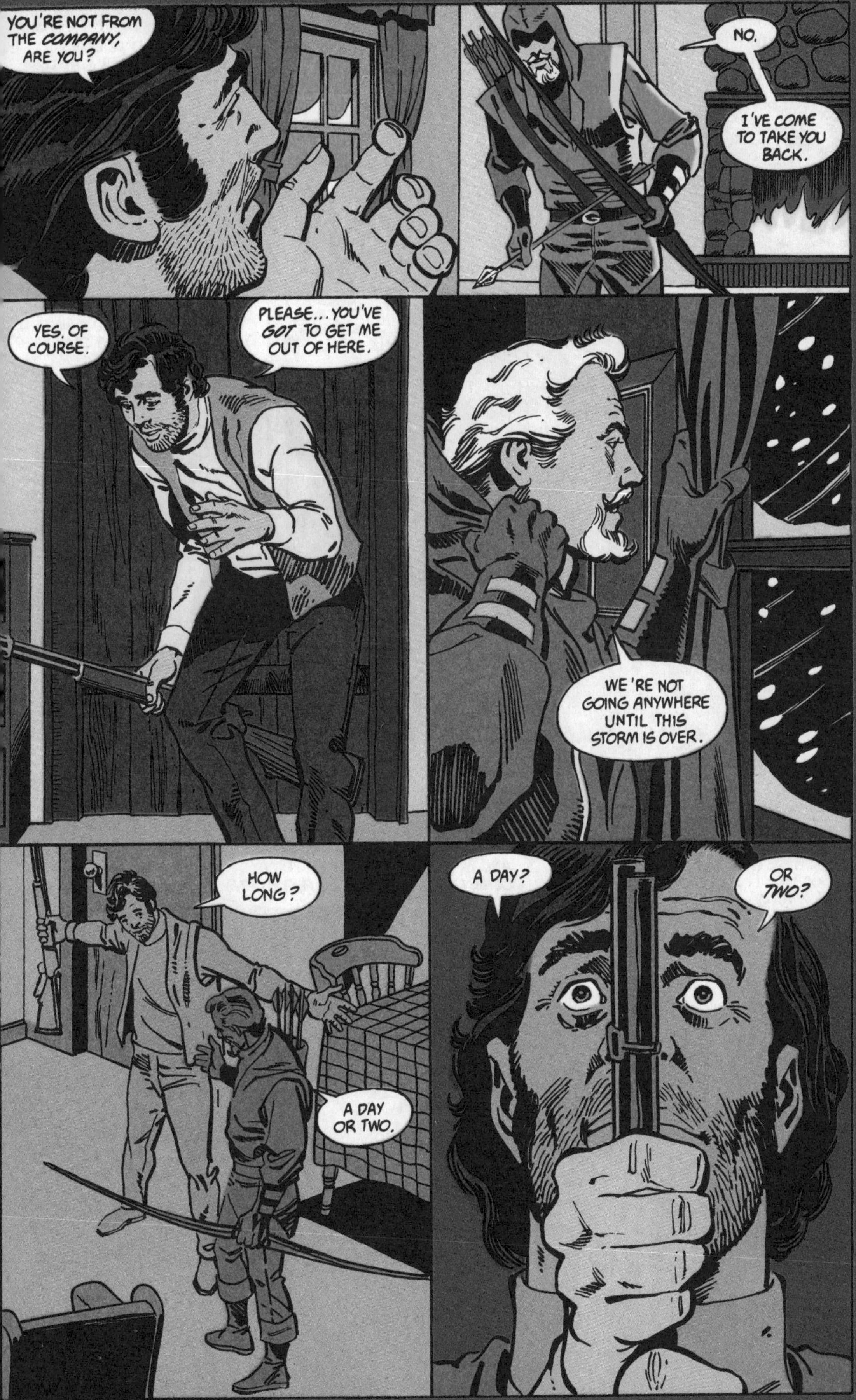
YOU'RE NOT FROM THE *COMPANY*, ARE YOU?
NO.
I'VE COME TO TAKE YOU BACK.
YES. OF COURSE.
PLEASE... YOU'VE *GOT* TO GET ME OUT OF HERE.
WE'RE NOT GOING ANYWHERE UNTIL THIS STORM IS OVER.
HOW LONG?
A DAY OR TWO.
A DAY?
OR *TWO?*

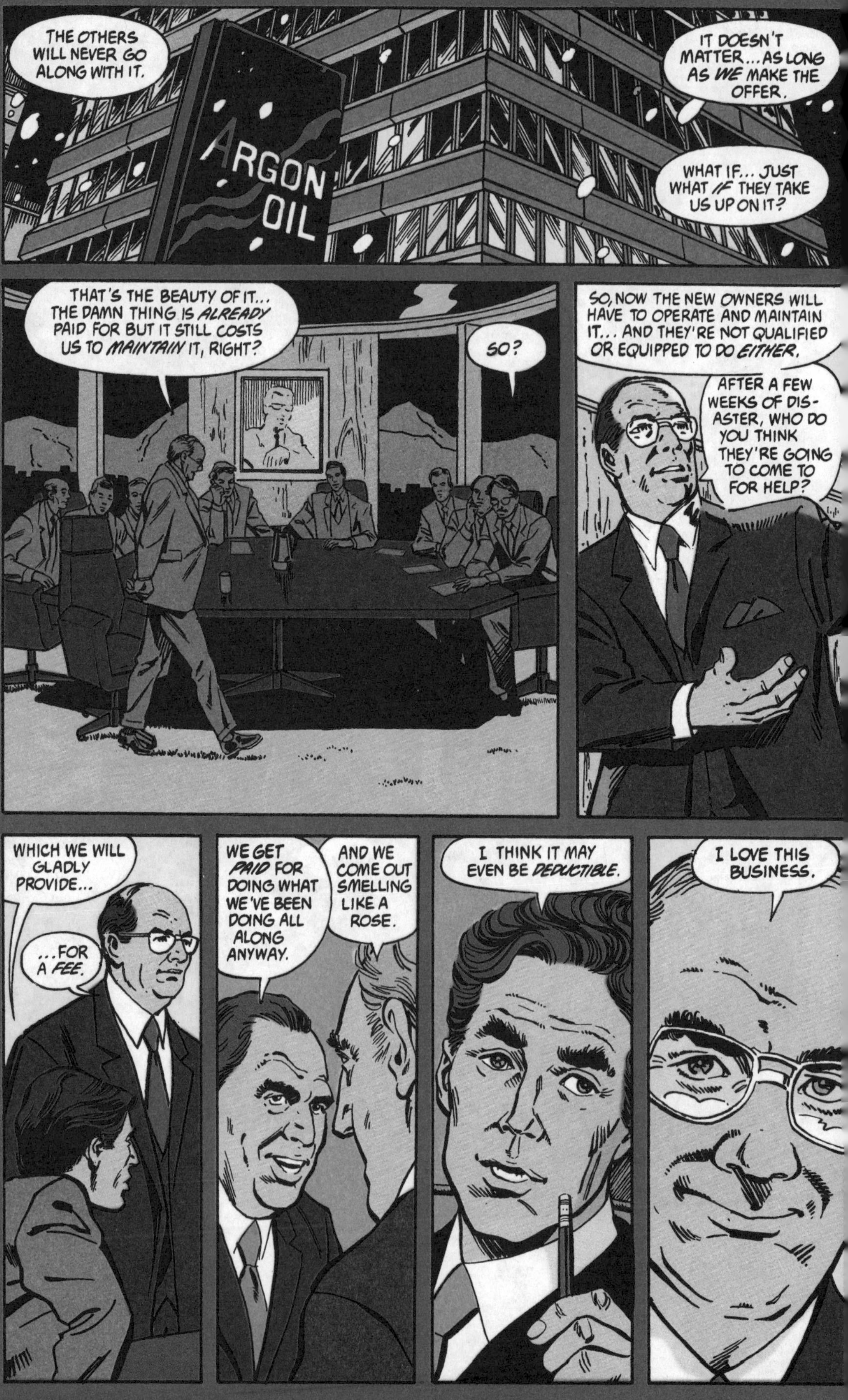
THE OTHERS WILL NEVER GO ALONG WITH IT.
IT DOESN'T MATTER... AS LONG AS WE MAKE THE OFFER.
ARGON OIL
WHAT IF... JUST WHAT IF THEY TAKE US UP ON IT?
THAT'S THE BEAUTY OF IT... THE DAMN THING IS ALREADY PAID FOR BUT IT STILL COSTS US TO MAINTAIN IT, RIGHT?
SO?
SO, NOW THE NEW OWNERS WILL HAVE TO OPERATE AND MAINTAIN IT... AND THEY'RE NOT QUALIFIED OR EQUIPPED TO DO EITHER.
AFTER A FEW WEEKS OF DIS-ASTER, WHO DO YOU THINK THEY'RE GOING TO COME TO FOR HELP?
WHICH WE WILL GLADLY PROVIDE...
...FOR A FEE.
WE GET PAID FOR DOING WHAT WE'VE BEEN DOING ALL ALONG ANYWAY.
AND WE COME OUT SMELLING LIKE A ROSE.
I THINK IT MAY EVEN BE DEDUCTIBLE.
I LOVE THIS BUSINESS.

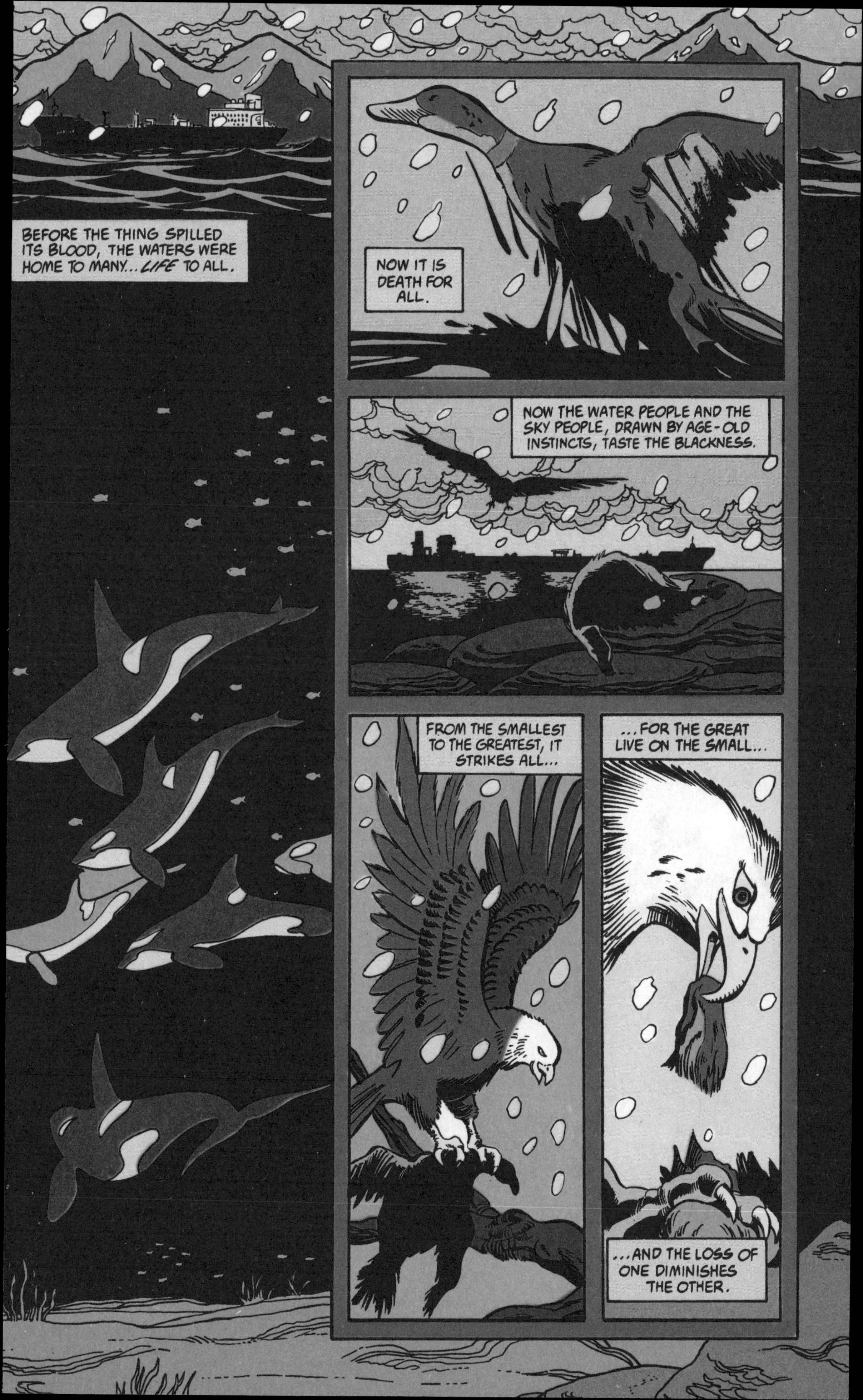
BEFORE THE THING SPILLED ITS BLOOD, THE WATERS WERE HOME TO MANY... *LIFE* TO ALL.
NOW IT IS DEATH FOR ALL.
NOW THE WATER PEOPLE AND THE SKY PEOPLE, DRAWN BY AGE-OLD INSTINCTS, TASTE THE BLACKNESS.
FROM THE SMALLEST TO THE GREATEST, IT STRIKES ALL...
...FOR THE GREAT LIVE ON THE SMALL...
...AND THE LOSS OF ONE DIMINISHES THE OTHER.

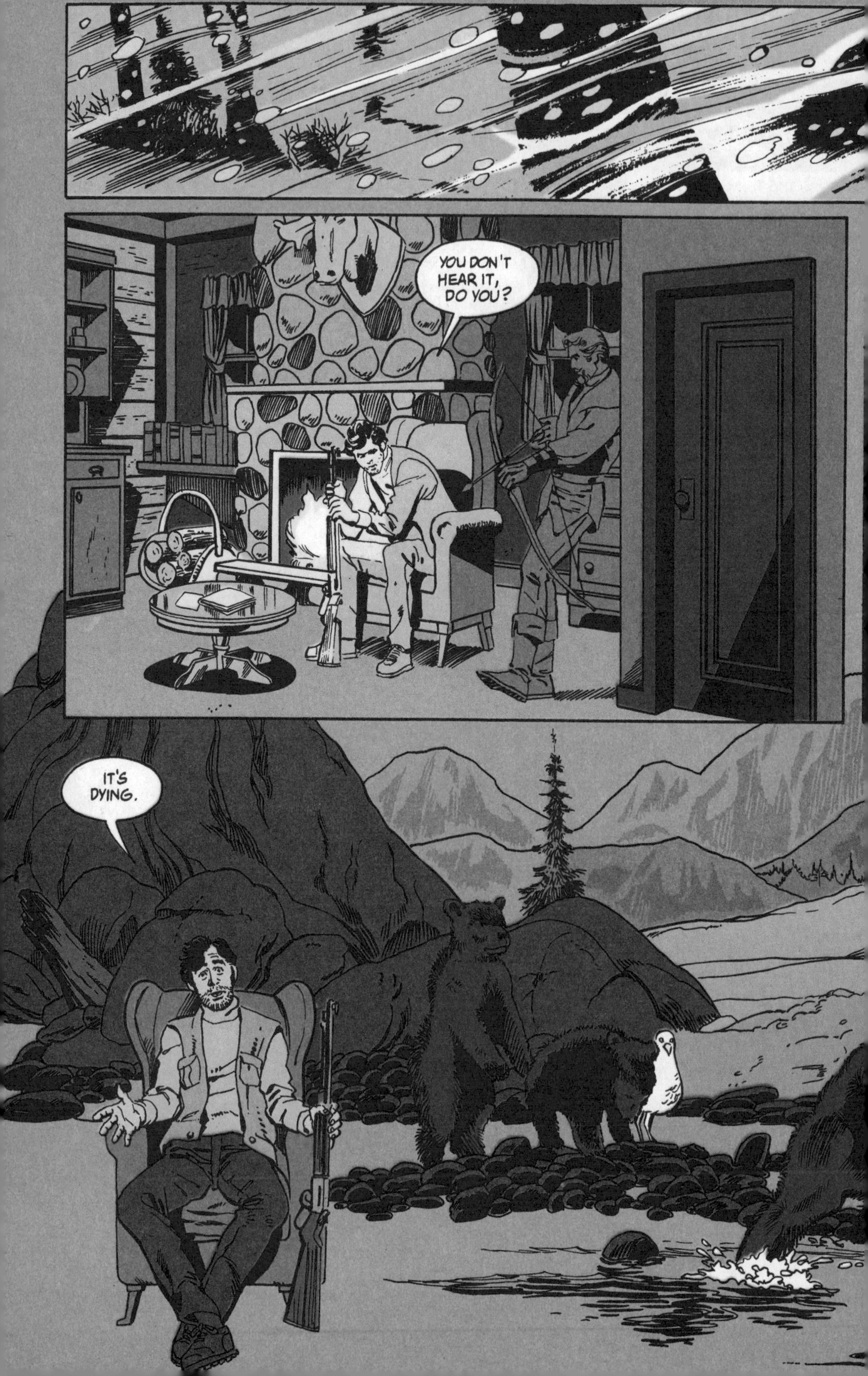
YOU DON'T HEAR IT, DO YOU?
IT'S DYING.

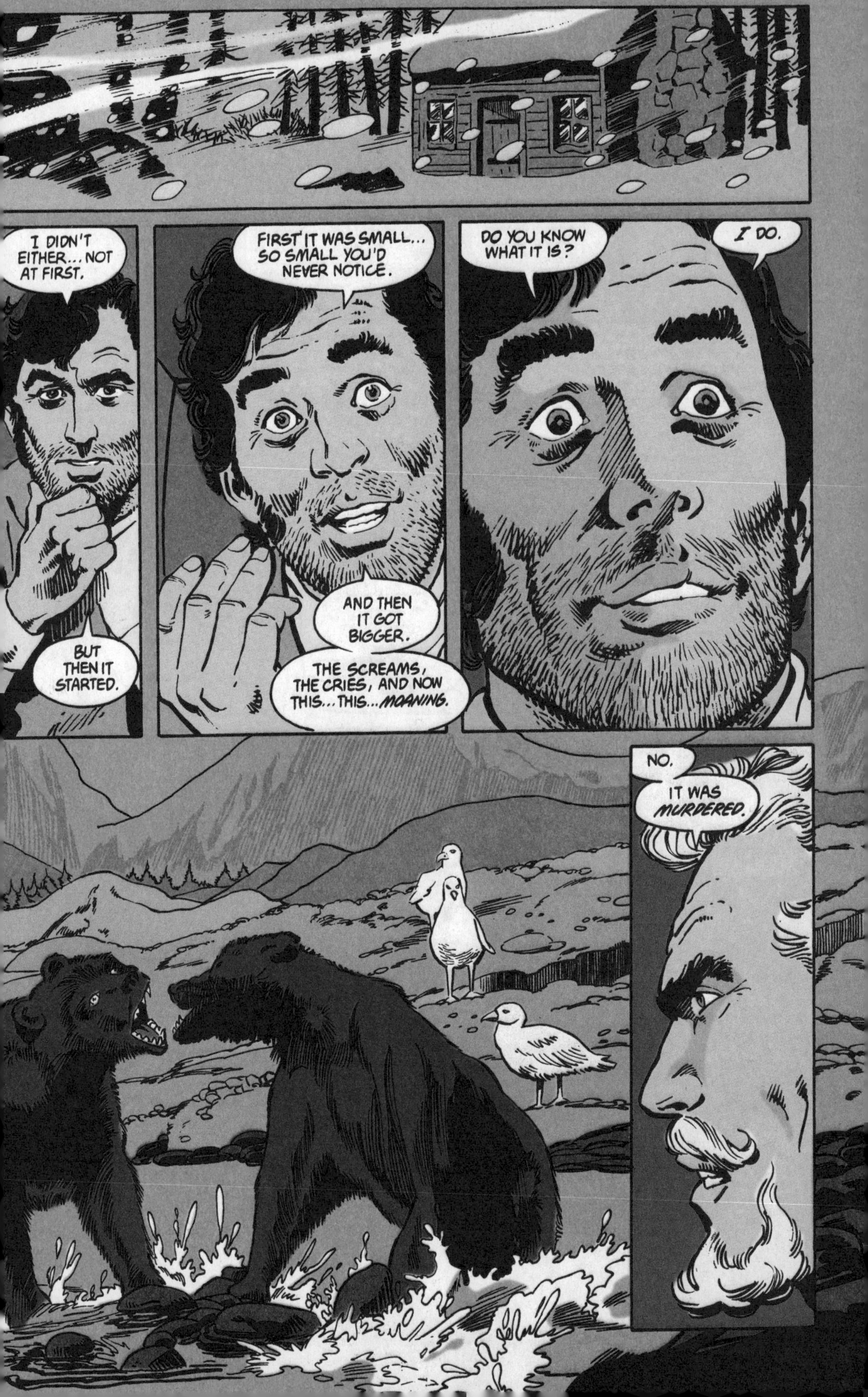
I DIDN'T EITHER... NOT AT FIRST.
BUT THEN IT STARTED.
FIRST IT WAS SMALL... SO SMALL YOU'D NEVER NOTICE.
AND THEN IT GOT BIGGER.
THE SCREAMS, THE CRIES, AND NOW THIS... THIS... *MOANING*.
DO YOU KNOW WHAT IT IS?
*I* DO.
NO.
IT WAS *MURDERED*.

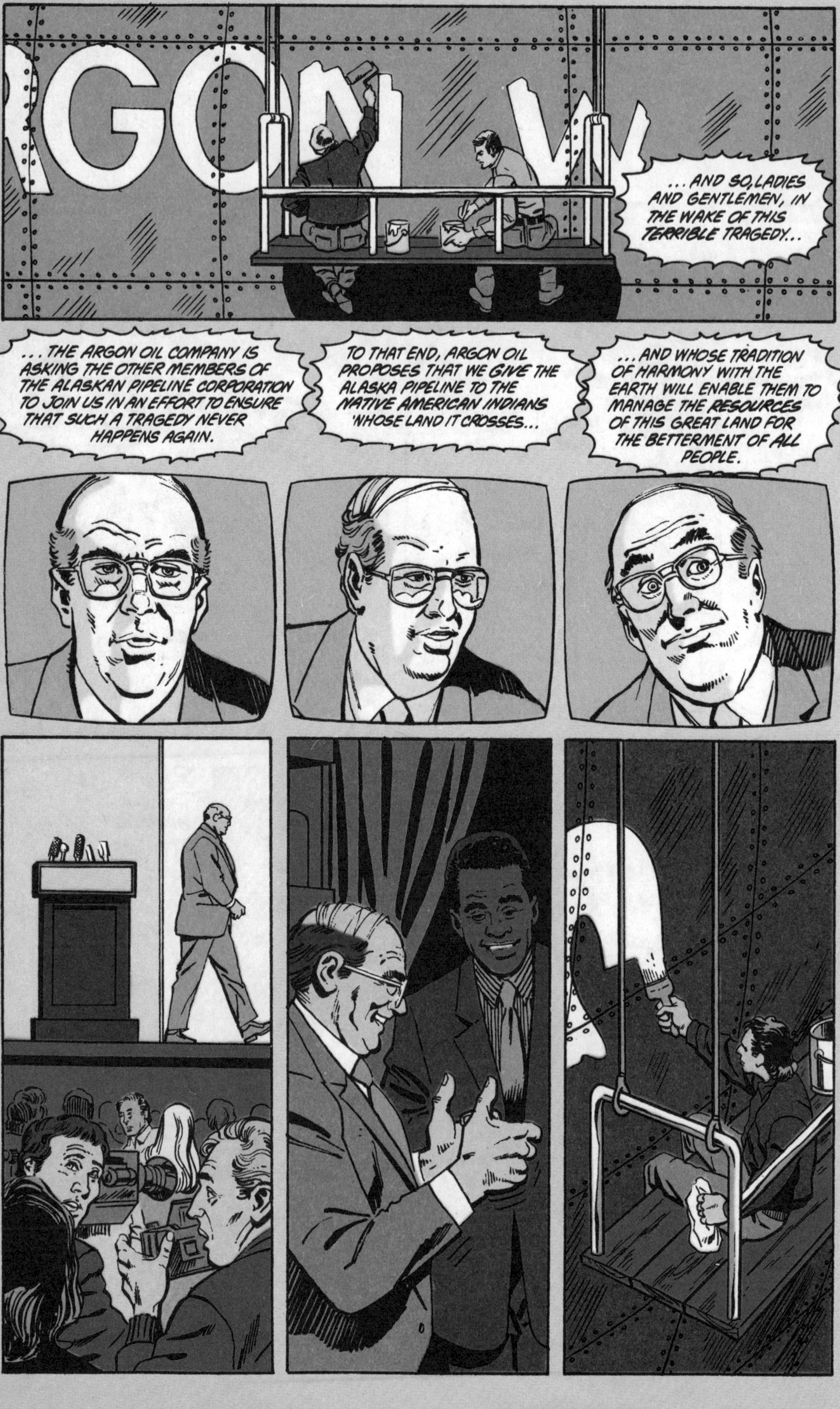

RGON
... AND SO, LADIES AND GENTLEMEN, IN THE WAKE OF THIS TERRIBLE TRAGEDY...
... THE ARGON OIL COMPANY IS ASKING THE OTHER MEMBERS OF THE ALASKAN PIPELINE CORPORATION TO JOIN US IN AN EFFORT TO ENSURE THAT SUCH A TRAGEDY NEVER HAPPENS AGAIN.
TO THAT END, ARGON OIL PROPOSES THAT WE GIVE THE ALASKA PIPELINE TO THE NATIVE AMERICAN INDIANS WHOSE LAND IT CROSSES...
... AND WHOSE TRADITION OF HARMONY WITH THE EARTH WILL ENABLE THEM TO MANAGE THE RESOURCES OF THIS GREAT LAND FOR THE BETTERMENT OF ALL PEOPLE.

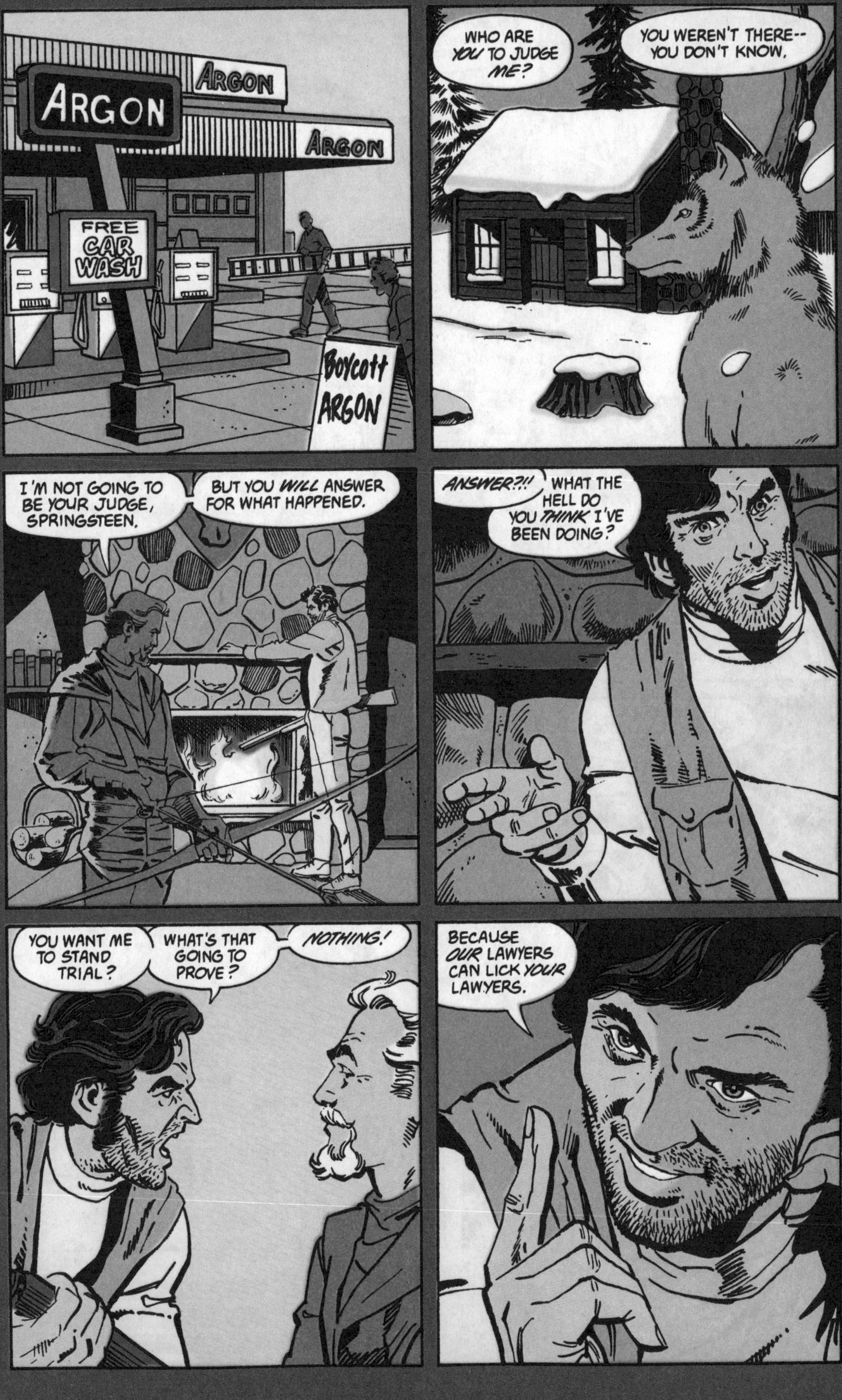
ARGON
ARGON
ARGON
FREE CAR WASH
Boycott ARGON
WHO ARE YOU TO JUDGE ME?
YOU WEREN'T THERE-- YOU DON'T KNOW.
I'M NOT GOING TO BE YOUR JUDGE, SPRINGSTEEN.
BUT YOU WILL ANSWER FOR WHAT HAPPENED.
ANSWER?!!
WHAT THE HELL DO YOU THINK I'VE BEEN DOING?
YOU WANT ME TO STAND TRIAL?
WHAT'S THAT GOING TO PROVE?
NOTHING!
BECAUSE OUR LAWYERS CAN LICK YOUR LAWYERS.

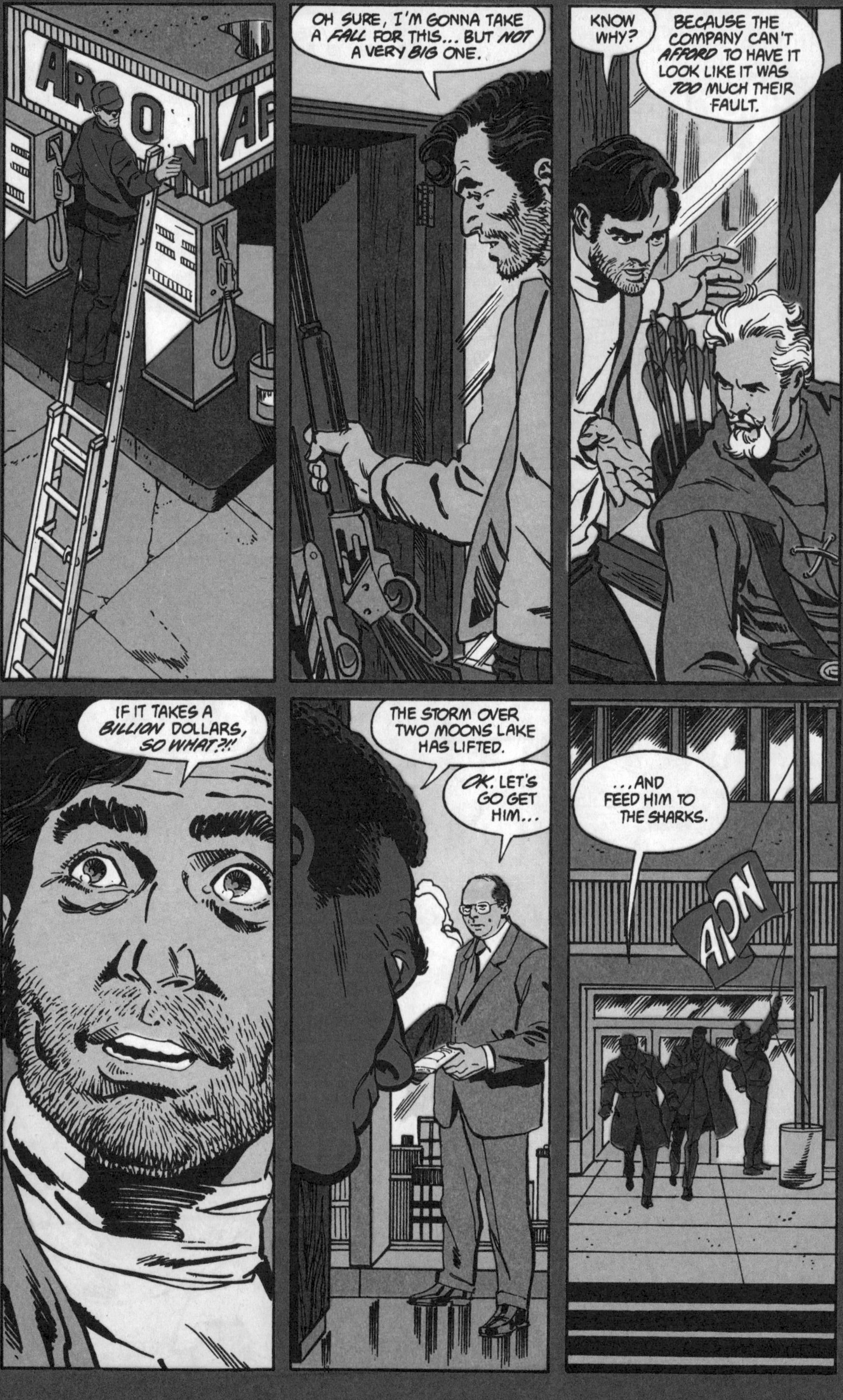
OH SURE, I'M GONNA TAKE A FALL FOR THIS... BUT NOT A VERY BIG ONE.
KNOW WHY?
BECAUSE THE COMPANY CAN'T AFFORD TO HAVE IT LOOK LIKE IT WAS TOO MUCH THEIR FAULT.
IF IT TAKES A BILLION DOLLARS, SO WHAT?!!
THE STORM OVER TWO MOONS LAKE HAS LIFTED.
OK. LET'S GO GET HIM...
...AND FEED HIM TO THE SHARKS.

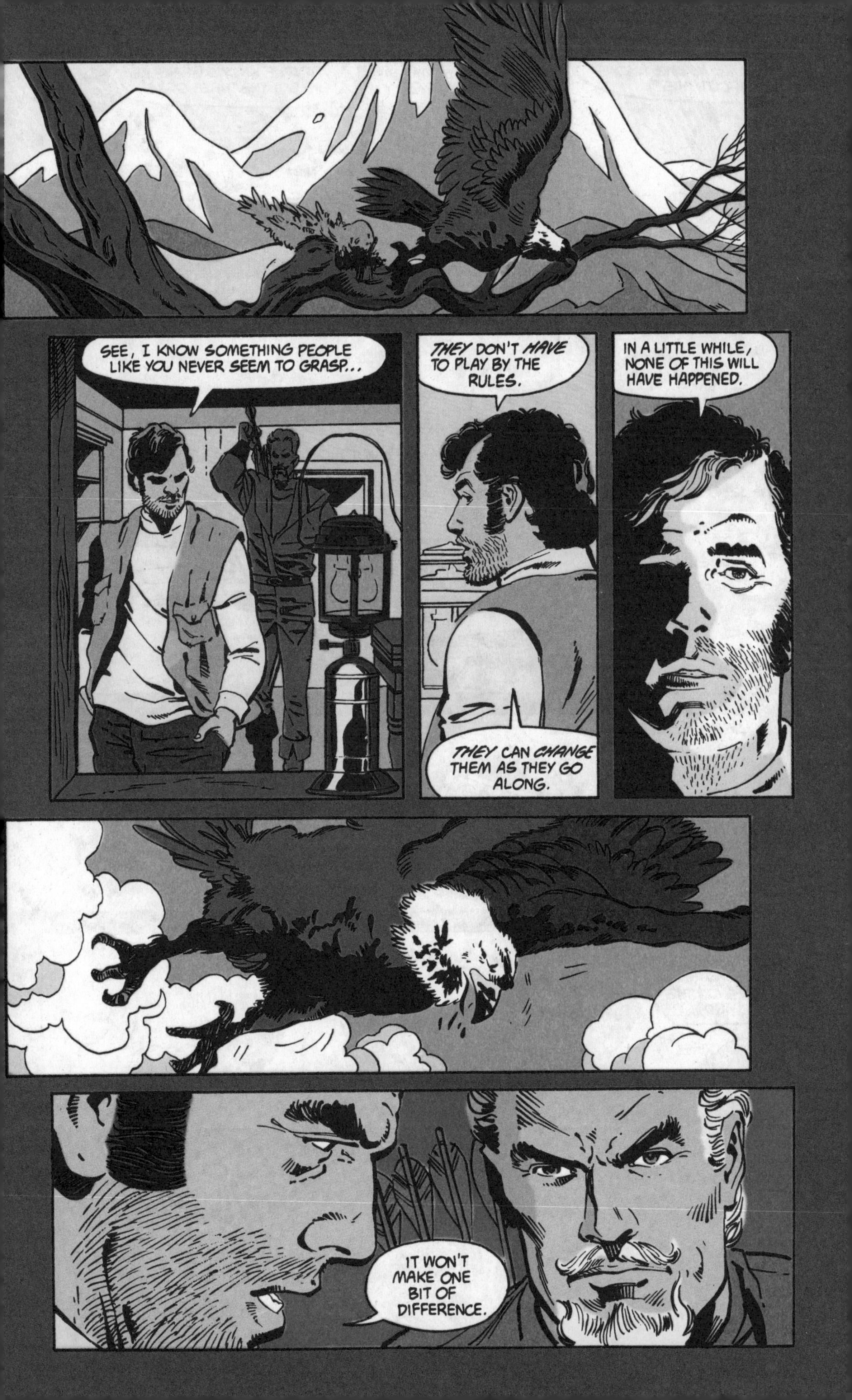
SEE, I KNOW SOMETHING PEOPLE LIKE YOU NEVER SEEM TO GRASP...
THEY DON'T HAVE TO PLAY BY THE RULES.
THEY CAN CHANGE THEM AS THEY GO ALONG.
IN A LITTLE WHILE, NONE OF THIS WILL HAVE HAPPENED.
IT WON'T MAKE ONE BIT OF DIFFERENCE.

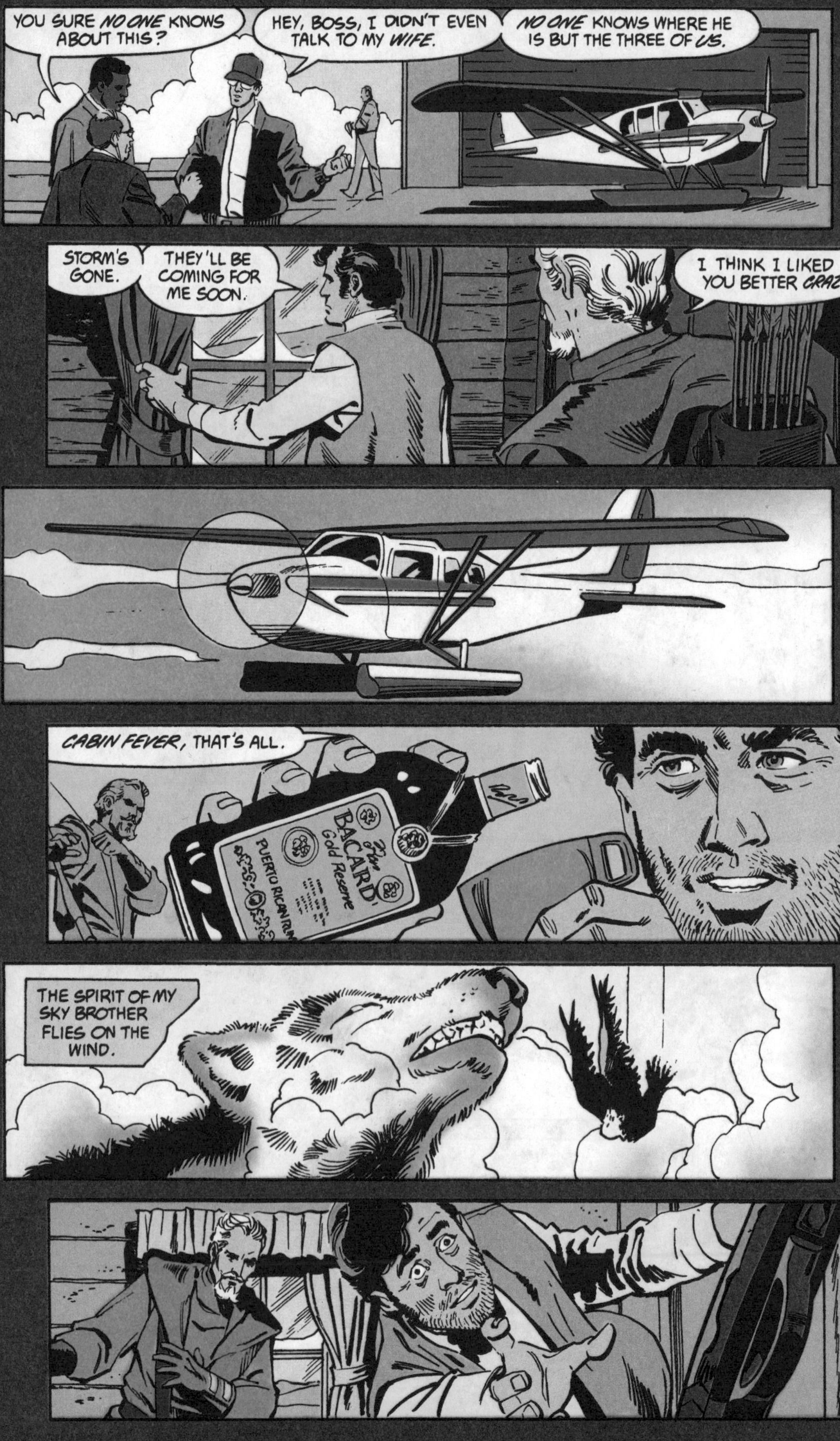
YOU SURE NO ONE KNOWS ABOUT THIS?
HEY, BOSS, I DIDN'T EVEN TALK TO MY WIFE.
NO ONE KNOWS WHERE HE IS BUT THE THREE OF US.
STORM'S GONE.
THEY'LL BE COMING FOR ME SOON.
I THINK I LIKED YOU BETTER CRAZY.
CABIN FEVER, THAT'S ALL.
THE SPIRIT OF MY SKY BROTHER FLIES ON THE WIND.

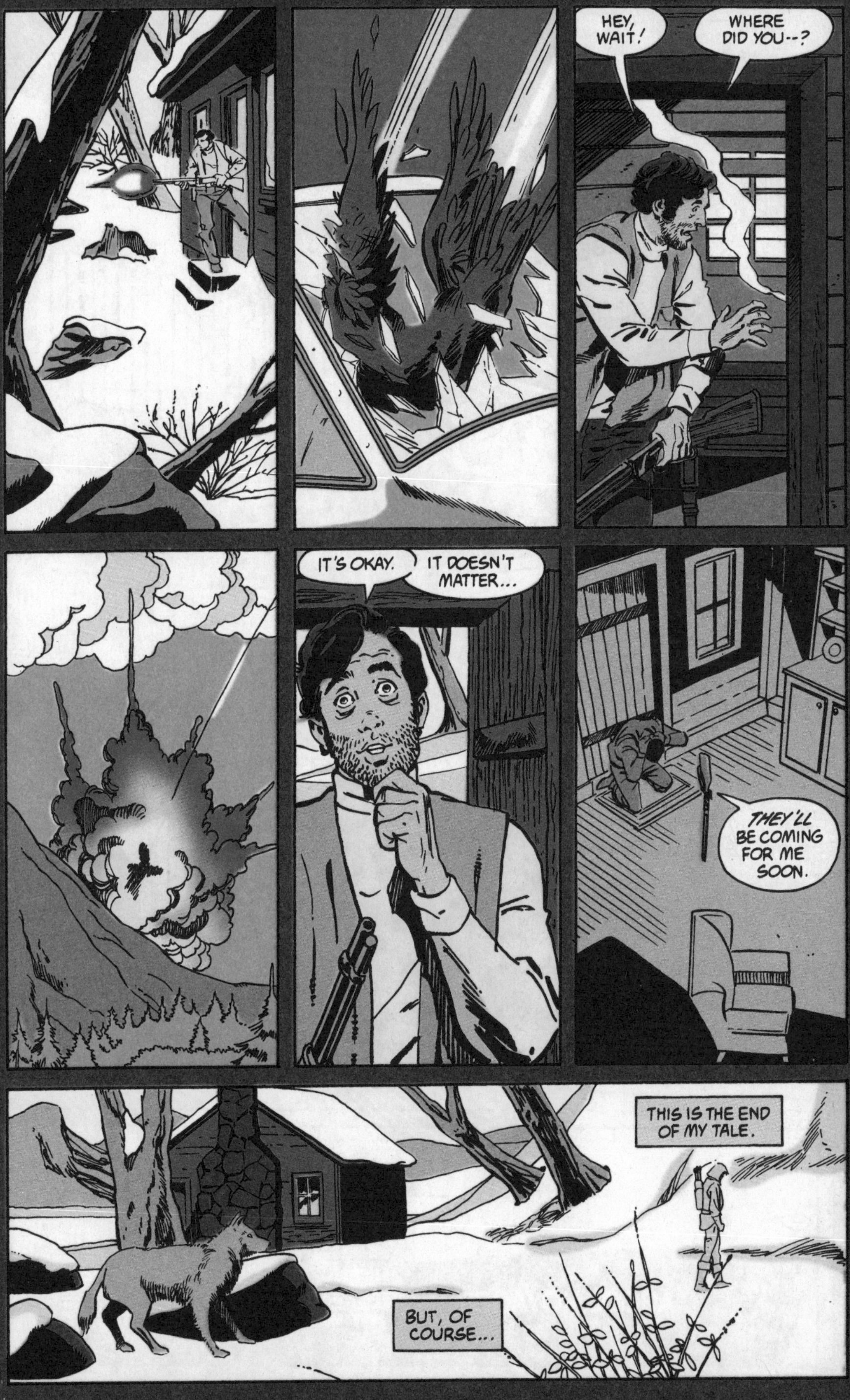
HEY, WAIT!
WHERE DID YOU--?
IT'S OKAY.
IT DOESN'T MATTER...
THEY'LL BE COMING FOR ME SOON.
THIS IS THE END OF MY TALE.
BUT, OF COURSE...

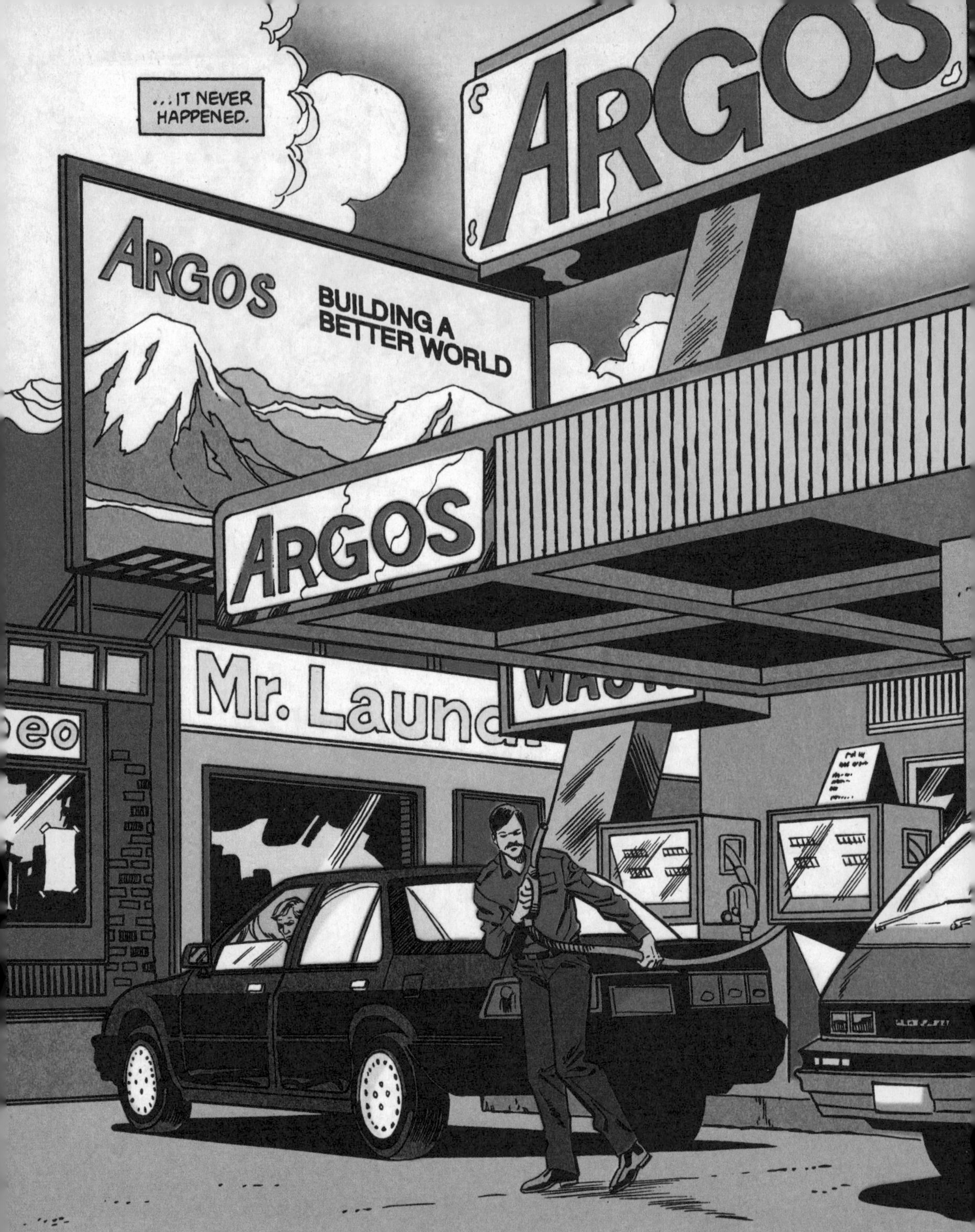
...IT NEVER HAPPENED.
ARGOS
ARGOS
BUILDING A BETTER WORLD
ARGOS
Mr. Laund

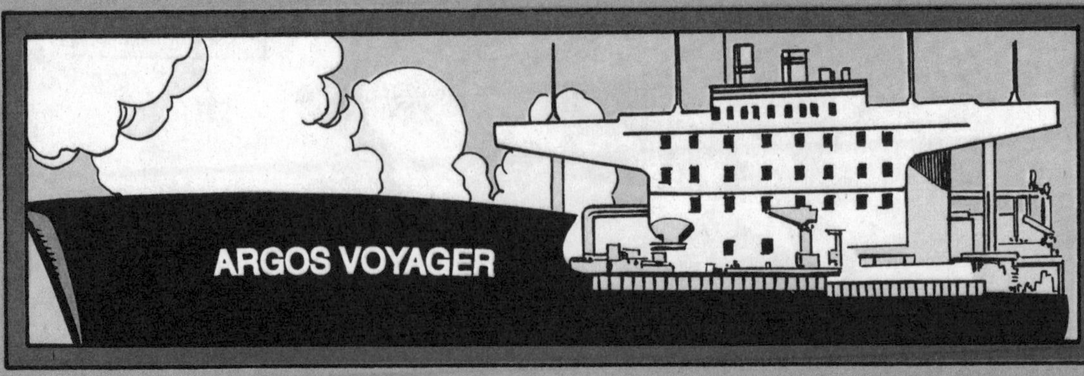
ARGOS VOYAGER

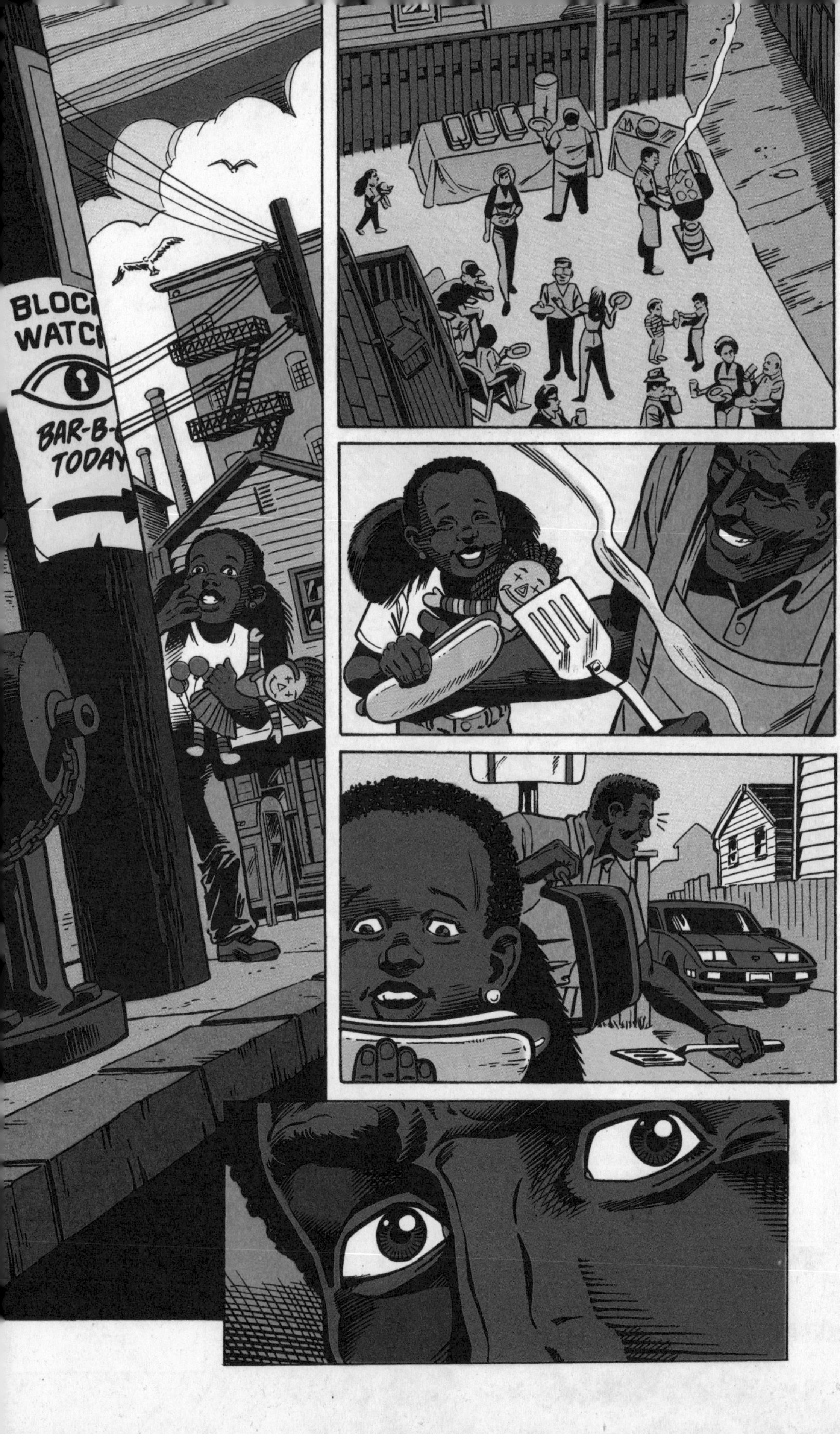
BLOCK WATCH
BAR-B-
TODAY

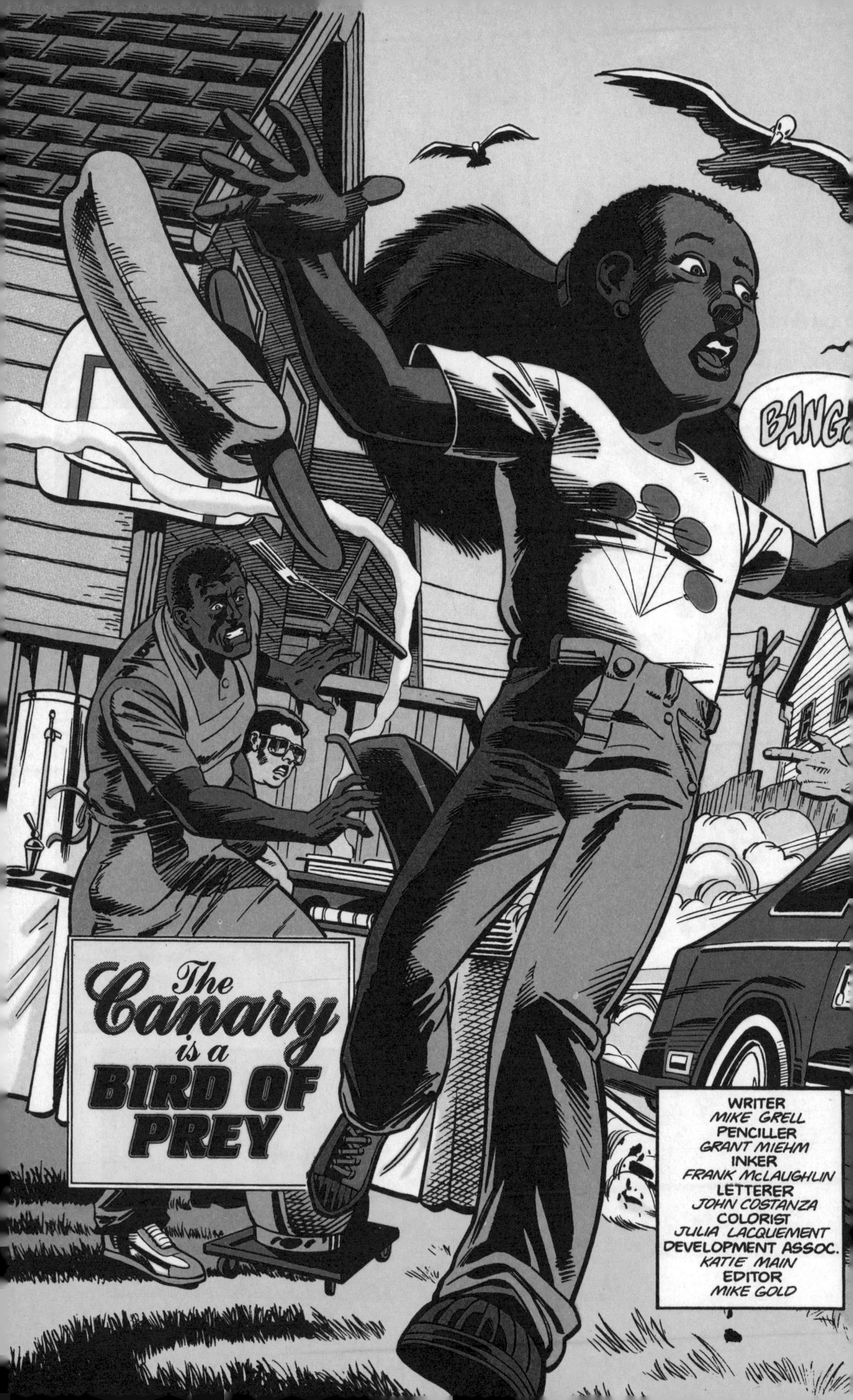
BANG!
The Canary is a BIRD OF PREY
WRITER
MIKE GRELL
PENCILLER
GRANT MIEHM
INKER
FRANK McLAUGHLIN
LETTERER
JOHN COSTANZA
COLORIST
JULIA LACQUEMENT
DEVELOPMENT ASSOC.
KATIE MAIN
EDITOR
MIKE GOLD

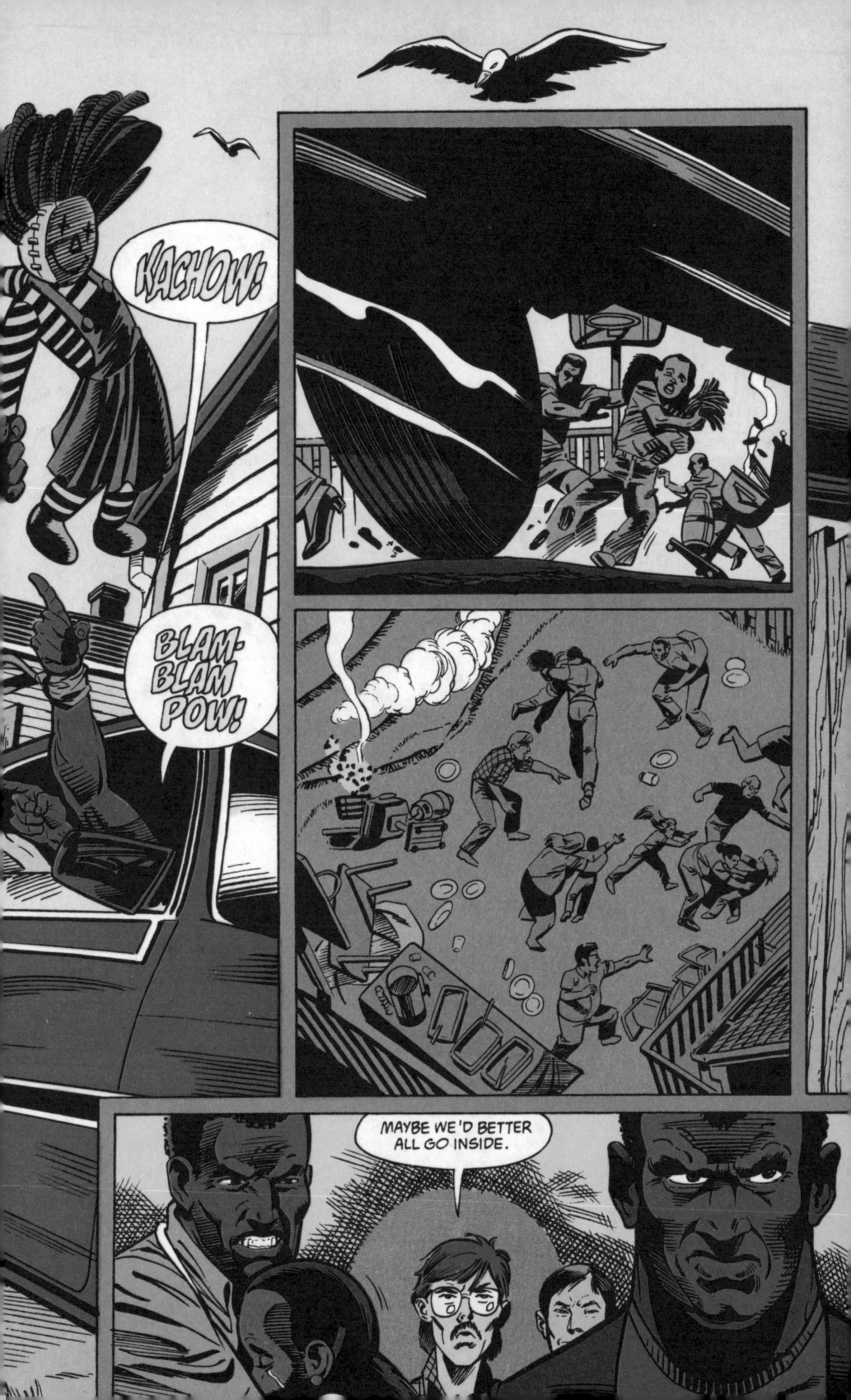
KACHOW!
BLAM-BLAM POW!
MAYBE WE'D BETTER ALL GO INSIDE.

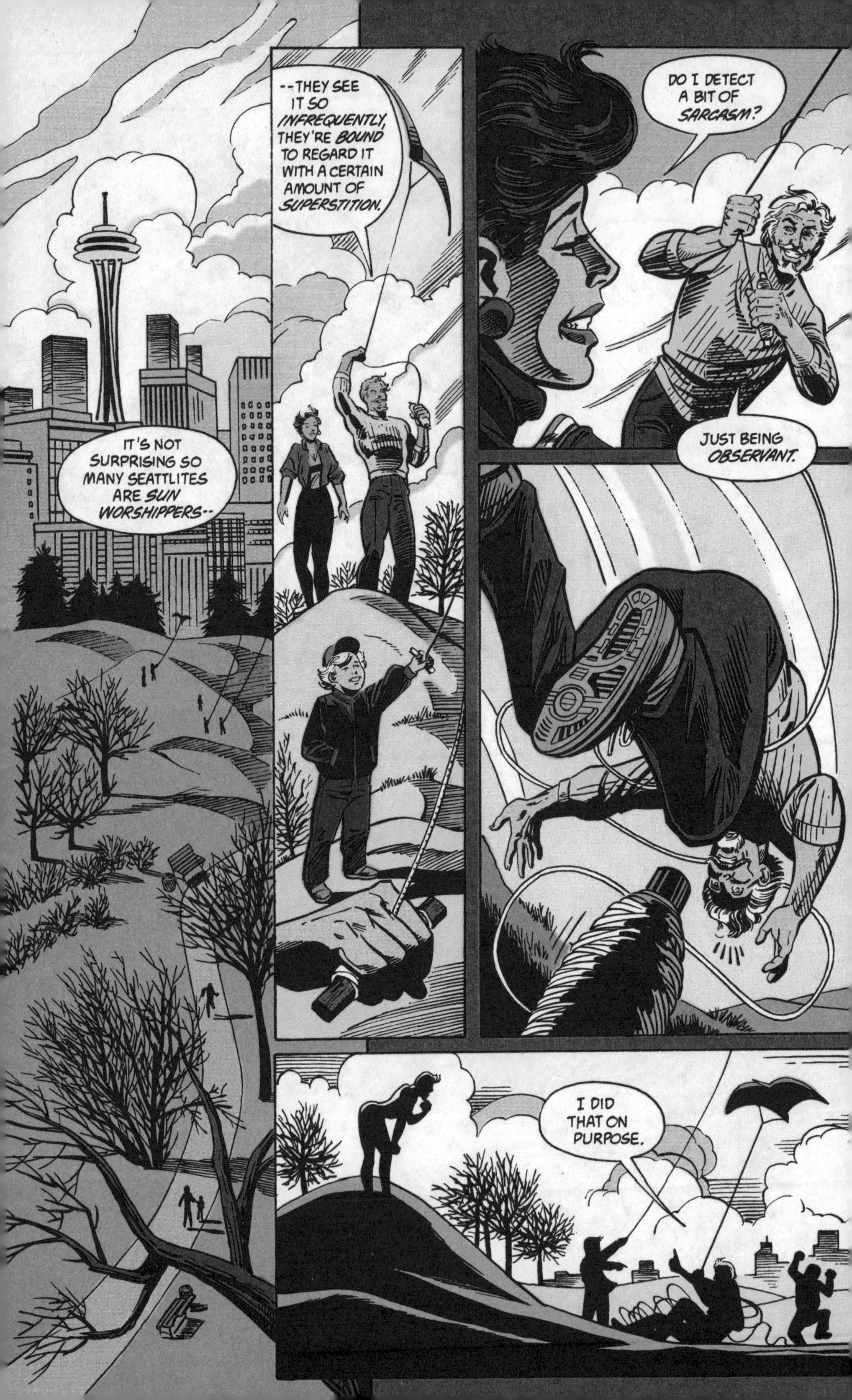
IT'S NOT SURPRISING SO MANY SEATTLITES ARE SUN WORSHIPPERS--
--THEY SEE IT SO INFREQUENTLY, THEY'RE BOUND TO REGARD IT WITH A CERTAIN AMOUNT OF SUPERSTITION.
DO I DETECT A BIT OF SARCASM?
JUST BEING OBSERVANT.
I DID THAT ON PURPOSE.

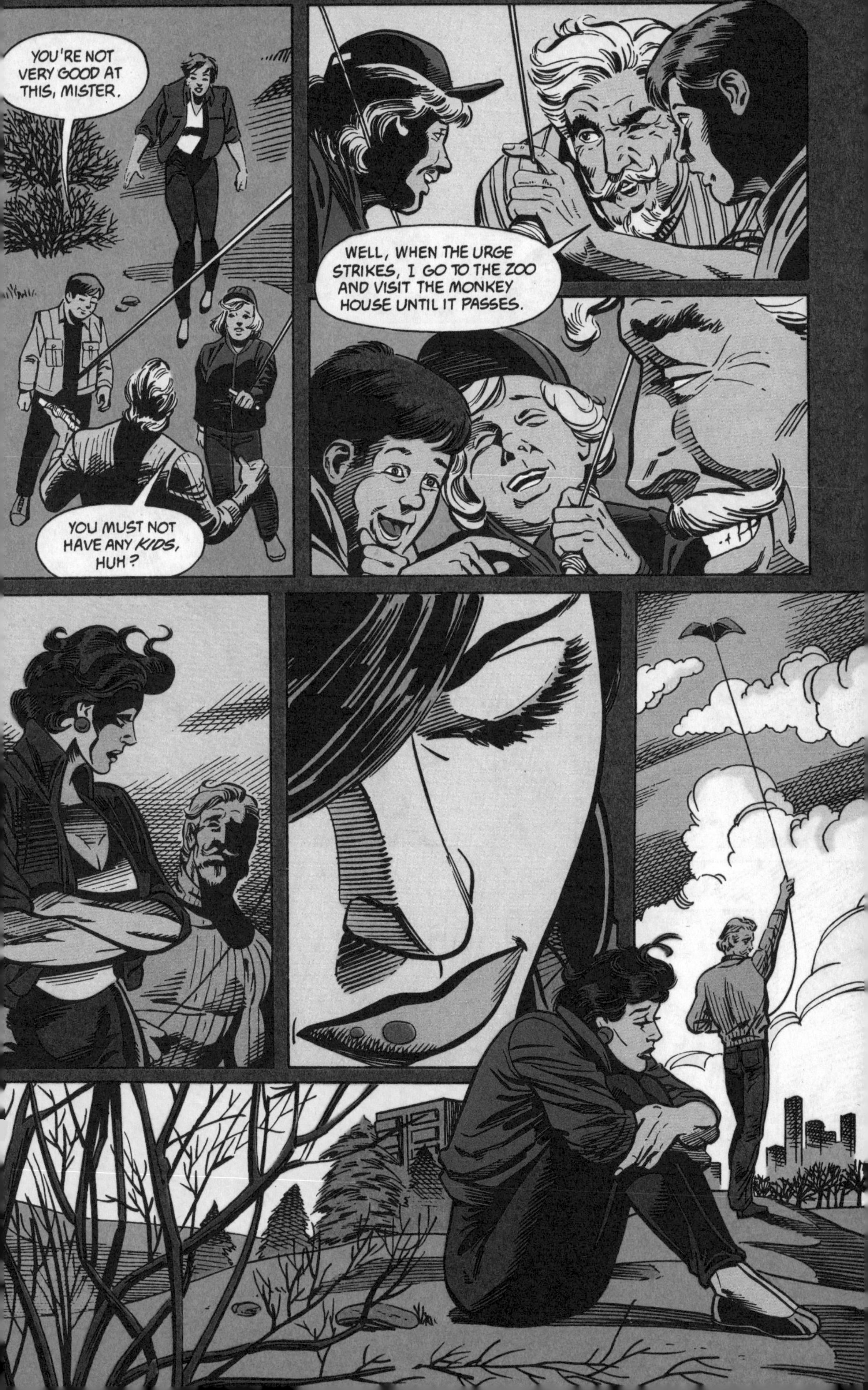
YOU'RE NOT VERY GOOD AT THIS, MISTER.
YOU MUST NOT HAVE ANY KIDS, HUH?
WELL, WHEN THE URGE STRIKES, I GO TO THE ZOO AND VISIT THE MONKEY HOUSE UNTIL IT PASSES.

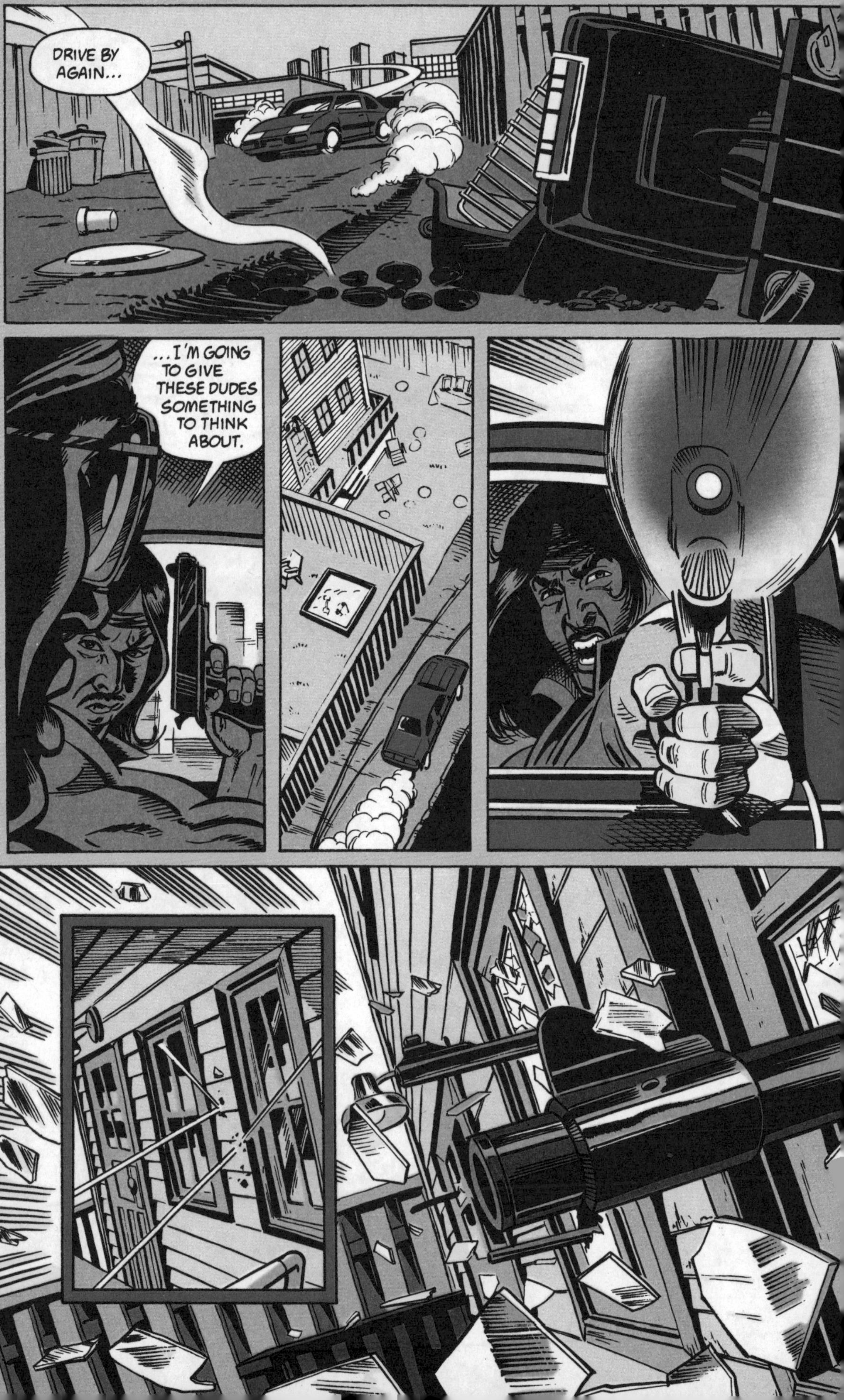
DRIVE BY AGAIN...
...I'M GOING TO GIVE THESE DUDES SOMETHING TO THINK ABOUT.

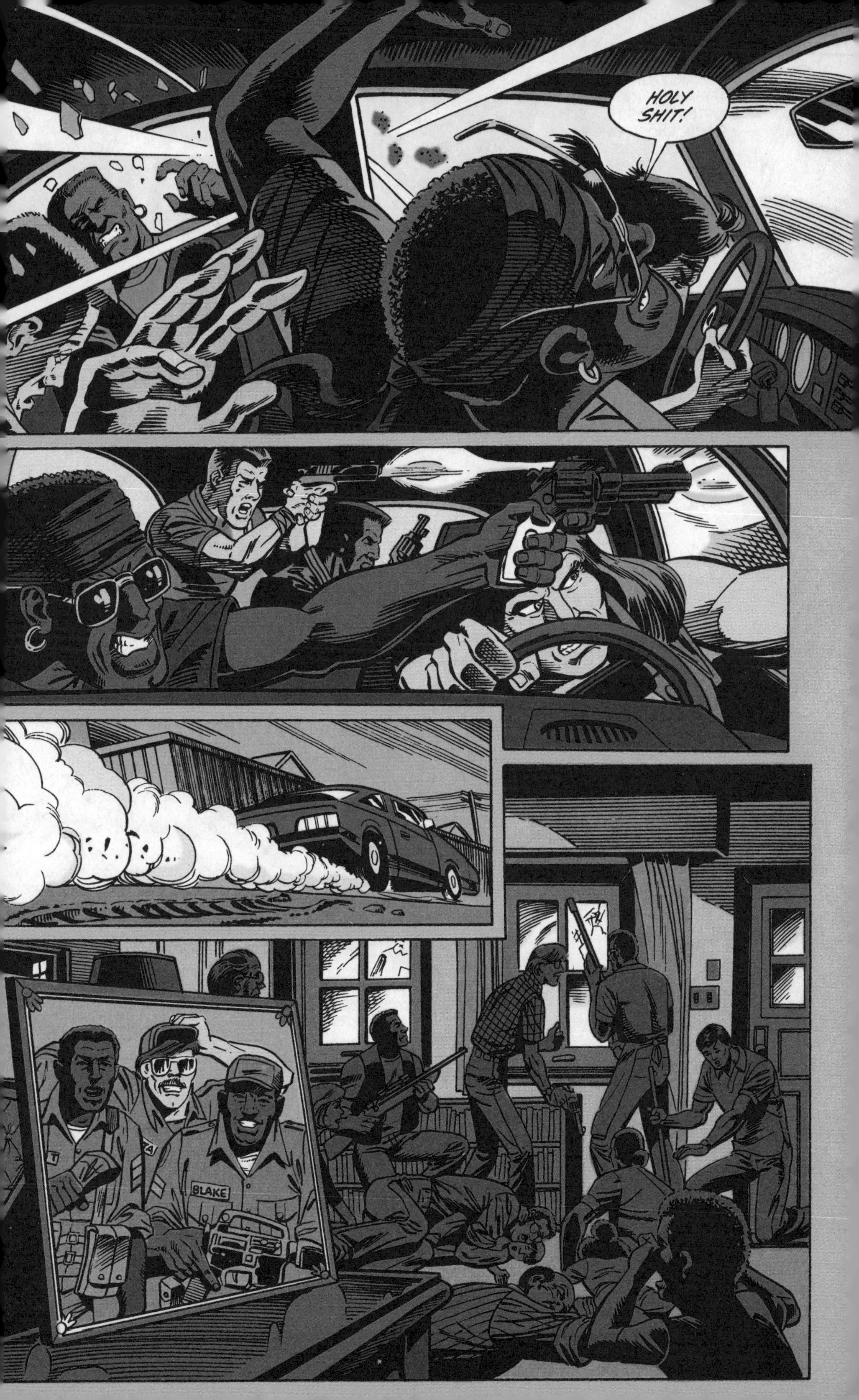
HOLY SHIT!
BLAKE

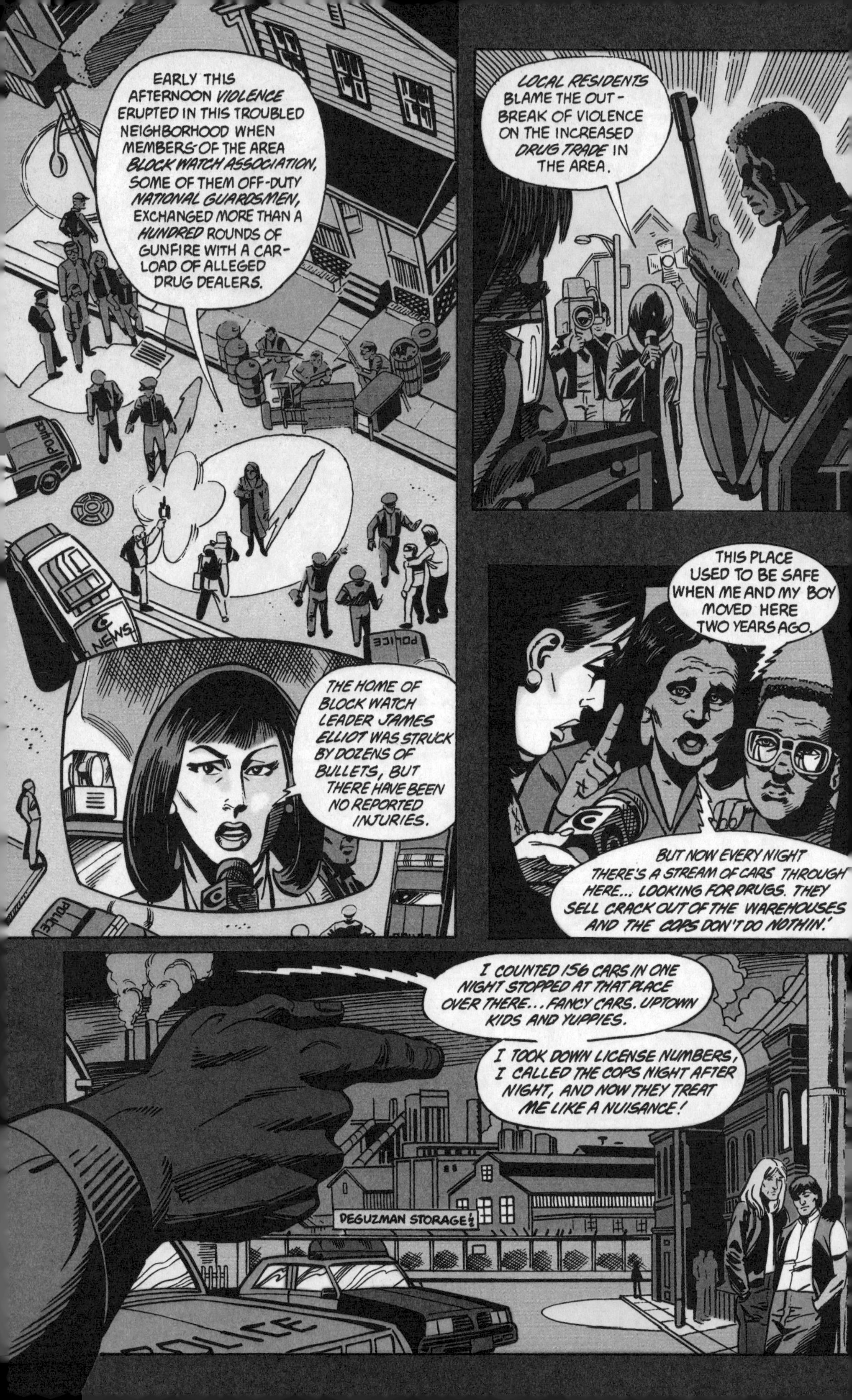
EARLY THIS AFTERNOON VIOLENCE ERUPTED IN THIS TROUBLED NEIGHBORHOOD WHEN MEMBERS OF THE AREA BLOCK WATCH ASSOCIATION, SOME OF THEM OFF-DUTY NATIONAL GUARDSMEN, EXCHANGED MORE THAN A HUNDRED ROUNDS OF GUNFIRE WITH A CAR-LOAD OF ALLEGED DRUG DEALERS.
POLICE
NEWS
POLICE
THE HOME OF BLOCK WATCH LEADER JAMES ELLIOT WAS STRUCK BY DOZENS OF BULLETS, BUT THERE HAVE BEEN NO REPORTED INJURIES.
LOCAL RESIDENTS BLAME THE OUT-BREAK OF VIOLENCE ON THE INCREASED DRUG TRADE IN THE AREA.
THIS PLACE USED TO BE SAFE WHEN ME AND MY BOY MOVED HERE TWO YEARS AGO.
BUT NOW EVERY NIGHT THERE'S A STREAM OF CARS THROUGH HERE... LOOKING FOR DRUGS. THEY SELL CRACK OUT OF THE WAREHOUSES AND THE COPS DON'T DO NOTHIN'.
I COUNTED 156 CARS IN ONE NIGHT STOPPED AT THAT PLACE OVER THERE... FANCY CARS. UPTOWN KIDS AND YUPPIES.
I TOOK DOWN LICENSE NUMBERS, I CALLED THE COPS NIGHT AFTER NIGHT, AND NOW THEY TREAT ME LIKE A NUISANCE!
DEGUZMAN STORAGE
POLICE

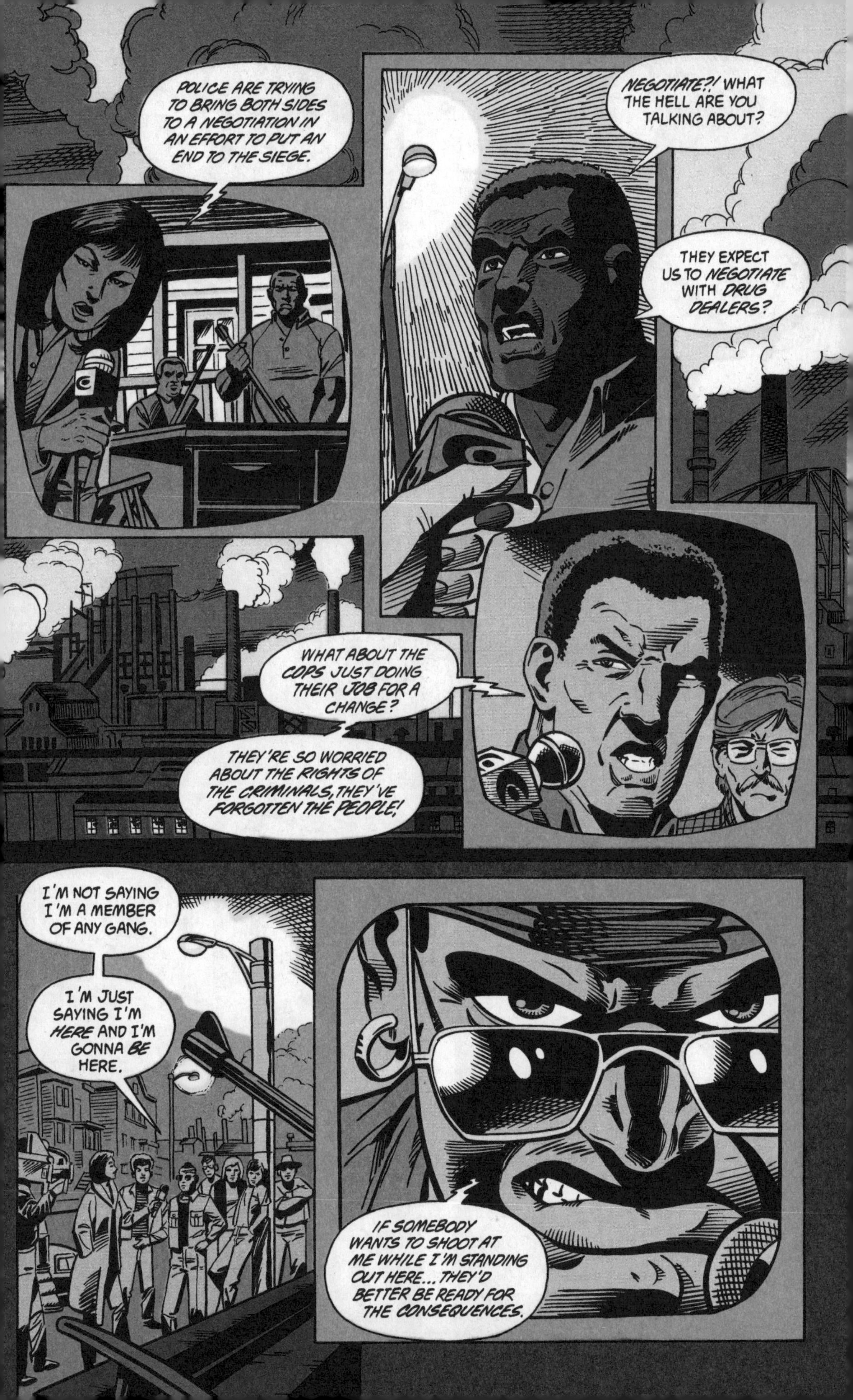
POLICE ARE TRYING TO BRING BOTH SIDES TO A NEGOTIATION IN AN EFFORT TO PUT AN END TO THE SIEGE.
NEGOTIATE?! WHAT THE HELL ARE YOU TALKING ABOUT?
THEY EXPECT US TO NEGOTIATE WITH DRUG DEALERS?
WHAT ABOUT THE COPS JUST DOING THEIR JOB FOR A CHANGE?
THEY'RE SO WORRIED ABOUT THE RIGHTS OF THE CRIMINALS, THEY'VE FORGOTTEN THE PEOPLE!
I'M NOT SAYING I'M A MEMBER OF ANY GANG.
I'M JUST SAYING I'M HERE AND I'M GONNA BE HERE.
IF SOMEBODY WANTS TO SHOOT AT ME WHILE I'M STANDING OUT HERE... THEY'D BETTER BE READY FOR THE CONSEQUENCES.

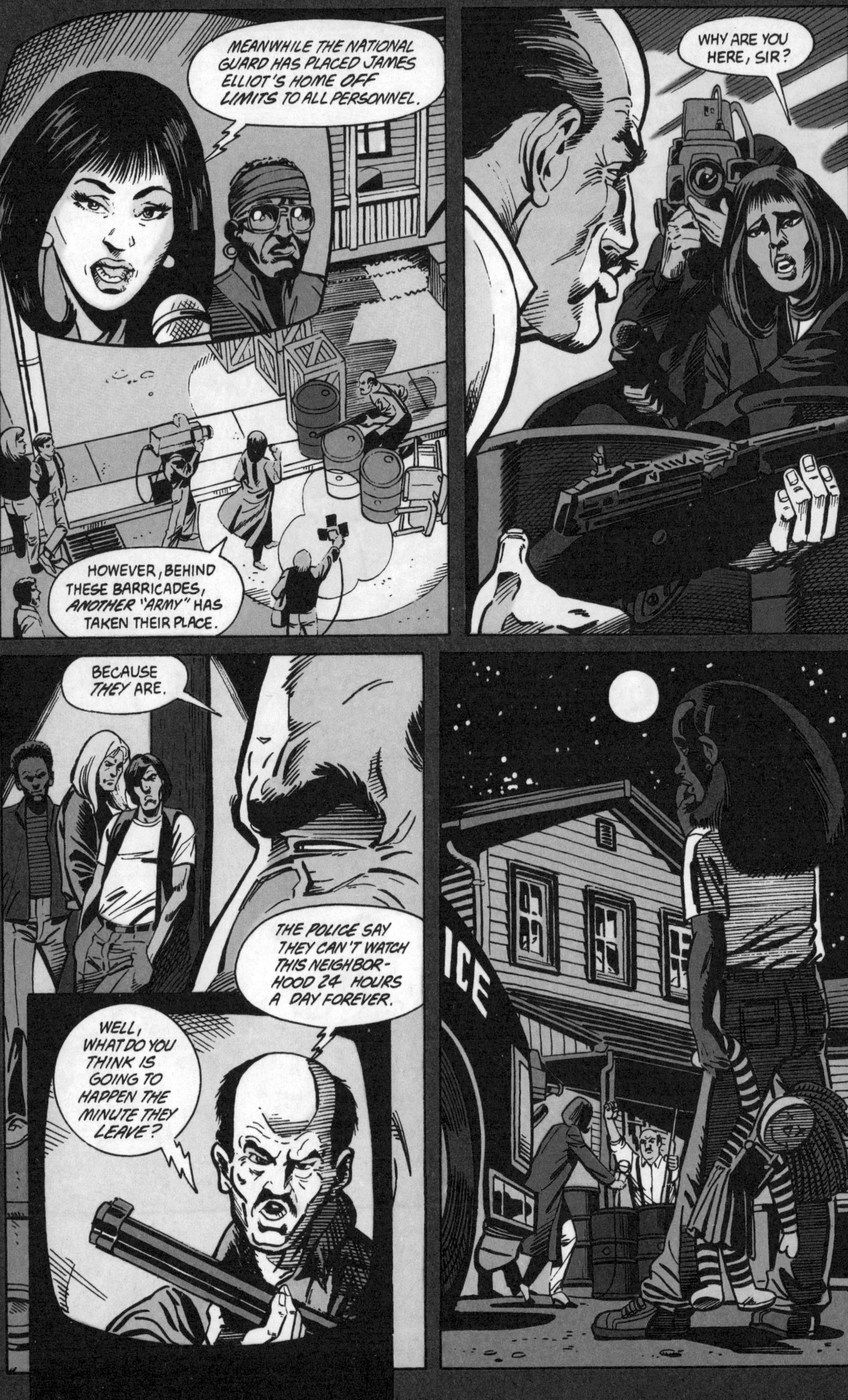
MEANWHILE THE NATIONAL GUARD HAS PLACED JAMES ELLIOT'S HOME OFF LIMITS TO ALL PERSONNEL.
HOWEVER, BEHIND THESE BARRICADES, ANOTHER "ARMY" HAS TAKEN THEIR PLACE.
WHY ARE YOU HERE, SIR?
BECAUSE THEY ARE.
THE POLICE SAY THEY CAN'T WATCH THIS NEIGHBOR-HOOD 24 HOURS A DAY FOREVER.
WELL, WHAT DO YOU THINK IS GOING TO HAPPEN THE MINUTE THEY LEAVE?
ICE

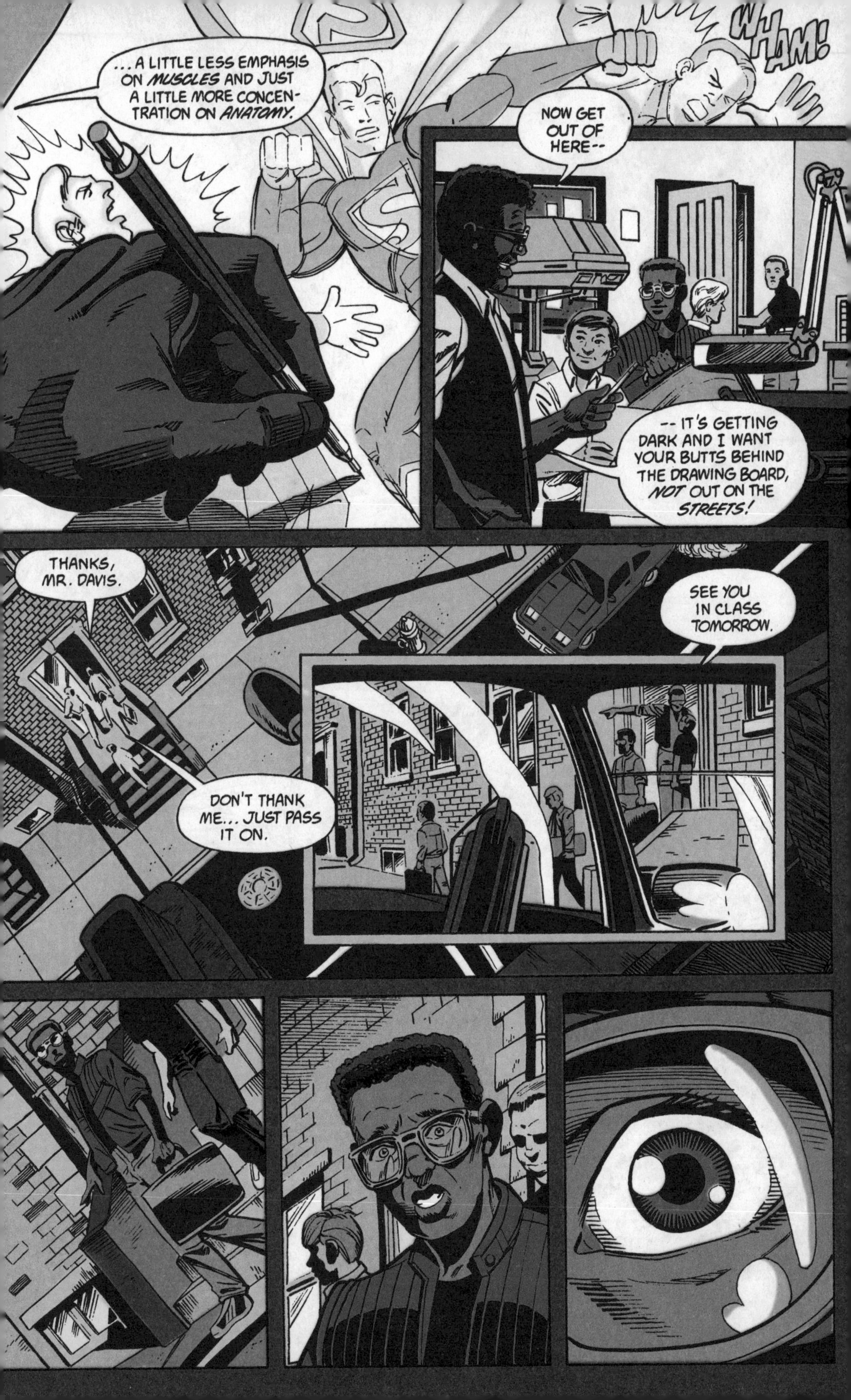
...A LITTLE LESS EMPHASIS ON MUSCLES AND JUST A LITTLE MORE CONCENTRATION ON ANATOMY.
WHAM!
NOW GET OUT OF HERE--
-- IT'S GETTING DARK AND I WANT YOUR BUTTS BEHIND THE DRAWING BOARD, NOT OUT ON THE STREETS!
THANKS, MR. DAVIS.
SEE YOU IN CLASS TOMORROW.
DON'T THANK ME... JUST PASS IT ON.

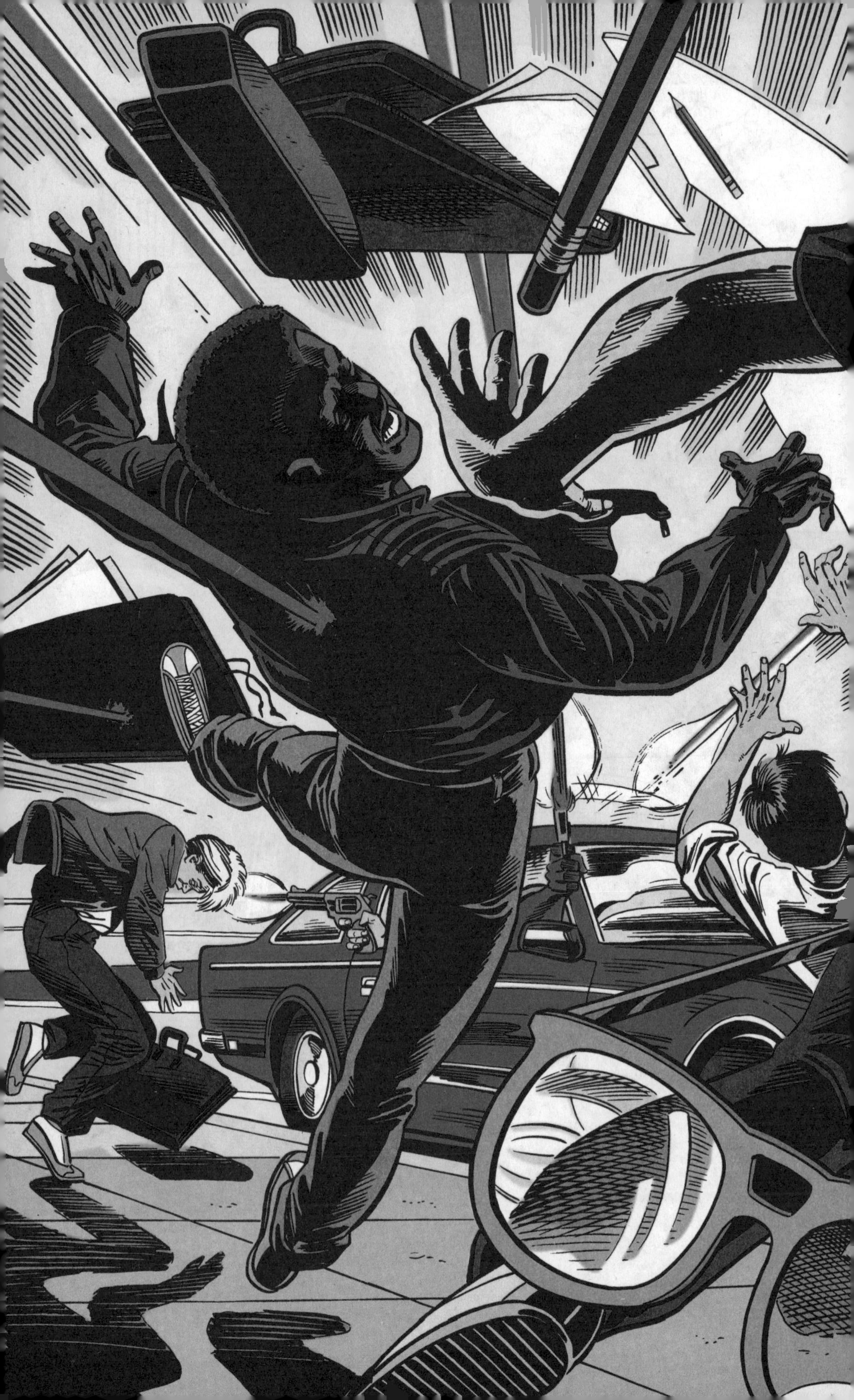

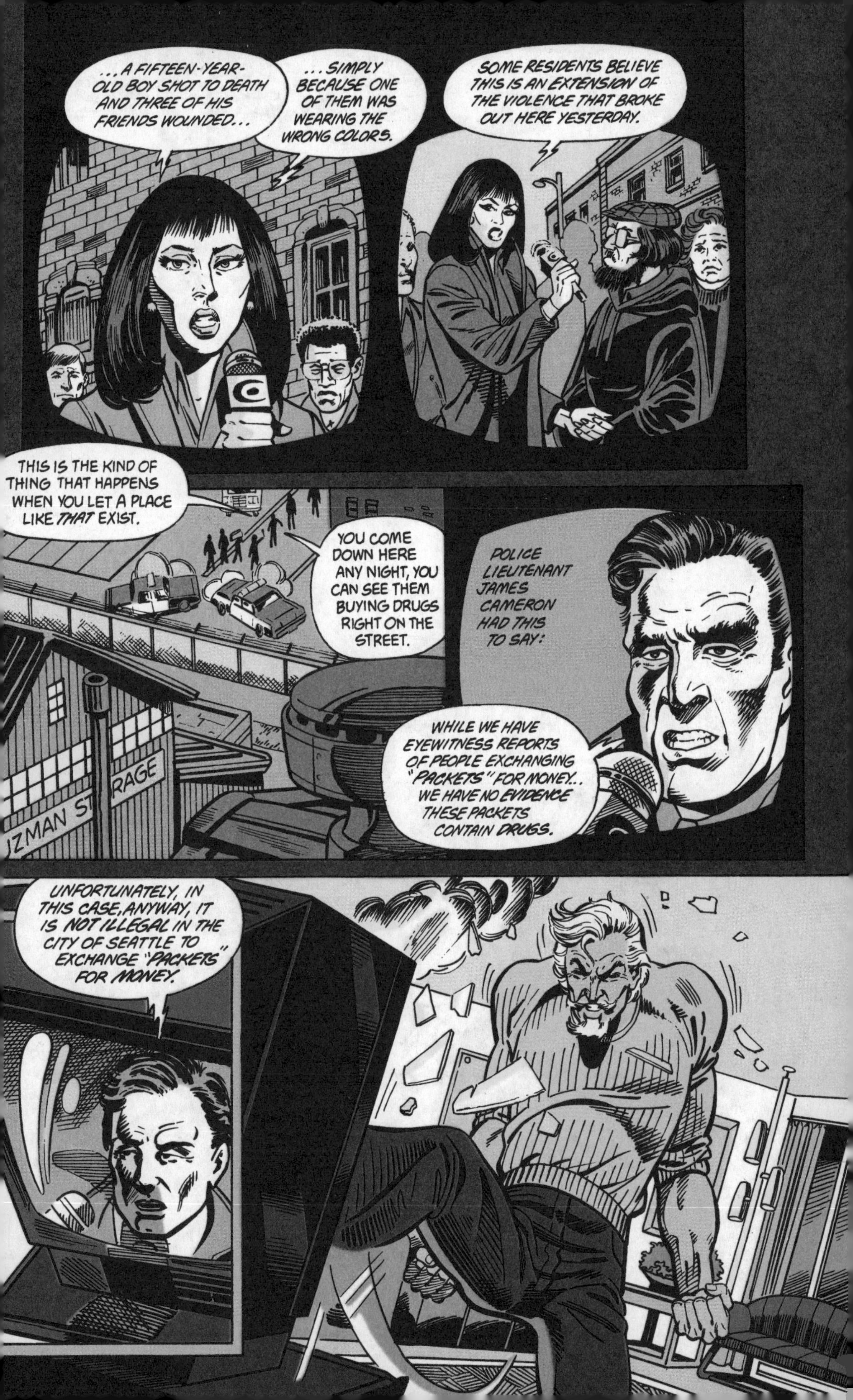
. . . A FIFTEEN-YEAR-OLD BOY SHOT TO DEATH AND THREE OF HIS FRIENDS WOUNDED . . .
. . . SIMPLY BECAUSE ONE OF THEM WAS WEARING THE WRONG COLORS.
SOME RESIDENTS BELIEVE THIS IS AN EXTENSION OF THE VIOLENCE THAT BROKE OUT HERE YESTERDAY.
THIS IS THE KIND OF THING THAT HAPPENS WHEN YOU LET A PLACE LIKE *THAT* EXIST.
YOU COME DOWN HERE ANY NIGHT, YOU CAN SEE THEM BUYING DRUGS RIGHT ON THE STREET.
ZMAN ST RAGE
POLICE LIEUTENANT JAMES CAMERON HAD THIS TO SAY:
WHILE WE HAVE EYEWITNESS REPORTS OF PEOPLE EXCHANGING "PACKETS" FOR MONEY... WE HAVE NO *EVIDENCE* THESE PACKETS CONTAIN *DRUGS*.
UNFORTUNATELY, IN THIS CASE, ANYWAY, IT IS *NOT ILLEGAL* IN THE CITY OF SEATTLE TO EXCHANGE "*PACKETS*" FOR *MONEY*.

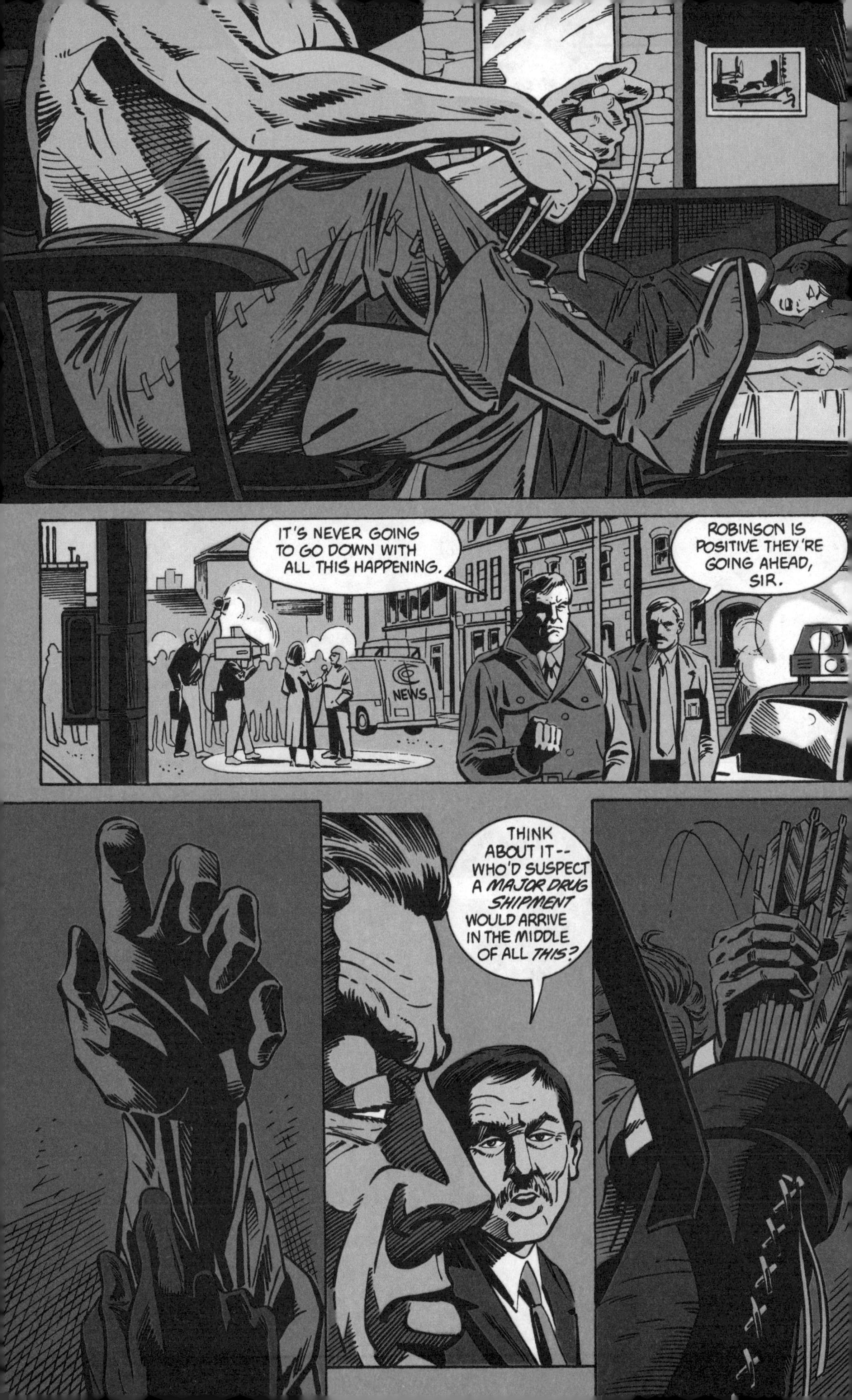
IT'S NEVER GOING TO GO DOWN WITH ALL THIS HAPPENING.
ROBINSON IS POSITIVE THEY'RE GOING AHEAD, SIR.
NEWS
THINK ABOUT IT-- WHO'D SUSPECT A *MAJOR DRUG SHIPMENT* WOULD ARRIVE IN THE MIDDLE OF ALL *THIS*?

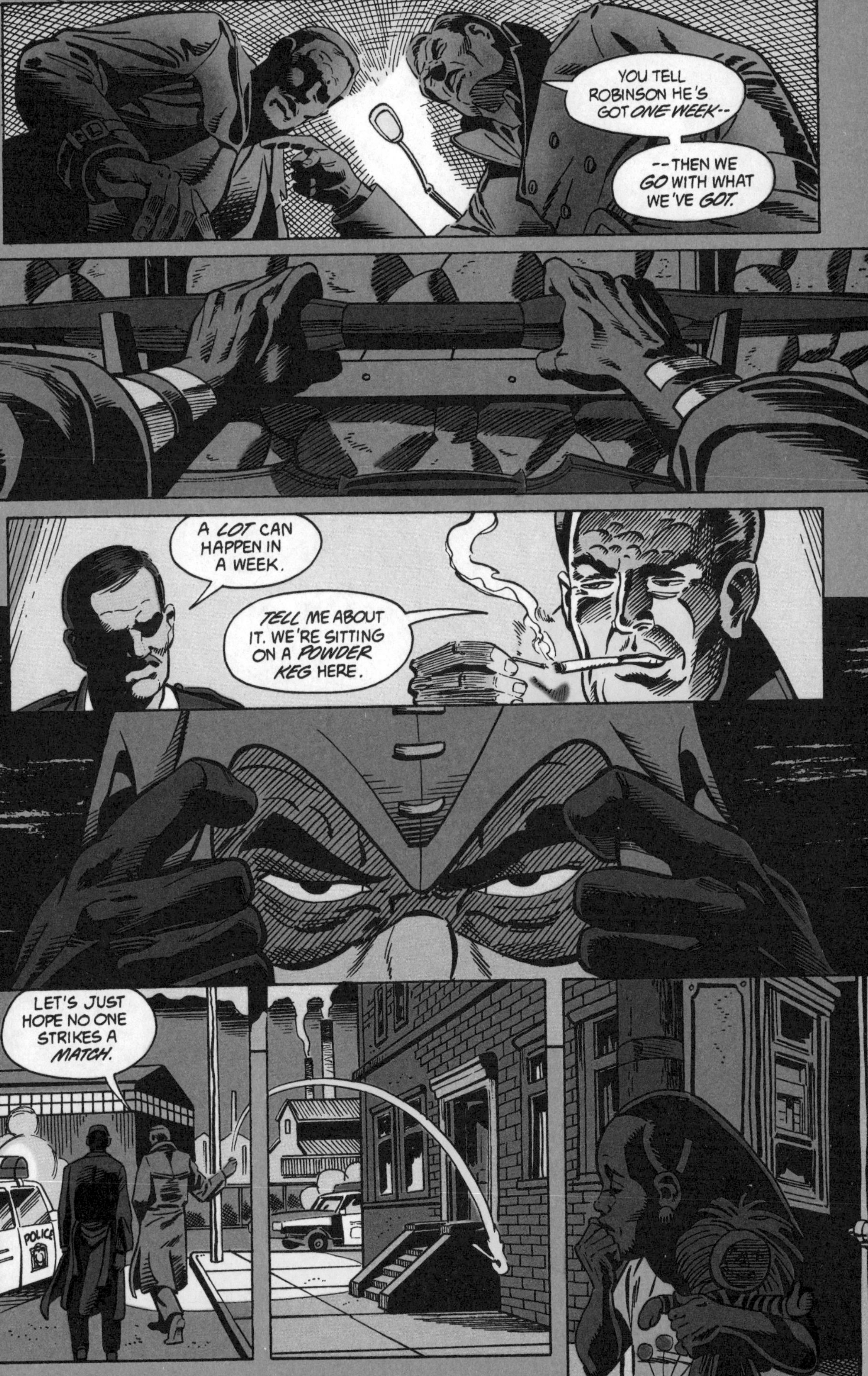
YOU TELL ROBINSON HE'S GOT ONE WEEK--
--THEN WE GO WITH WHAT WE'VE GOT.
A LOT CAN HAPPEN IN A WEEK.
TELL ME ABOUT IT. WE'RE SITTING ON A POWDER KEG HERE.
LET'S JUST HOPE NO ONE STRIKES A MATCH.
POLICE

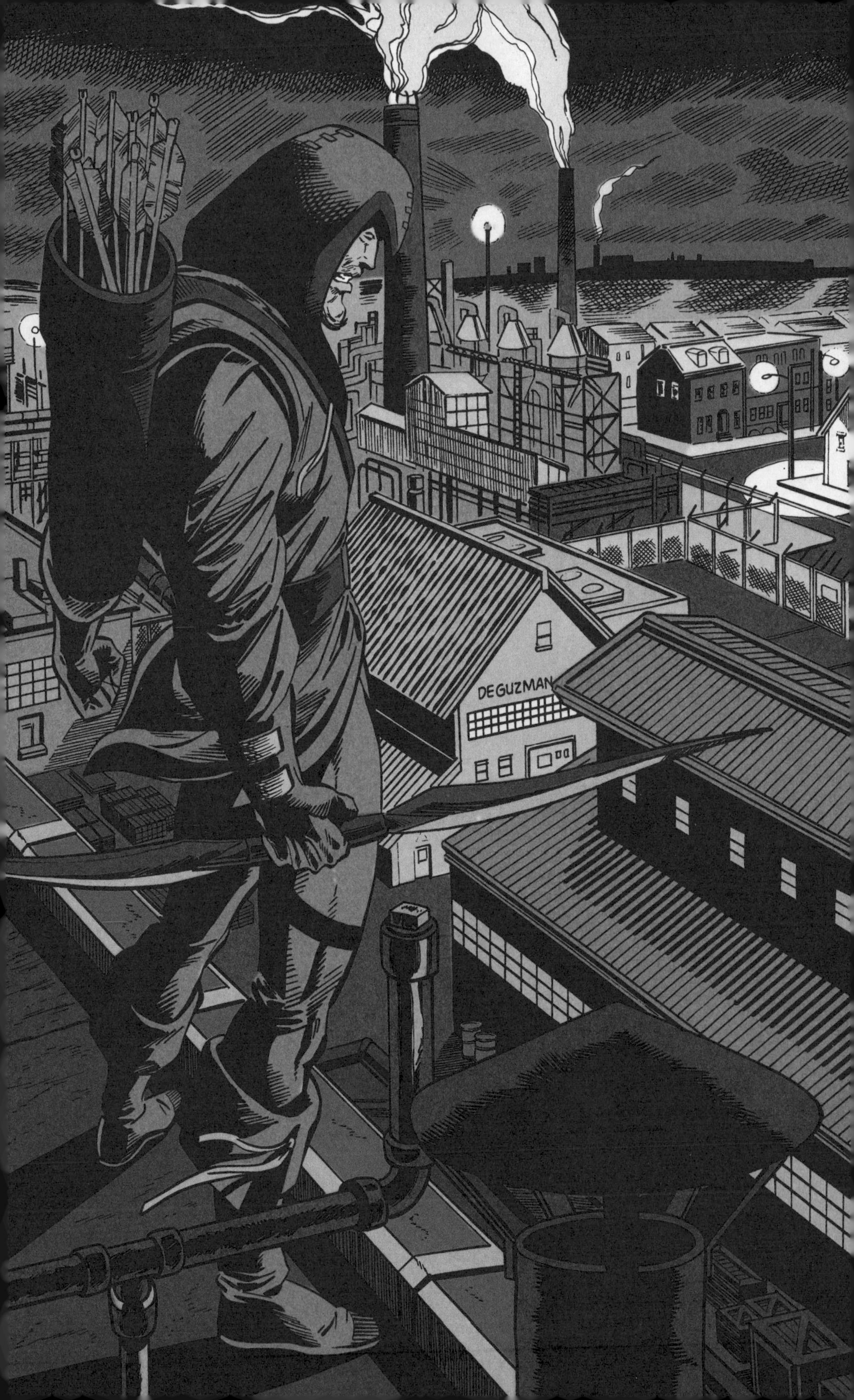
DEGUZMAN

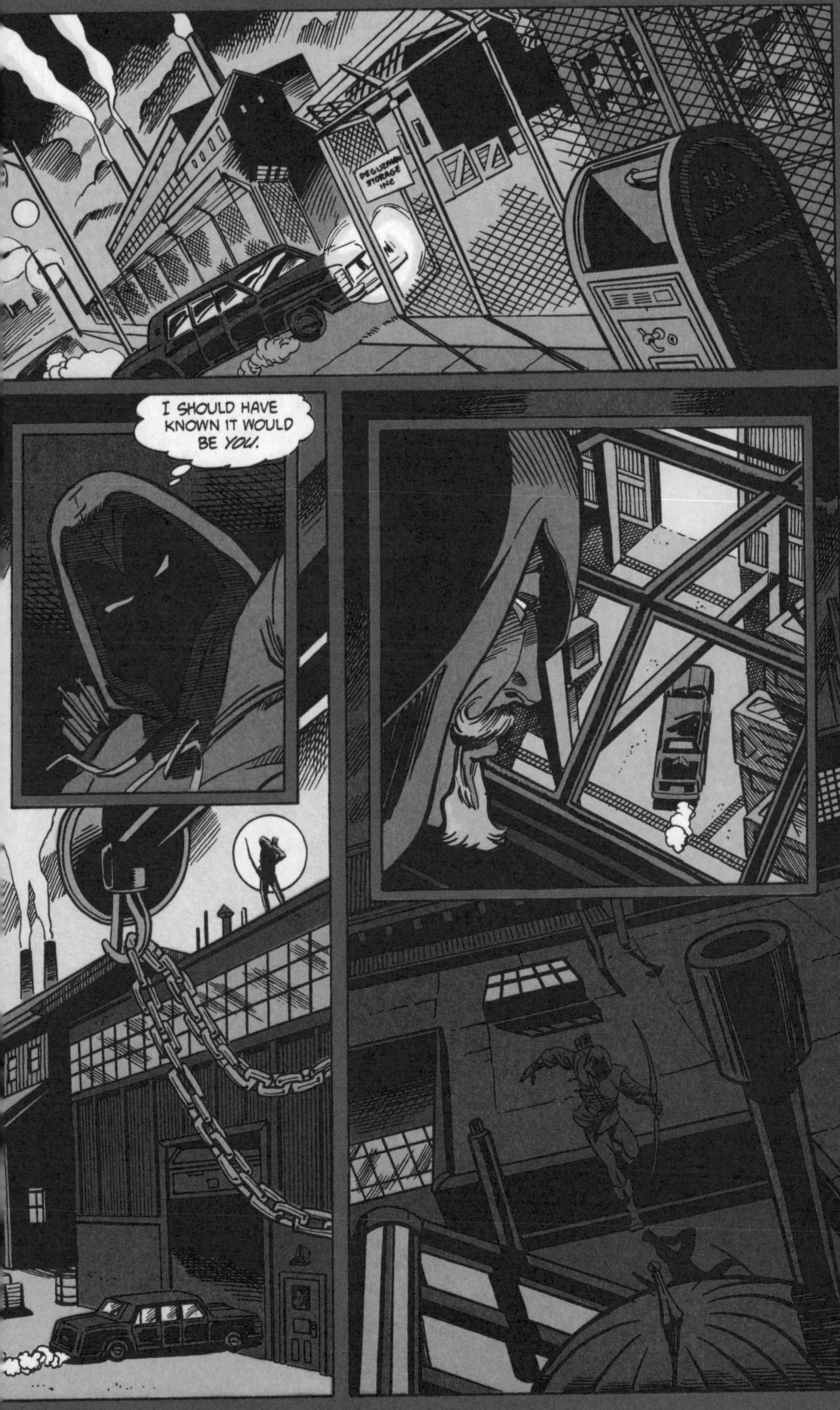
DEGUZMAN STORAGE INC
U.S. MAIL
I SHOULD HAVE KNOWN IT WOULD BE *YOU*.

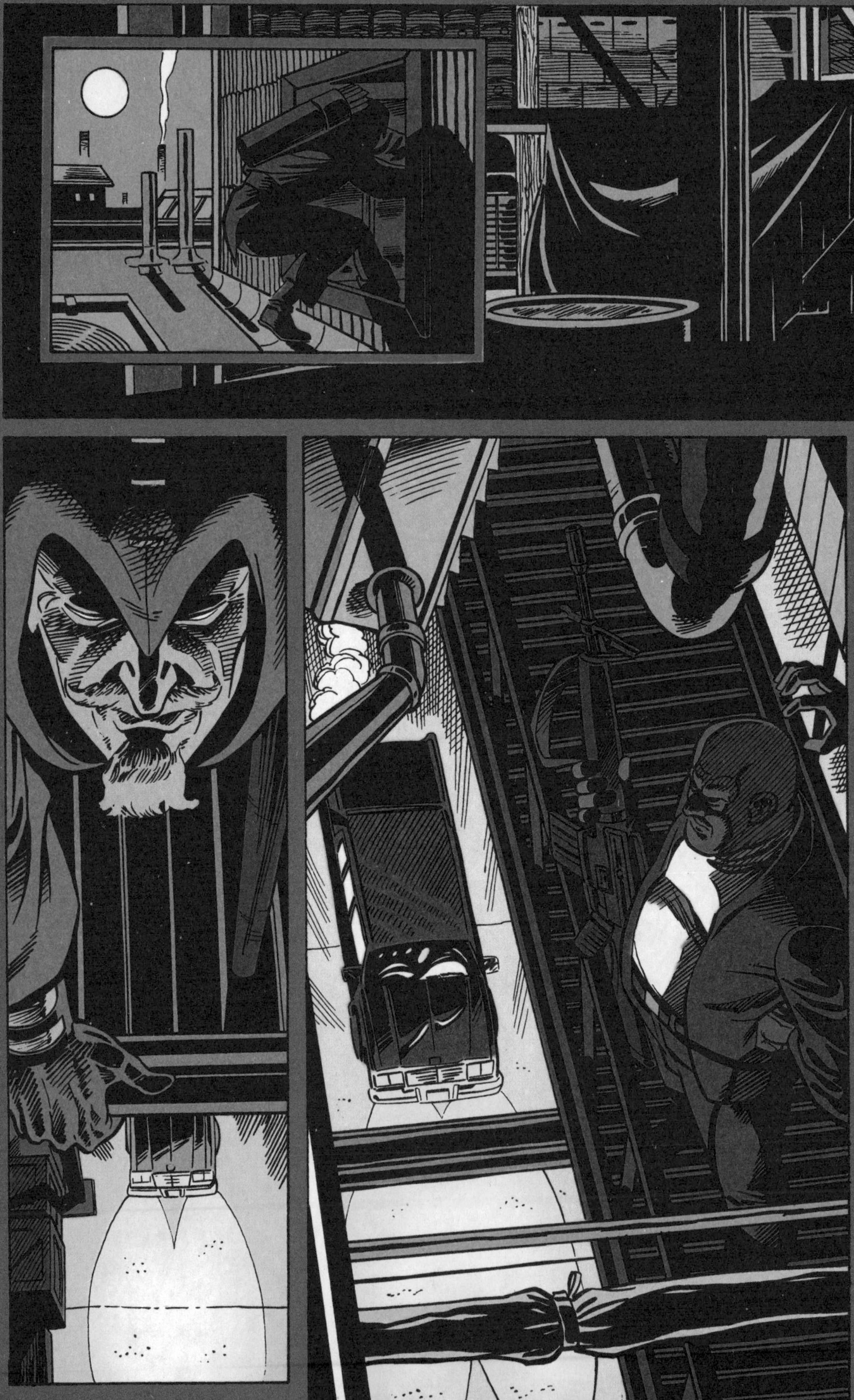

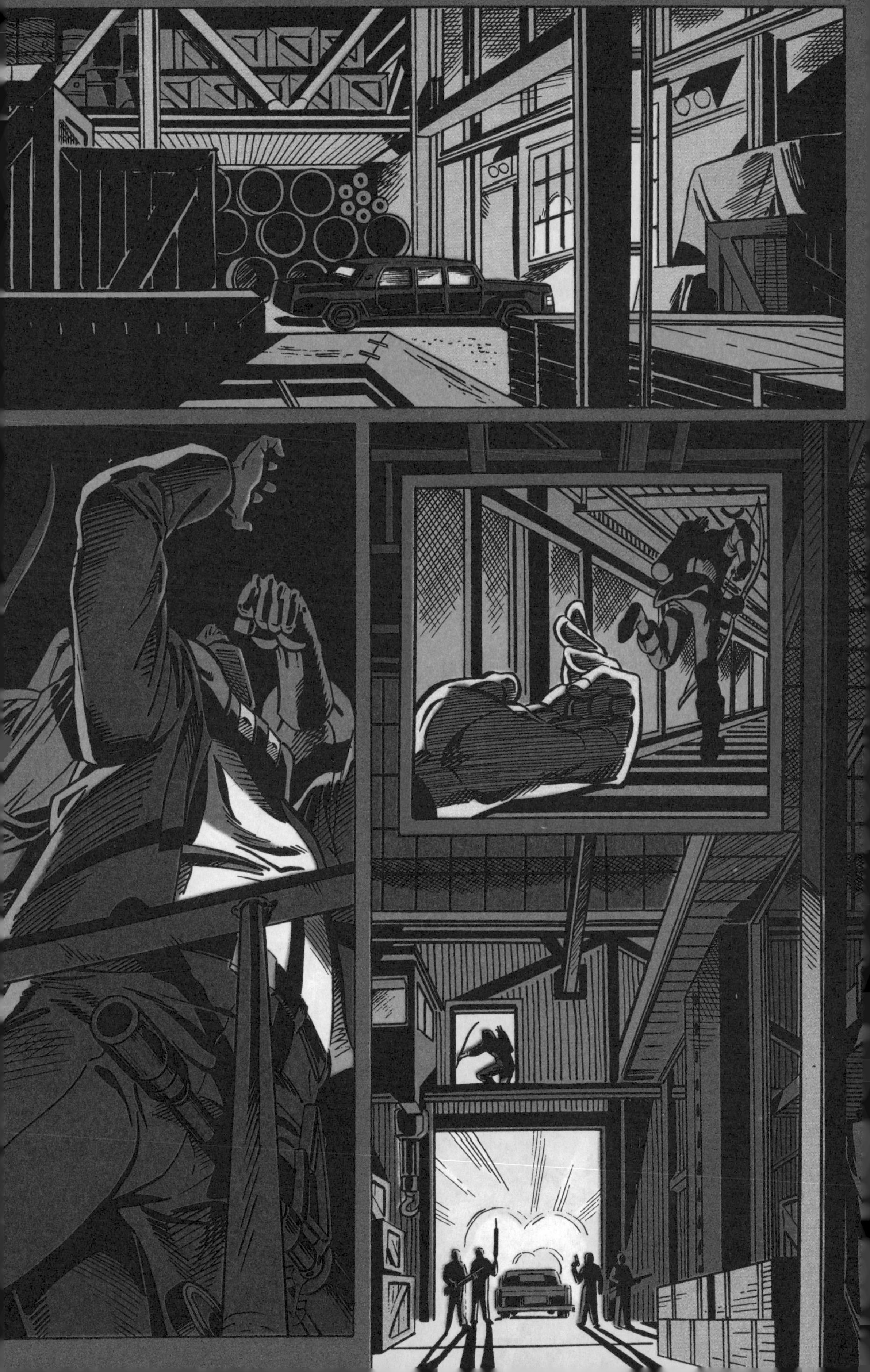

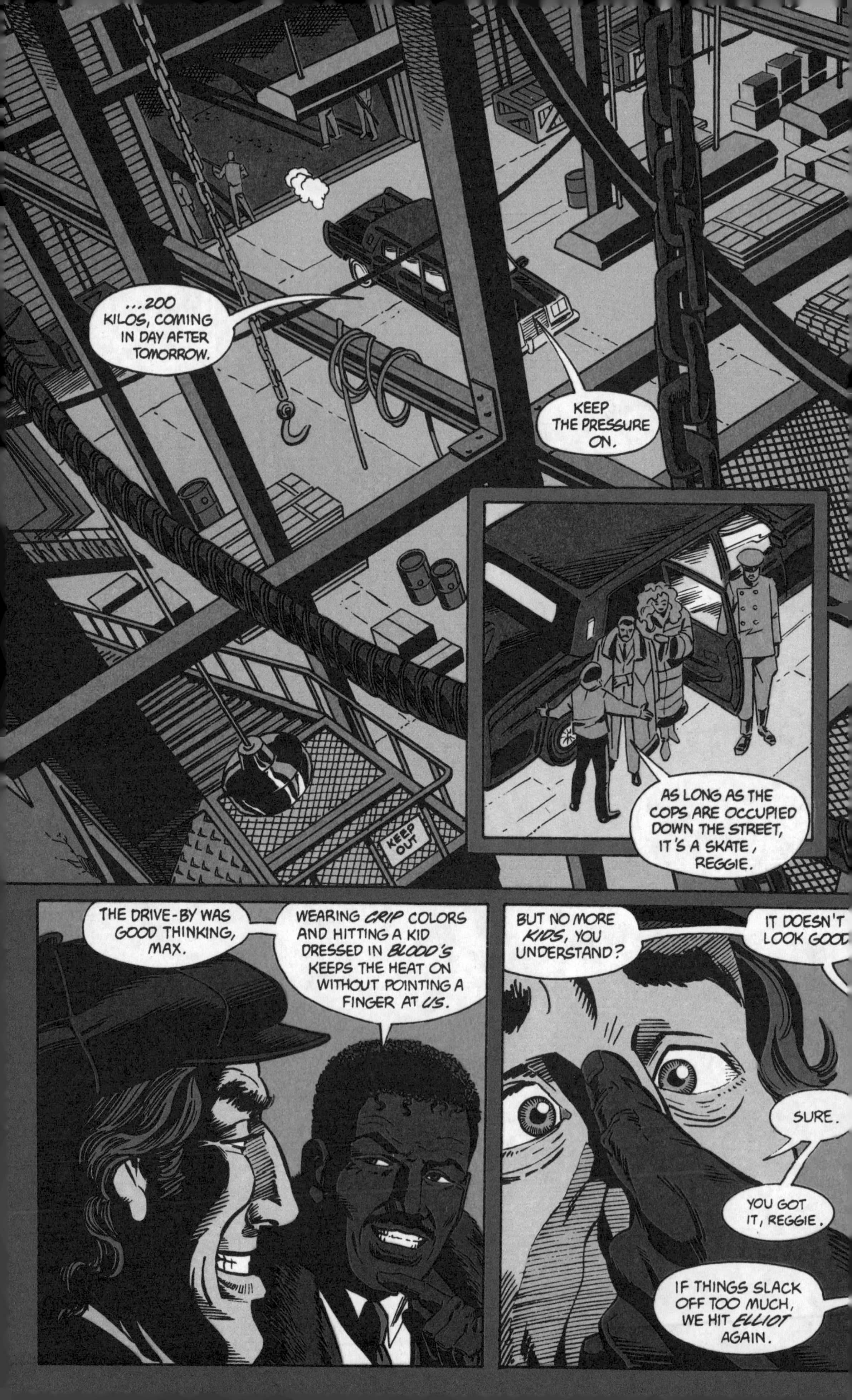
...200 KILOS, COMING IN DAY AFTER TOMORROW.
KEEP THE PRESSURE ON.
AS LONG AS THE COPS ARE OCCUPIED DOWN THE STREET, IT'S A SKATE, REGGIE.
THE DRIVE-BY WAS GOOD THINKING, MAX.
WEARING CRIP COLORS AND HITTING A KID DRESSED IN BLOOD'S KEEPS THE HEAT ON WITHOUT POINTING A FINGER AT US.
BUT NO MORE KIDS, YOU UNDERSTAND?
IT DOESN'T LOOK GOOD
SURE.
YOU GOT IT, REGGIE.
IF THINGS SLACK OFF TOO MUCH, WE HIT ELLIOT AGAIN.
KEEP OUT

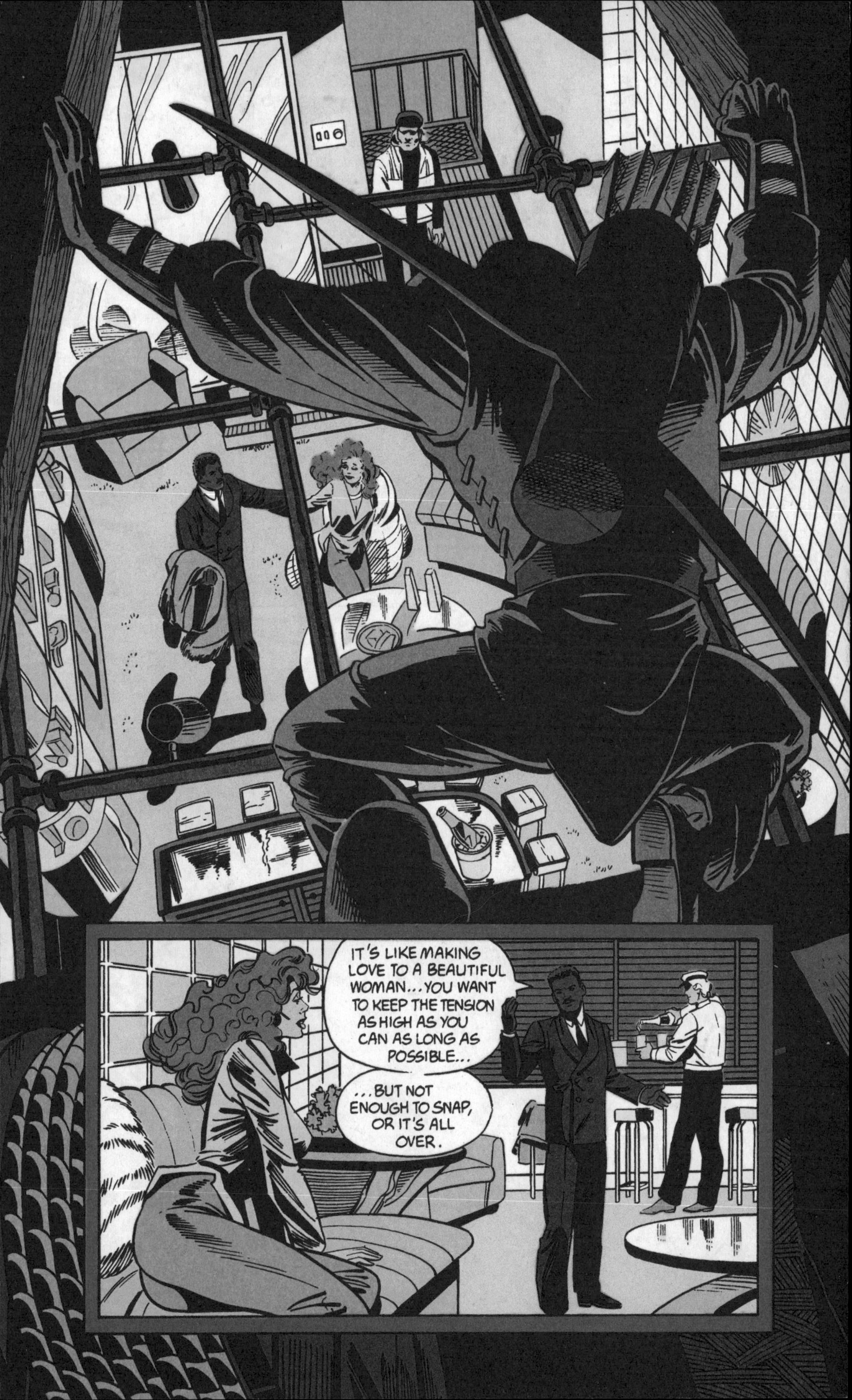
IT'S LIKE MAKING LOVE TO A BEAUTIFUL WOMAN... YOU WANT TO KEEP THE TENSION AS HIGH AS YOU CAN AS LONG AS POSSIBLE...
...BUT NOT ENOUGH TO SNAP, OR IT'S ALL OVER.

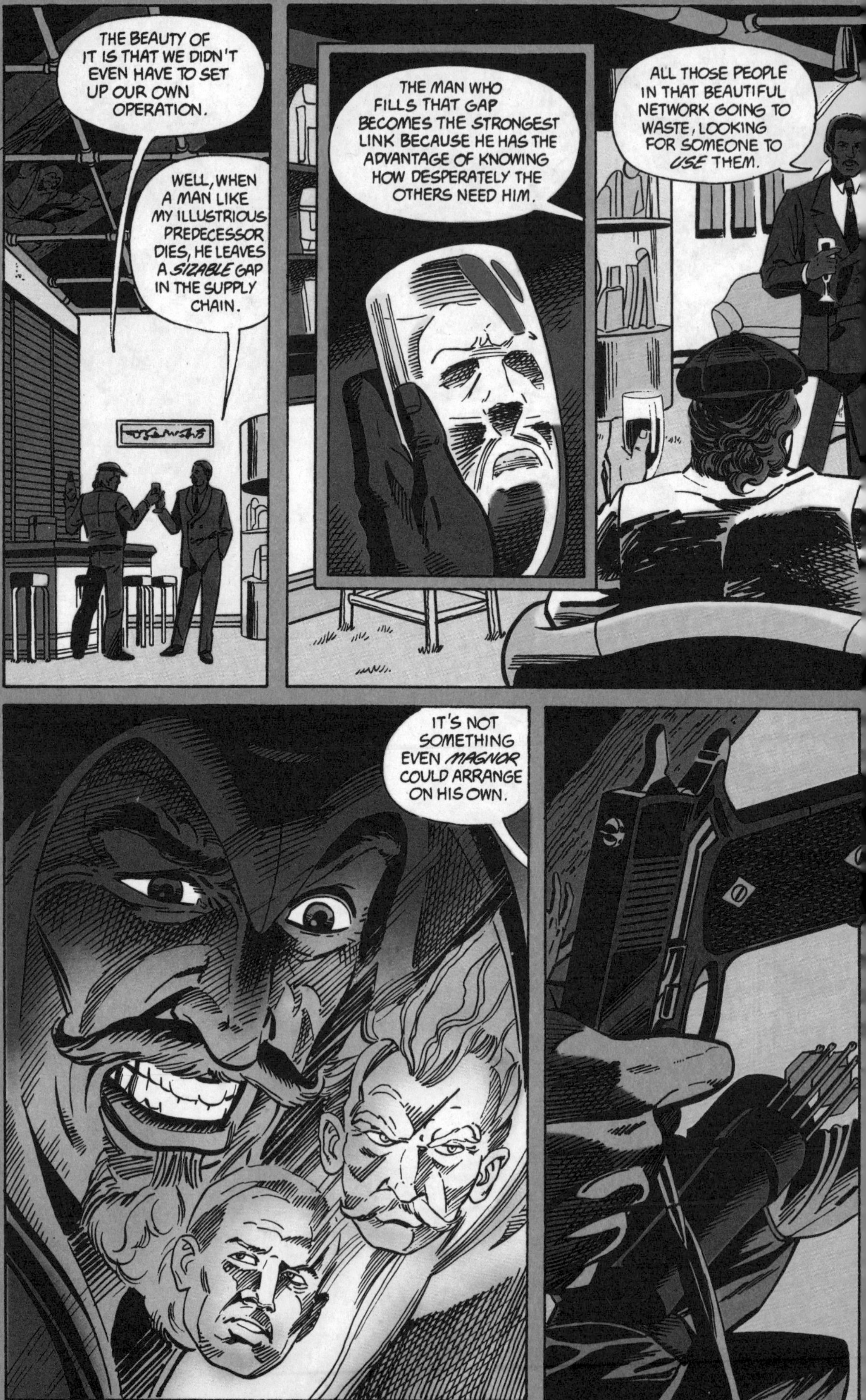
THE BEAUTY OF IT IS THAT WE DIDN'T EVEN HAVE TO SET UP OUR OWN OPERATION.
WELL, WHEN A MAN LIKE MY ILLUSTRIOUS PREDECESSOR DIES, HE LEAVES A SIZABLE GAP IN THE SUPPLY CHAIN.
THE MAN WHO FILLS THAT GAP BECOMES THE STRONGEST LINK BECAUSE HE HAS THE ADVANTAGE OF KNOWING HOW DESPERATELY THE OTHERS NEED HIM.
ALL THOSE PEOPLE IN THAT BEAUTIFUL NETWORK GOING TO WASTE, LOOKING FOR SOMEONE TO USE THEM.
IT'S NOT SOMETHING EVEN MAGNOR COULD ARRANGE ON HIS OWN.

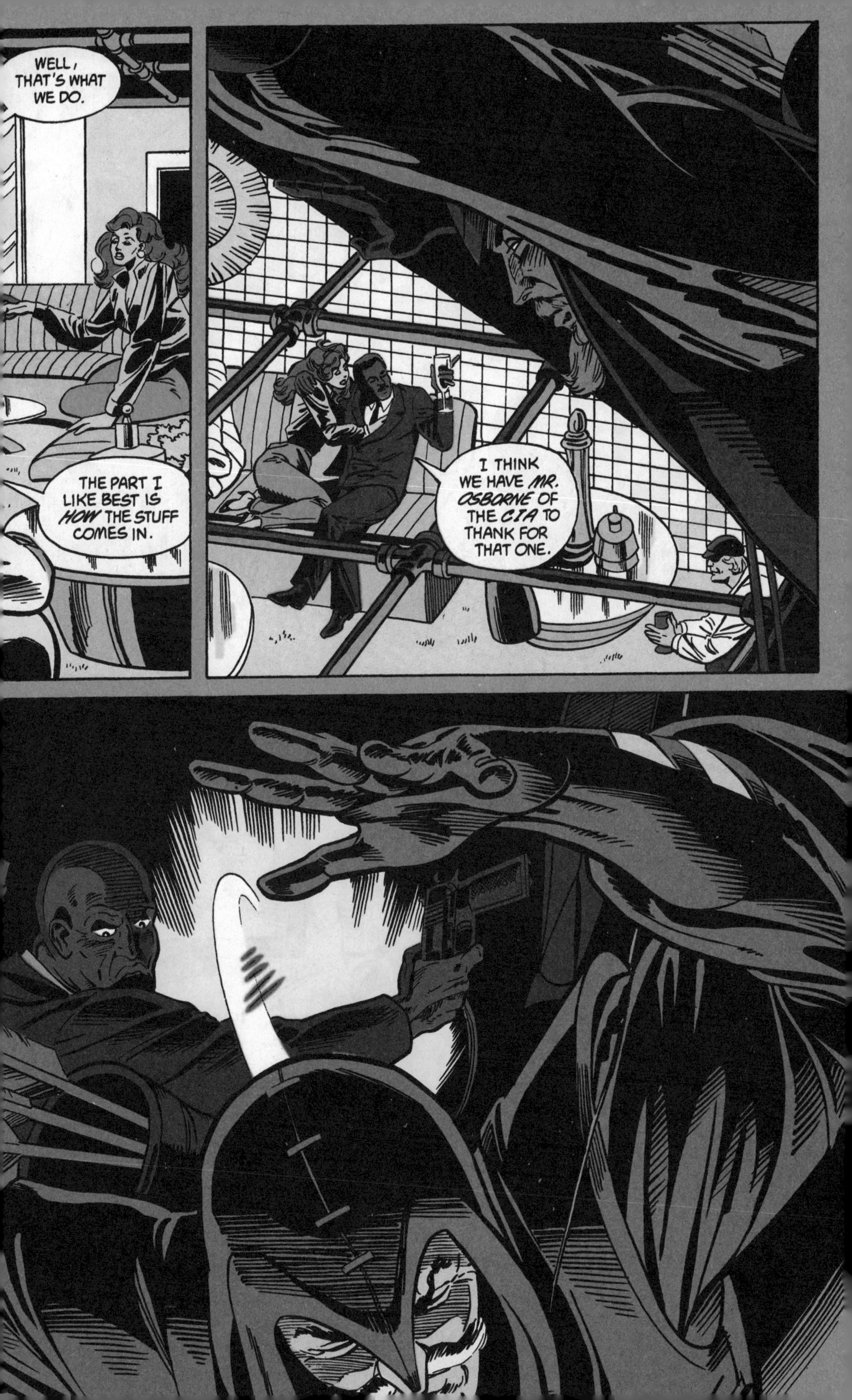

WELL, THAT'S WHAT WE DO.
THE PART I LIKE BEST IS *HOW* THE STUFF COMES IN.
I THINK WE HAVE *MR. OSBORNE* OF THE *CIA* TO THANK FOR THAT ONE.

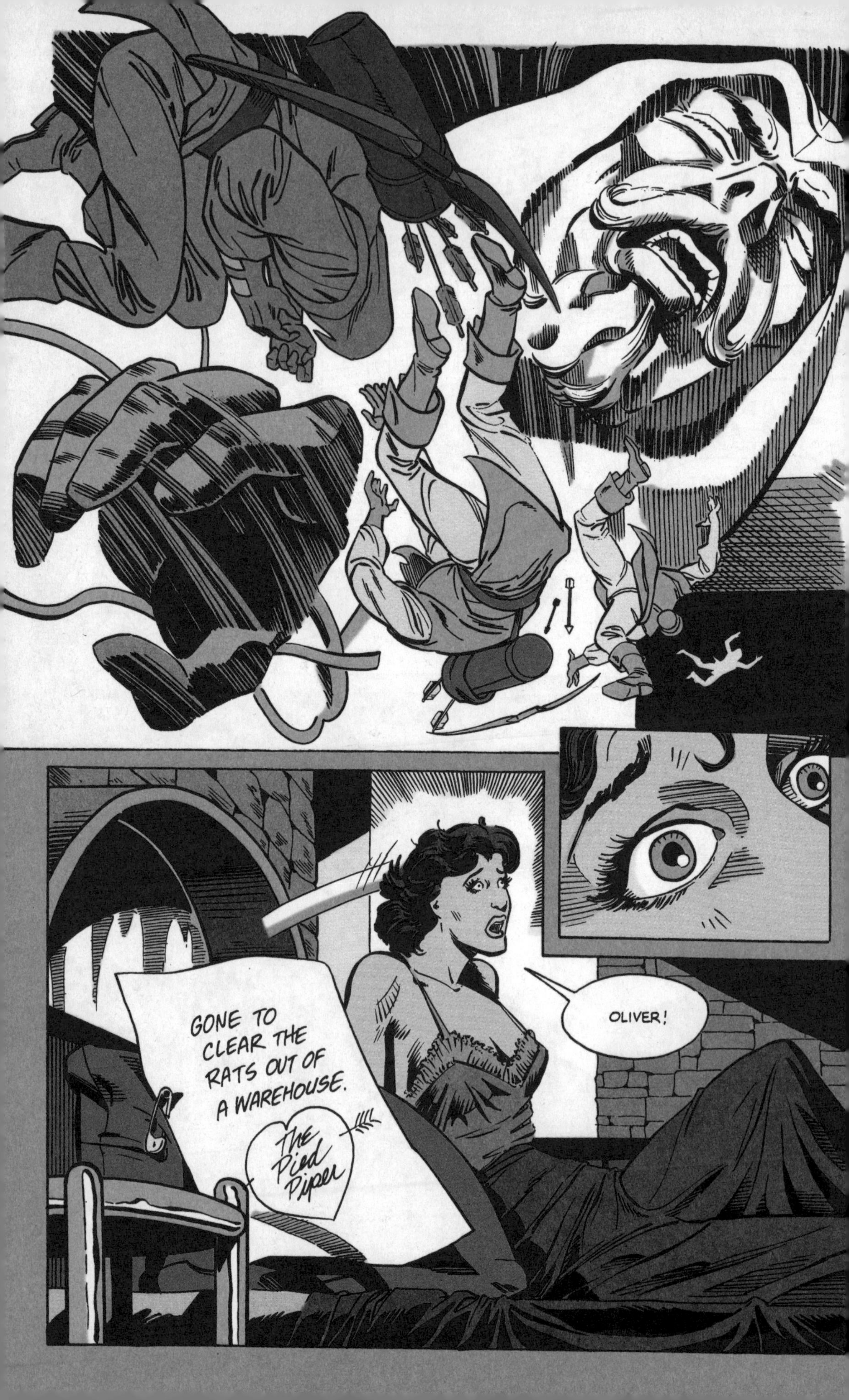
GONE TO CLEAR THE RATS OUT OF A WAREHOUSE.
The Pied Piper
OLIVER!

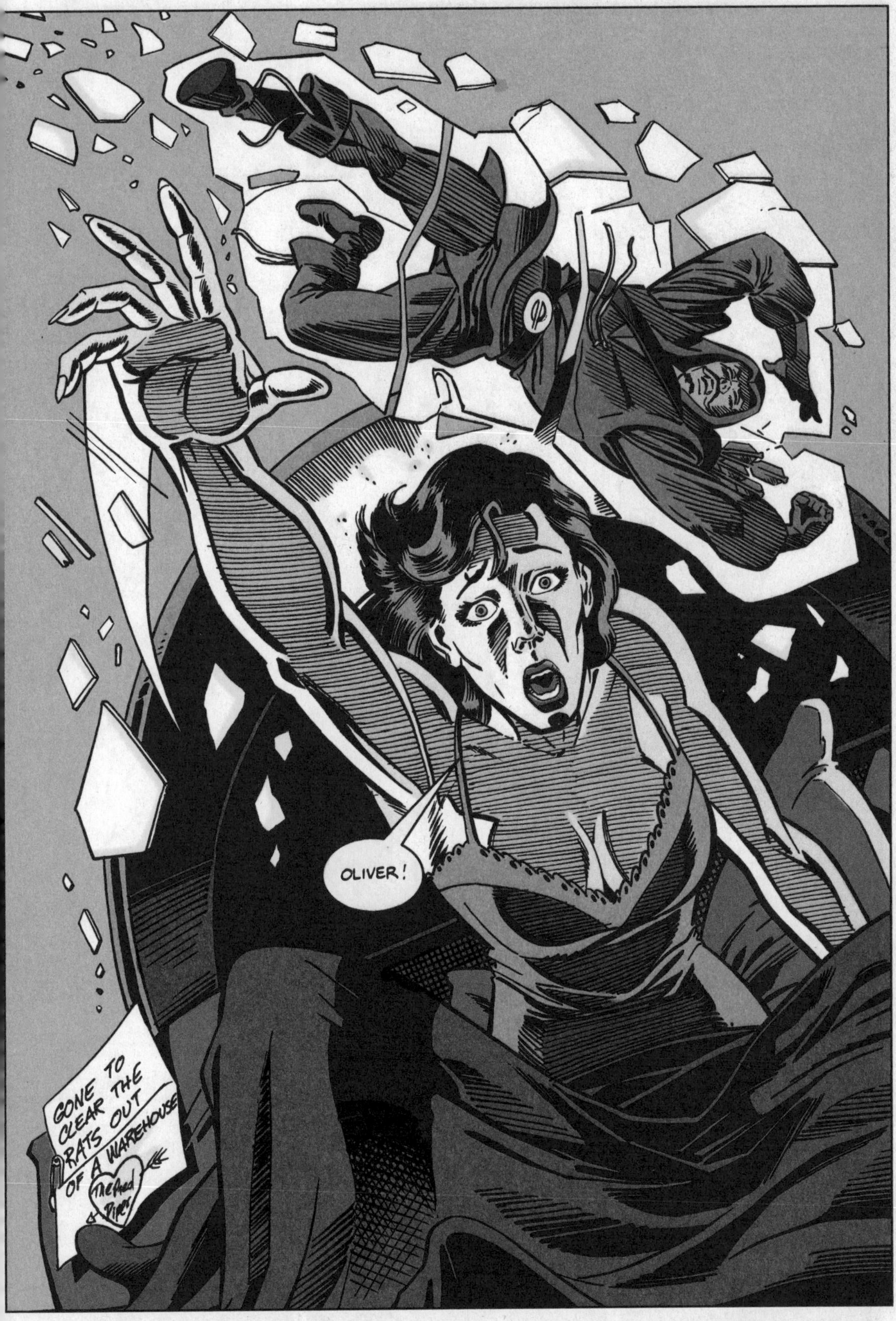
OLIVER!
GONE TO CLEAR THE RATS OUT OF A WAREHOUSE
The Pied Piper

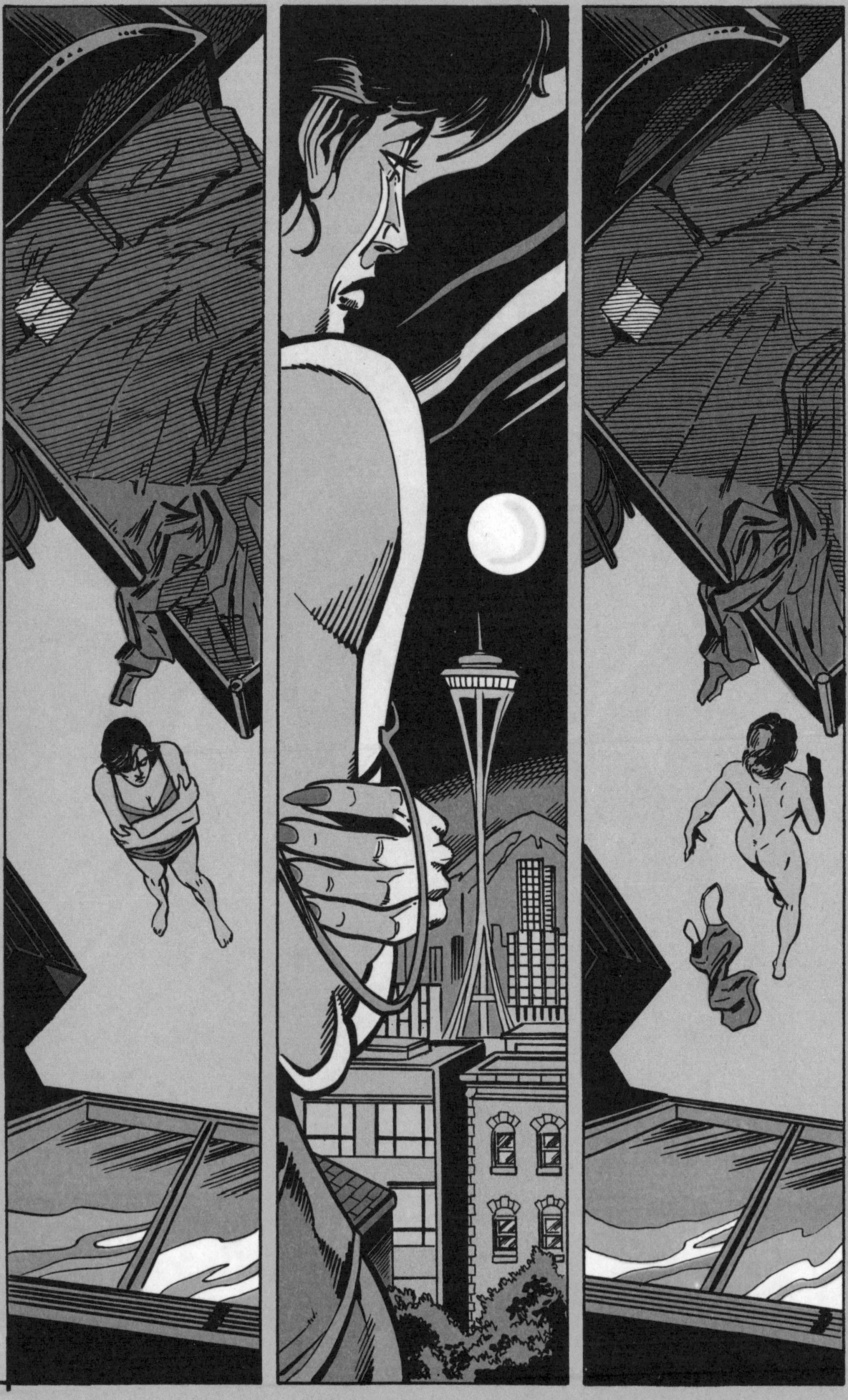

Part Two
The CANARY is a
BIRD of PREY

| | |
|---|---|
| GRELL | script |
| MIEHM | pencils |
| McLAUGHLIN | inks |
| COSTANZA | letters |
| LACQUEMENT | colors |
| MAIN | development assoc. |
| GOLD | editor |

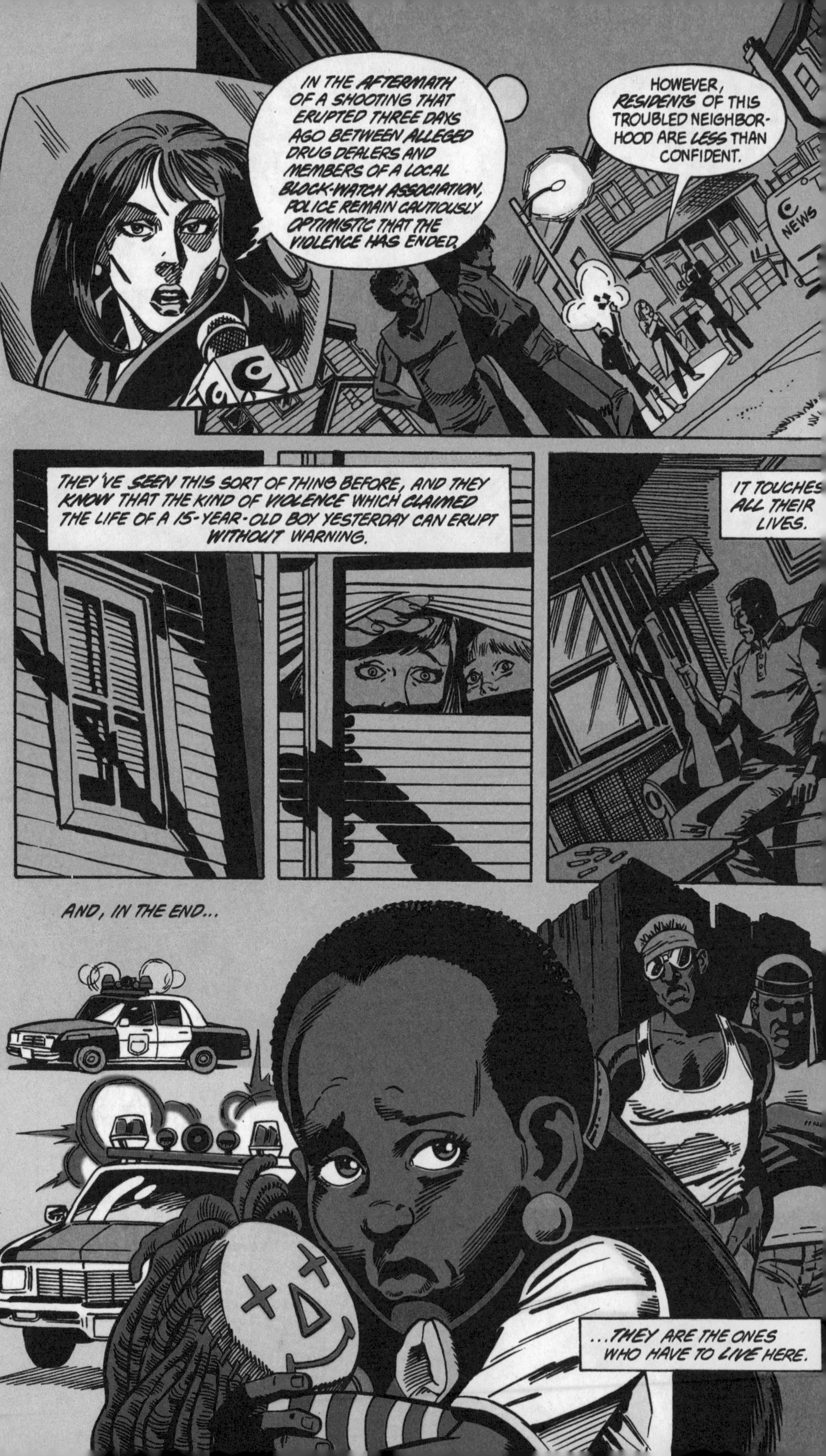
IN THE AFTERMATH OF A SHOOTING THAT ERUPTED THREE DAYS AGO BETWEEN ALLEGED DRUG DEALERS AND MEMBERS OF A LOCAL BLOCK-WATCH ASSOCIATION, POLICE REMAIN CAUTIOUSLY OPTIMISTIC THAT THE VIOLENCE HAS ENDED.
HOWEVER, RESIDENTS OF THIS TROUBLED NEIGHBOR-HOOD ARE LESS THAN CONFIDENT.
NEWS
THEY'VE SEEN THIS SORT OF THING BEFORE, AND THEY KNOW THAT THE KIND OF VIOLENCE WHICH CLAIMED THE LIFE OF A 15-YEAR-OLD BOY YESTERDAY CAN ERUPT WITHOUT WARNING.
IT TOUCHES ALL THEIR LIVES.
AND, IN THE END...
...THEY ARE THE ONES WHO HAVE TO LIVE HERE.

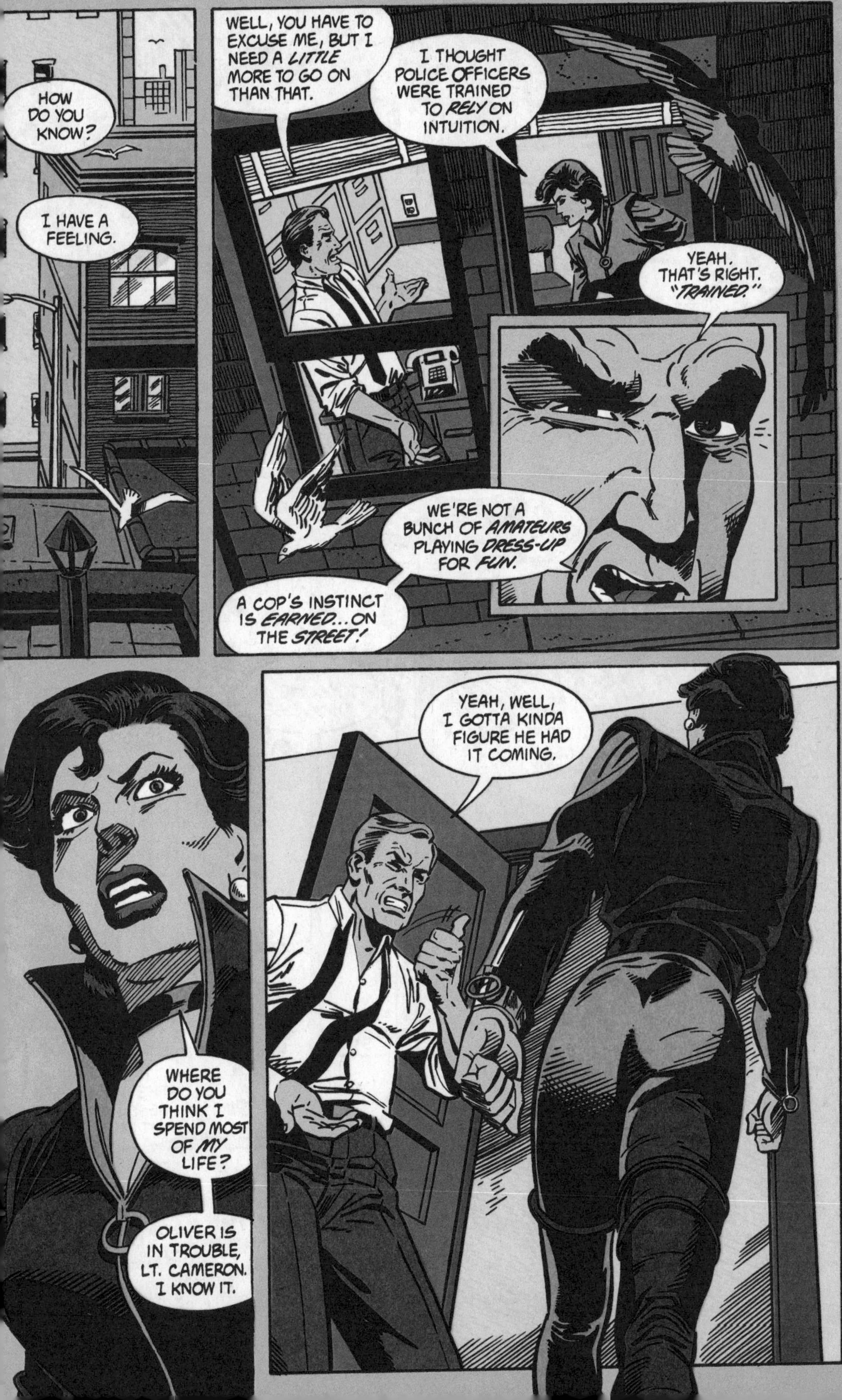
HOW DO YOU KNOW?
I HAVE A FEELING.
WELL, YOU HAVE TO EXCUSE ME, BUT I NEED A LITTLE MORE TO GO ON THAN THAT.
I THOUGHT POLICE OFFICERS WERE TRAINED TO RELY ON INTUITION.
YEAH. THAT'S RIGHT. "TRAINED."
WE'RE NOT A BUNCH OF AMATEURS PLAYING DRESS-UP FOR FUN.
A COP'S INSTINCT IS EARNED... ON THE STREET!
WHERE DO YOU THINK I SPEND MOST OF MY LIFE?
OLIVER IS IN TROUBLE, LT. CAMERON. I KNOW IT.
YEAH, WELL, I GOTTA KINDA FIGURE HE HAD IT COMING.

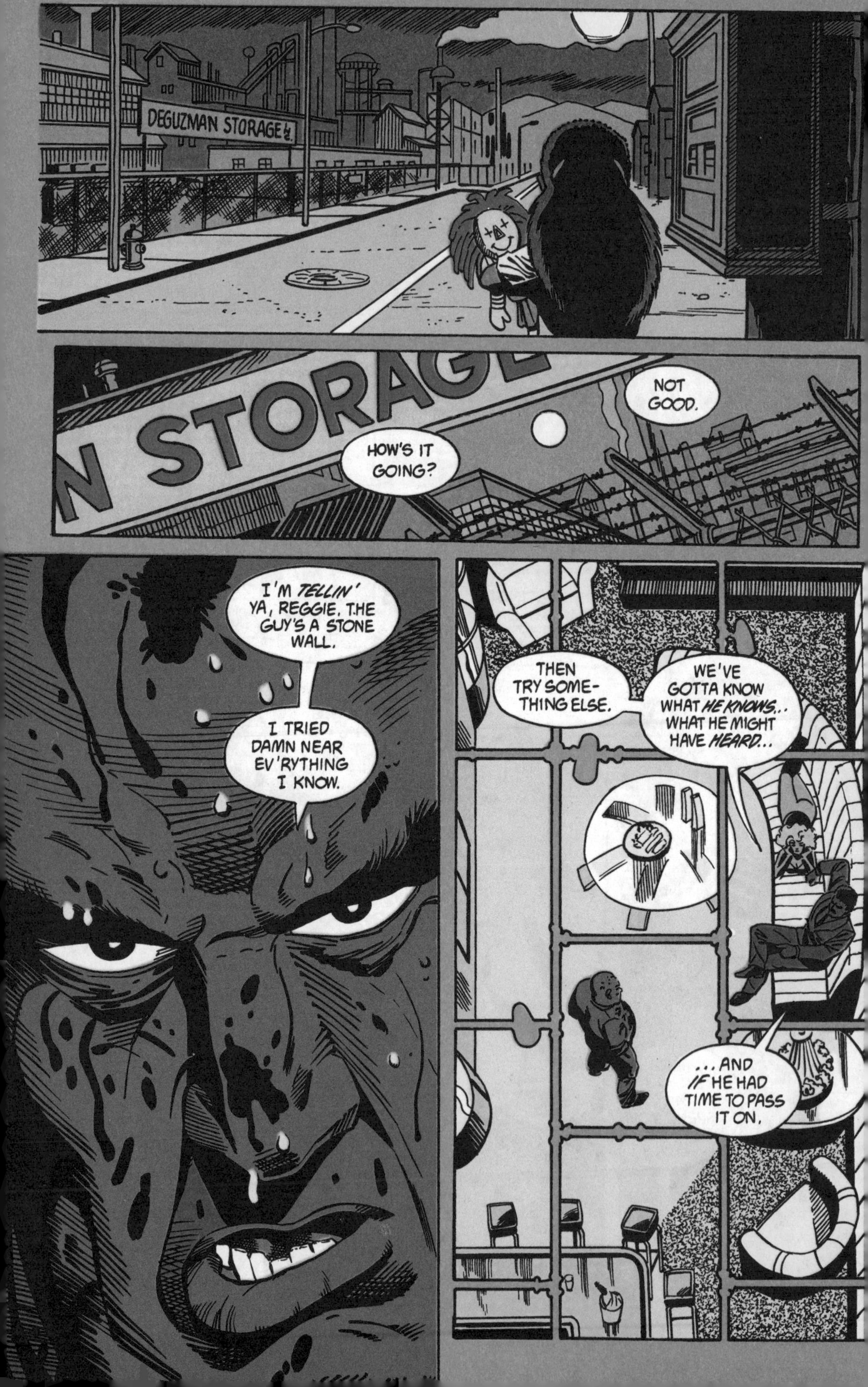
DEGUZMAN STORAGE
STORAGE
HOW'S IT GOING?
NOT GOOD.
I'M TELLIN' YA, REGGIE. THE GUY'S A STONE WALL.
I TRIED DAMN NEAR EV'RYTHING I KNOW.
THEN TRY SOME-THING ELSE.
WE'VE GOTTA KNOW WHAT HE KNOWS... WHAT HE MIGHT HAVE HEARD...
...AND IF HE HAD TIME TO PASS IT ON.

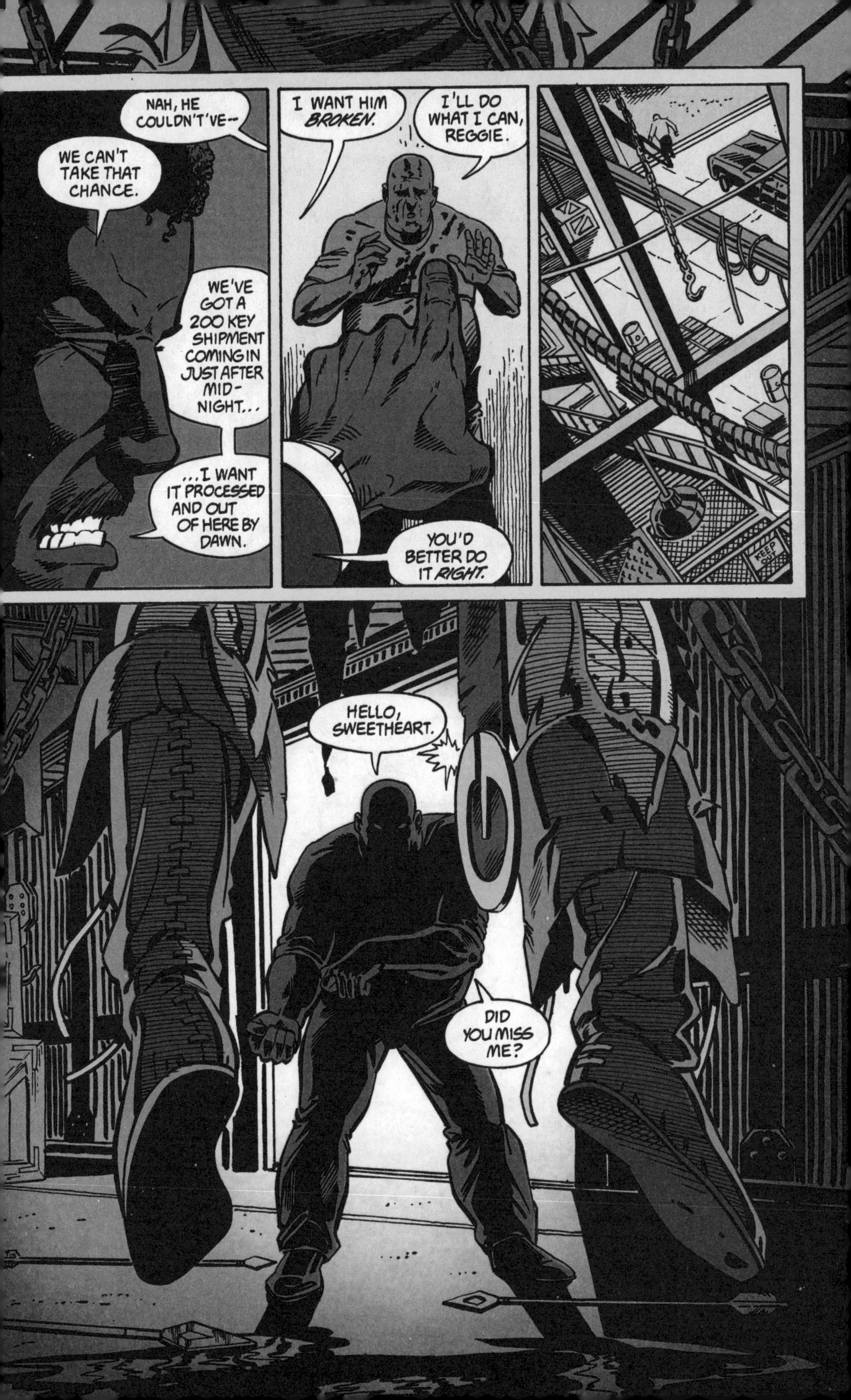
NAH, HE COULDN'T'VE--
WE CAN'T TAKE THAT CHANCE.
WE'VE GOT A 200 KEY SHIPMENT COMING IN JUST AFTER MID-NIGHT...
...I WANT IT PROCESSED AND OUT OF HERE BY DAWN.
I WANT HIM BROKEN.
I'LL DO WHAT I CAN, REGGIE.
YOU'D BETTER DO IT RIGHT.
KEEP OUT
HELLO, SWEETHEART.
DID YOU MISS ME?

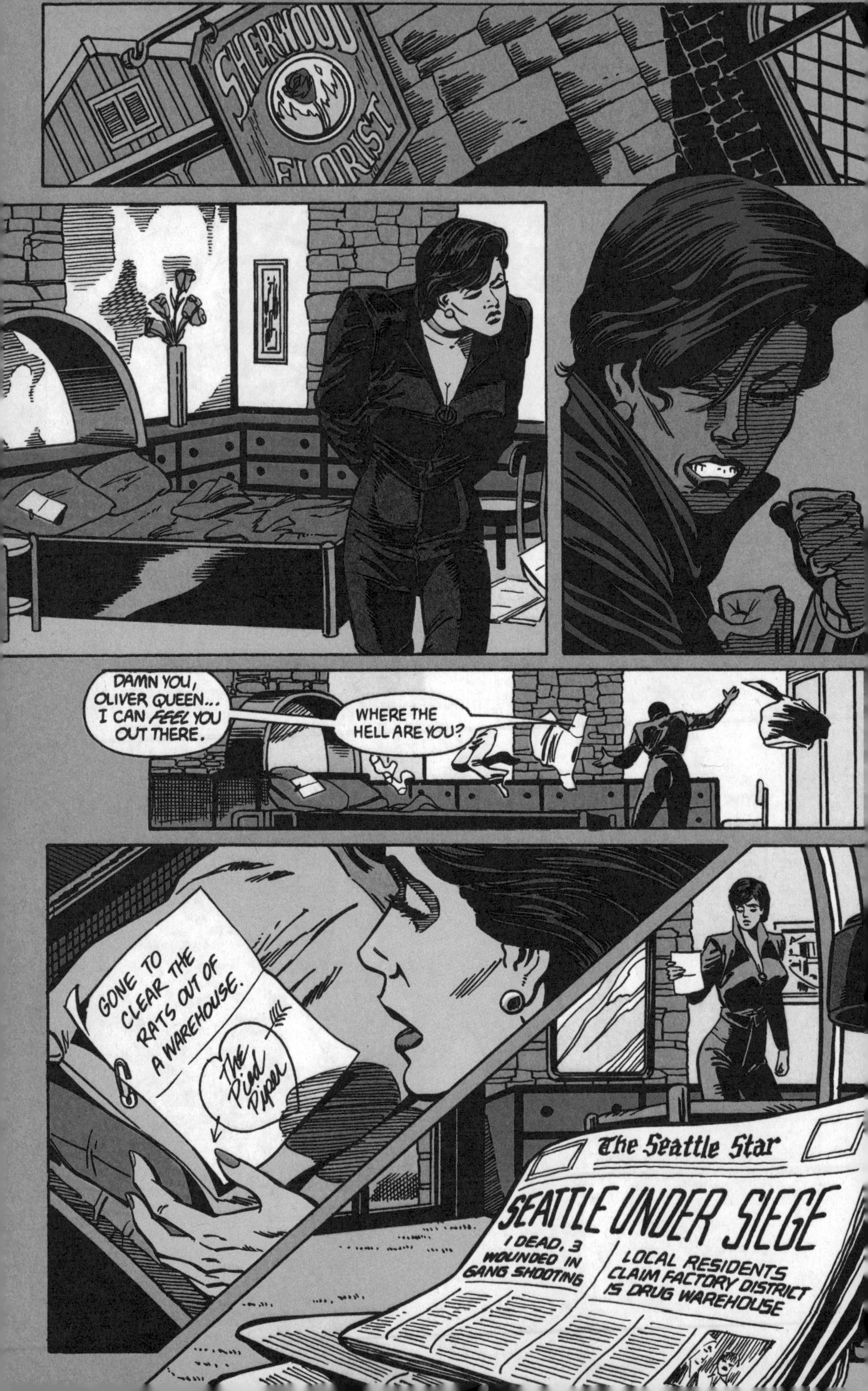
SHERWOOD FLORIST
DAMN YOU, OLIVER QUEEN... I CAN FEEL YOU OUT THERE.
WHERE THE HELL ARE YOU?
GONE TO CLEAR THE RATS OUT OF A WAREHOUSE.
The Pied Piper
The Seattle Star
SEATTLE UNDER SIEGE
1 DEAD, 3 WOUNDED IN GANG SHOOTING
LOCAL RESIDENTS CLAIM FACTORY DISTRICT IS DRUG WAREHOUSE

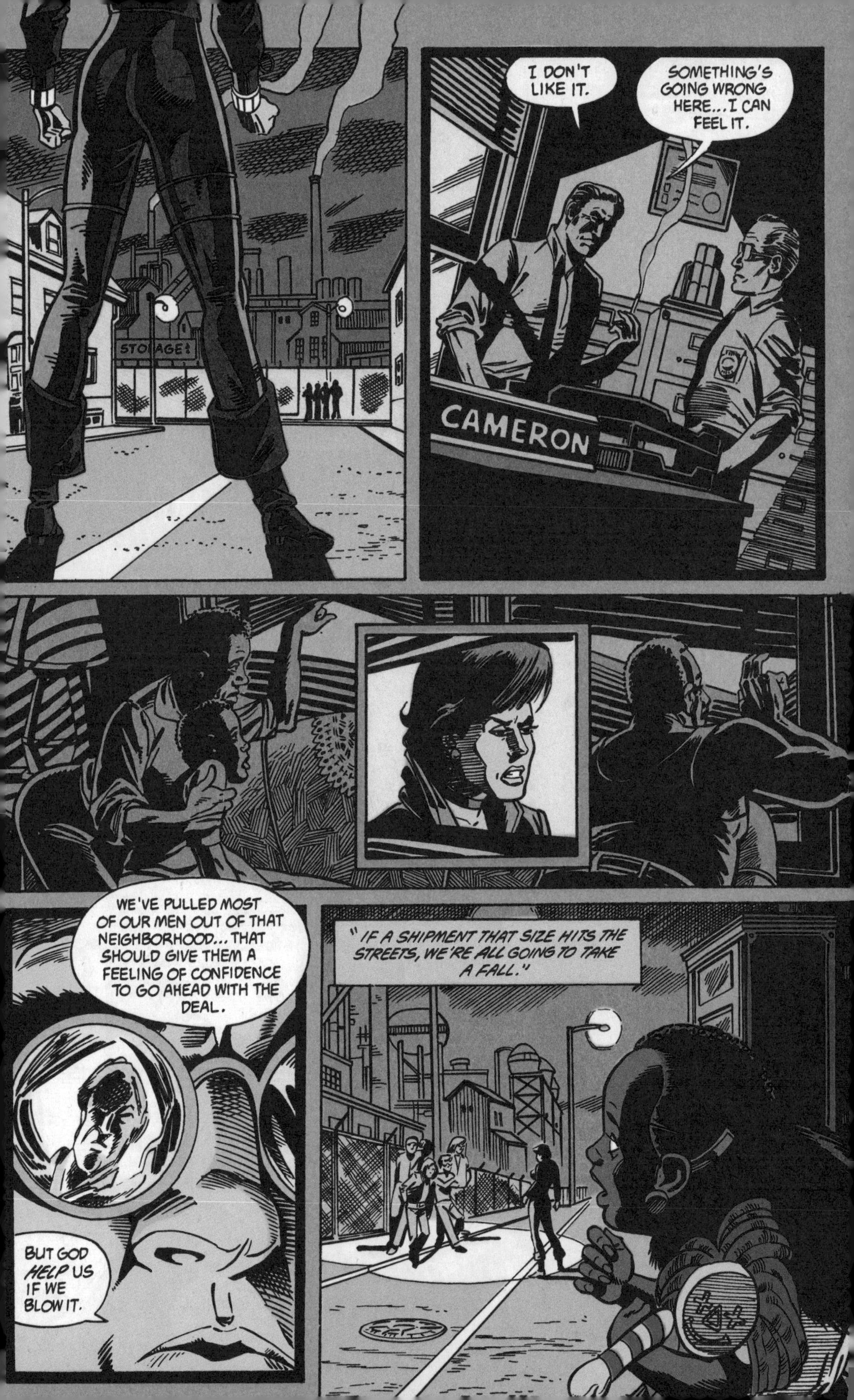

STORAGE
I DON'T LIKE IT.
SOMETHING'S GOING WRONG HERE... I CAN FEEL IT.
CAMERON
WE'VE PULLED MOST OF OUR MEN OUT OF THAT NEIGHBORHOOD... THAT SHOULD GIVE THEM A FEELING OF CONFIDENCE TO GO AHEAD WITH THE DEAL.
BUT GOD *HELP* US IF WE BLOW IT.
"IF A SHIPMENT THAT SIZE HITS THE STREETS, WE'RE ALL GOING TO TAKE A FALL."

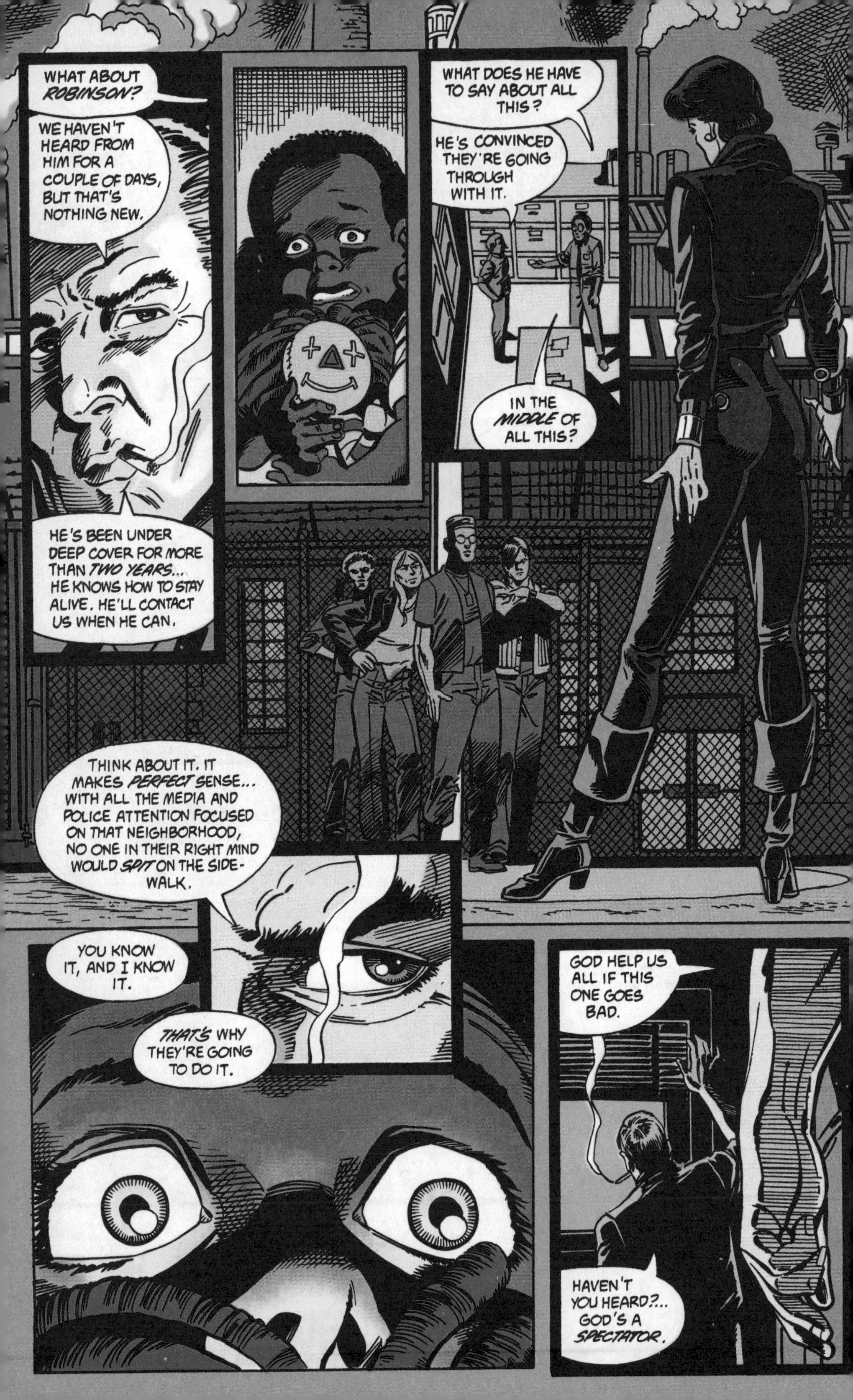
WHAT ABOUT ROBINSON?
WE HAVEN'T HEARD FROM HIM FOR A COUPLE OF DAYS, BUT THAT'S NOTHING NEW.
HE'S BEEN UNDER DEEP COVER FOR MORE THAN TWO YEARS... HE KNOWS HOW TO STAY ALIVE. HE'LL CONTACT US WHEN HE CAN.
WHAT DOES HE HAVE TO SAY ABOUT ALL THIS?
HE'S CONVINCED THEY'RE GOING THROUGH WITH IT.
IN THE MIDDLE OF ALL THIS?
THINK ABOUT IT. IT MAKES PERFECT SENSE... WITH ALL THE MEDIA AND POLICE ATTENTION FOCUSED ON THAT NEIGHBORHOOD, NO ONE IN THEIR RIGHT MIND WOULD SPIT ON THE SIDE-WALK.
YOU KNOW IT, AND I KNOW IT.
THAT'S WHY THEY'RE GOING TO DO IT.
GOD HELP US ALL IF THIS ONE GOES BAD.
HAVEN'T YOU HEARD?... GOD'S A SPECTATOR.

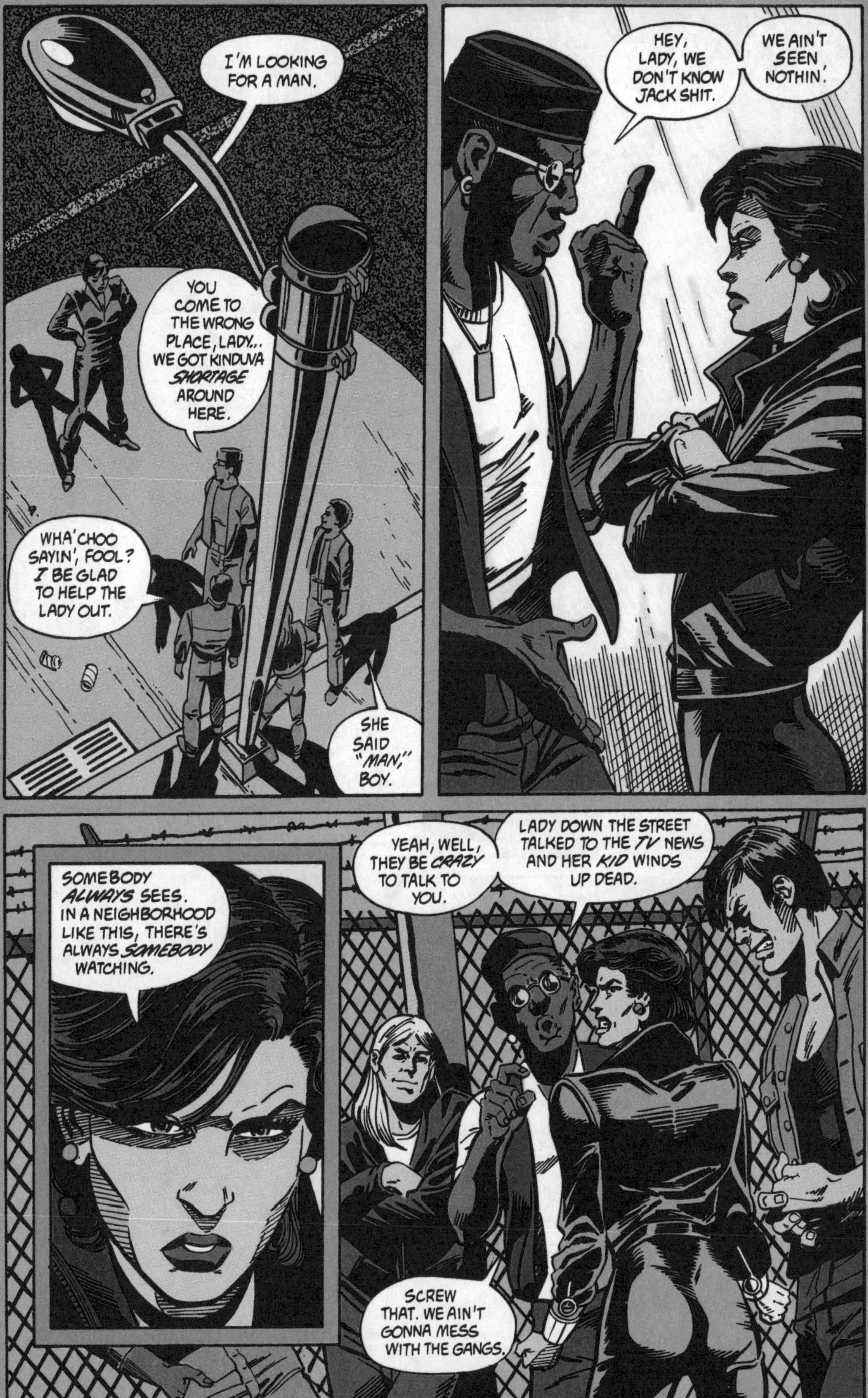
I'M LOOKING FOR A MAN.
YOU COME TO THE WRONG PLACE, LADY.. WE GOT KINDUVA SHORTAGE AROUND HERE.
WHA'CHOO SAYIN', FOOL? I BE GLAD TO HELP THE LADY OUT.
SHE SAID "MAN," BOY.
HEY, LADY, WE DON'T KNOW JACK SHIT.
WE AIN'T SEEN NOTHIN'.
SOMEBODY ALWAYS SEES. IN A NEIGHBORHOOD LIKE THIS, THERE'S ALWAYS SOMEBODY WATCHING.
YEAH, WELL, THEY BE CRAZY TO TALK TO YOU.
LADY DOWN THE STREET TALKED TO THE TV NEWS AND HER KID WINDS UP DEAD.
SCREW THAT. WE AIN'T GONNA MESS WITH THE GANGS.

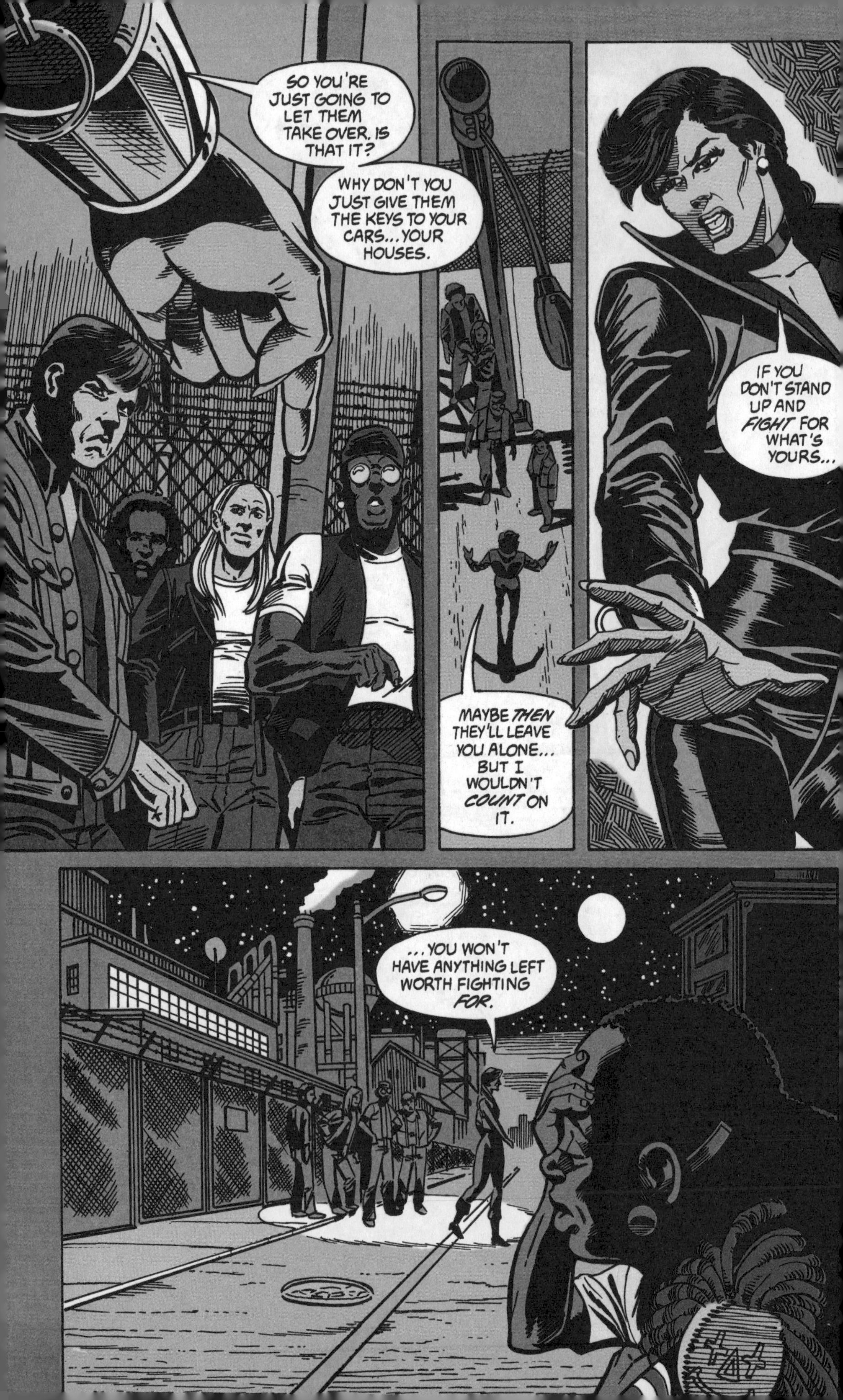
SO YOU'RE JUST GOING TO LET THEM TAKE OVER. IS THAT IT?
WHY DON'T YOU JUST GIVE THEM THE KEYS TO YOUR CARS... YOUR HOUSES.
MAYBE *THEN* THEY'LL LEAVE YOU ALONE... BUT I WOULDN'T *COUNT* ON IT.
IF YOU DON'T STAND UP AND *FIGHT* FOR WHAT'S YOURS...
...YOU WON'T HAVE ANYTHING LEFT WORTH FIGHTING *FOR*.

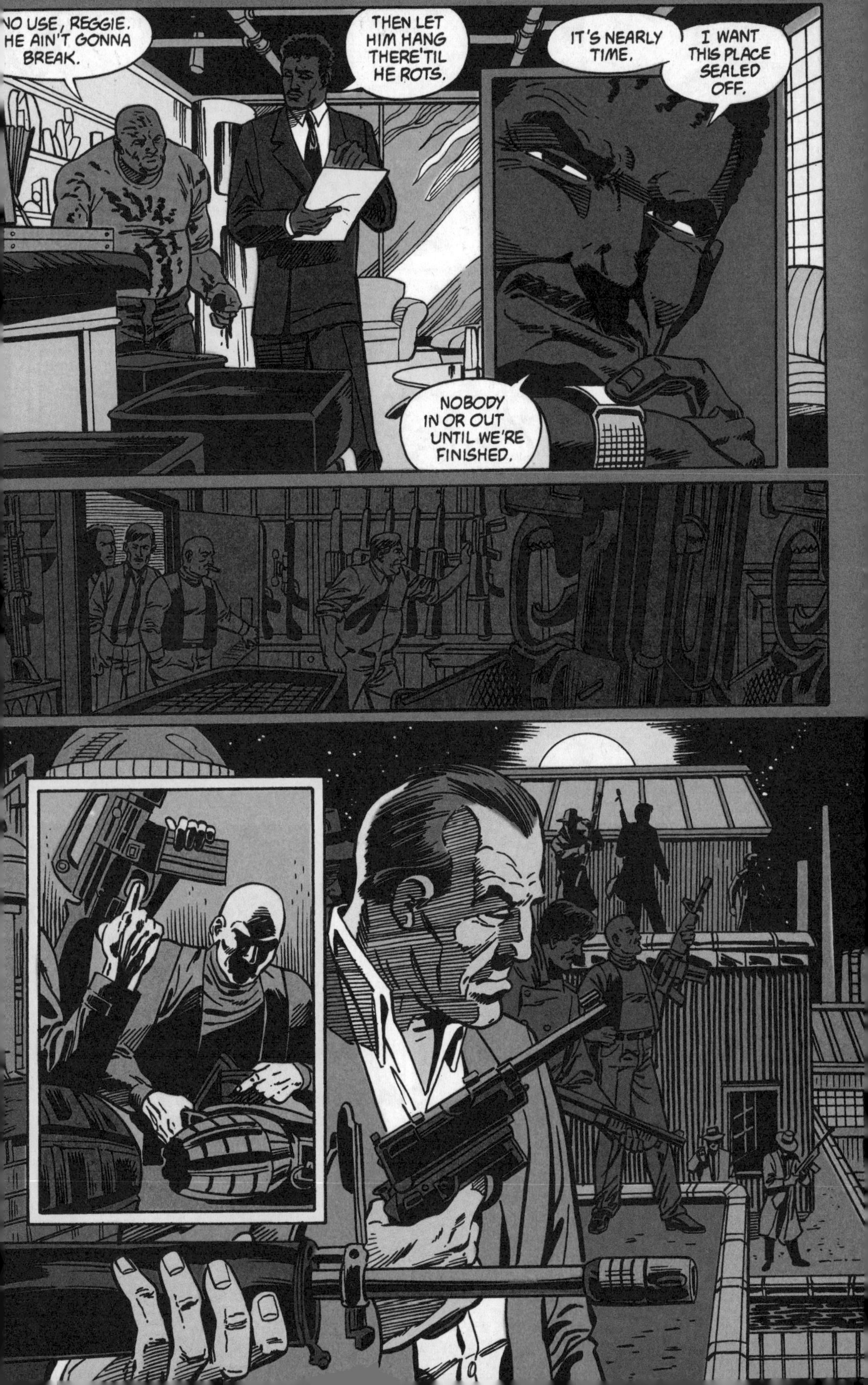
NO USE, REGGIE. HE AIN'T GONNA BREAK.
THEN LET HIM HANG THERE 'TIL HE ROTS.
IT'S NEARLY TIME.
I WANT THIS PLACE SEALED OFF.
NOBODY IN OR OUT UNTIL WE'RE FINISHED.

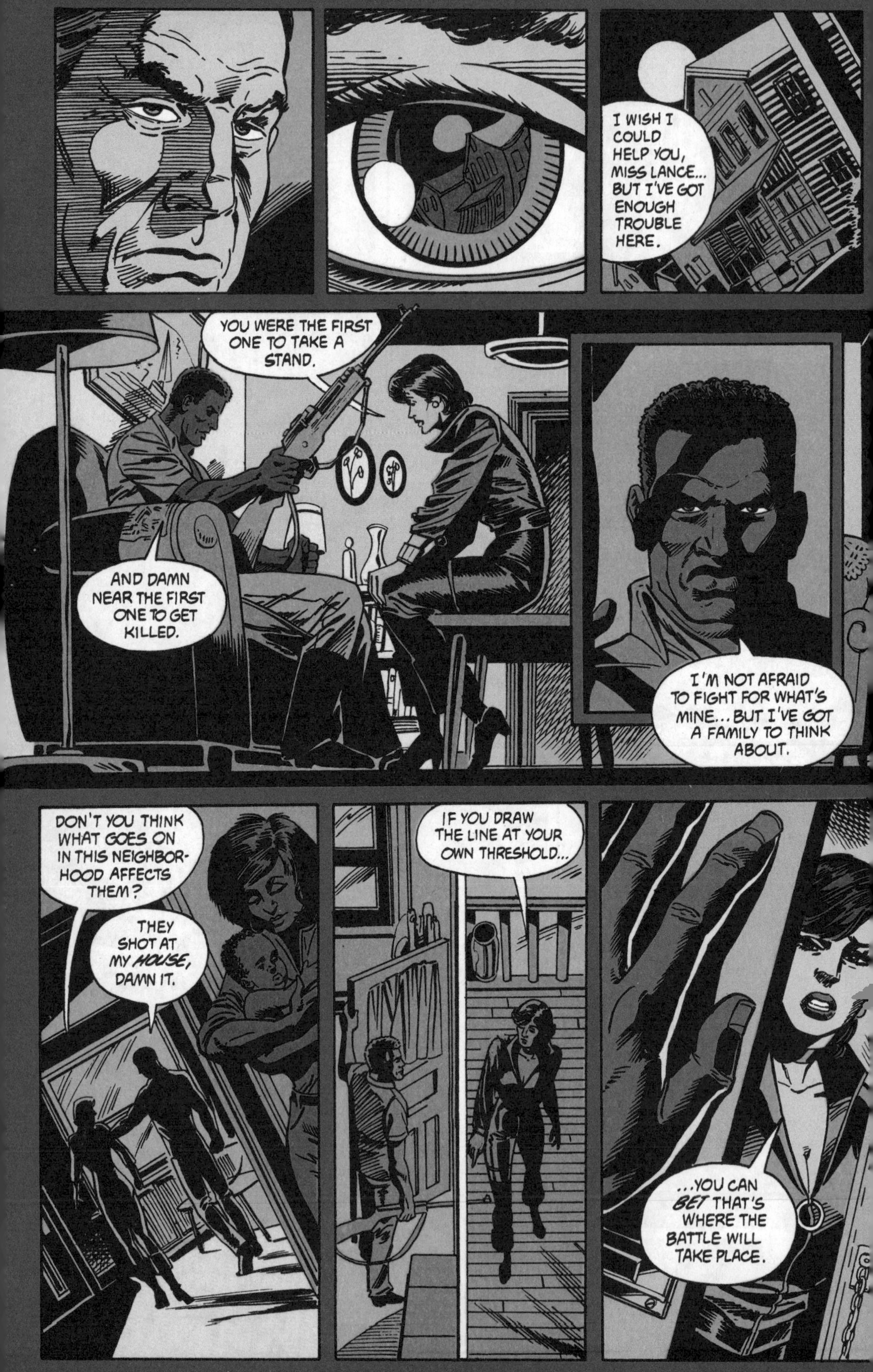
I WISH I COULD HELP YOU, MISS LANCE... BUT I'VE GOT ENOUGH TROUBLE HERE.
YOU WERE THE FIRST ONE TO TAKE A STAND.
AND DAMN NEAR THE FIRST ONE TO GET KILLED.
I'M NOT AFRAID TO FIGHT FOR WHAT'S MINE... BUT I'VE GOT A FAMILY TO THINK ABOUT.
DON'T YOU THINK WHAT GOES ON IN THIS NEIGHBOR-HOOD AFFECTS THEM?
THEY SHOT AT MY *HOUSE*, DAMN IT.
IF YOU DRAW THE LINE AT YOUR OWN THRESHOLD...
...YOU CAN *BET* THAT'S WHERE THE BATTLE WILL TAKE PLACE.

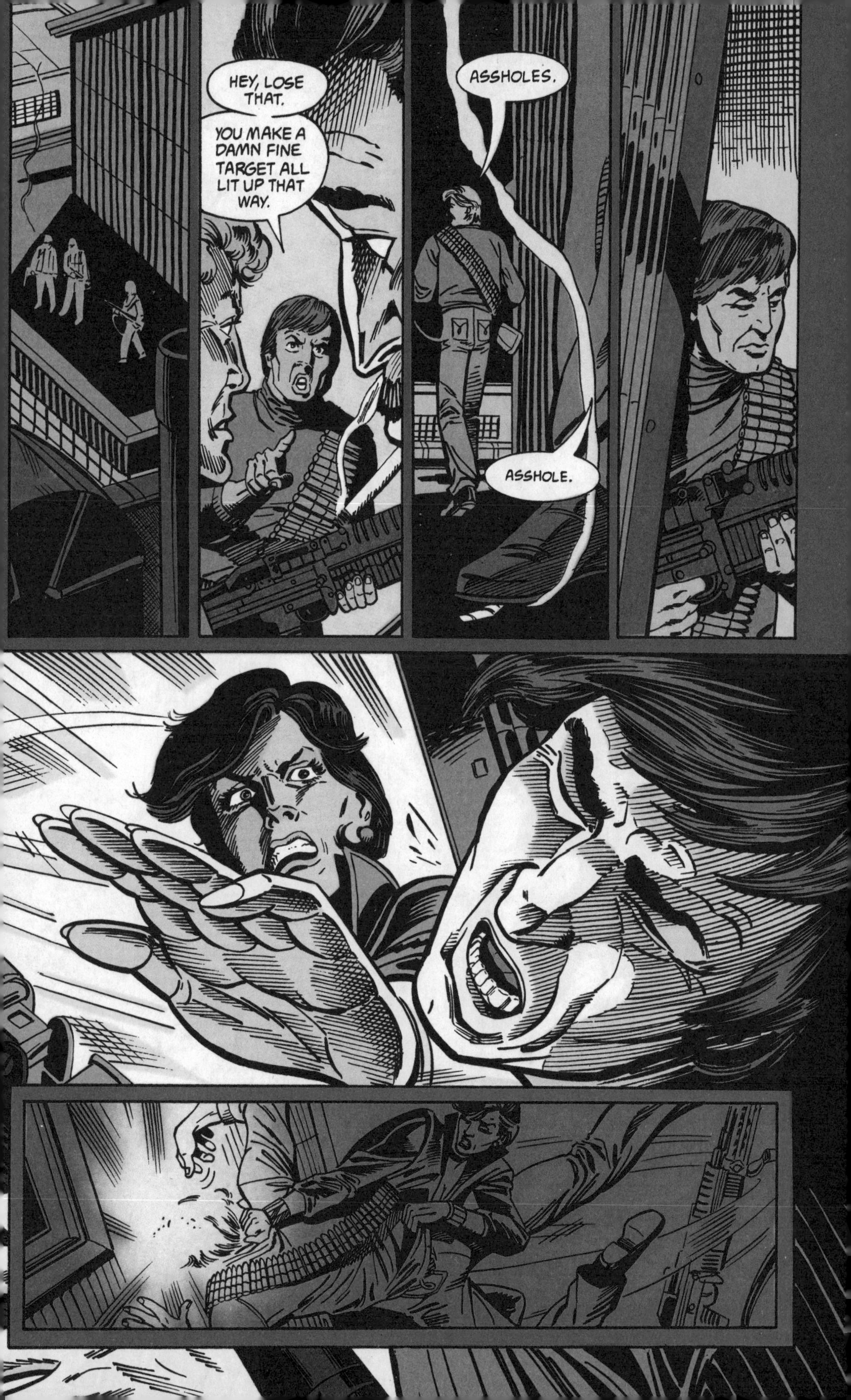
HEY, LOSE THAT.
YOU MAKE A DAMN FINE TARGET ALL LIT UP THAT WAY.
ASSHOLES.
ASSHOLE.

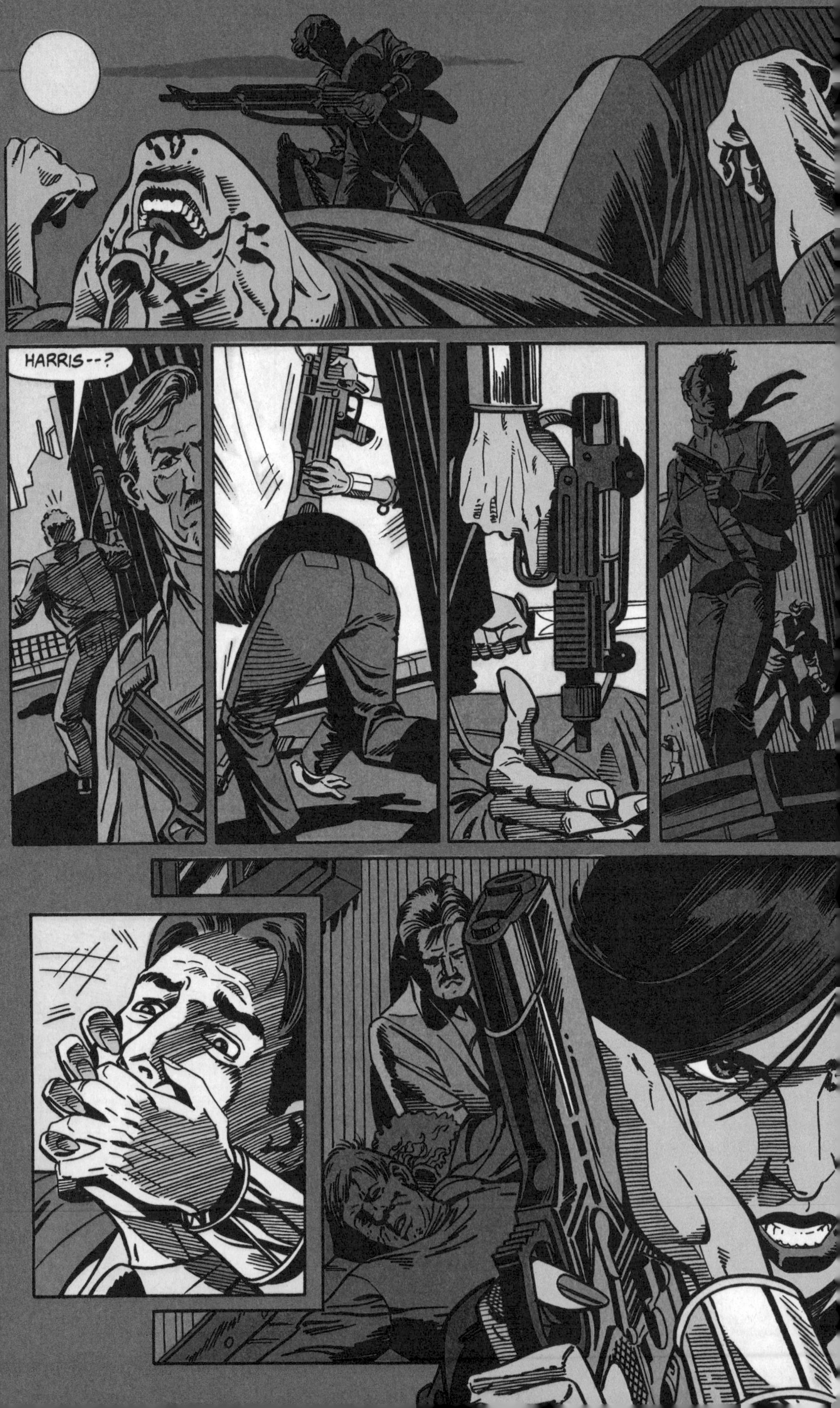
HARRIS--?

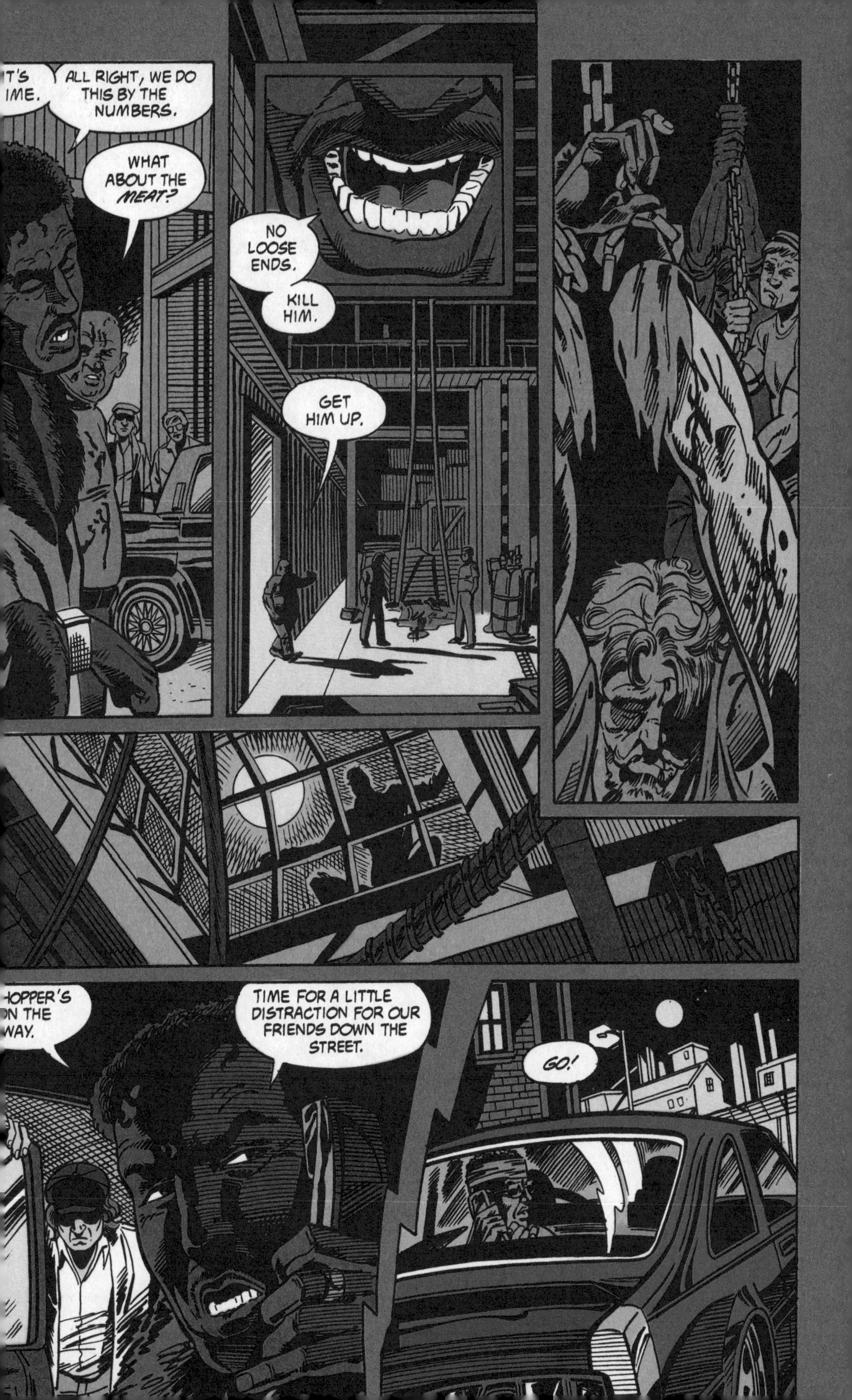

T'S
IME.
ALL RIGHT, WE DO THIS BY THE NUMBERS.
WHAT ABOUT THE *MEAT?*
NO LOOSE ENDS.
KILL HIM.
GET HIM UP.
OPPER'S
N THE
WAY.
TIME FOR A LITTLE DISTRACTION FOR OUR FRIENDS DOWN THE STREET.
GO!

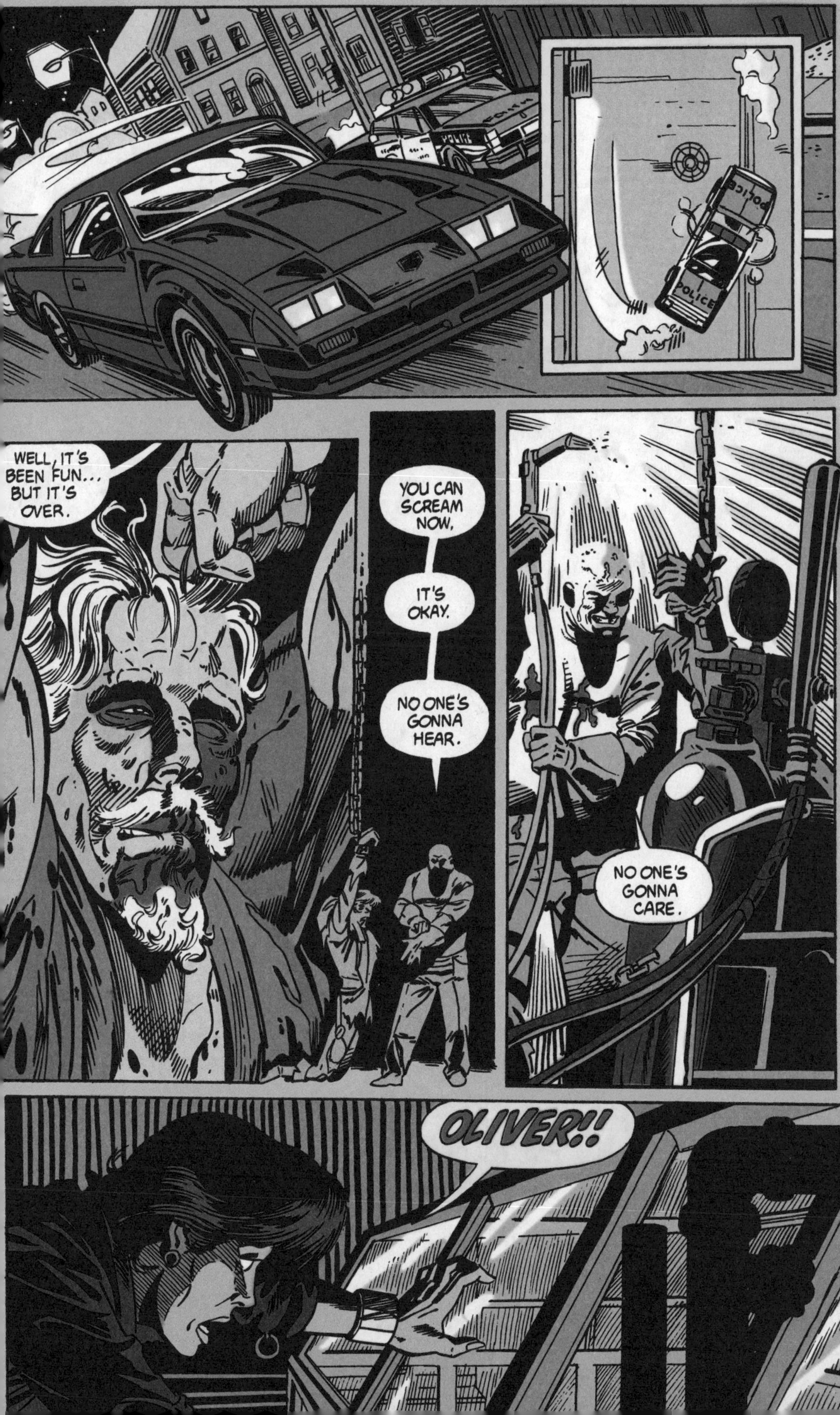
POLICE
POLICE
POLICE
WELL, IT'S BEEN FUN... BUT IT'S OVER.
YOU CAN SCREAM NOW.
IT'S OKAY.
NO ONE'S GONNA HEAR.
NO ONE'S GONNA CARE.
OLIVER!!

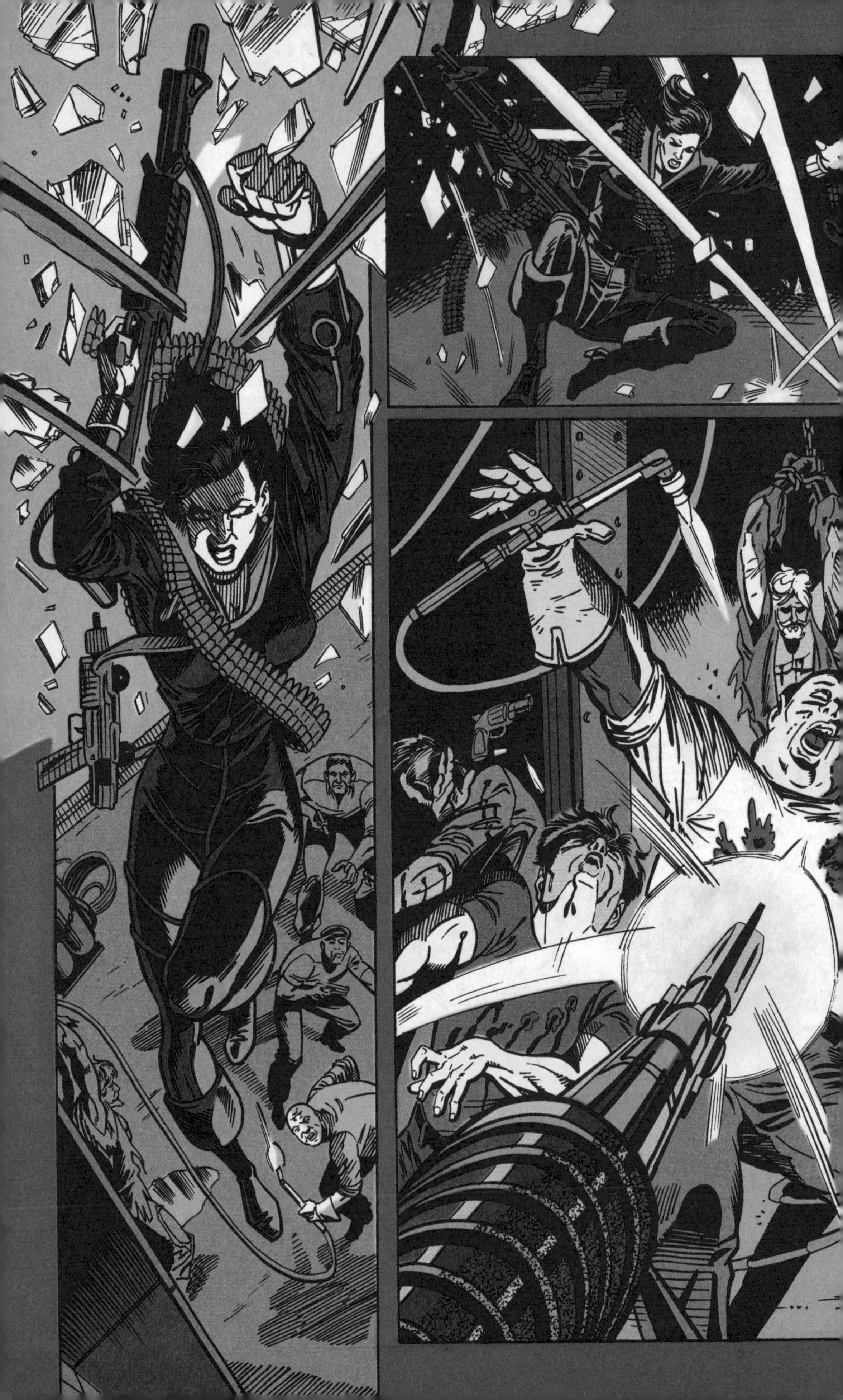

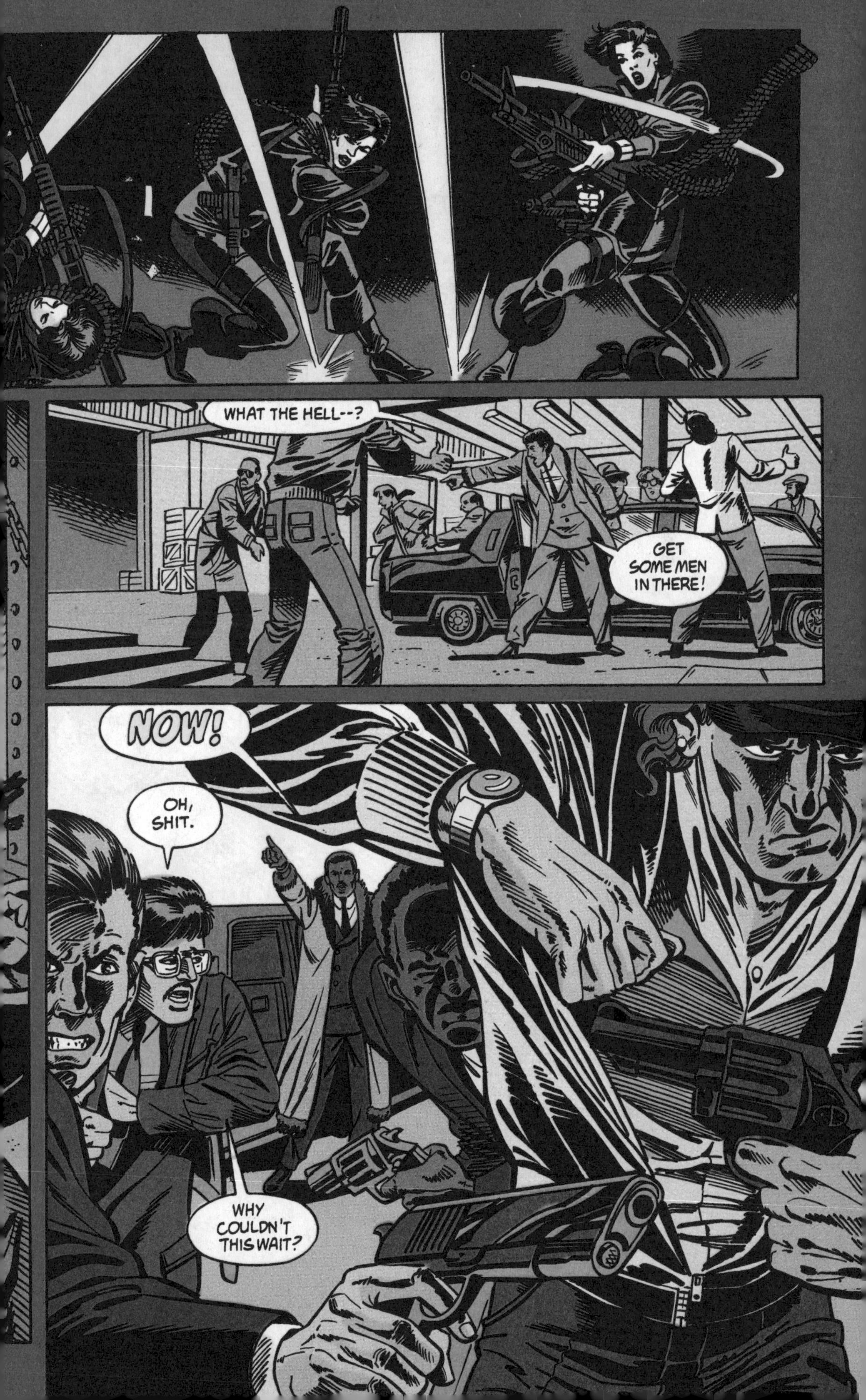
WHAT THE HELL--?
GET SOME MEN IN THERE!
NOW!
OH, SHIT.
WHY COULDN'T THIS WAIT?

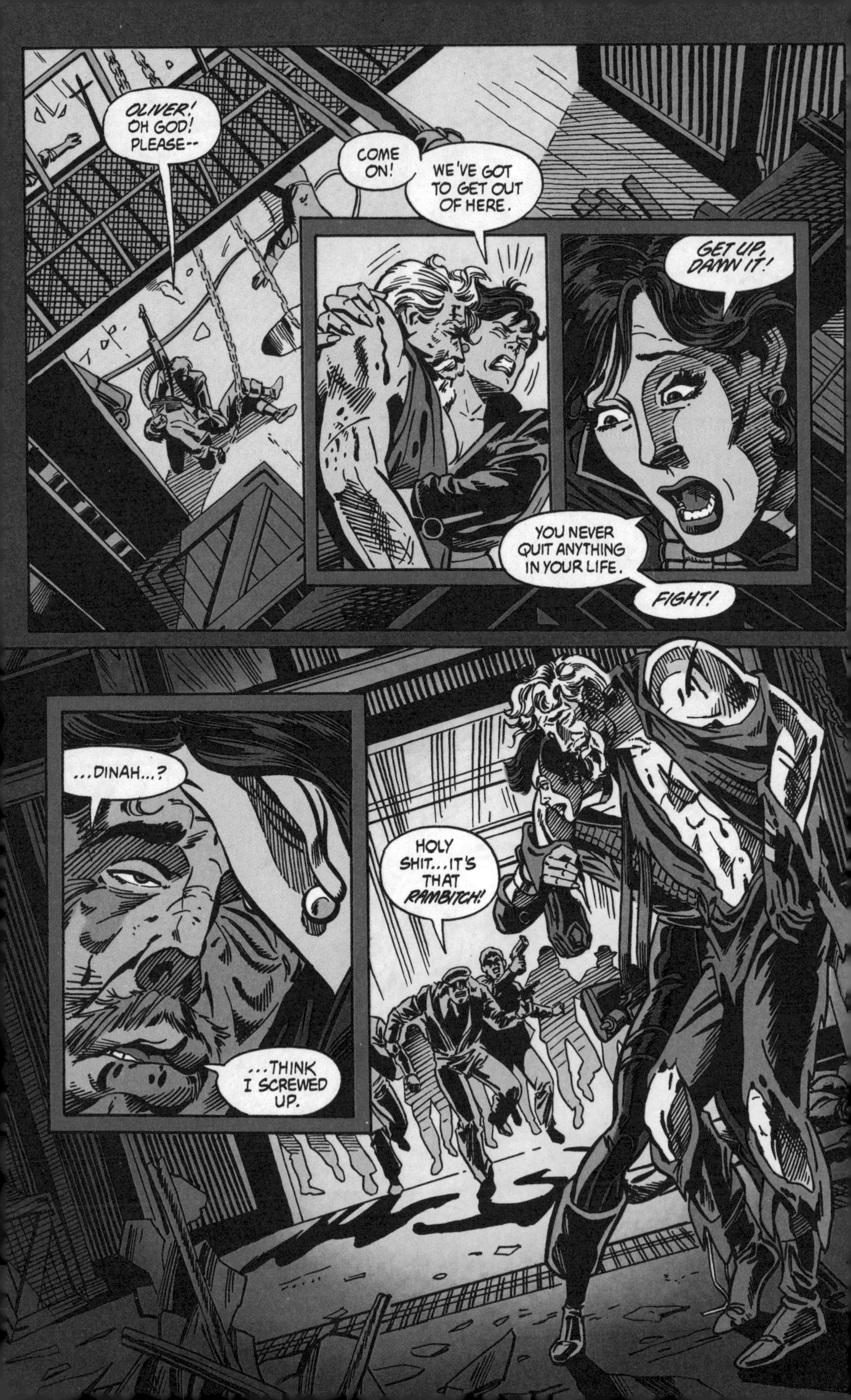
OLIVER! OH GOD! PLEASE--
COME ON!
WE'VE GOT TO GET OUT OF HERE.
GET UP, DAMN IT!
YOU NEVER QUIT ANYTHING IN YOUR LIFE.
FIGHT!
...DINAH...?
...THINK I SCREWED UP.
HOLY SHIT...IT'S THAT RAMBITCH!

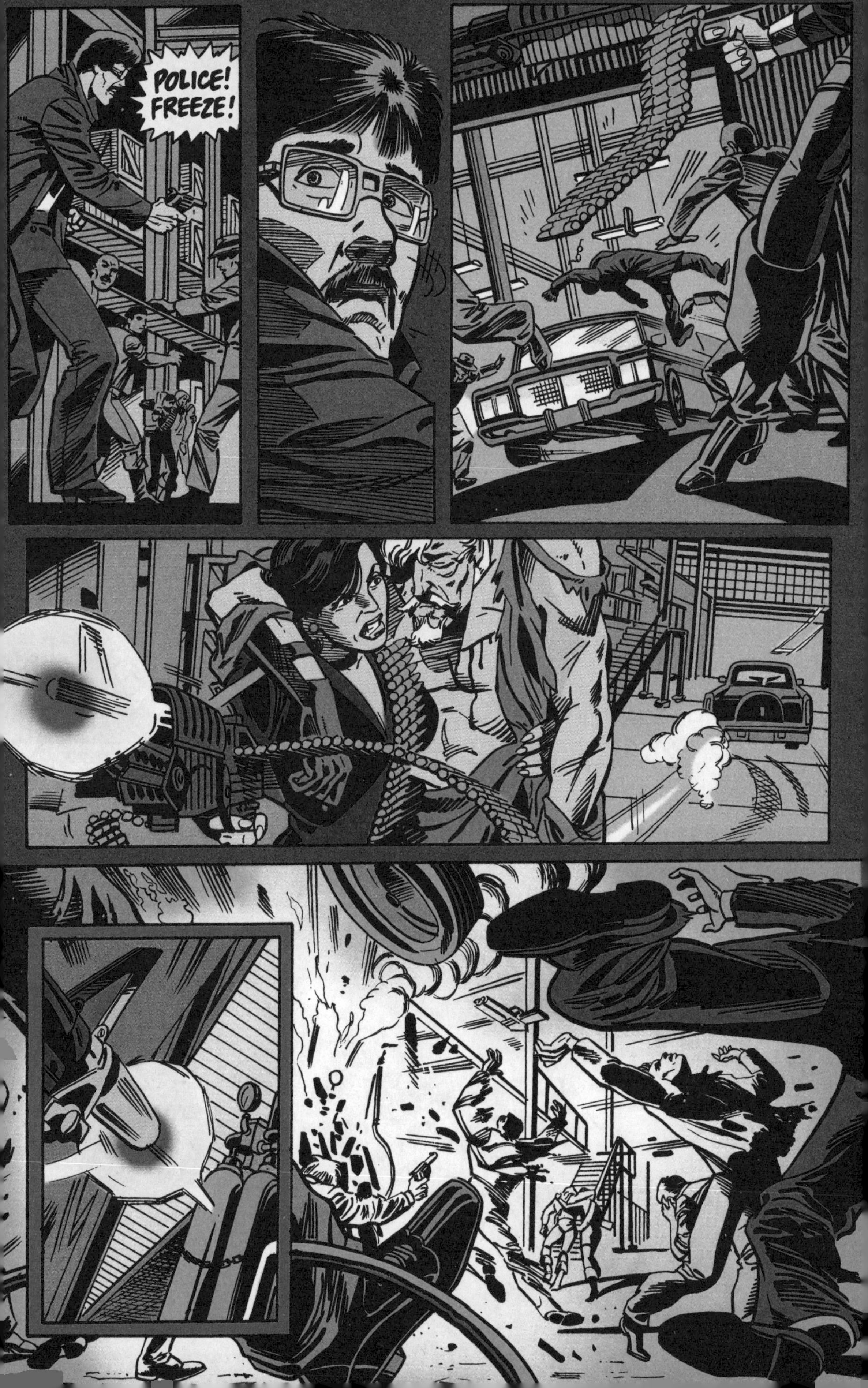
POLICE! FREEZE!

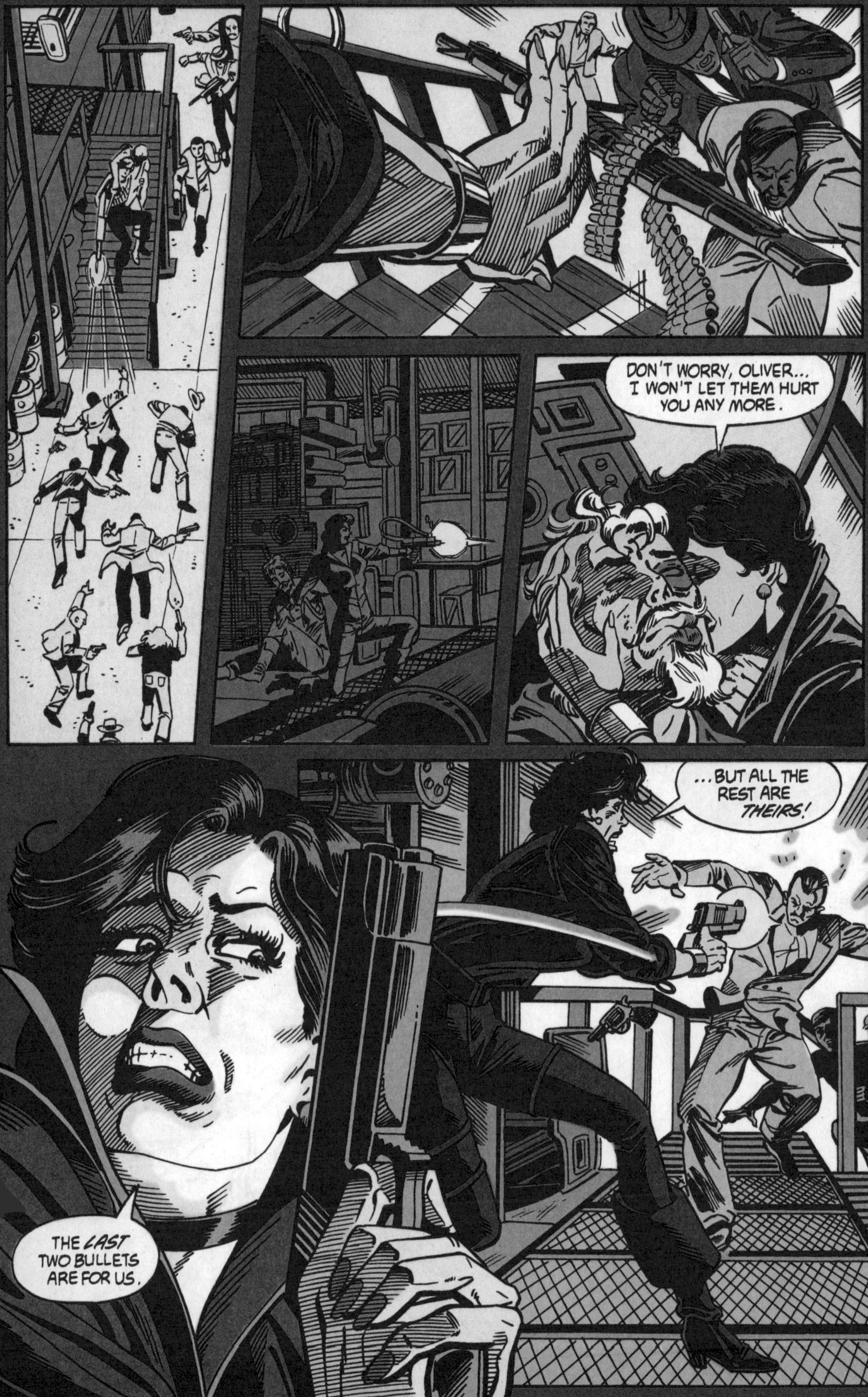
DON'T WORRY, OLIVER... I WON'T LET THEM HURT YOU ANY MORE.
...BUT ALL THE REST ARE THEIRS!
THE LAST TWO BULLETS ARE FOR US.

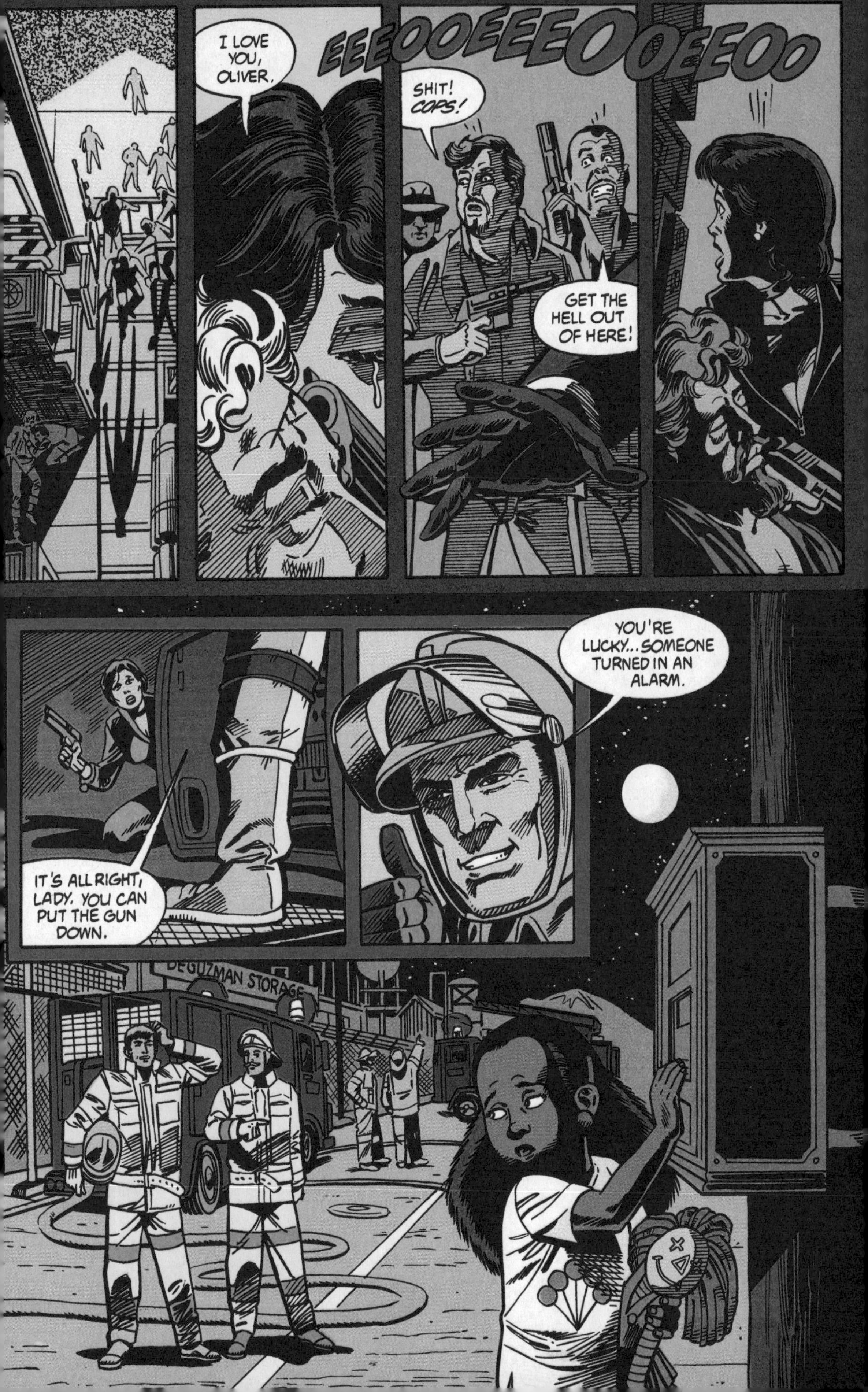
I LOVE YOU, OLIVER.
EEEOOEEEEOOEEOO
SHIT! COPS!
GET THE HELL OUT OF HERE!
IT'S ALL RIGHT, LADY. YOU CAN PUT THE GUN DOWN.
YOU'RE LUCKY... SOMEONE TURNED IN AN ALARM.
DEGUZMAN STORAGE

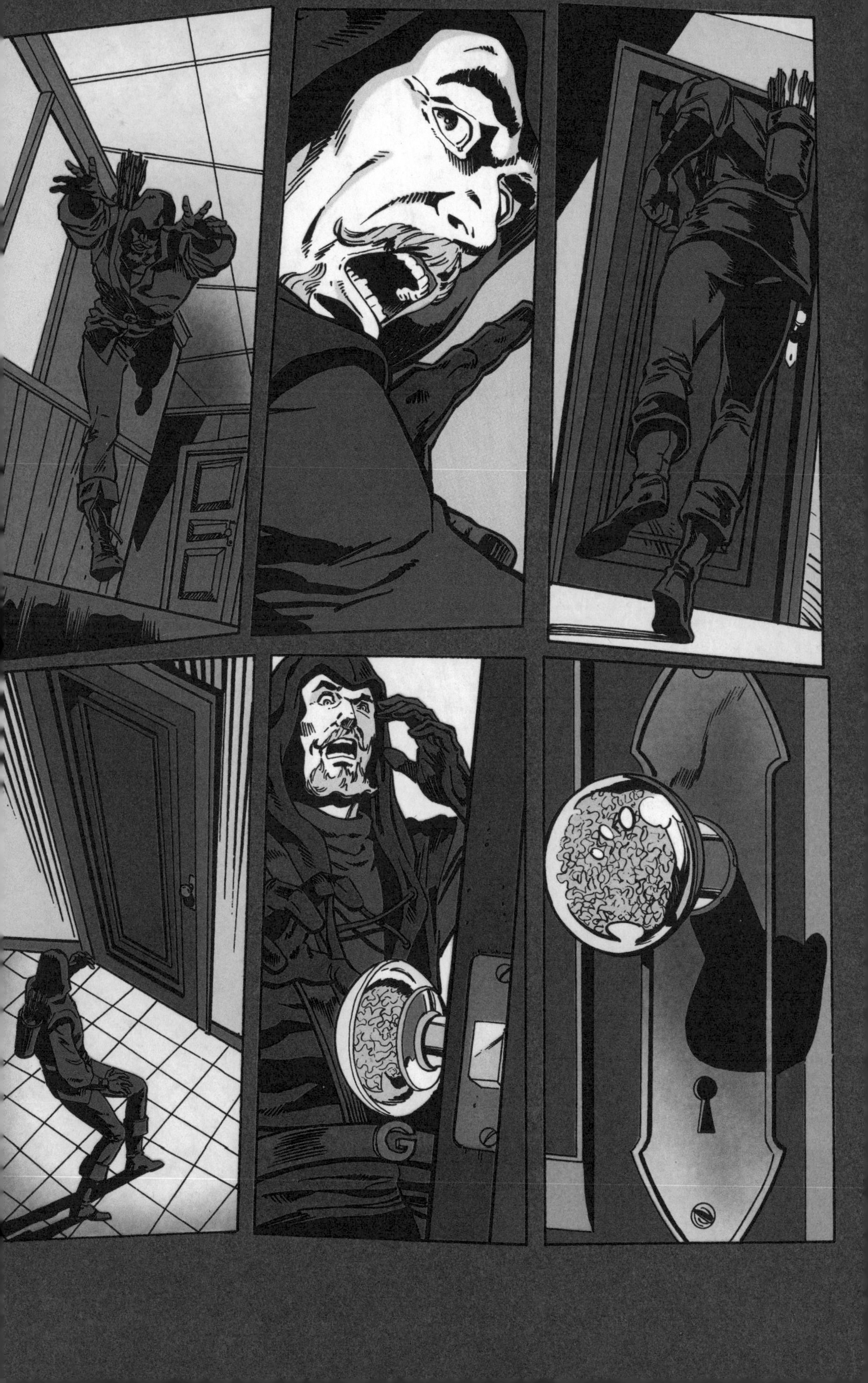

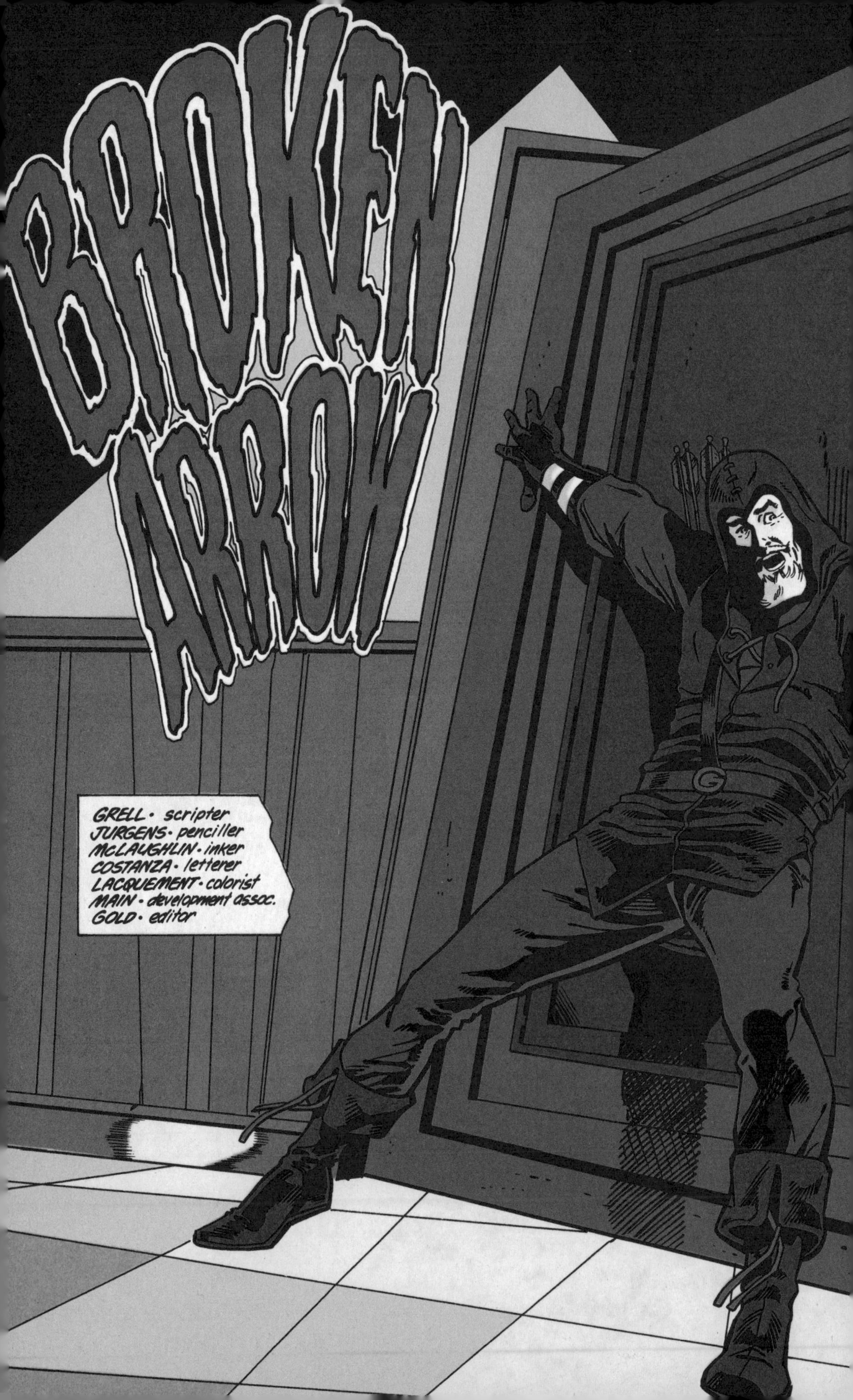
BROKEN ARROW
GRELL • scripter
JURGENS • penciller
McLAUGHLIN • inker
COSTANZA • letterer
LACQUEMENT • colorist
MAIN • development assoc.
GOLD • editor

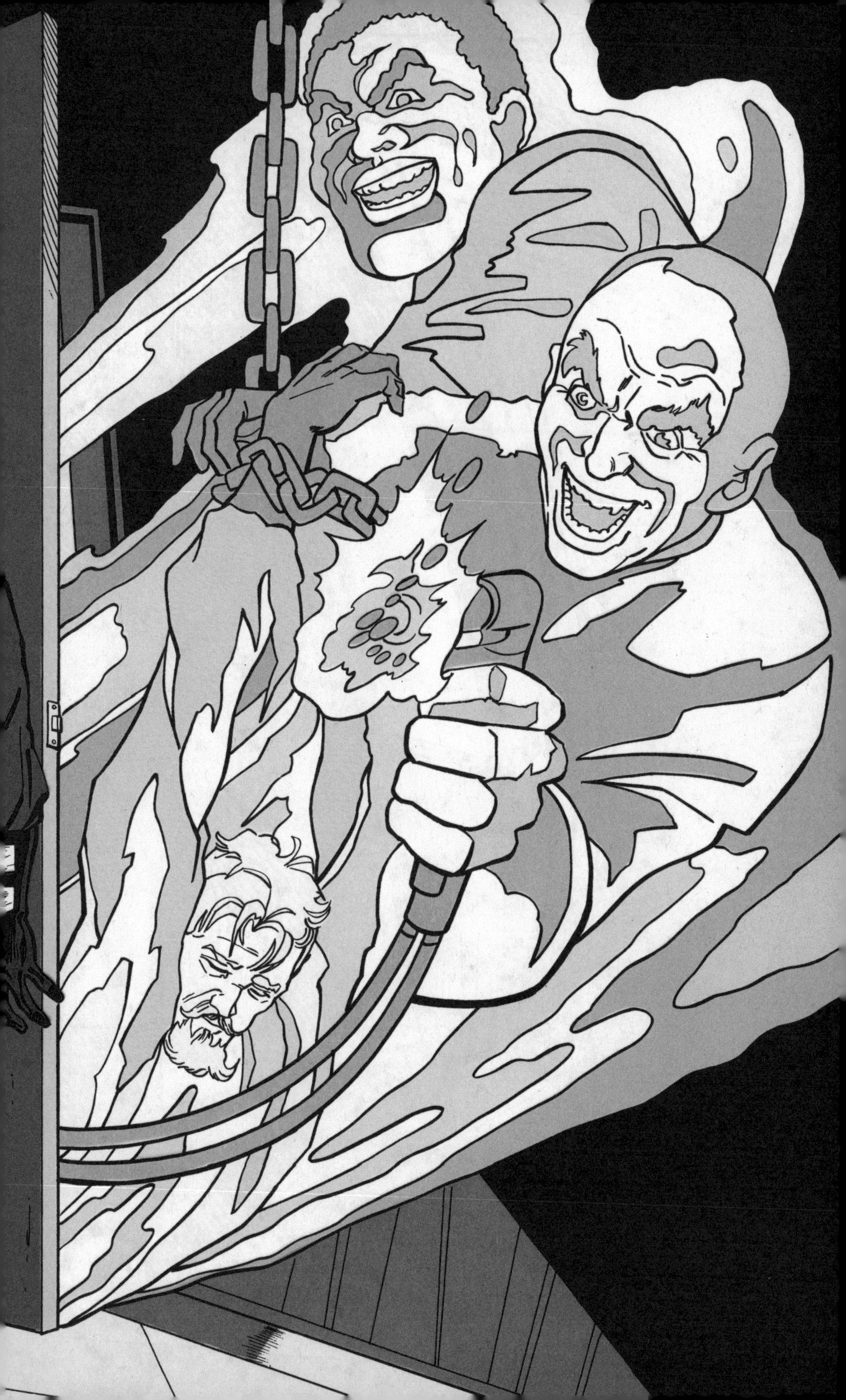

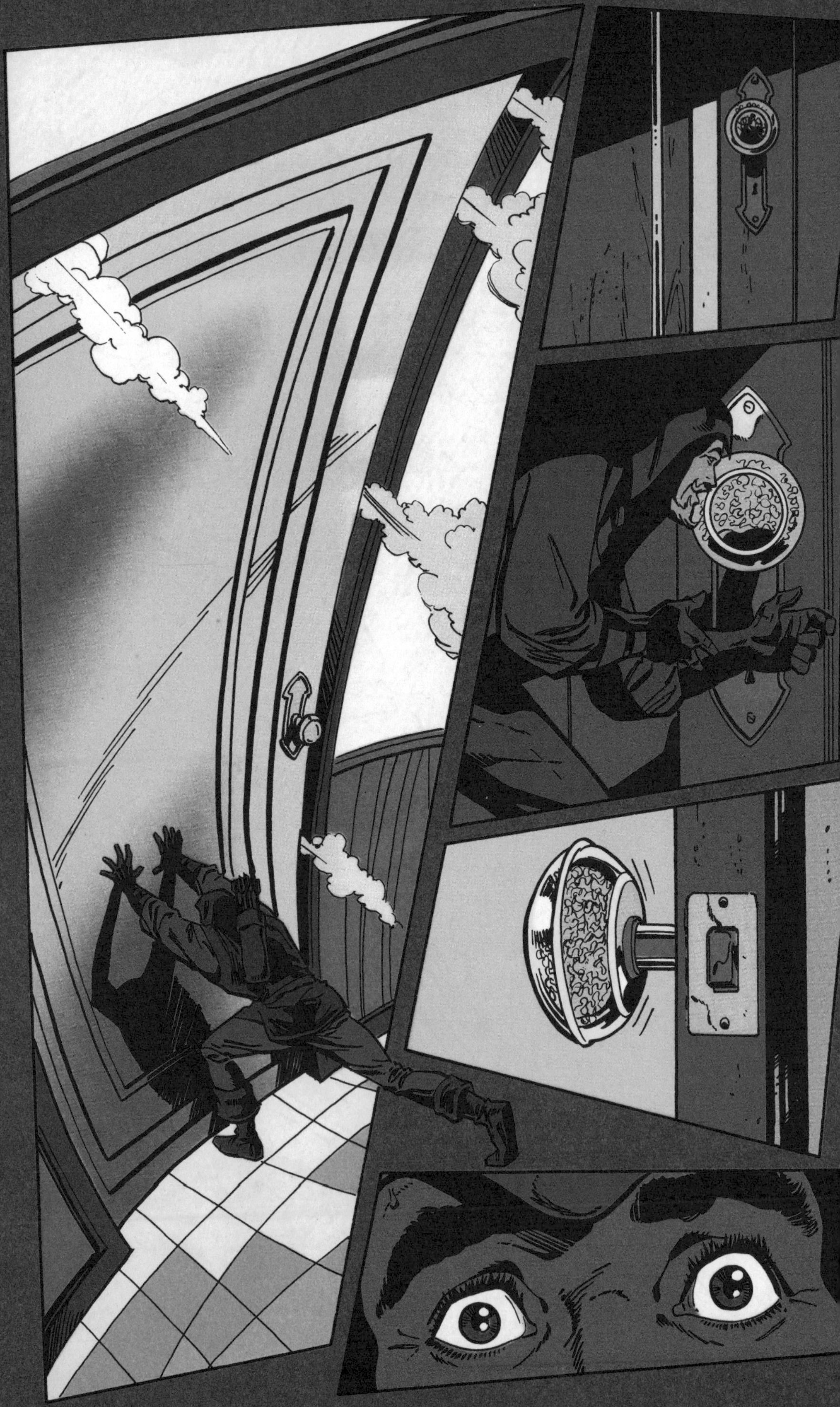

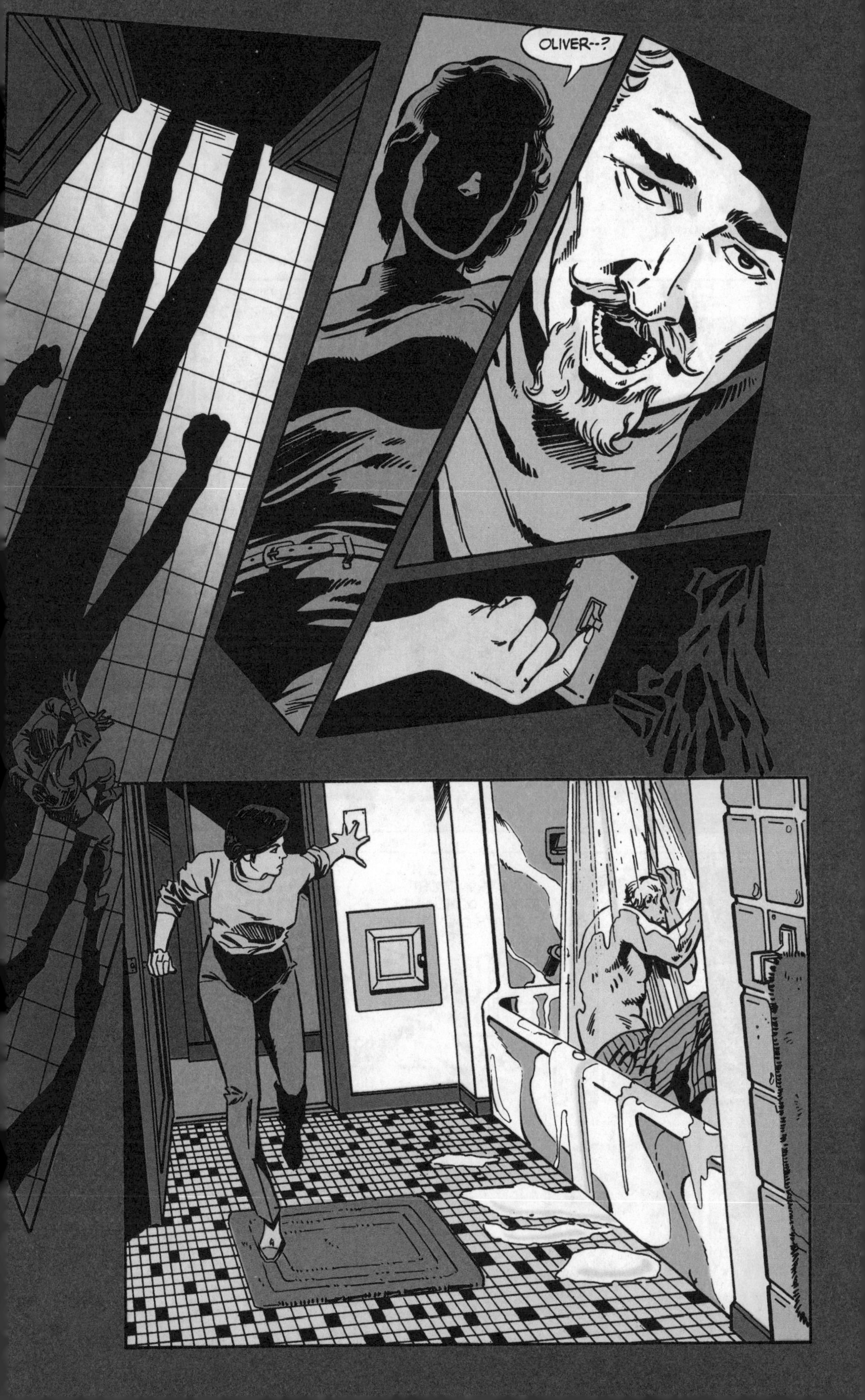
OLIVER--?

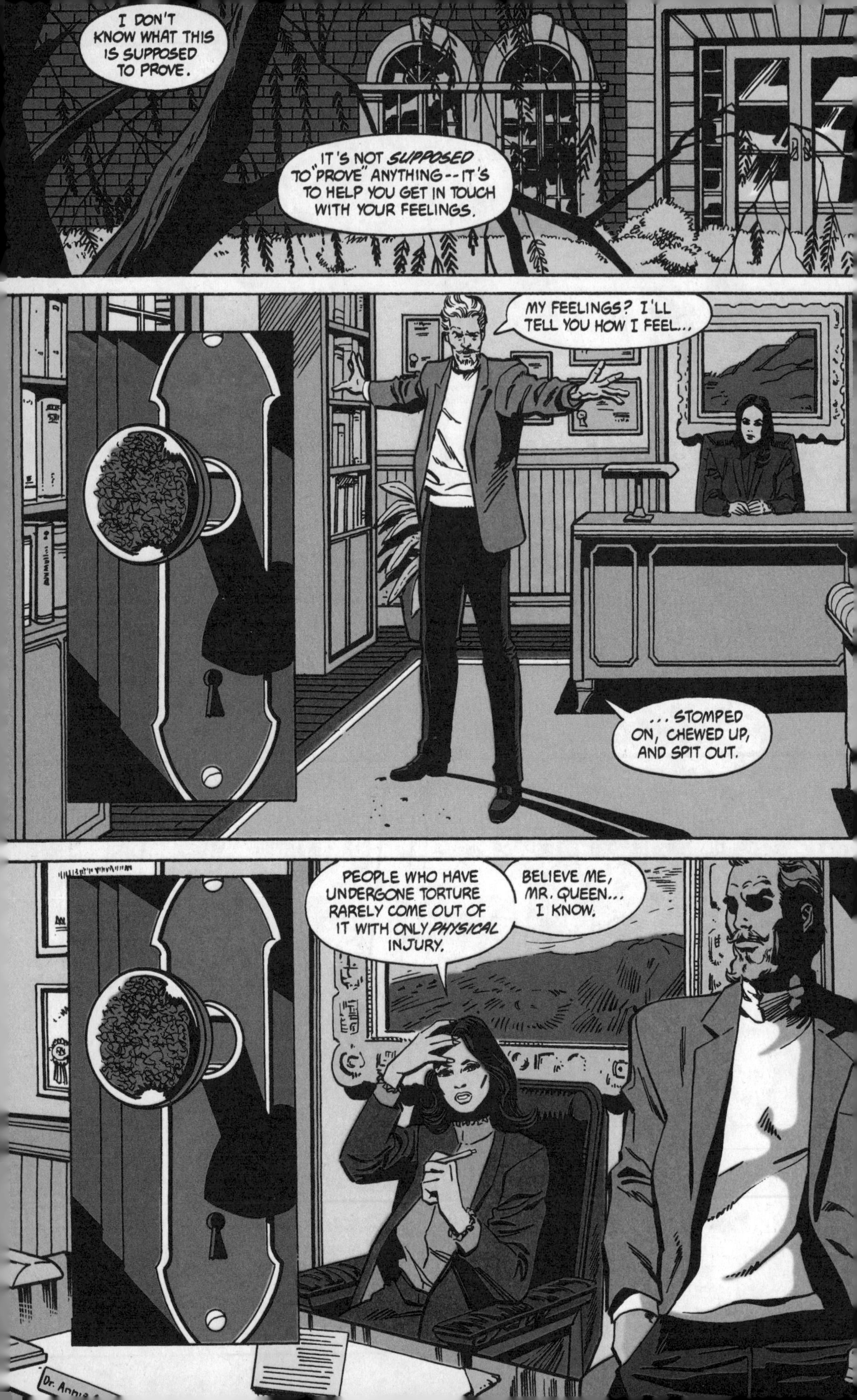
I DON'T KNOW WHAT THIS IS SUPPOSED TO PROVE.
IT'S NOT *SUPPOSED* TO "PROVE" ANYTHING--IT'S TO HELP YOU GET IN TOUCH WITH YOUR FEELINGS.
MY FEELINGS? I'LL TELL YOU HOW I FEEL...
...STOMPED ON, CHEWED UP, AND SPIT OUT.
PEOPLE WHO HAVE UNDERGONE TORTURE RARELY COME OUT OF IT WITH ONLY *PHYSICAL* INJURY.
BELIEVE ME, MR. QUEEN... I KNOW.

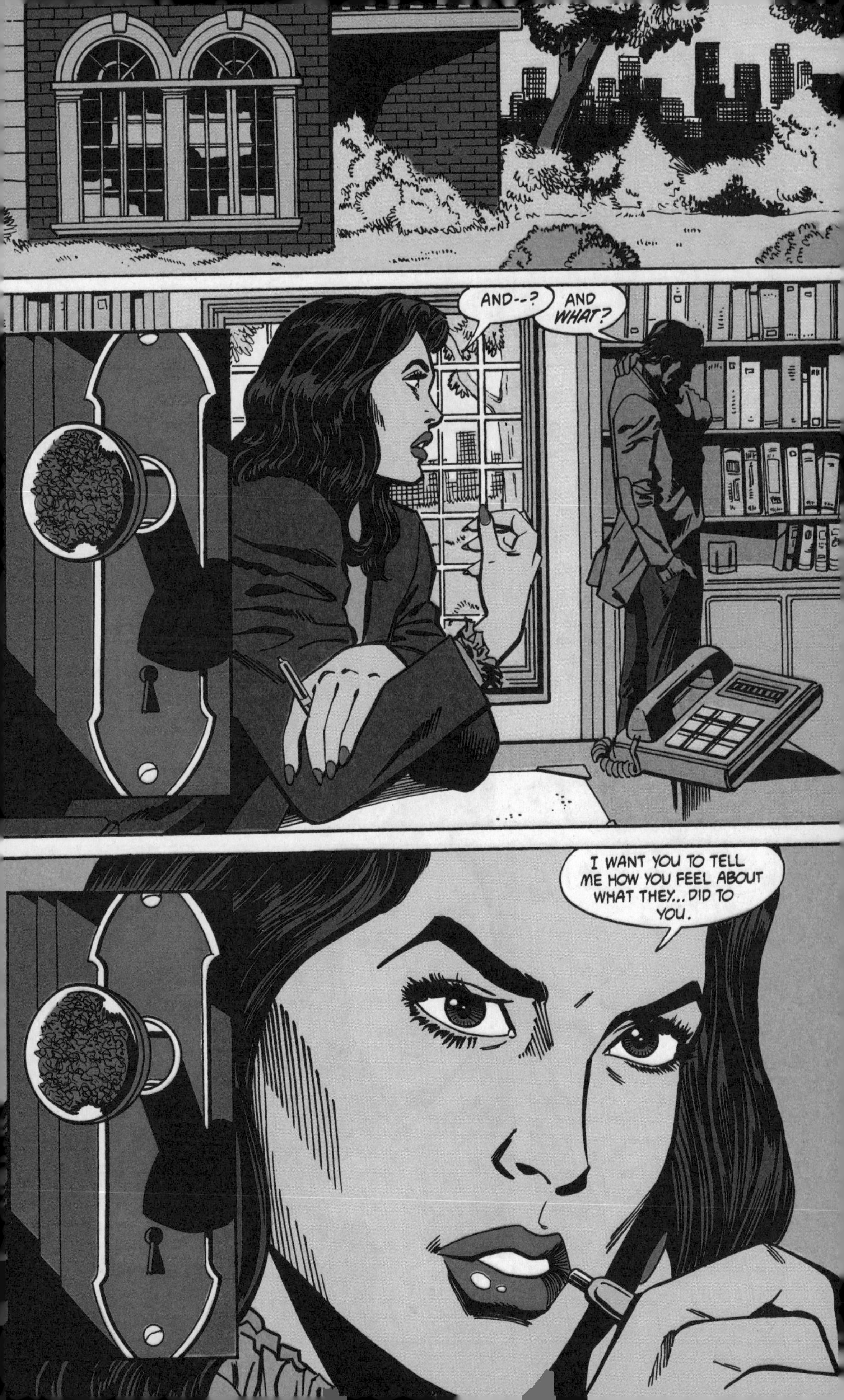
AND--?
AND WHAT?
I WANT YOU TO TELL ME HOW YOU FEEL ABOUT WHAT THEY... DID TO YOU.

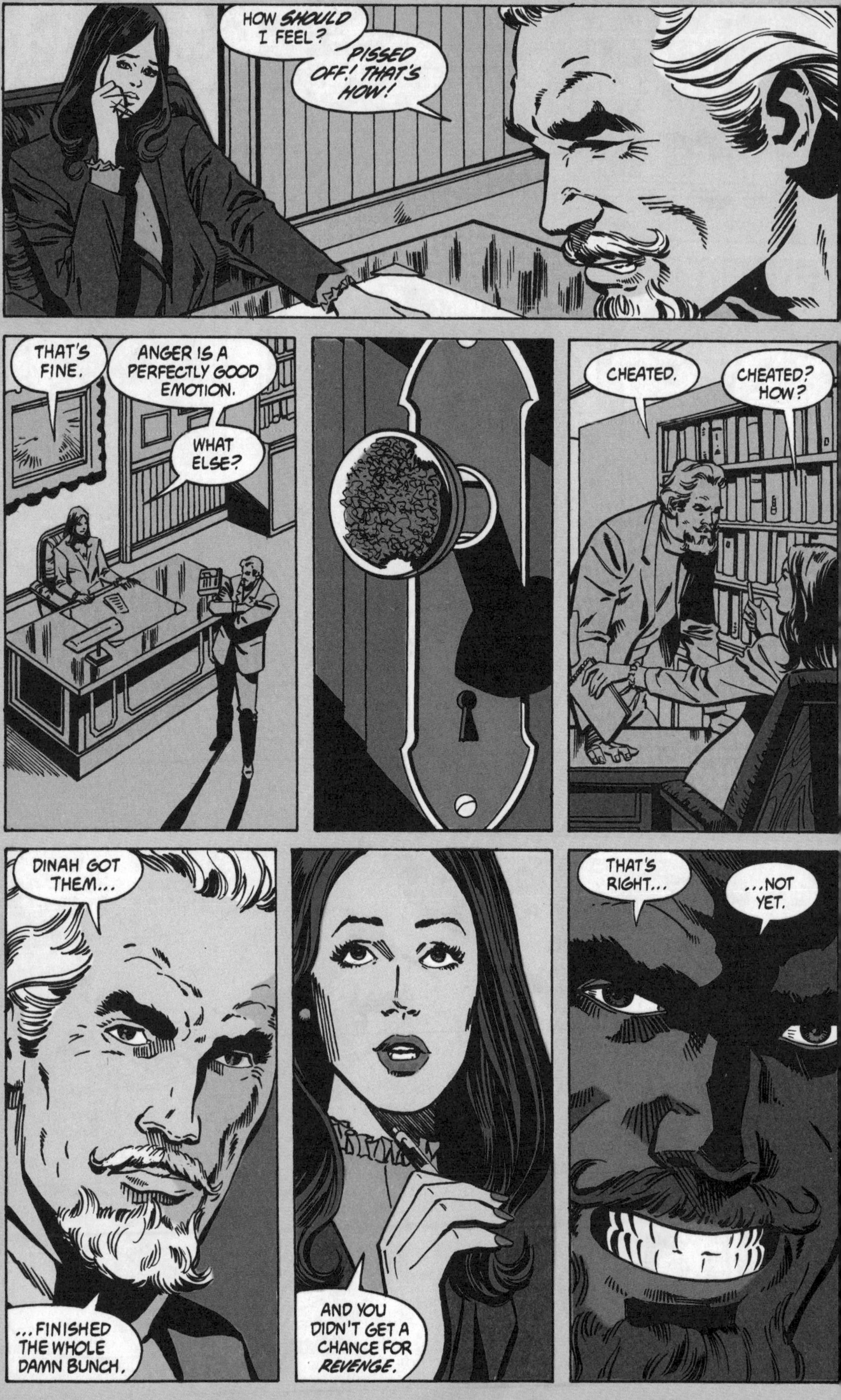
HOW SHOULD I FEEL?
PISSED OFF! THAT'S HOW!
THAT'S FINE.
ANGER IS A PERFECTLY GOOD EMOTION.
WHAT ELSE?
CHEATED.
CHEATED? HOW?
DINAH GOT THEM...
...FINISHED THE WHOLE DAMN BUNCH.
AND YOU DIDN'T GET A CHANCE FOR REVENGE.
THAT'S RIGHT...
...NOT YET.

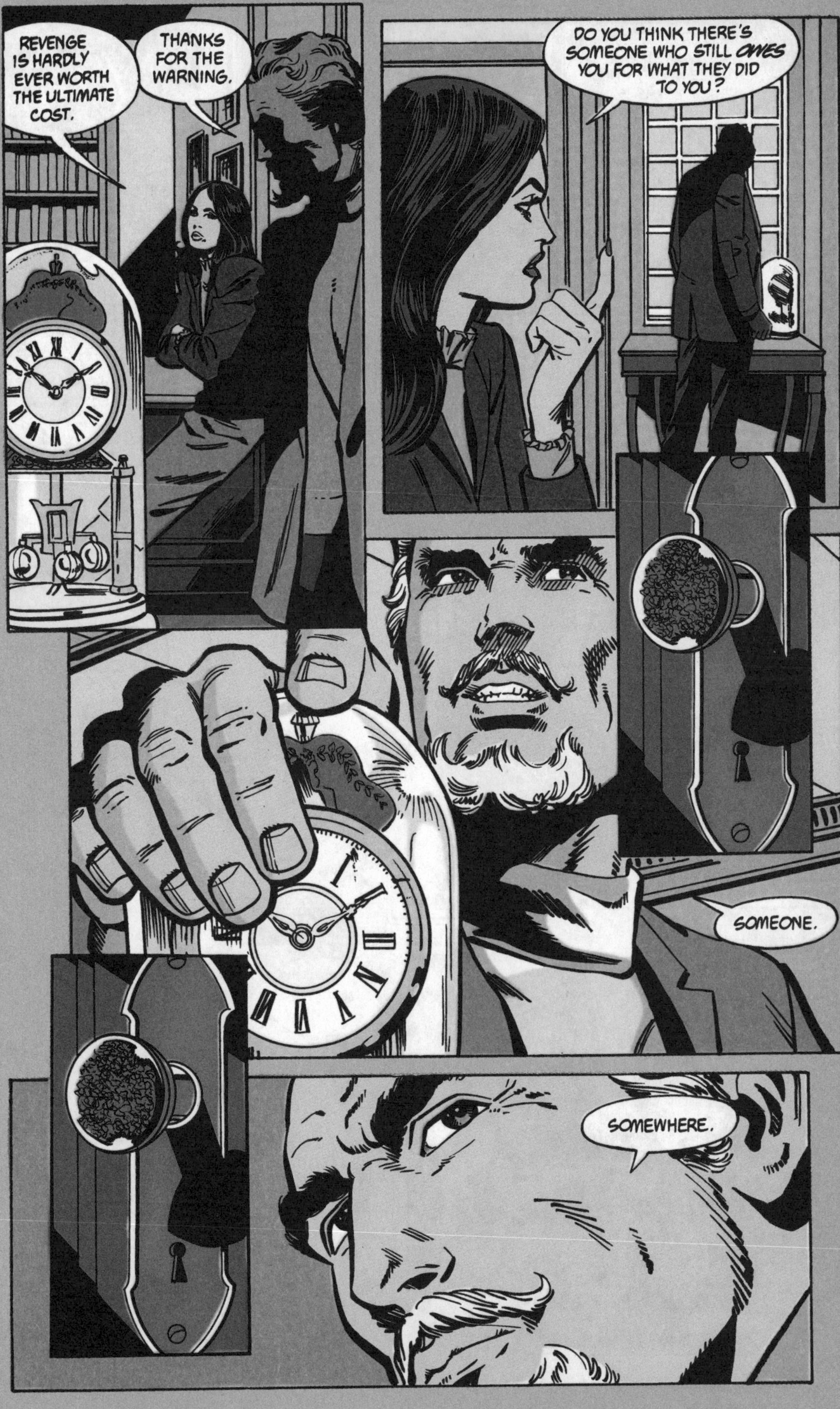
REVENGE IS HARDLY EVER WORTH THE ULTIMATE COST.
THANKS FOR THE WARNING.
DO YOU THINK THERE'S SOMEONE WHO STILL *OWES* YOU FOR WHAT THEY DID TO YOU?
SOMEONE.
SOMEWHERE.

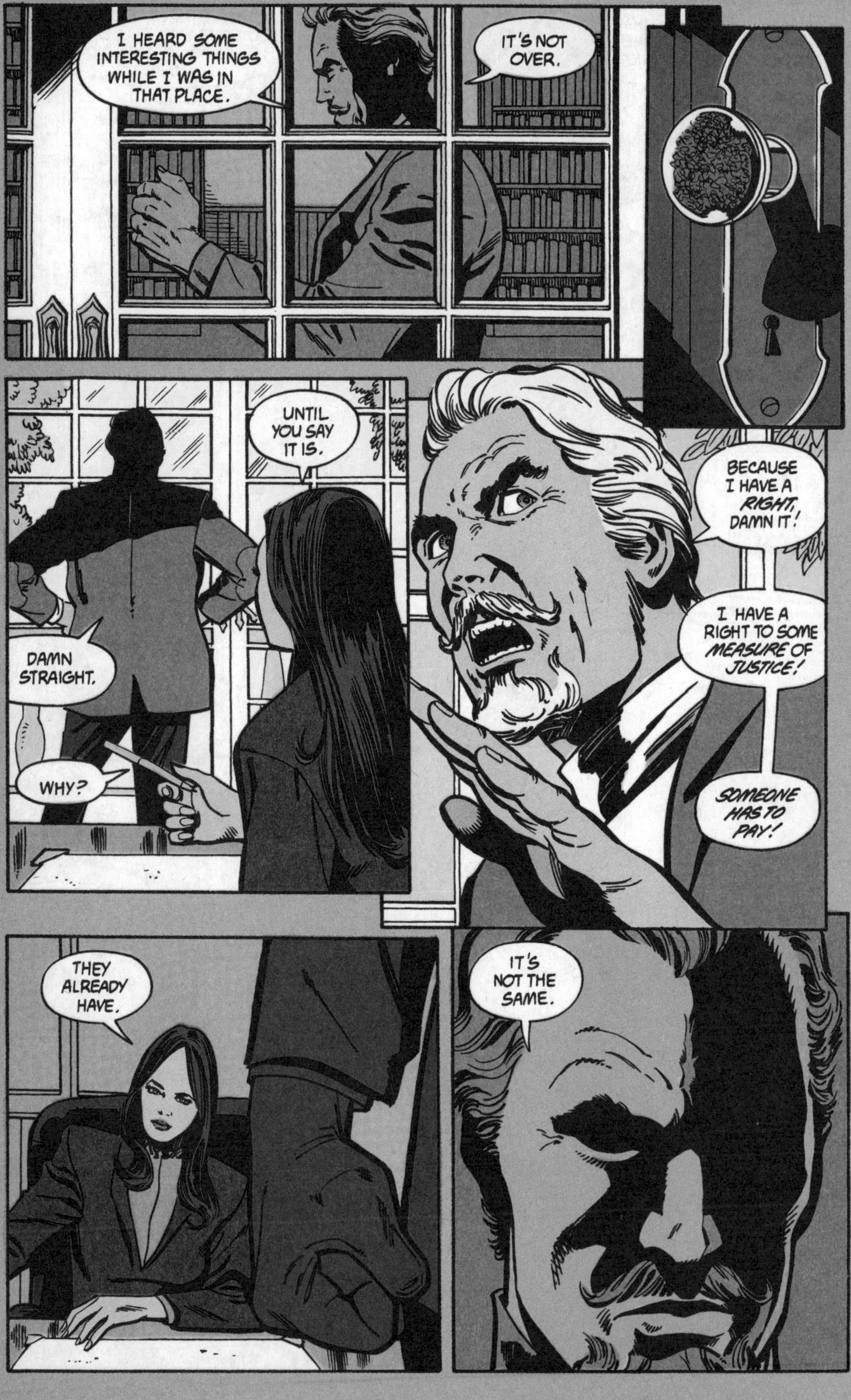
I HEARD SOME INTERESTING THINGS WHILE I WAS IN THAT PLACE.
IT'S NOT OVER.
UNTIL YOU SAY IT IS.
DAMN STRAIGHT.
WHY?
BECAUSE I HAVE A *RIGHT*, DAMN IT!
I HAVE A RIGHT TO SOME *MEASURE* OF *JUSTICE*!
*SOMEONE HAS TO PAY!*
THEY ALREADY HAVE.
IT'S NOT THE SAME.

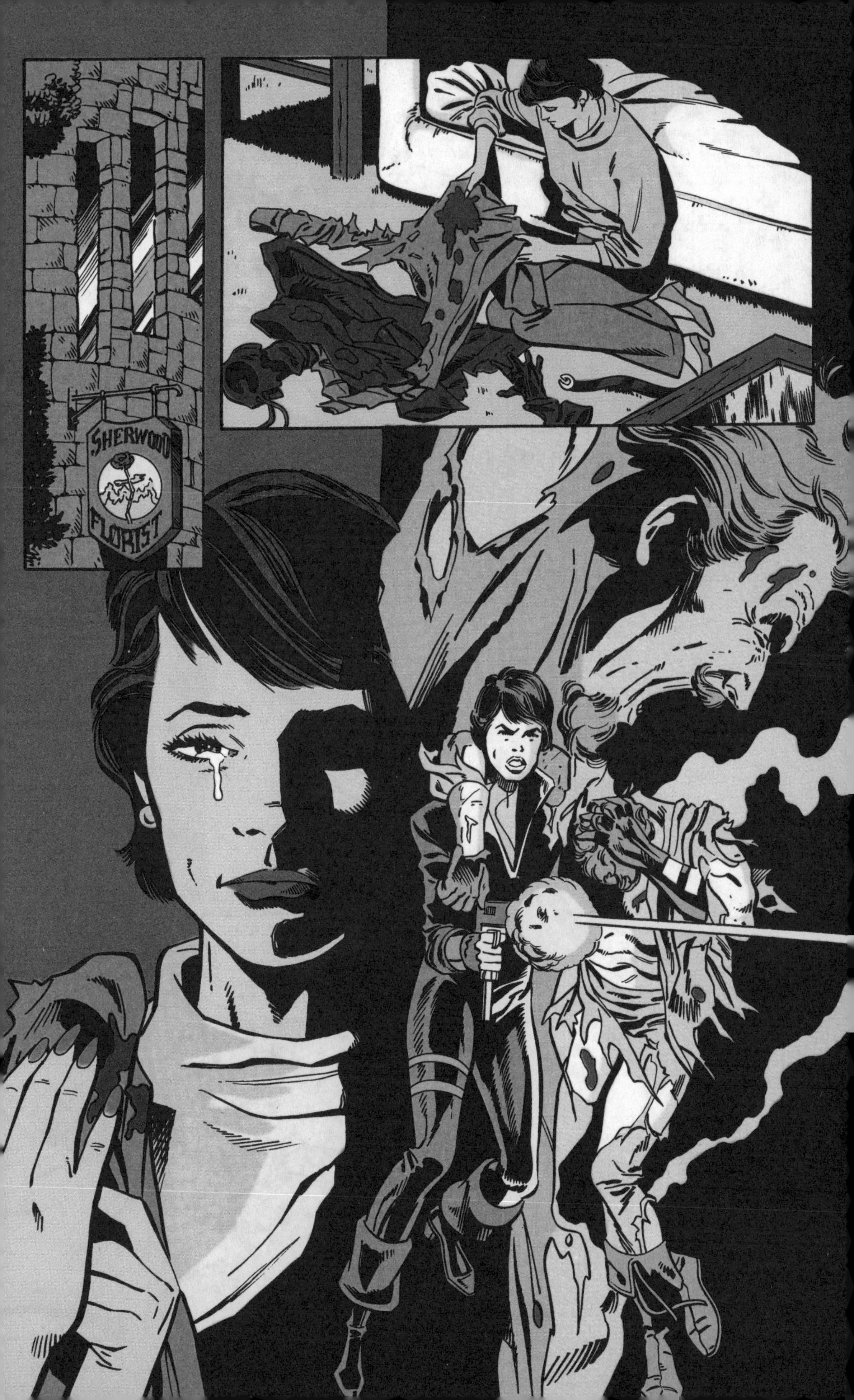
SHERWOOD
FLORIST

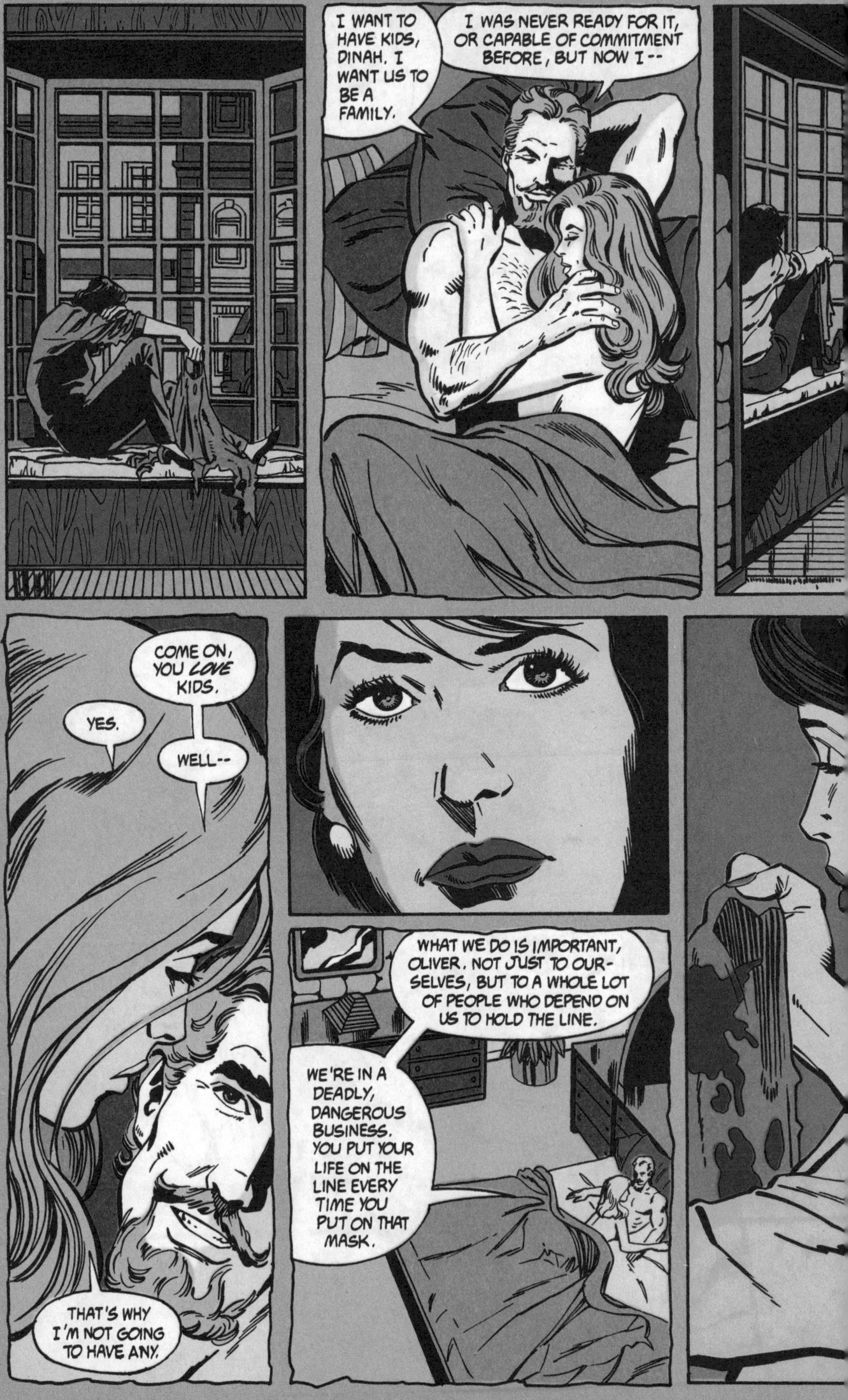
I WANT TO HAVE KIDS, DINAH. I WANT US TO BE A FAMILY.
I WAS NEVER READY FOR IT, OR CAPABLE OF COMMITMENT BEFORE, BUT NOW I--
YES.
COME ON, YOU LOVE KIDS.
WELL--
THAT'S WHY I'M NOT GOING TO HAVE ANY.
WHAT WE DO IS IMPORTANT, OLIVER. NOT JUST TO OURSELVES, BUT TO A WHOLE LOT OF PEOPLE WHO DEPEND ON US TO HOLD THE LINE.
WE'RE IN A DEADLY, DANGEROUS BUSINESS. YOU PUT YOUR LIFE ON THE LINE EVERY TIME YOU PUT ON THAT MASK.

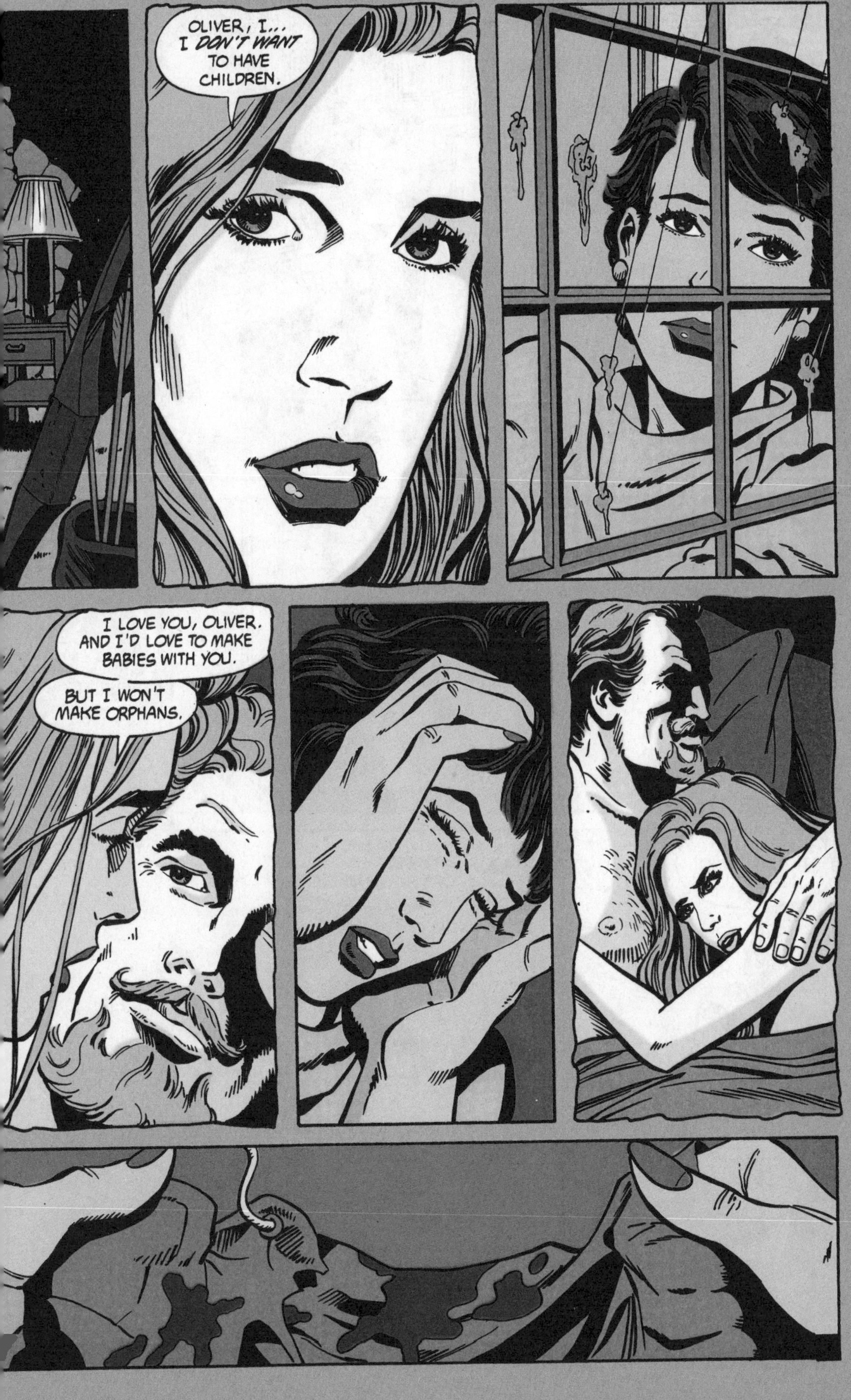
OLIVER, I... I *DON'T WANT* TO HAVE CHILDREN.
I LOVE YOU, OLIVER. AND I'D LOVE TO MAKE BABIES WITH YOU.
BUT I WON'T MAKE ORPHANS.

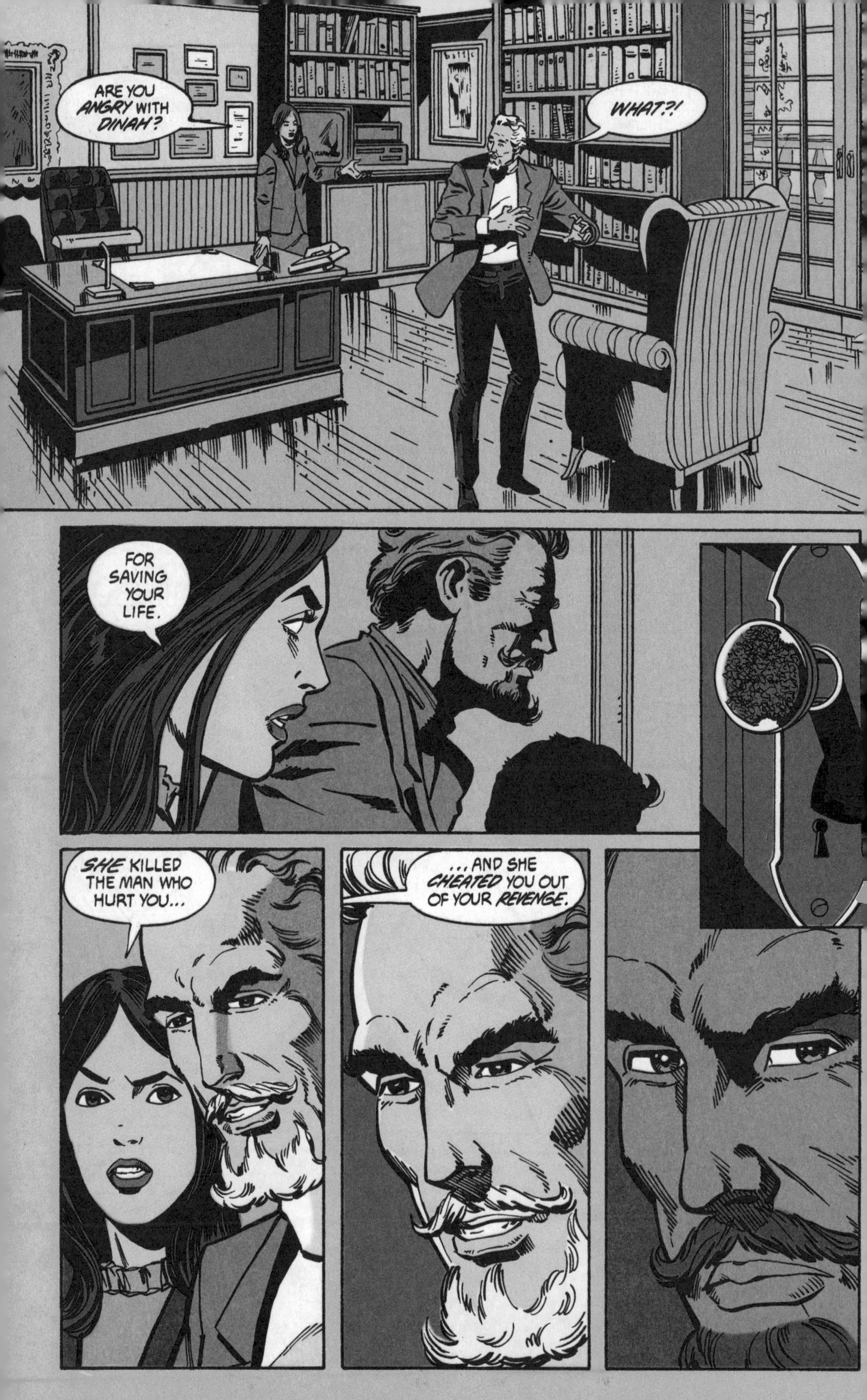
ARE YOU ANGRY WITH DINAH?
WHAT?!
FOR SAVING YOUR LIFE.
SHE KILLED THE MAN WHO HURT YOU...
...AND SHE CHEATED YOU OUT OF YOUR REVENGE.

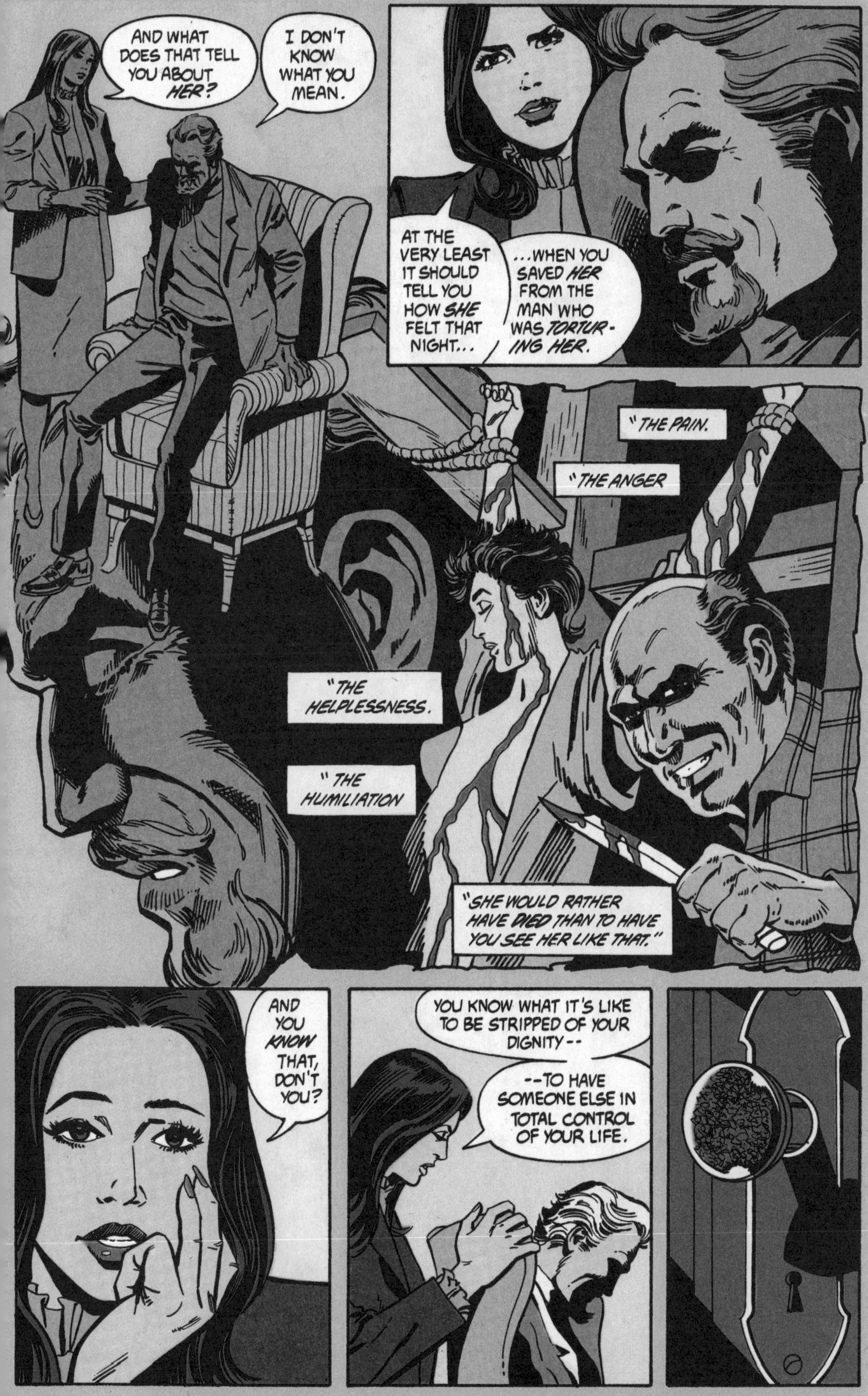
AND WHAT DOES THAT TELL YOU ABOUT HER?
I DON'T KNOW WHAT YOU MEAN.
AT THE VERY LEAST IT SHOULD TELL YOU HOW SHE FELT THAT NIGHT...
...WHEN YOU SAVED HER FROM THE MAN WHO WAS TORTURING HER.
"THE PAIN.
"THE ANGER
"THE HELPLESSNESS.
"THE HUMILIATION
"SHE WOULD RATHER HAVE DIED THAN TO HAVE YOU SEE HER LIKE THAT."
AND YOU KNOW THAT, DON'T YOU?
YOU KNOW WHAT IT'S LIKE TO BE STRIPPED OF YOUR DIGNITY--
--TO HAVE SOMEONE ELSE IN TOTAL CONTROL OF YOUR LIFE.

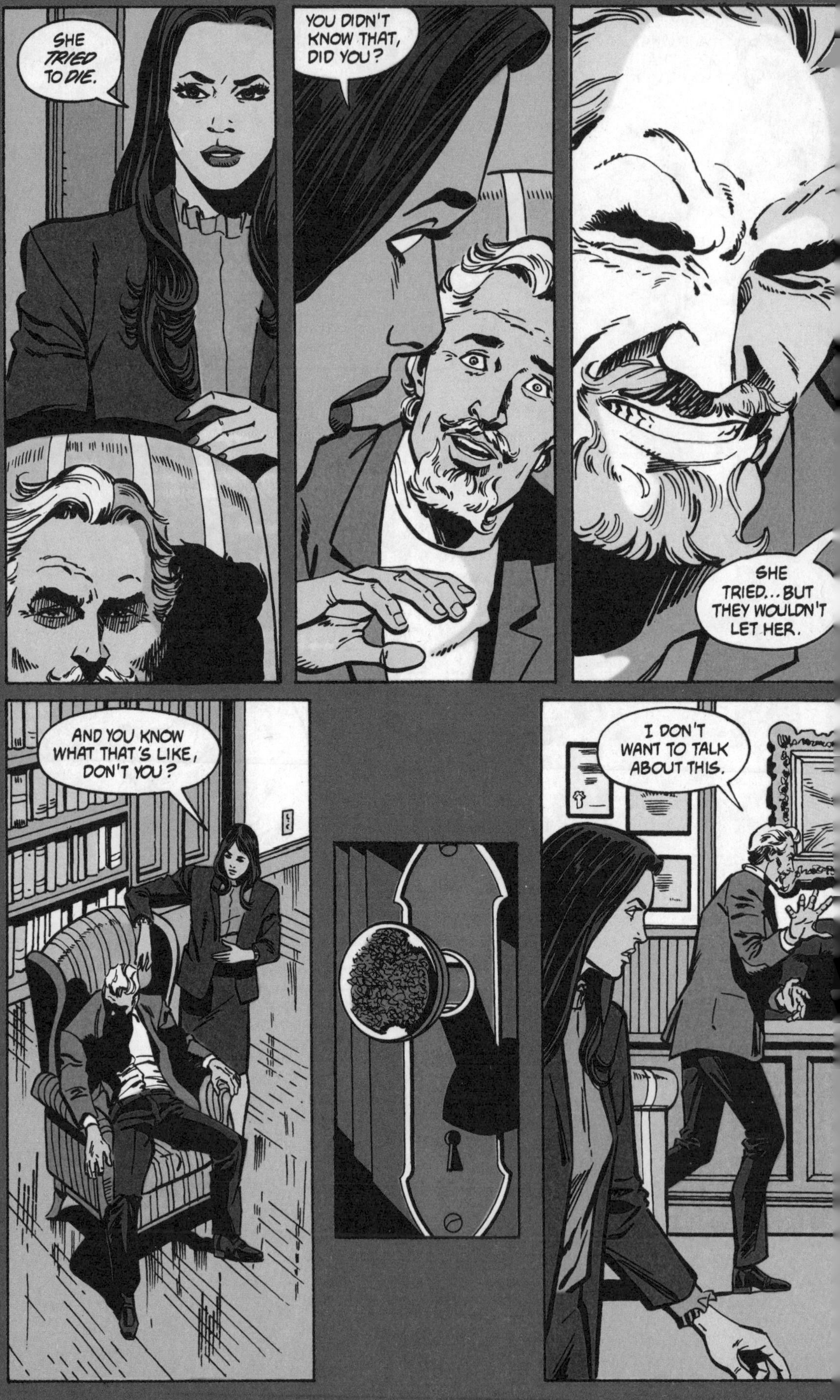
SHE TRIED TO DIE.
YOU DIDN'T KNOW THAT, DID YOU?
SHE TRIED... BUT THEY WOULDN'T LET HER.
AND YOU KNOW WHAT THAT'S LIKE, DON'T YOU?
I DON'T WANT TO TALK ABOUT THIS.

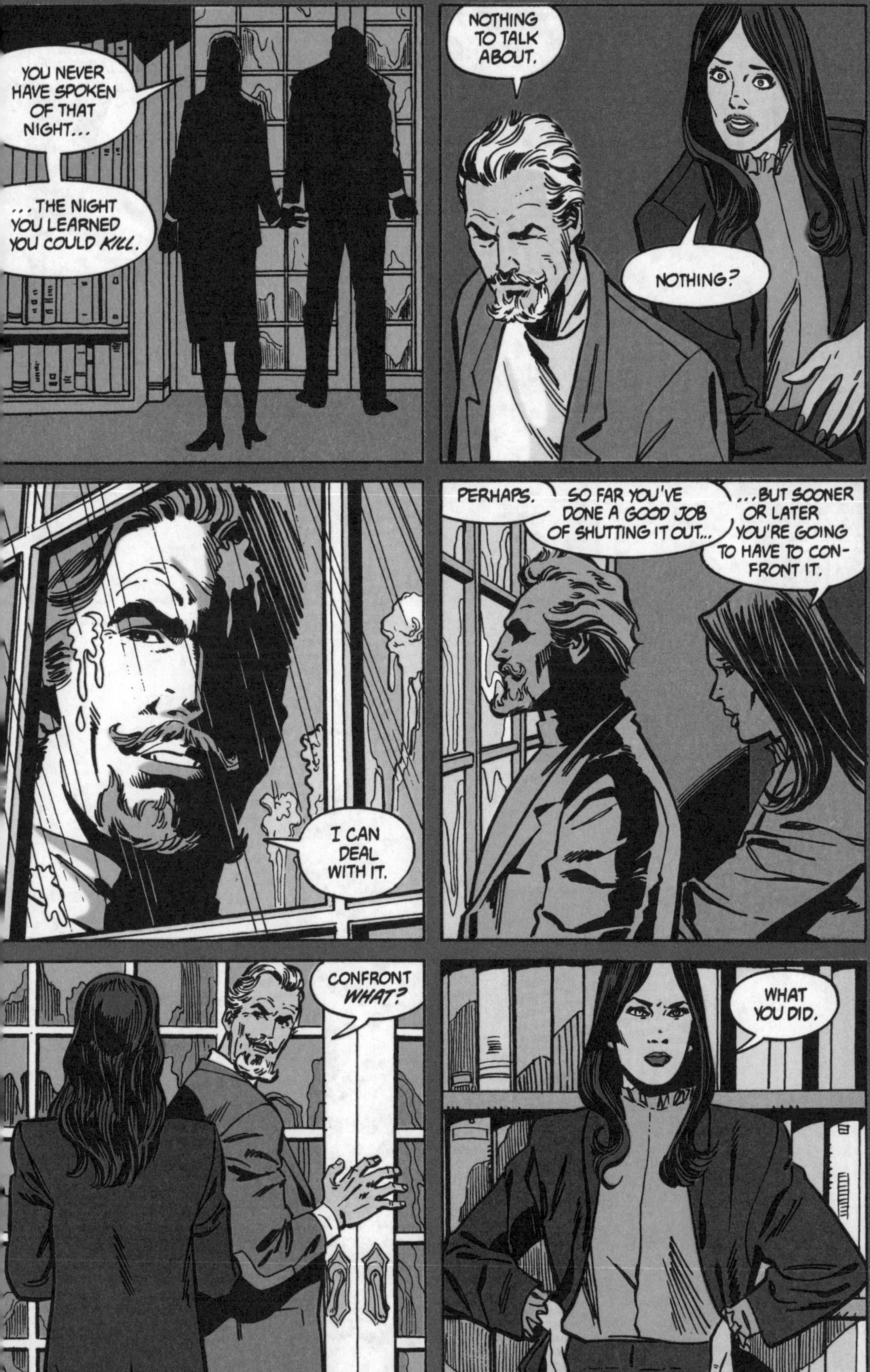
YOU NEVER HAVE SPOKEN OF THAT NIGHT...
...THE NIGHT YOU LEARNED YOU COULD KILL.
NOTHING TO TALK ABOUT.
NOTHING?
I CAN DEAL WITH IT.
PERHAPS.
SO FAR YOU'VE DONE A GOOD JOB OF SHUTTING IT OUT...
...BUT SOONER OR LATER YOU'RE GOING TO HAVE TO CONFRONT IT.
CONFRONT WHAT?
WHAT YOU DID.

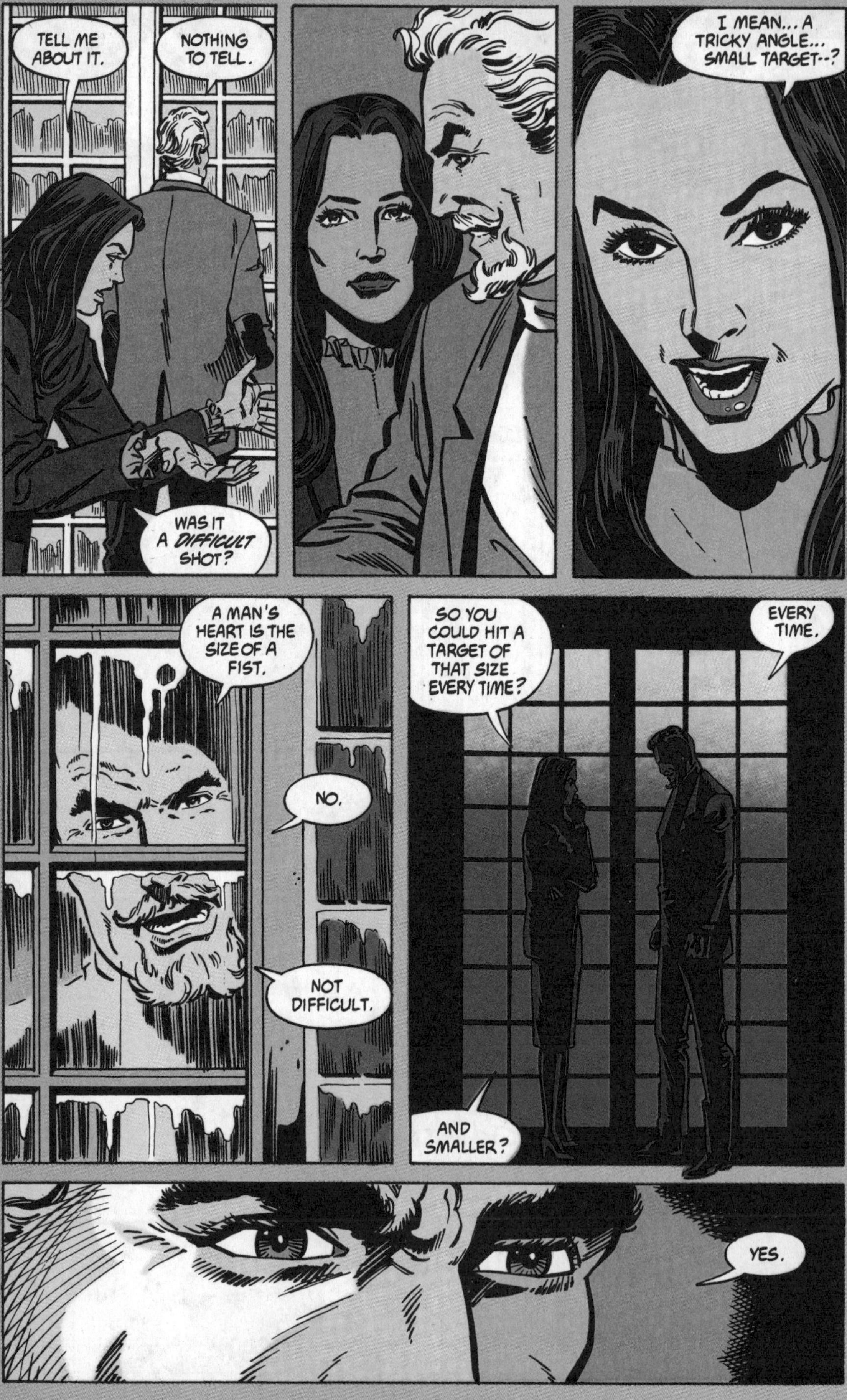
TELL ME ABOUT IT.
NOTHING TO TELL.
WAS IT A DIFFICULT SHOT?
I MEAN... A TRICKY ANGLE... SMALL TARGET--?
A MAN'S HEART IS THE SIZE OF A FIST.
NO.
NOT DIFFICULT.
SO YOU COULD HIT A TARGET OF THAT SIZE EVERY TIME?
EVERY TIME.
AND SMALLER?
YES.

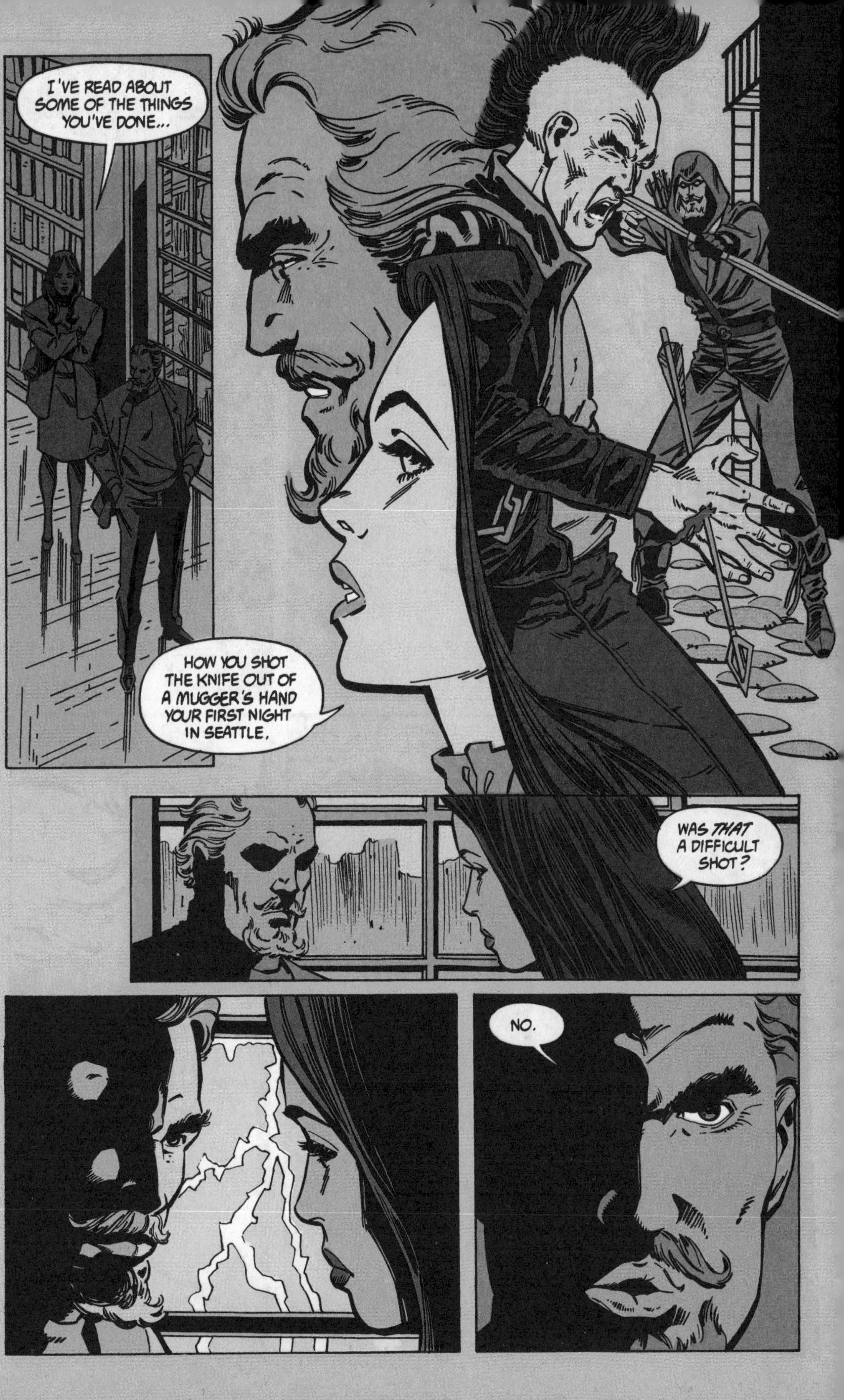
I'VE READ ABOUT SOME OF THE THINGS YOU'VE DONE...
HOW YOU SHOT THE KNIFE OUT OF A MUGGER'S HAND YOUR FIRST NIGHT IN SEATTLE.
WAS *THAT* A DIFFICULT SHOT?
NO.

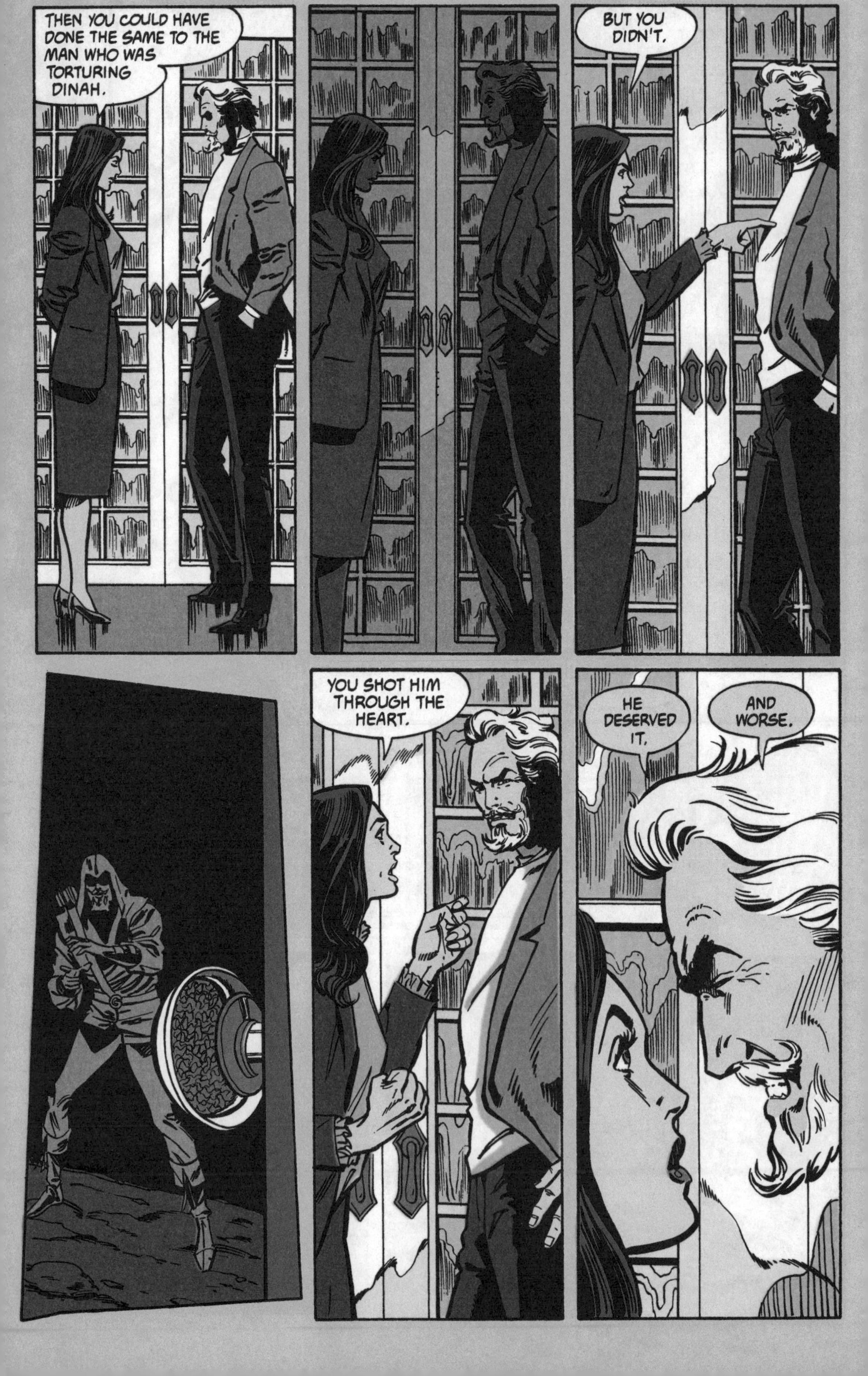
THEN YOU COULD HAVE DONE THE SAME TO THE MAN WHO WAS TORTURING DINAH.
BUT YOU DIDN'T.
YOU SHOT HIM THROUGH THE HEART.
HE DESERVED IT.
AND WORSE.

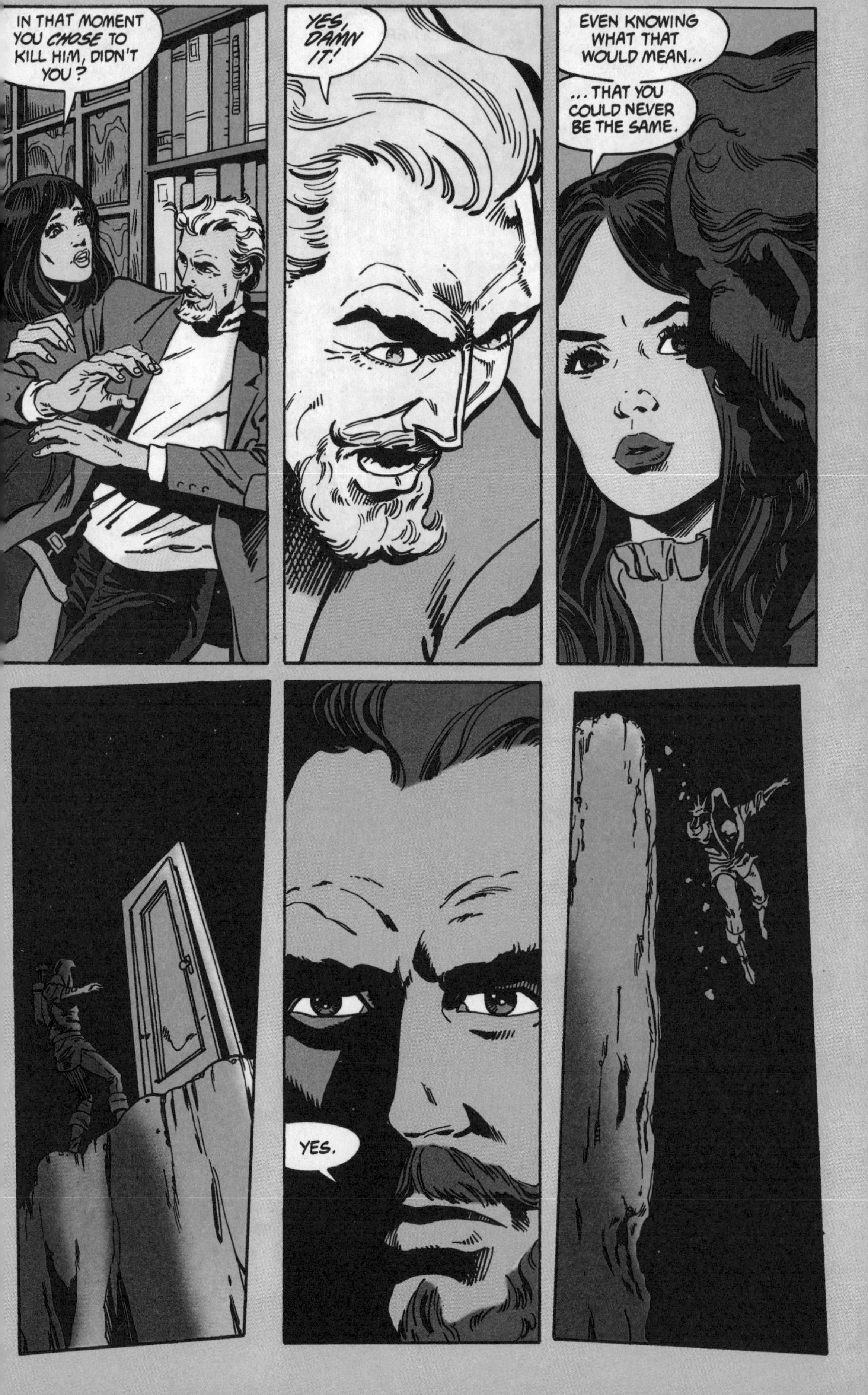
IN THAT MOMENT YOU CHOSE TO KILL HIM, DIDN'T YOU?
YES, DAMN IT!
EVEN KNOWING WHAT THAT WOULD MEAN...
...THAT YOU COULD NEVER BE THE SAME.
YES.

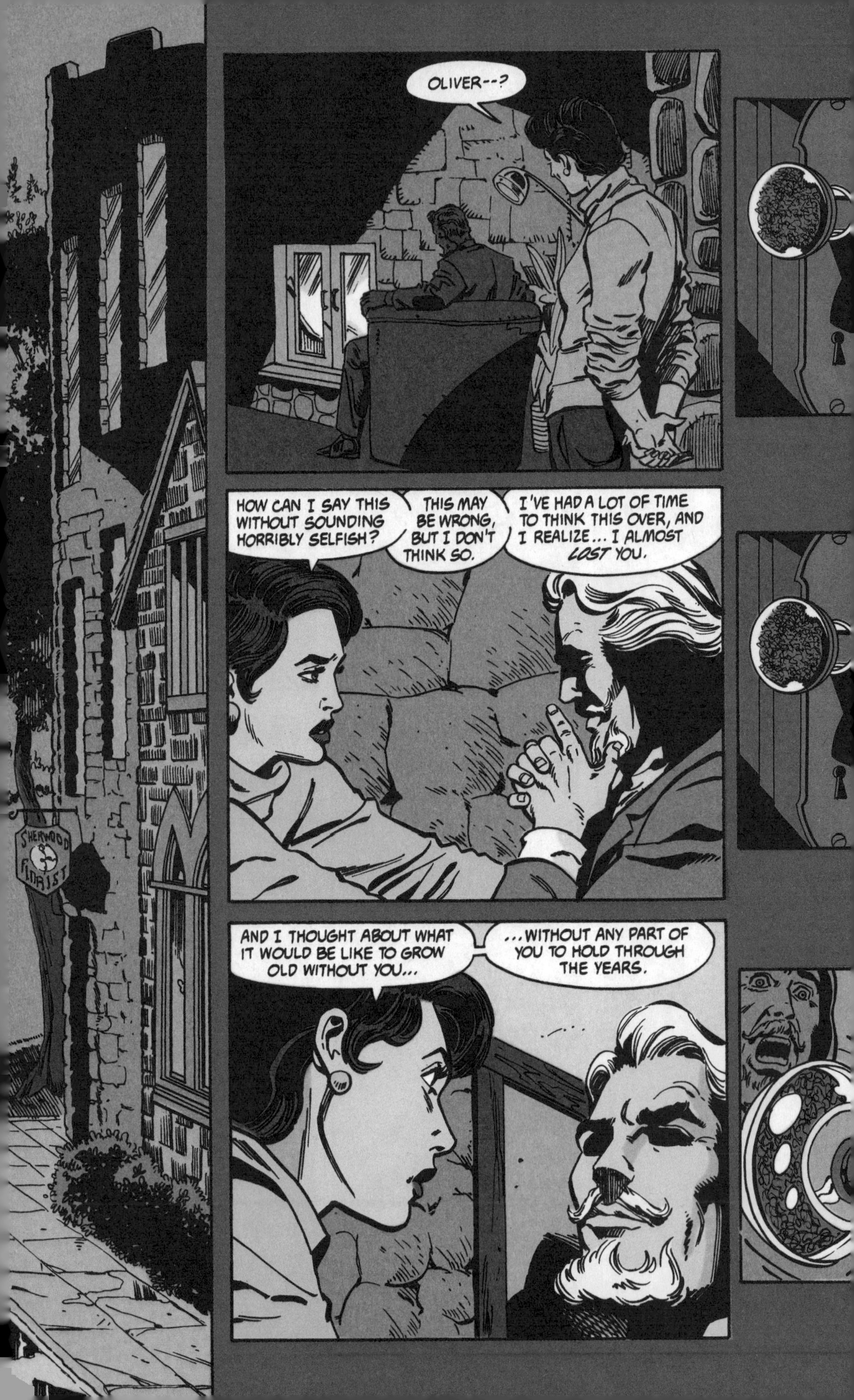
SHERWOOD FLORIST
OLIVER--?
HOW CAN I SAY THIS WITHOUT SOUNDING HORRIBLY SELFISH?
THIS MAY BE WRONG, BUT I DON'T THINK SO.
I'VE HAD A LOT OF TIME TO THINK THIS OVER, AND I REALIZE... I ALMOST LOST YOU.
AND I THOUGHT ABOUT WHAT IT WOULD BE LIKE TO GROW OLD WITHOUT YOU...
...WITHOUT ANY PART OF YOU TO HOLD THROUGH THE YEARS.

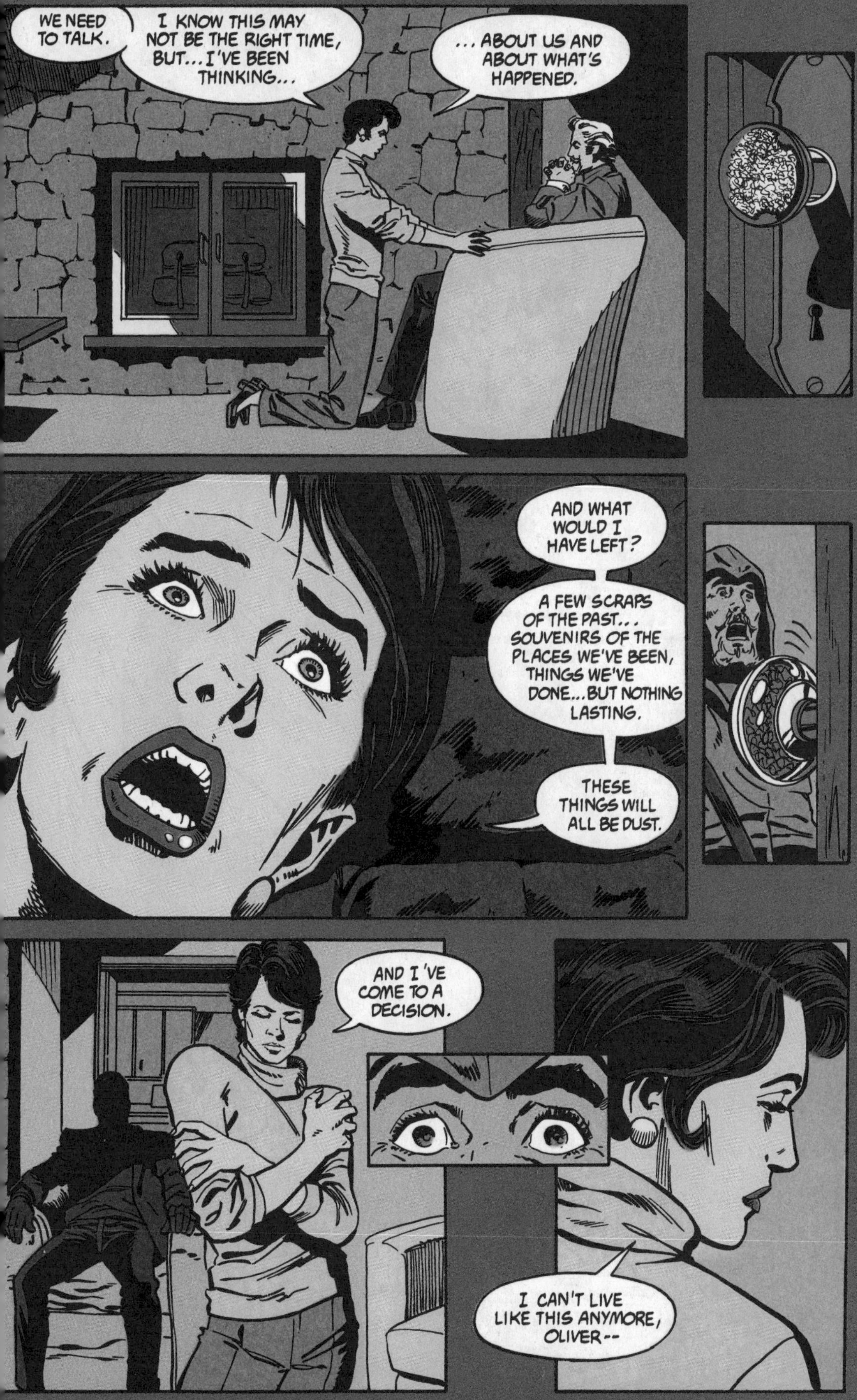
WE NEED TO TALK.
I KNOW THIS MAY NOT BE THE RIGHT TIME, BUT... I'VE BEEN THINKING...
... ABOUT US AND ABOUT WHAT'S HAPPENED.
AND WHAT WOULD I HAVE LEFT?
A FEW SCRAPS OF THE PAST... SOUVENIRS OF THE PLACES WE'VE BEEN, THINGS WE'VE DONE... BUT NOTHING LASTING.
THESE THINGS WILL ALL BE DUST.
AND I'VE COME TO A DECISION.
I CAN'T LIVE LIKE THIS ANYMORE, OLIVER--

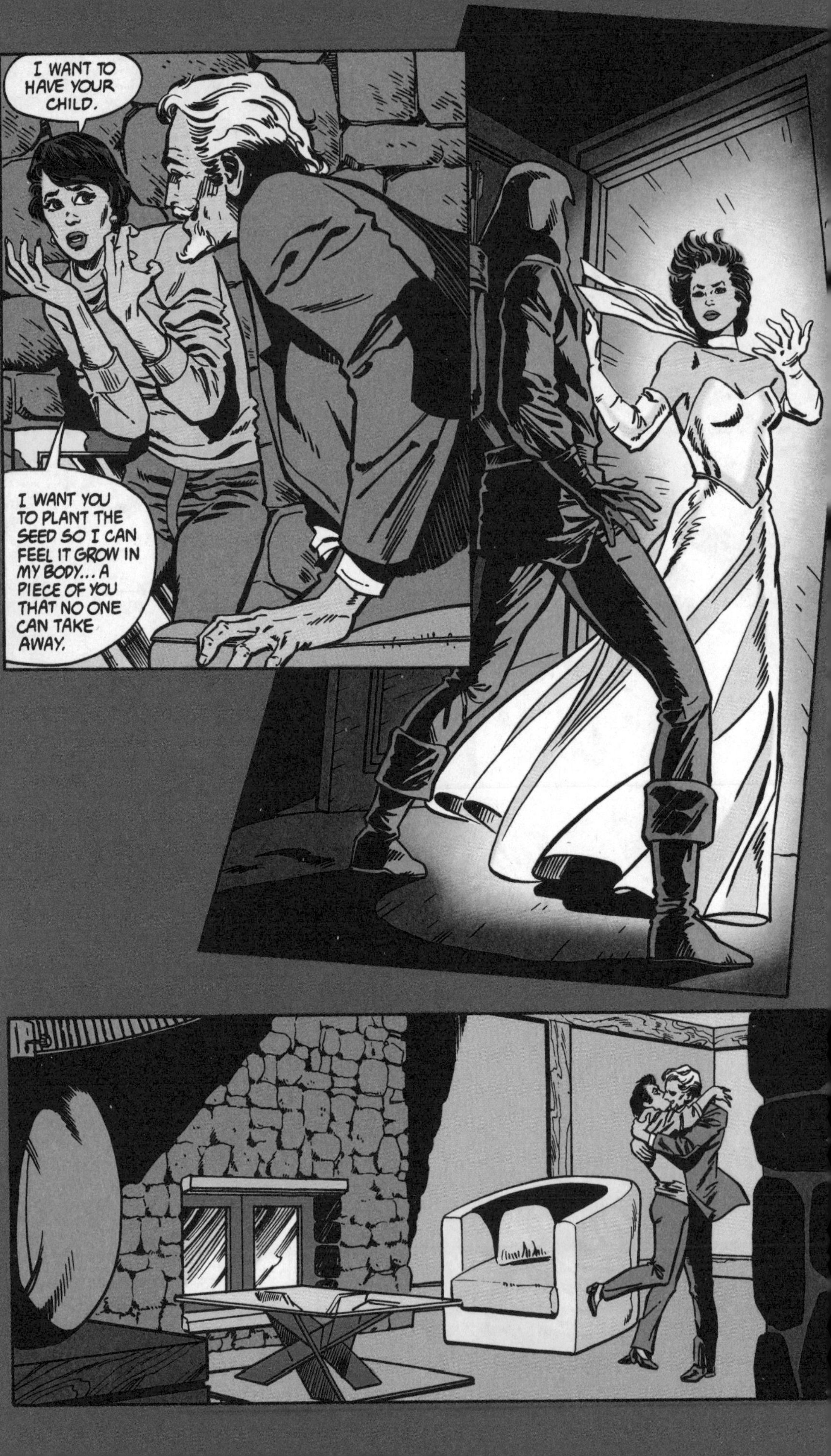
I WANT TO HAVE YOUR CHILD.
I WANT YOU TO PLANT THE SEED SO I CAN FEEL IT GROW IN MY BODY... A PIECE OF YOU THAT NO ONE CAN TAKE AWAY.

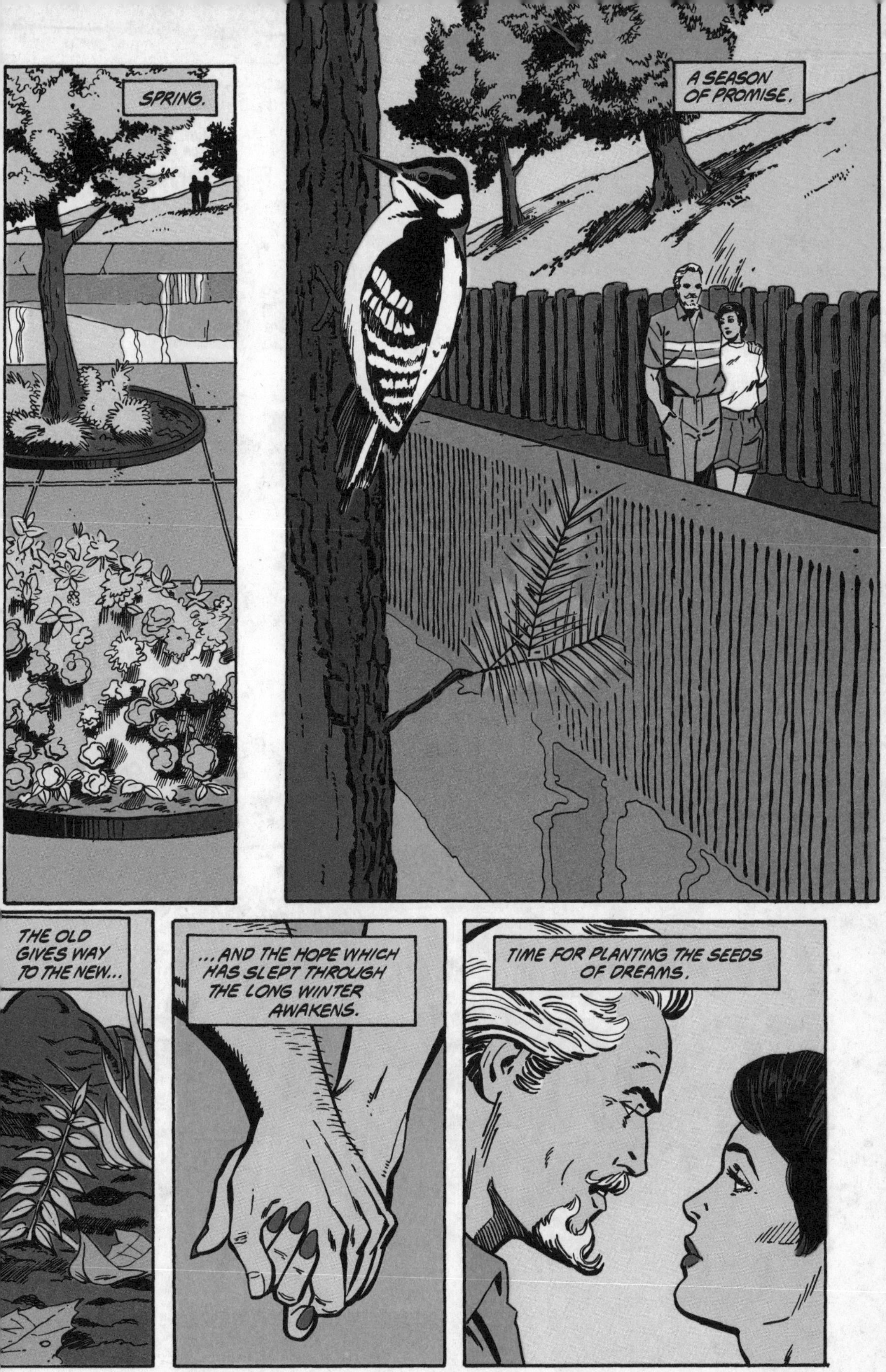
SPRING.
A SEASON OF PROMISE.
THE OLD GIVES WAY TO THE NEW...
...AND THE HOPE WHICH HAS SLEPT THROUGH THE LONG WINTER AWAKENS.
TIME FOR PLANTING THE SEEDS OF DREAMS.

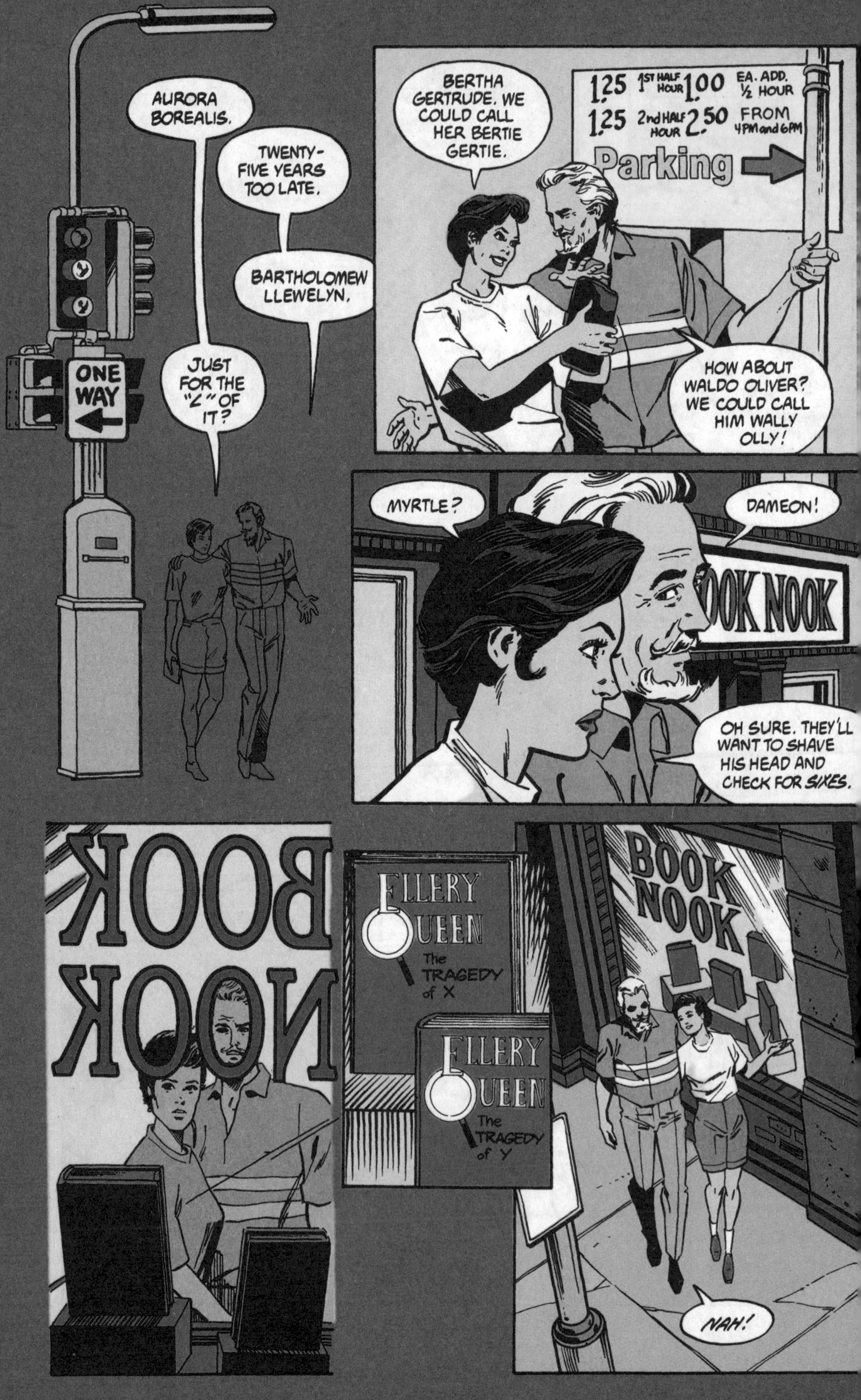
AURORA BOREALIS.
TWENTY-FIVE YEARS TOO LATE.
BARTHOLOMEW LLEWELYN.
JUST FOR THE "L" OF IT?
ONE WAY
BERTHA GERTRUDE. WE COULD CALL HER BERTIE GERTIE.
1.25 1ST HALF HOUR 1.00 EA. ADD. 1/2 HOUR
1.25 2nd HALF HOUR 2.50 FROM 4PM and 6PM
Parking
HOW ABOUT WALDO OLIVER? WE COULD CALL HIM WALLY OLLY!
MYRTLE?
DAMEON!
OOK NOOK
OH SURE. THEY'LL WANT TO SHAVE HIS HEAD AND CHECK FOR SIXES.
BOOK NOOK
ELLERY QUEEN The TRAGEDY of X
ELLERY QUEEN The TRAGEDY of Y
BOOK NOOK
NAH!

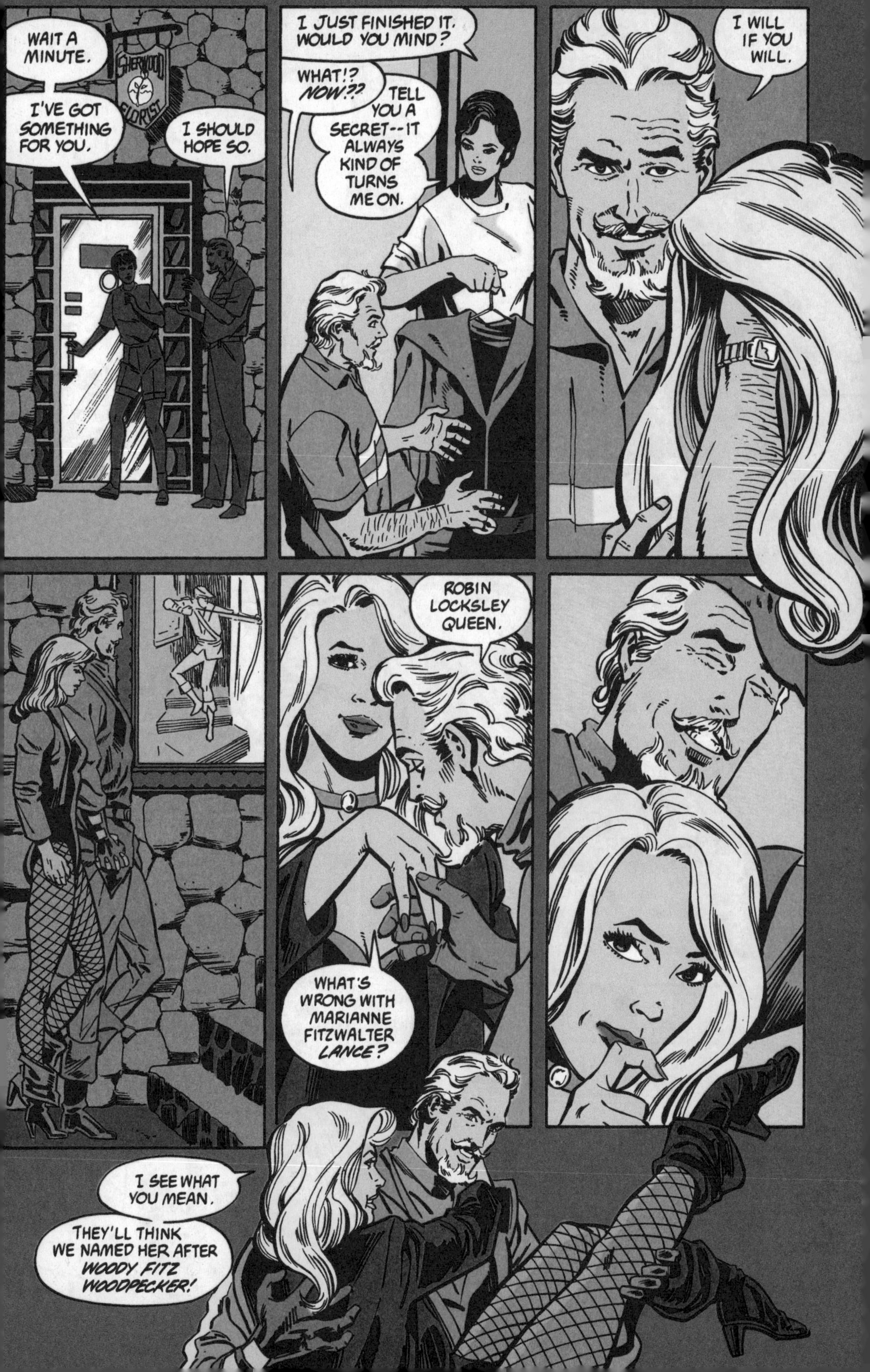
WAIT A MINUTE.
I'VE GOT SOMETHING FOR YOU.
SHERWOOD FLORIST
I SHOULD HOPE SO.
I JUST FINISHED IT. WOULD YOU MIND?
WHAT!? NOW??
TELL YOU A SECRET--IT ALWAYS KIND OF TURNS ME ON.
I WILL IF YOU WILL.
ROBIN LOCKSLEY QUEEN.
WHAT'S WRONG WITH MARIANNE FITZWALTER LANCE?
I SEE WHAT YOU MEAN.
THEY'LL THINK WE NAMED HER AFTER WOODY FITZ WOODPECKER!

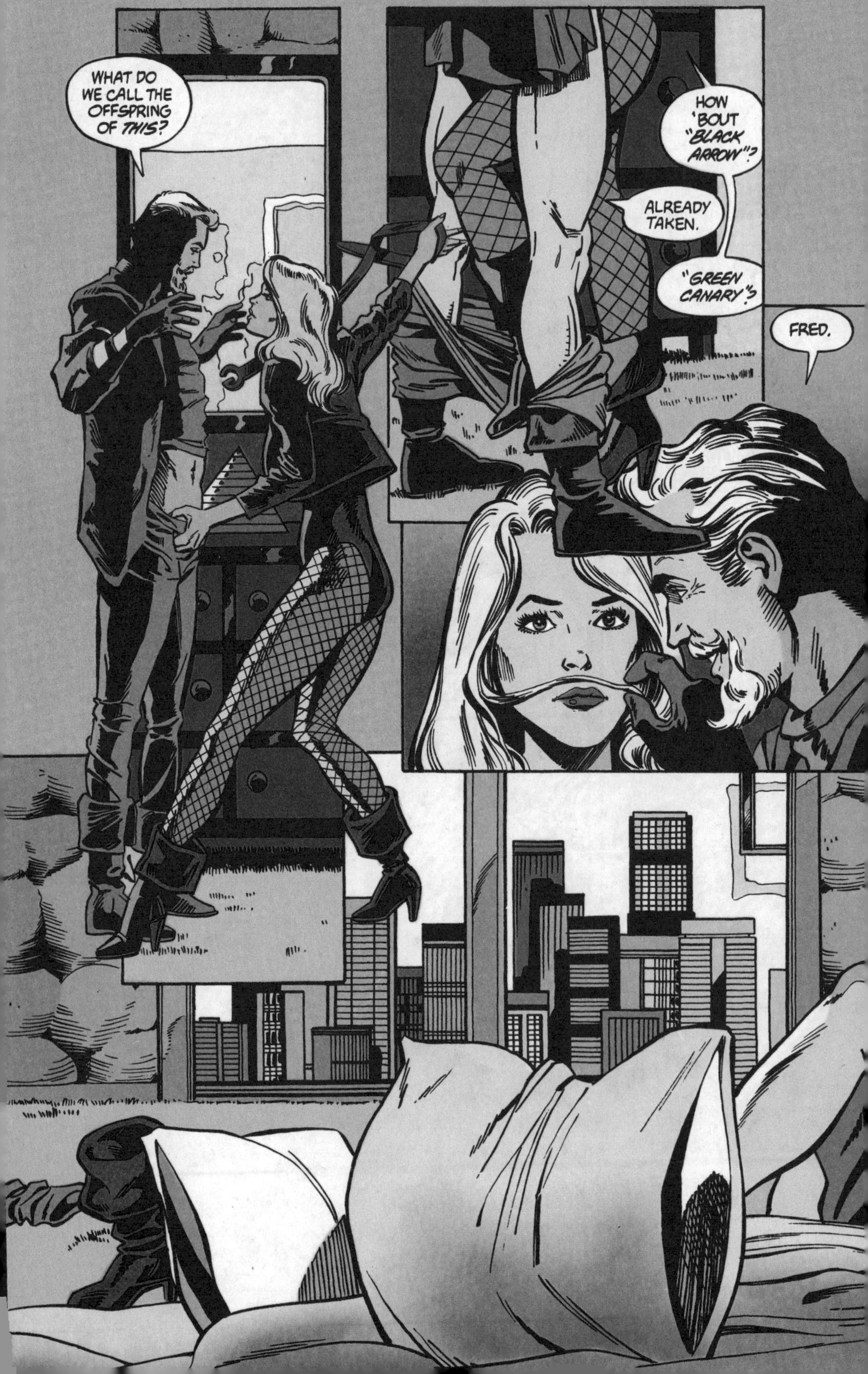
WHAT DO WE CALL THE OFFSPRING OF THIS?
HOW 'BOUT "BLACK ARROW"?
ALREADY TAKEN.
"GREEN CANARY"?
FRED.

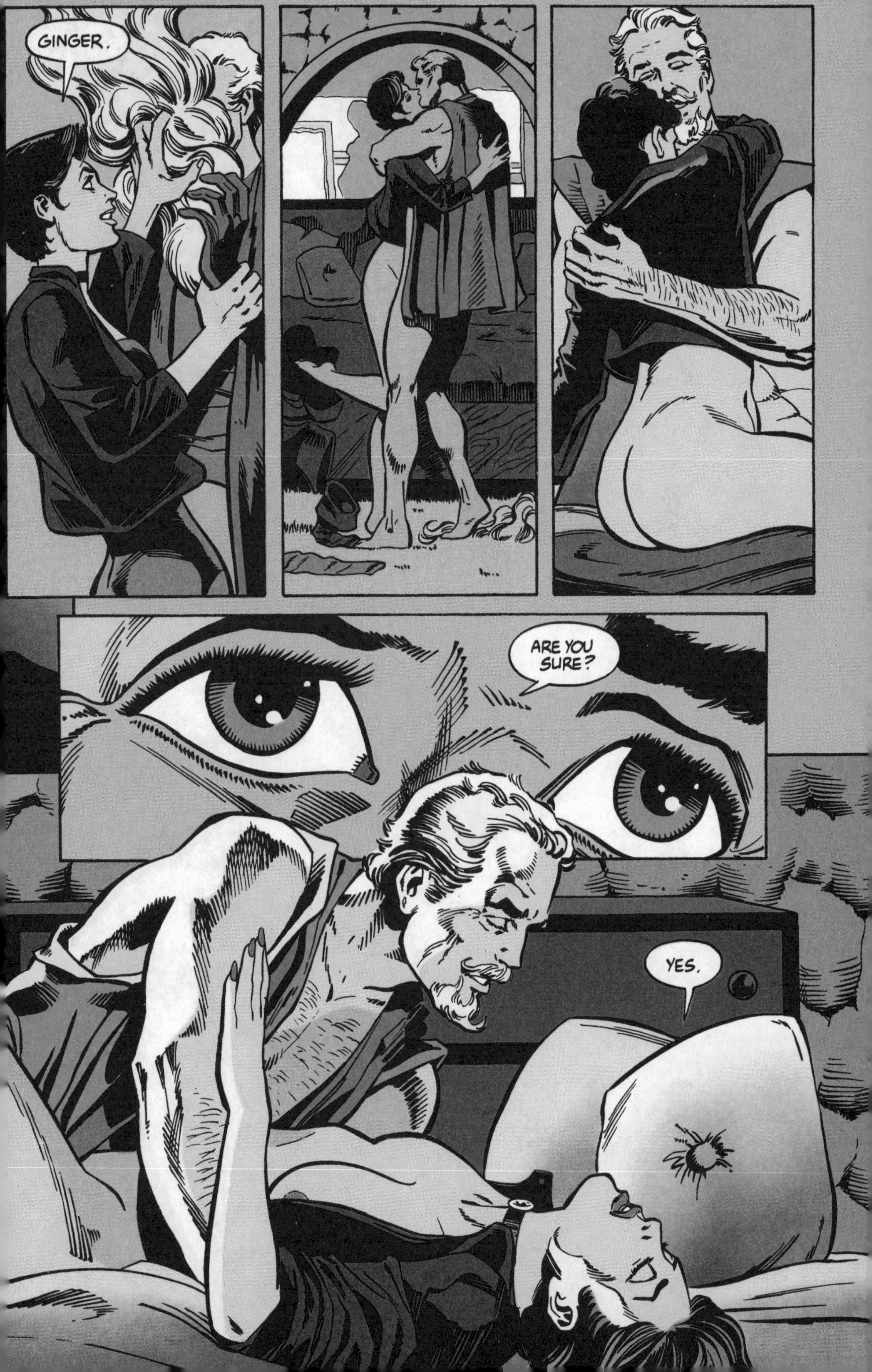
GINGER.
ARE YOU SURE?
YES.

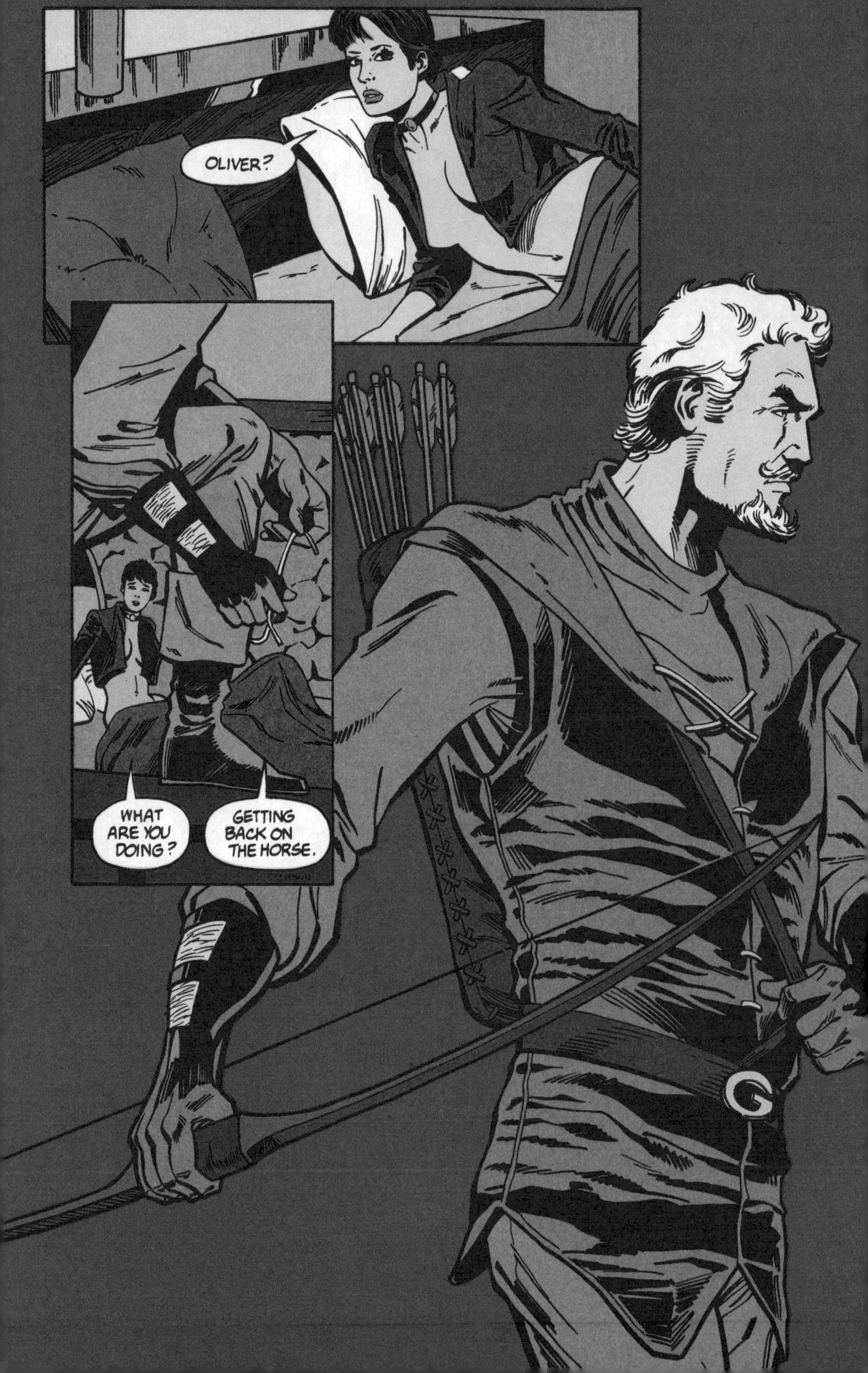
OLIVER?
WHAT ARE YOU DOING?
GETTING BACK ON THE HORSE.

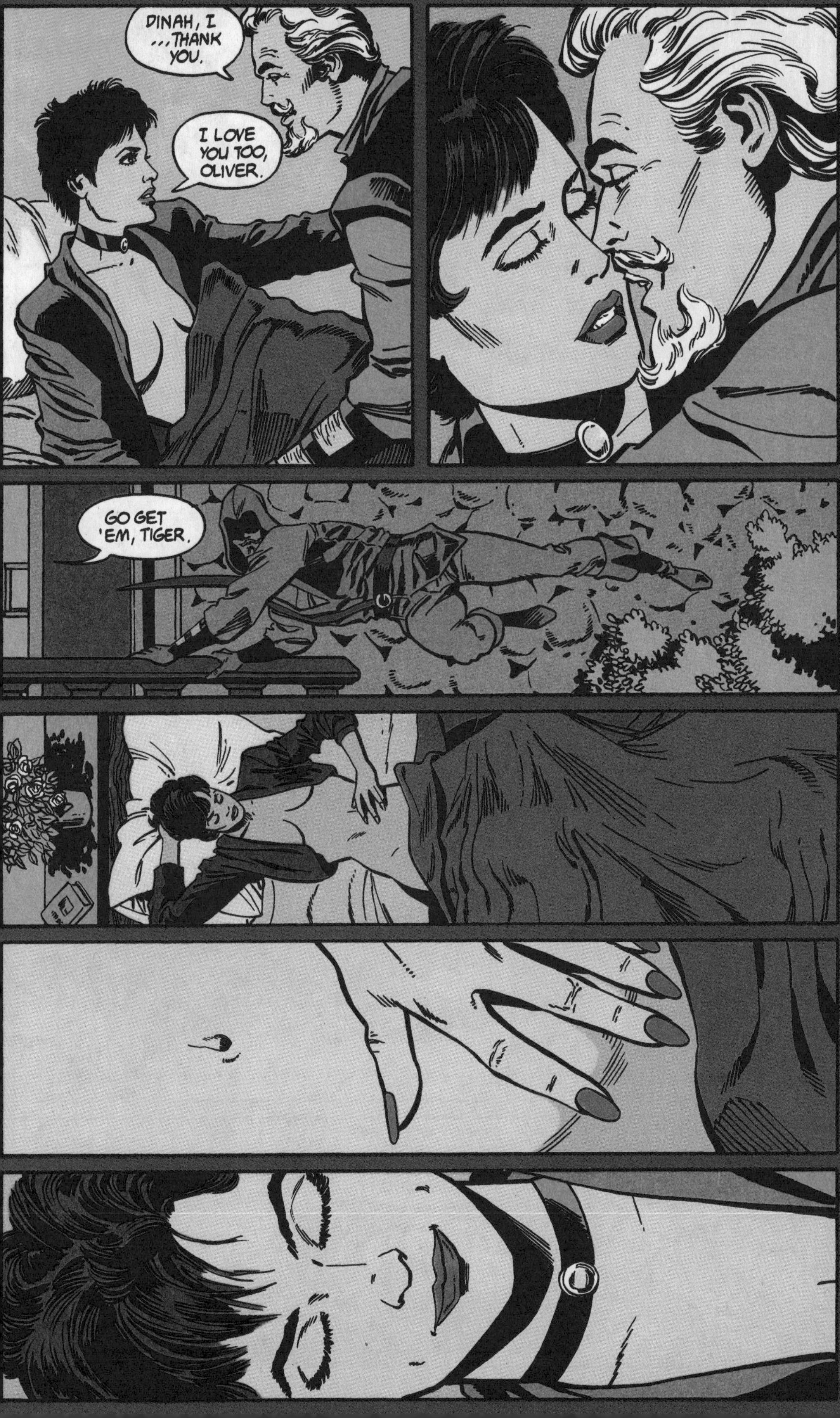
DINAH, I ...THANK YOU.
I LOVE YOU TOO, OLIVER.
GO GET 'EM, TIGER.

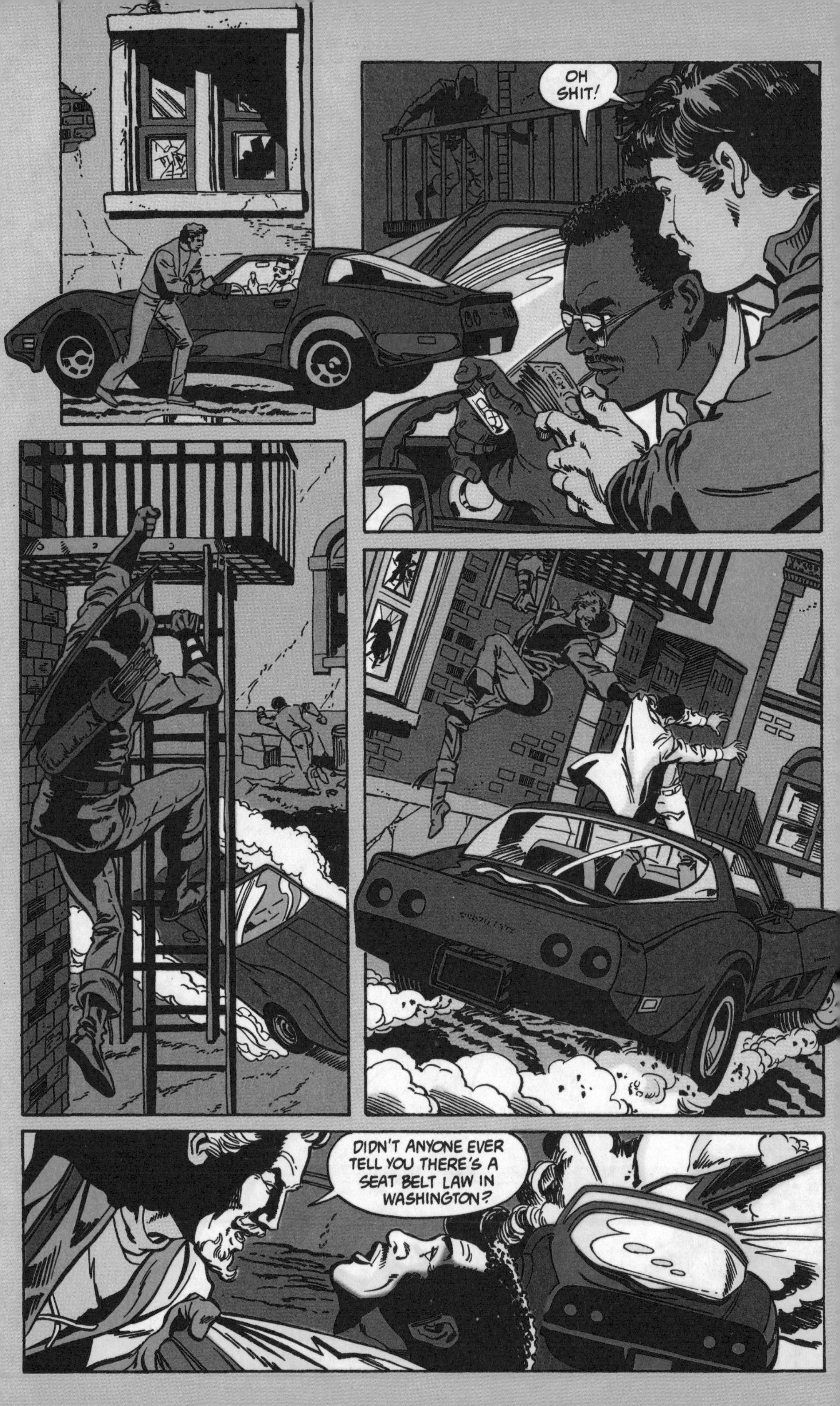
OH SHIT!
DIDN'T ANYONE EVER TELL YOU THERE'S A SEAT BELT LAW IN WASHINGTON?

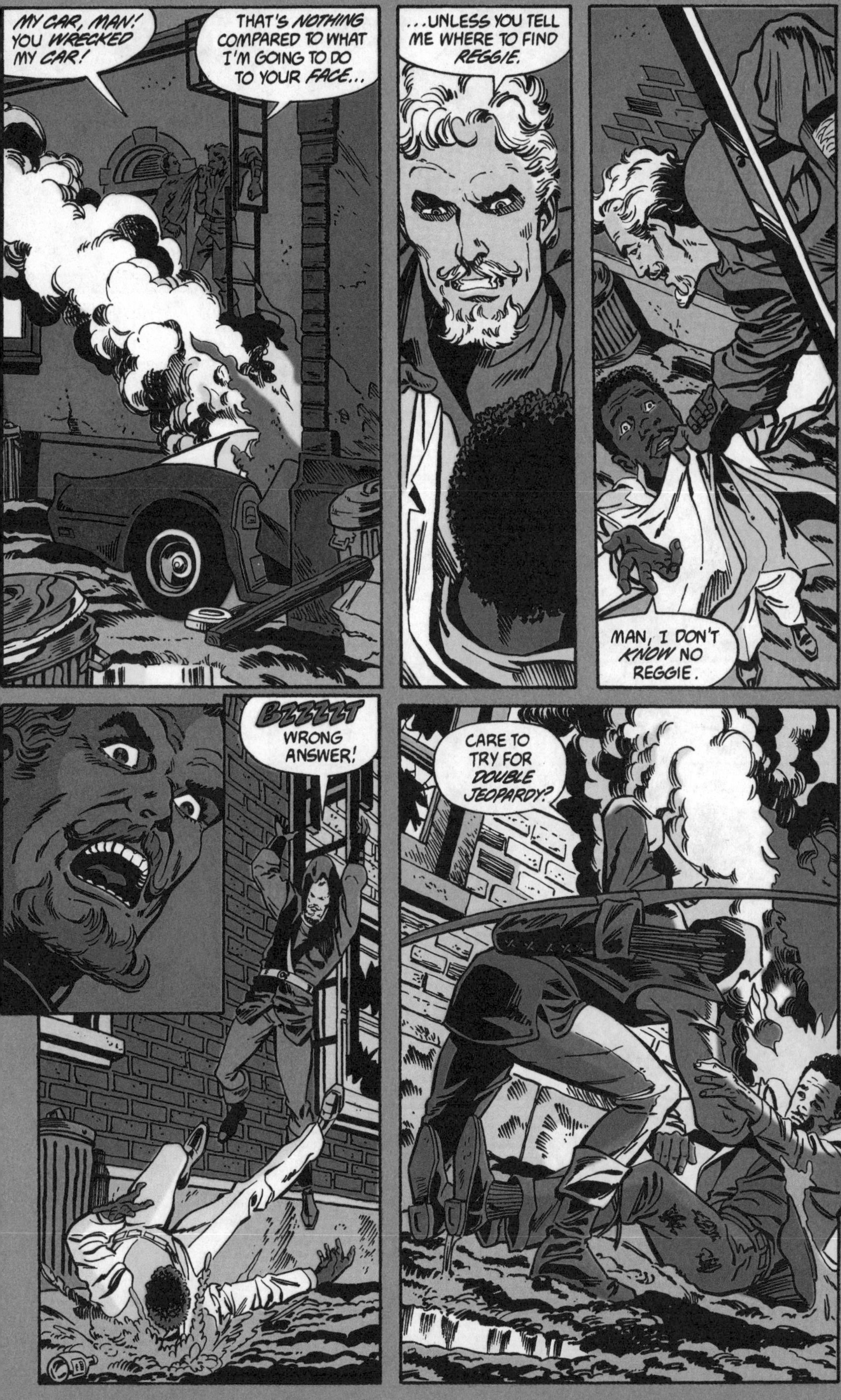
MY CAR, MAN! YOU WRECKED MY CAR!
THAT'S NOTHING COMPARED TO WHAT I'M GOING TO DO TO YOUR FACE...
...UNLESS YOU TELL ME WHERE TO FIND REGGIE.
MAN, I DON'T KNOW NO REGGIE.
BZZZZT WRONG ANSWER!
CARE TO TRY FOR DOUBLE JEOPARDY?

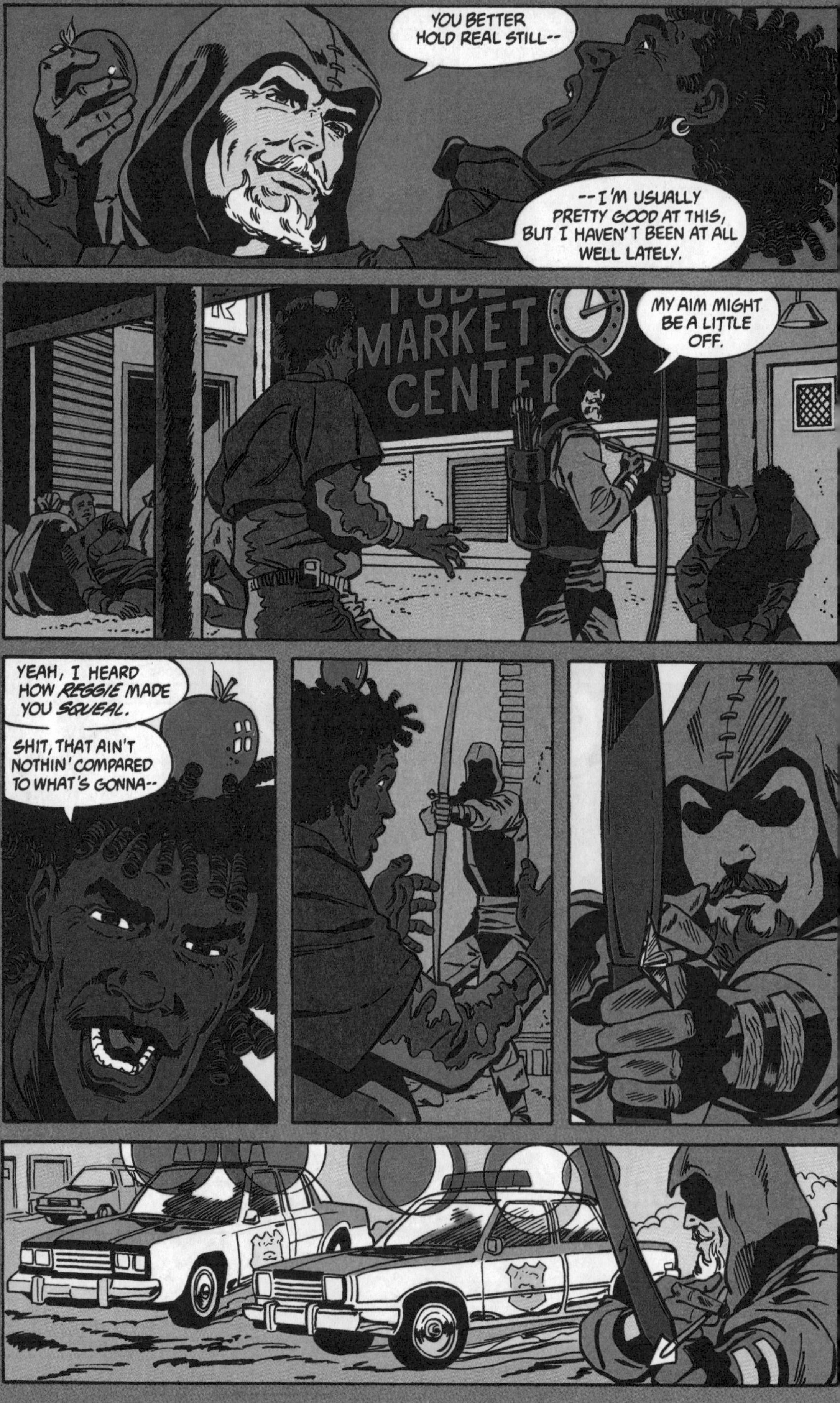
YOU BETTER HOLD REAL STILL--
--I'M USUALLY PRETTY GOOD AT THIS, BUT I HAVEN'T BEEN AT ALL WELL LATELY.
MARKET CENTER
MY AIM MIGHT BE A LITTLE OFF.
YEAH, I HEARD HOW *REGGIE* MADE YOU *SQUEAL*.
SHIT, THAT AIN'T NOTHIN' COMPARED TO WHAT'S GONNA--

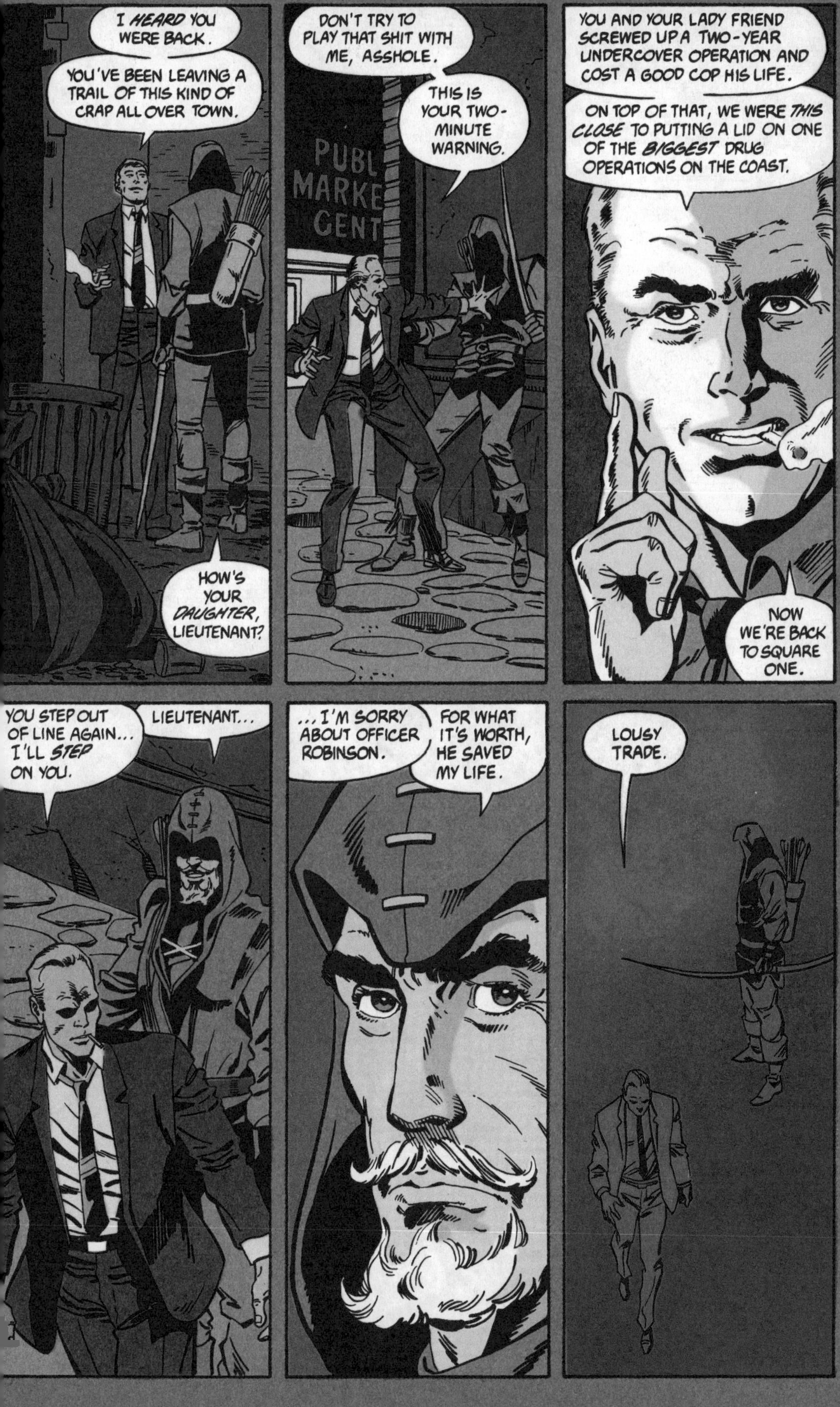
I HEARD YOU WERE BACK.
YOU'VE BEEN LEAVING A TRAIL OF THIS KIND OF CRAP ALL OVER TOWN.
HOW'S YOUR DAUGHTER, LIEUTENANT?
DON'T TRY TO PLAY THAT SHIT WITH ME, ASSHOLE.
THIS IS YOUR TWO-MINUTE WARNING.
PUBL
MARKE
CENT
YOU AND YOUR LADY FRIEND SCREWED UP A TWO-YEAR UNDERCOVER OPERATION AND COST A GOOD COP HIS LIFE.
ON TOP OF THAT, WE WERE THIS CLOSE TO PUTTING A LID ON ONE OF THE BIGGEST DRUG OPERATIONS ON THE COAST.
NOW WE'RE BACK TO SQUARE ONE.
YOU STEP OUT OF LINE AGAIN... I'LL STEP ON YOU.
LIEUTENANT...
...I'M SORRY ABOUT OFFICER ROBINSON.
FOR WHAT IT'S WORTH, HE SAVED MY LIFE.
LOUSY TRADE.

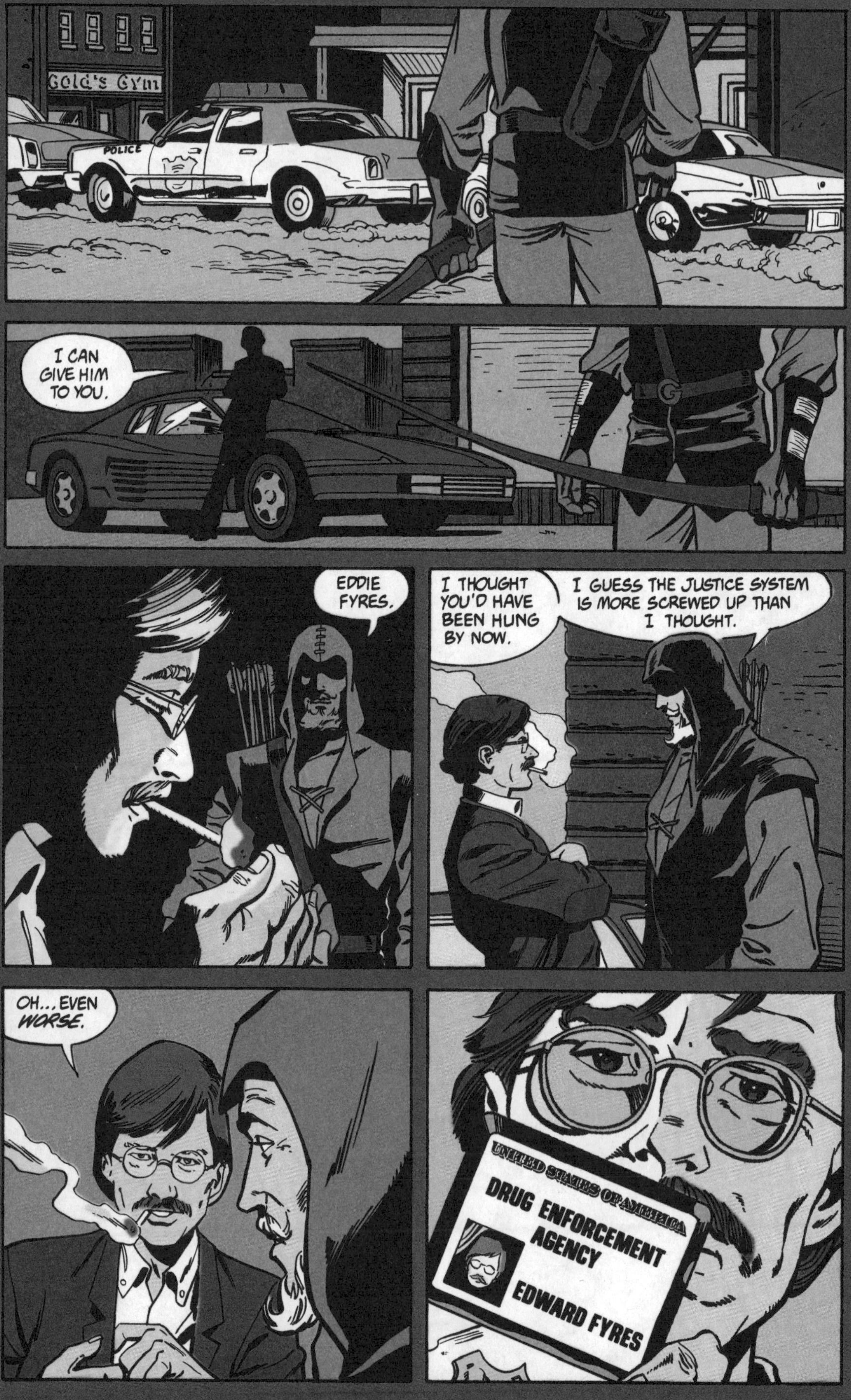
Gold's Gym
POLICE
I CAN GIVE HIM TO YOU.
EDDIE FYRES.
I THOUGHT YOU'D HAVE BEEN HUNG BY NOW.
I GUESS THE JUSTICE SYSTEM IS MORE SCREWED UP THAN I THOUGHT.
OH... EVEN WORSE.
UNITED STATES OF AMERICA
DRUG ENFORCEMENT AGENCY
EDWARD FYRES

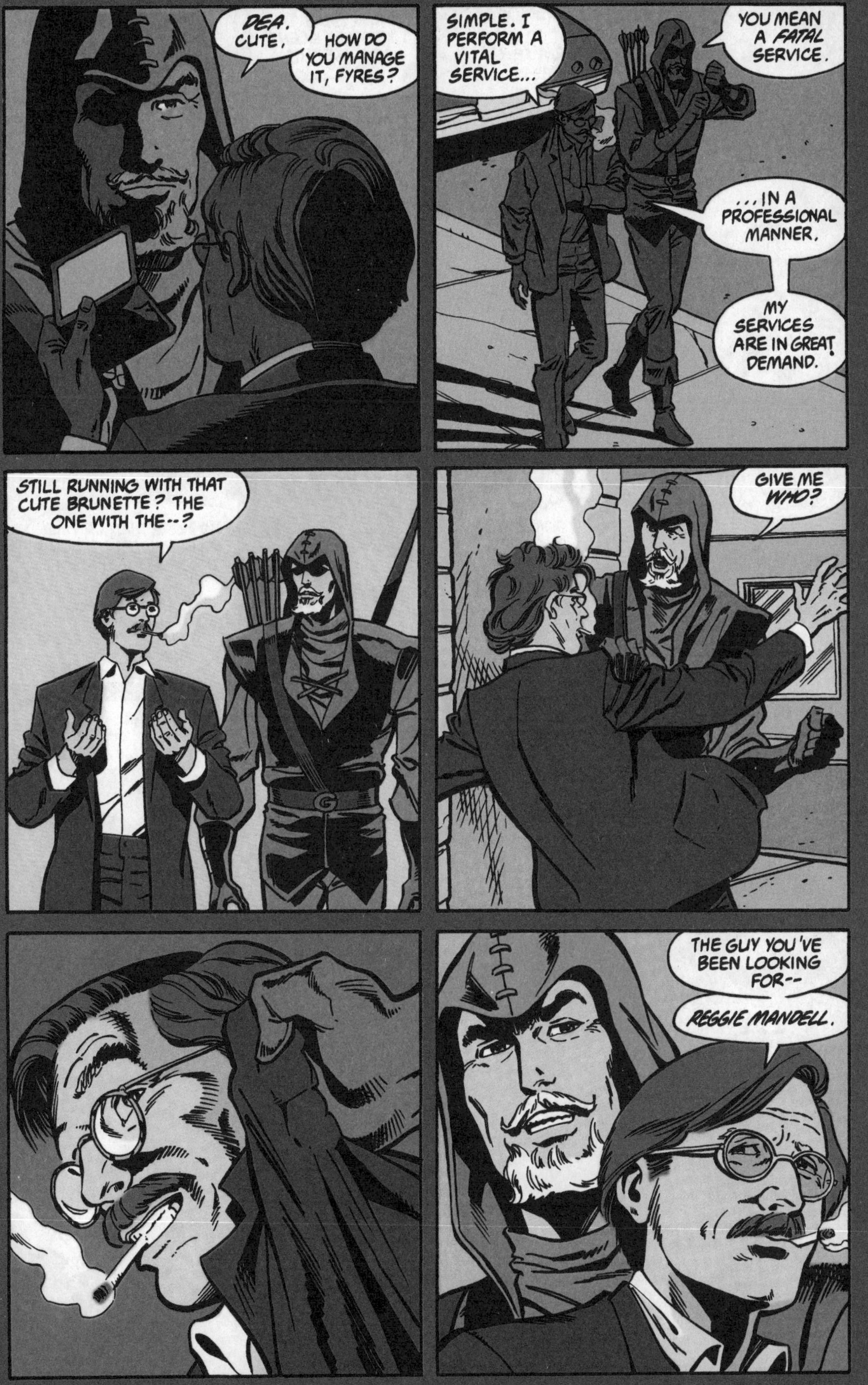
DEA. CUTE.
HOW DO YOU MANAGE IT, FYRES?
SIMPLE. I PERFORM A VITAL SERVICE...
YOU MEAN A FATAL SERVICE.
...IN A PROFESSIONAL MANNER.
MY SERVICES ARE IN GREAT DEMAND.
STILL RUNNING WITH THAT CUTE BRUNETTE? THE ONE WITH THE--?
GIVE ME WHO?
THE GUY YOU'VE BEEN LOOKING FOR--
REGGIE MANDELL.

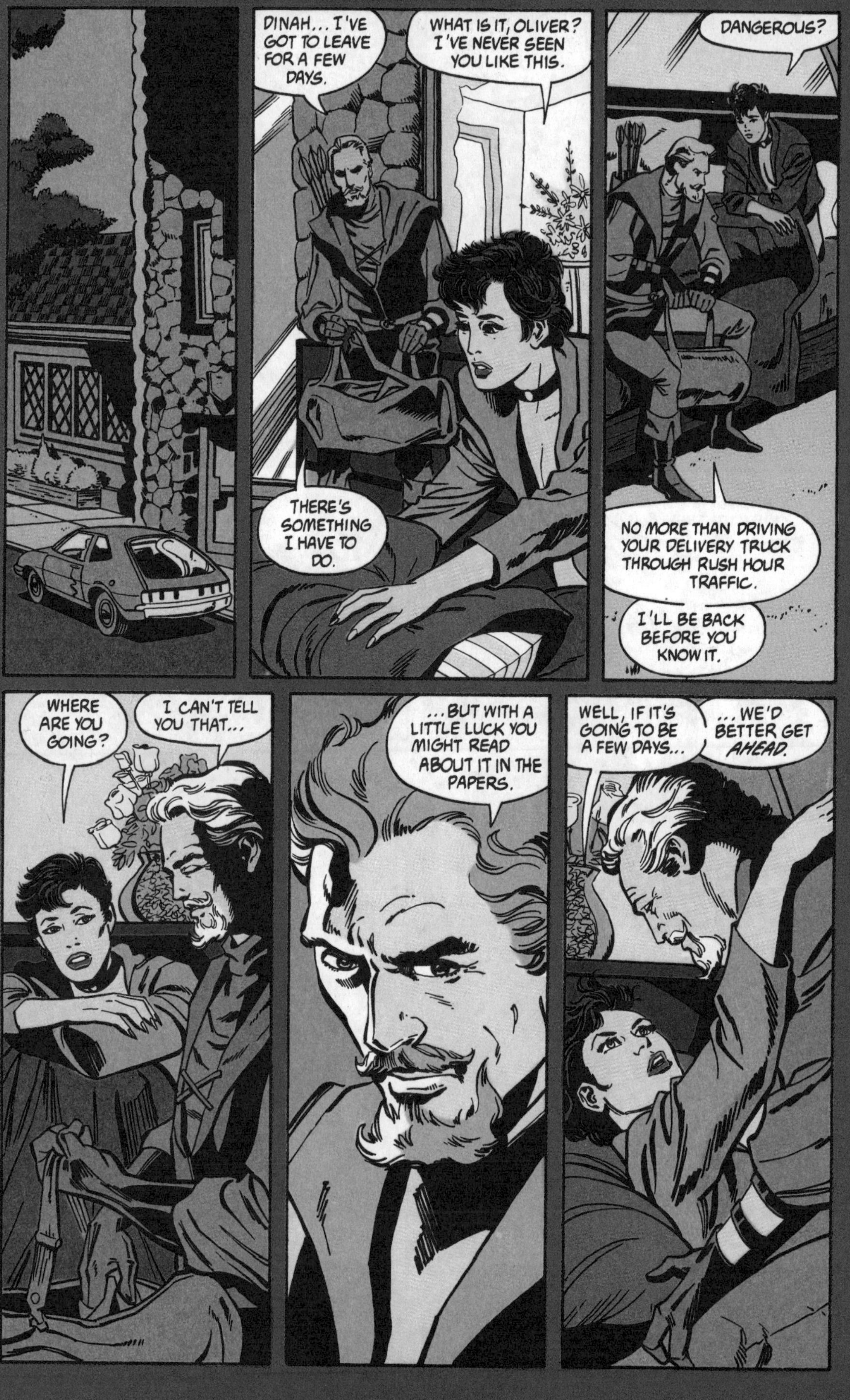
DINAH... I'VE GOT TO LEAVE FOR A FEW DAYS.
WHAT IS IT, OLIVER? I'VE NEVER SEEN YOU LIKE THIS.
THERE'S SOMETHING I HAVE TO DO.
DANGEROUS?
NO MORE THAN DRIVING YOUR DELIVERY TRUCK THROUGH RUSH HOUR TRAFFIC.
I'LL BE BACK BEFORE YOU KNOW IT.
WHERE ARE YOU GOING?
I CAN'T TELL YOU THAT...
...BUT WITH A LITTLE LUCK YOU MIGHT READ ABOUT IT IN THE PAPERS.
WELL, IF IT'S GOING TO BE A FEW DAYS...
...WE'D BETTER GET *AHEAD*.

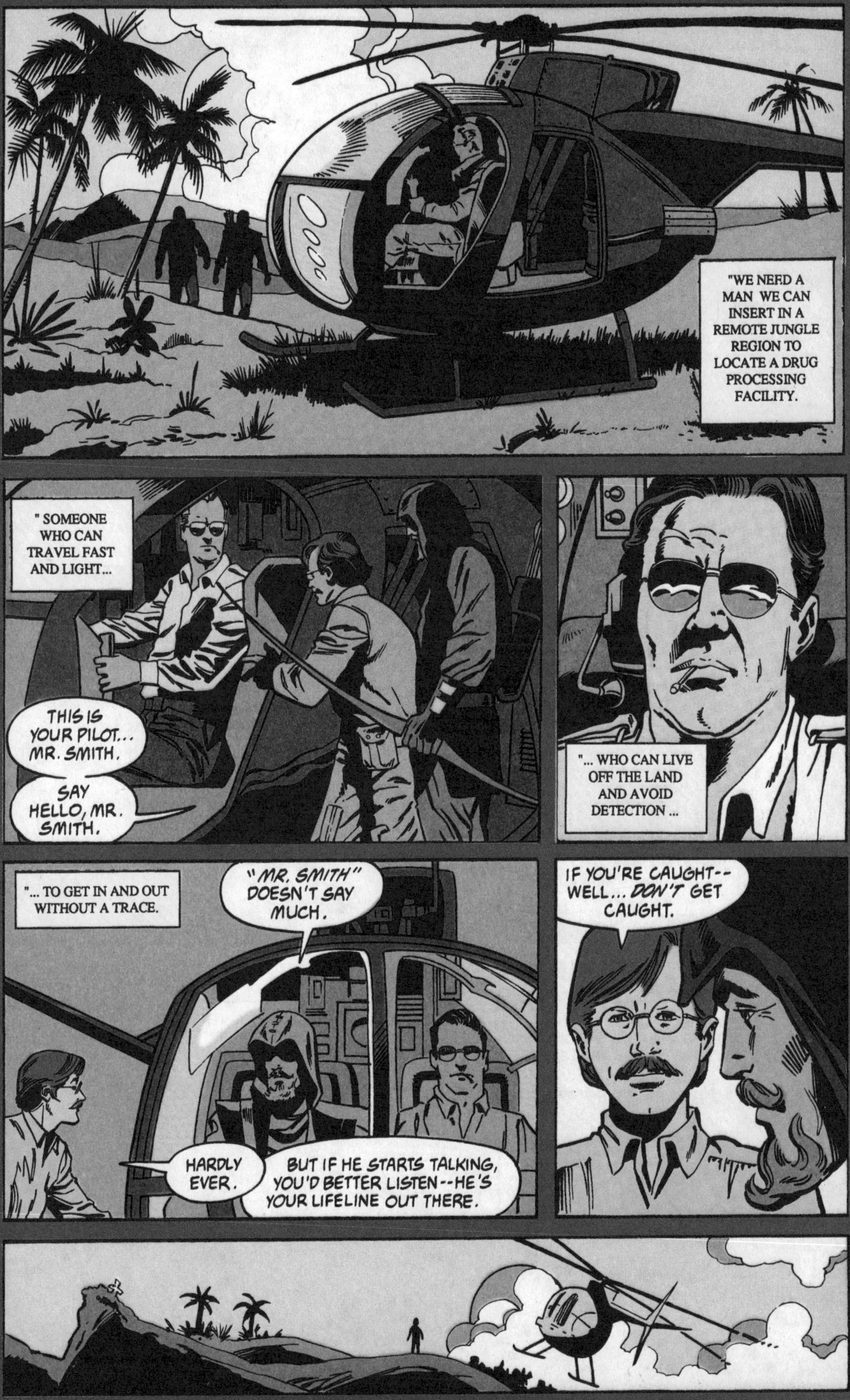
"WE NEED A MAN WE CAN INSERT IN A REMOTE JUNGLE REGION TO LOCATE A DRUG PROCESSING FACILITY.
" SOMEONE WHO CAN TRAVEL FAST AND LIGHT...
THIS IS YOUR PILOT... MR. SMITH.
SAY HELLO, MR. SMITH.
"... WHO CAN LIVE OFF THE LAND AND AVOID DETECTION ...
"... TO GET IN AND OUT WITHOUT A TRACE.
"MR. SMITH" DOESN'T SAY MUCH.
HARDLY EVER.
BUT IF HE STARTS TALKING, YOU'D BETTER LISTEN--HE'S YOUR LIFELINE OUT THERE.
IF YOU'RE CAUGHT--WELL... DON'T GET CAUGHT.

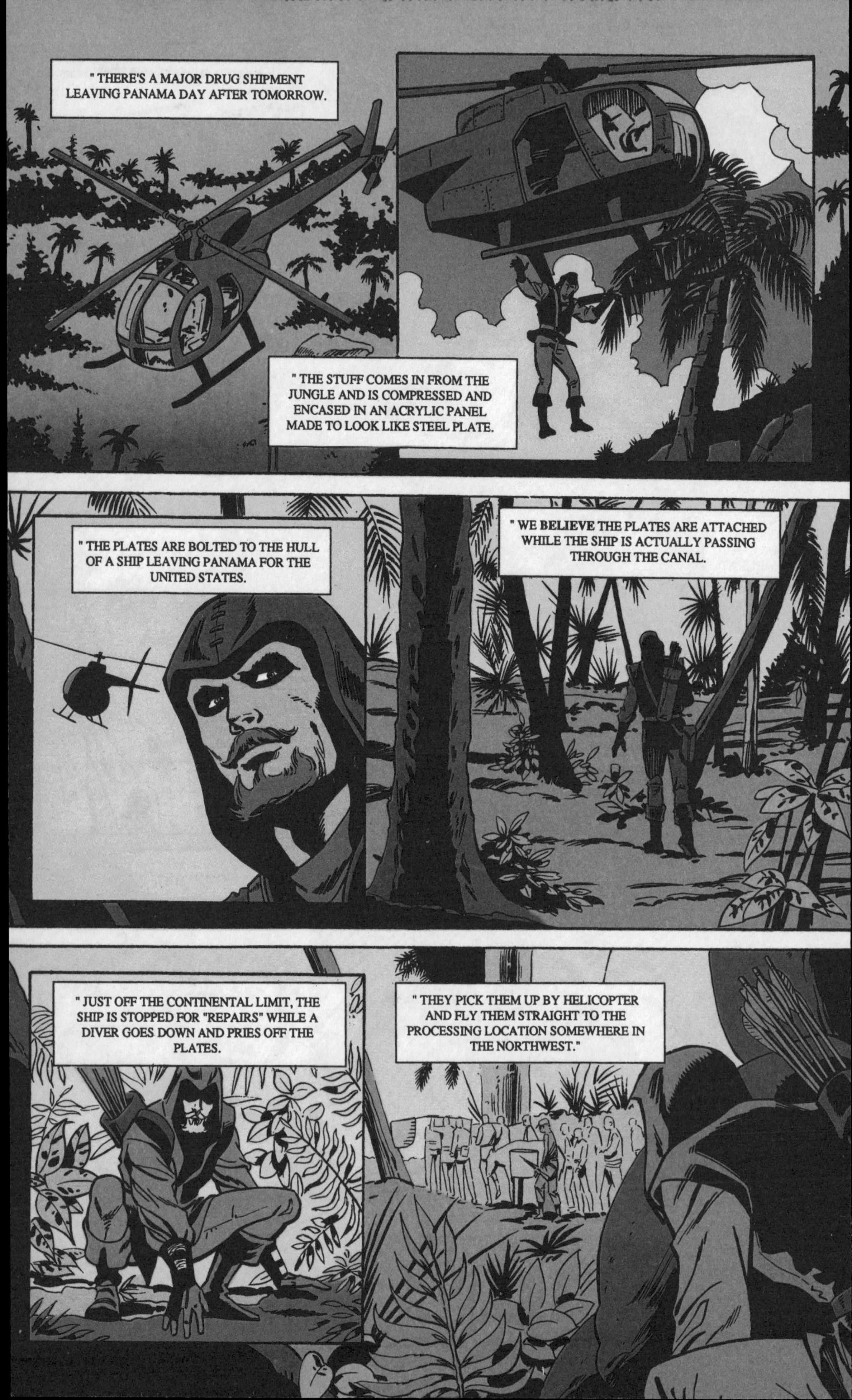
" THERE'S A MAJOR DRUG SHIPMENT LEAVING PANAMA DAY AFTER TOMORROW.
" THE STUFF COMES IN FROM THE JUNGLE AND IS COMPRESSED AND ENCASED IN AN ACRYLIC PANEL MADE TO LOOK LIKE STEEL PLATE.
" THE PLATES ARE BOLTED TO THE HULL OF A SHIP LEAVING PANAMA FOR THE UNITED STATES.
" WE **BELIEVE** THE PLATES ARE ATTACHED WHILE THE SHIP IS ACTUALLY PASSING THROUGH THE CANAL.
" JUST OFF THE CONTINENTAL LIMIT, THE SHIP IS STOPPED FOR "REPAIRS" WHILE A DIVER GOES DOWN AND PRIES OFF THE PLATES.
" THEY PICK THEM UP BY HELICOPTER AND FLY THEM STRAIGHT TO THE PROCESSING LOCATION SOMEWHERE IN THE NORTHWEST."

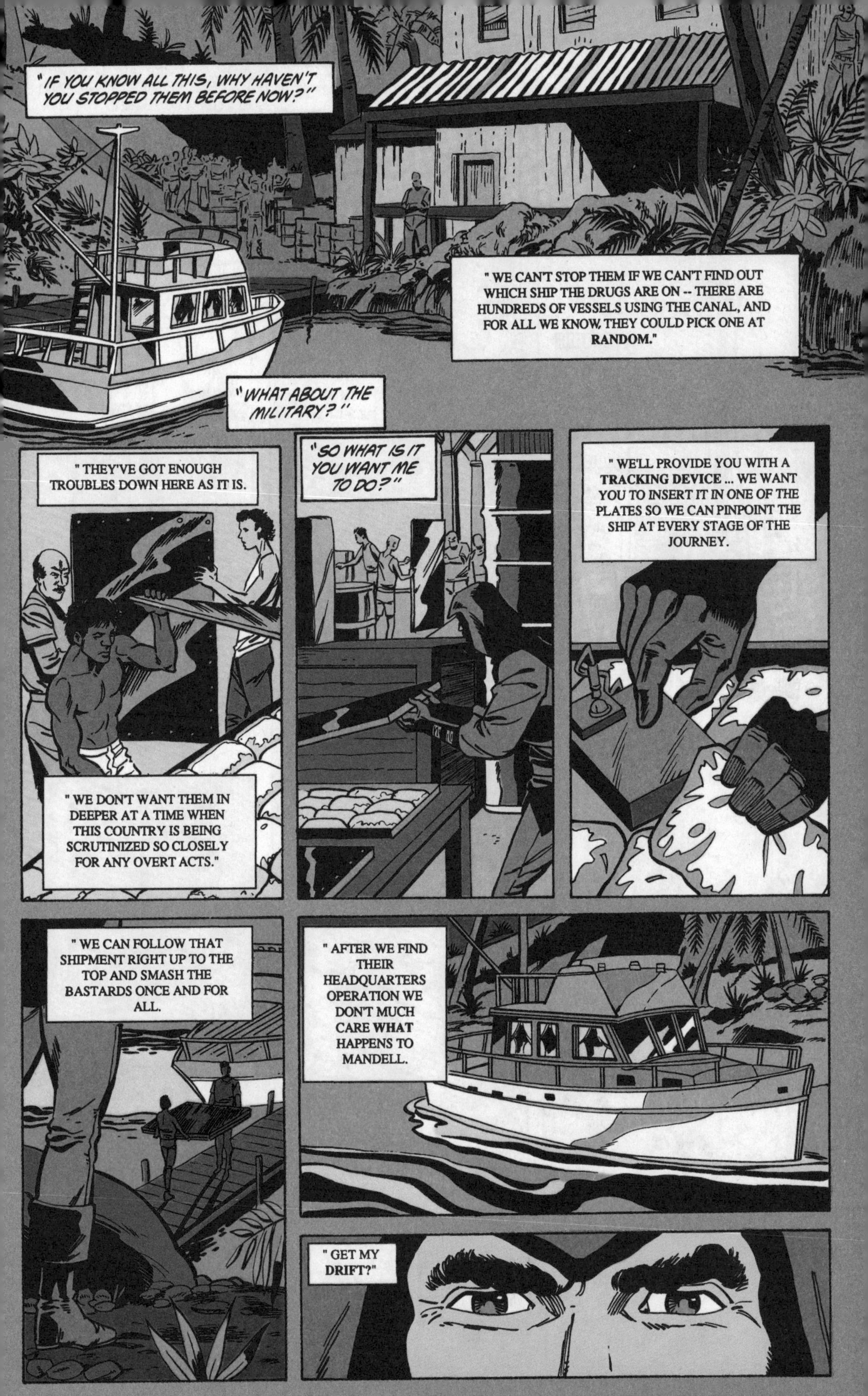
"IF YOU KNOW ALL THIS, WHY HAVEN'T YOU STOPPED THEM BEFORE NOW?"
" WE CAN'T STOP THEM IF WE CAN'T FIND OUT WHICH SHIP THE DRUGS ARE ON -- THERE ARE HUNDREDS OF VESSELS USING THE CANAL, AND FOR ALL WE KNOW, THEY COULD PICK ONE AT RANDOM."
"WHAT ABOUT THE MILITARY?"
" THEY'VE GOT ENOUGH TROUBLES DOWN HERE AS IT IS.
" WE DON'T WANT THEM IN DEEPER AT A TIME WHEN THIS COUNTRY IS BEING SCRUTINIZED SO CLOSELY FOR ANY OVERT ACTS."
"SO WHAT IS IT YOU WANT ME TO DO?"
" WE'LL PROVIDE YOU WITH A TRACKING DEVICE ... WE WANT YOU TO INSERT IT IN ONE OF THE PLATES SO WE CAN PINPOINT THE SHIP AT EVERY STAGE OF THE JOURNEY.
" WE CAN FOLLOW THAT SHIPMENT RIGHT UP TO THE TOP AND SMASH THE BASTARDS ONCE AND FOR ALL.
" AFTER WE FIND THEIR HEADQUARTERS OPERATION WE DON'T MUCH CARE WHAT HAPPENS TO MANDELL.
" GET MY DRIFT?"

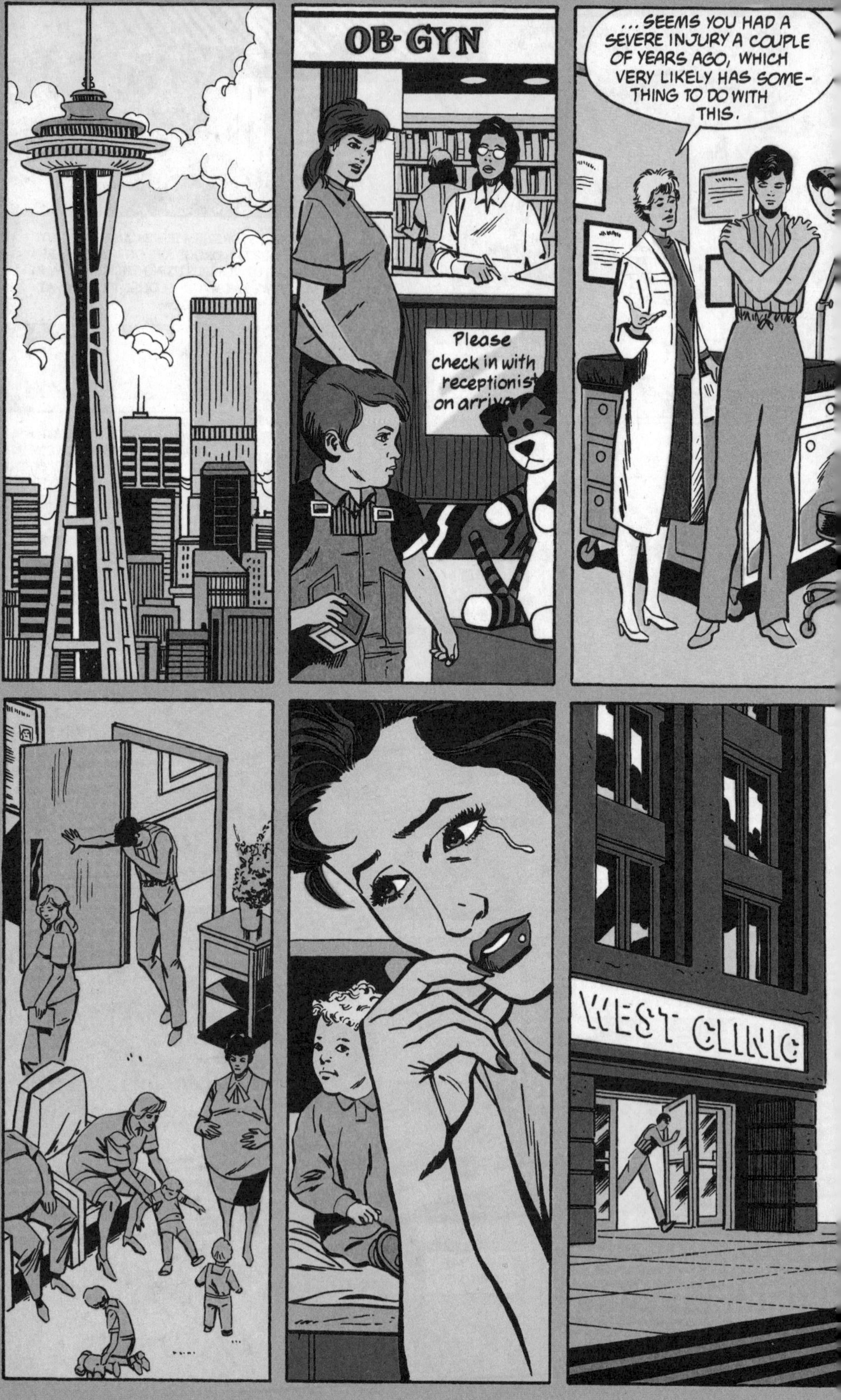
OB-GYN
Please check in with receptionist on arriva
...SEEMS YOU HAD A SEVERE INJURY A COUPLE OF YEARS AGO, WHICH VERY LIKELY HAS SOME-THING TO DO WITH THIS.
WEST CLINIC

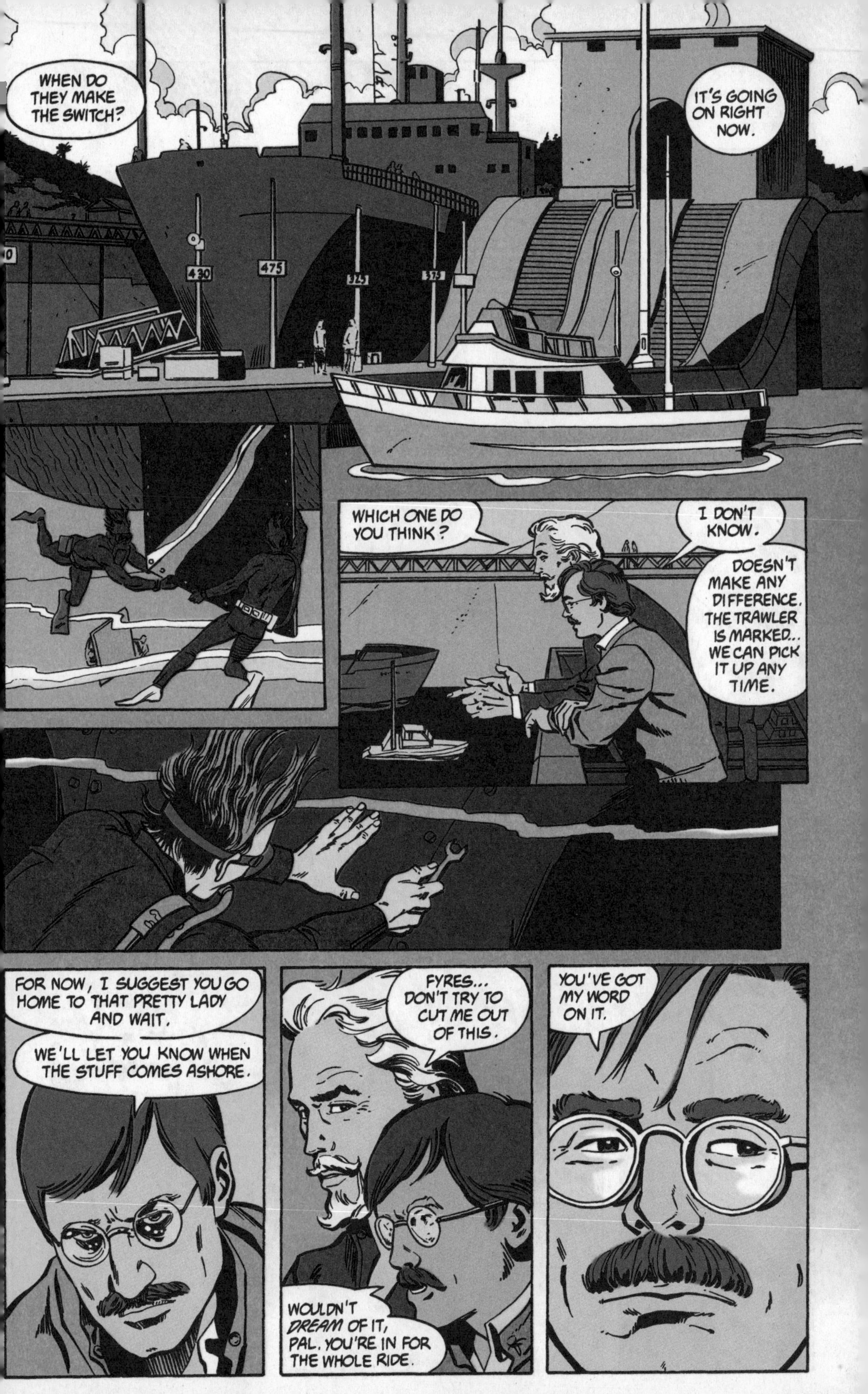
WHEN DO THEY MAKE THE SWITCH?
IT'S GOING ON RIGHT NOW.
430
475
WHICH ONE DO YOU THINK?
I DON'T KNOW.
DOESN'T MAKE ANY DIFFERENCE. THE TRAWLER IS MARKED... WE CAN PICK IT UP ANY TIME.
FOR NOW, I SUGGEST YOU GO HOME TO THAT PRETTY LADY AND WAIT.
WE'LL LET YOU KNOW WHEN THE STUFF COMES ASHORE.
FYRES... DON'T TRY TO CUT ME OUT OF THIS.
WOULDN'T *DREAM* OF IT, PAL. YOU'RE IN FOR THE WHOLE RIDE.
YOU'VE GOT MY WORD ON IT.

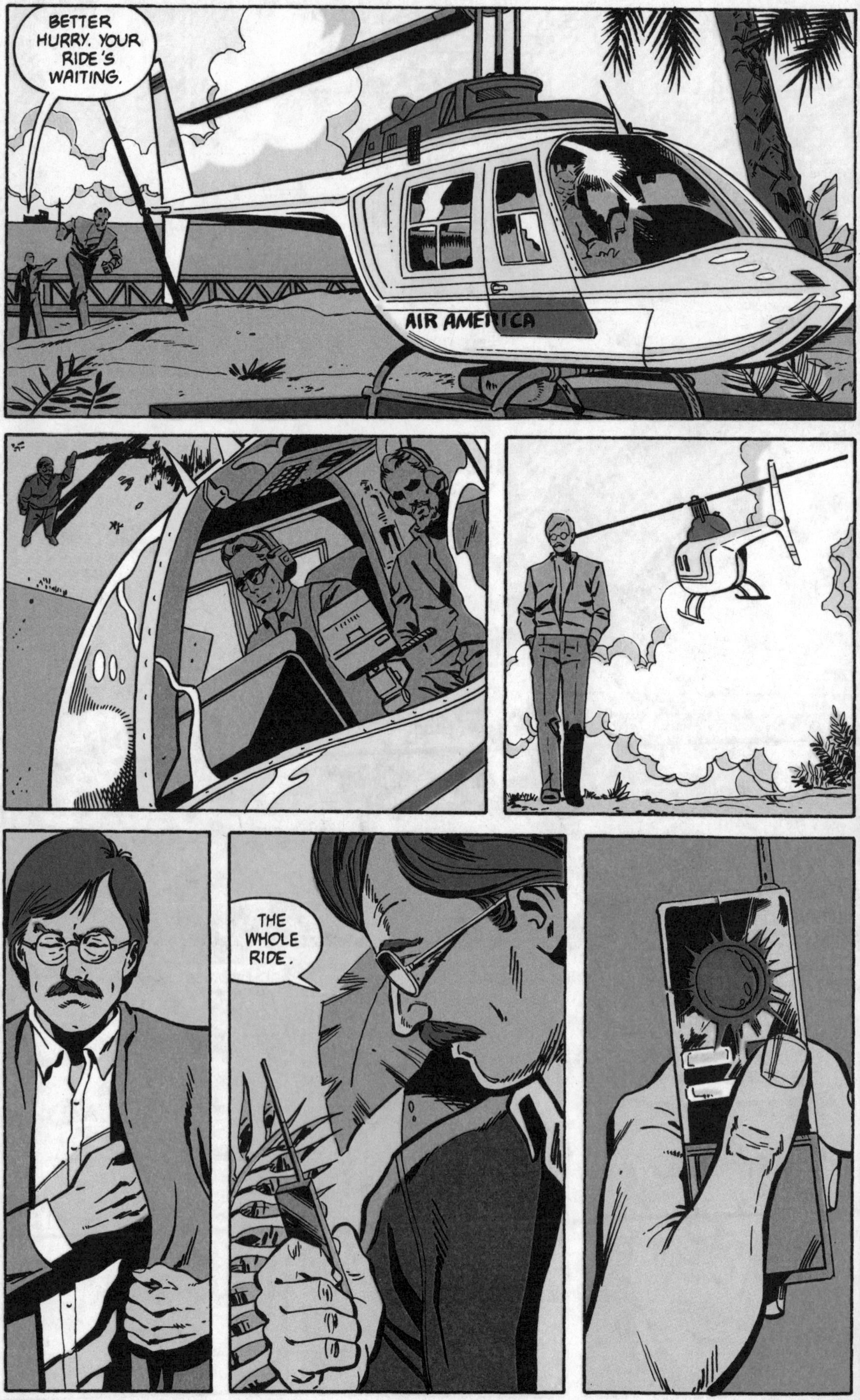
BETTER HURRY. YOUR RIDE'S WAITING.
AIR AMERICA
THE WHOLE RIDE.

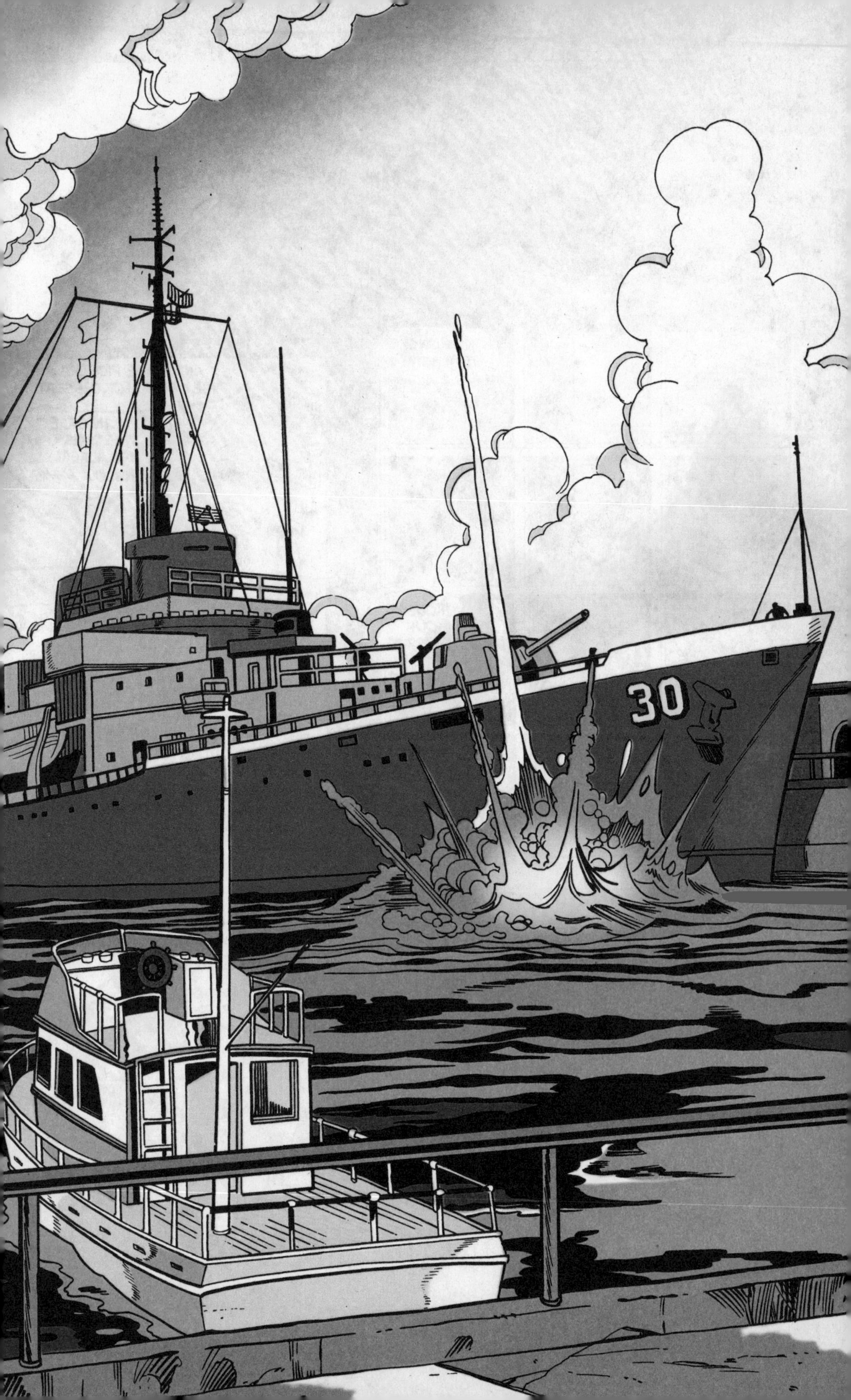
30

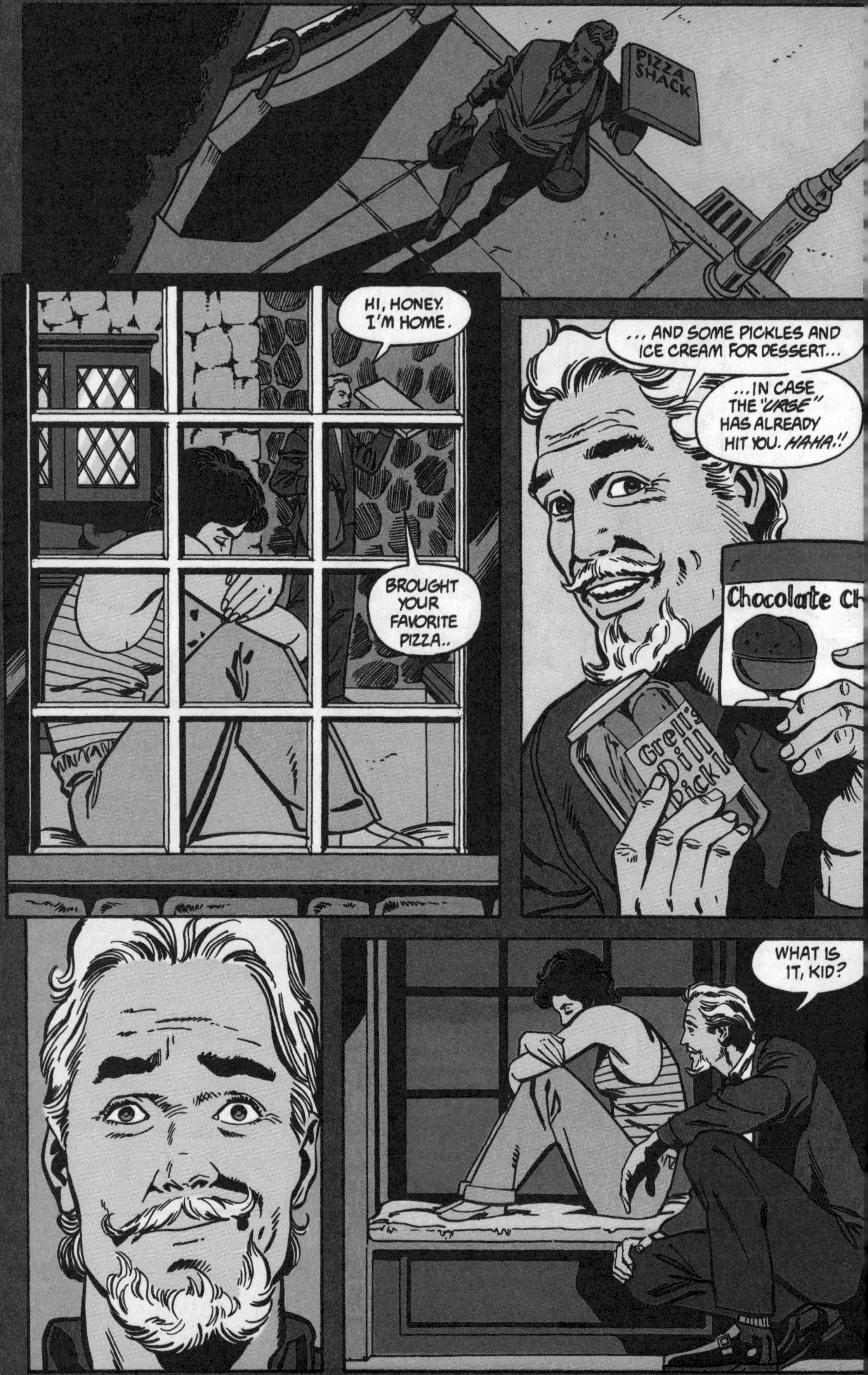
PIZZA SHACK
HI, HONEY. I'M HOME.
BROUGHT YOUR FAVORITE PIZZA..
... AND SOME PICKLES AND ICE CREAM FOR DESSERT...
...IN CASE THE "URGE" HAS ALREADY HIT YOU. HAHA!!
Chocolate Ch
Grell's Dill Pickl
WHAT IS IT, KID?

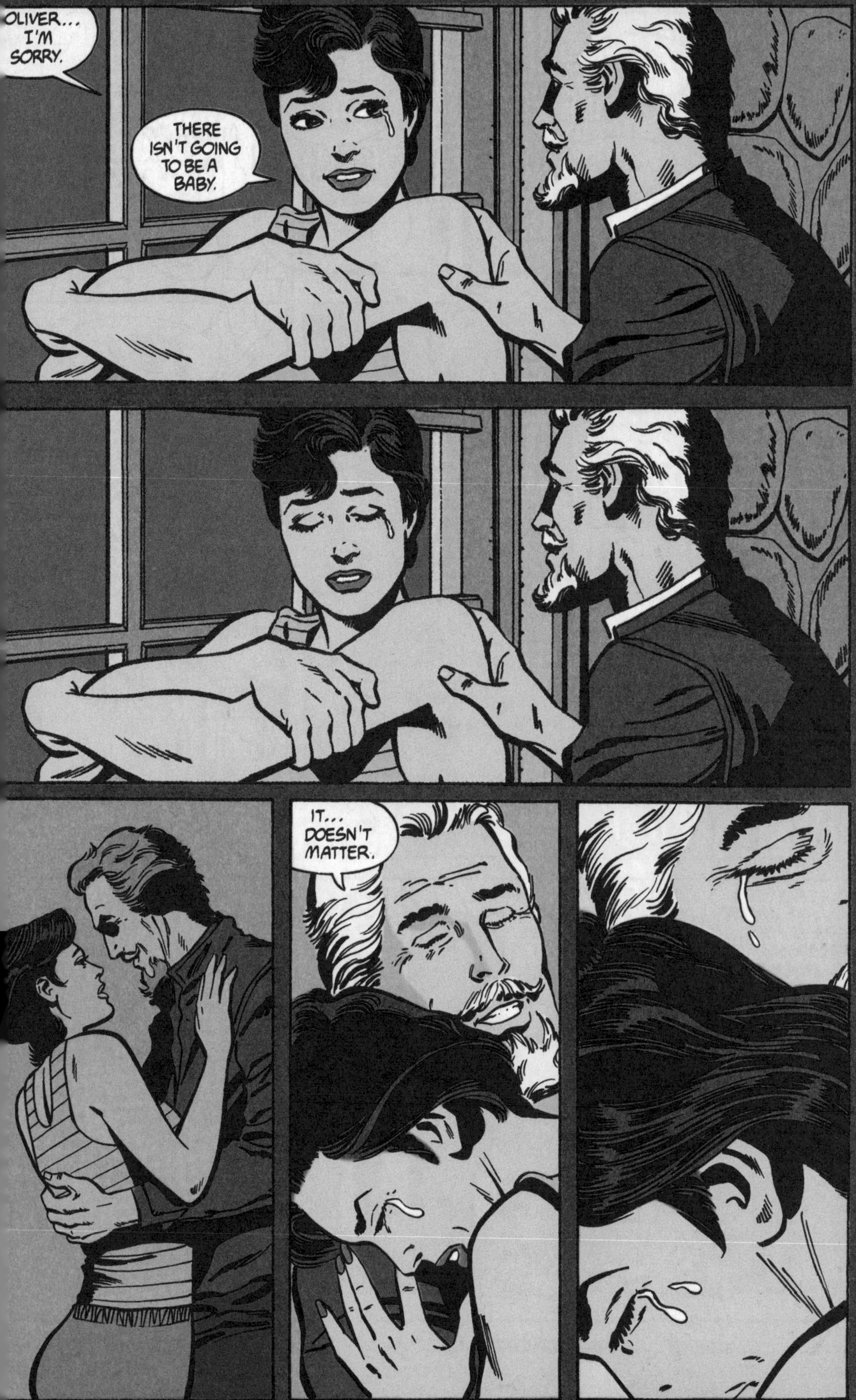
OLIVER... I'M SORRY.
THERE ISN'T GOING TO BE A BABY.
IT... DOESN'T MATTER.

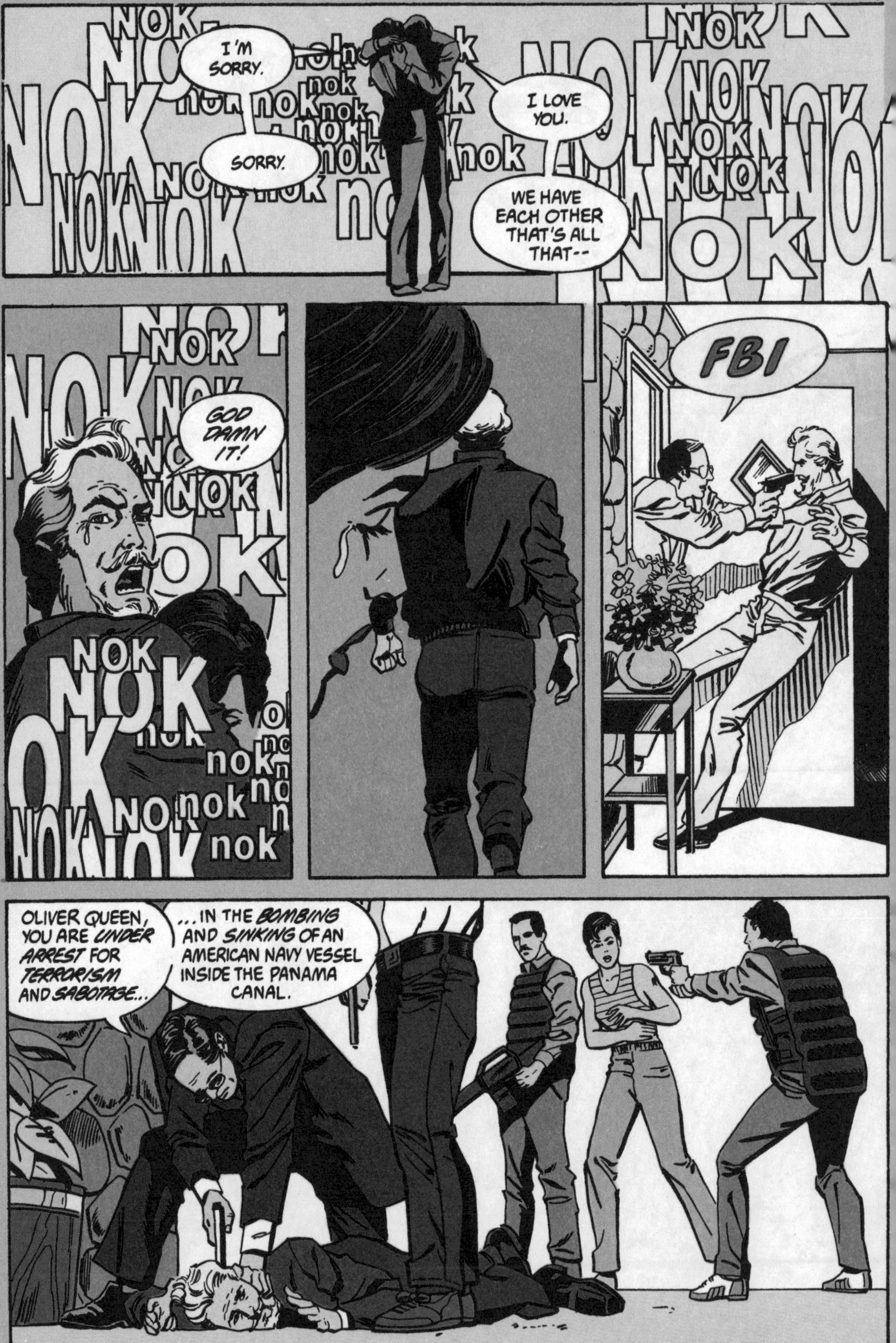
I'M SORRY.
SORRY.
I LOVE YOU.
WE HAVE EACH OTHER THAT'S ALL THAT--
GOD DAMN IT!
FBI
OLIVER QUEEN, YOU ARE UNDER ARREST FOR TERRORISM AND SABOTAGE...
...IN THE BOMBING AND SINKING OF AN AMERICAN NAVY VESSEL INSIDE THE PANAMA CANAL.

GRELL WRITER · JURGENS PENCILLER · McLAUGHLIN INKER · COSTANZA LETTERER · LACQUEMENT COLORIST · MAIN ASSOC. EDITOR · GOLD EDITOR

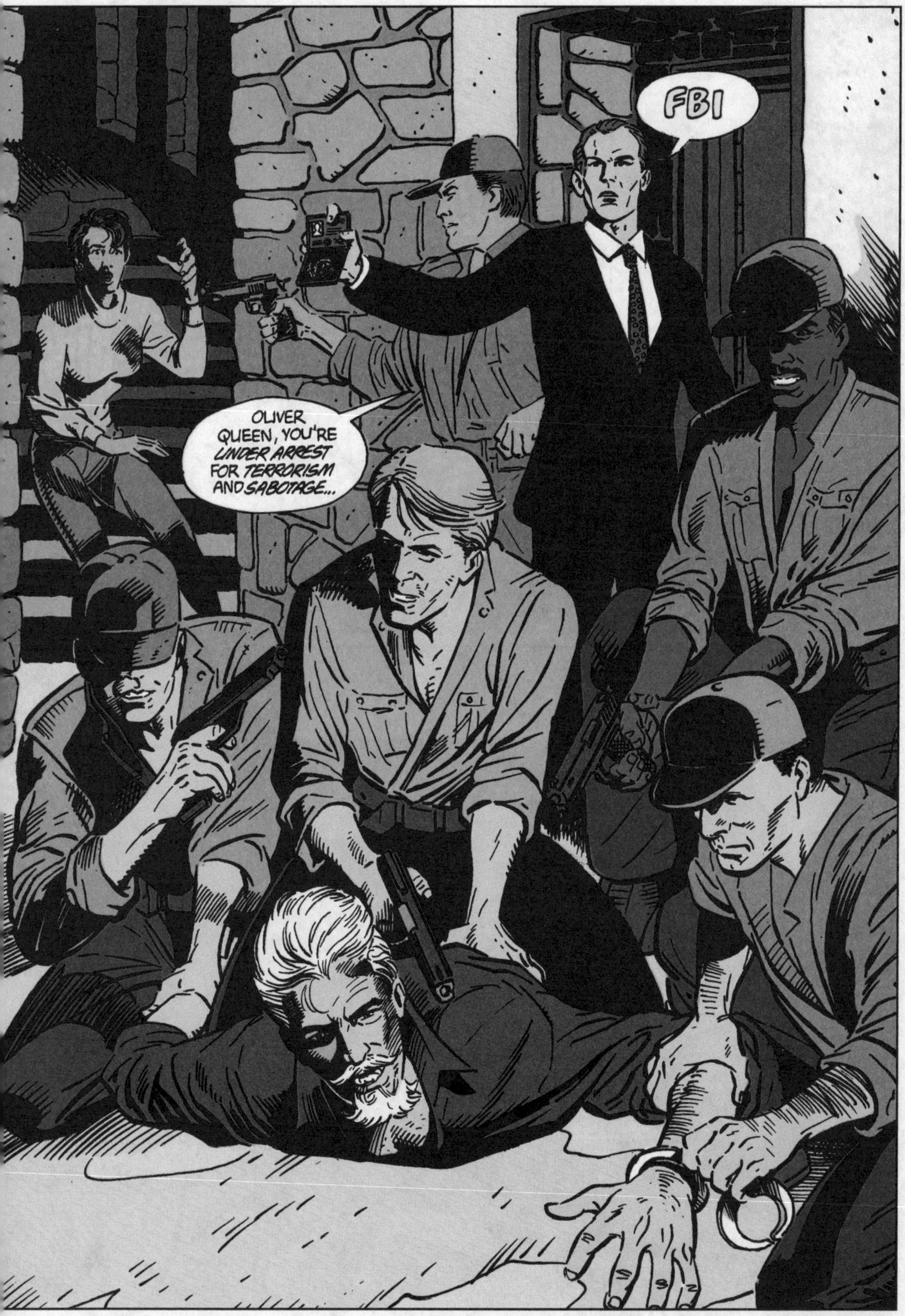
FBI
OLIVER QUEEN, YOU'RE UNDER ARREST FOR TERRORISM AND SABOTAGE...

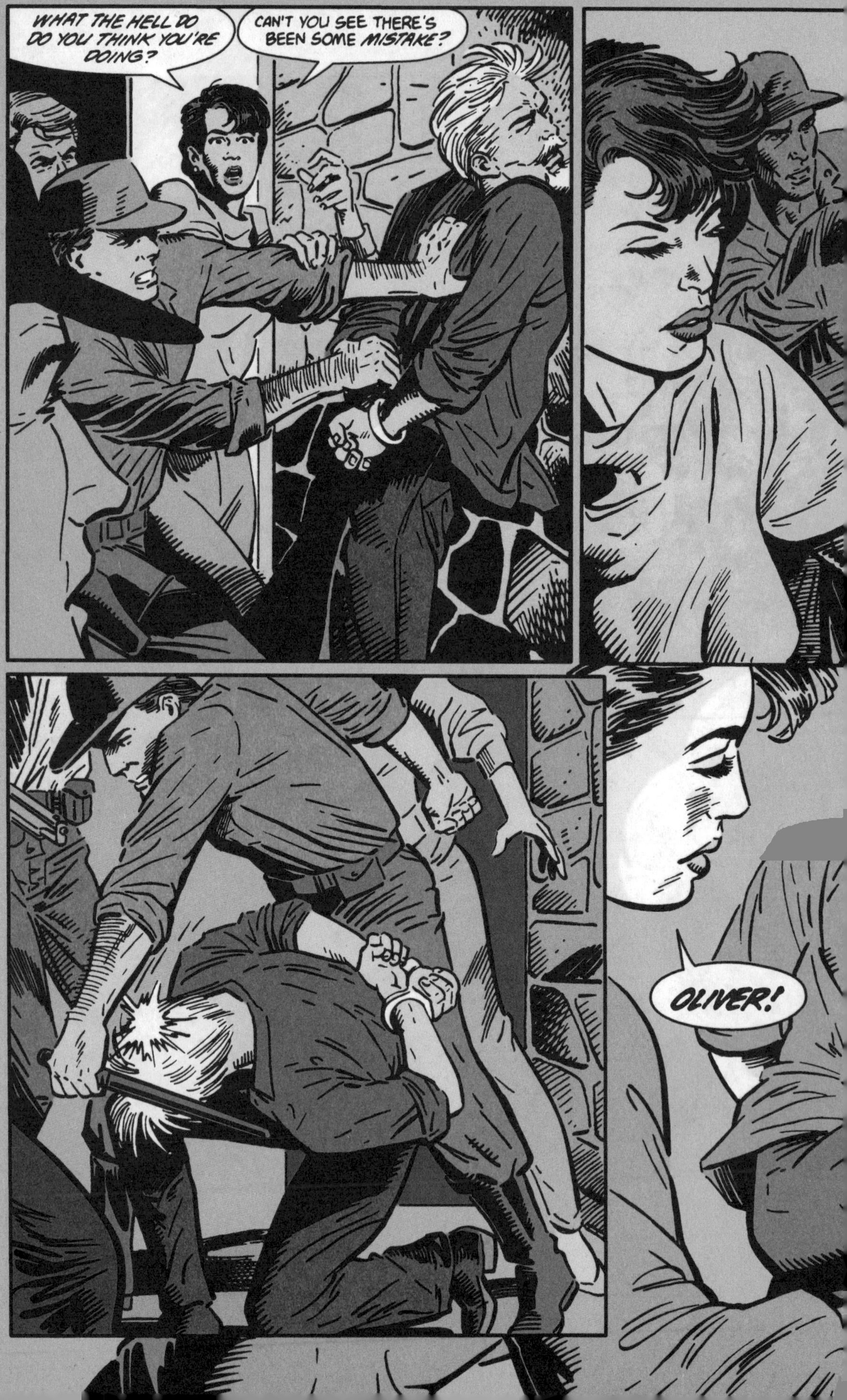
WHAT THE HELL DO DO YOU THINK YOU'RE DOING?
CAN'T YOU SEE THERE'S BEEN SOME MISTAKE?
OLIVER!

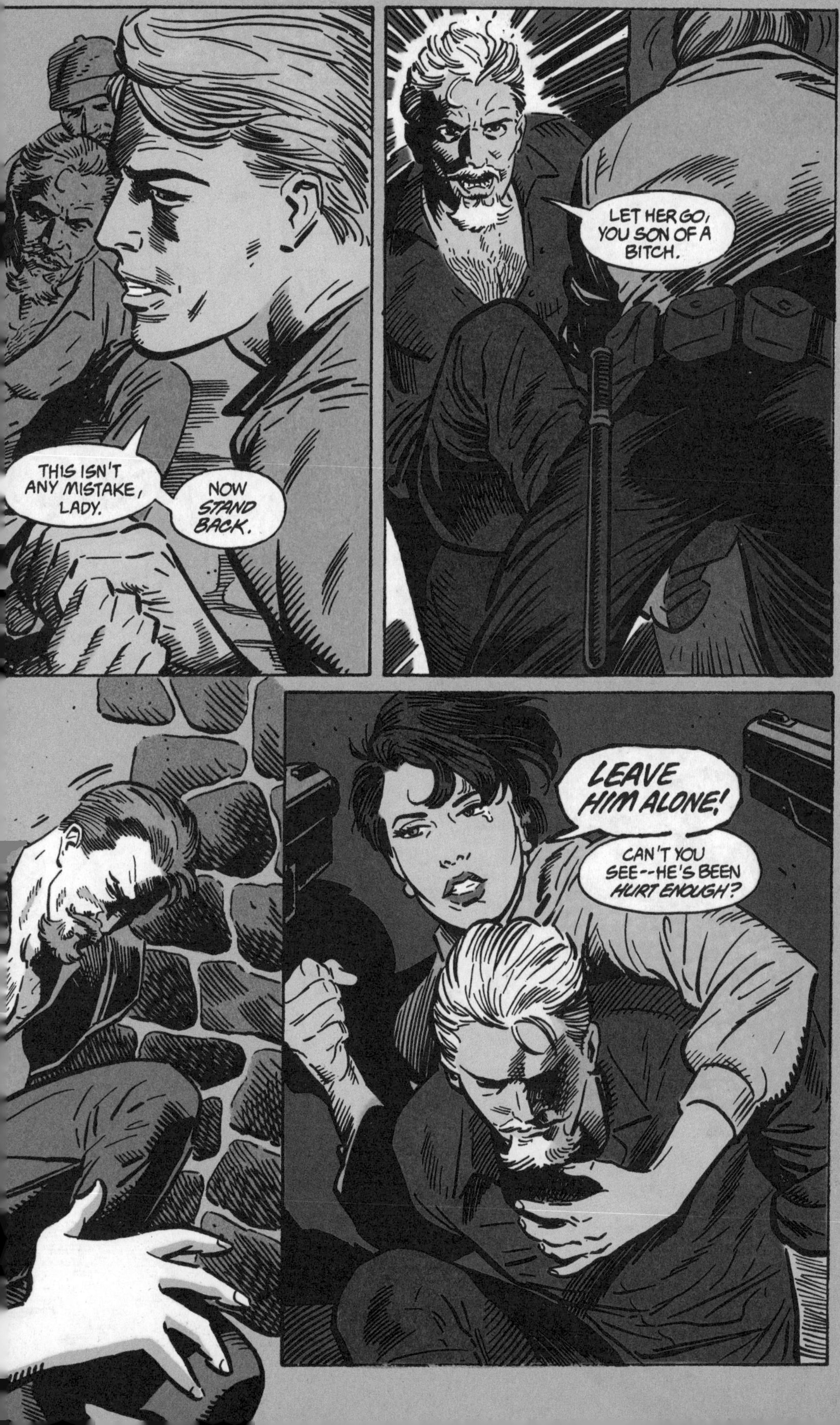
THIS ISN'T ANY MISTAKE, LADY.
NOW STAND BACK.
LET HER GO, YOU SON OF A BITCH.
LEAVE HIM ALONE!
CAN'T YOU SEE--HE'S BEEN HURT ENOUGH?

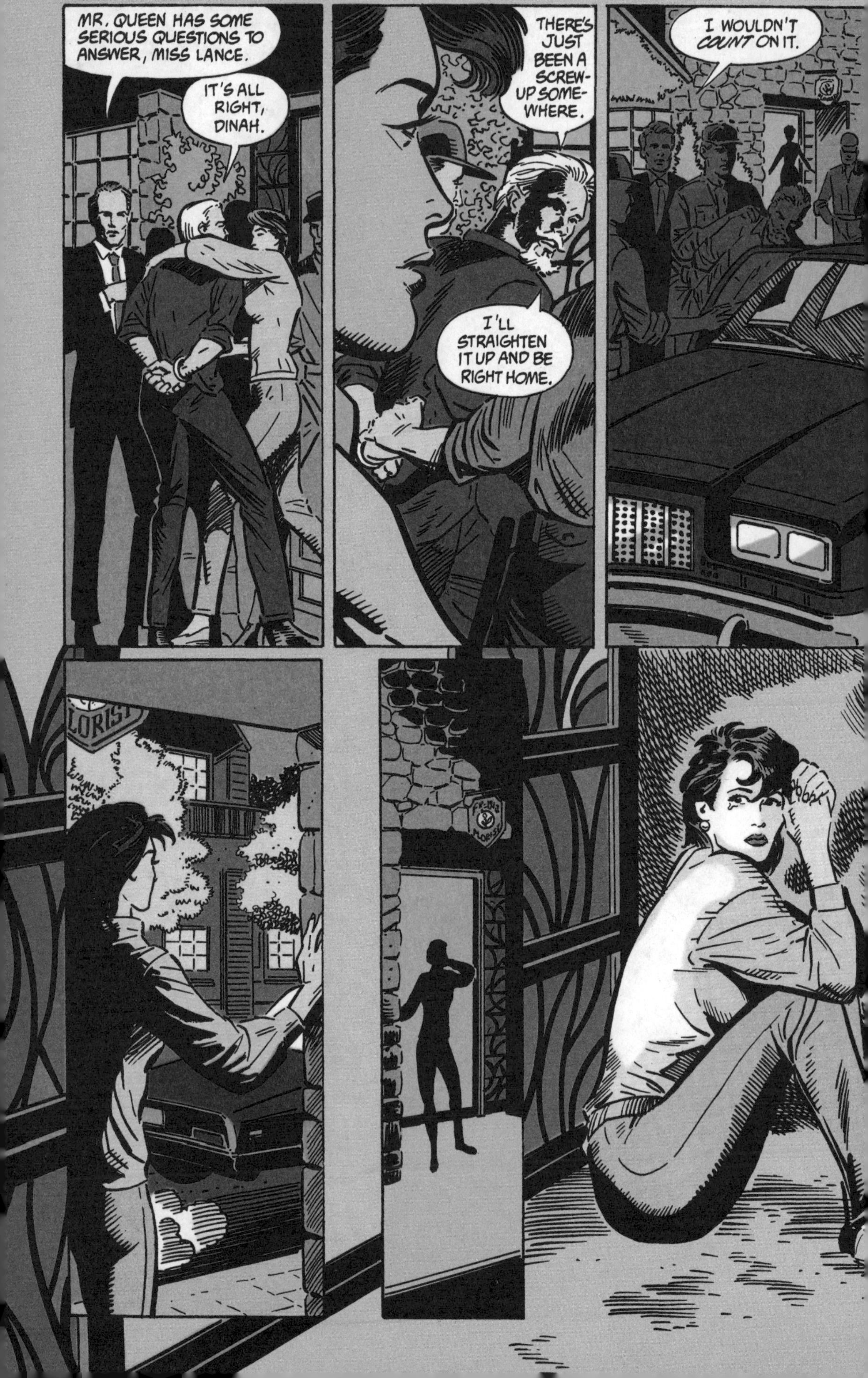
MR. QUEEN HAS SOME SERIOUS QUESTIONS TO ANSWER, MISS LANCE.
IT'S ALL RIGHT, DINAH.
THERE'S JUST BEEN A SCREW-UP SOME-WHERE.
I'LL STRAIGHTEN IT UP AND BE RIGHT HOME.
I WOULDN'T COUNT ON IT.

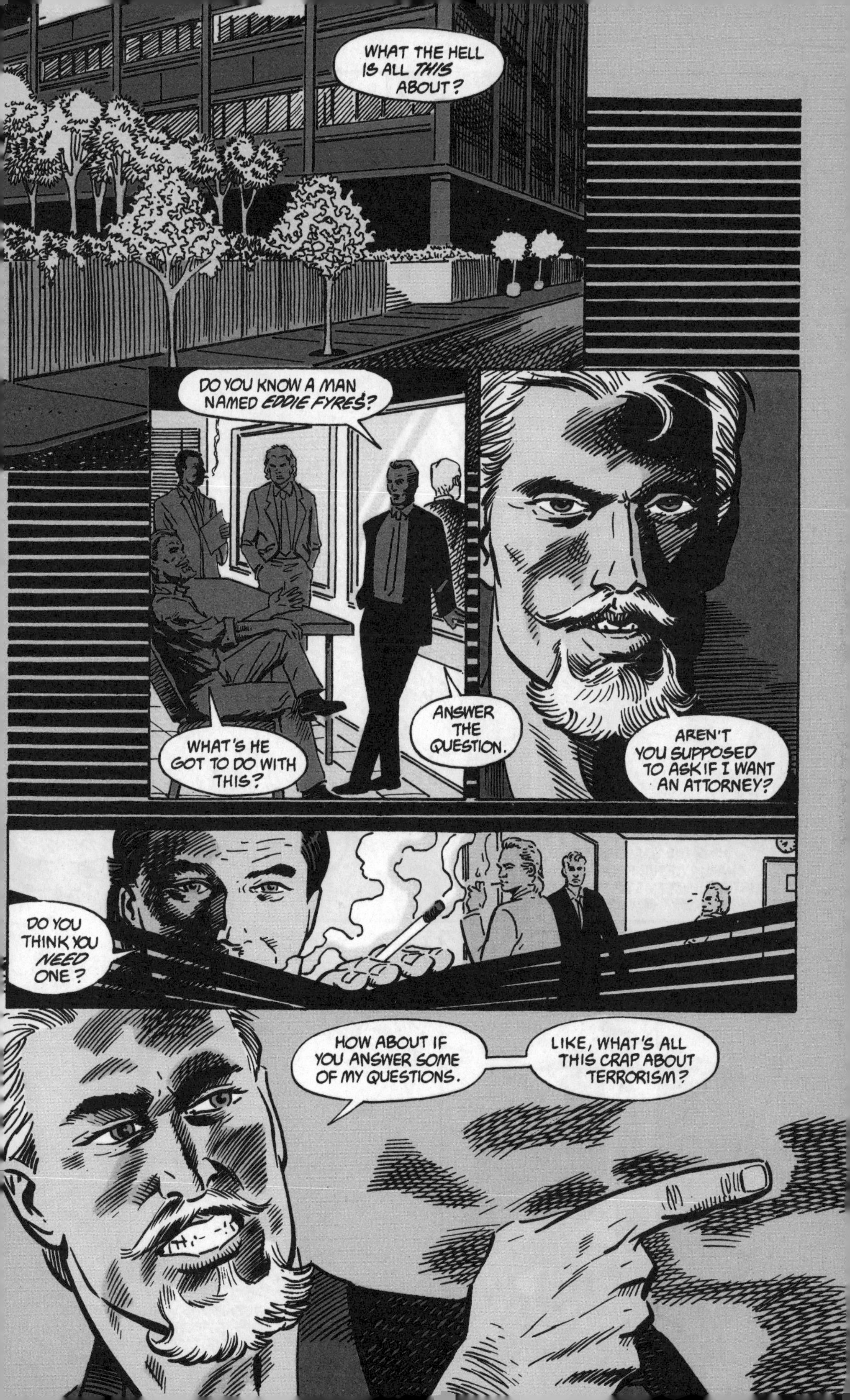
WHAT THE HELL IS ALL THIS ABOUT?
DO YOU KNOW A MAN NAMED EDDIE FYRES?
WHAT'S HE GOT TO DO WITH THIS?
ANSWER THE QUESTION.
AREN'T YOU SUPPOSED TO ASK IF I WANT AN ATTORNEY?
DO YOU THINK YOU NEED ONE?
HOW ABOUT IF YOU ANSWER SOME OF MY QUESTIONS.
LIKE, WHAT'S ALL THIS CRAP ABOUT TERRORISM?

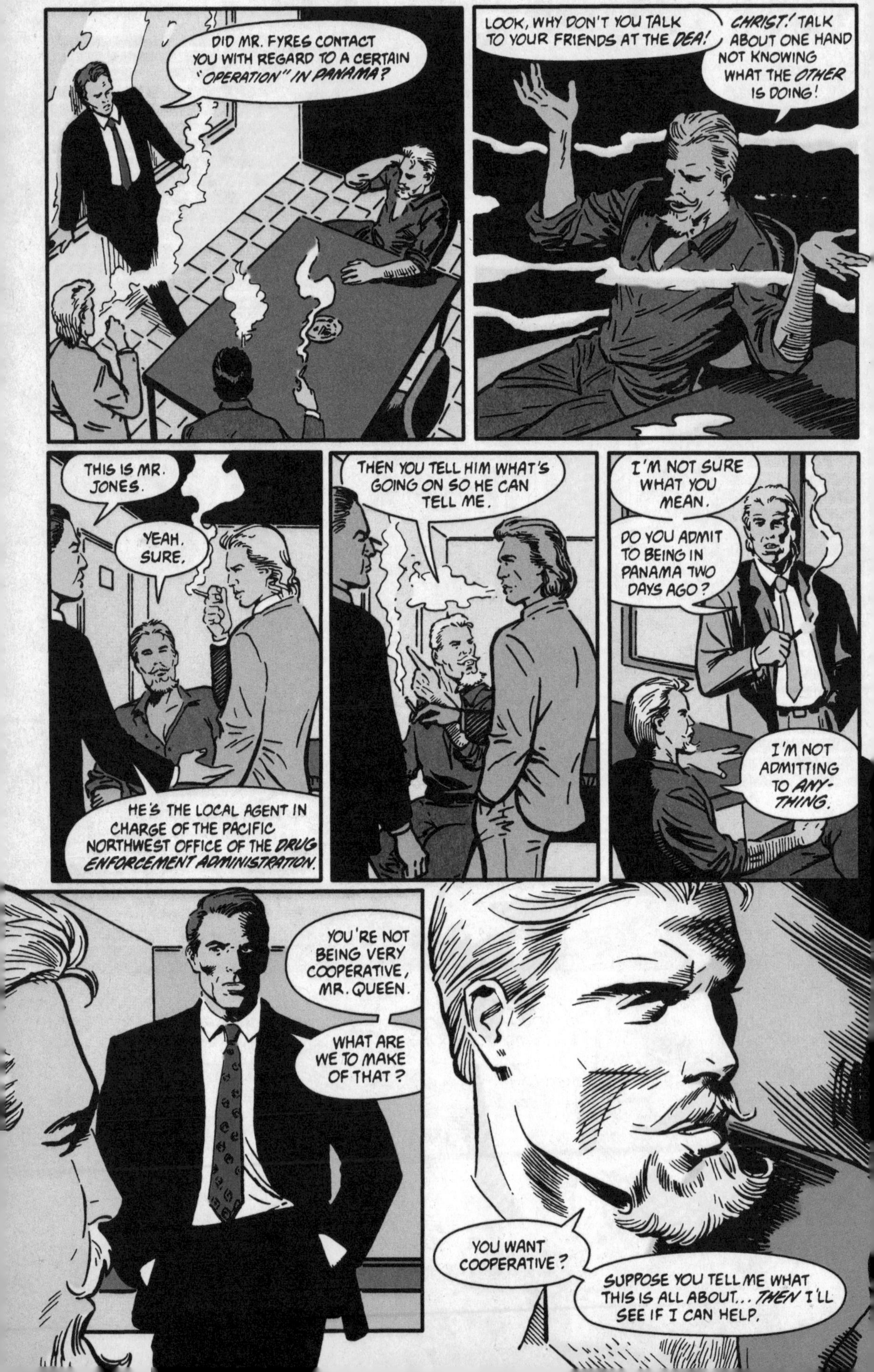
DID MR. FYRES CONTACT YOU WITH REGARD TO A CERTAIN "OPERATION" IN PANAMA?
LOOK, WHY DON'T YOU TALK TO YOUR FRIENDS AT THE DEA!
CHRIST! TALK ABOUT ONE HAND NOT KNOWING WHAT THE OTHER IS DOING!
THIS IS MR. JONES.
YEAH. SURE.
HE'S THE LOCAL AGENT IN CHARGE OF THE PACIFIC NORTHWEST OFFICE OF THE DRUG ENFORCEMENT ADMINISTRATION.
THEN YOU TELL HIM WHAT'S GOING ON SO HE CAN TELL ME.
I'M NOT SURE WHAT YOU MEAN.
DO YOU ADMIT TO BEING IN PANAMA TWO DAYS AGO?
I'M NOT ADMITTING TO ANY-THING.
YOU'RE NOT BEING VERY COOPERATIVE, MR. QUEEN.
WHAT ARE WE TO MAKE OF THAT?
YOU WANT COOPERATIVE?
SUPPOSE YOU TELL ME WHAT THIS IS ALL ABOUT... THEN I'LL SEE IF I CAN HELP.

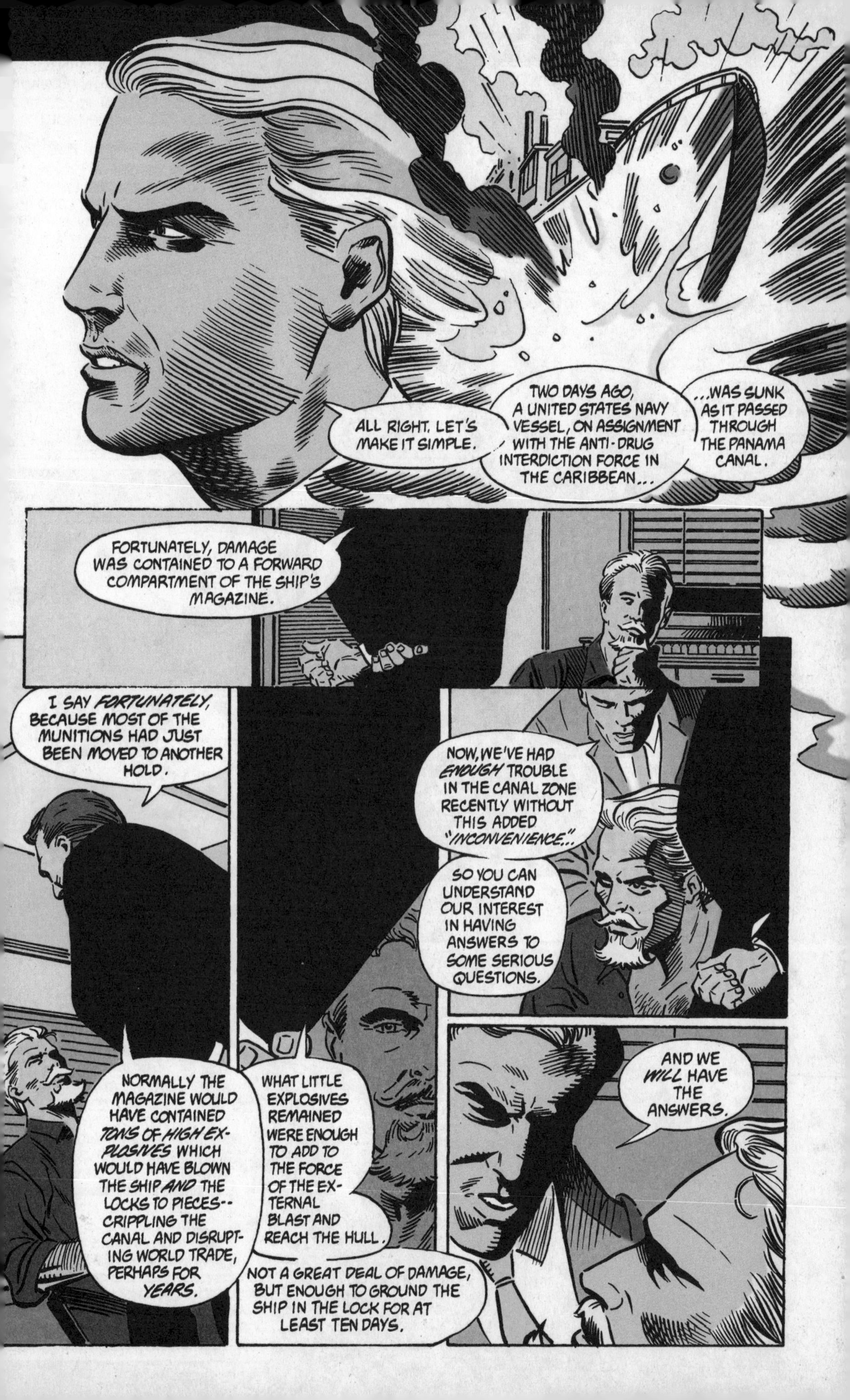
ALL RIGHT. LET'S MAKE IT SIMPLE.
TWO DAYS AGO, A UNITED STATES NAVY VESSEL, ON ASSIGNMENT WITH THE ANTI-DRUG INTERDICTION FORCE IN THE CARIBBEAN...
...WAS SUNK AS IT PASSED THROUGH THE PANAMA CANAL.
FORTUNATELY, DAMAGE WAS CONTAINED TO A FORWARD COMPARTMENT OF THE SHIP'S MAGAZINE.
I SAY *FORTUNATELY,* BECAUSE MOST OF THE MUNITIONS HAD JUST BEEN *MOVED* TO ANOTHER HOLD.
NOW, WE'VE HAD *ENOUGH* TROUBLE IN THE CANAL ZONE RECENTLY WITHOUT THIS ADDED *"INCONVENIENCE."*
SO YOU CAN UNDERSTAND OUR INTEREST IN HAVING ANSWERS TO SOME SERIOUS QUESTIONS.
NORMALLY THE MAGAZINE WOULD HAVE CONTAINED *TONS OF HIGH EXPLOSIVES* WHICH WOULD HAVE BLOWN THE SHIP *AND* THE LOCKS TO PIECES-- CRIPPLING THE CANAL AND DISRUPTING WORLD TRADE, PERHAPS FOR *YEARS.*
WHAT LITTLE EXPLOSIVES REMAINED WERE ENOUGH TO ADD TO THE FORCE OF THE EXTERNAL BLAST AND REACH THE HULL.
NOT A GREAT DEAL OF DAMAGE, BUT ENOUGH TO GROUND THE SHIP IN THE LOCK FOR AT LEAST TEN DAYS.
AND WE *WILL* HAVE THE ANSWERS.

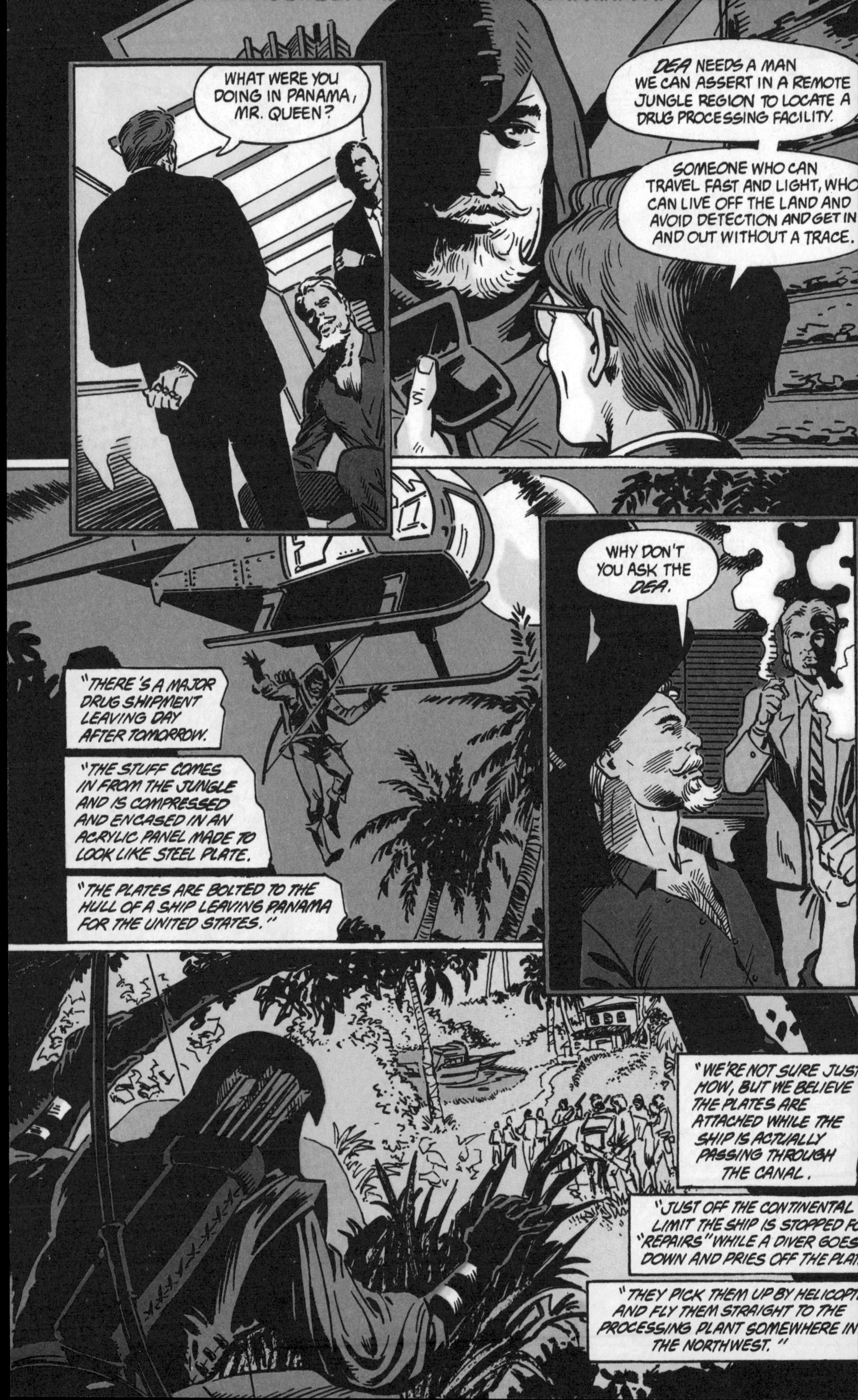
WHAT WERE YOU DOING IN PANAMA, MR. QUEEN?
DEA NEEDS A MAN WE CAN ASSERT IN A REMOTE JUNGLE REGION TO LOCATE A DRUG PROCESSING FACILITY.
SOMEONE WHO CAN TRAVEL FAST AND LIGHT, WHO CAN LIVE OFF THE LAND AND AVOID DETECTION AND GET IN AND OUT WITHOUT A TRACE.
WHY DON'T YOU ASK THE DEA.
"THERE'S A MAJOR DRUG SHIPMENT LEAVING DAY AFTER TOMORROW.
"THE STUFF COMES IN FROM THE JUNGLE AND IS COMPRESSED AND ENCASED IN AN ACRYLIC PANEL MADE TO LOOK LIKE STEEL PLATE.
"THE PLATES ARE BOLTED TO THE HULL OF A SHIP LEAVING PANAMA FOR THE UNITED STATES."
"WE'RE NOT SURE JUST HOW, BUT WE BELIEVE THE PLATES ARE ATTACHED WHILE THE SHIP IS ACTUALLY PASSING THROUGH THE CANAL.
"JUST OFF THE CONTINENTAL LIMIT THE SHIP IS STOPPED FOR "REPAIRS" WHILE A DIVER GOES DOWN AND PRIES OFF THE PLATES.
"THEY PICK THEM UP BY HELICOPTER AND FLY THEM STRAIGHT TO THE PROCESSING PLANT SOMEWHERE IN THE NORTHWEST."

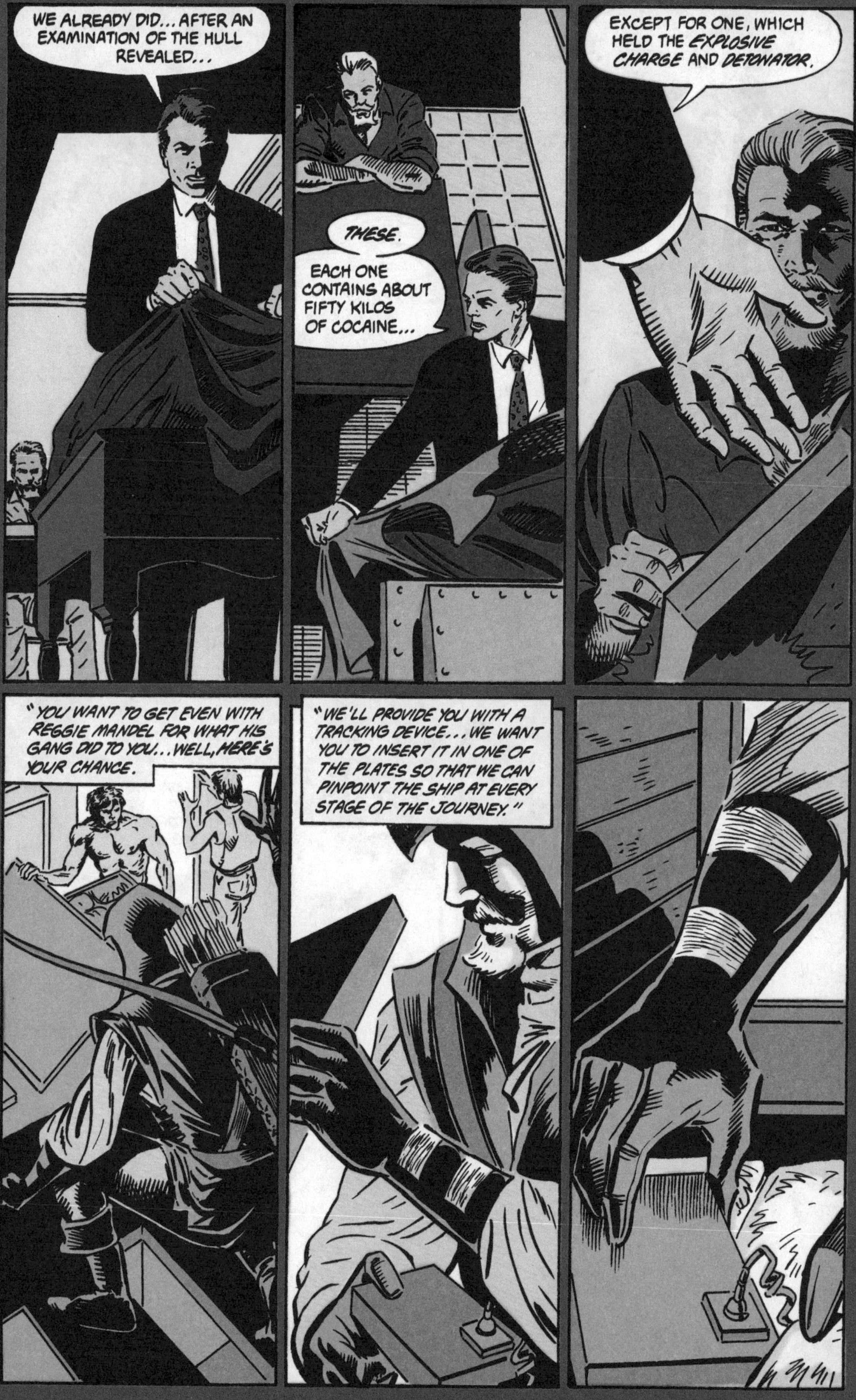
WE ALREADY DID... AFTER AN EXAMINATION OF THE HULL REVEALED...
THESE.
EACH ONE CONTAINS ABOUT FIFTY KILOS OF COCAINE...
EXCEPT FOR ONE, WHICH HELD THE *EXPLOSIVE CHARGE* AND *DETONATOR*.
"YOU WANT TO GET EVEN WITH REGGIE MANDEL FOR WHAT HIS GANG DID TO YOU... WELL, HERE'S YOUR CHANCE.
"WE'LL PROVIDE YOU WITH A TRACKING DEVICE... WE WANT YOU TO INSERT IT IN ONE OF THE PLATES SO THAT WE CAN PINPOINT THE SHIP AT EVERY STAGE OF THE JOURNEY."

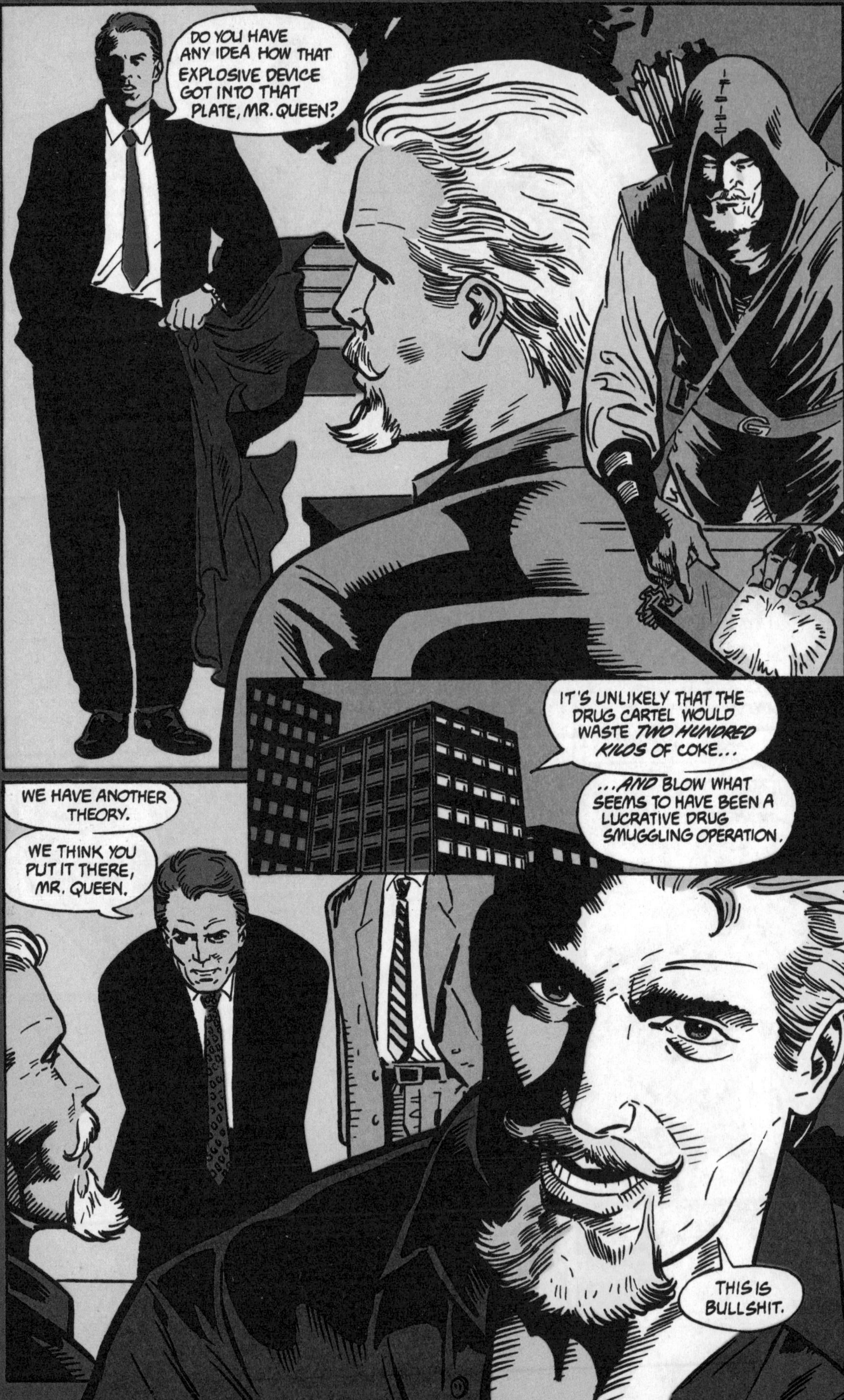
DO YOU HAVE ANY IDEA HOW THAT EXPLOSIVE DEVICE GOT INTO THAT PLATE, MR. QUEEN?
IT'S UNLIKELY THAT THE DRUG CARTEL WOULD WASTE *TWO HUNDRED KILOS* OF COKE...
...*AND* BLOW WHAT SEEMS TO HAVE BEEN A LUCRATIVE DRUG SMUGGLING OPERATION.
WE HAVE ANOTHER THEORY.
WE THINK YOU PUT IT THERE, MR. QUEEN.
THIS IS BULLSHIT.

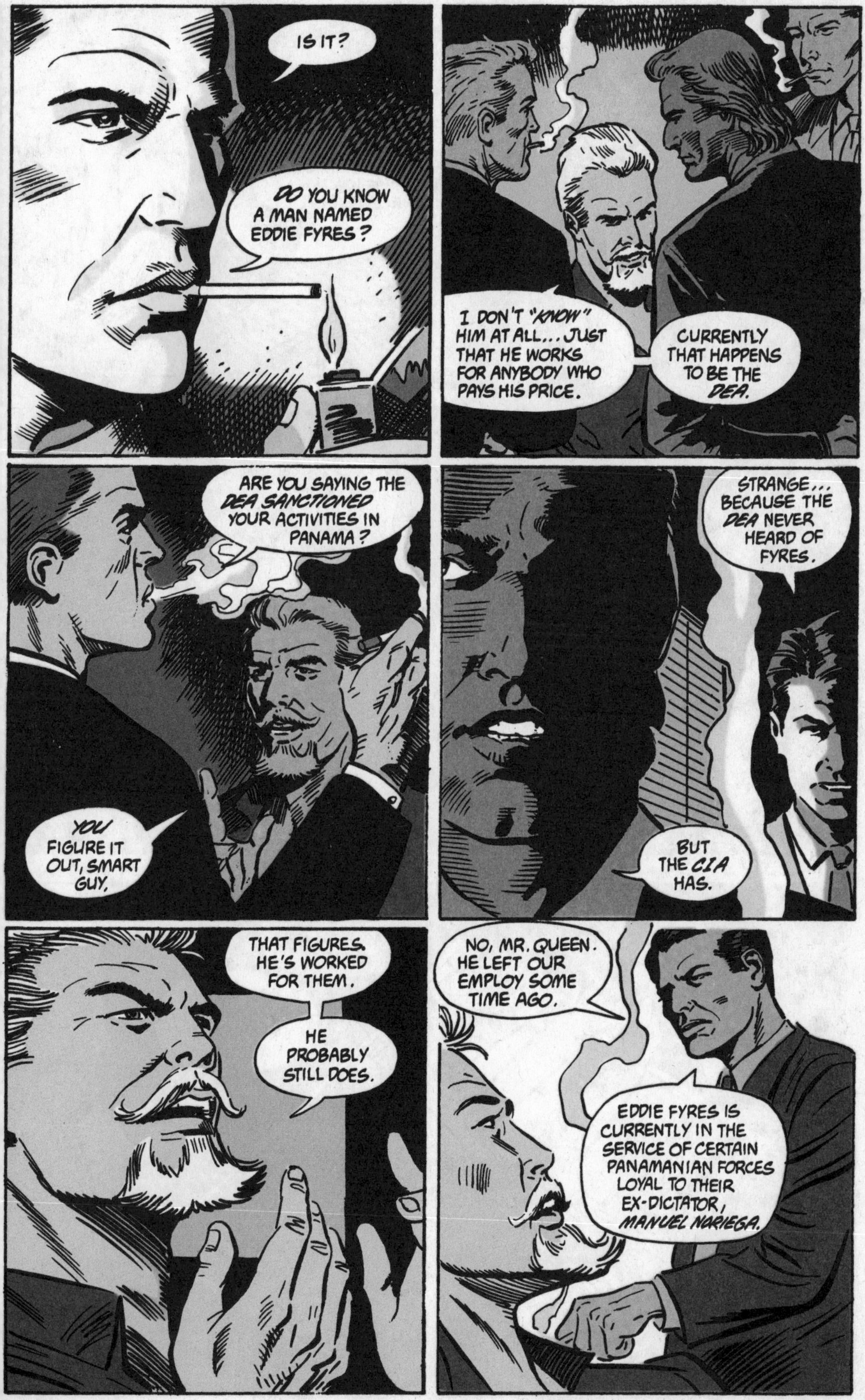
IS IT?
DO YOU KNOW A MAN NAMED EDDIE FYRES?
I DON'T "KNOW" HIM AT ALL... JUST THAT HE WORKS FOR ANYBODY WHO PAYS HIS PRICE.
CURRENTLY THAT HAPPENS TO BE THE DEA.
ARE YOU SAYING THE DEA SANCTIONED YOUR ACTIVITIES IN PANAMA?
YOU FIGURE IT OUT, SMART GUY.
STRANGE... BECAUSE THE DEA NEVER HEARD OF FYRES.
BUT THE CIA HAS.
THAT FIGURES. HE'S WORKED FOR THEM.
HE PROBABLY STILL DOES.
NO, MR. QUEEN. HE LEFT OUR EMPLOY SOME TIME AGO.
EDDIE FYRES IS CURRENTLY IN THE SERVICE OF CERTAIN PANAMANIAN FORCES LOYAL TO THEIR EX-DICTATOR, MANUEL NARIEGA.

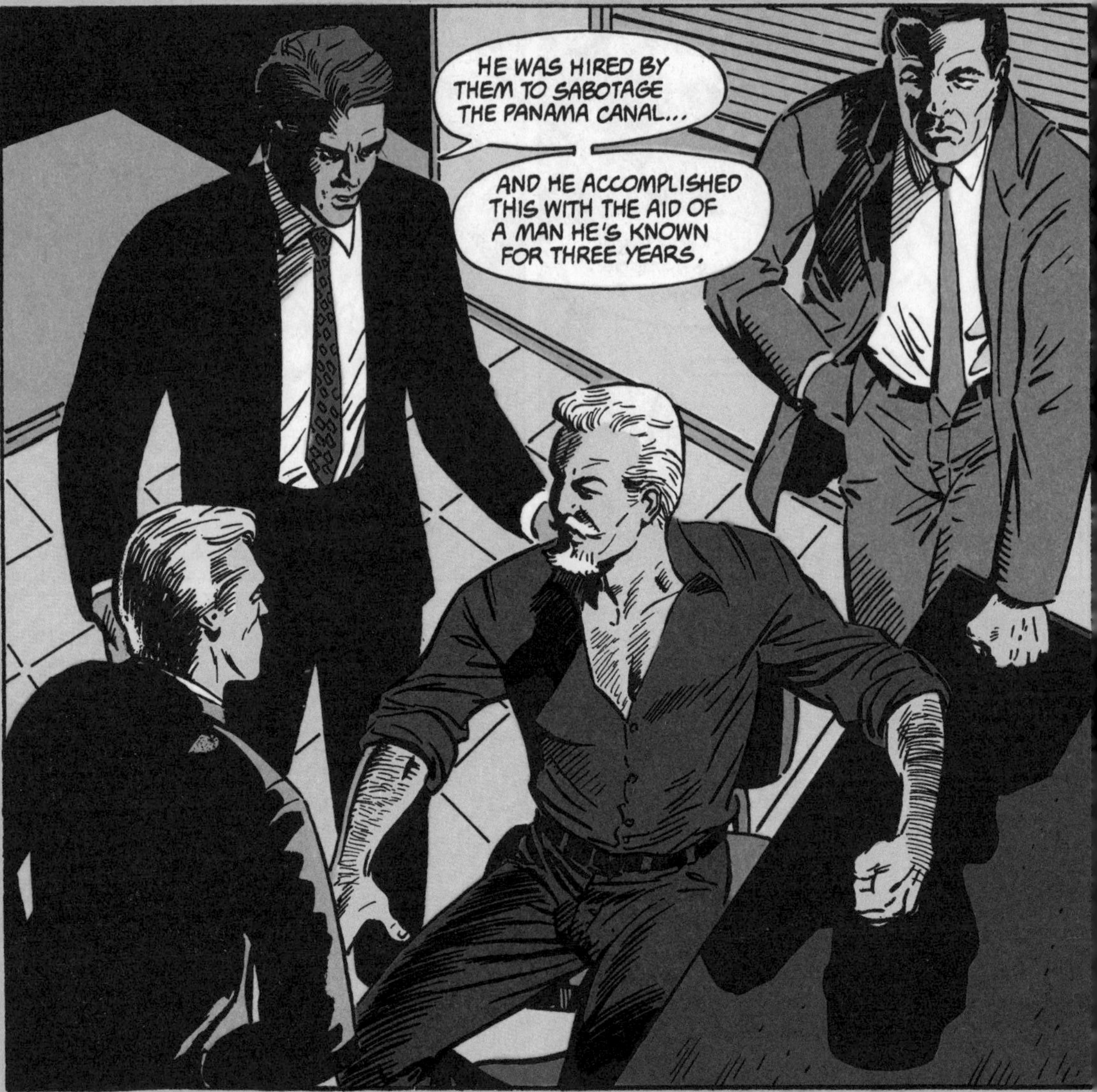
HE WAS HIRED BY THEM TO SABOTAGE THE PANAMA CANAL...
AND HE ACCOMPLISHED THIS WITH THE AID OF A MAN HE'S KNOWN FOR THREE YEARS.

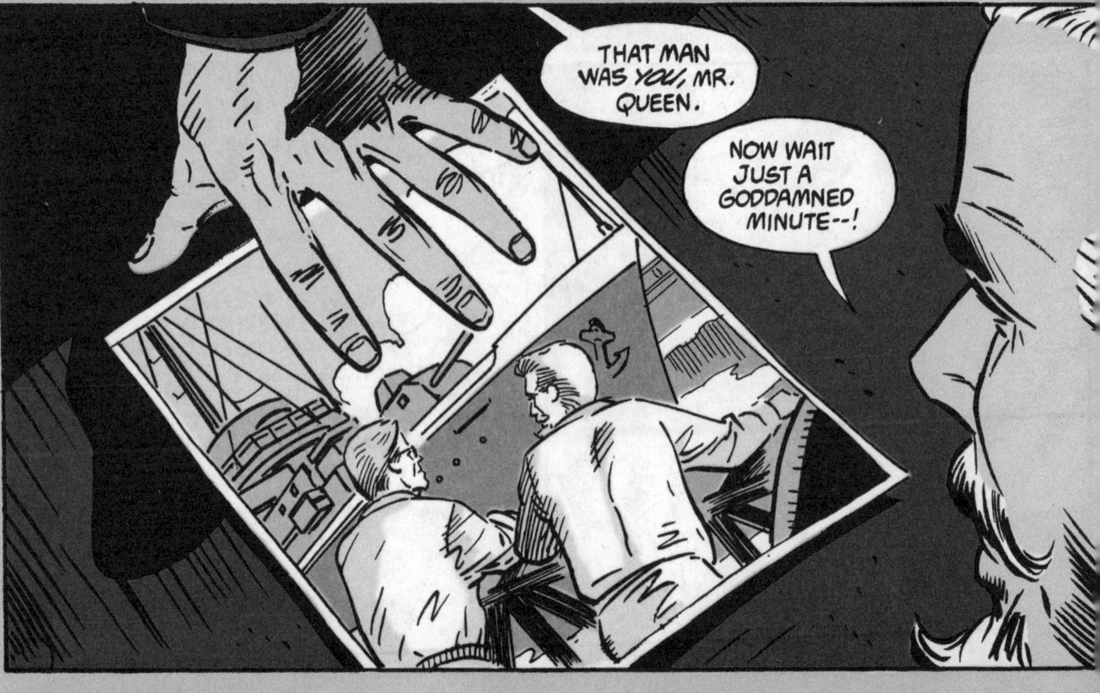
THAT MAN WAS *YOU*, MR. QUEEN.
NOW WAIT JUST A GODDAMNED MINUTE--!

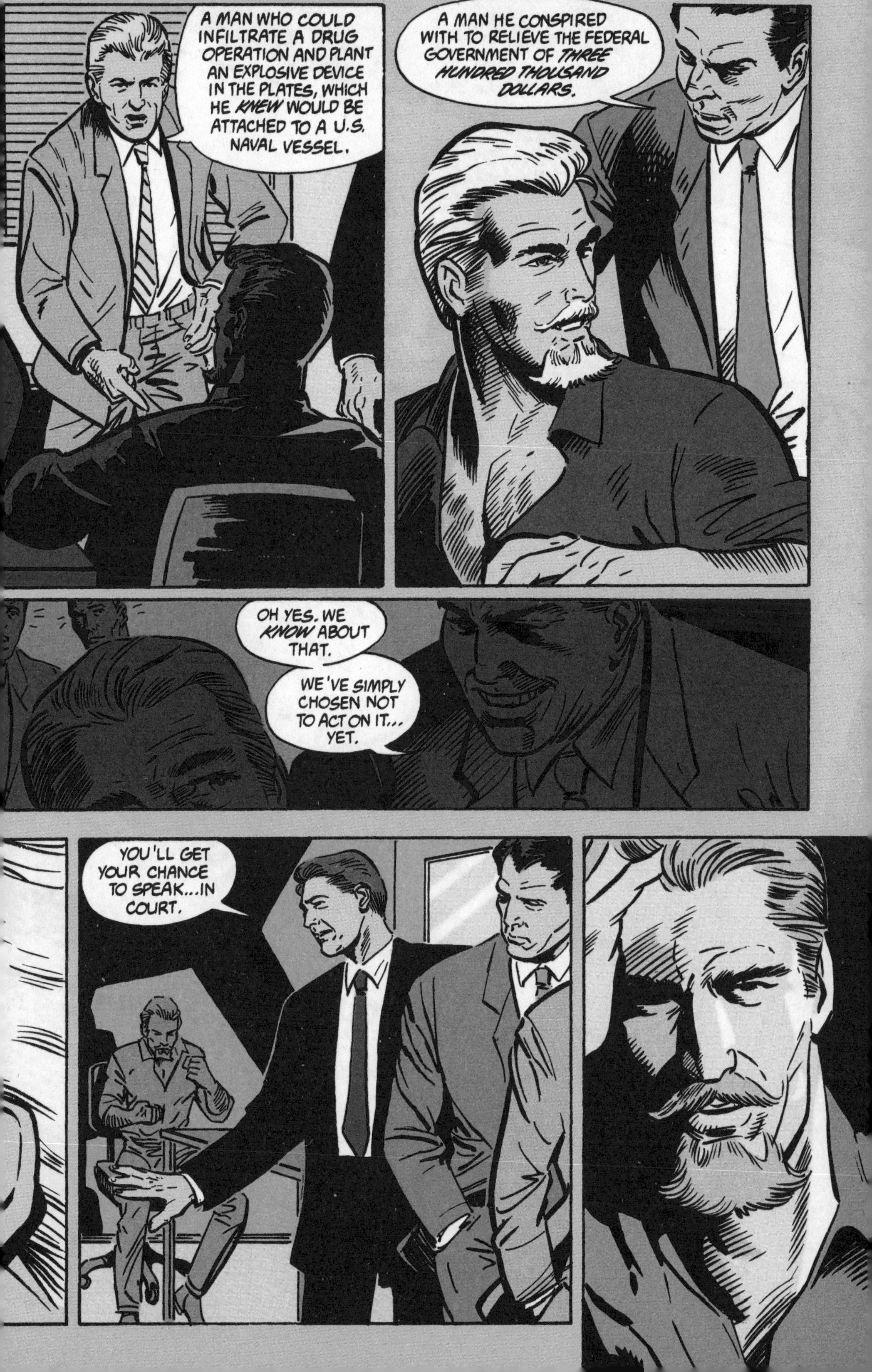
A MAN WHO COULD INFILTRATE A DRUG OPERATION AND PLANT AN EXPLOSIVE DEVICE IN THE PLATES, WHICH HE *KNEW* WOULD BE ATTACHED TO A U.S. NAVAL VESSEL.
A MAN HE CONSPIRED WITH TO RELIEVE THE FEDERAL GOVERNMENT OF *THREE HUNDRED THOUSAND DOLLARS.*
OH YES. WE *KNOW* ABOUT THAT.
WE'VE SIMPLY CHOSEN NOT TO ACT ON IT... YET.
YOU'LL GET YOUR CHANCE TO SPEAK...IN COURT.

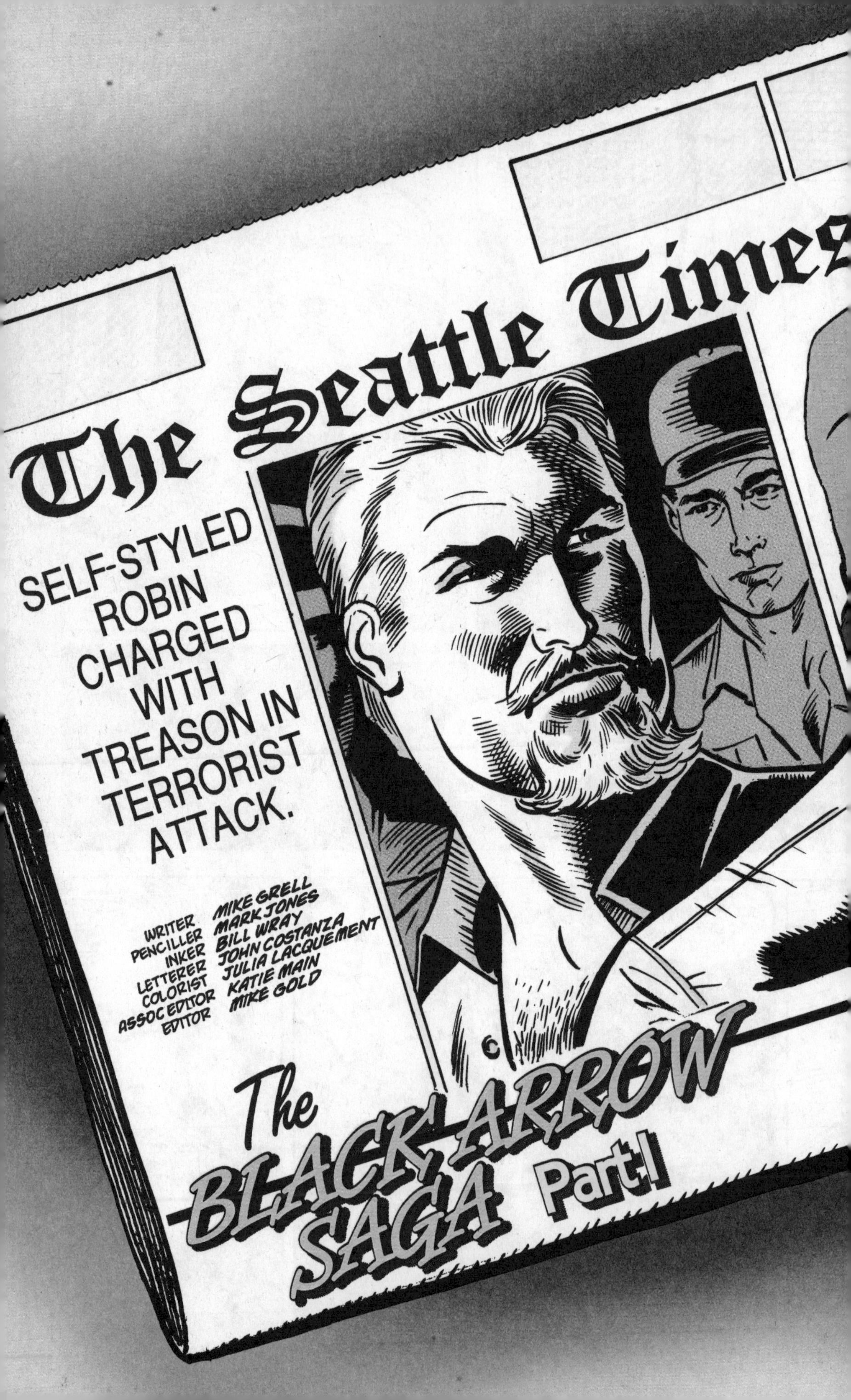

The Seattle Times
SELF-STYLED ROBIN CHARGED WITH TREASON IN TERRORIST ATTACK.
WRITER MIKE GRELL
PENCILLER MARK JONES
INKER BILL WRAY
LETTERER JOHN COSTANZA
COLORIST JULIA LACQUEMENT
ASSOC EDITOR KATIE MAIN
EDITOR MIKE GOLD
The BLACK ARROW SAGA Part I

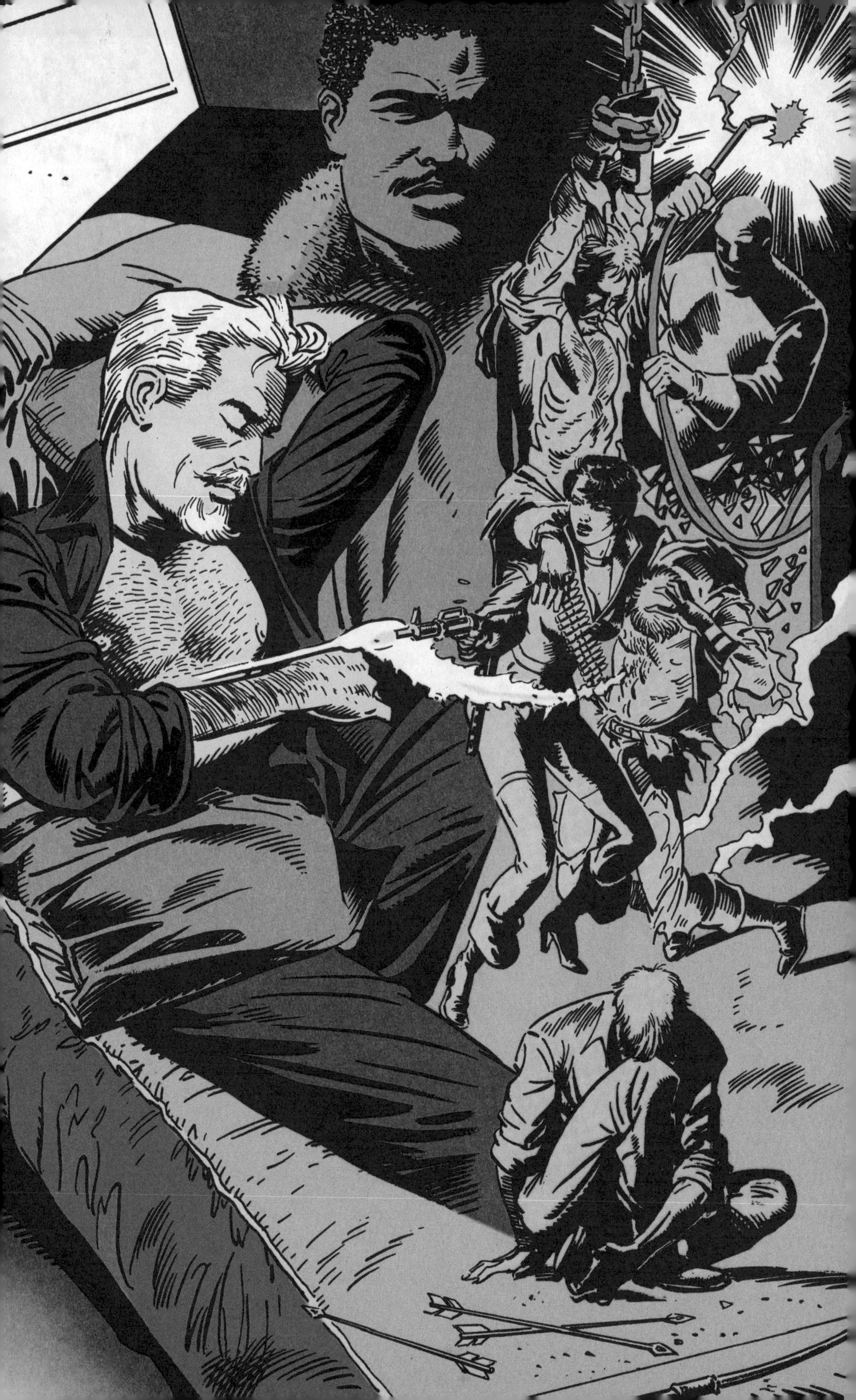

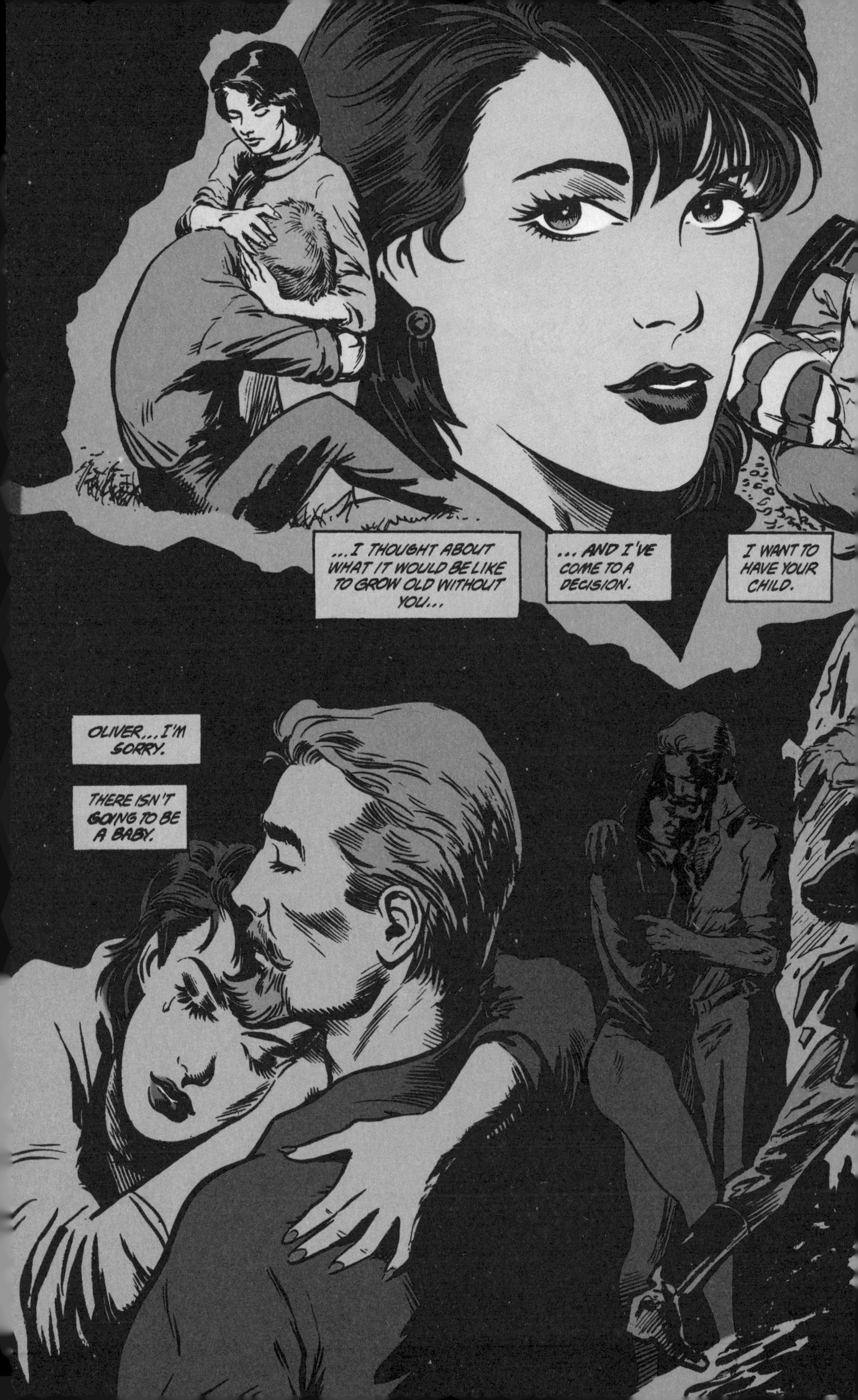
...I THOUGHT ABOUT WHAT IT WOULD BE LIKE TO GROW OLD WITHOUT YOU...
...AND I'VE COME TO A DECISION.
I WANT TO HAVE YOUR CHILD.
OLIVER...I'M SORRY.
THERE ISN'T GOING TO BE A BABY.

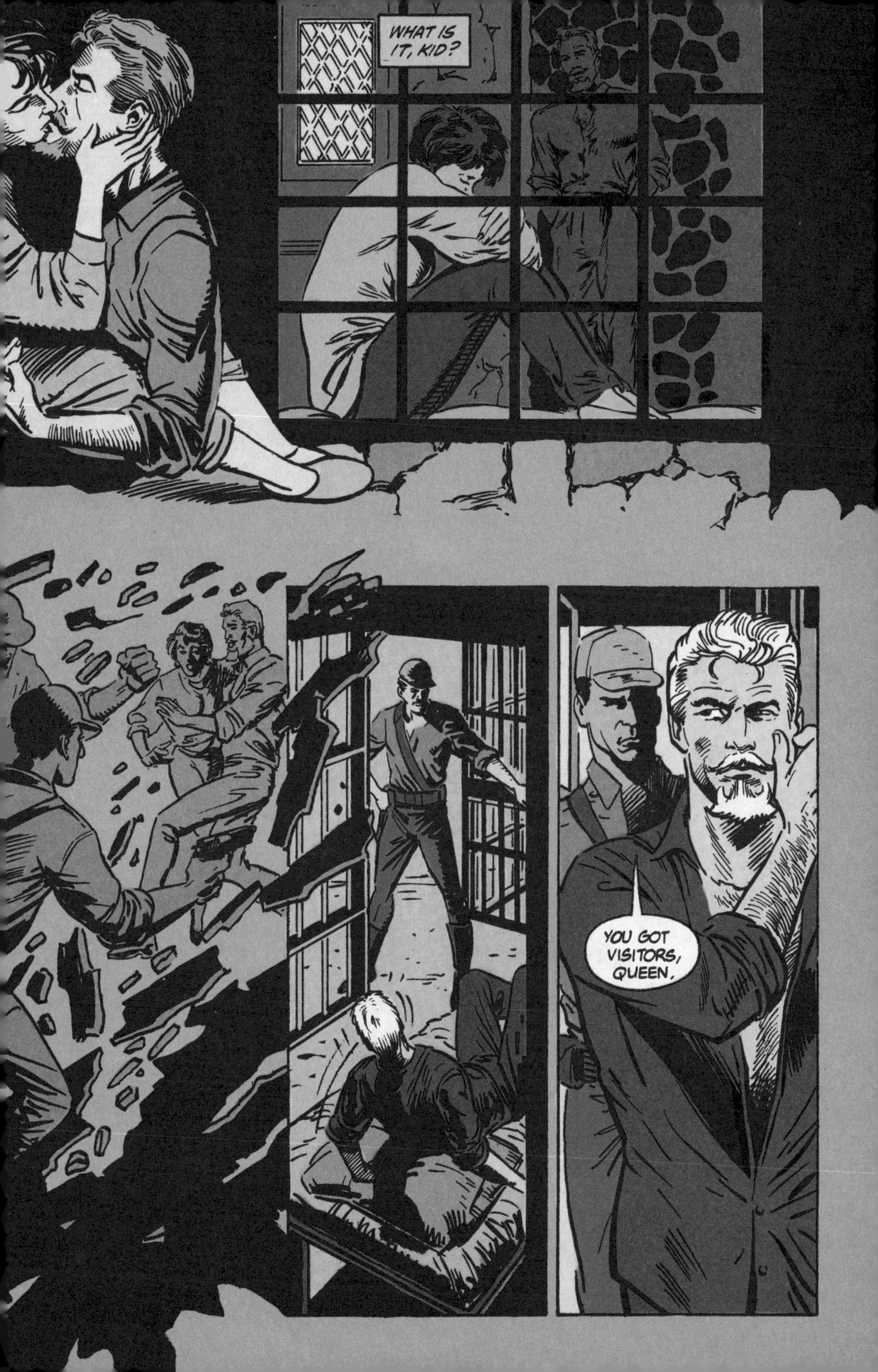
WHAT IS IT, KID?
YOU GOT VISITORS, QUEEN.

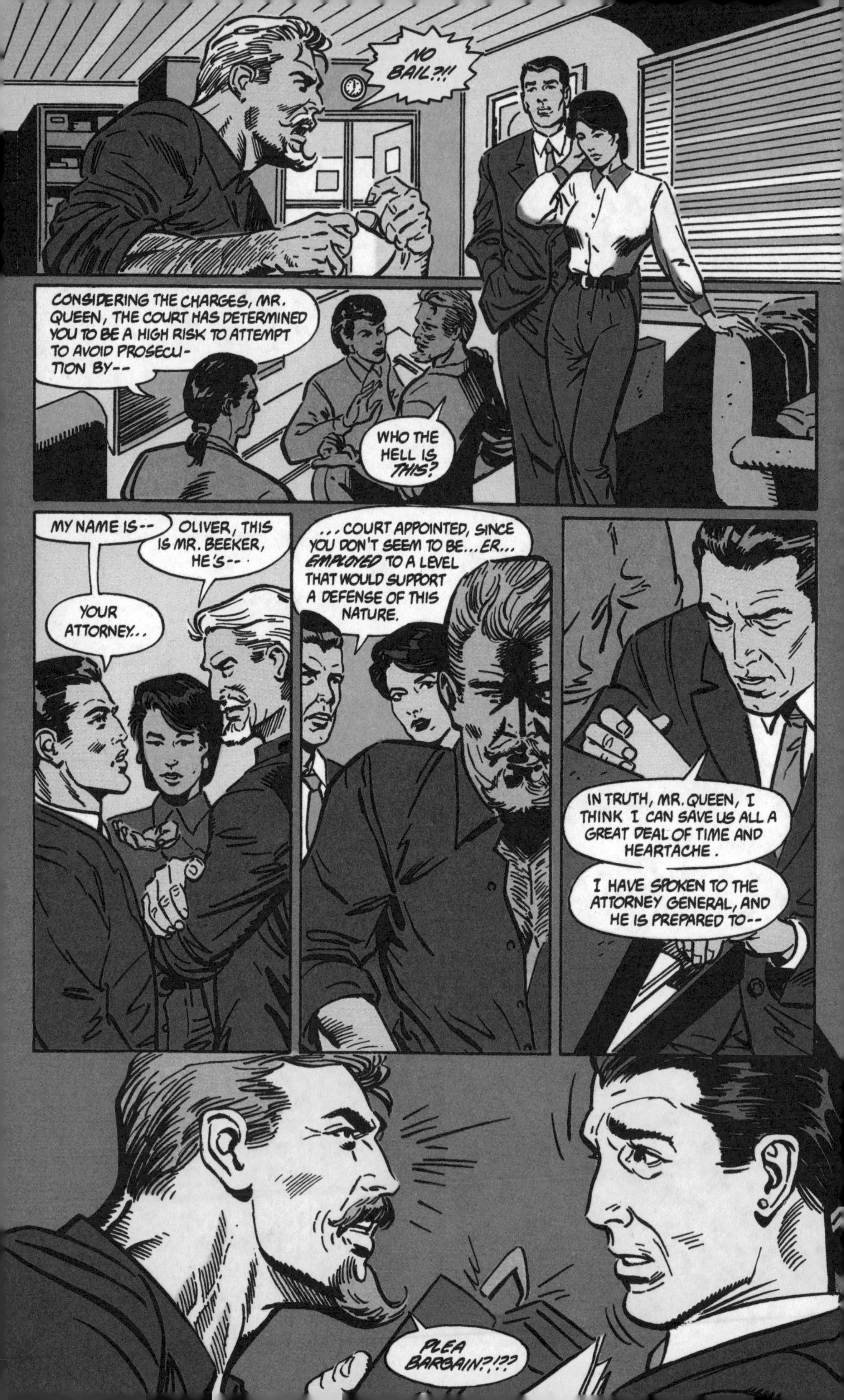
NO BAIL?!!
CONSIDERING THE CHARGES, MR. QUEEN, THE COURT HAS DETERMINED YOU TO BE A HIGH RISK TO ATTEMPT TO AVOID PROSECUTION BY--
WHO THE HELL IS THIS?
MY NAME IS--
OLIVER, THIS IS MR. BEEKER, HE'S--
YOUR ATTORNEY...
...COURT APPOINTED, SINCE YOU DON'T SEEM TO BE...ER... EMPLOYED TO A LEVEL THAT WOULD SUPPORT A DEFENSE OF THIS NATURE.
IN TRUTH, MR. QUEEN, I THINK I CAN SAVE US ALL A GREAT DEAL OF TIME AND HEARTACHE.
I HAVE SPOKEN TO THE ATTORNEY GENERAL, AND HE IS PREPARED TO--
PLEA BARGAIN?!??

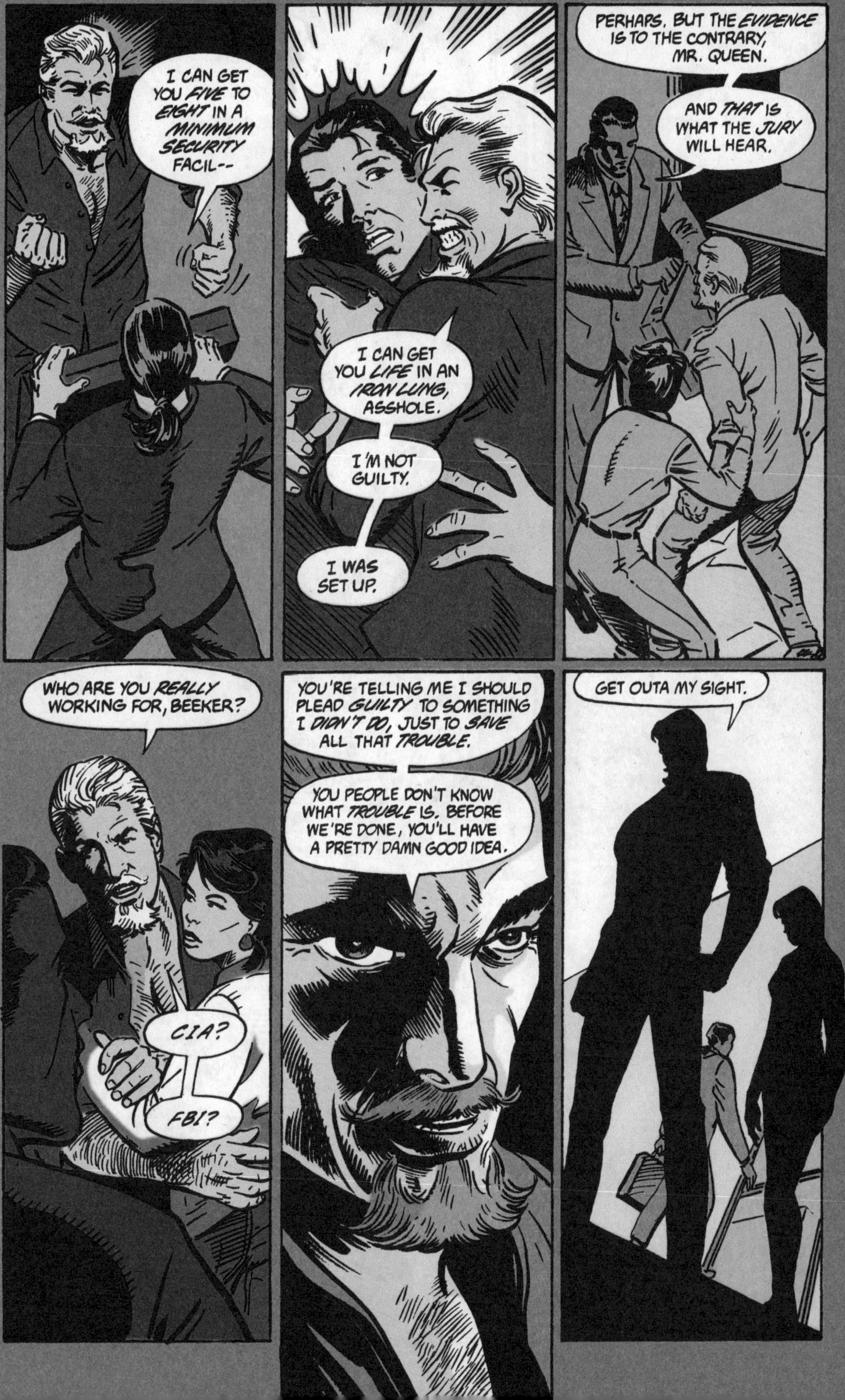
I CAN GET YOU FIVE TO EIGHT IN A MINIMUM SECURITY FACIL--
I CAN GET YOU LIFE IN AN IRON LUNG, ASSHOLE.
I'M NOT GUILTY.
I WAS SET UP.
PERHAPS, BUT THE EVIDENCE IS TO THE CONTRARY, MR. QUEEN.
AND THAT IS WHAT THE JURY WILL HEAR.
WHO ARE YOU REALLY WORKING FOR, BEEKER?
CIA?
FBI?
YOU'RE TELLING ME I SHOULD PLEAD GUILTY TO SOMETHING I DIDN'T DO, JUST TO SAVE ALL THAT TROUBLE.
YOU PEOPLE DON'T KNOW WHAT TROUBLE IS. BEFORE WE'RE DONE, YOU'LL HAVE A PRETTY DAMN GOOD IDEA.
GET OUTA MY SIGHT.

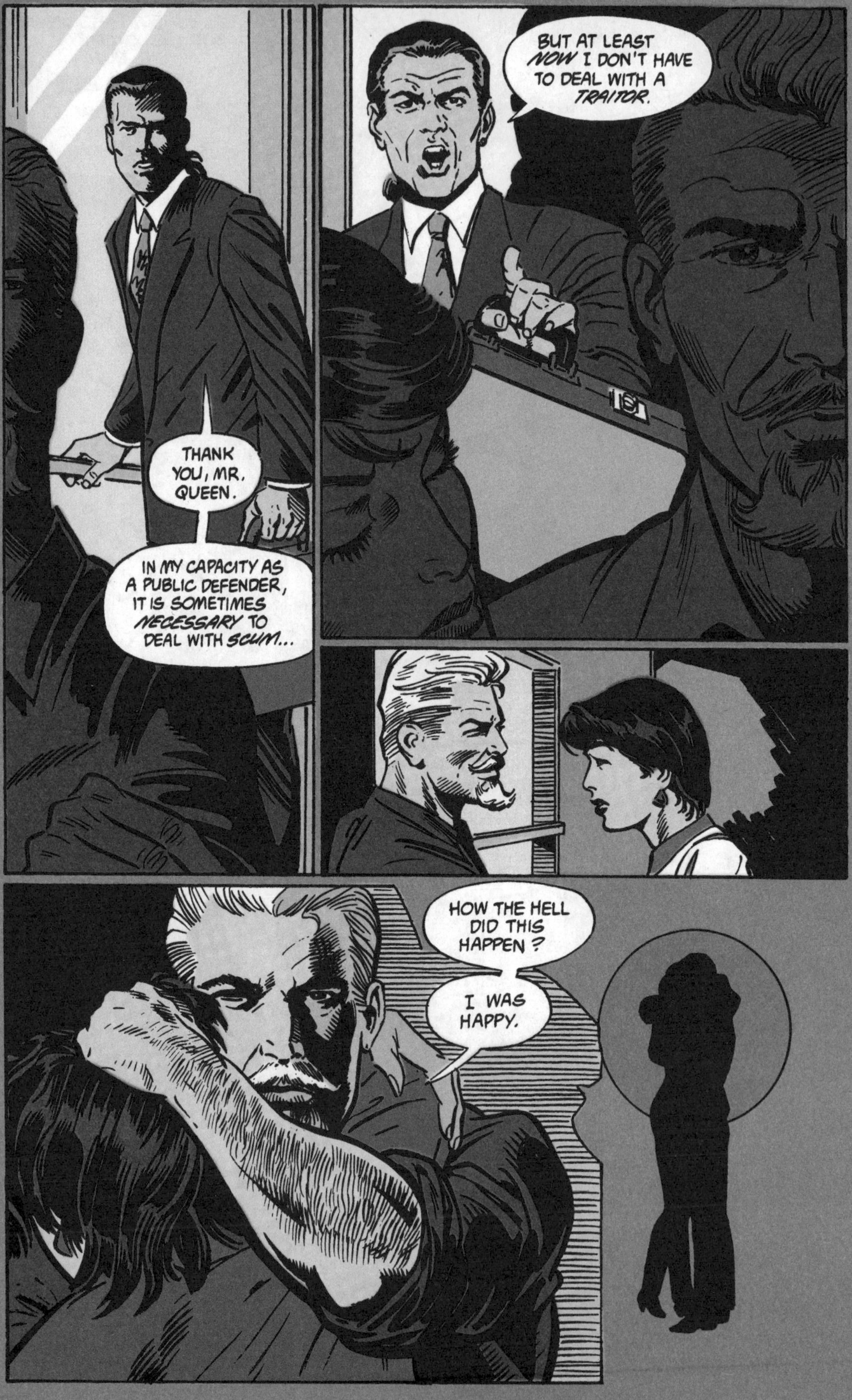
THANK YOU, MR. QUEEN.
IN MY CAPACITY AS A PUBLIC DEFENDER, IT IS SOMETIMES NECESSARY TO DEAL WITH SCUM...
BUT AT LEAST NOW I DON'T HAVE TO DEAL WITH A TRAITOR.
HOW THE HELL DID THIS HAPPEN?
I WAS HAPPY.

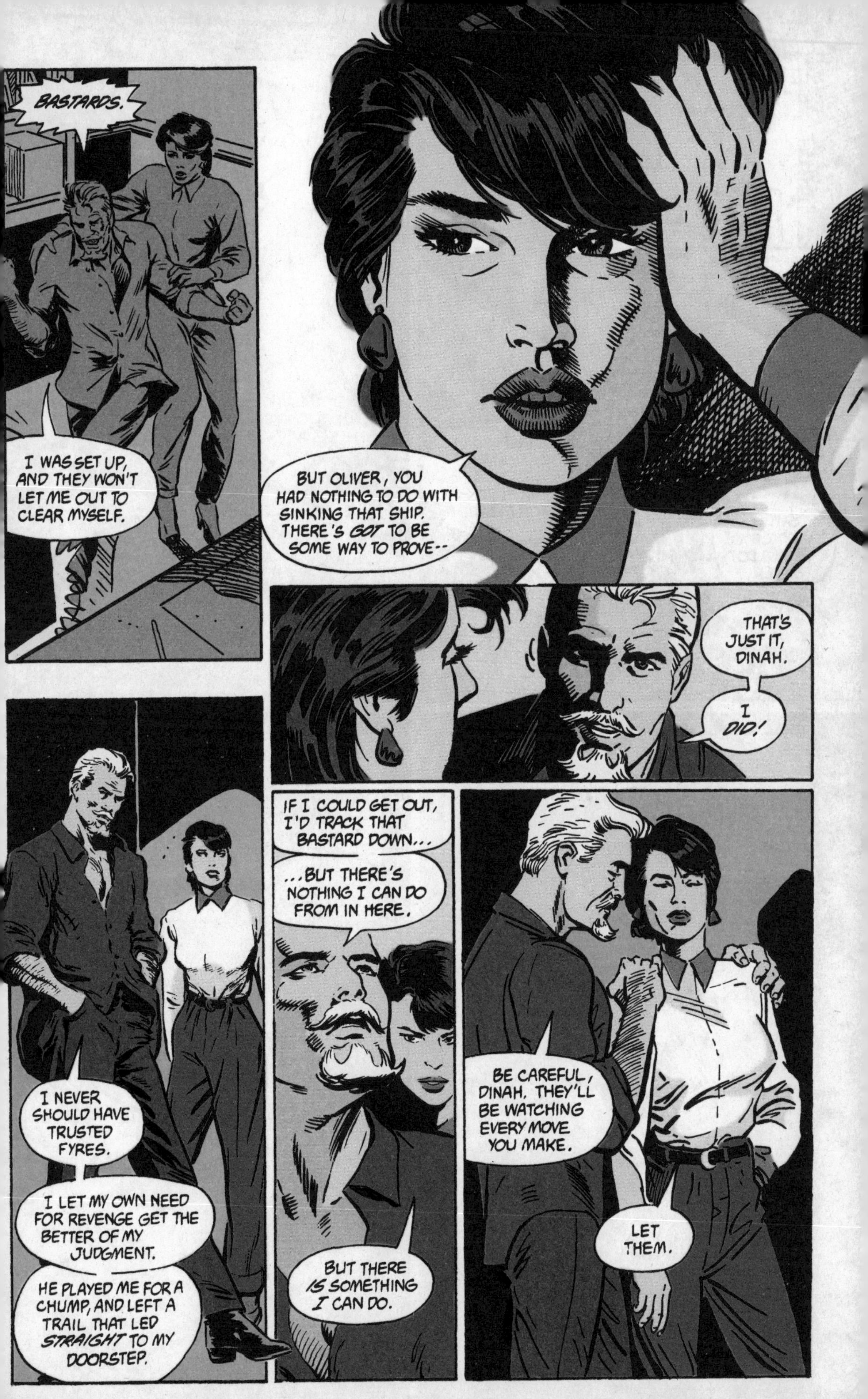
BASTARDS.
I WAS SET UP, AND THEY WON'T LET ME OUT TO CLEAR MYSELF.
BUT OLIVER, YOU HAD NOTHING TO DO WITH SINKING THAT SHIP. THERE'S GOT TO BE SOME WAY TO PROVE--
THAT'S JUST IT, DINAH.
I DID!
I NEVER SHOULD HAVE TRUSTED FYRES.
I LET MY OWN NEED FOR REVENGE GET THE BETTER OF MY JUDGMENT.
HE PLAYED ME FOR A CHUMP, AND LEFT A TRAIL THAT LED STRAIGHT TO MY DOORSTEP.
IF I COULD GET OUT, I'D TRACK THAT BASTARD DOWN...
...BUT THERE'S NOTHING I CAN DO FROM IN HERE.
BUT THERE IS SOMETHING I CAN DO.
BE CAREFUL, DINAH. THEY'LL BE WATCHING EVERY MOVE YOU MAKE.
LET THEM.

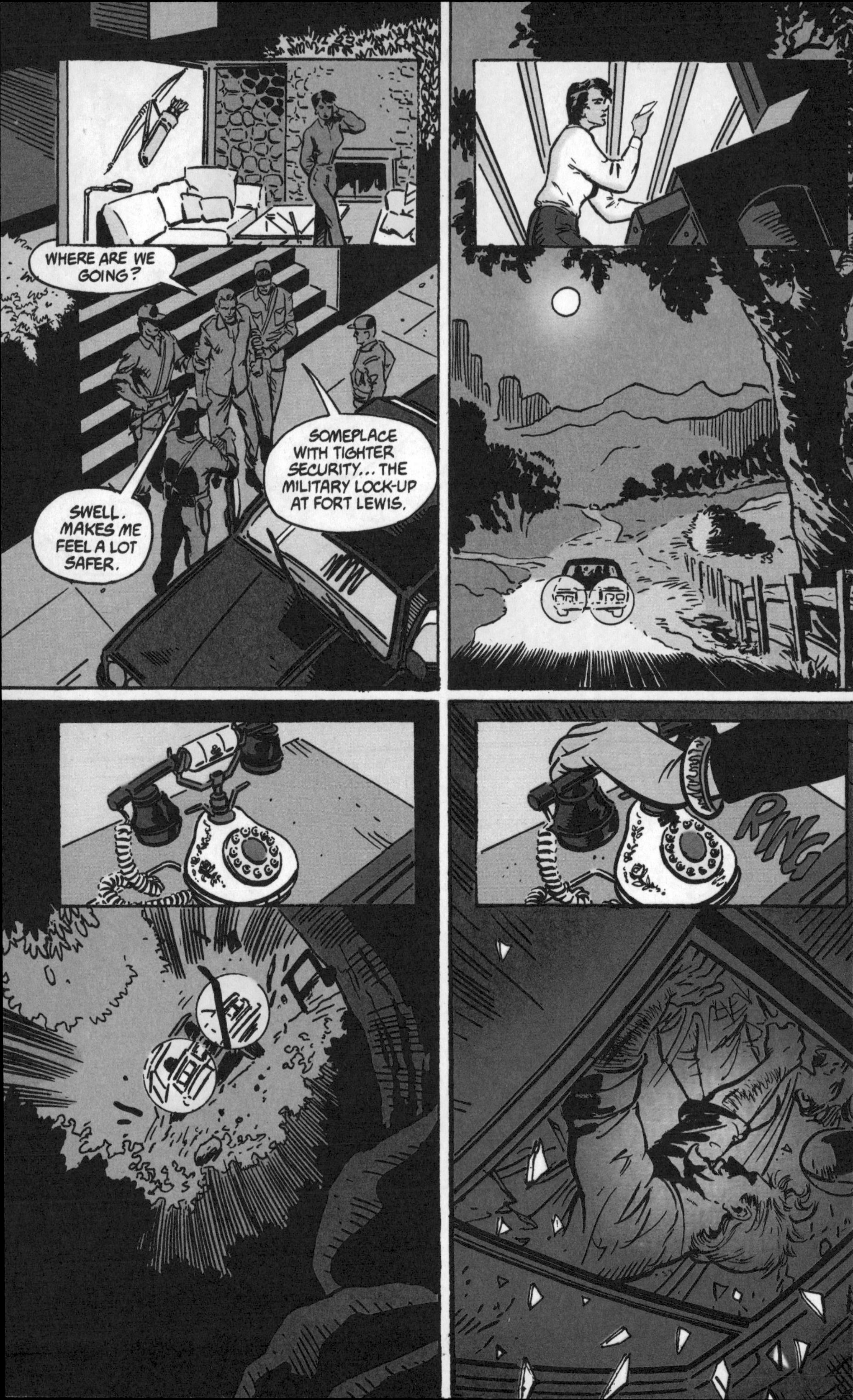
WHERE ARE WE GOING?
SOMEPLACE WITH TIGHTER SECURITY... THE MILITARY LOCK-UP AT FORT LEWIS.
SWELL. MAKES ME FEEL A LOT SAFER.
RING

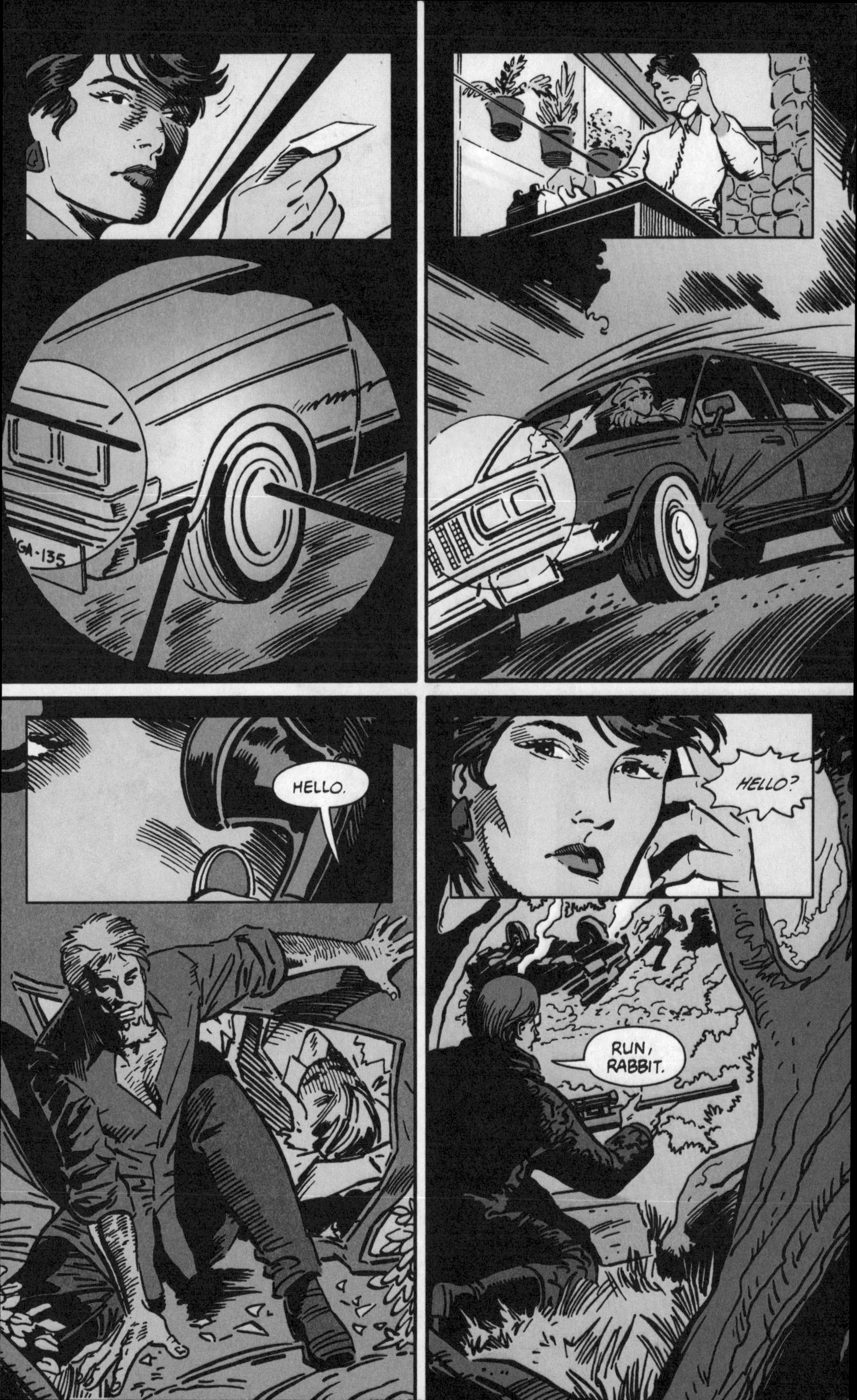
GA-135
HELLO.
HELLO?
RUN, RABBIT.

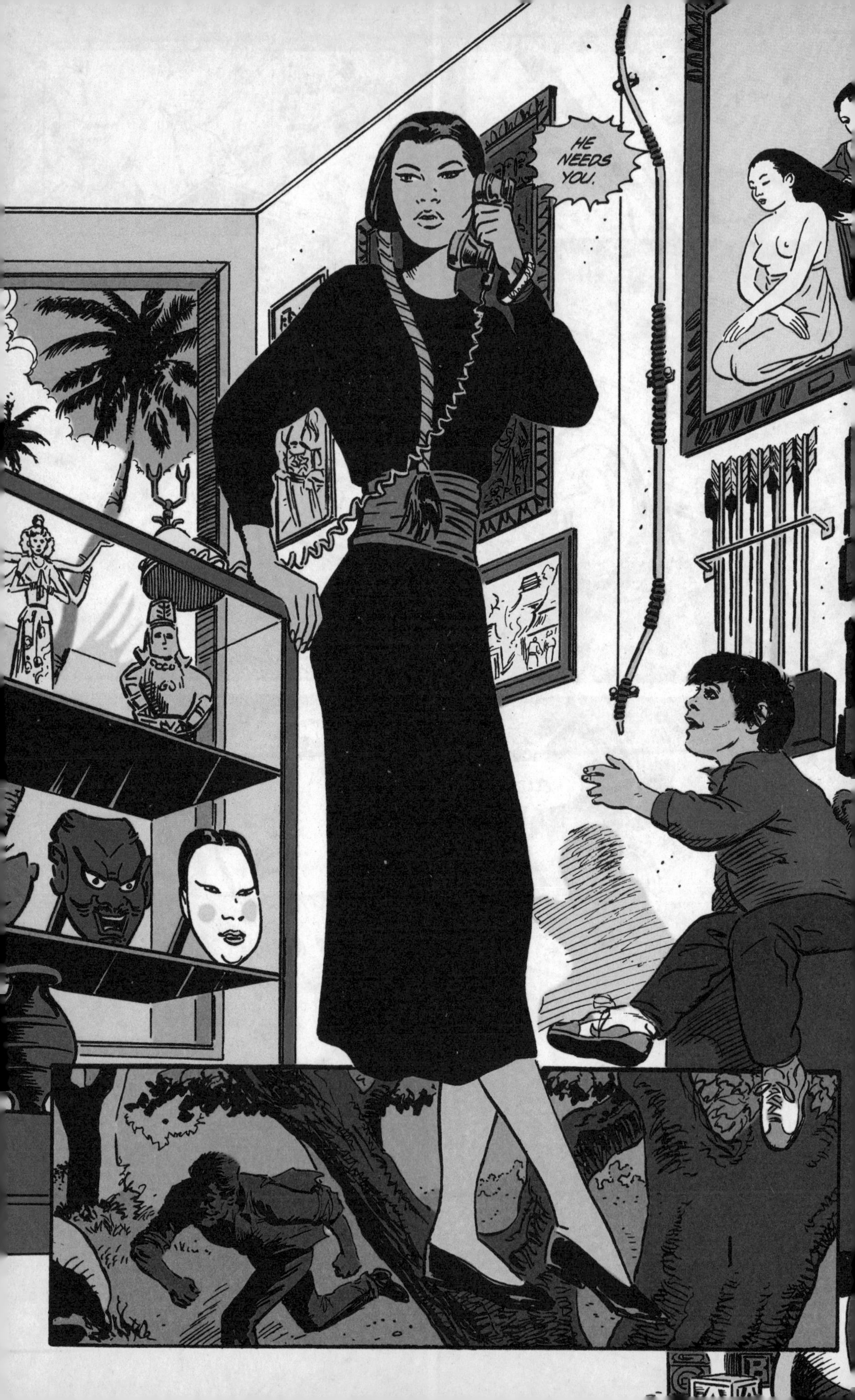
HE NEEDS YOU.

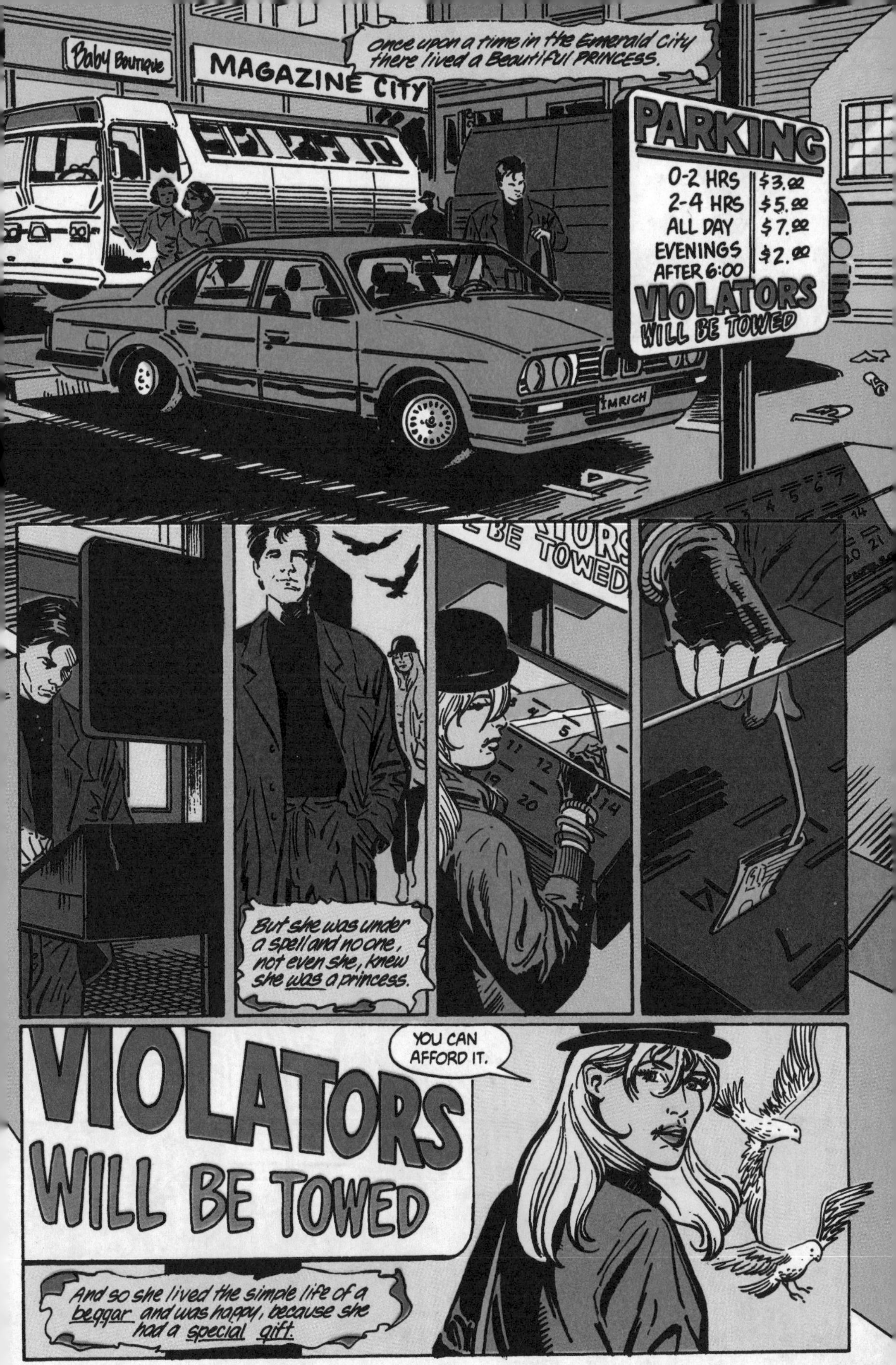
Once upon a time in the Emerald City there lived a Beautiful PRINCESS.
Baby Boutique
MAGAZINE CITY
PARKING
0-2 HRS $3.00
2-4 HRS $5.00
ALL DAY $7.00
EVENINGS AFTER 6:00 $2.00
VIOLATORS WILL BE TOWED
IMRICH
But she was under a spell and no one, not even she, knew she was a princess.
YOU CAN AFFORD IT.
VIOLATORS WILL BE TOWED
And so she lived the simple life of a beggar and was happy, because she had a special gift.

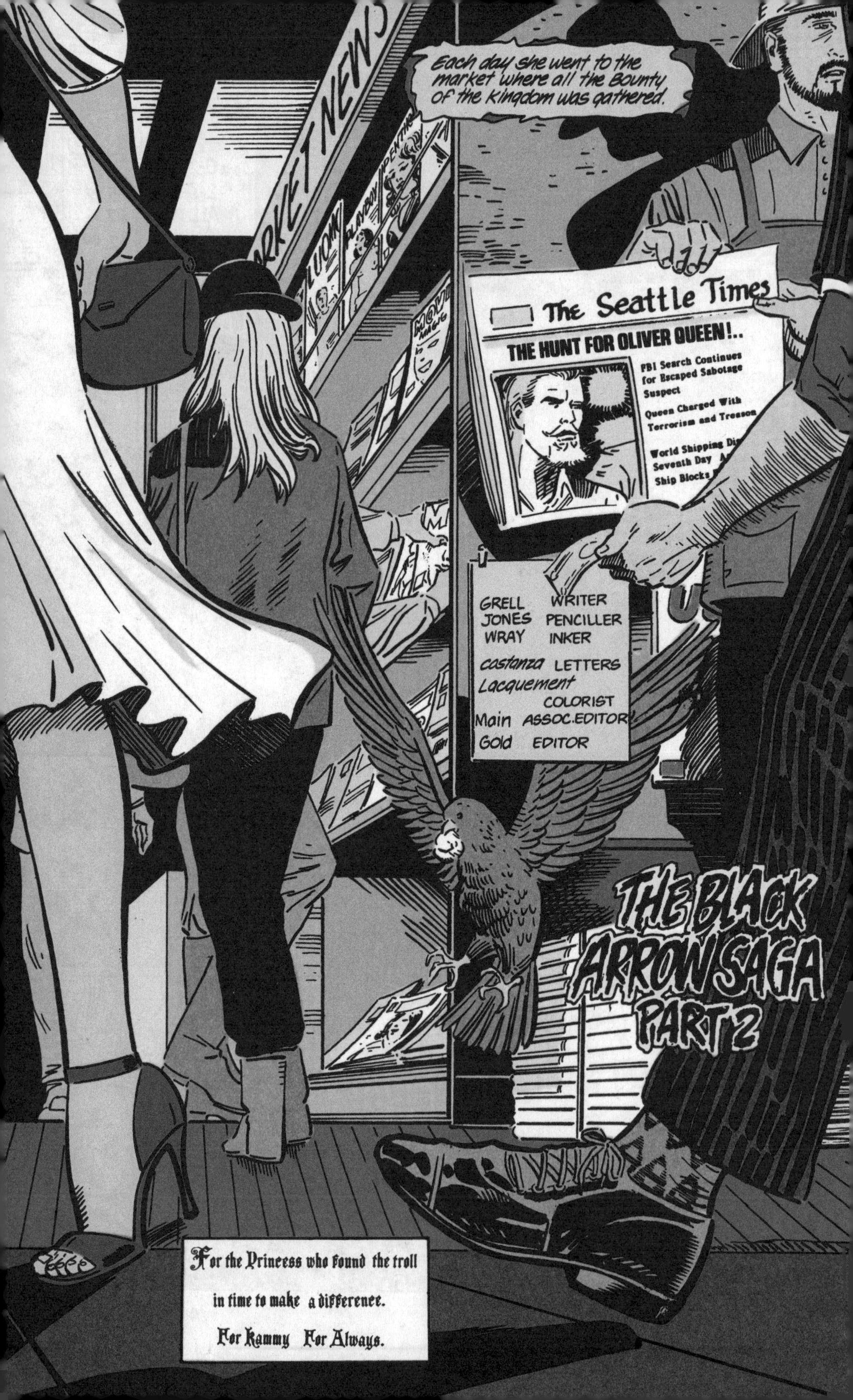

Each day she went to the market where all the Bounty of the Kingdom was gathered.
MARKET NEWS
PLAYBOY
PENTHOUSE
MOVIE MAGIC
The Seattle Times
THE HUNT FOR OLIVER QUEEN!..
FBI Search Continues for Escaped Sabotage Suspect
Queen Charged With Terrorism and Treason
GRELL WRITER
JONES PENCILLER
WRAY INKER
costanza LETTERS
Lacquement COLORIST
Main ASSOC.EDITOR
Gold EDITOR
THE BLACK ARROW SAGA PART 2
For the Princess who found the troll in time to make a difference.
For Kammy For Always.

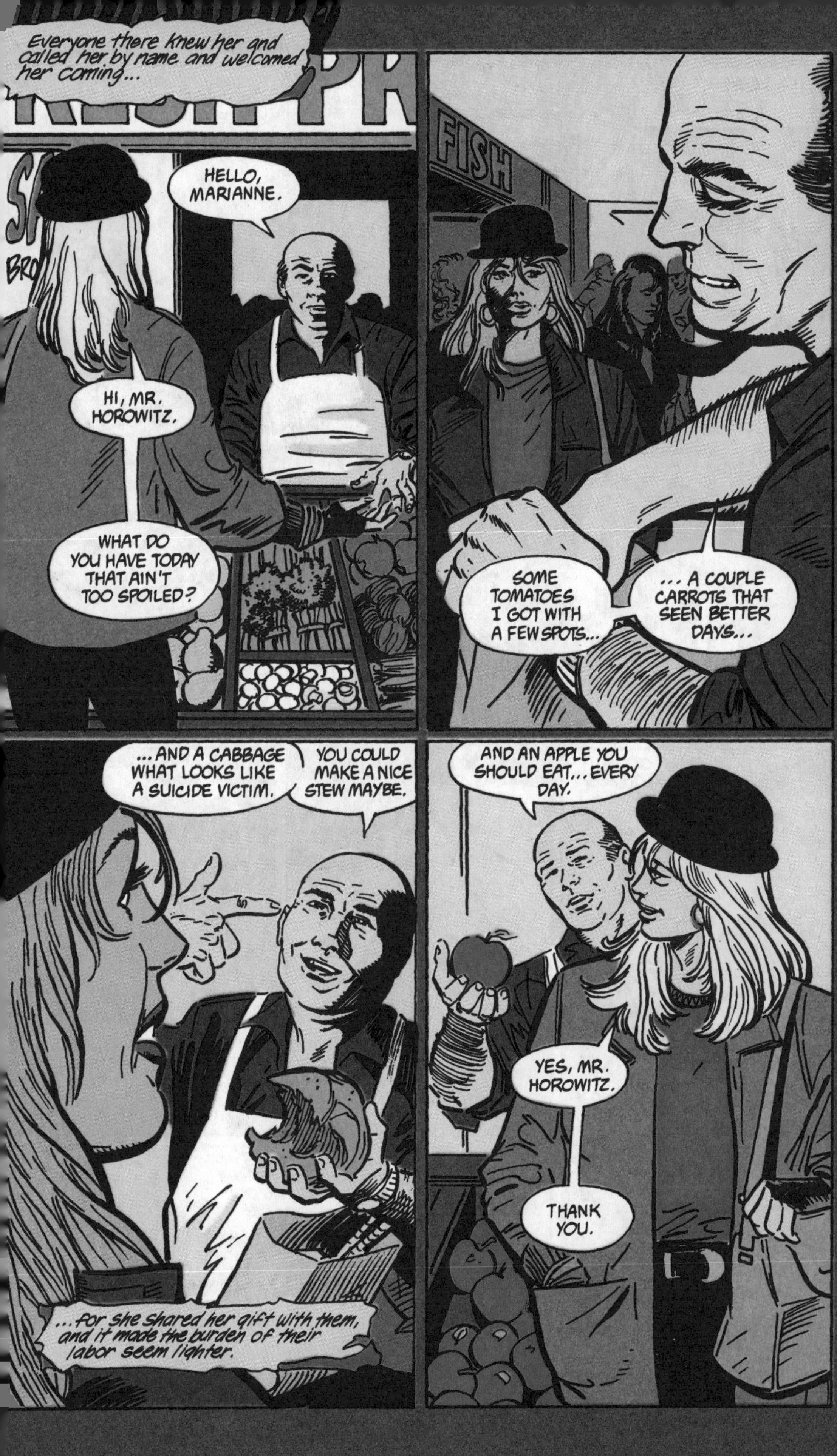
Everyone there knew her and called her by name and welcomed her coming...
HELLO, MARIANNE.
HI, MR. HOROWITZ.
WHAT DO YOU HAVE TODAY THAT AIN'T TOO SPOILED?
FISH
SOME TOMATOES I GOT WITH A FEW SPOTS...
... A COUPLE CARROTS THAT SEEN BETTER DAYS...
...AND A CABBAGE WHAT LOOKS LIKE A SUICIDE VICTIM.
YOU COULD MAKE A NICE STEW MAYBE.
...for she shared her gift with them, and it made the burden of their labor seem lighter.
AND AN APPLE YOU SHOULD EAT... EVERY DAY.
YES, MR. HOROWITZ.
THANK YOU.

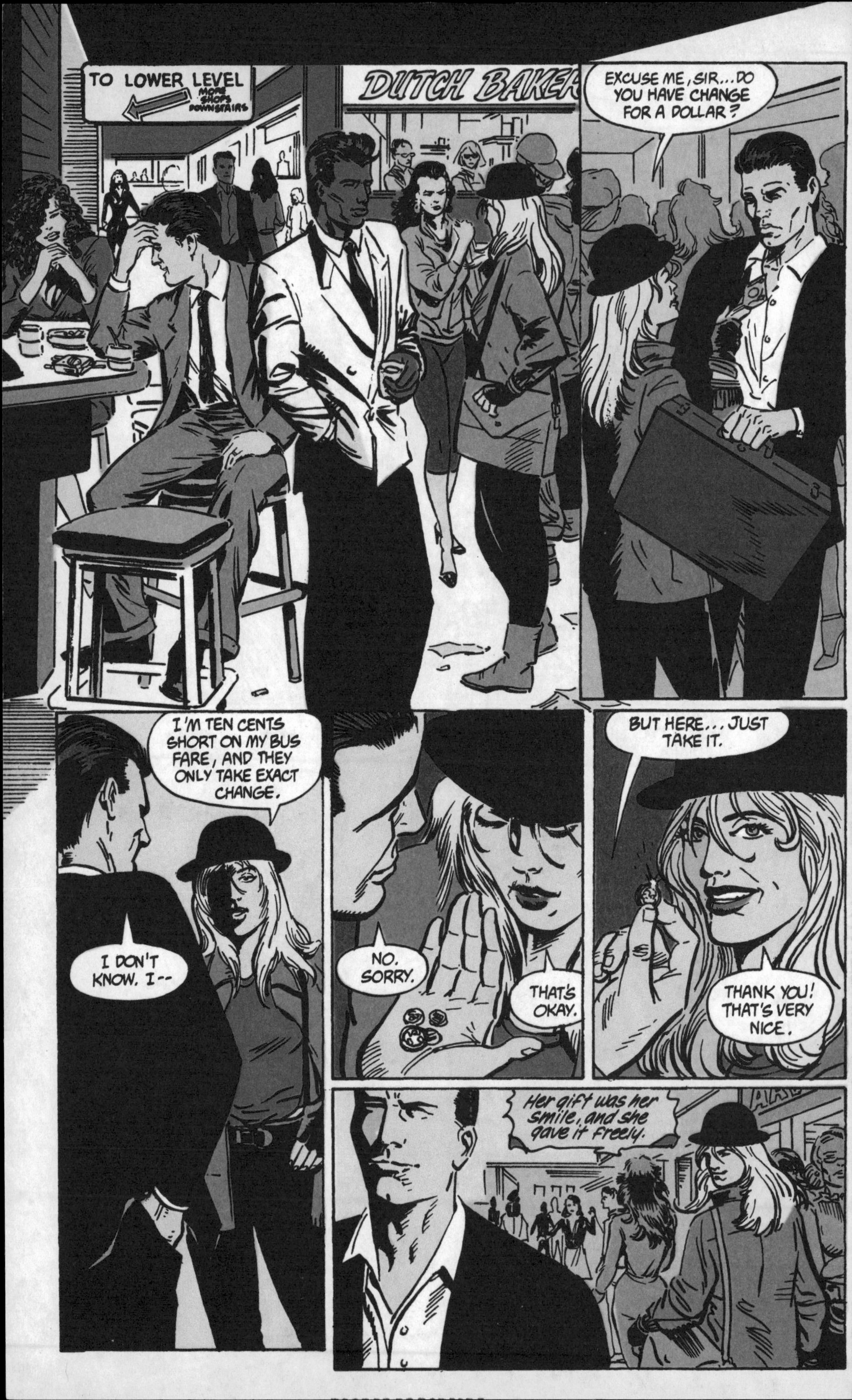
TO LOWER LEVEL
MORE SHOPS DOWNSTAIRS
DUTCH BAKER
EXCUSE ME, SIR... DO YOU HAVE CHANGE FOR A DOLLAR?
I'M TEN CENTS SHORT ON MY BUS FARE, AND THEY ONLY TAKE EXACT CHANGE.
I DON'T KNOW. I--
NO. SORRY.
THAT'S OKAY.
BUT HERE... JUST TAKE IT.
THANK YOU! THAT'S VERY NICE.
Her gift was her smile, and she gave it freely.

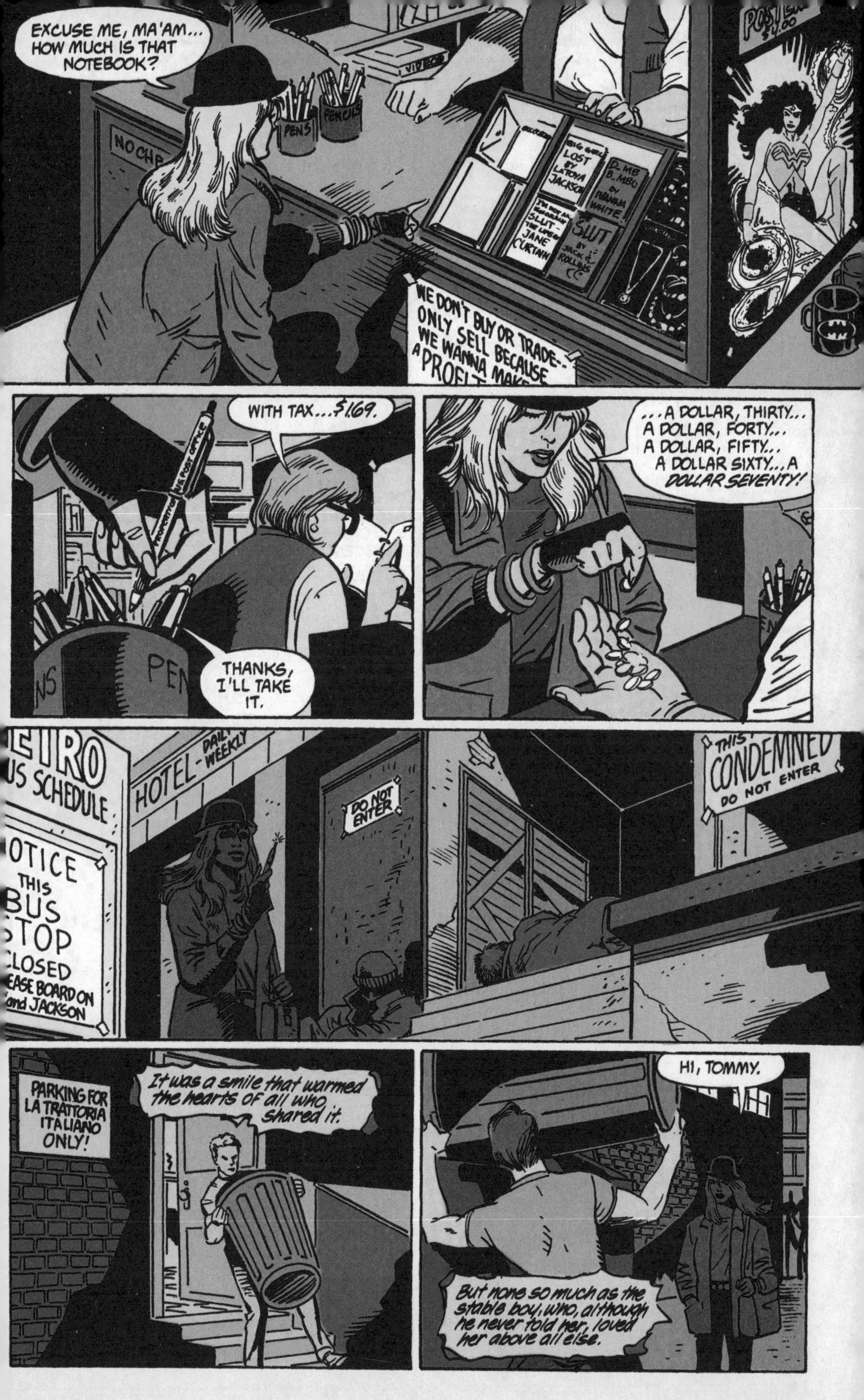
EXCUSE ME, MA'AM... HOW MUCH IS THAT NOTEBOOK?
PENS
PENCILS
LOST BY LATOYA JACKSON
SLUT
WE DON'T BUY OR TRADE- ONLY SELL BECAUSE WE WANNA MAKE A PROFI
WITH TAX...$1.69.
THANKS, I'LL TAKE IT.
...A DOLLAR, THIRTY... A DOLLAR, FORTY... A DOLLAR, FIFTY... A DOLLAR SIXTY... A DOLLAR SEVENTY!
US SCHEDULE
OTICE THIS BUS TOP CLOSED
HOTEL-DAILY-WEEKLY
DO NOT ENTER
CONDEMNED DO NOT ENTER
PARKING FOR LA TRATTORIA ITALIANO ONLY!
It was a smile that warmed the hearts of all who shared it.
HI, TOMMY.
But none so much as the stable boy, who, although he never told her, loved her above all else.

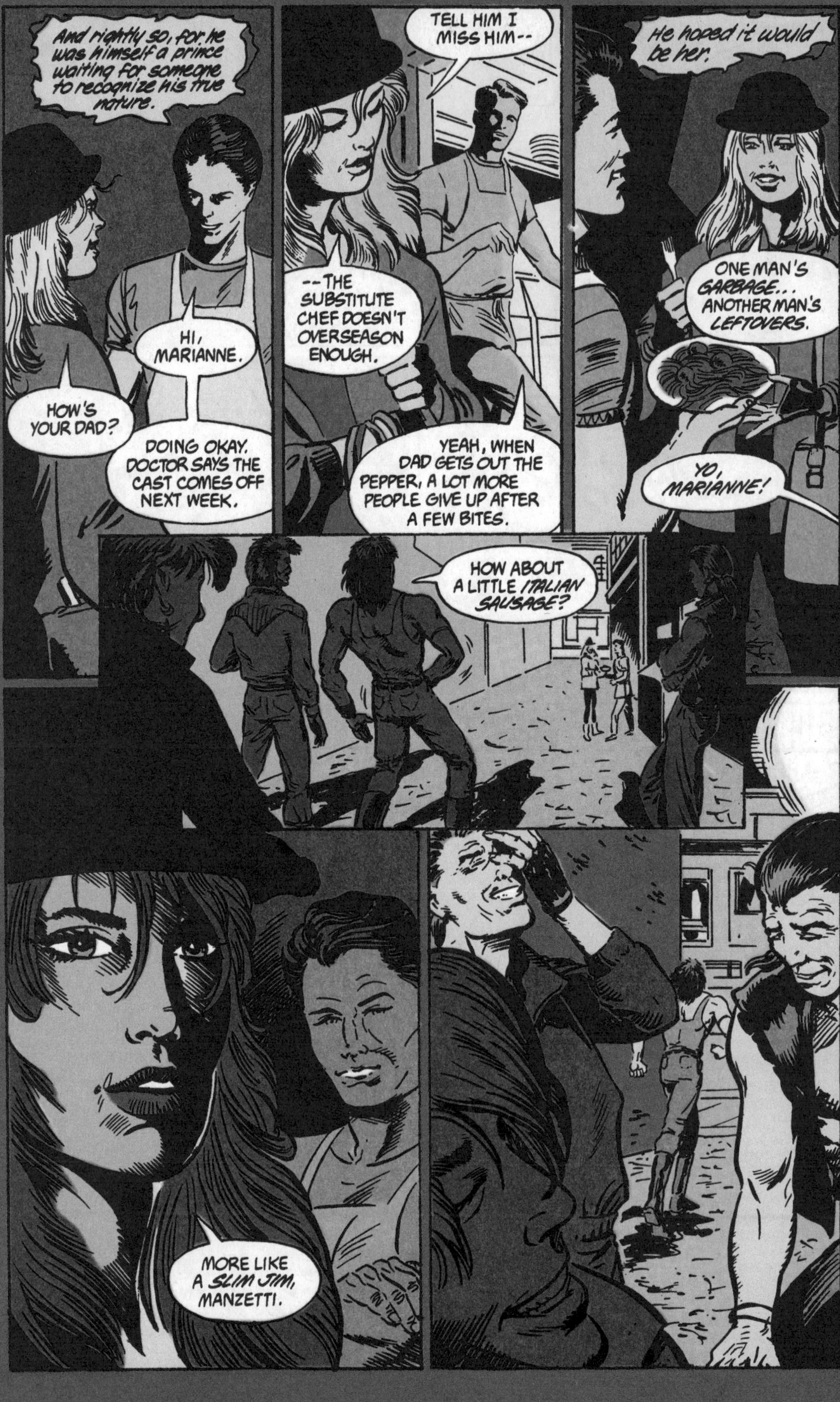
And rightly so, for he was himself a prince waiting for someone to recognize his true nature.
HI, MARIANNE.
HOW'S YOUR DAD?
DOING OKAY. DOCTOR SAYS THE CAST COMES OFF NEXT WEEK.
TELL HIM I MISS HIM--
--THE SUBSTITUTE CHEF DOESN'T OVERSEASON ENOUGH.
YEAH, WHEN DAD GETS OUT THE PEPPER, A LOT MORE PEOPLE GIVE UP AFTER A FEW BITES.
He hoped it would be her.
ONE MAN'S GARBAGE... ANOTHER MAN'S LEFTOVERS.
YO, MARIANNE!
HOW ABOUT A LITTLE ITALIAN SAUSAGE?
MORE LIKE A SLIM JIM, MANZETTI.

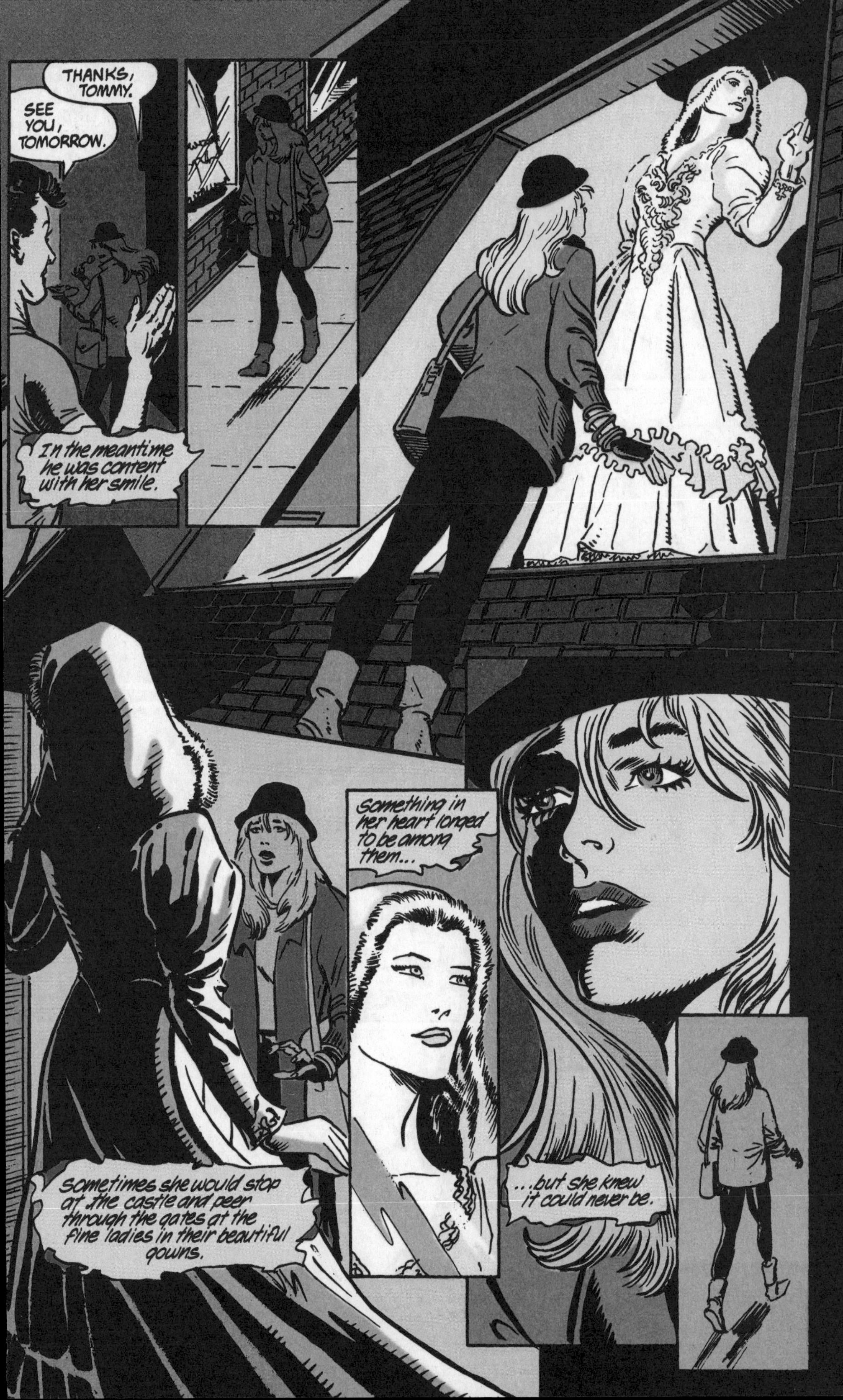
THANKS, TOMMY.
SEE YOU, TOMORROW.
In the meantime he was content with her smile.
Sometimes she would stop at the castle and peer through the gates at the fine ladies in their beautiful gowns.
Something in her heart longed to be among them...
...but she knew it could never be.

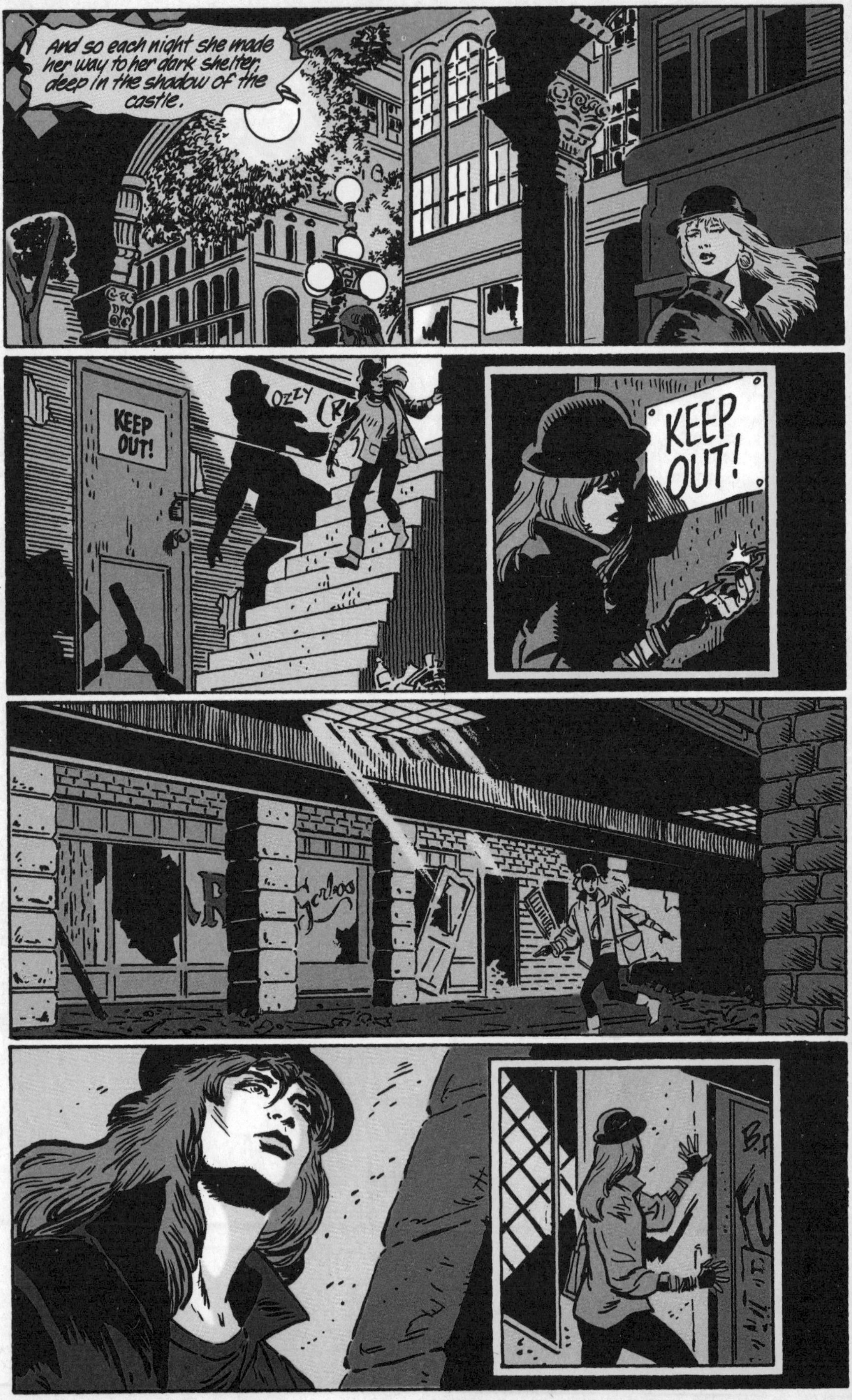
And so each night she made her way to her dark shelter, deep in the shadow of the castle.
KEEP OUT!
KEEP OUT!

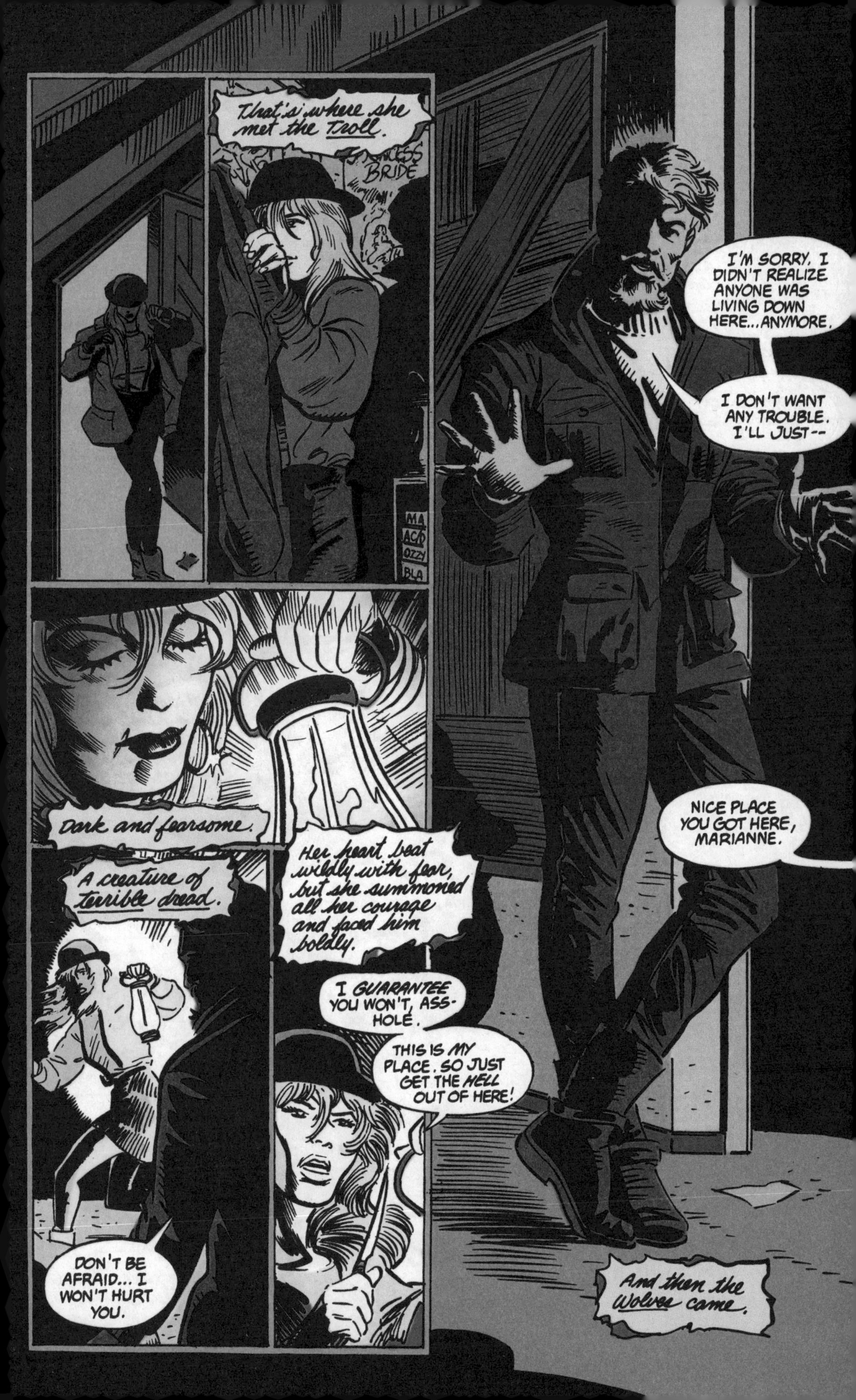
That's where she met the Troll.
I'M SORRY. I DIDN'T REALIZE ANYONE WAS LIVING DOWN HERE...ANYMORE.
I DON'T WANT ANY TROUBLE. I'LL JUST--
Dark and fearsome.
A creature of terrible dread.
DON'T BE AFRAID... I WON'T HURT YOU.
Her heart beat wildly with fear, but she summoned all her courage and faced him boldly.
I GUARANTEE YOU WON'T, ASS-HOLE.
THIS IS MY PLACE. SO JUST GET THE HELL OUT OF HERE!
NICE PLACE YOU GOT HERE, MARIANNE.
And then the Wolves came.

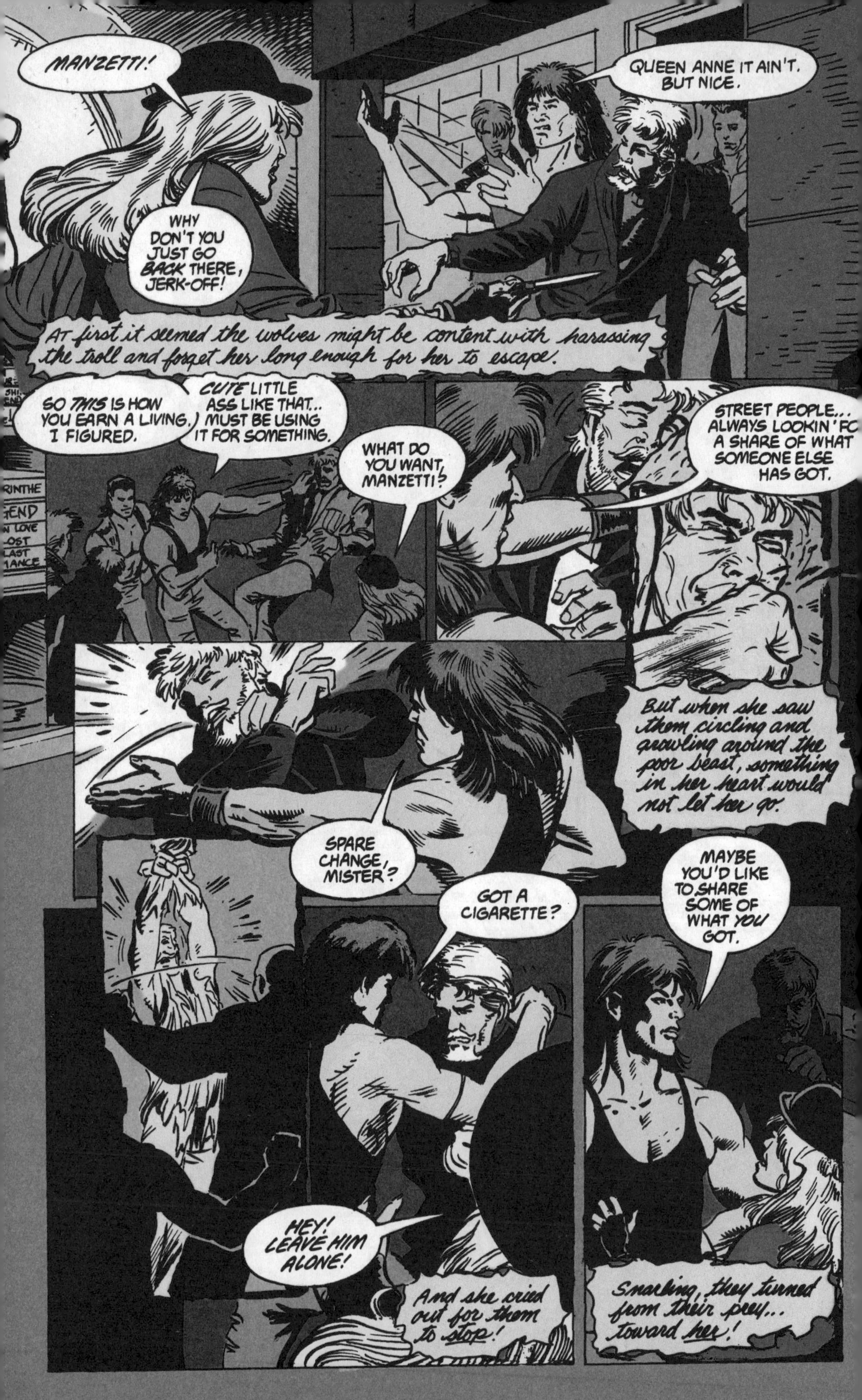
MANZETTI!
QUEEN ANNE IT AIN'T. BUT NICE.
WHY DON'T YOU JUST GO BACK THERE, JERK-OFF!
At first it seemed the wolves might be content with harassing the troll and forget her long enough for her to escape.
SO THIS IS HOW YOU EARN A LIVING. I FIGURED.
CUTE LITTLE ASS LIKE THAT... MUST BE USING IT FOR SOMETHING.
WHAT DO YOU WANT, MANZETTI?
STREET PEOPLE... ALWAYS LOOKIN' FO A SHARE OF WHAT SOMEONE ELSE HAS GOT.
But when she saw them circling and growling around the poor beast, something in her heart would not let her go.
SPARE CHANGE, MISTER?
GOT A CIGARETTE?
MAYBE YOU'D LIKE TO SHARE SOME OF WHAT YOU GOT.
HEY! LEAVE HIM ALONE!
And she cried out for them to stop!
Snarling, they turned from their prey... toward her!

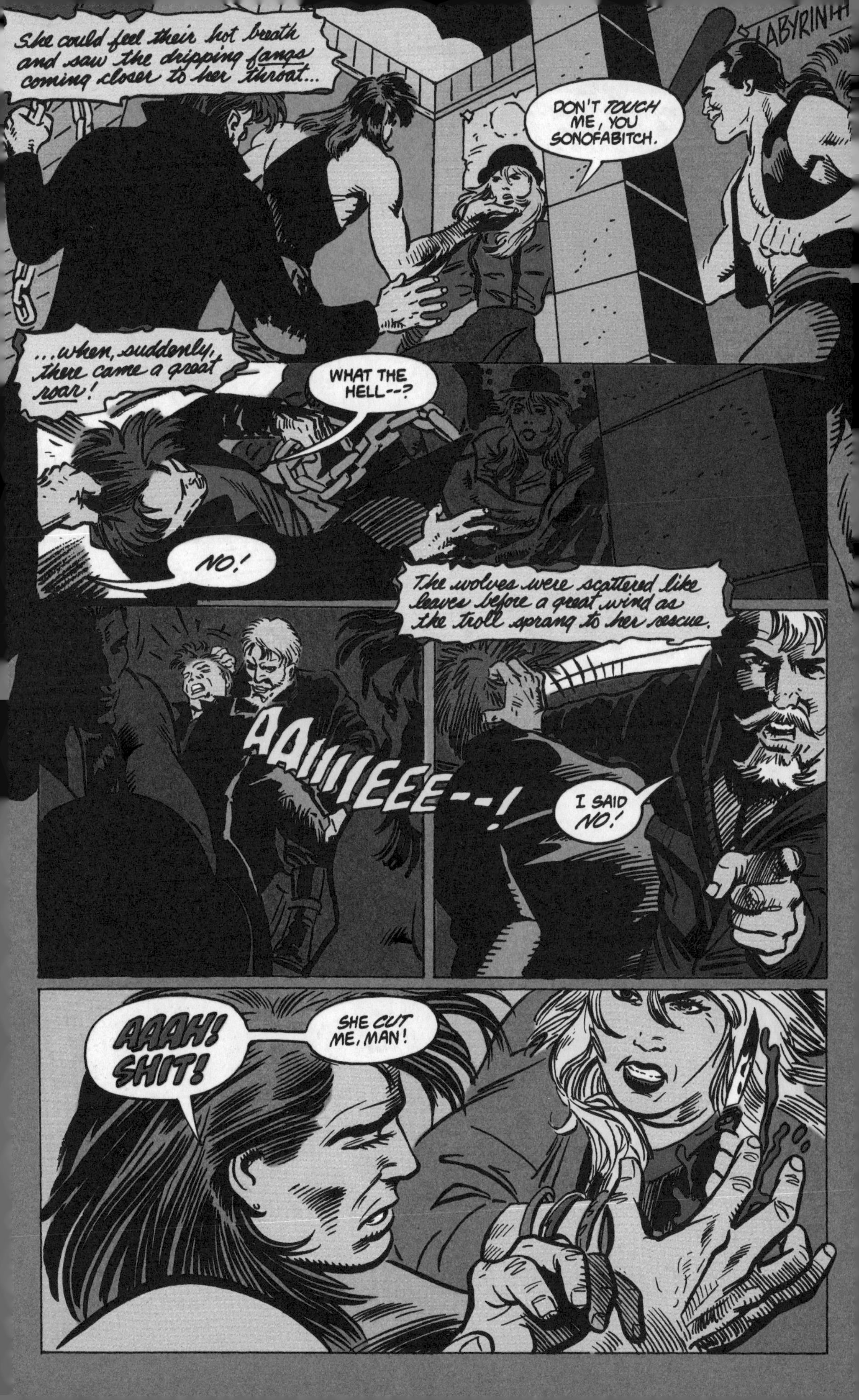
She could feel their hot breath and saw the dripping fangs coming closer to her throat...
DON'T TOUCH ME, YOU SONOFABITCH.
...when, suddenly, there came a great roar!
WHAT THE HELL--?
NO!
The wolves were scattered like leaves before a great wind as the troll sprang to her rescue.
AAIIIEEE--!
I SAID NO!
AAAH! SHIT!
SHE CUT ME, MAN!

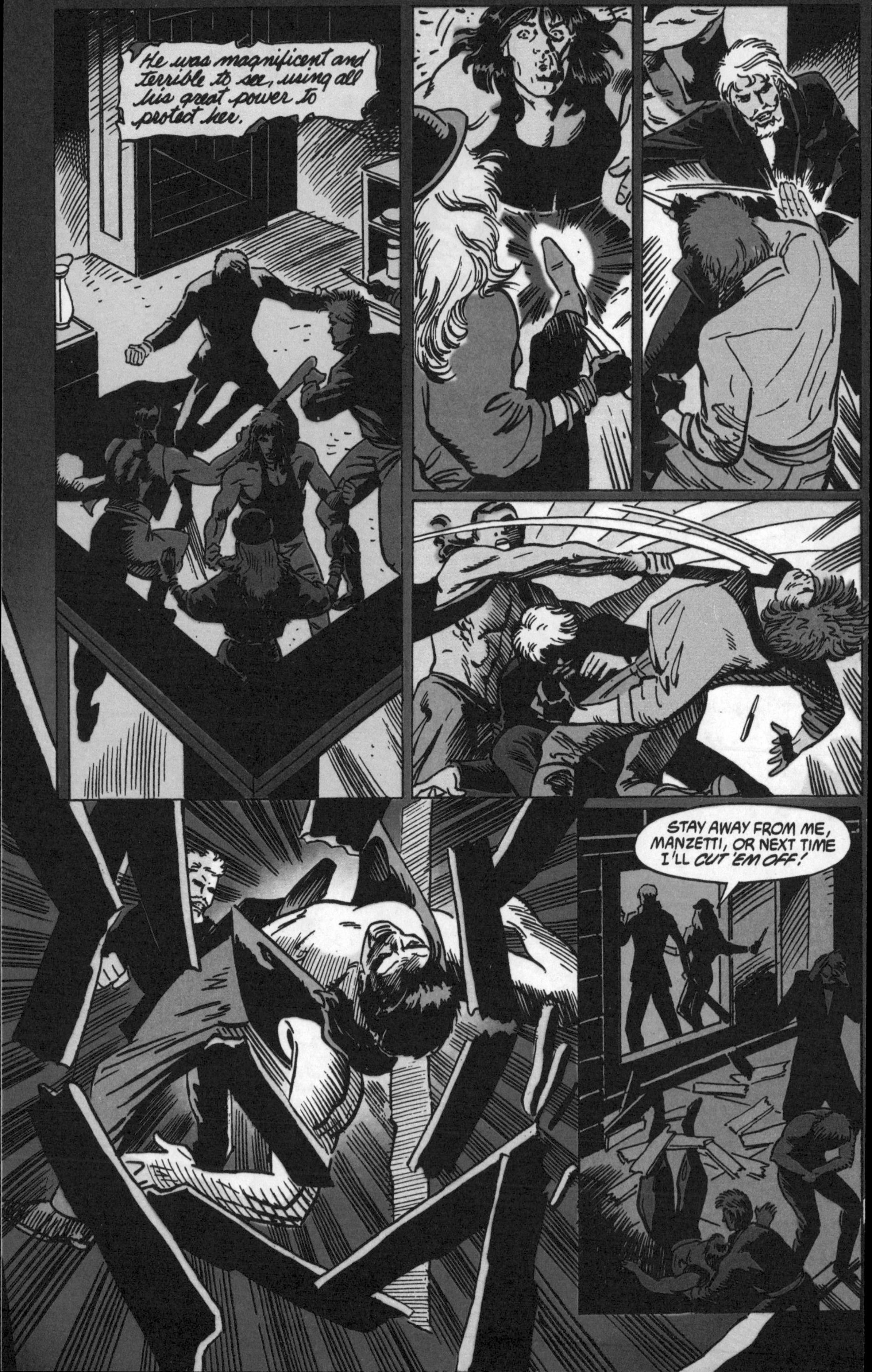
He was magnificent and terrible to see, using all his great power to protect her.
STAY AWAY FROM ME, MANZETTI, OR NEXT TIME I'LL CUT 'EM OFF!

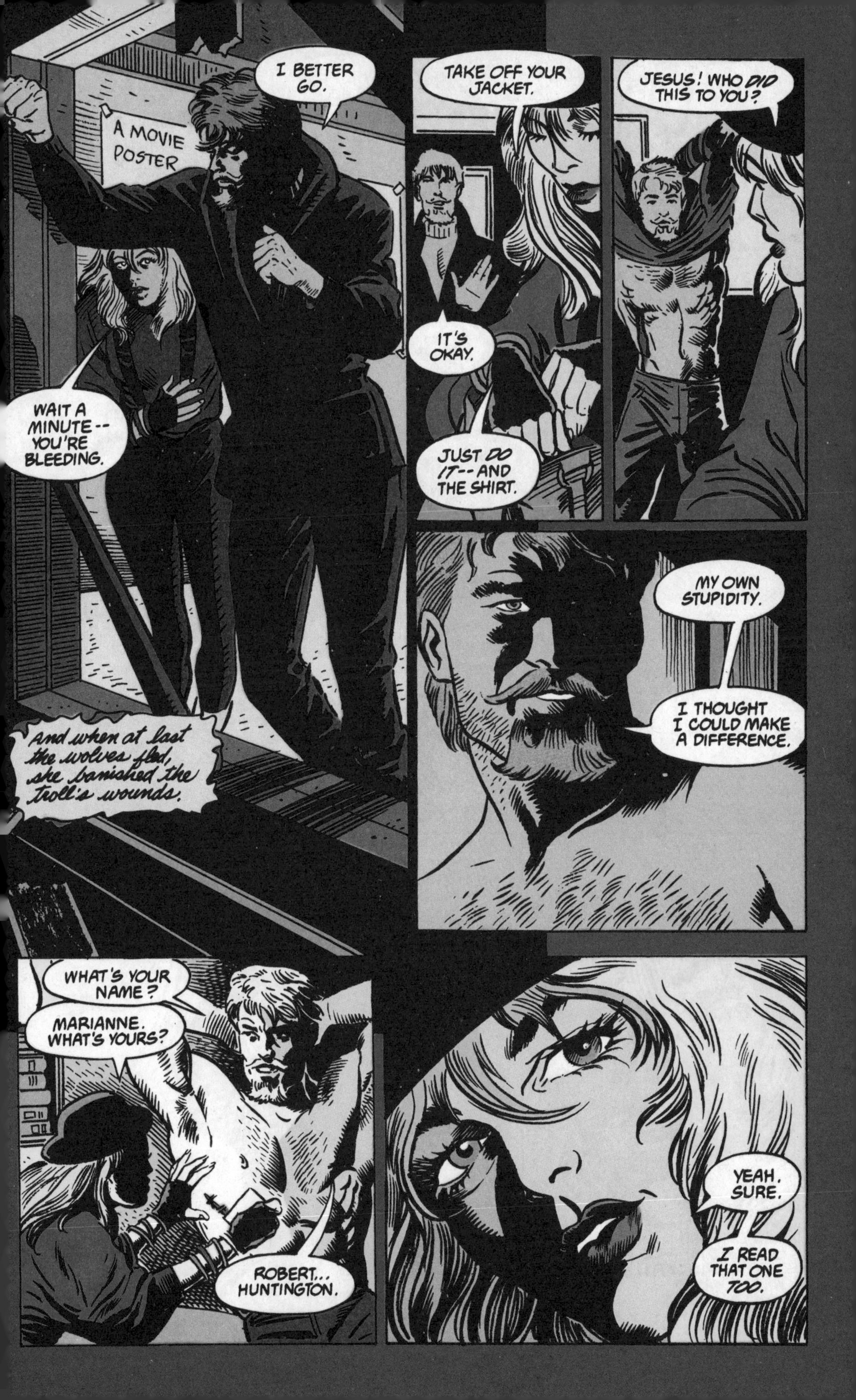
I BETTER GO.
A MOVIE POSTER
WAIT A MINUTE-- YOU'RE BLEEDING.
And when at last the wolves fled, she banished the troll's wounds.
TAKE OFF YOUR JACKET.
IT'S OKAY.
JUST DO IT-- AND THE SHIRT.
JESUS! WHO DID THIS TO YOU?
MY OWN STUPIDITY.
I THOUGHT I COULD MAKE A DIFFERENCE.
WHAT'S YOUR NAME?
MARIANNE. WHAT'S YOURS?
ROBERT... HUNTINGTON.
YEAH. SURE.
I READ THAT ONE TOO.

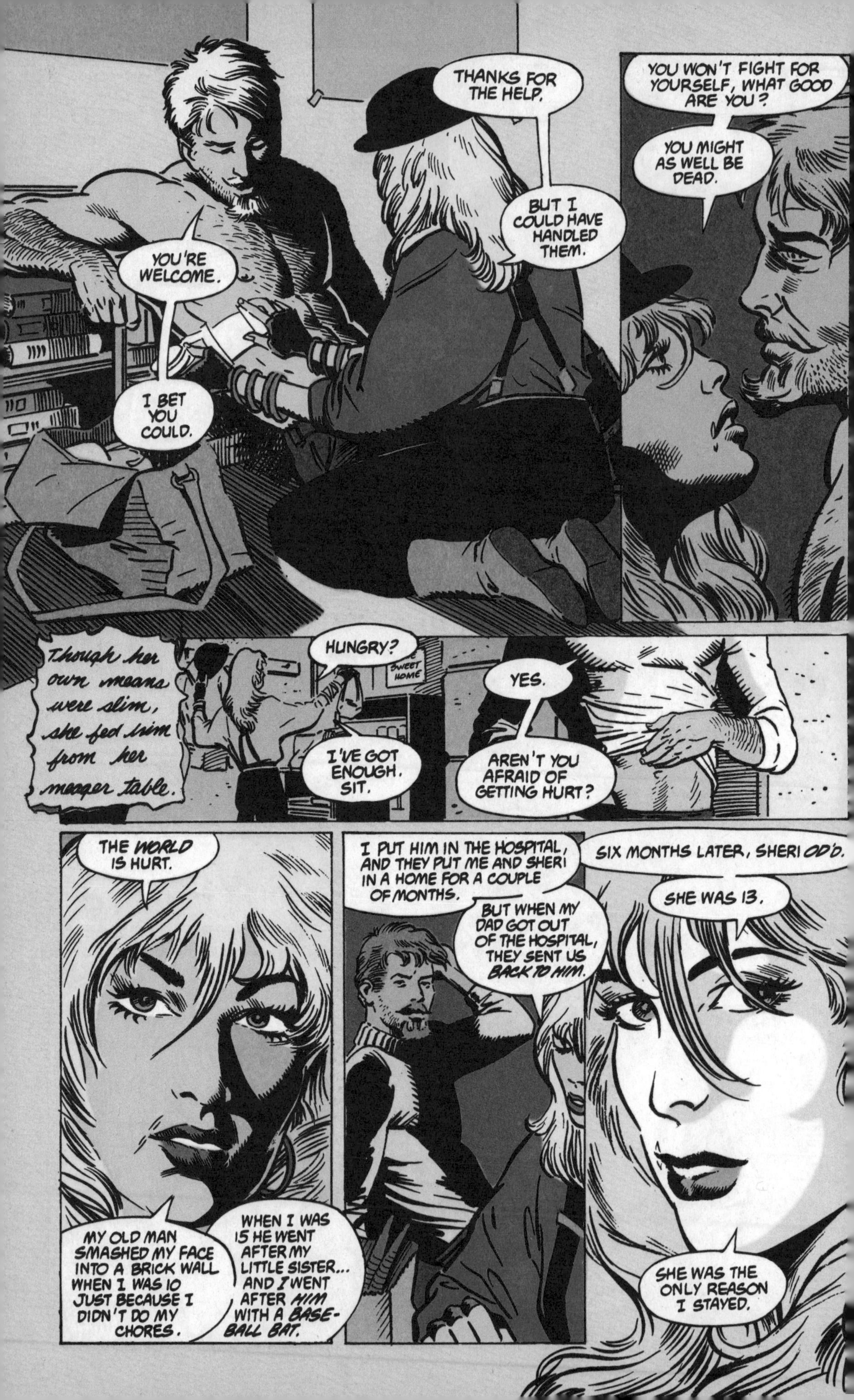

THANKS FOR THE HELP,
BUT I COULD HAVE HANDLED THEM.
YOU'RE WELCOME.
I BET YOU COULD.
YOU WON'T FIGHT FOR YOURSELF, WHAT GOOD ARE YOU?
YOU MIGHT AS WELL BE DEAD.
Though her own means were slim, she fed him from her meager table.
HUNGRY?
I'VE GOT ENOUGH. SIT.
YES.
AREN'T YOU AFRAID OF GETTING HURT?
THE WORLD IS HURT.
MY OLD MAN SMASHED MY FACE INTO A BRICK WALL WHEN I WAS 10 JUST BECAUSE I DIDN'T DO MY CHORES.
WHEN I WAS 15 HE WENT AFTER MY LITTLE SISTER... AND I WENT AFTER HIM WITH A BASE-BALL BAT.
I PUT HIM IN THE HOSPITAL, AND THEY PUT ME AND SHERI IN A HOME FOR A COUPLE OF MONTHS.
BUT WHEN MY DAD GOT OUT OF THE HOSPITAL, THEY SENT US BACK TO HIM.
SIX MONTHS LATER, SHERI OD'D.
SHE WAS 13.
SHE WAS THE ONLY REASON I STAYED.

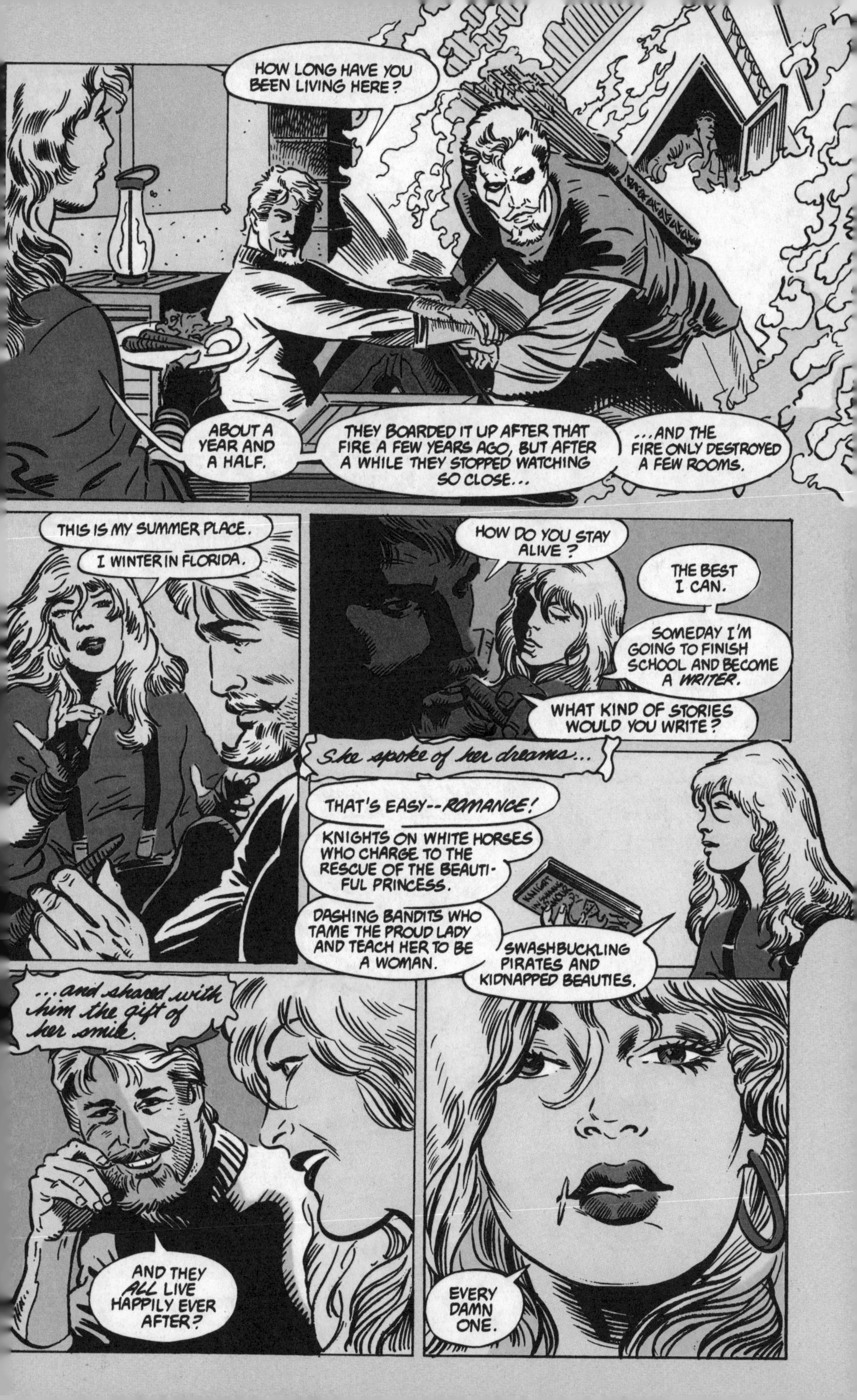
HOW LONG HAVE YOU BEEN LIVING HERE?
ABOUT A YEAR AND A HALF.
THEY BOARDED IT UP AFTER THAT FIRE A FEW YEARS AGO, BUT AFTER A WHILE THEY STOPPED WATCHING SO CLOSE...
...AND THE FIRE ONLY DESTROYED A FEW ROOMS.
THIS IS MY SUMMER PLACE.
I WINTER IN FLORIDA.
HOW DO YOU STAY ALIVE?
THE BEST I CAN.
SOMEDAY I'M GOING TO FINISH SCHOOL AND BECOME A *WRITER*.
WHAT KIND OF STORIES WOULD YOU WRITE?
She spoke of her dreams...
THAT'S EASY--*ROMANCE!*
KNIGHTS ON WHITE HORSES WHO CHARGE TO THE RESCUE OF THE BEAUTIFUL PRINCESS.
DASHING BANDITS WHO TAME THE PROUD LADY AND TEACH HER TO BE A WOMAN.
SWASHBUCKLING PIRATES AND KIDNAPPED BEAUTIES.
...and shared with him the gift of her smile.
AND THEY *ALL* LIVE HAPPILY EVER AFTER?
EVERY DAMN ONE.

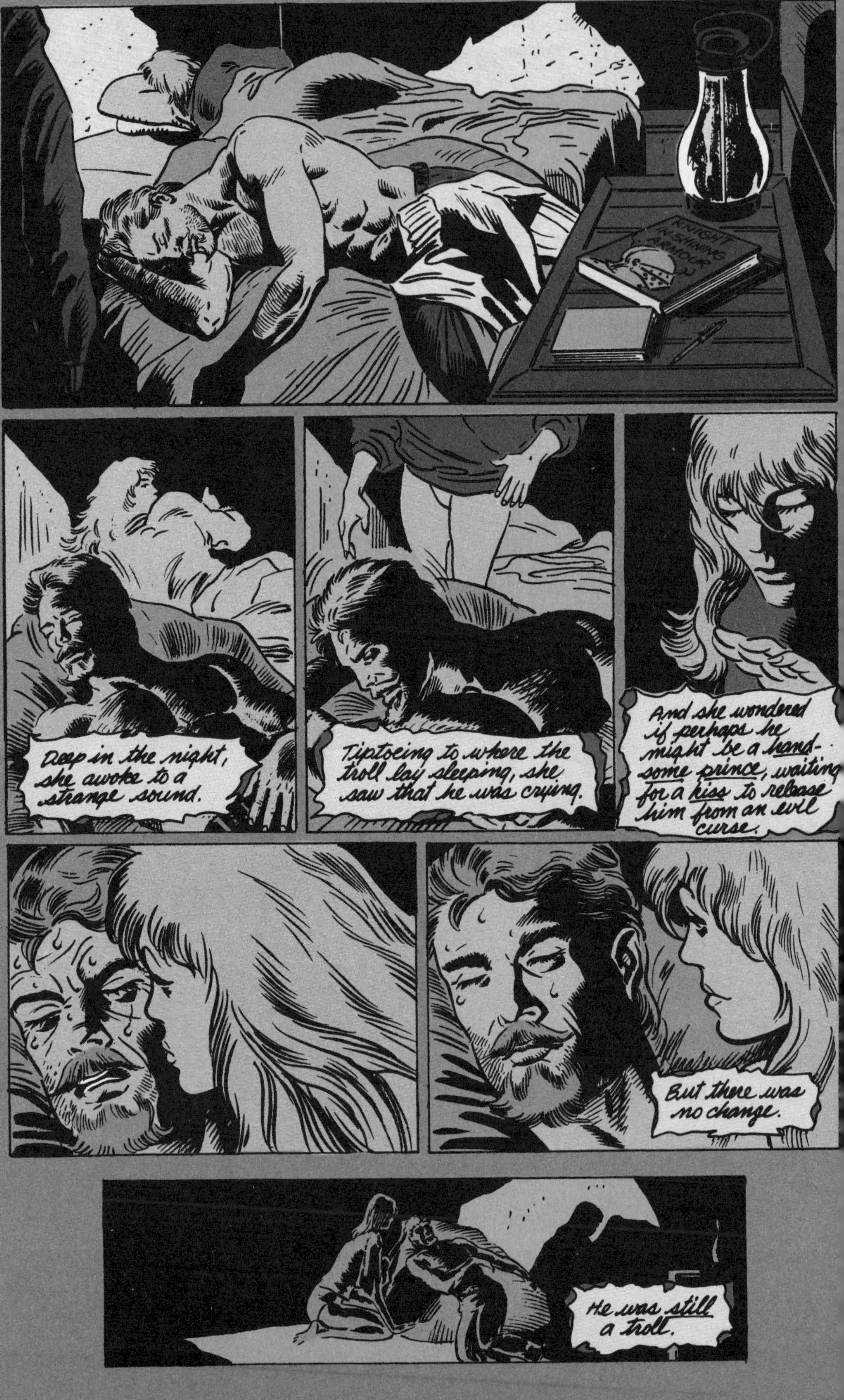
KNIGHT IN SHINING ARMOUR
Deep in the night, she awoke to a strange sound.
Tiptoeing to where the troll lay sleeping, she saw that he was crying.
And she wondered if perhaps he might be a handsome prince, waiting for a kiss to release him from an evil curse.
But there was no change.
He was still a troll.

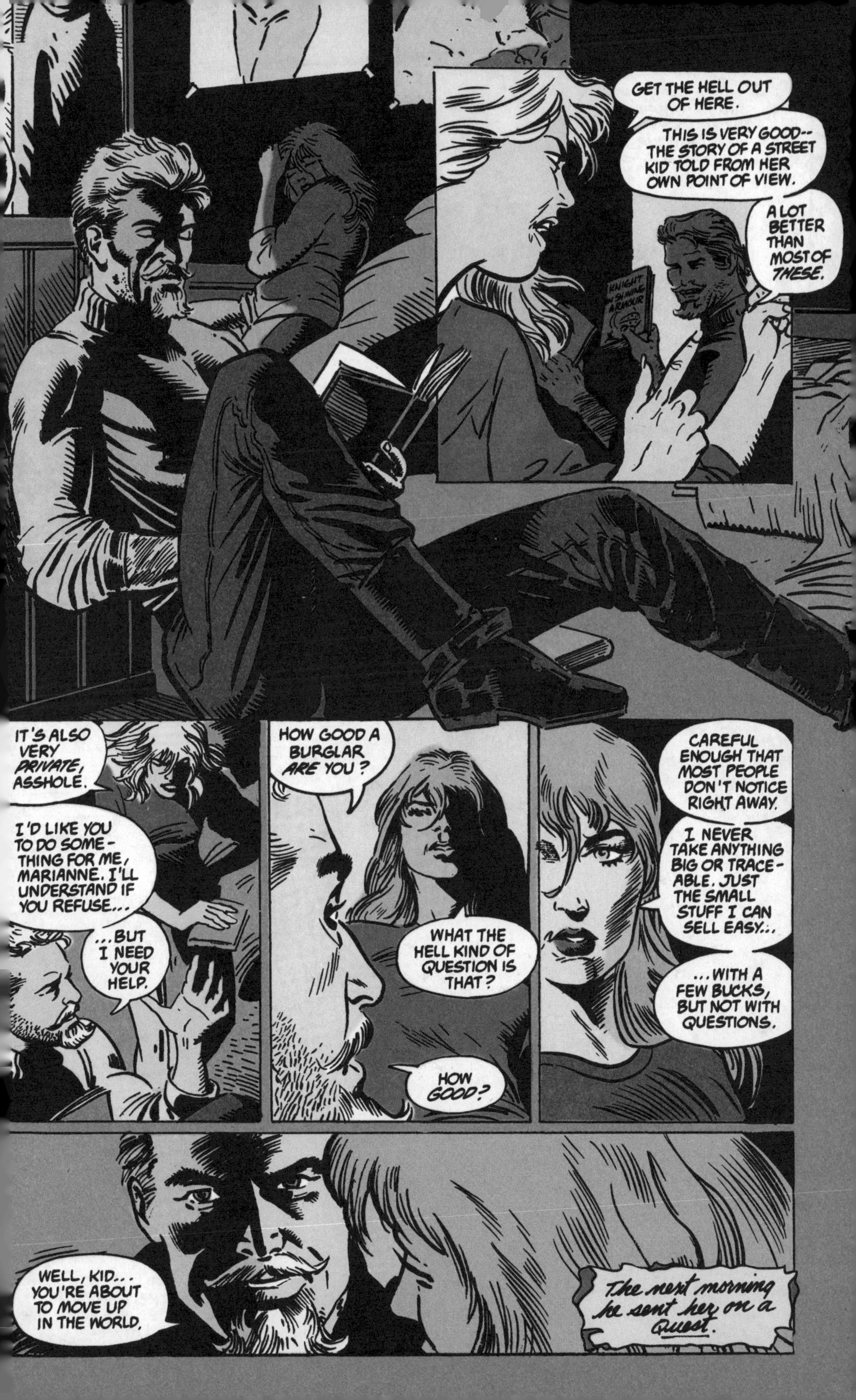
GET THE HELL OUT OF HERE.
THIS IS VERY GOOD-- THE STORY OF A STREET KID TOLD FROM HER OWN POINT OF VIEW.
A LOT BETTER THAN MOST OF THESE.
KNIGHT IN SHINING ARMOUR
IT'S ALSO VERY PRIVATE, ASSHOLE.
I'D LIKE YOU TO DO SOME-THING FOR ME, MARIANNE. I'LL UNDERSTAND IF YOU REFUSE...
...BUT I NEED YOUR HELP.
HOW GOOD A BURGLAR ARE YOU?
WHAT THE HELL KIND OF QUESTION IS THAT?
HOW GOOD?
CAREFUL ENOUGH THAT MOST PEOPLE DON'T NOTICE RIGHT AWAY.
I NEVER TAKE ANYTHING BIG OR TRACE-ABLE. JUST THE SMALL STUFF I CAN SELL EASY...
...WITH A FEW BUCKS, BUT NOT WITH QUESTIONS.
WELL, KID... YOU'RE ABOUT TO MOVE UP IN THE WORLD.
The next morning he sent her on a Quest.

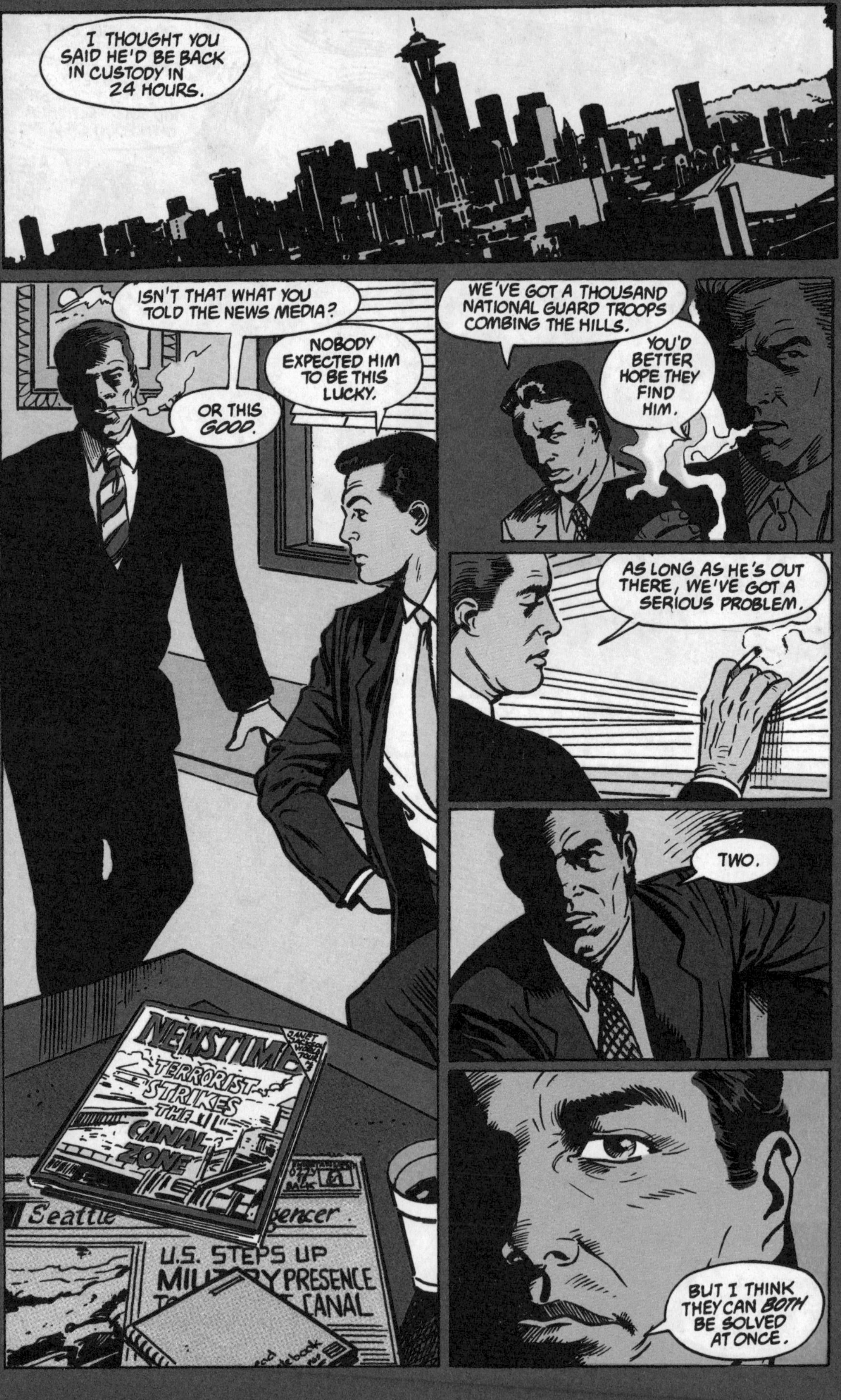
I THOUGHT YOU SAID HE'D BE BACK IN CUSTODY IN 24 HOURS.
ISN'T THAT WHAT YOU TOLD THE NEWS MEDIA?
NOBODY EXPECTED HIM TO BE THIS LUCKY.
OR THIS GOOD.
NEWSTIME
TERRORIST STRIKES THE CANAL ZONE
U.S. STEPS UP
WE'VE GOT A THOUSAND NATIONAL GUARD TROOPS COMBING THE HILLS.
YOU'D BETTER HOPE THEY FIND HIM.
AS LONG AS HE'S OUT THERE, WE'VE GOT A SERIOUS PROBLEM.
TWO.
BUT I THINK THEY CAN BOTH BE SOLVED AT ONCE.

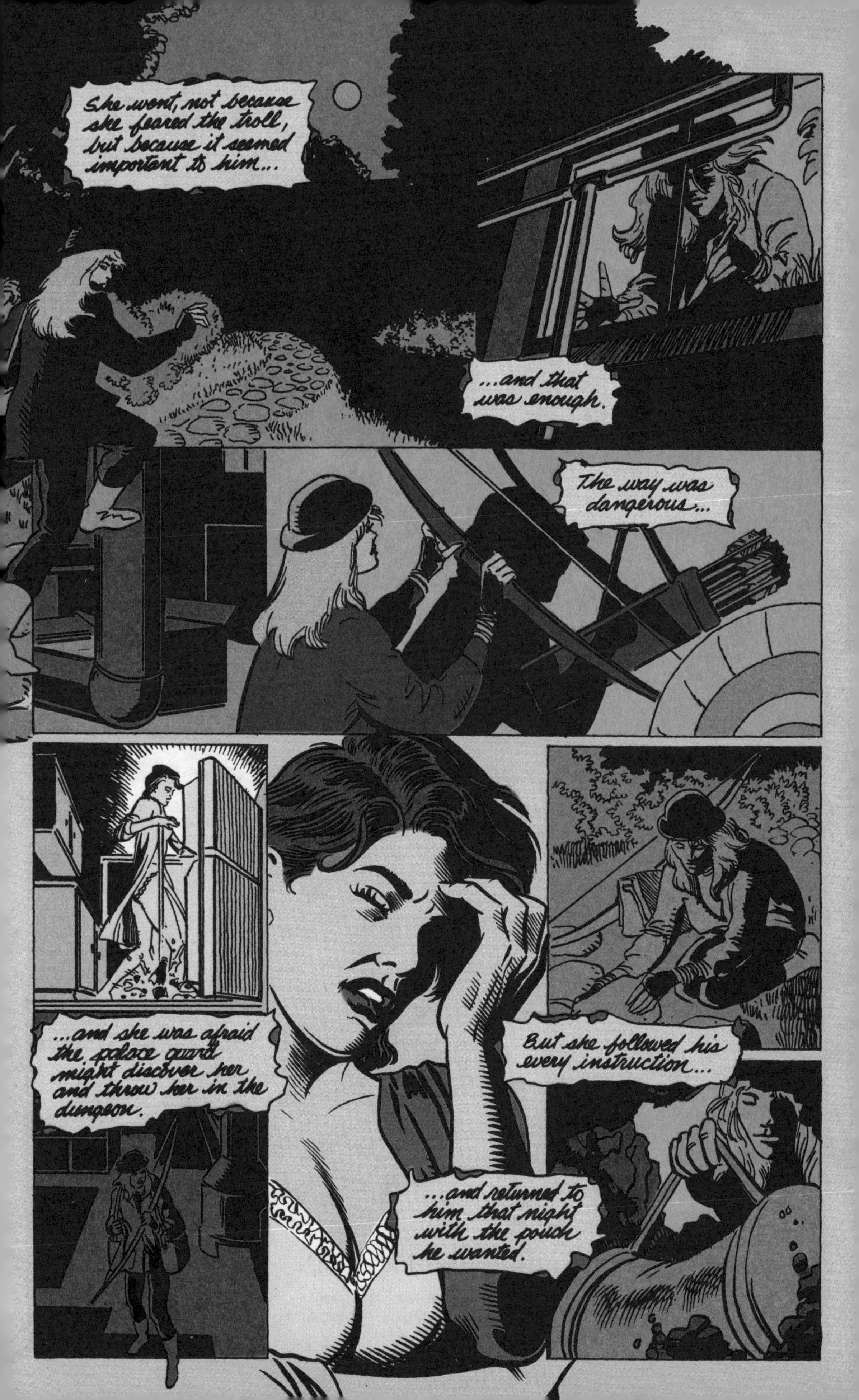
She went, not because she feared the troll, but because it seemed important to him...
...and that was enough.
The way was dangerous...
...and she was afraid the palace guard might discover her and throw her in the dungeon.
But she followed his every instruction...
...and returned to him that night with the pouch he wanted.

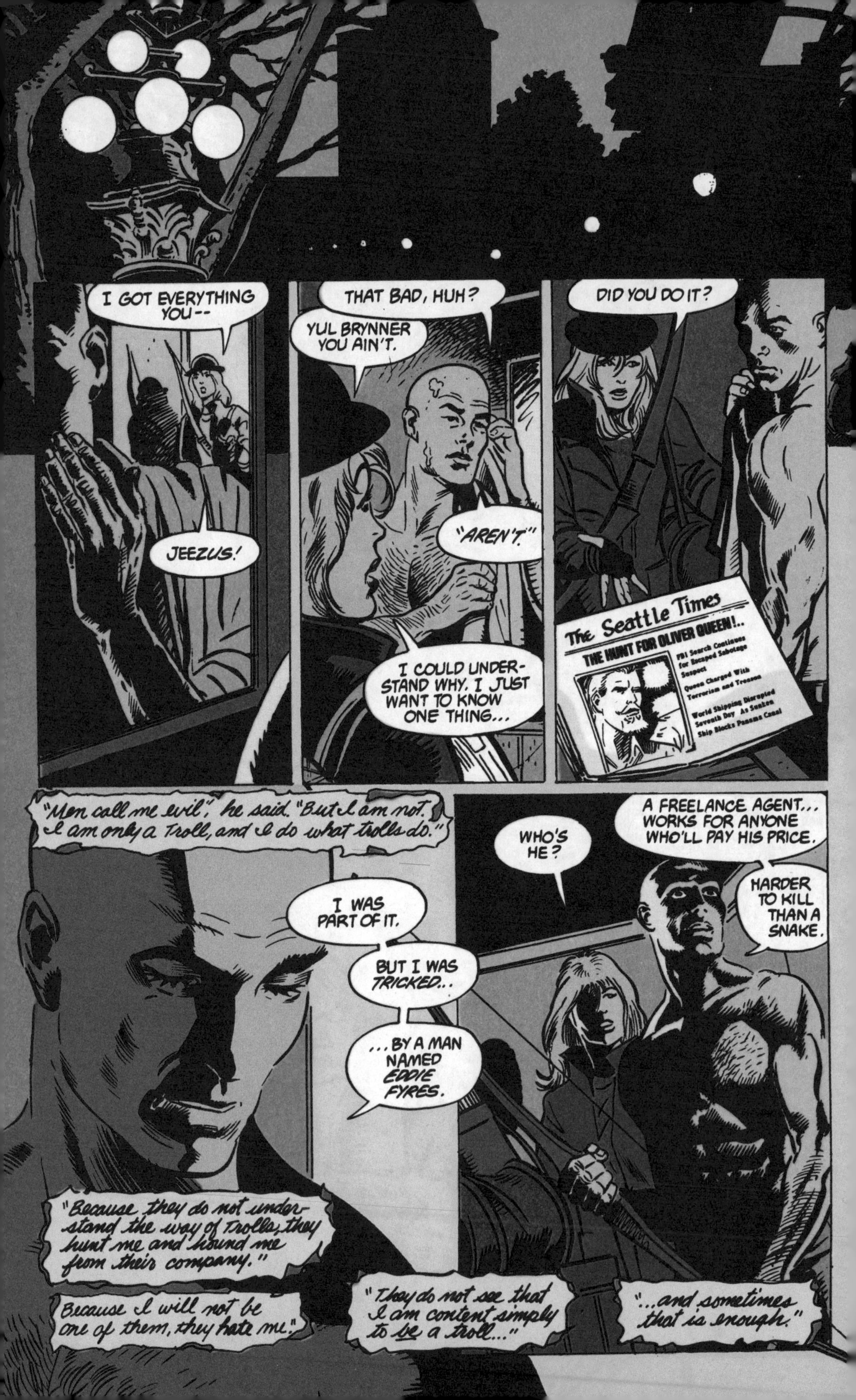
I GOT EVERYTHING YOU--
JEEZUS!
THAT BAD, HUH?
YUL BRYNNER YOU AIN'T.
"AREN'T."
I COULD UNDERSTAND WHY. I JUST WANT TO KNOW ONE THING...
DID YOU DO IT?
The Seattle Times
THE HUNT FOR OLIVER QUEEN!..
FBI Search Continues for Escaped Sabotage Suspect
Queen Charged With Terrorism and Treason
World Shipping Disrupted Seventh Day As Sunken Ship Blocks Panama Canal
"Men call me evil," he said. "But I am not. I am only a Troll, and I do what trolls do."
I WAS PART OF IT.
BUT I WAS TRICKED...
...BY A MAN NAMED EDDIE FYRES.
"Because they do not understand the way of Trolls, they hunt me and hound me from their company."
Because I will not be one of them, they hate me."
WHO'S HE?
A FREELANCE AGENT... WORKS FOR ANYONE WHO'LL PAY HIS PRICE.
HARDER TO KILL THAN A SNAKE.
"They do not see that I am content simply to be a troll..."
"...and sometimes that is enough."

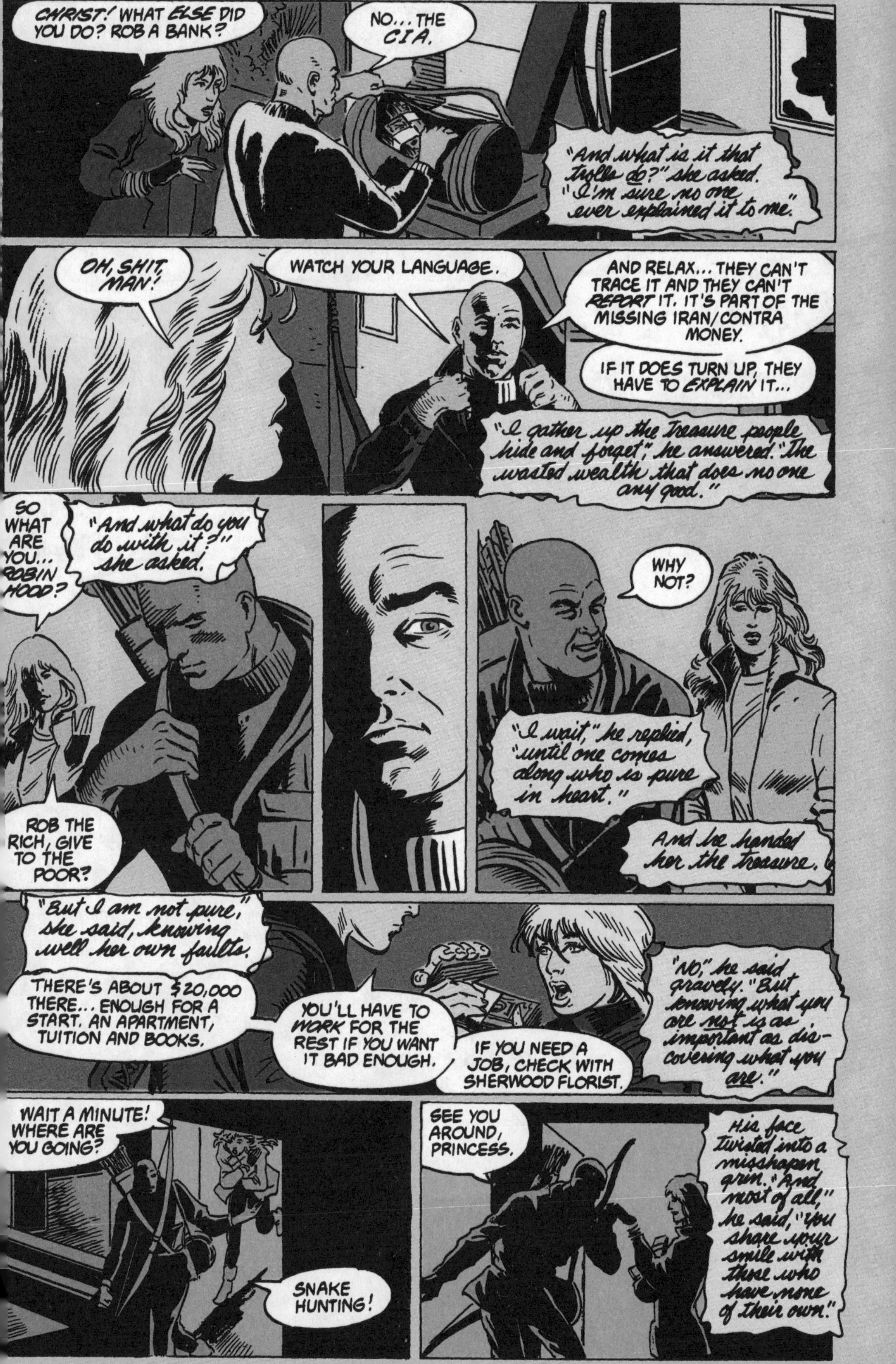
CHRIST! WHAT ELSE DID YOU DO? ROB A BANK?
NO... THE CIA.
"And what is it that trolls do?" she asked. "I'm sure no one ever explained it to me."
OH, SHIT, MAN!
WATCH YOUR LANGUAGE.
AND RELAX... THEY CAN'T TRACE IT AND THEY CAN'T REPORT IT. IT'S PART OF THE MISSING IRAN/CONTRA MONEY.
IF IT DOES TURN UP, THEY HAVE TO EXPLAIN IT...
"I gather up the Treasure people hide and forget," he answered. "The wasted wealth that does no one any good."
SO WHAT ARE YOU... ROBIN HOOD?
"And what do you do with it?" she asked.
ROB THE RICH, GIVE TO THE POOR?
WHY NOT?
"I wait," he replied, "until one comes along who is pure in heart."
And he handed her the treasure.
"But I am not pure," she said, knowing well her own faults.
THERE'S ABOUT $20,000 THERE... ENOUGH FOR A START. AN APARTMENT, TUITION AND BOOKS.
YOU'LL HAVE TO WORK FOR THE REST IF YOU WANT IT BAD ENOUGH.
IF YOU NEED A JOB, CHECK WITH SHERWOOD FLORIST.
"No," he said gravely. "But knowing what you are not is as important as discovering what you are."
WAIT A MINUTE! WHERE ARE YOU GOING?
SNAKE HUNTING!
SEE YOU AROUND, PRINCESS.
His face twisted into a misshapen grin. "And most of all," he said, "you share your smile with those who have none of their own."

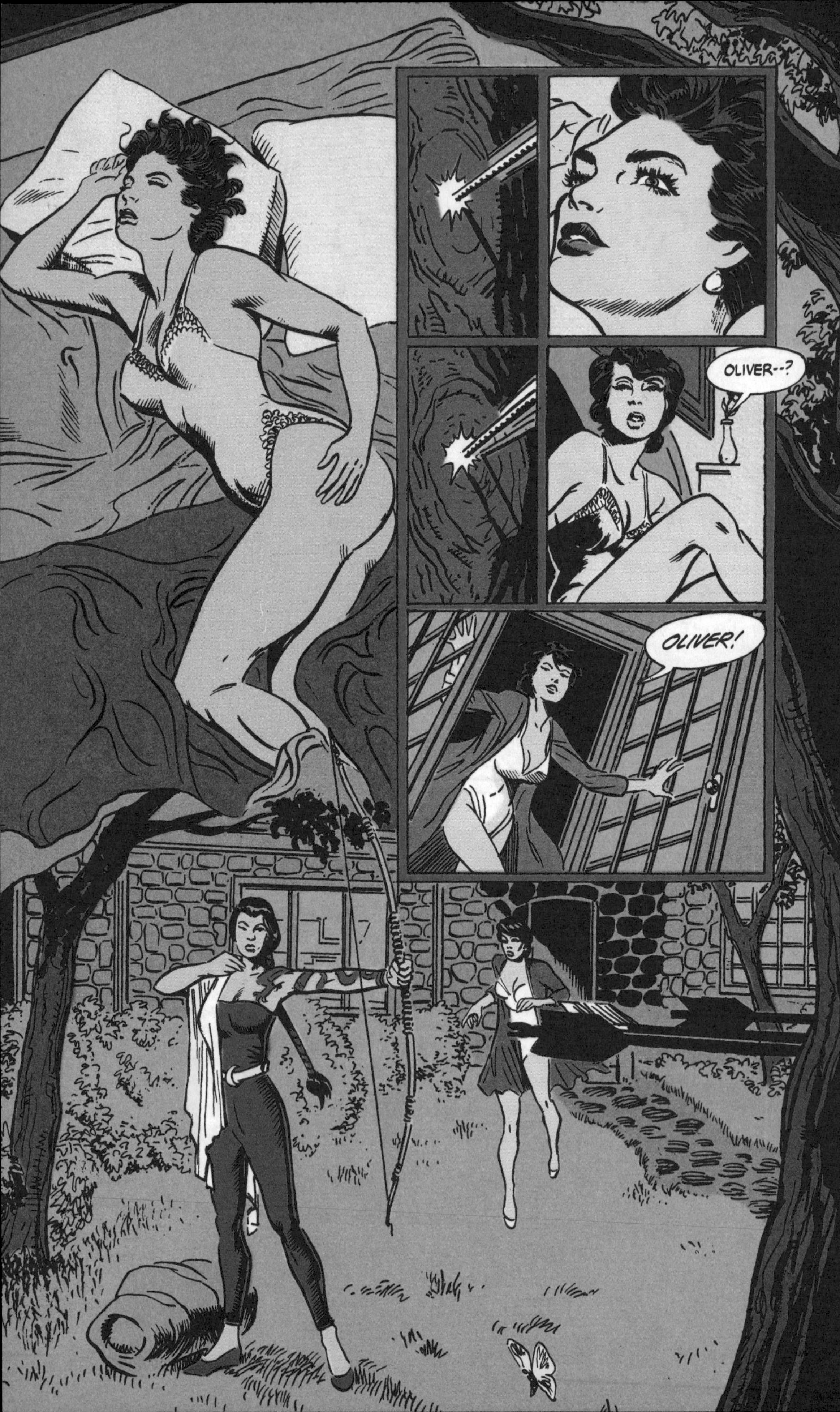
OLIVER--?
OLIVER!

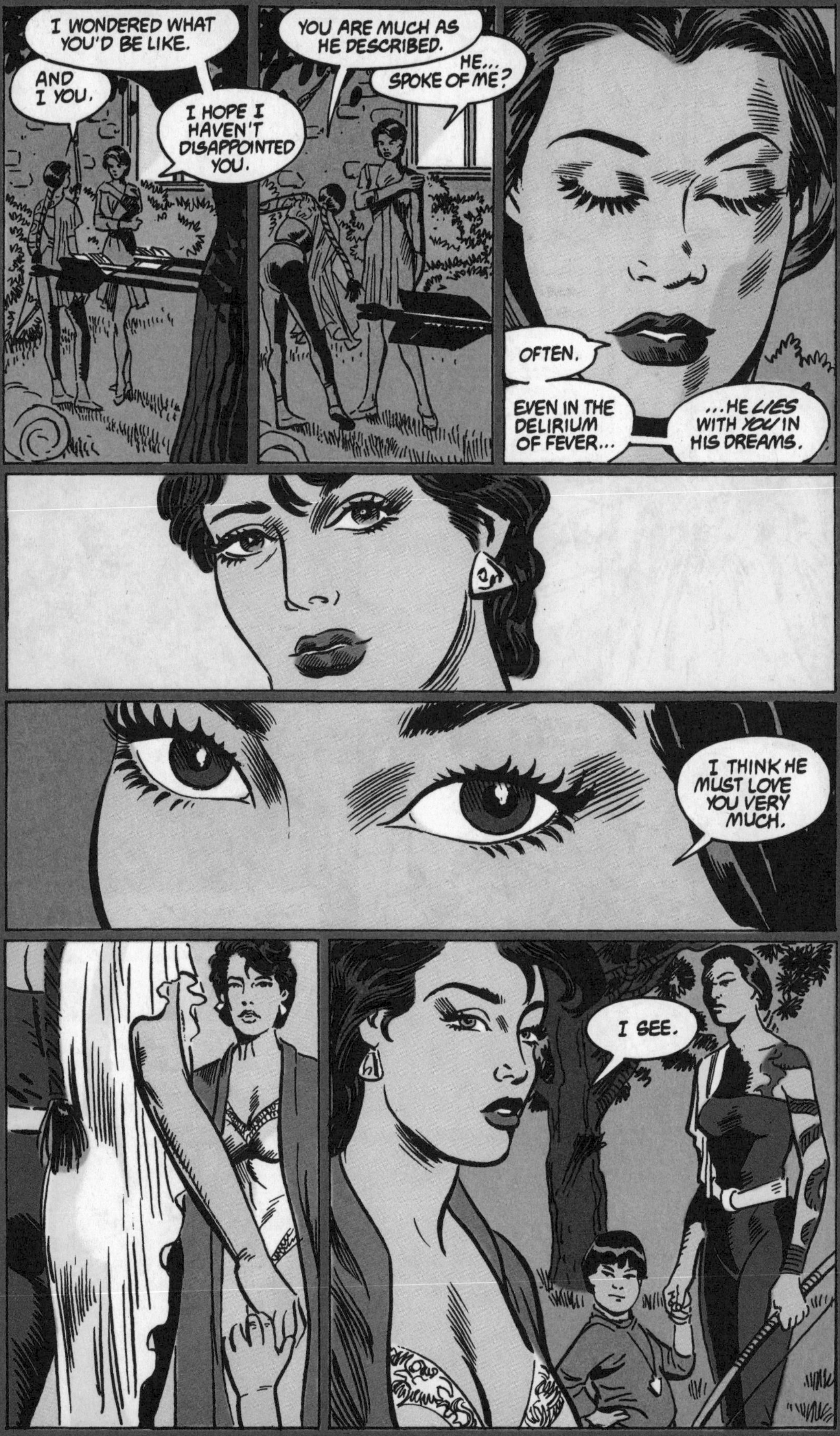
I WONDERED WHAT YOU'D BE LIKE.
AND I YOU.
I HOPE I HAVEN'T DISAPPOINTED YOU.
YOU ARE MUCH AS HE DESCRIBED.
HE... SPOKE OF ME?
OFTEN.
EVEN IN THE DELIRIUM OF FEVER...
...HE *LIES* WITH *YOU* IN HIS DREAMS.
I THINK HE MUST LOVE YOU VERY MUCH.
I SEE.

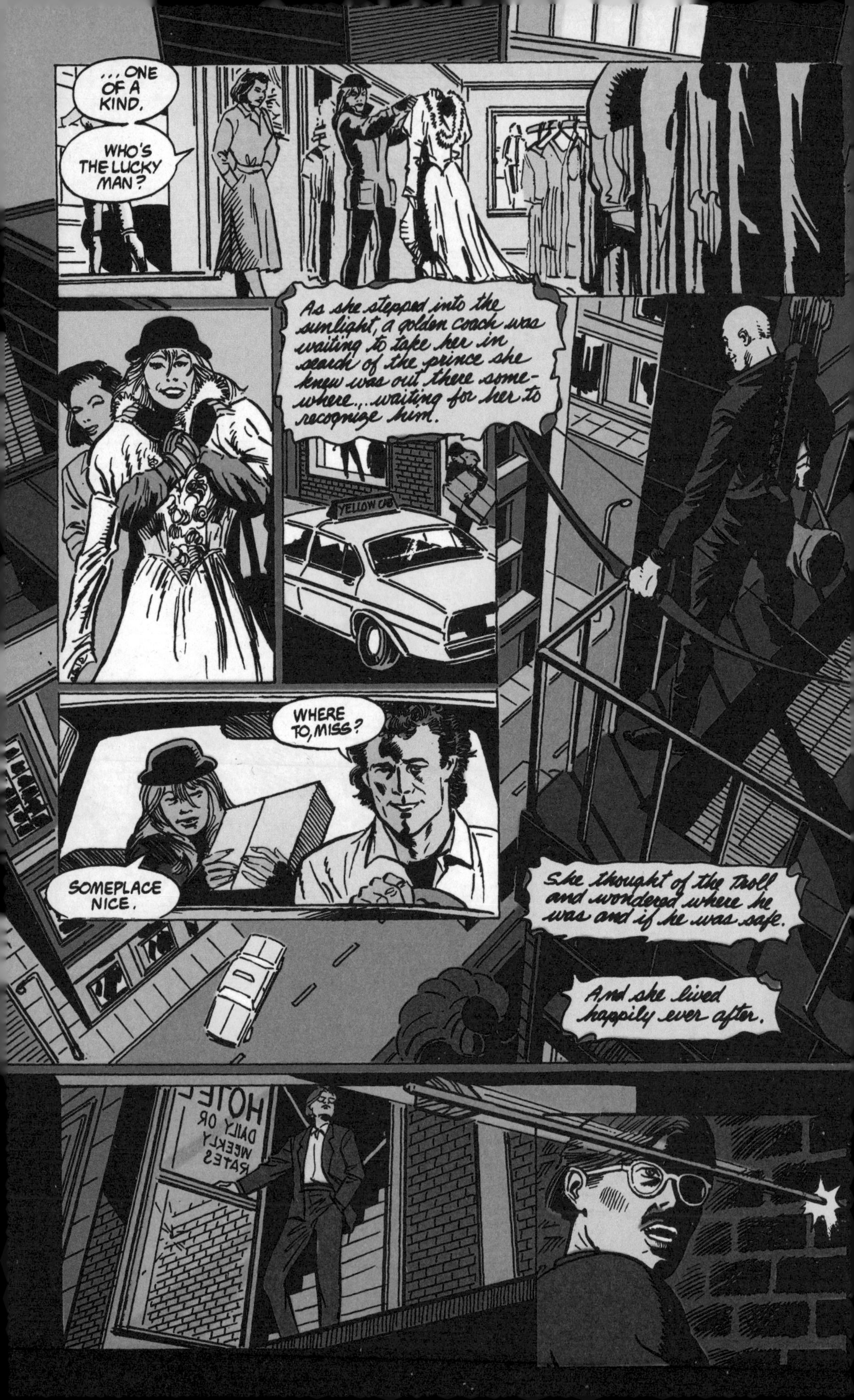
...ONE OF A KIND.
WHO'S THE LUCKY MAN?
As she stepped into the sunlight, a golden coach was waiting to take her in search of the prince she knew was out there somewhere... waiting for her to recognize him.
YELLOW CAB
WHERE TO, MISS?
SOMEPLACE NICE.
She thought of the Troll and wondered where he was and if he was safe.
And she lived happily ever after.
HOTEL
DAILY OR WEEKLY RATES

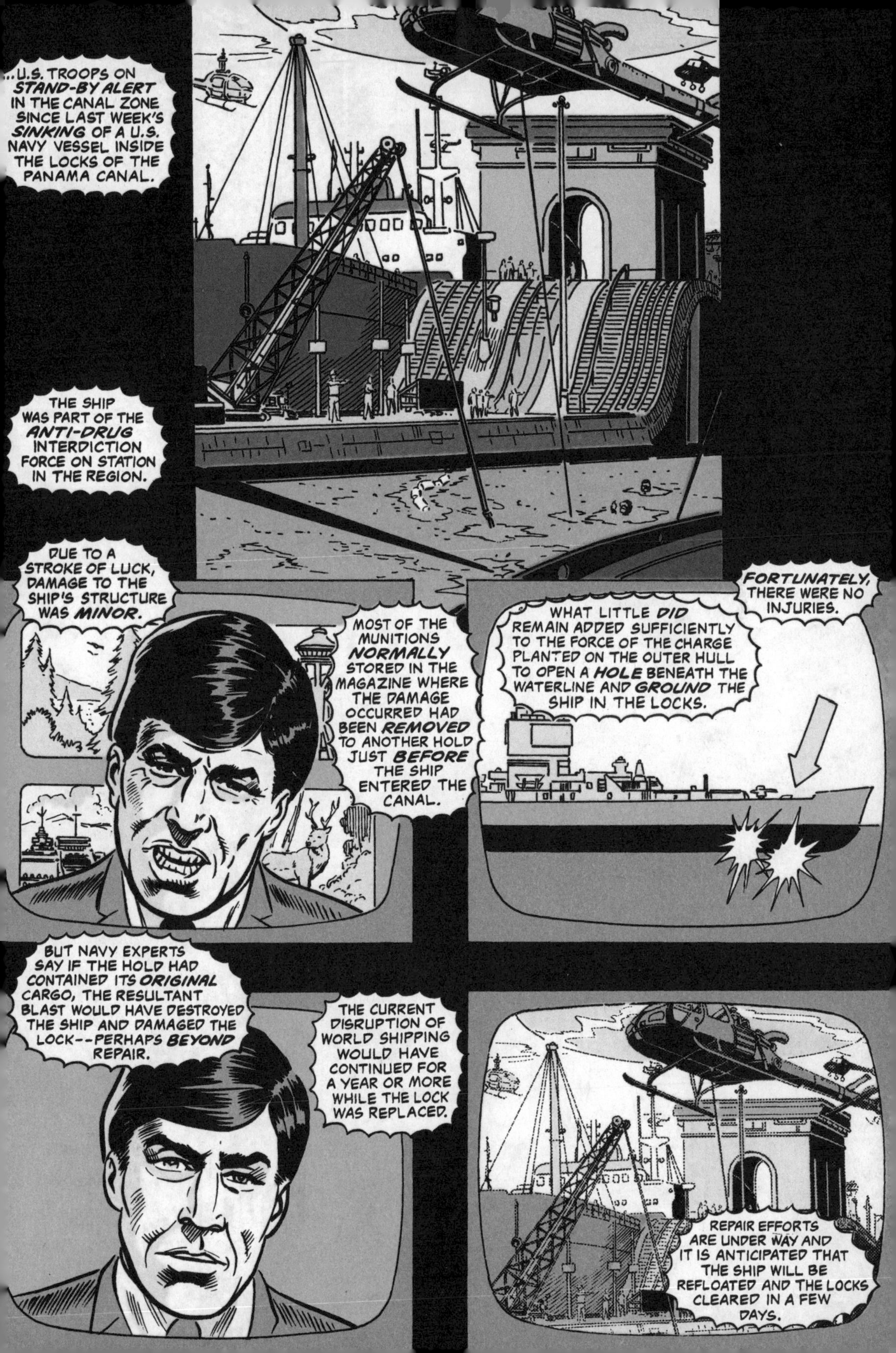

...U.S. TROOPS ON STAND-BY ALERT IN THE CANAL ZONE SINCE LAST WEEK'S SINKING OF A U.S. NAVY VESSEL INSIDE THE LOCKS OF THE PANAMA CANAL.
THE SHIP WAS PART OF THE ANTI-DRUG INTERDICTION FORCE ON STATION IN THE REGION.
DUE TO A STROKE OF LUCK, DAMAGE TO THE SHIP'S STRUCTURE WAS MINOR.
MOST OF THE MUNITIONS NORMALLY STORED IN THE MAGAZINE WHERE THE DAMAGE OCCURRED HAD BEEN REMOVED TO ANOTHER HOLD JUST BEFORE THE SHIP ENTERED THE CANAL.
WHAT LITTLE DID REMAIN ADDED SUFFICIENTLY TO THE FORCE OF THE CHARGE PLANTED ON THE OUTER HULL TO OPEN A HOLE BENEATH THE WATERLINE AND GROUND THE SHIP IN THE LOCKS.
FORTUNATELY, THERE WERE NO INJURIES.
BUT NAVY EXPERTS SAY IF THE HOLD HAD CONTAINED ITS ORIGINAL CARGO, THE RESULTANT BLAST WOULD HAVE DESTROYED THE SHIP AND DAMAGED THE LOCK--PERHAPS BEYOND REPAIR.
THE CURRENT DISRUPTION OF WORLD SHIPPING WOULD HAVE CONTINUED FOR A YEAR OR MORE WHILE THE LOCK WAS REPLACED.
REPAIR EFFORTS ARE UNDER WAY AND IT IS ANTICIPATED THAT THE SHIP WILL BE REFLOATED AND THE LOCKS CLEARED IN A FEW DAYS.

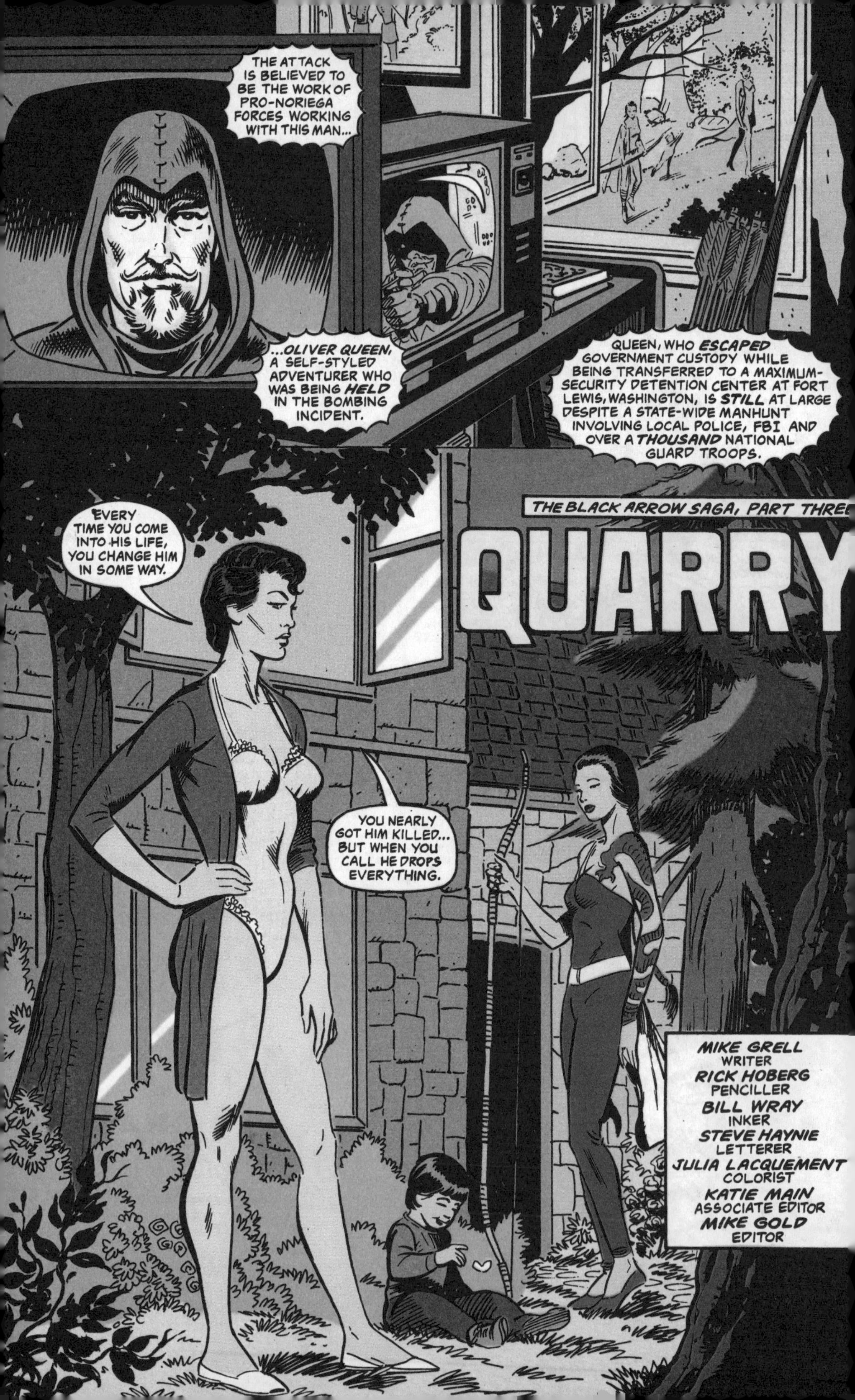
THE ATTACK IS BELIEVED TO BE THE WORK OF PRO-NORIEGA FORCES WORKING WITH THIS MAN...
...OLIVER QUEEN, A SELF-STYLED ADVENTURER WHO WAS BEING HELD IN THE BOMBING INCIDENT.
QUEEN, WHO ESCAPED GOVERNMENT CUSTODY WHILE BEING TRANSFERRED TO A MAXIMUM-SECURITY DETENTION CENTER AT FORT LEWIS, WASHINGTON, IS STILL AT LARGE DESPITE A STATE-WIDE MANHUNT INVOLVING LOCAL POLICE, FBI AND OVER A THOUSAND NATIONAL GUARD TROOPS.
THE BLACK ARROW SAGA, PART THREE
QUARRY
EVERY TIME YOU COME INTO HIS LIFE, YOU CHANGE HIM IN SOME WAY.
YOU NEARLY GOT HIM KILLED... BUT WHEN YOU CALL HE DROPS EVERYTHING.
MIKE GRELL WRITER
RICK HOBERG PENCILLER
BILL WRAY INKER
STEVE HAYNIE LETTERER
JULIA LACQUEMENT COLORIST
KATIE MAIN ASSOCIATE EDITOR
MIKE GOLD EDITOR

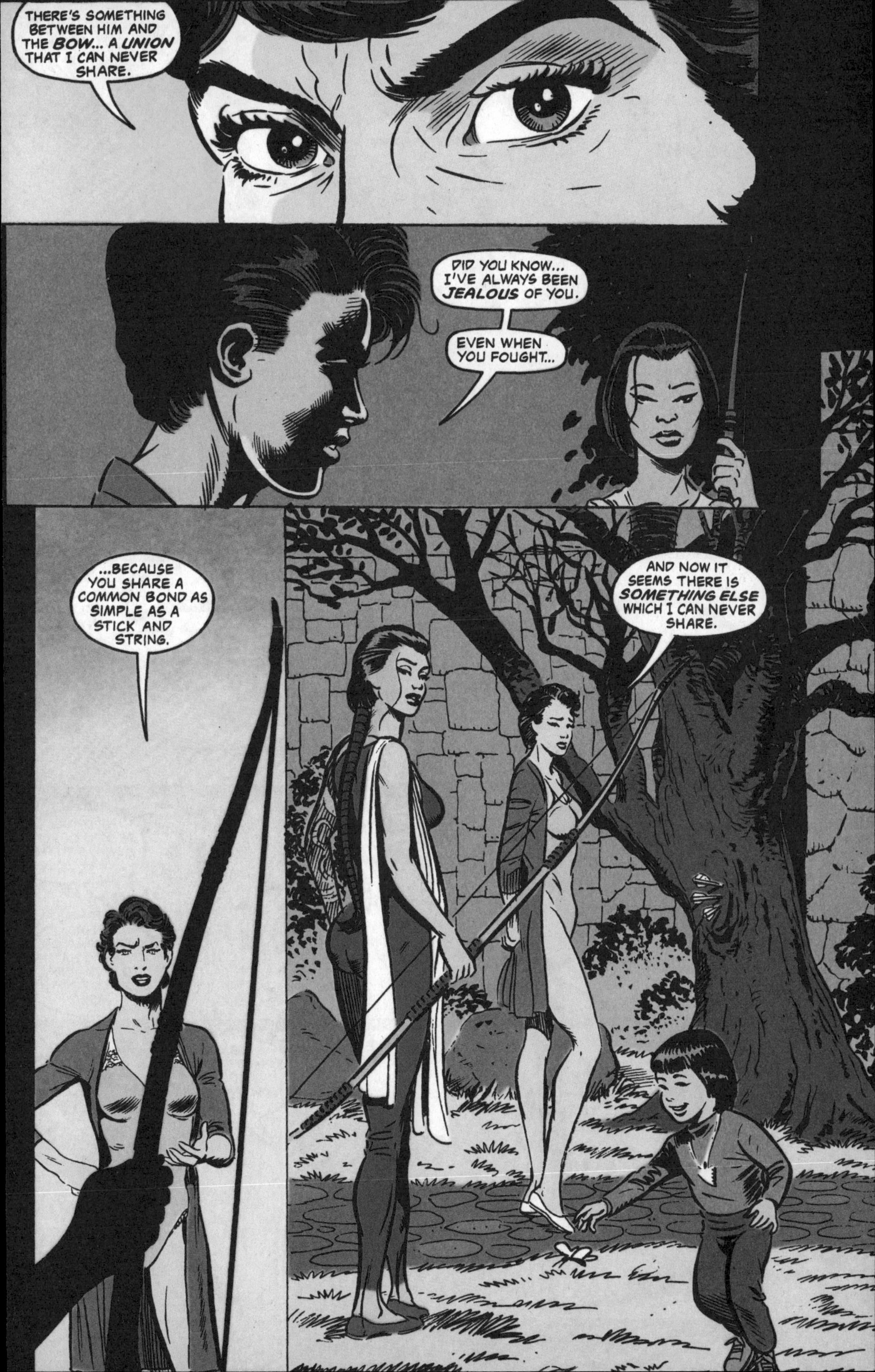
THERE'S SOMETHING BETWEEN HIM AND THE BOW... A UNION THAT I CAN NEVER SHARE.
DID YOU KNOW... I'VE ALWAYS BEEN JEALOUS OF YOU.
EVEN WHEN YOU FOUGHT...
...BECAUSE YOU SHARE A COMMON BOND AS SIMPLE AS A STICK AND STRING.
AND NOW IT SEEMS THERE IS SOMETHING ELSE WHICH I CAN NEVER SHARE.

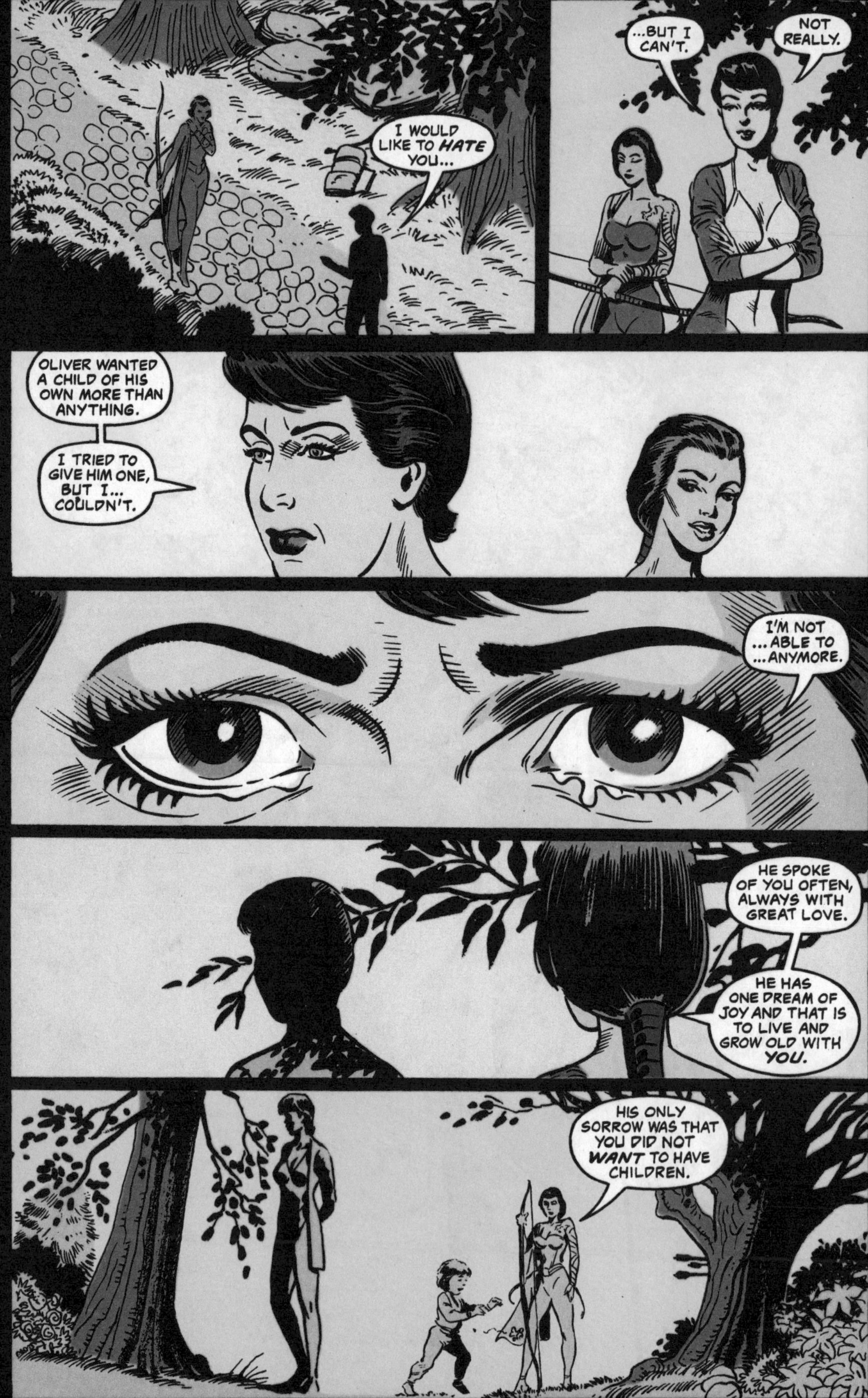
I WOULD LIKE TO HATE YOU...
...BUT I CAN'T.
NOT REALLY.
OLIVER WANTED A CHILD OF HIS OWN MORE THAN ANYTHING.
I TRIED TO GIVE HIM ONE, BUT I... COULDN'T.
I'M NOT ...ABLE TO ...ANYMORE.
HE SPOKE OF YOU OFTEN, ALWAYS WITH GREAT LOVE.
HE HAS ONE DREAM OF JOY AND THAT IS TO LIVE AND GROW OLD WITH YOU.
HIS ONLY SORROW WAS THAT YOU DID NOT WANT TO HAVE CHILDREN.

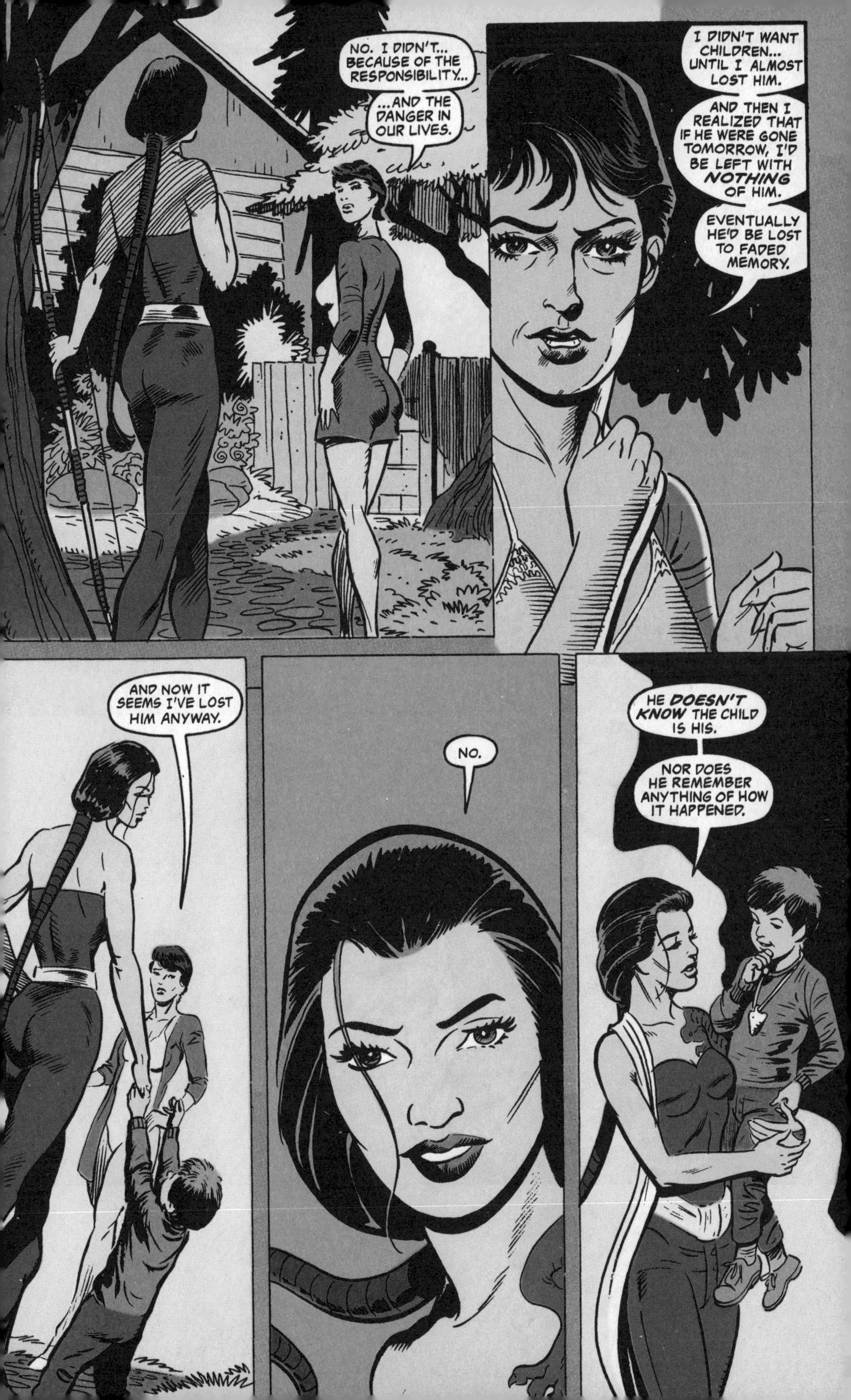
NO. I DIDN'T... BECAUSE OF THE RESPONSIBILITY...
...AND THE DANGER IN OUR LIVES.
I DIDN'T WANT CHILDREN... UNTIL I ALMOST LOST HIM.
AND THEN I REALIZED THAT IF HE WERE GONE TOMORROW, I'D BE LEFT WITH NOTHING OF HIM.
EVENTUALLY HE'D BE LOST TO FADED MEMORY.
AND NOW IT SEEMS I'VE LOST HIM ANYWAY.
NO.
HE DOESN'T KNOW THE CHILD IS HIS.
NOR DOES HE REMEMBER ANYTHING OF HOW IT HAPPENED.

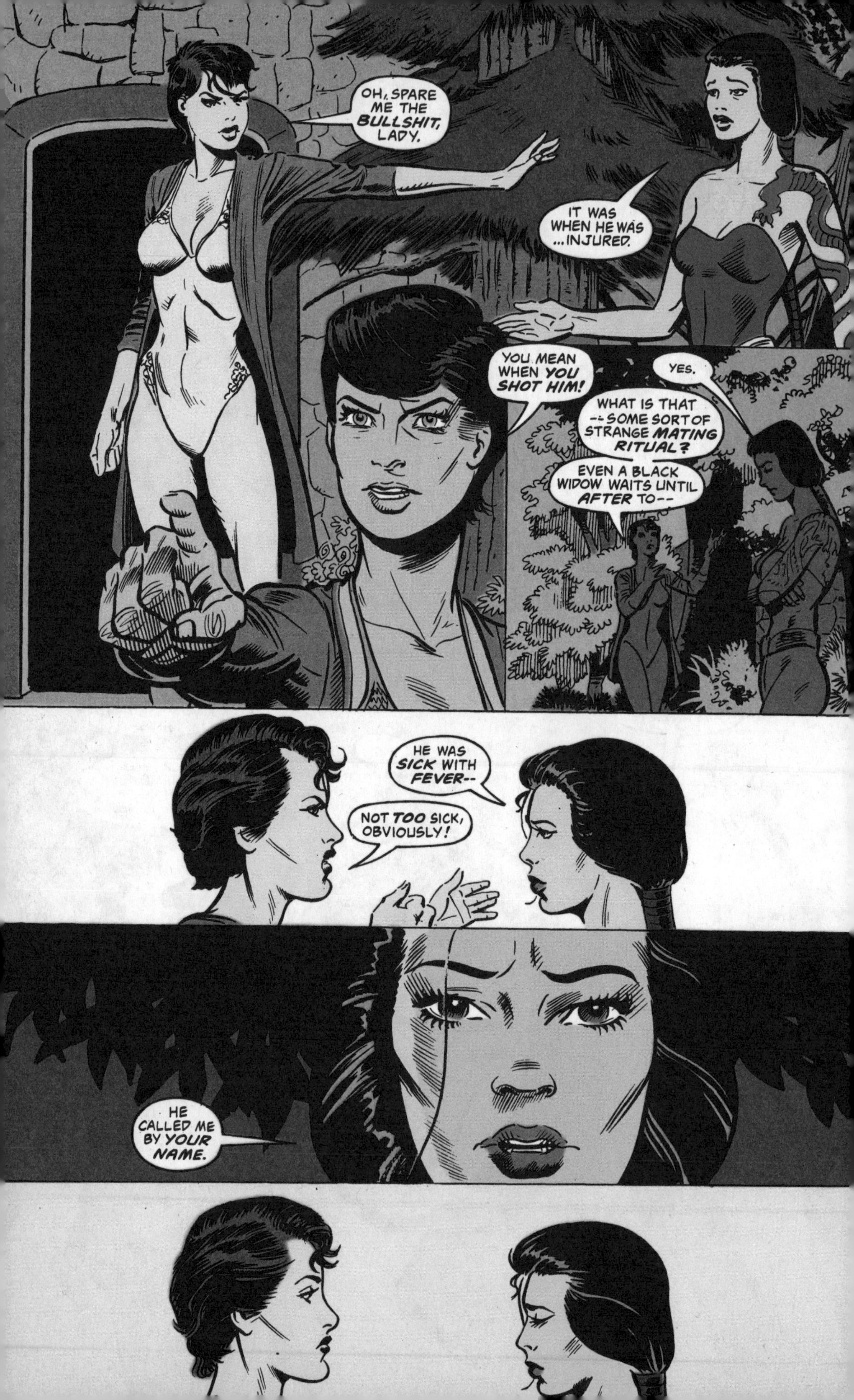
OH, SPARE ME THE BULLSHIT, LADY.
IT WAS WHEN HE WAS ...INJURED.
YOU MEAN WHEN YOU SHOT HIM!
YES.
WHAT IS THAT -- SOME SORT OF STRANGE MATING RITUAL?
EVEN A BLACK WIDOW WAITS UNTIL AFTER TO--
HE WAS SICK WITH FEVER--
NOT TOO SICK, OBVIOUSLY!
HE CALLED ME BY YOUR NAME.

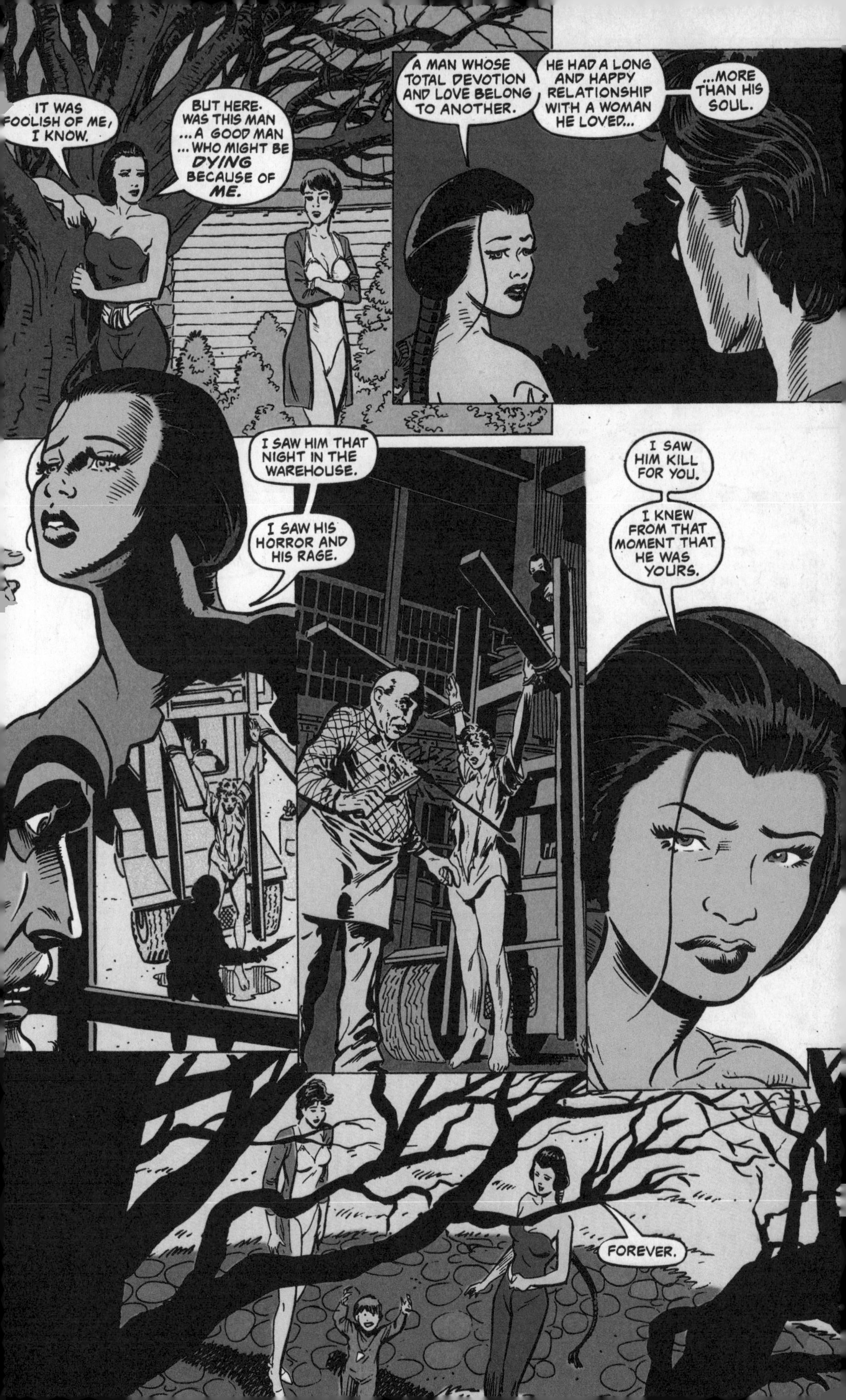
IT WAS FOOLISH OF ME, I KNOW.
BUT HERE WAS THIS MAN ...A GOOD MAN ...WHO MIGHT BE DYING BECAUSE OF ME.
A MAN WHOSE TOTAL DEVOTION AND LOVE BELONG TO ANOTHER.
HE HAD A LONG AND HAPPY RELATIONSHIP WITH A WOMAN HE LOVED...
...MORE THAN HIS SOUL.
I SAW HIM THAT NIGHT IN THE WAREHOUSE.
I SAW HIS HORROR AND HIS RAGE.
I SAW HIM KILL FOR YOU.
I KNEW FROM THAT MOMENT THAT HE WAS YOURS.
FOREVER.

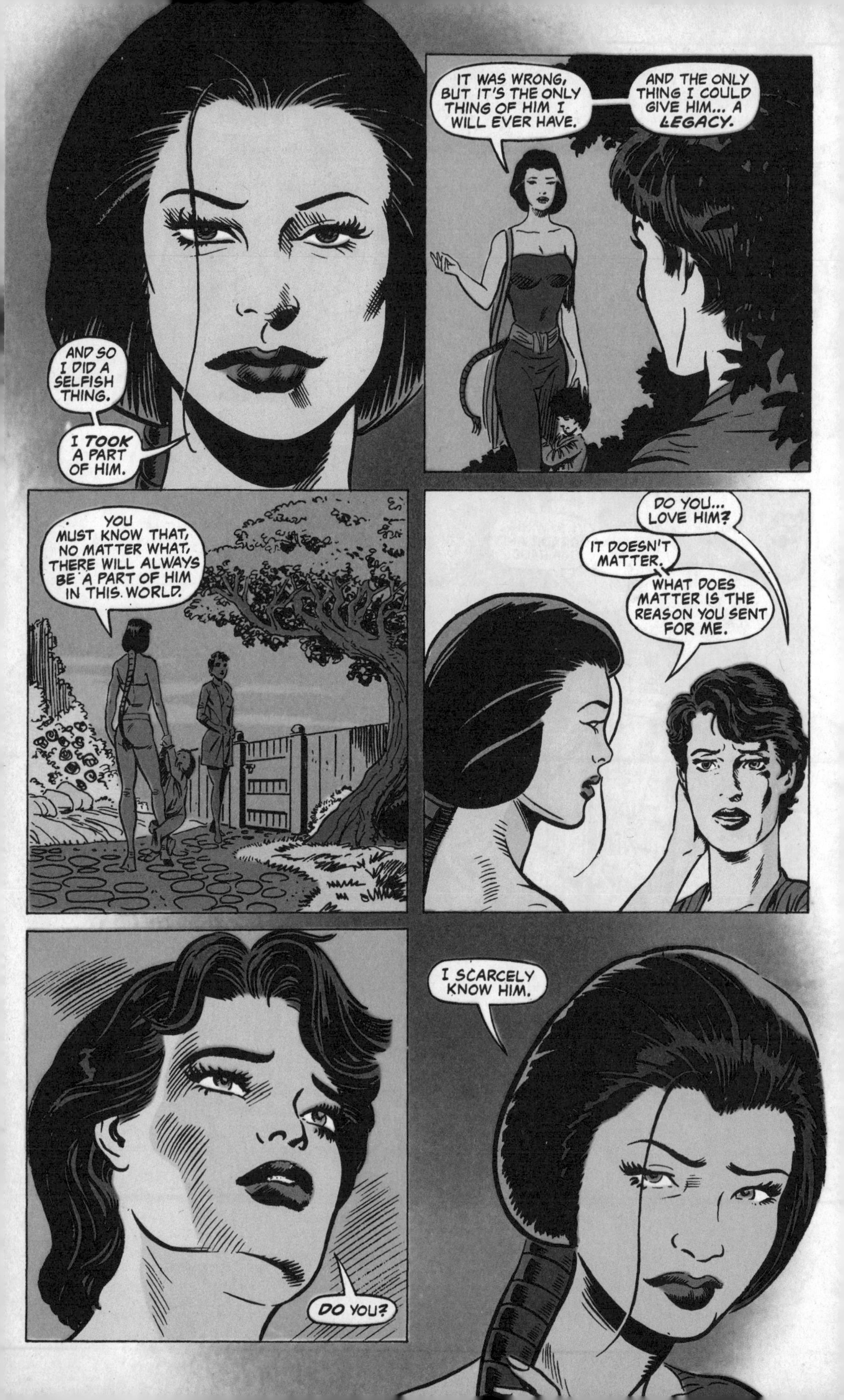
AND SO I DID A SELFISH THING.
I *TOOK* A PART OF HIM.
IT WAS WRONG, BUT IT'S THE ONLY THING OF HIM I WILL EVER HAVE.
AND THE ONLY THING I COULD GIVE HIM... A *LEGACY.*
YOU MUST KNOW THAT, NO MATTER WHAT, THERE WILL ALWAYS BE A PART OF HIM IN THIS WORLD.
DO YOU... LOVE HIM?
IT DOESN'T MATTER.
WHAT DOES MATTER IS THE REASON YOU SENT FOR ME.
*DO* YOU?
I SCARCELY KNOW HIM.

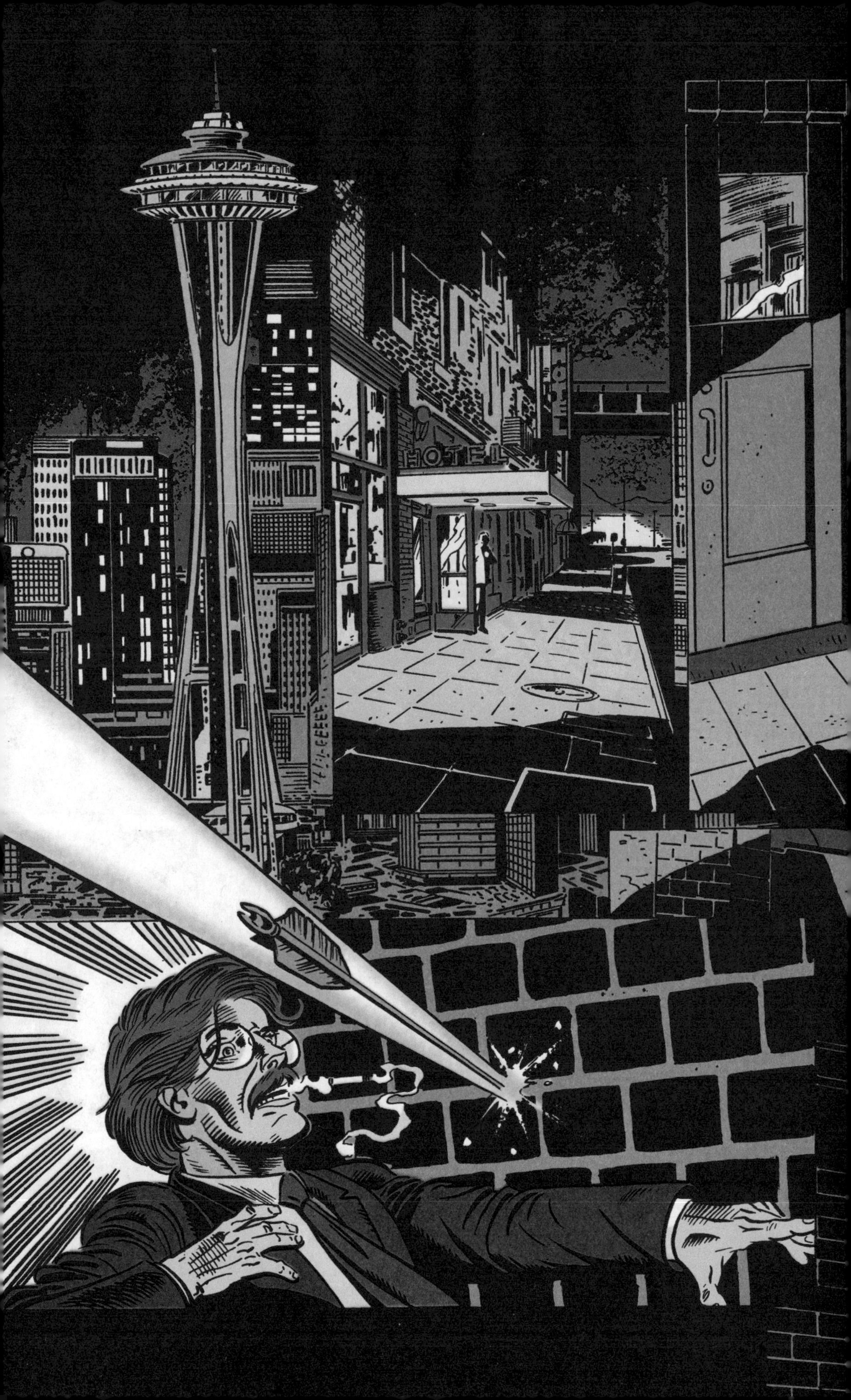
HOTEL

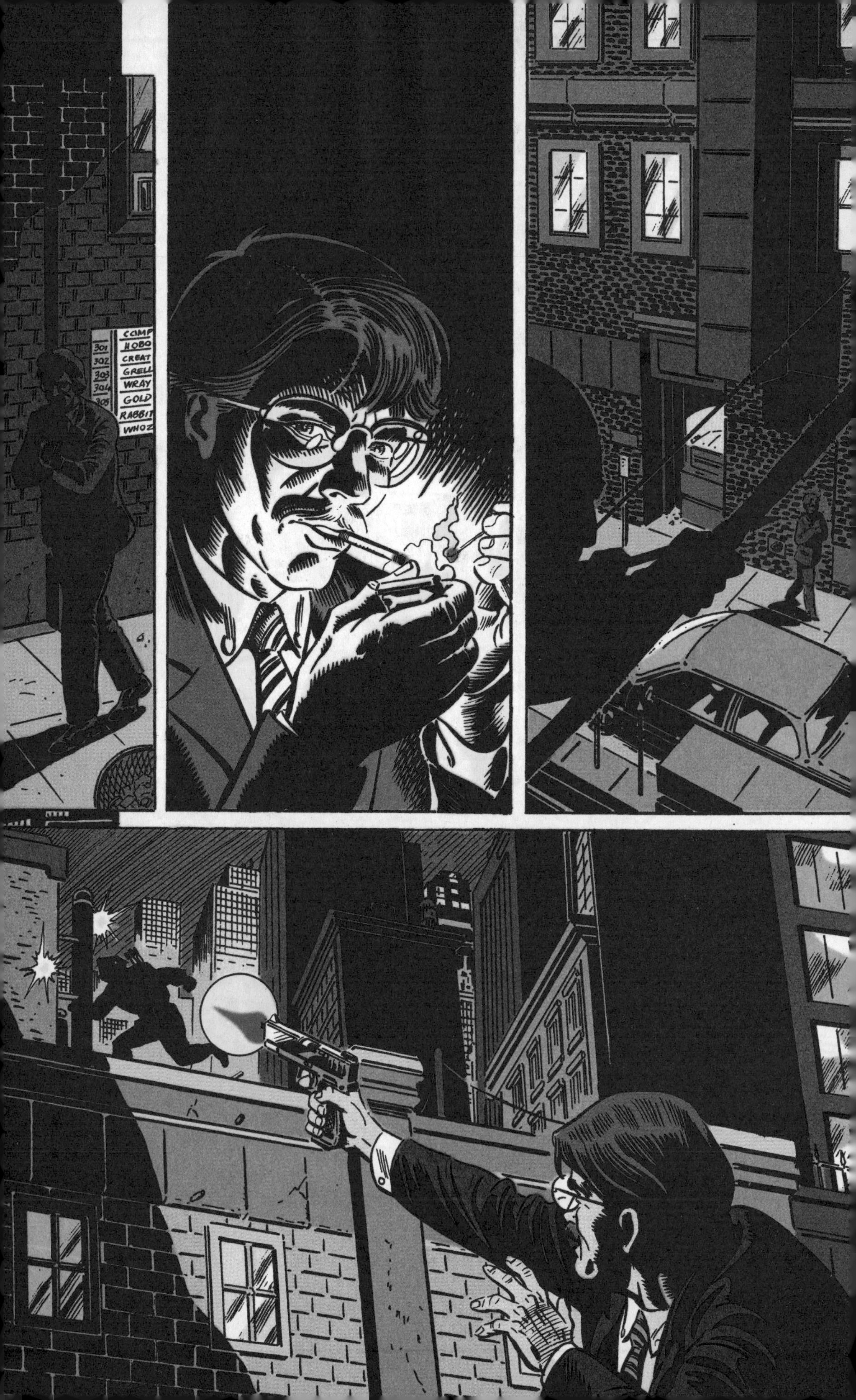

CCMP
301 HOBO
302 CREAT
303 GRELL
304 WRAY
305 GOLD
RABBIT
WHOZ

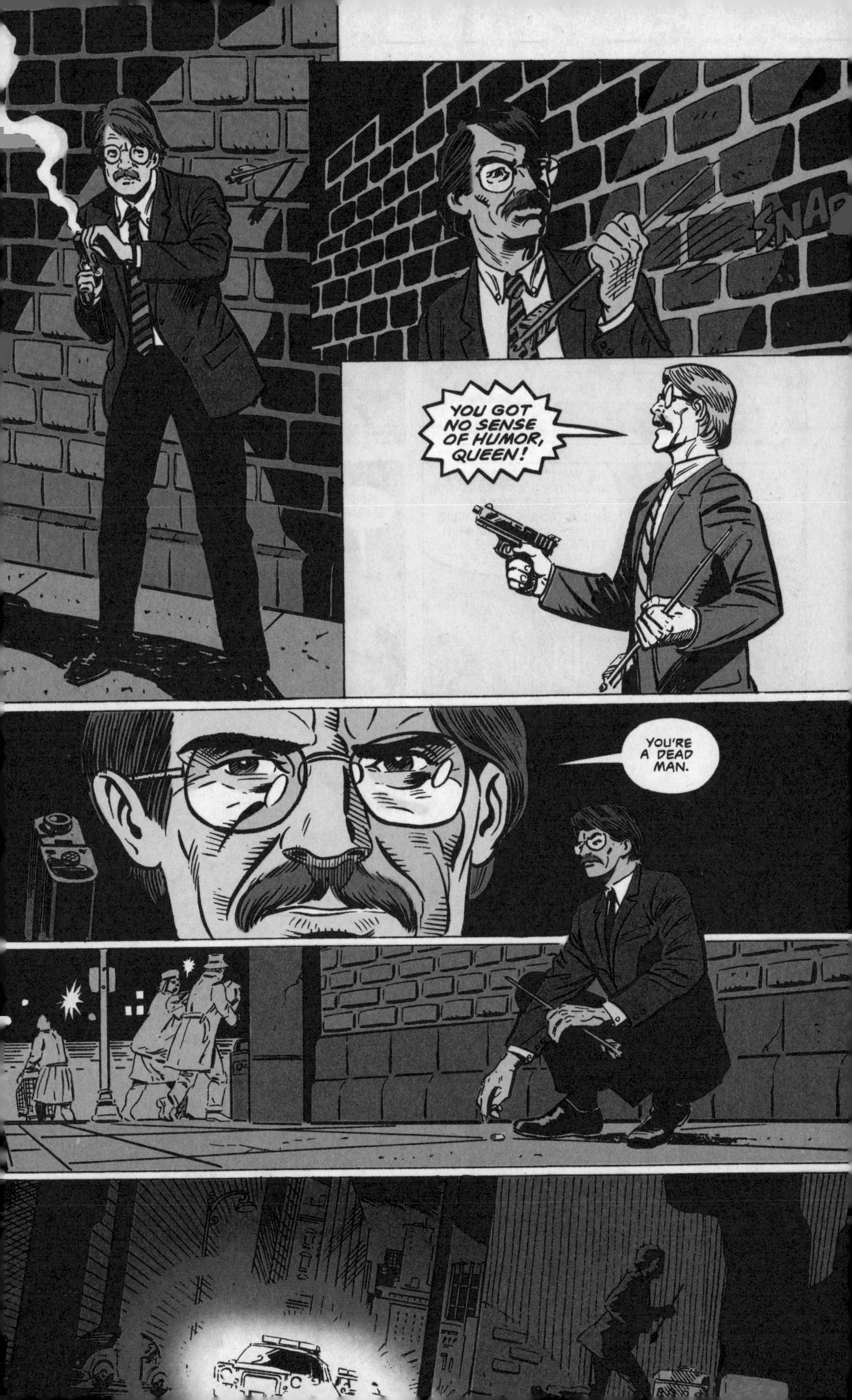
SNAP
YOU GOT NO SENSE OF HUMOR, QUEEN!
YOU'RE A DEAD MAN.

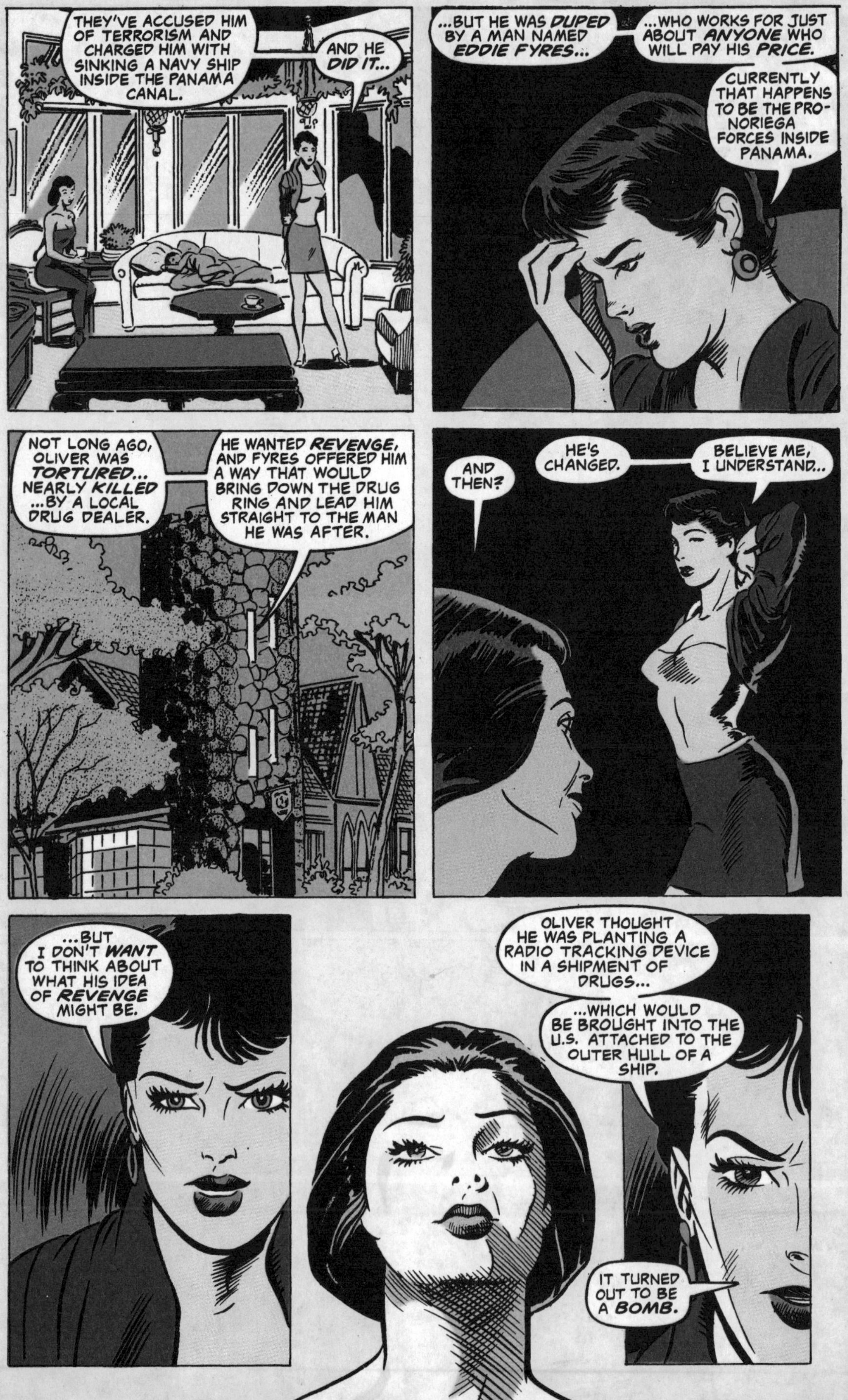
THEY'VE ACCUSED HIM OF TERRORISM AND CHARGED HIM WITH SINKING A NAVY SHIP INSIDE THE PANAMA CANAL.
AND HE DID IT...
...BUT HE WAS DUPED BY A MAN NAMED EDDIE FYRES...
...WHO WORKS FOR JUST ABOUT ANYONE WHO WILL PAY HIS PRICE.
CURRENTLY THAT HAPPENS TO BE THE PRO-NORIEGA FORCES INSIDE PANAMA.
NOT LONG AGO, OLIVER WAS TORTURED... NEARLY KILLED ...BY A LOCAL DRUG DEALER.
HE WANTED REVENGE, AND FYRES OFFERED HIM A WAY THAT WOULD BRING DOWN THE DRUG RING AND LEAD HIM STRAIGHT TO THE MAN HE WAS AFTER.
AND THEN?
HE'S CHANGED.
BELIEVE ME, I UNDERSTAND...
...BUT I DON'T WANT TO THINK ABOUT WHAT HIS IDEA OF REVENGE MIGHT BE.
OLIVER THOUGHT HE WAS PLANTING A RADIO TRACKING DEVICE IN A SHIPMENT OF DRUGS...
...WHICH WOULD BE BROUGHT INTO THE U.S. ATTACHED TO THE OUTER HULL OF A SHIP.
IT TURNED OUT TO BE A BOMB.

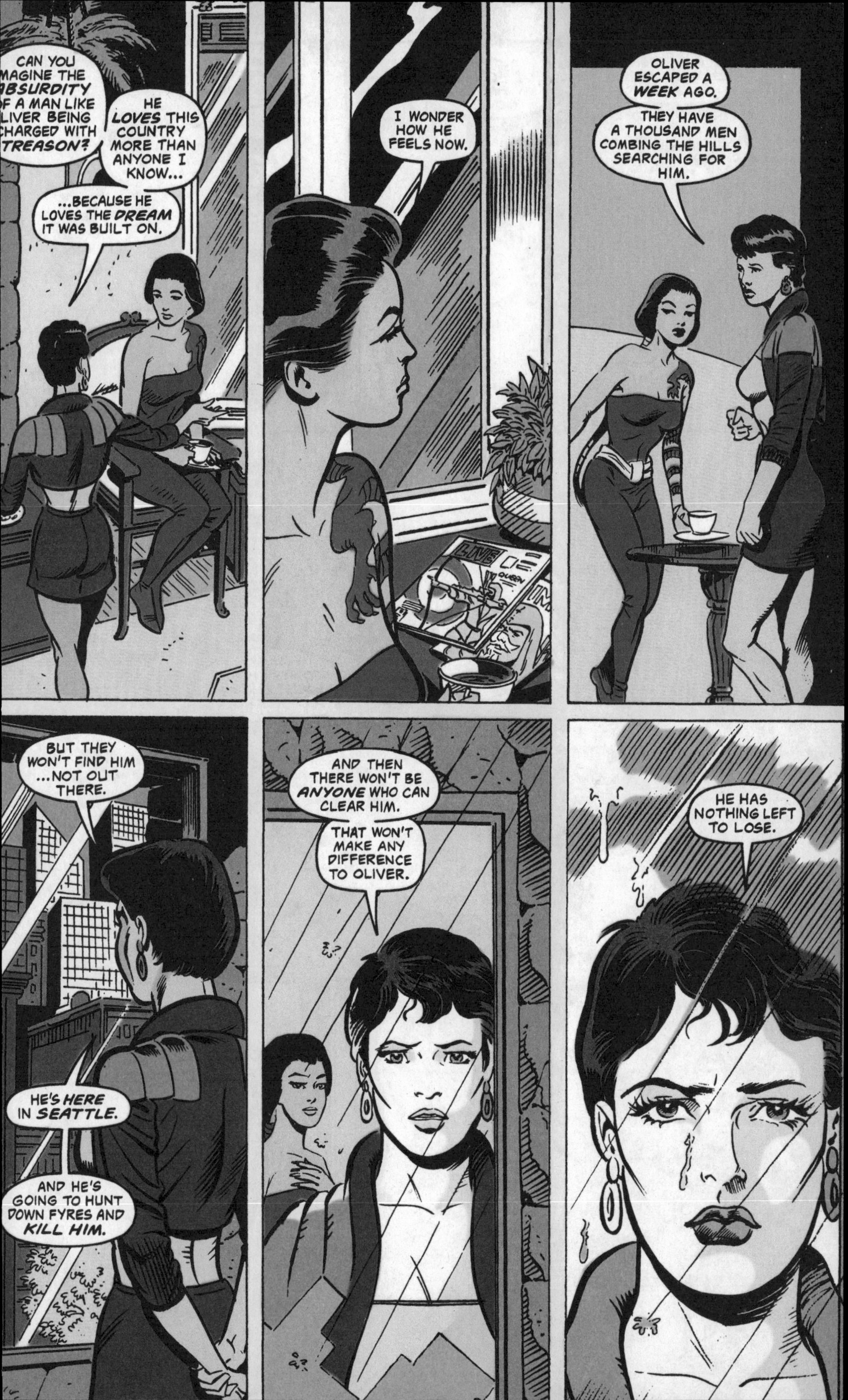
CAN YOU MAGINE THE ABSURDITY OF A MAN LIKE LIVER BEING CHARGED WITH TREASON?
HE LOVES THIS COUNTRY MORE THAN ANYONE I KNOW...
...BECAUSE HE LOVES THE DREAM IT WAS BUILT ON.
I WONDER HOW HE FEELS NOW.
OLIVER ESCAPED A WEEK AGO.
THEY HAVE A THOUSAND MEN COMBING THE HILLS SEARCHING FOR HIM.
BUT THEY WON'T FIND HIM ...NOT OUT THERE.
HE'S HERE IN SEATTLE.
AND HE'S GOING TO HUNT DOWN FYRES AND KILL HIM.
AND THEN THERE WON'T BE ANYONE WHO CAN CLEAR HIM.
THAT WON'T MAKE ANY DIFFERENCE TO OLIVER.
HE HAS NOTHING LEFT TO LOSE.

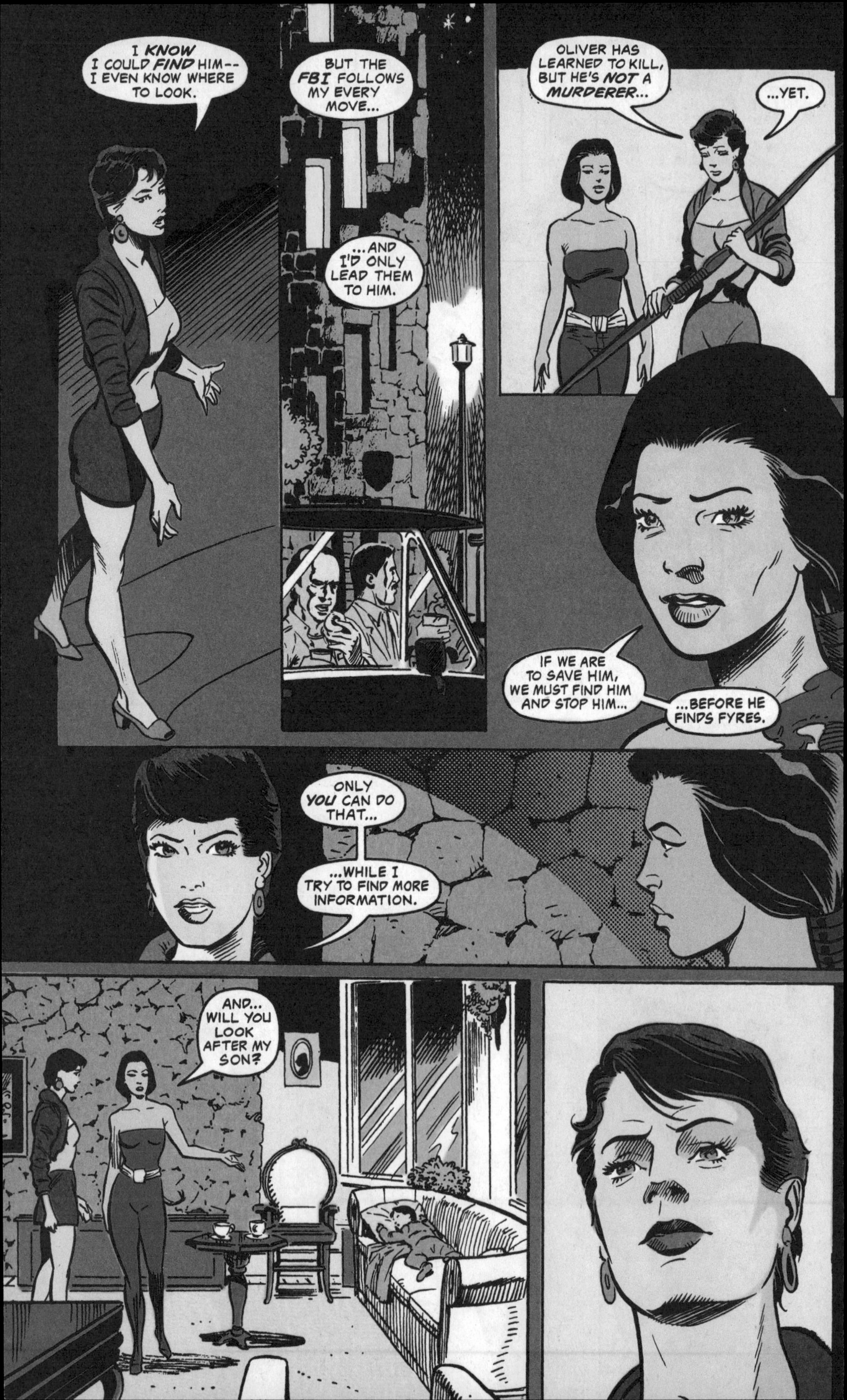
I KNOW I COULD FIND HIM-- I EVEN KNOW WHERE TO LOOK.
BUT THE FBI FOLLOWS MY EVERY MOVE...
...AND I'D ONLY LEAD THEM TO HIM.
OLIVER HAS LEARNED TO KILL, BUT HE'S NOT A MURDERER...
...YET.
IF WE ARE TO SAVE HIM, WE MUST FIND HIM AND STOP HIM...
...BEFORE HE FINDS FYRES.
ONLY YOU CAN DO THAT...
...WHILE I TRY TO FIND MORE INFORMATION.
AND... WILL YOU LOOK AFTER MY SON?

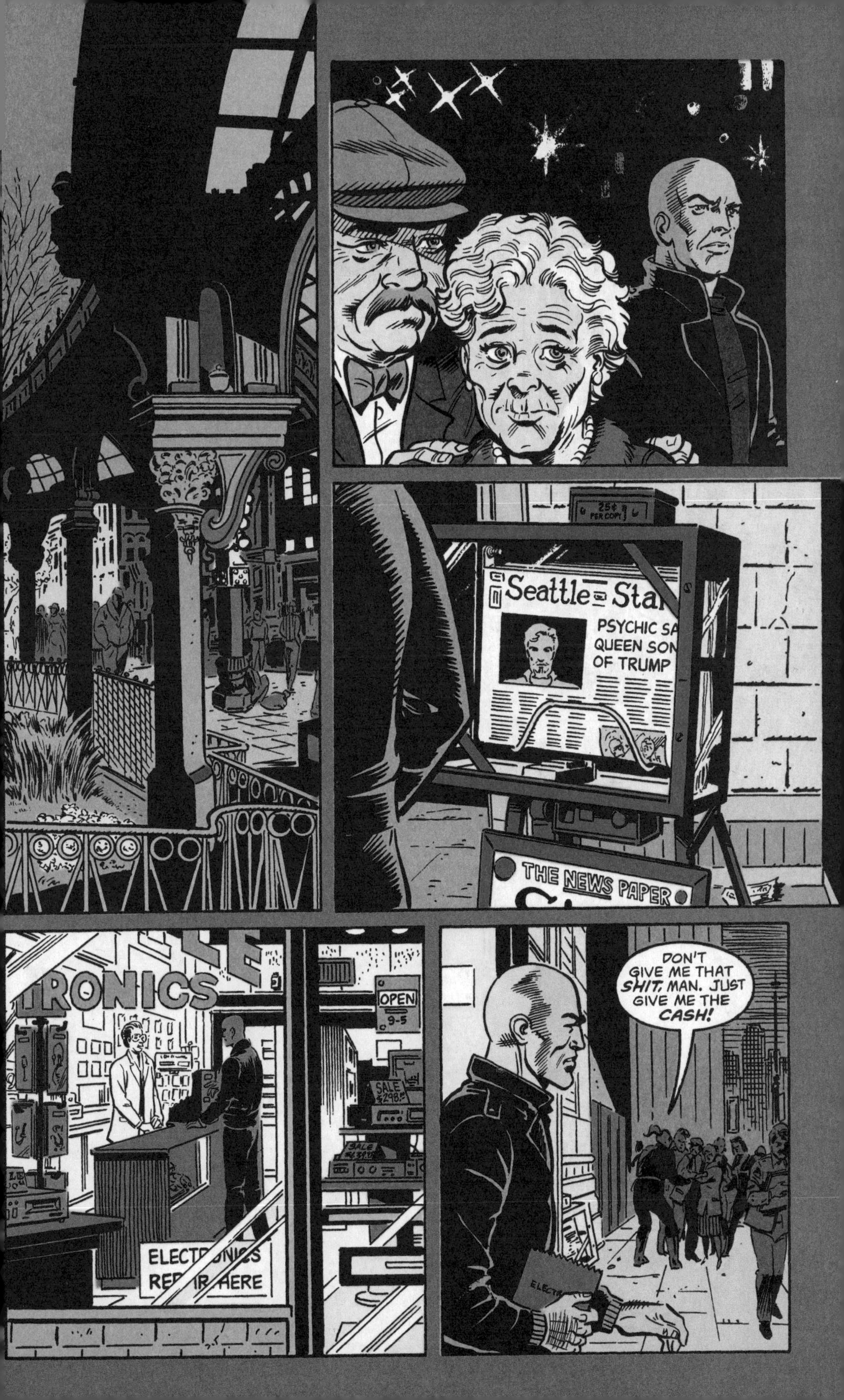

25¢ PER COPY
Seattle Star
PSYCHIC SA
QUEEN SON
OF TRUMP
THE NEWS PAPER
RONICS
OPEN
9-5
SALE
ELECTRONICS
REPAIR HERE
DON'T GIVE ME THAT *SHIT,* MAN. JUST GIVE ME THE *CASH!*

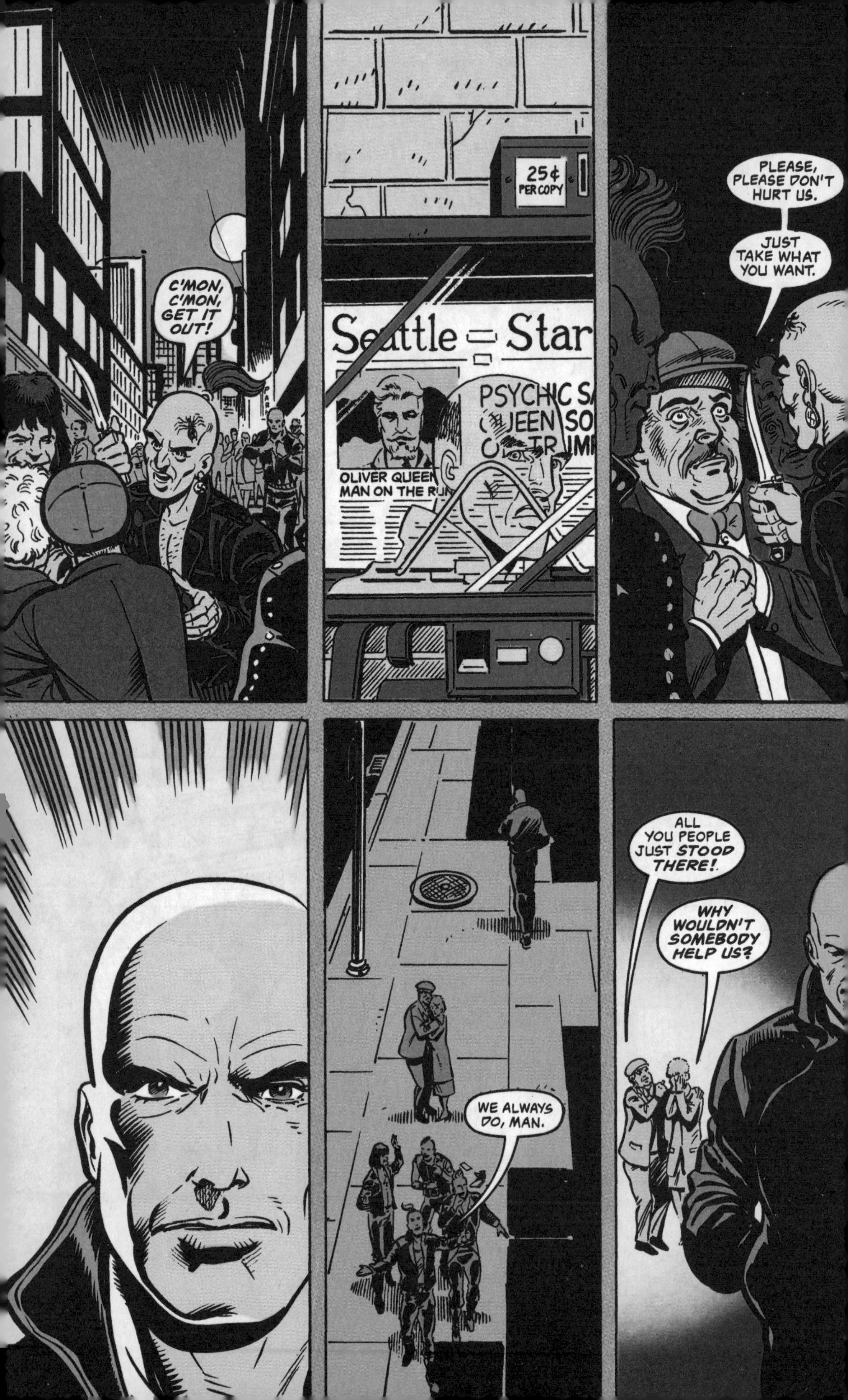
C'MON, C'MON, GET IT OUT!
25¢ PER COPY
Seattle Star
PSYCHIC SA
QUEEN SO
TRIUMP
OLIVER QUEEN MAN ON THE RUN
PLEASE, PLEASE DON'T HURT US.
JUST TAKE WHAT YOU WANT.
WE ALWAYS DO, MAN.
ALL YOU PEOPLE JUST STOOD THERE!
WHY WOULDN'T SOMEBODY HELP US?

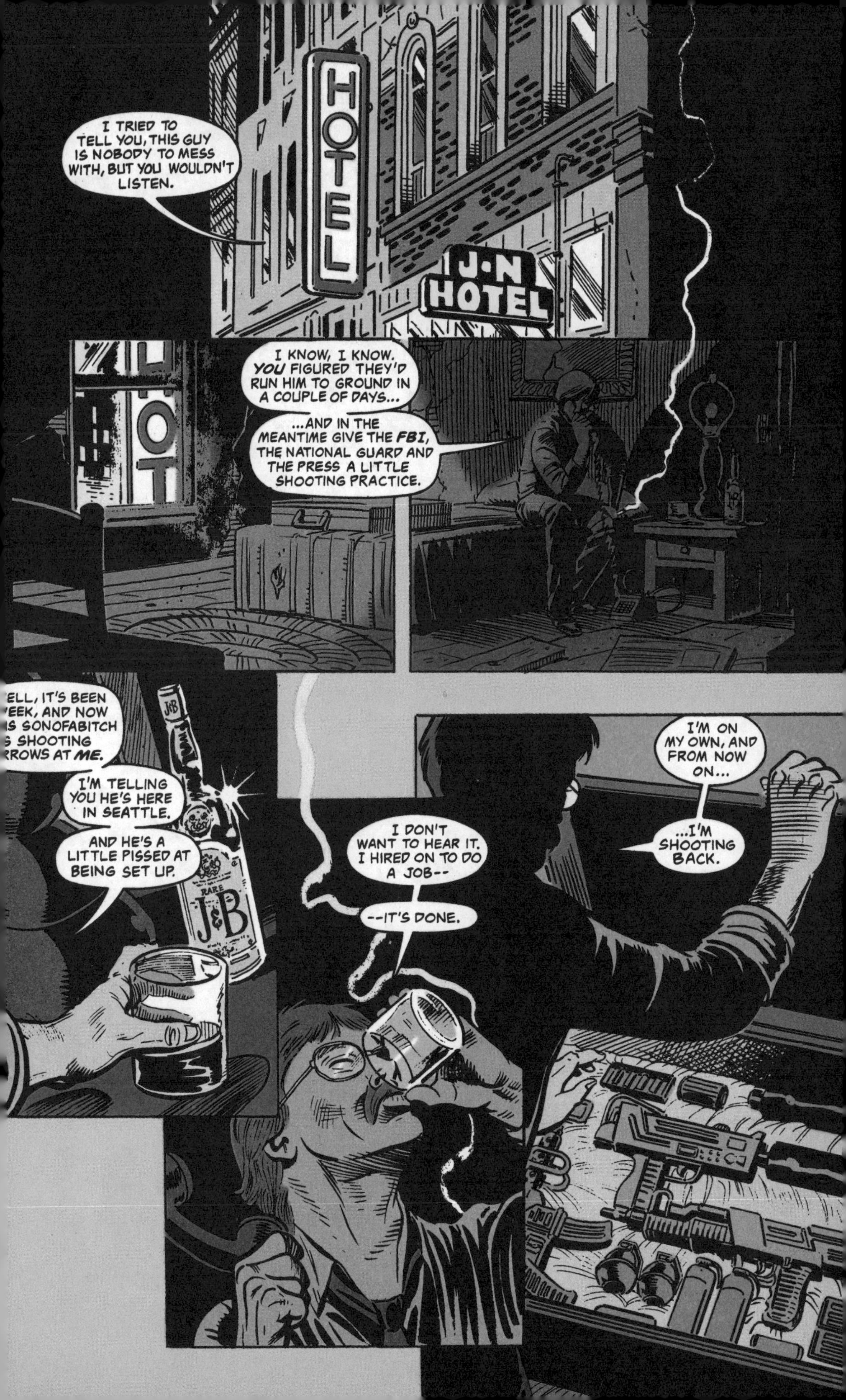
I TRIED TO TELL YOU, THIS GUY IS NOBODY TO MESS WITH, BUT YOU WOULDN'T LISTEN.
J·N HOTEL
I KNOW, I KNOW. YOU FIGURED THEY'D RUN HIM TO GROUND IN A COUPLE OF DAYS...
...AND IN THE MEANTIME GIVE THE FBI, THE NATIONAL GUARD AND THE PRESS A LITTLE SHOOTING PRACTICE.
ELL, IT'S BEEN EEK, AND NOW S SONOFABITCH SHOOTING RROWS AT ME.
I'M TELLING YOU HE'S HERE IN SEATTLE.
AND HE'S A LITTLE PISSED AT BEING SET UP.
I DON'T WANT TO HEAR IT. I HIRED ON TO DO A JOB--
--IT'S DONE.
I'M ON MY OWN, AND FROM NOW ON...
...I'M SHOOTING BACK.

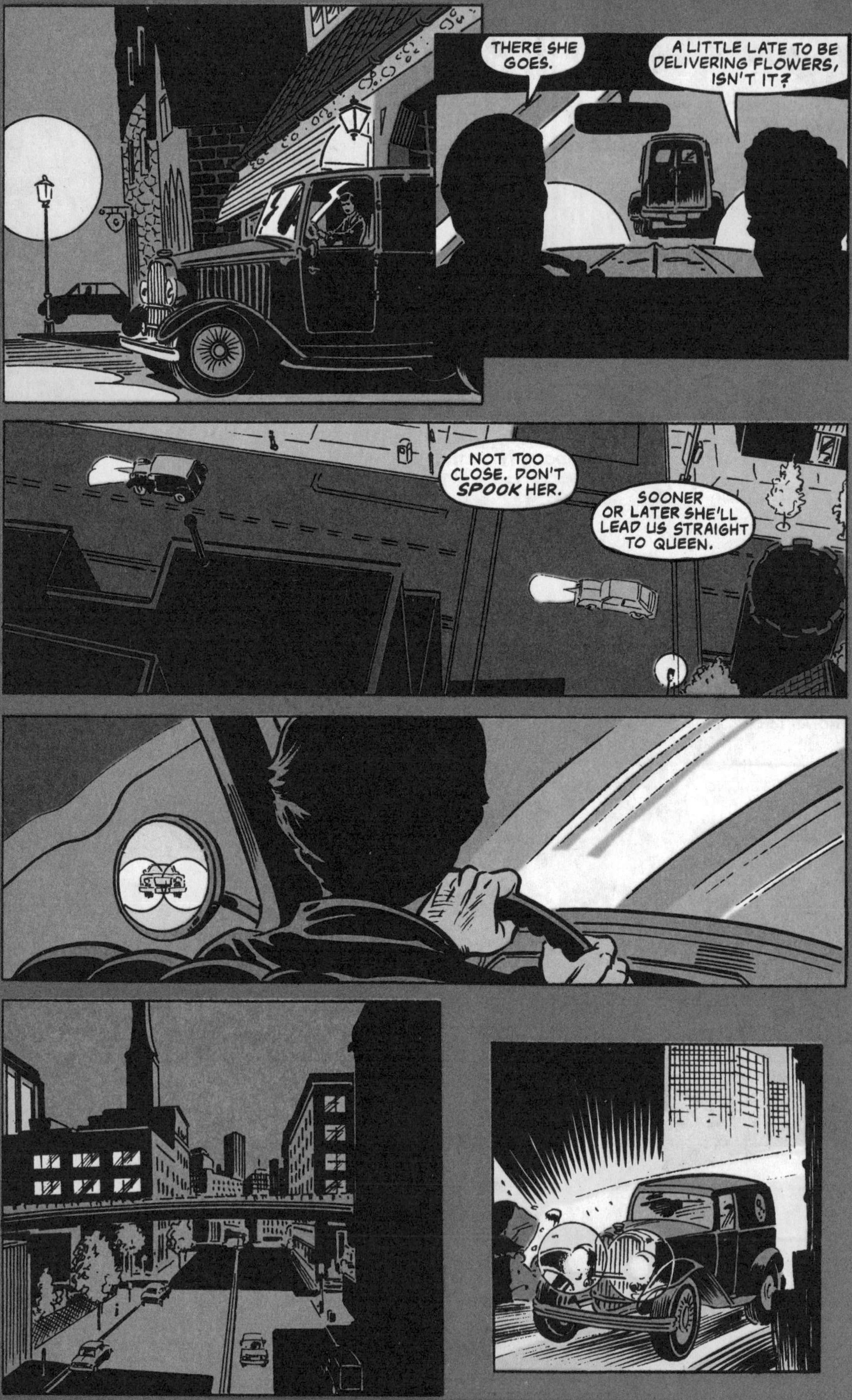
THERE SHE GOES.
A LITTLE LATE TO BE DELIVERING FLOWERS, ISN'T IT?
NOT TOO CLOSE. DON'T SPOOK HER.
SOONER OR LATER SHE'LL LEAD US STRAIGHT TO QUEEN.

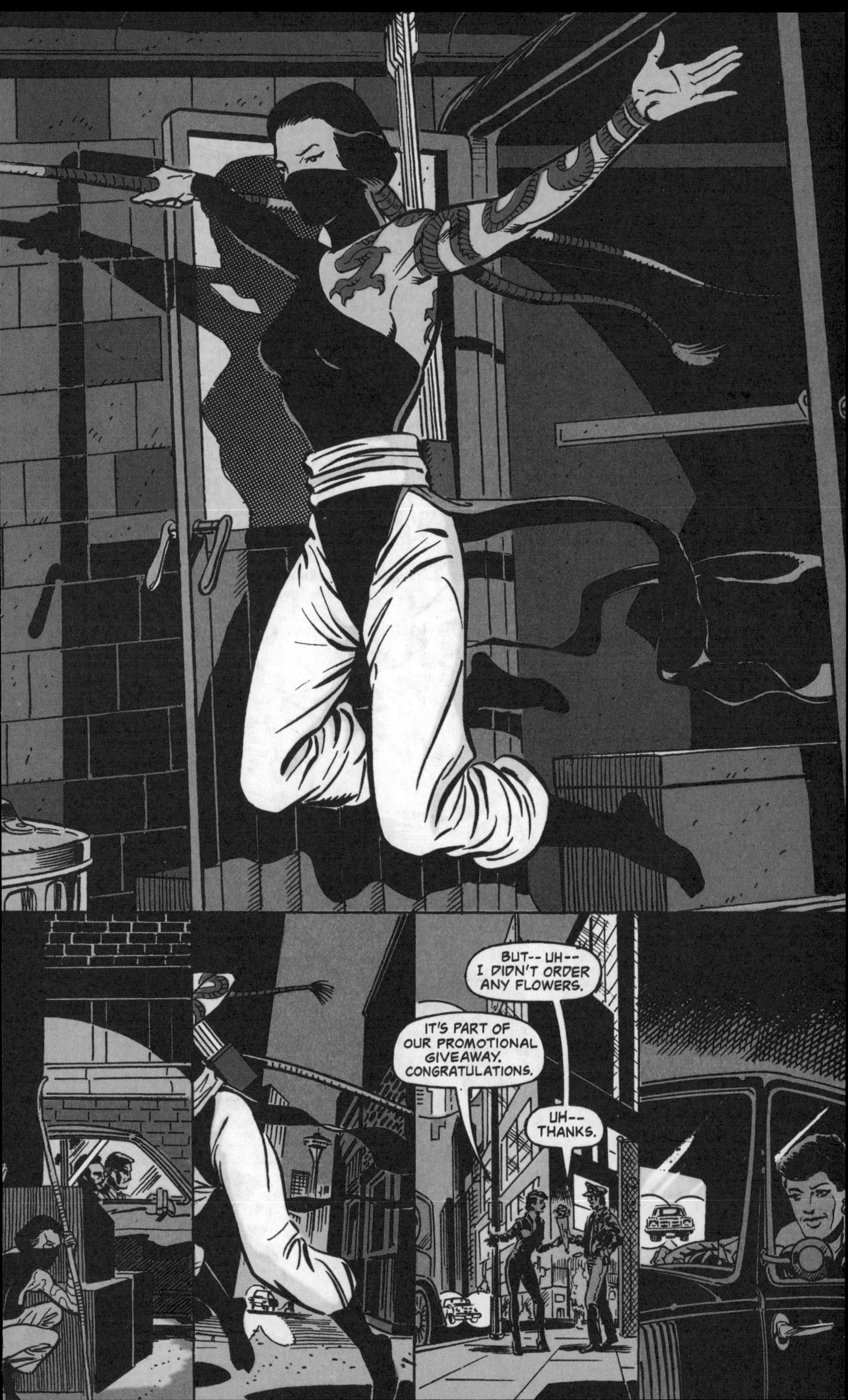
BUT-- UH-- I DIDN'T ORDER ANY FLOWERS.
IT'S PART OF OUR PROMOTIONAL GIVEAWAY. CONGRATULATIONS.
UH-- THANKS.

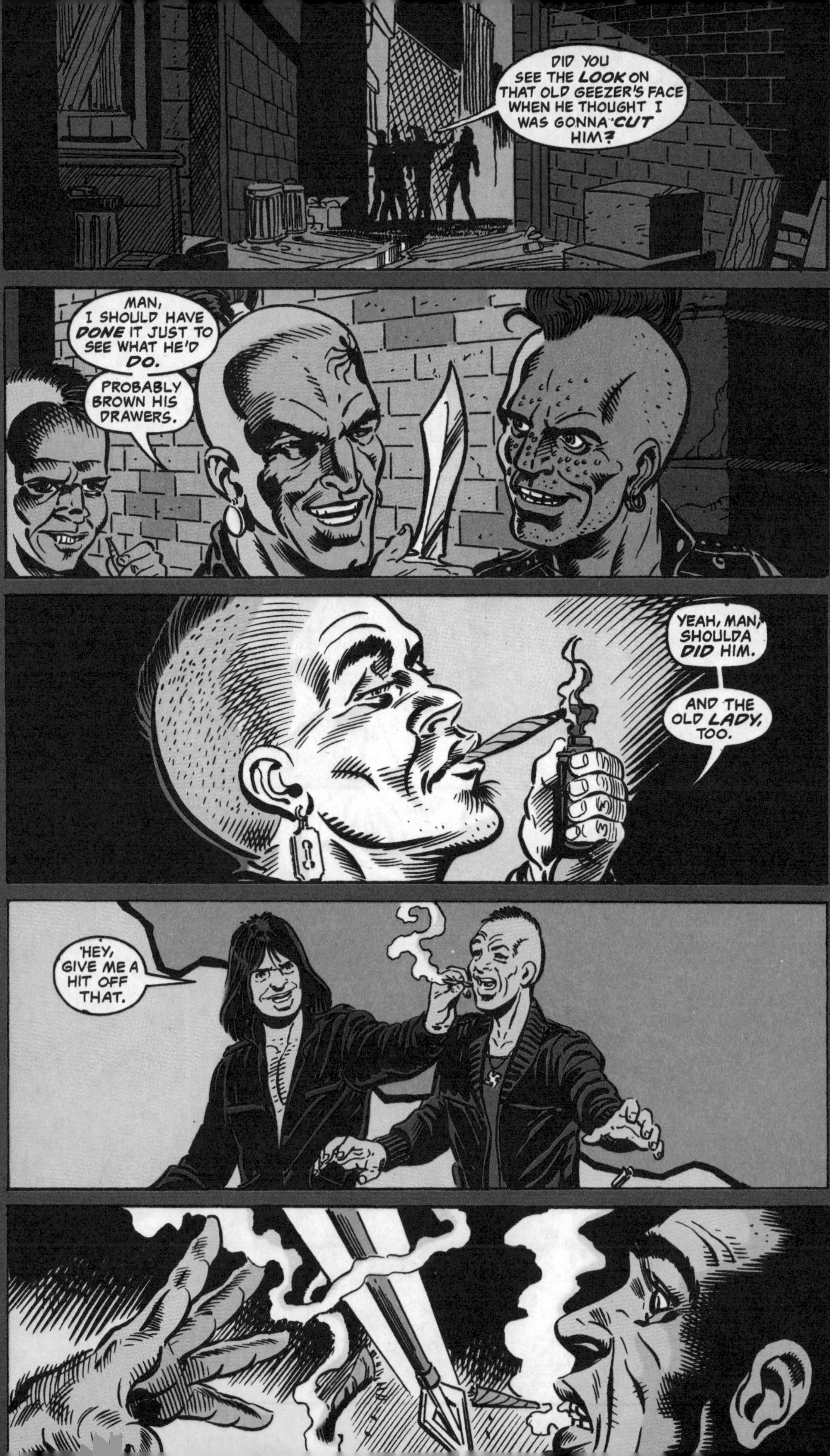
DID YOU SEE THE LOOK ON THAT OLD GEEZER'S FACE WHEN HE THOUGHT I WAS GONNA CUT HIM?
MAN, I SHOULD HAVE DONE IT JUST TO SEE WHAT HE'D DO.
PROBABLY BROWN HIS DRAWERS.
YEAH, MAN, SHOULDA DID HIM.
AND THE OLD LADY, TOO.
HEY, GIVE ME A HIT OFF THAT.

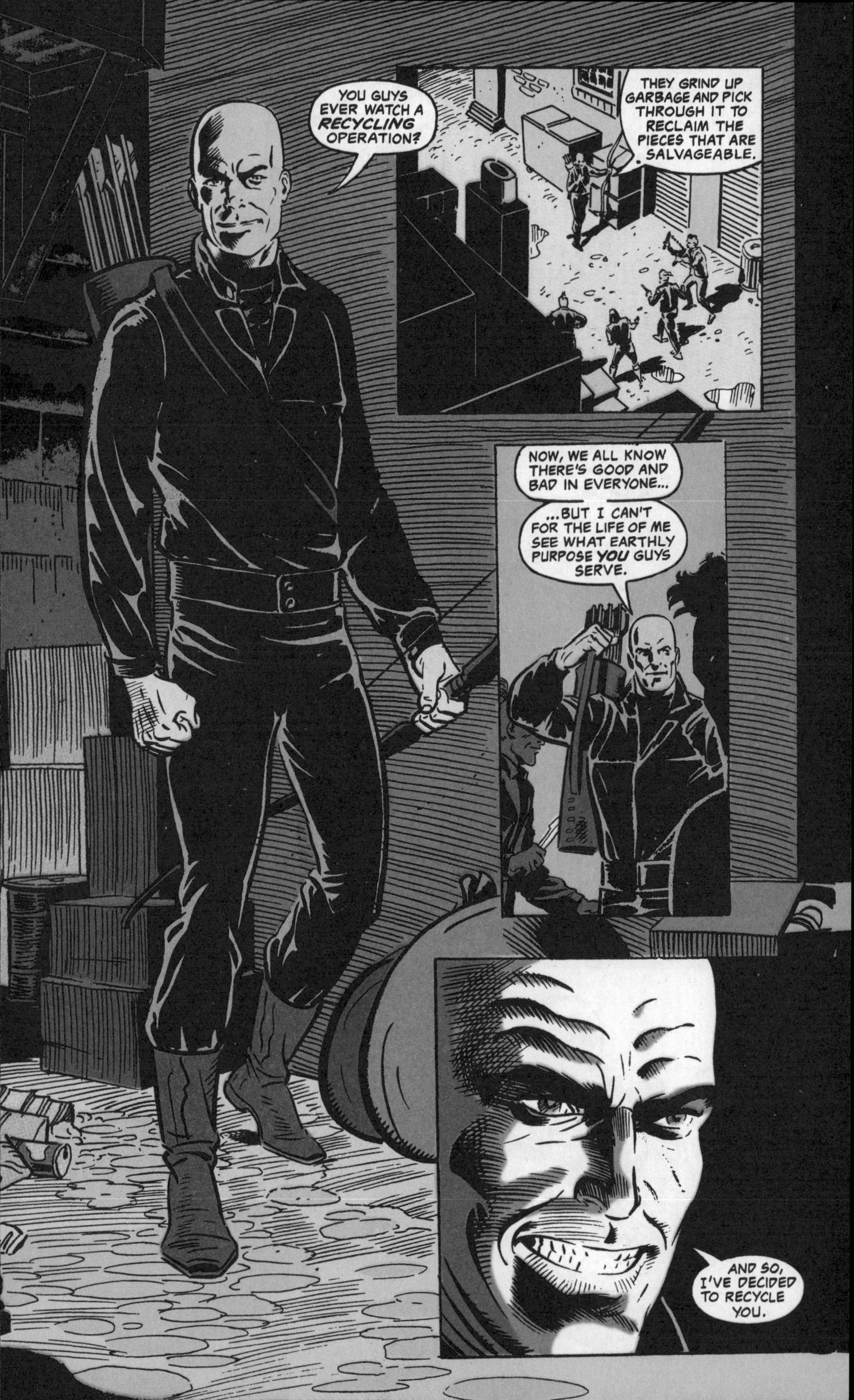
YOU GUYS EVER WATCH A RECYCLING OPERATION?
THEY GRIND UP GARBAGE AND PICK THROUGH IT TO RECLAIM THE PIECES THAT ARE SALVAGEABLE.
NOW, WE ALL KNOW THERE'S GOOD AND BAD IN EVERYONE...
...BUT I CAN'T FOR THE LIFE OF ME SEE WHAT EARTHLY PURPOSE YOU GUYS SERVE.
AND SO, I'VE DECIDED TO RECYCLE YOU.

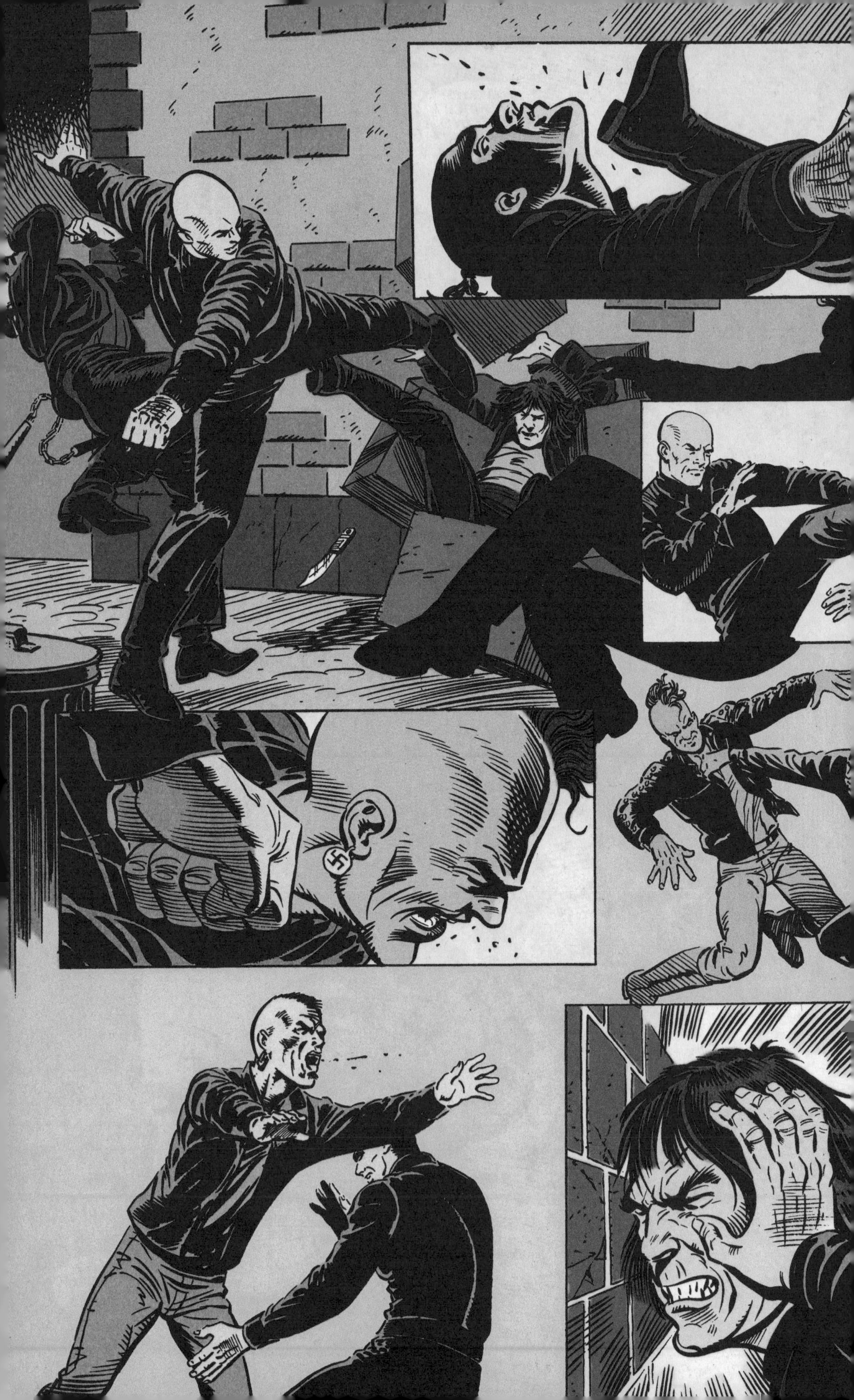

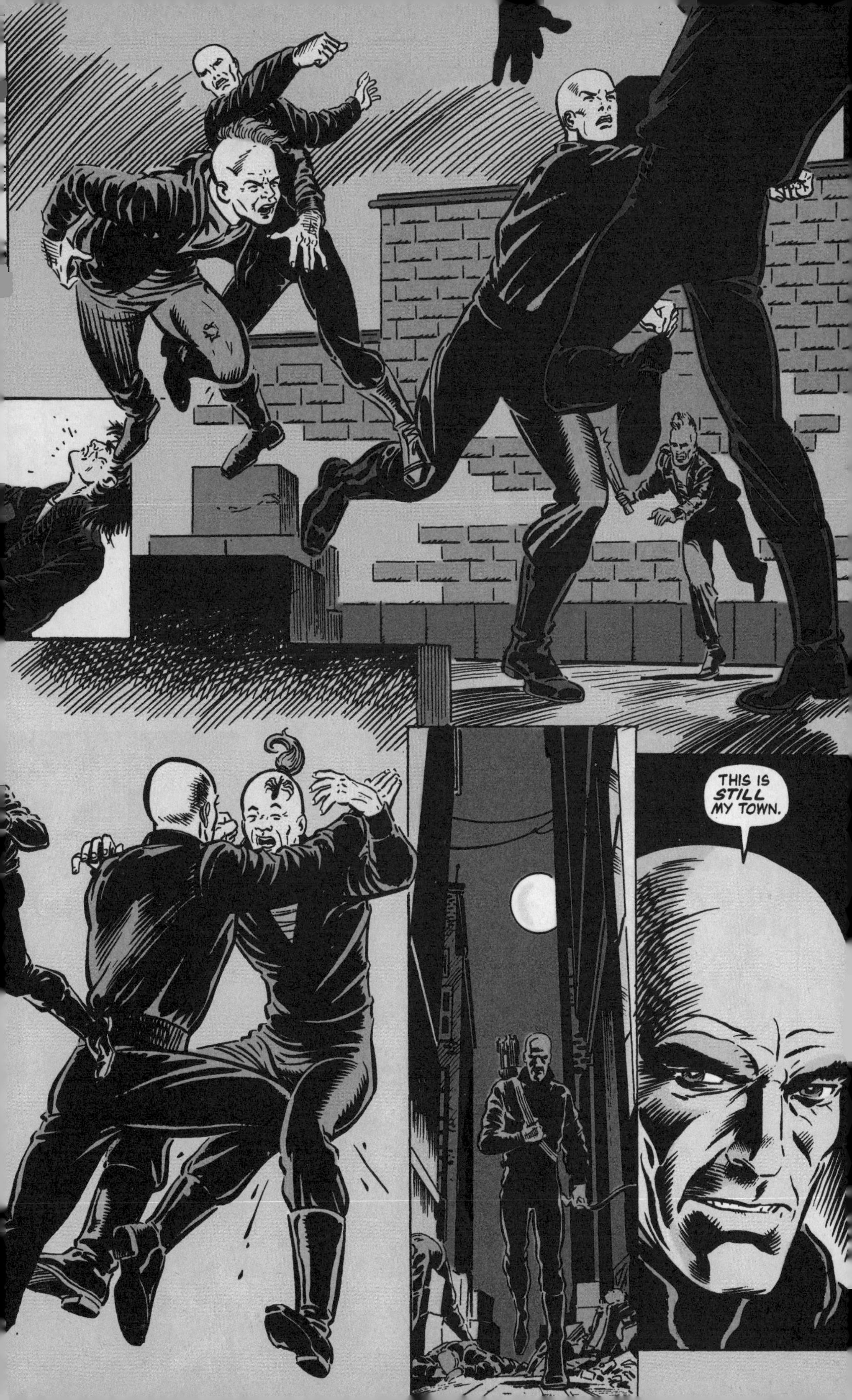
THIS IS *STILL* MY TOWN.

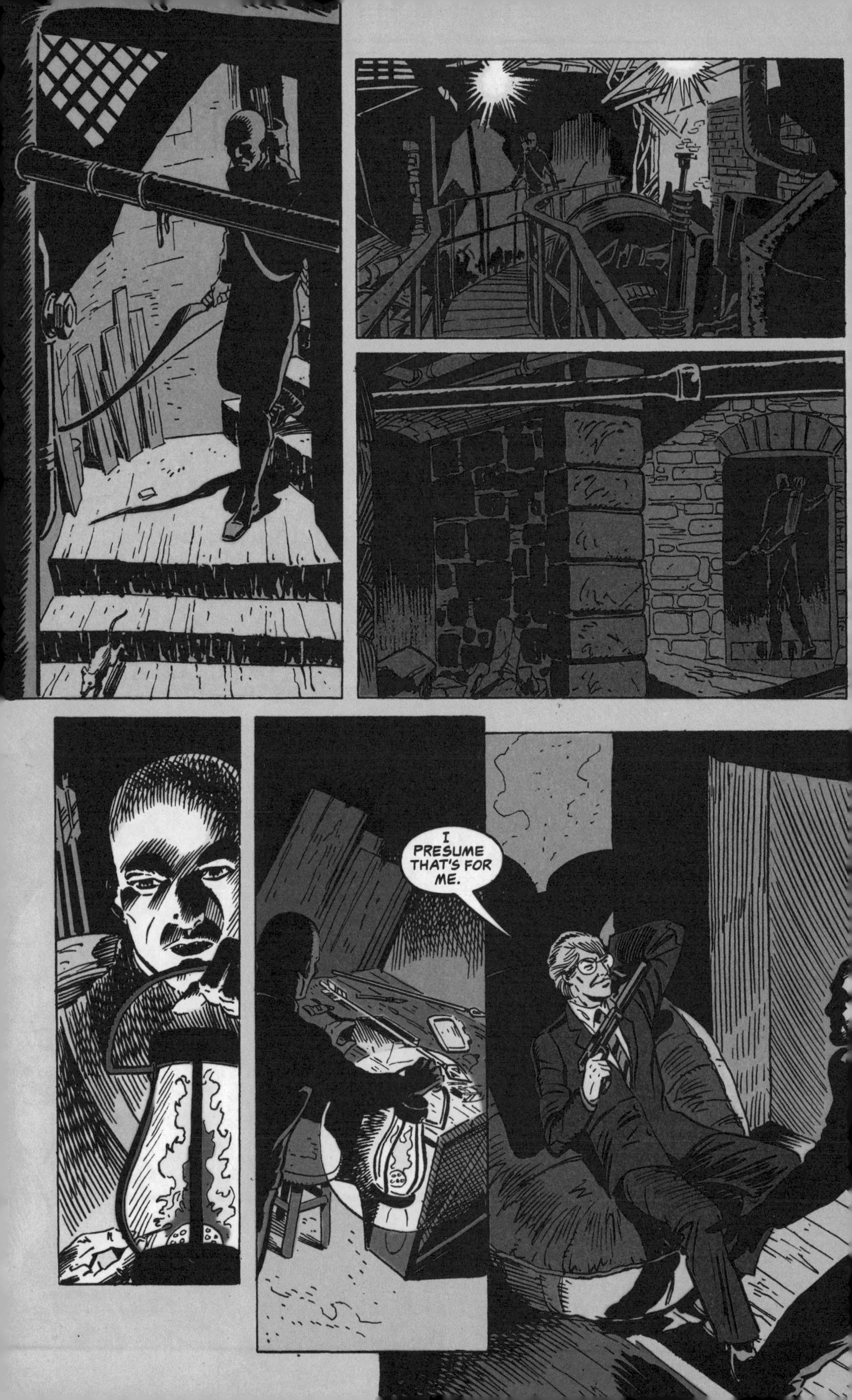
I PRESUME THAT'S FOR ME.

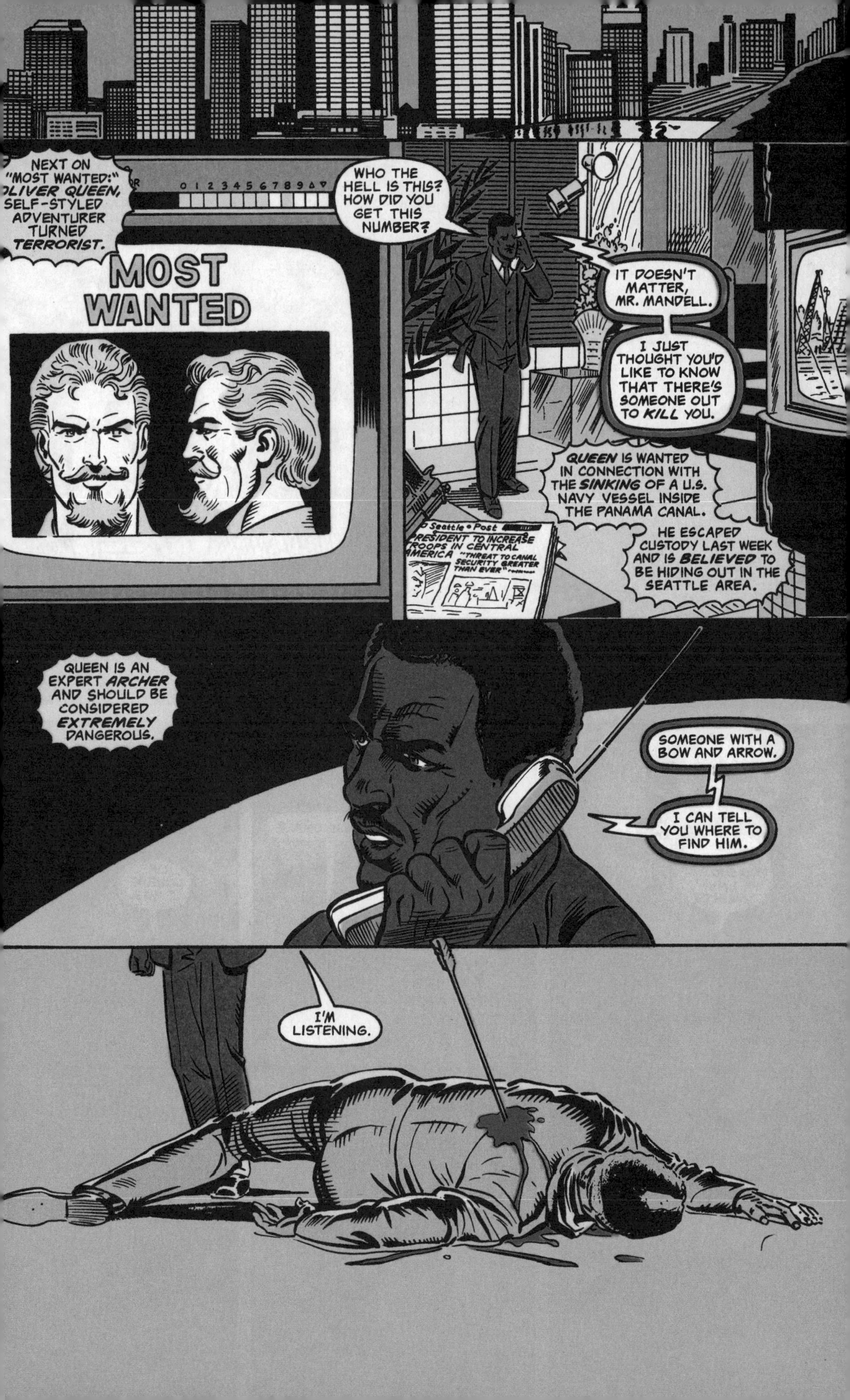

NEXT ON "MOST WANTED:" OLIVER QUEEN, SELF-STYLED ADVENTURER TURNED TERRORIST.
MOST WANTED
WHO THE HELL IS THIS? HOW DID YOU GET THIS NUMBER?
IT DOESN'T MATTER, MR. MANDELL.
I JUST THOUGHT YOU'D LIKE TO KNOW THAT THERE'S SOMEONE OUT TO KILL YOU.
QUEEN IS WANTED IN CONNECTION WITH THE SINKING OF A U.S. NAVY VESSEL INSIDE THE PANAMA CANAL.
Seattle • Post
PRESIDENT TO INCREASE TROOPS IN CENTRAL AMERICA
"THREAT TO CANAL SECURITY GREATER THAN EVER"
HE ESCAPED CUSTODY LAST WEEK AND IS BELIEVED TO BE HIDING OUT IN THE SEATTLE AREA.
QUEEN IS AN EXPERT ARCHER AND SHOULD BE CONSIDERED EXTREMELY DANGEROUS.
SOMEONE WITH A BOW AND ARROW.
I CAN TELL YOU WHERE TO FIND HIM.
I'M LISTENING.

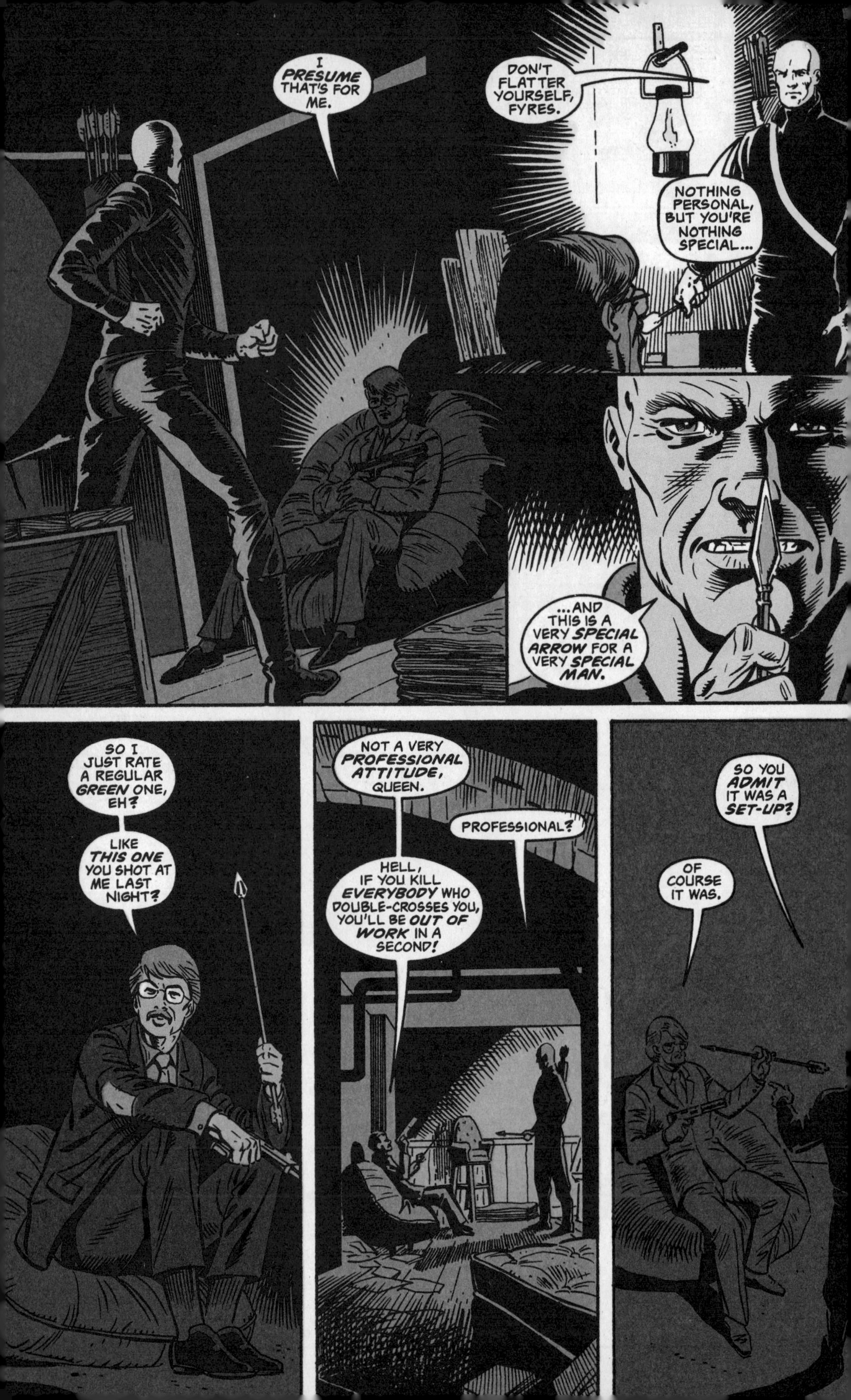
I PRESUME THAT'S FOR ME.
DON'T FLATTER YOURSELF, FYRES.
NOTHING PERSONAL, BUT YOU'RE NOTHING SPECIAL...
...AND THIS IS A VERY SPECIAL ARROW FOR A VERY SPECIAL MAN.
SO I JUST RATE A REGULAR GREEN ONE, EH?
LIKE THIS ONE YOU SHOT AT ME LAST NIGHT?
NOT A VERY PROFESSIONAL ATTITUDE, QUEEN.
PROFESSIONAL?
HELL, IF YOU KILL EVERYBODY WHO DOUBLE-CROSSES YOU, YOU'LL BE OUT OF WORK IN A SECOND!
SO YOU ADMIT IT WAS A SET-UP?
OF COURSE IT WAS.

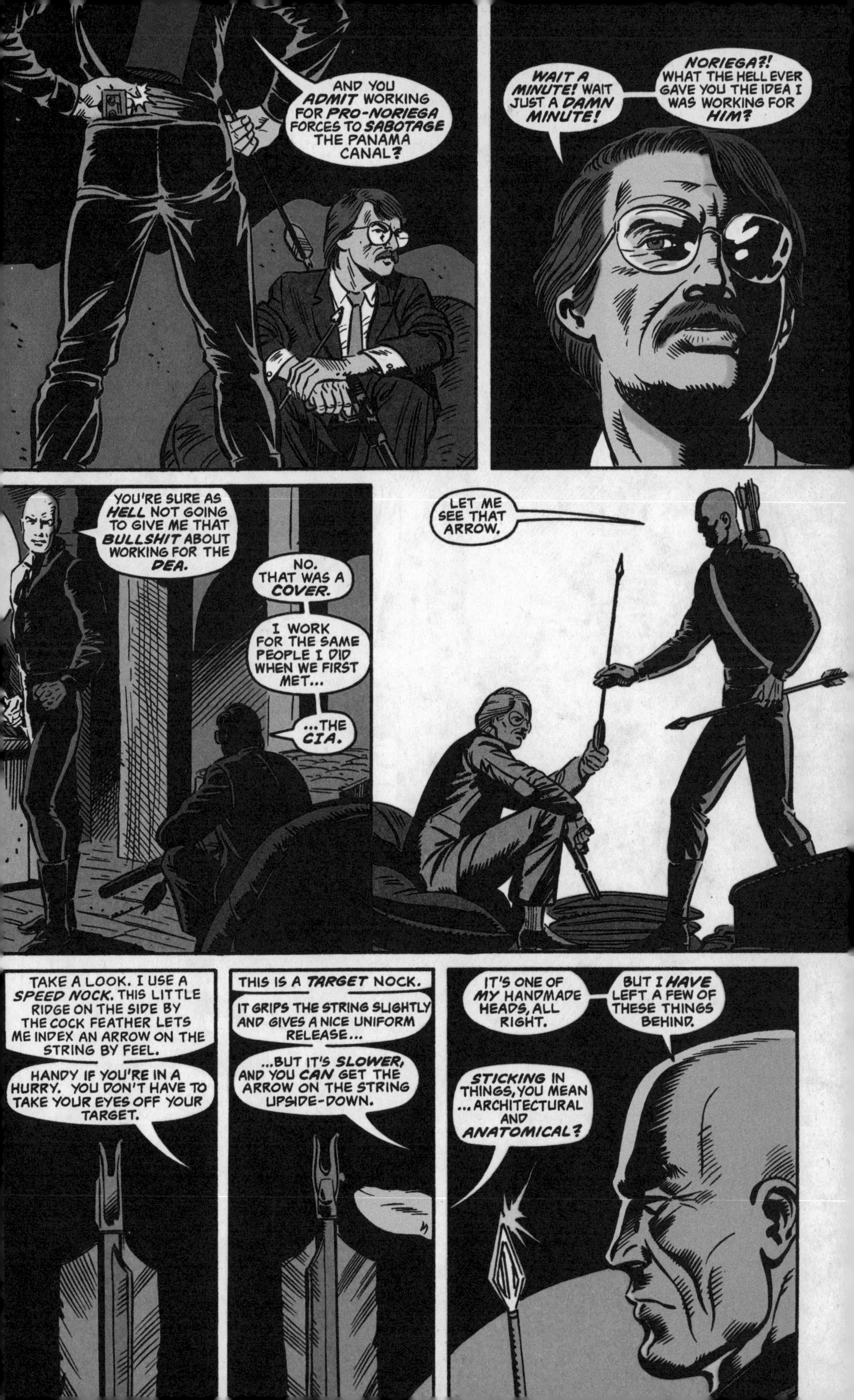
AND YOU ADMIT WORKING FOR PRO-NORIEGA FORCES TO SABOTAGE THE PANAMA CANAL?
WAIT A MINUTE! WAIT JUST A DAMN MINUTE!
NORIEGA?! WHAT THE HELL EVER GAVE YOU THE IDEA I WAS WORKING FOR HIM?
YOU'RE SURE AS HELL NOT GOING TO GIVE ME THAT BULLSHIT ABOUT WORKING FOR THE DEA.
NO. THAT WAS A COVER.
I WORK FOR THE SAME PEOPLE I DID WHEN WE FIRST MET...
...THE CIA.
LET ME SEE THAT ARROW.
TAKE A LOOK. I USE A SPEED NOCK. THIS LITTLE RIDGE ON THE SIDE BY THE COCK FEATHER LETS ME INDEX AN ARROW ON THE STRING BY FEEL.
HANDY IF YOU'RE IN A HURRY. YOU DON'T HAVE TO TAKE YOUR EYES OFF YOUR TARGET.
THIS IS A TARGET NOCK.
IT GRIPS THE STRING SLIGHTLY AND GIVES A NICE UNIFORM RELEASE...
...BUT IT'S SLOWER, AND YOU CAN GET THE ARROW ON THE STRING UPSIDE-DOWN.
IT'S ONE OF MY HANDMADE HEADS, ALL RIGHT.
BUT I HAVE LEFT A FEW OF THESE THINGS BEHIND.
STICKING IN THINGS, YOU MEAN ...ARCHITECTURAL AND ANATOMICAL?

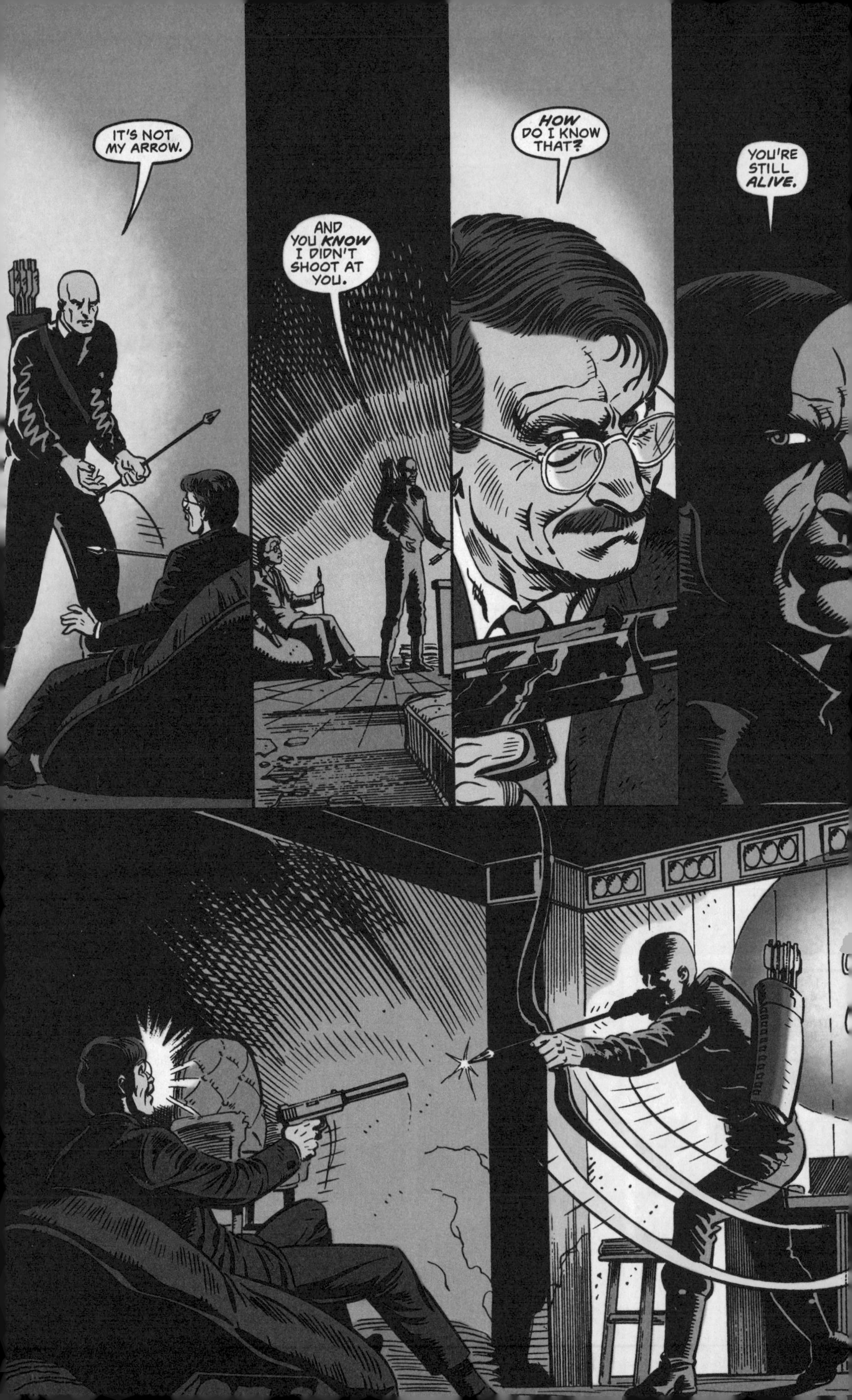
IT'S NOT MY ARROW.
AND YOU KNOW I DIDN'T SHOOT AT YOU.
HOW DO I KNOW THAT?
YOU'RE STILL ALIVE.

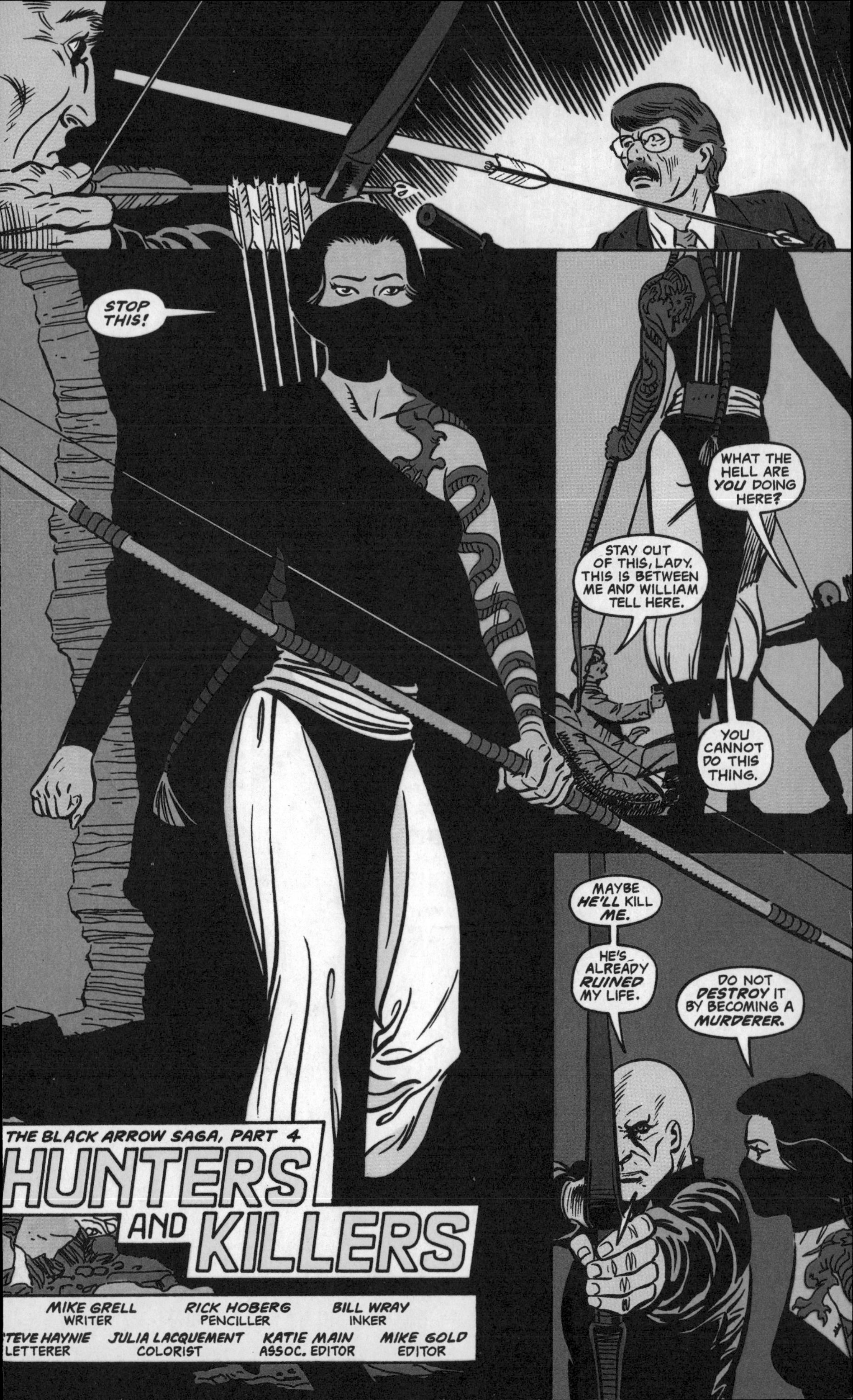
STOP THIS!
WHAT THE HELL ARE YOU DOING HERE?
STAY OUT OF THIS, LADY. THIS IS BETWEEN ME AND WILLIAM TELL HERE.
YOU CANNOT DO THIS THING.
MAYBE HE'LL KILL ME.
HE'S ALREADY RUINED MY LIFE.
DO NOT DESTROY IT BY BECOMING A MURDERER.
THE BLACK ARROW SAGA, PART 4
HUNTERS AND KILLERS
MIKE GRELL WRITER
RICK HOBERG PENCILLER
BILL WRAY INKER
STEVE HAYNIE LETTERER
JULIA LACQUEMENT COLORIST
KATIE MAIN ASSOC. EDITOR
MIKE GOLD EDITOR

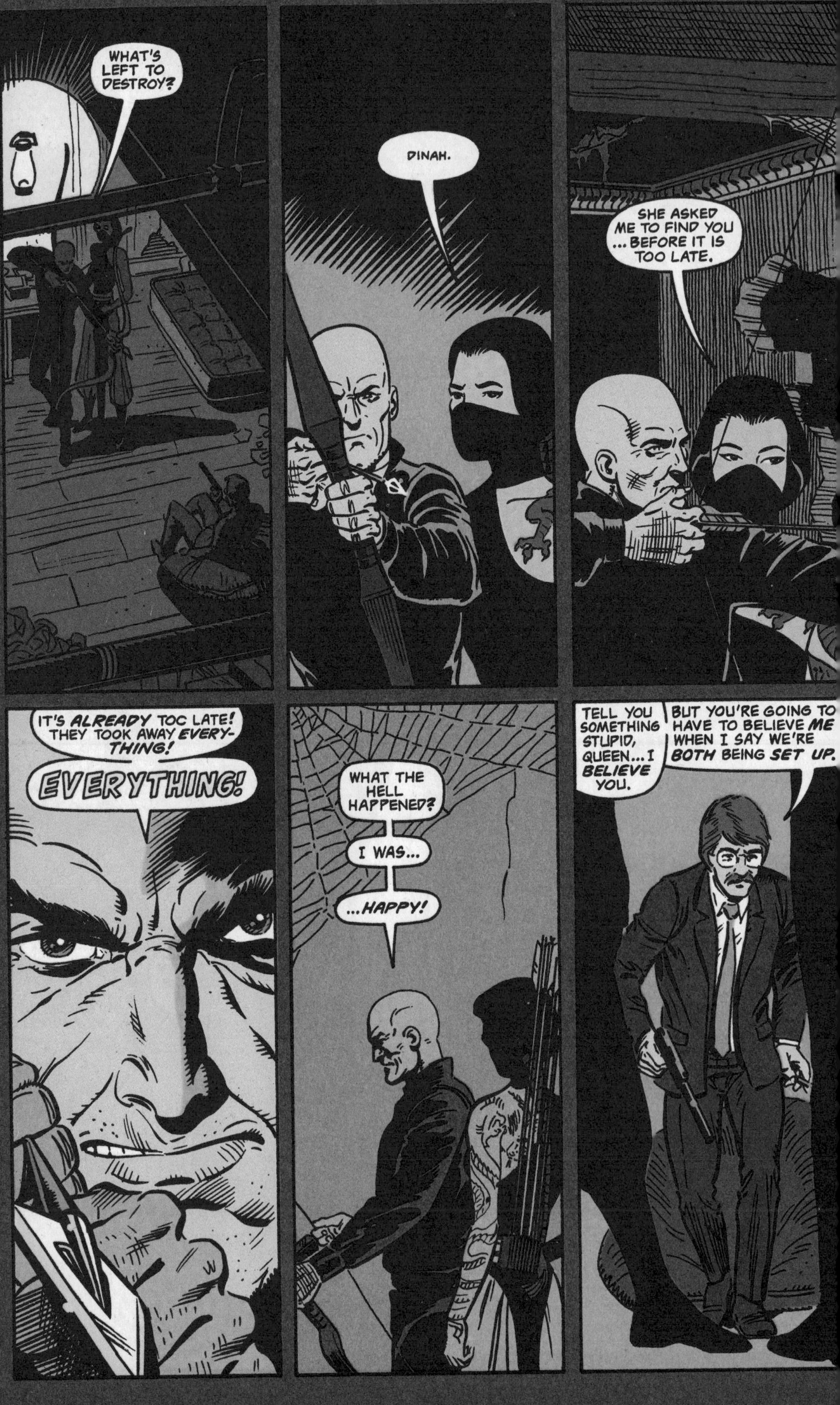
WHAT'S LEFT TO DESTROY?
DINAH.
SHE ASKED ME TO FIND YOU ...BEFORE IT IS TOO LATE.
IT'S ALREADY TOO LATE! THEY TOOK AWAY EVERYTHING!
EVERYTHING!
WHAT THE HELL HAPPENED?
I WAS...
...HAPPY!
TELL YOU SOMETHING STUPID, QUEEN... I BELIEVE YOU.
BUT YOU'RE GOING TO HAVE TO BELIEVE ME WHEN I SAY WE'RE BOTH BEING SET UP.

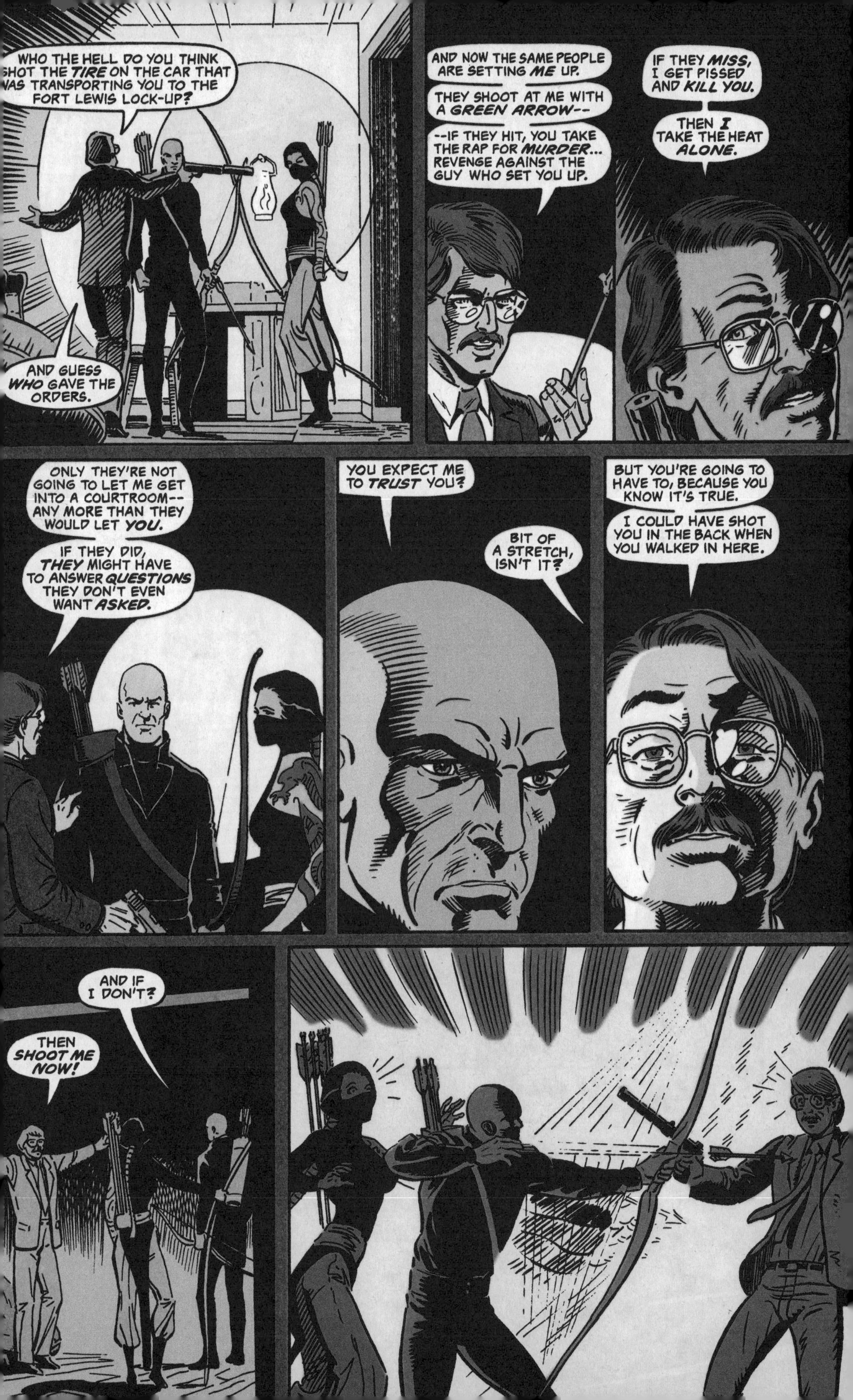
WHO THE HELL DO YOU THINK SHOT THE TIRE ON THE CAR THAT WAS TRANSPORTING YOU TO THE FORT LEWIS LOCK-UP?
AND GUESS WHO GAVE THE ORDERS.
AND NOW THE SAME PEOPLE ARE SETTING ME UP.
THEY SHOOT AT ME WITH A GREEN ARROW--
--IF THEY HIT, YOU TAKE THE RAP FOR MURDER... REVENGE AGAINST THE GUY WHO SET YOU UP.
IF THEY MISS, I GET PISSED AND KILL YOU.
THEN I TAKE THE HEAT ALONE.
ONLY THEY'RE NOT GOING TO LET ME GET INTO A COURTROOM-- ANY MORE THAN THEY WOULD LET YOU.
IF THEY DID, THEY MIGHT HAVE TO ANSWER QUESTIONS THEY DON'T EVEN WANT ASKED.
YOU EXPECT ME TO TRUST YOU?
BIT OF A STRETCH, ISN'T IT?
BUT YOU'RE GOING TO HAVE TO, BECAUSE YOU KNOW IT'S TRUE.
I COULD HAVE SHOT YOU IN THE BACK WHEN YOU WALKED IN HERE.
AND IF I DON'T?
THEN SHOOT ME NOW!

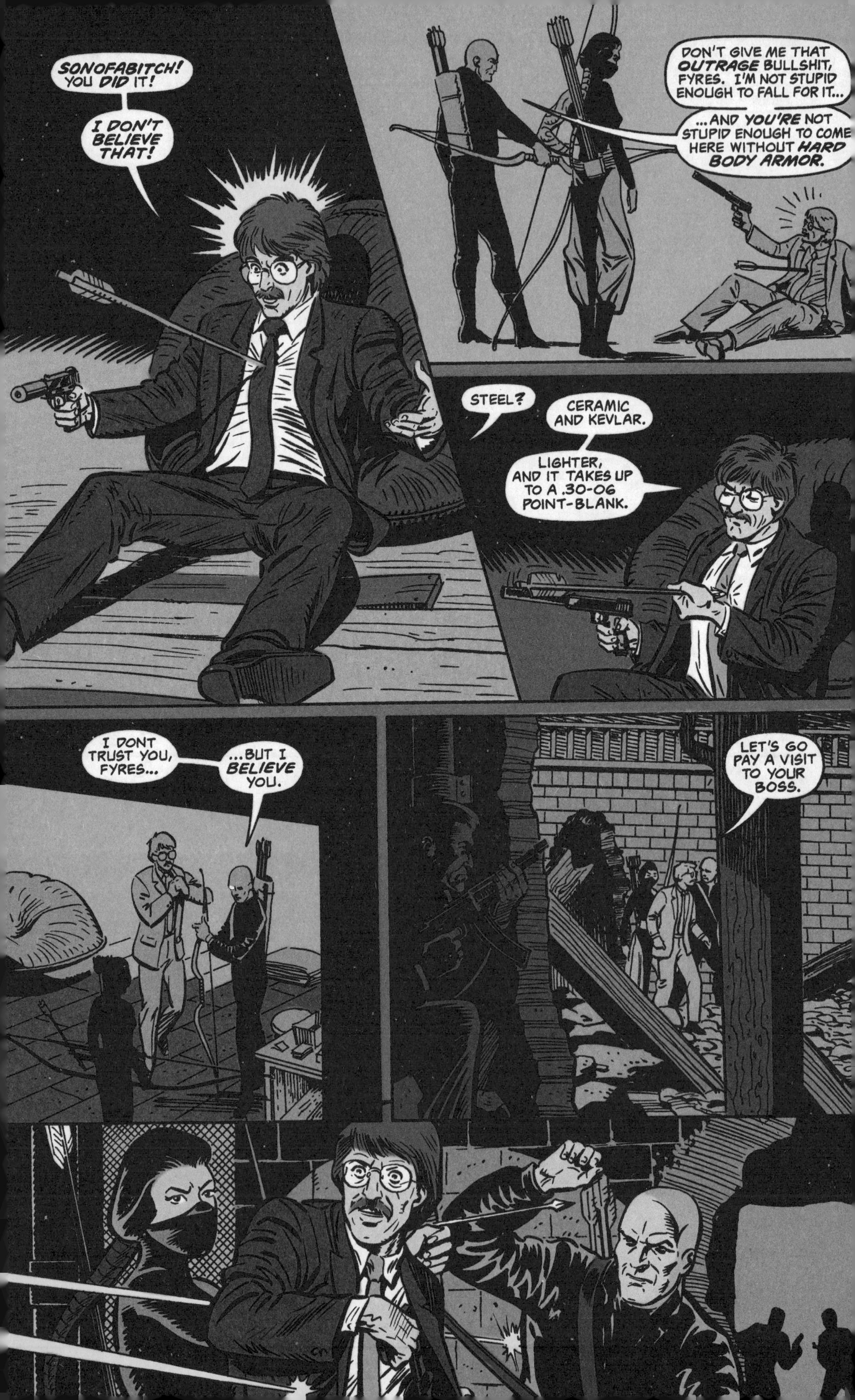
SONOFABITCH! YOU DID IT!
I DON'T BELIEVE THAT!
DON'T GIVE ME THAT OUTRAGE BULLSHIT, FYRES. I'M NOT STUPID ENOUGH TO FALL FOR IT...
...AND YOU'RE NOT STUPID ENOUGH TO COME HERE WITHOUT HARD BODY ARMOR.
STEEL?
CERAMIC AND KEVLAR.
LIGHTER, AND IT TAKES UP TO A .30-06 POINT-BLANK.
I DONT TRUST YOU, FYRES...
...BUT I BELIEVE YOU.
LET'S GO PAY A VISIT TO YOUR BOSS.

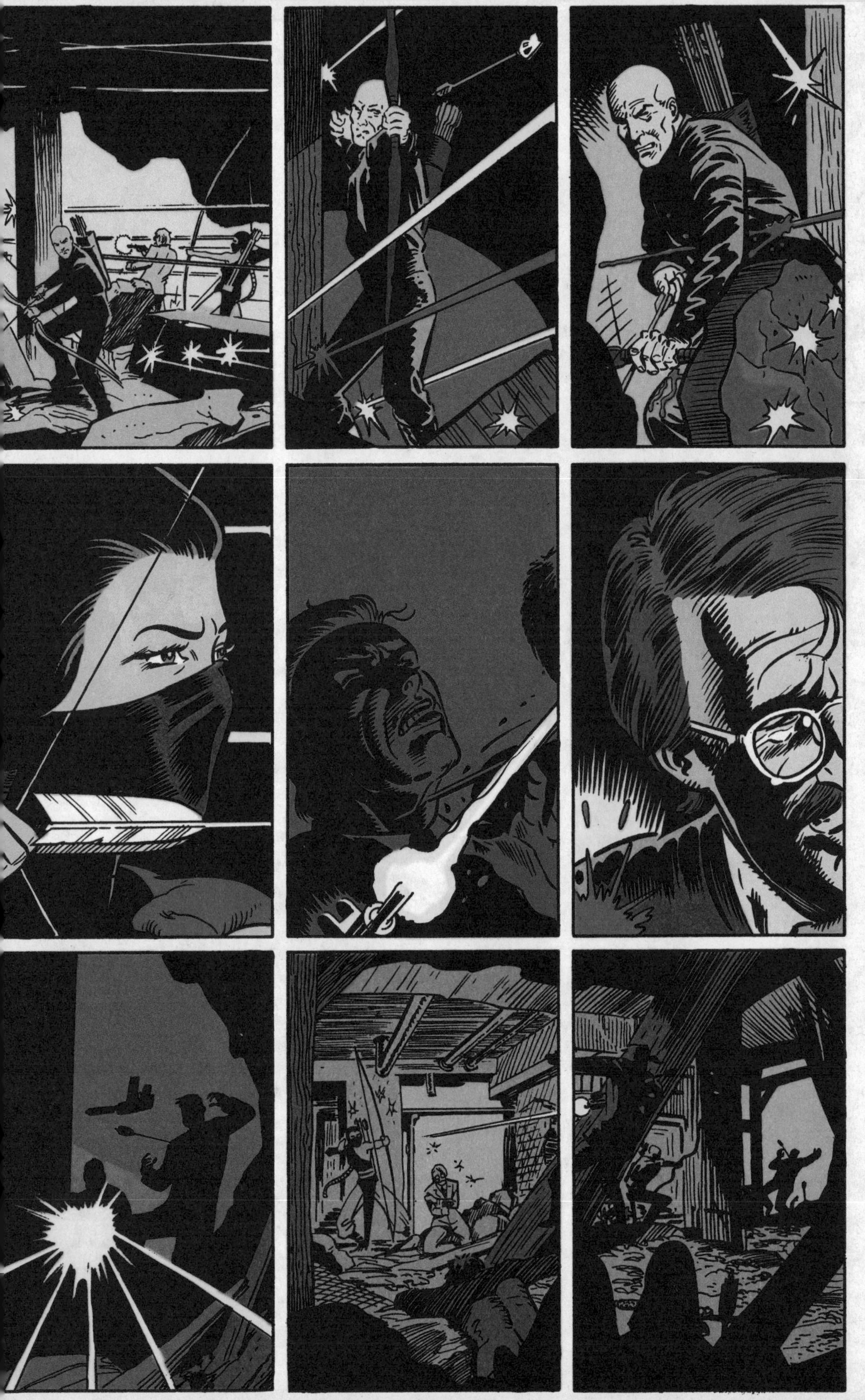

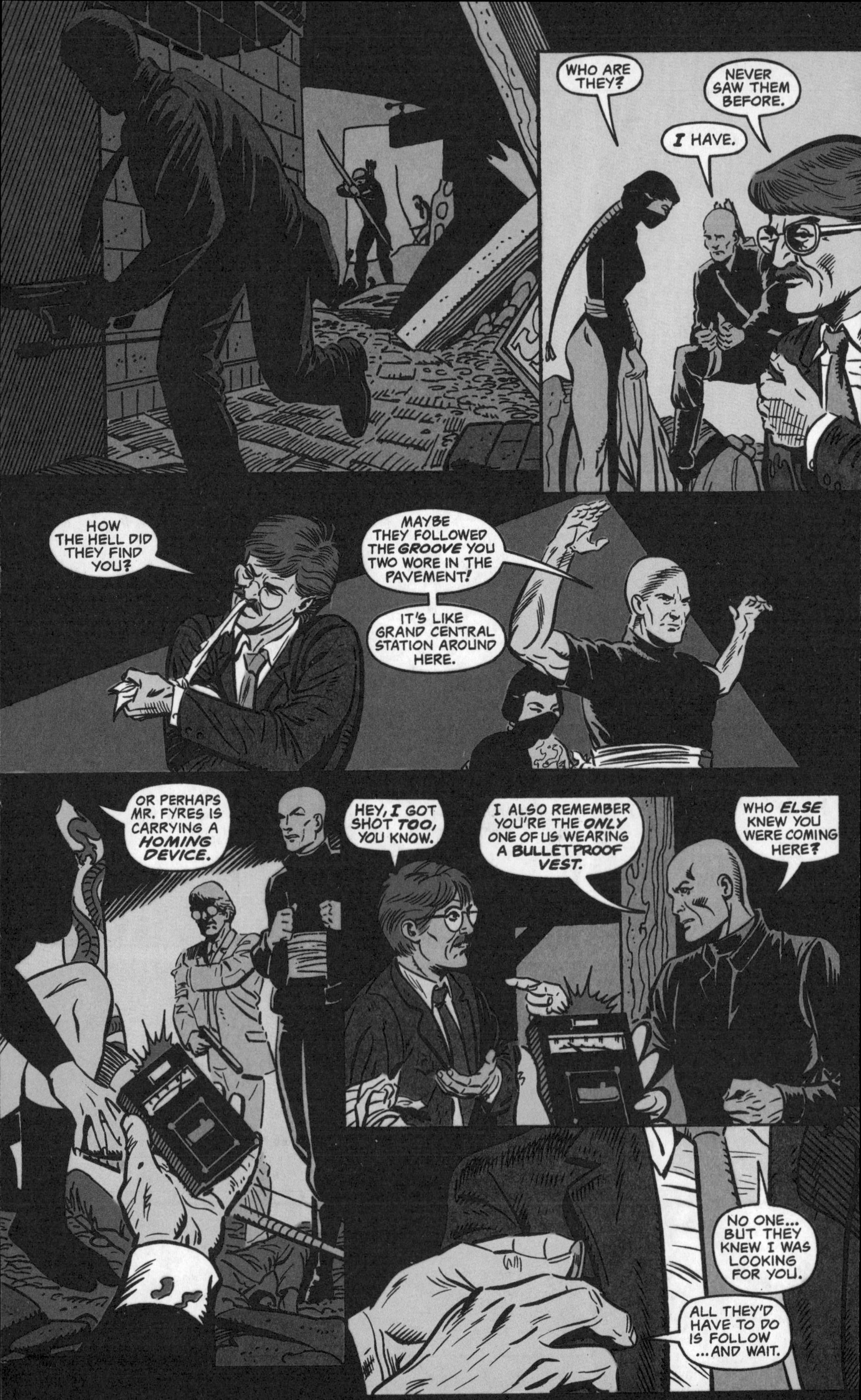
WHO ARE THEY?
NEVER SAW THEM BEFORE.
I HAVE.
HOW THE HELL DID THEY FIND YOU?
MAYBE THEY FOLLOWED THE GROOVE YOU TWO WORE IN THE PAVEMENT!
IT'S LIKE GRAND CENTRAL STATION AROUND HERE.
OR PERHAPS MR. FYRES IS CARRYING A HOMING DEVICE.
HEY, I GOT SHOT TOO, YOU KNOW.
I ALSO REMEMBER YOU'RE THE ONLY ONE OF US WEARING A BULLETPROOF VEST.
WHO ELSE KNEW YOU WERE COMING HERE?
NO ONE... BUT THEY KNEW I WAS LOOKING FOR YOU.
ALL THEY'D HAVE TO DO IS FOLLOW ...AND WAIT.

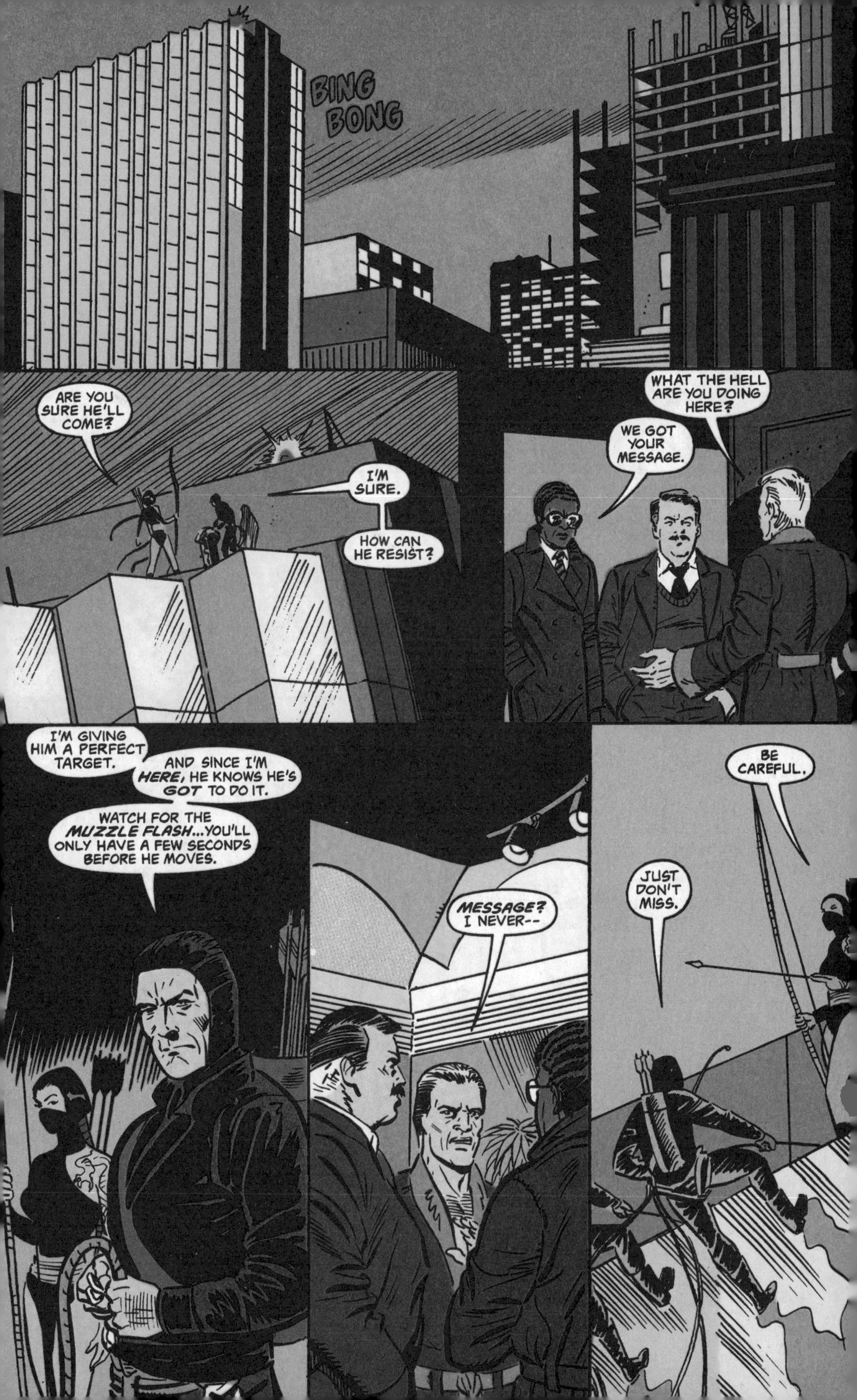
BING BONG
ARE YOU SURE HE'LL COME?
I'M SURE.
HOW CAN HE RESIST?
WHAT THE HELL ARE YOU DOING HERE?
WE GOT YOUR MESSAGE.
I'M GIVING HIM A PERFECT TARGET.
AND SINCE I'M *HERE*, HE KNOWS HE'S *GOT* TO DO IT.
WATCH FOR THE *MUZZLE FLASH*...YOU'LL ONLY HAVE A FEW SECONDS BEFORE HE MOVES.
*MESSAGE?* I NEVER--
BE CAREFUL.
JUST DON'T MISS.

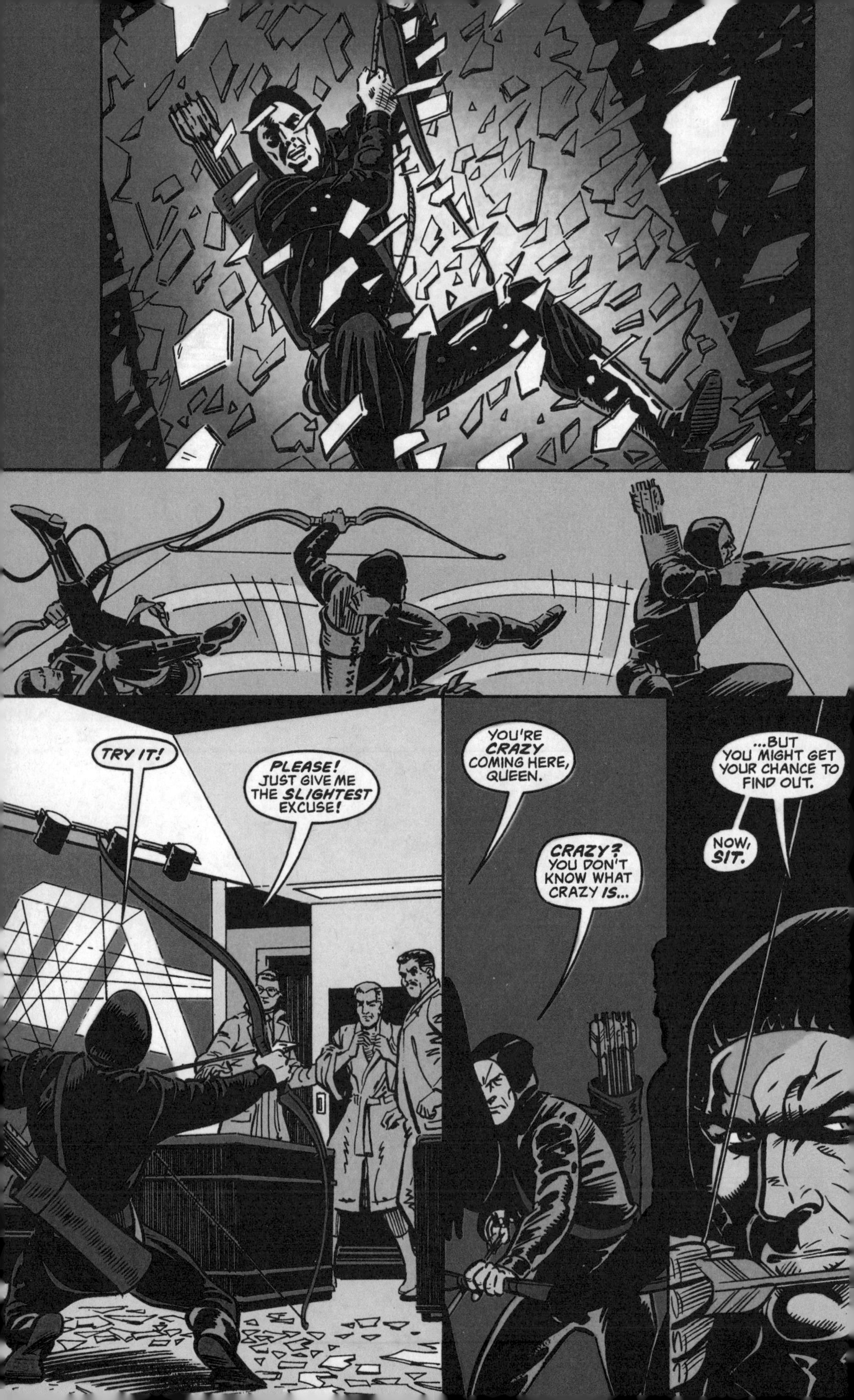
TRY IT!
PLEASE! JUST GIVE ME THE SLIGHTEST EXCUSE!
YOU'RE CRAZY COMING HERE, QUEEN.
CRAZY? YOU DON'T KNOW WHAT CRAZY IS...
...BUT YOU MIGHT GET YOUR CHANCE TO FIND OUT.
NOW, SIT.

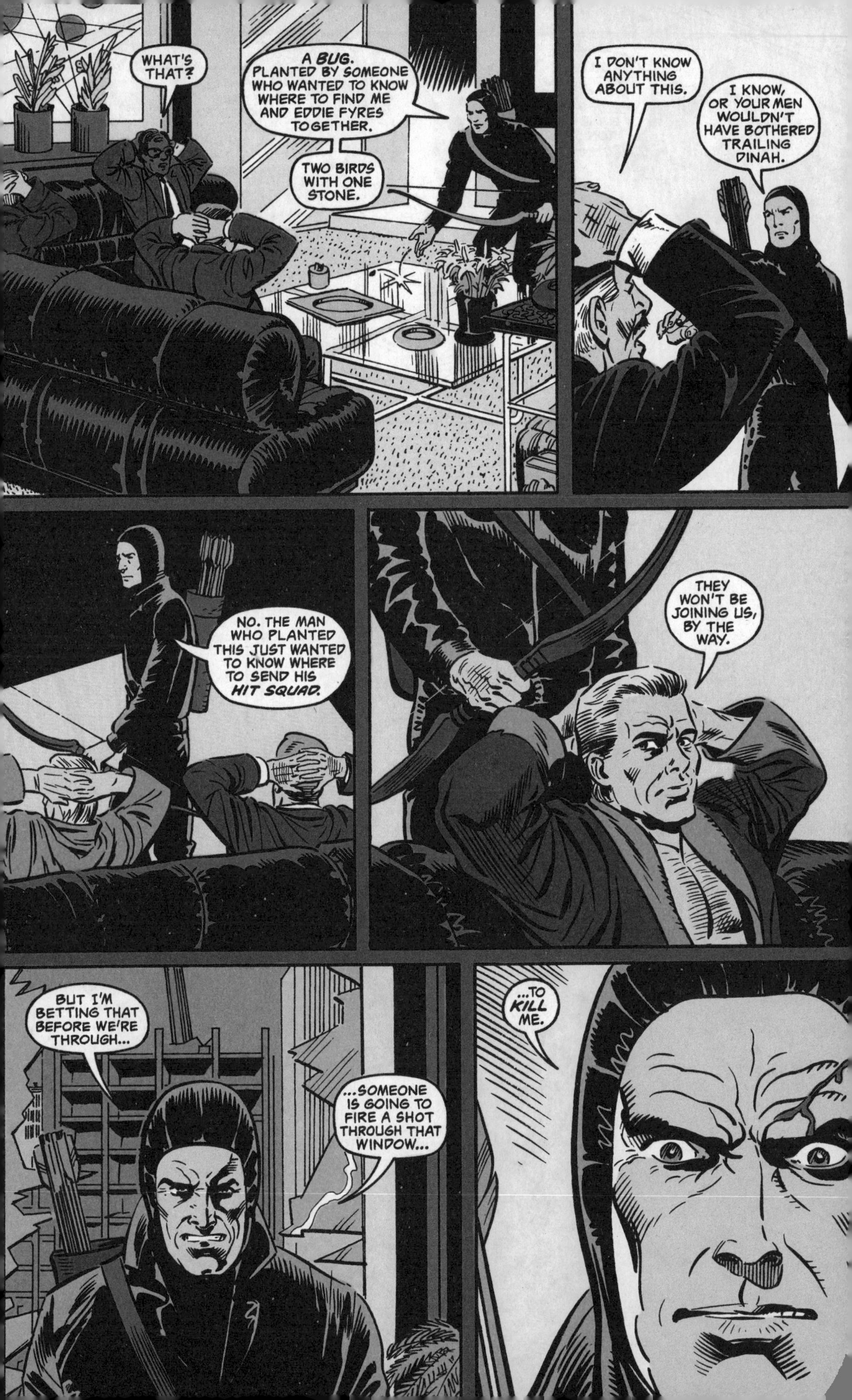
WHAT'S THAT?
A BUG. PLANTED BY SOMEONE WHO WANTED TO KNOW WHERE TO FIND ME AND EDDIE FYRES TOGETHER.
TWO BIRDS WITH ONE STONE.
I DON'T KNOW ANYTHING ABOUT THIS.
I KNOW, OR YOUR MEN WOULDN'T HAVE BOTHERED TRAILING DINAH.
NO. THE MAN WHO PLANTED THIS JUST WANTED TO KNOW WHERE TO SEND HIS HIT SQUAD.
THEY WON'T BE JOINING US, BY THE WAY.
BUT I'M BETTING THAT BEFORE WE'RE THROUGH...
...SOMEONE IS GOING TO FIRE A SHOT THROUGH THAT WINDOW...
...TO KILL ME.

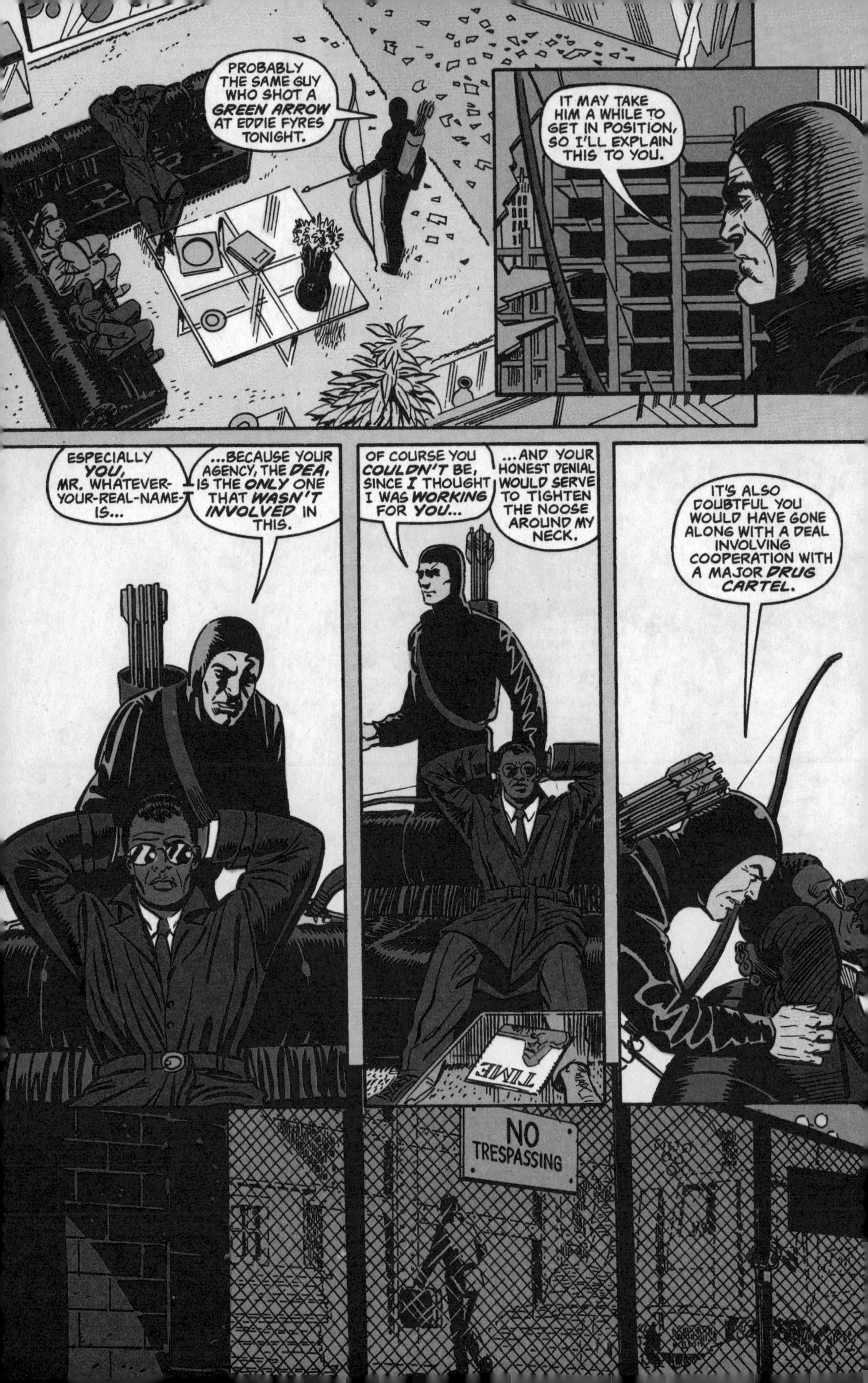

PROBABLY THE SAME GUY WHO SHOT A GREEN ARROW AT EDDIE FYRES TONIGHT.
IT MAY TAKE HIM A WHILE TO GET IN POSITION, SO I'LL EXPLAIN THIS TO YOU.
ESPECIALLY YOU, MR. WHATEVER-YOUR-REAL-NAME-IS...
...BECAUSE YOUR AGENCY, THE DEA, IS THE ONLY ONE THAT WASN'T INVOLVED IN THIS.
OF COURSE YOU COULDN'T BE, SINCE I THOUGHT I WAS WORKING FOR YOU...
...AND YOUR HONEST DENIAL WOULD SERVE TO TIGHTEN THE NOOSE AROUND MY NECK.
IT'S ALSO DOUBTFUL YOU WOULD HAVE GONE ALONG WITH A DEAL INVOLVING COOPERATION WITH A MAJOR DRUG CARTEL.
TIME
NO TRESPASSING

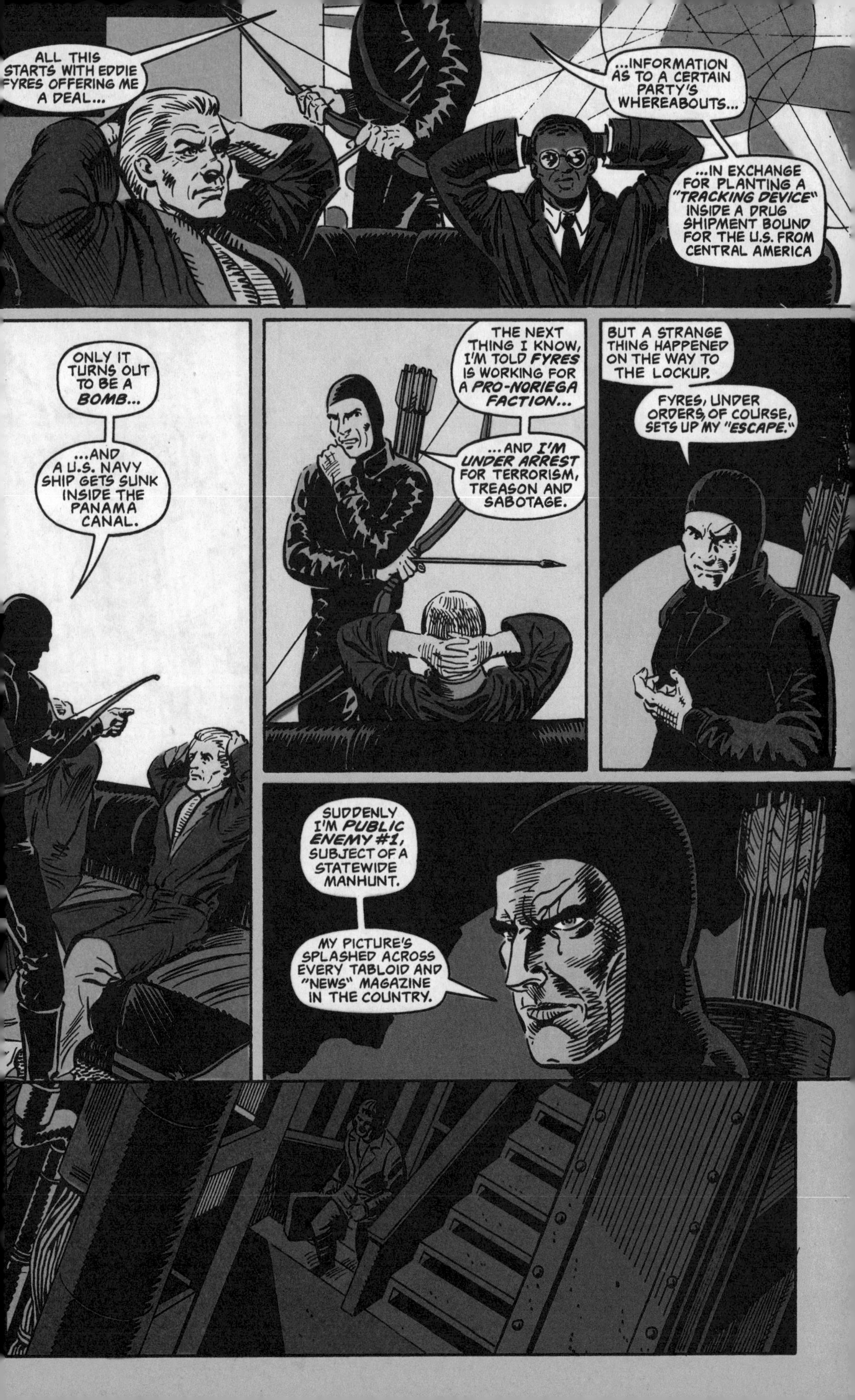
ALL THIS STARTS WITH EDDIE FYRES OFFERING ME A DEAL...
...INFORMATION AS TO A CERTAIN PARTY'S WHEREABOUTS...
...IN EXCHANGE FOR PLANTING A "TRACKING DEVICE" INSIDE A DRUG SHIPMENT BOUND FOR THE U.S. FROM CENTRAL AMERICA
ONLY IT TURNS OUT TO BE A BOMB...
...AND A U.S. NAVY SHIP GETS SUNK INSIDE THE PANAMA CANAL.
THE NEXT THING I KNOW, I'M TOLD FYRES IS WORKING FOR A PRO-NORIEGA FACTION...
...AND I'M UNDER ARREST FOR TERRORISM, TREASON AND SABOTAGE.
BUT A STRANGE THING HAPPENED ON THE WAY TO THE LOCKUP.
FYRES, UNDER ORDERS, OF COURSE, SETS UP MY "ESCAPE."
SUDDENLY I'M PUBLIC ENEMY #1, SUBJECT OF A STATEWIDE MANHUNT.
MY PICTURE'S SPLASHED ACROSS EVERY TABLOID AND "NEWS" MAGAZINE IN THE COUNTRY.

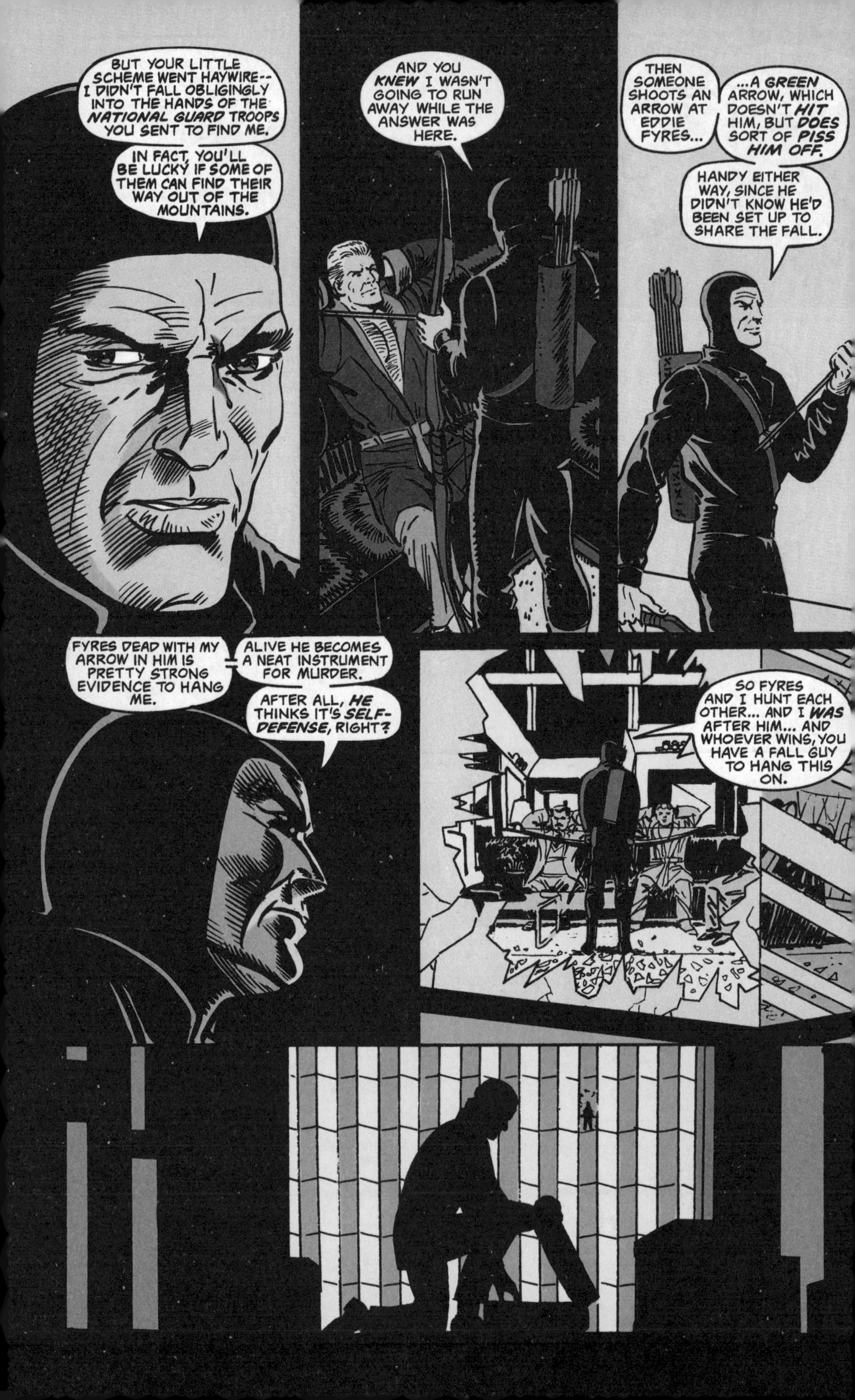
BUT YOUR LITTLE SCHEME WENT HAYWIRE-- I DIDN'T FALL OBLIGINGLY INTO THE HANDS OF THE NATIONAL GUARD TROOPS YOU SENT TO FIND ME.
IN FACT, YOU'LL BE LUCKY IF SOME OF THEM CAN FIND THEIR WAY OUT OF THE MOUNTAINS.
AND YOU KNEW I WASN'T GOING TO RUN AWAY WHILE THE ANSWER WAS HERE.
THEN SOMEONE SHOOTS AN ARROW AT EDDIE FYRES...
...A GREEN ARROW, WHICH DOESN'T HIT HIM, BUT DOES SORT OF PISS HIM OFF.
HANDY EITHER WAY, SINCE HE DIDN'T KNOW HE'D BEEN SET UP TO SHARE THE FALL.
FYRES DEAD WITH MY ARROW IN HIM IS PRETTY STRONG EVIDENCE TO HANG ME.
ALIVE HE BECOMES A NEAT INSTRUMENT FOR MURDER.
AFTER ALL, HE THINKS IT'S SELF-DEFENSE, RIGHT?
SO FYRES AND I HUNT EACH OTHER... AND I WAS AFTER HIM... AND WHOEVER WINS, YOU HAVE A FALL GUY TO HANG THIS ON.

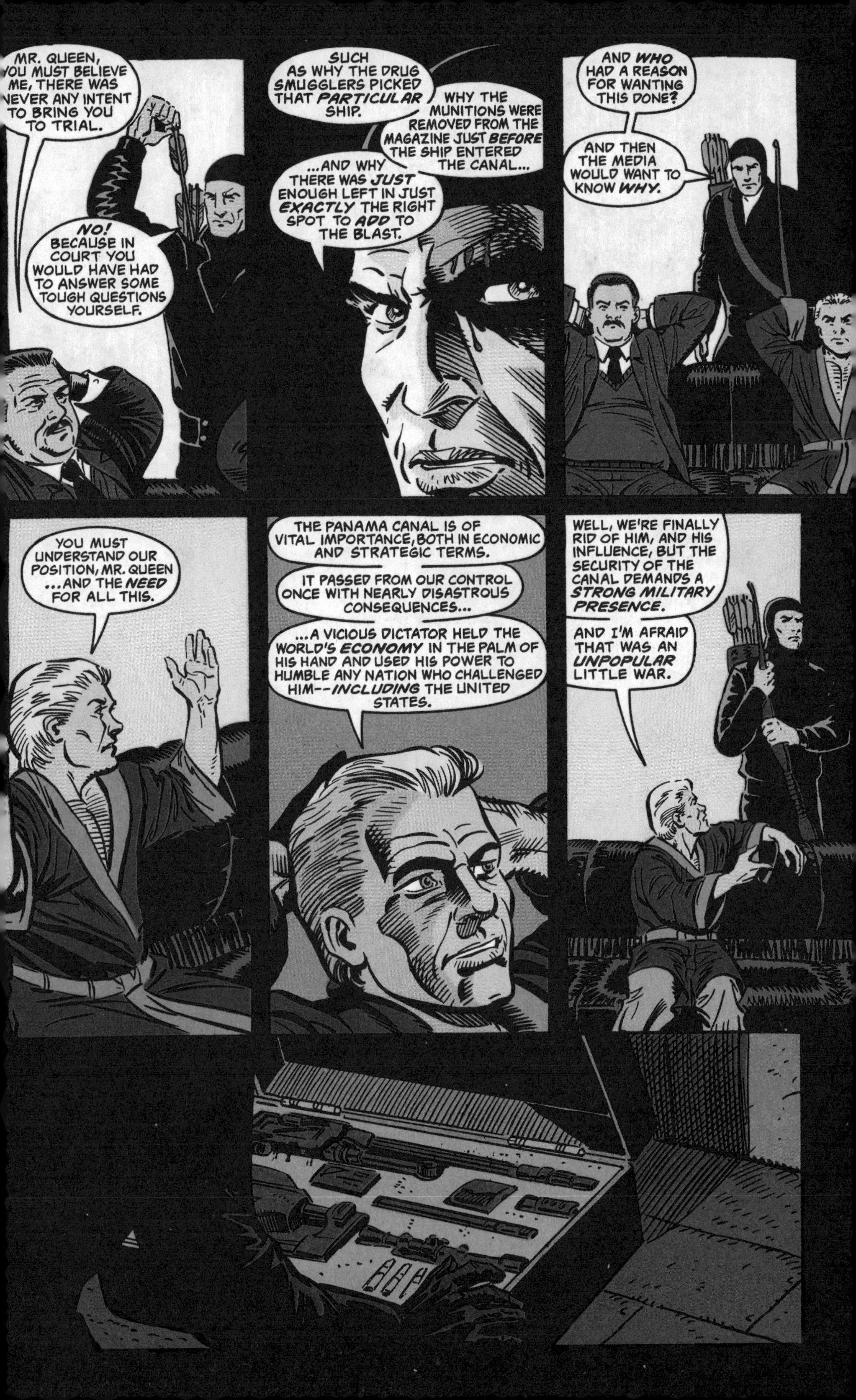
MR. QUEEN, YOU MUST BELIEVE ME, THERE WAS NEVER ANY INTENT TO BRING YOU TO TRIAL.
NO! BECAUSE IN COURT YOU WOULD HAVE HAD TO ANSWER SOME TOUGH QUESTIONS YOURSELF.
SUCH AS WHY THE DRUG SMUGGLERS PICKED THAT PARTICULAR SHIP.
WHY THE MUNITIONS WERE REMOVED FROM THE MAGAZINE JUST BEFORE THE SHIP ENTERED THE CANAL...
...AND WHY THERE WAS JUST ENOUGH LEFT IN JUST EXACTLY THE RIGHT SPOT TO ADD TO THE BLAST.
AND WHO HAD A REASON FOR WANTING THIS DONE?
AND THEN THE MEDIA WOULD WANT TO KNOW WHY.
YOU MUST UNDERSTAND OUR POSITION, MR. QUEEN ...AND THE NEED FOR ALL THIS.
THE PANAMA CANAL IS OF VITAL IMPORTANCE, BOTH IN ECONOMIC AND STRATEGIC TERMS.
IT PASSED FROM OUR CONTROL ONCE WITH NEARLY DISASTROUS CONSEQUENCES...
...A VICIOUS DICTATOR HELD THE WORLD'S ECONOMY IN THE PALM OF HIS HAND AND USED HIS POWER TO HUMBLE ANY NATION WHO CHALLENGED HIM--INCLUDING THE UNITED STATES.
WELL, WE'RE FINALLY RID OF HIM, AND HIS INFLUENCE, BUT THE SECURITY OF THE CANAL DEMANDS A STRONG MILITARY PRESENCE.
AND I'M AFRAID THAT WAS AN UNPOPULAR LITTLE WAR.

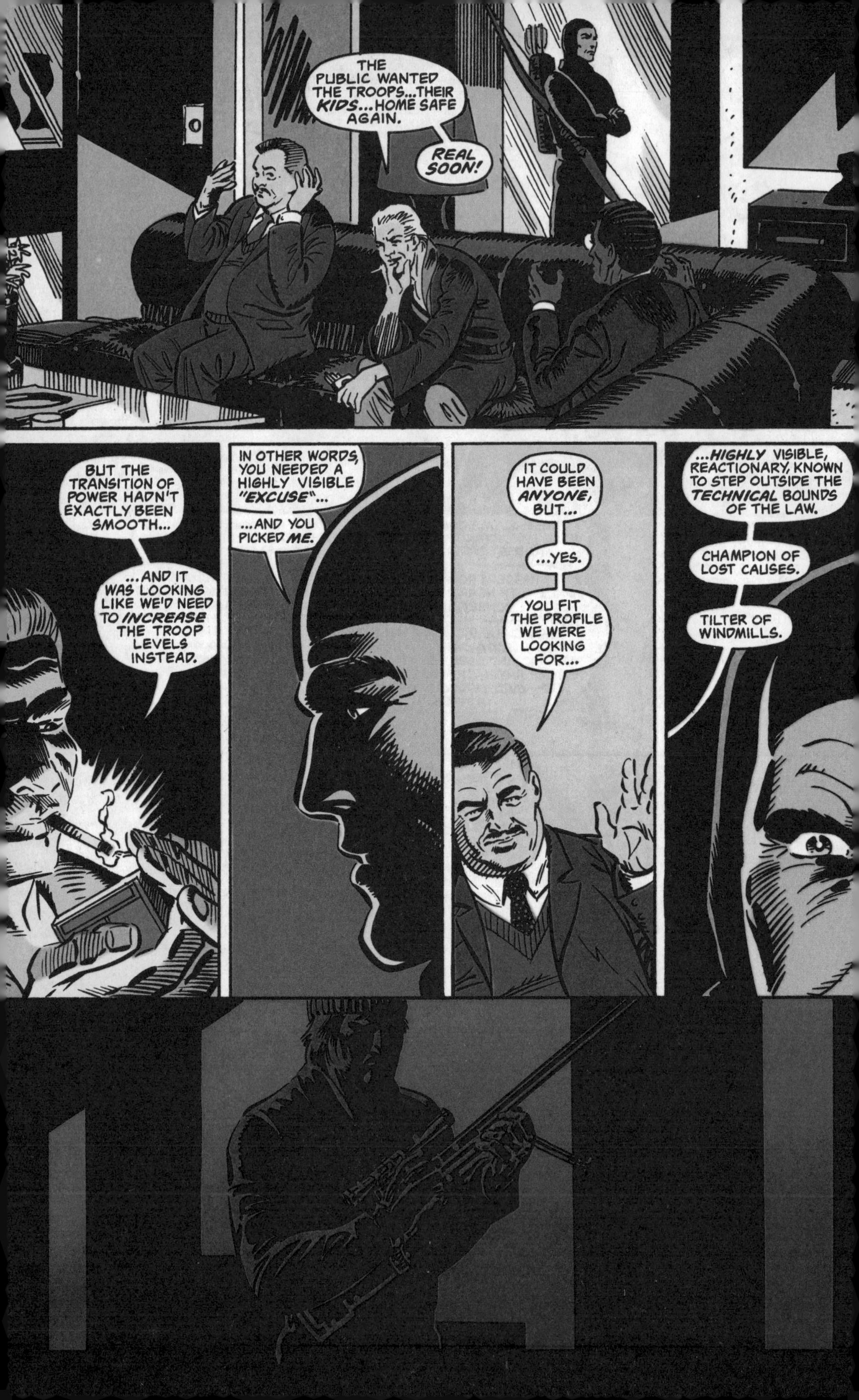
THE PUBLIC WANTED THE TROOPS...THEIR KIDS...HOME SAFE AGAIN.
REAL SOON!
BUT THE TRANSITION OF POWER HADN'T EXACTLY BEEN SMOOTH...
...AND IT WAS LOOKING LIKE WE'D NEED TO INCREASE THE TROOP LEVELS INSTEAD.
IN OTHER WORDS, YOU NEEDED A HIGHLY VISIBLE "EXCUSE"...
...AND YOU PICKED ME.
IT COULD HAVE BEEN ANYONE, BUT...
...YES.
YOU FIT THE PROFILE WE WERE LOOKING FOR...
...HIGHLY VISIBLE, REACTIONARY, KNOWN TO STEP OUTSIDE THE TECHNICAL BOUNDS OF THE LAW.
CHAMPION OF LOST CAUSES.
TILTER OF WINDMILLS.

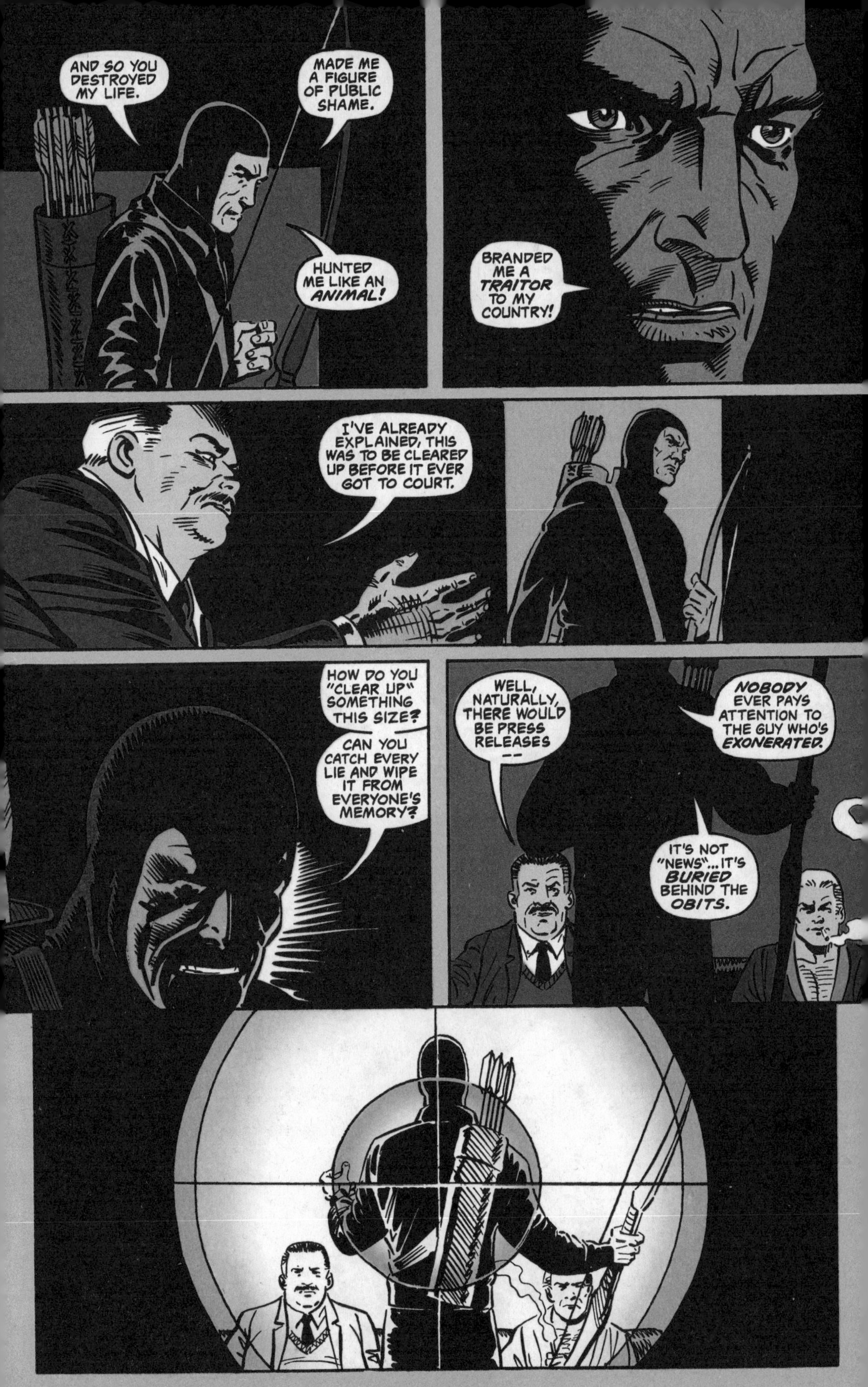

AND SO YOU DESTROYED MY LIFE.
MADE ME A FIGURE OF PUBLIC SHAME.
HUNTED ME LIKE AN ANIMAL!
BRANDED ME A TRAITOR TO MY COUNTRY!
I'VE ALREADY EXPLAINED, THIS WAS TO BE CLEARED UP BEFORE IT EVER GOT TO COURT.
HOW DO YOU "CLEAR UP" SOMETHING THIS SIZE?
CAN YOU CATCH EVERY LIE AND WIPE IT FROM EVERYONE'S MEMORY?
WELL, NATURALLY, THERE WOULD BE PRESS RELEASES --
NOBODY EVER PAYS ATTENTION TO THE GUY WHO'S EXONERATED.
IT'S NOT "NEWS"... IT'S BURIED BEHIND THE OBITS.

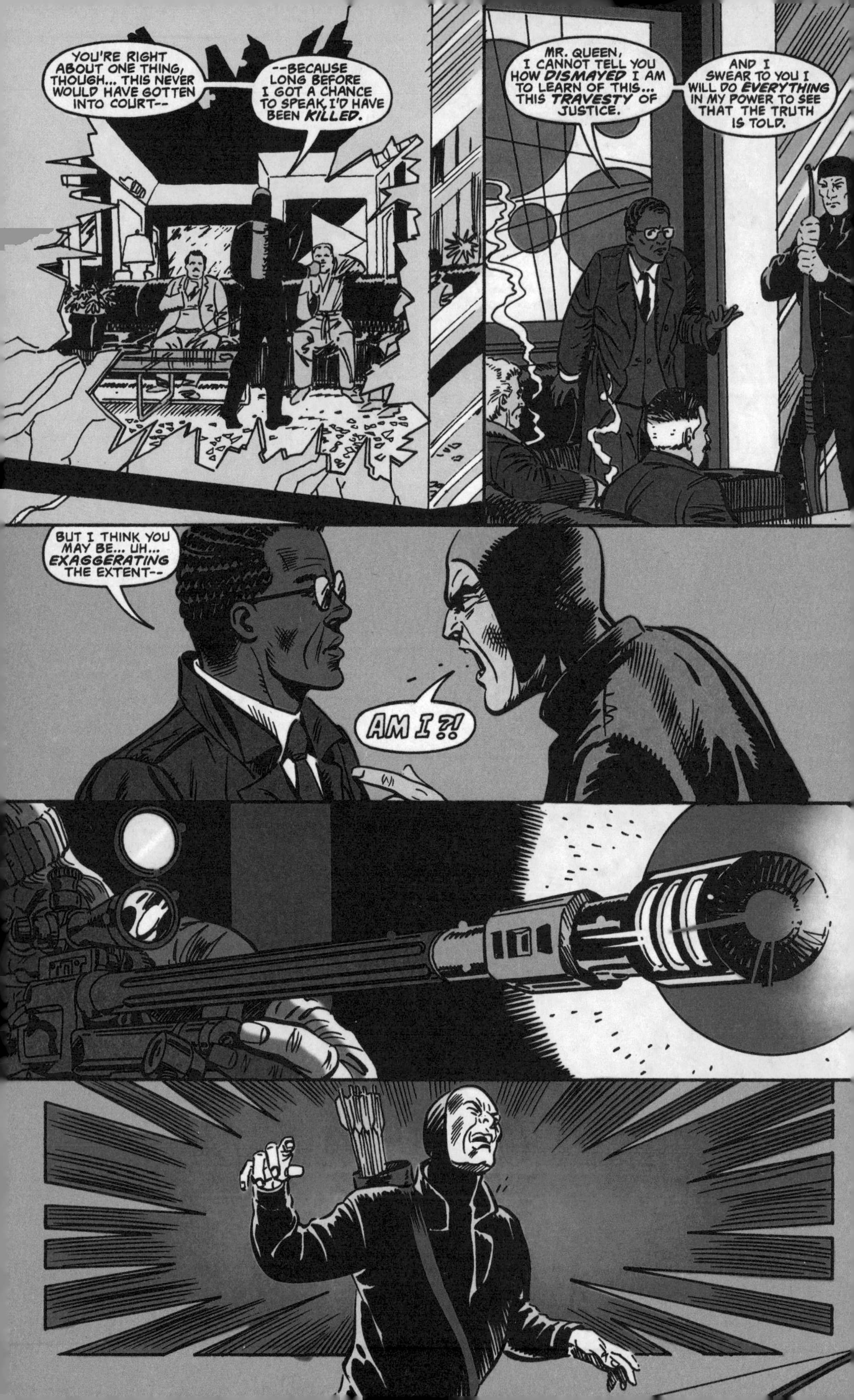
YOU'RE RIGHT ABOUT ONE THING, THOUGH... THIS NEVER WOULD HAVE GOTTEN INTO COURT--
--BECAUSE LONG BEFORE I GOT A CHANCE TO SPEAK, I'D HAVE BEEN KILLED.
MR. QUEEN, I CANNOT TELL YOU HOW DISMAYED I AM TO LEARN OF THIS... THIS TRAVESTY OF JUSTICE.
AND I SWEAR TO YOU I WILL DO EVERYTHING IN MY POWER TO SEE THAT THE TRUTH IS TOLD.
BUT I THINK YOU MAY BE... UH... EXAGGERATING THE EXTENT--
AM I?!

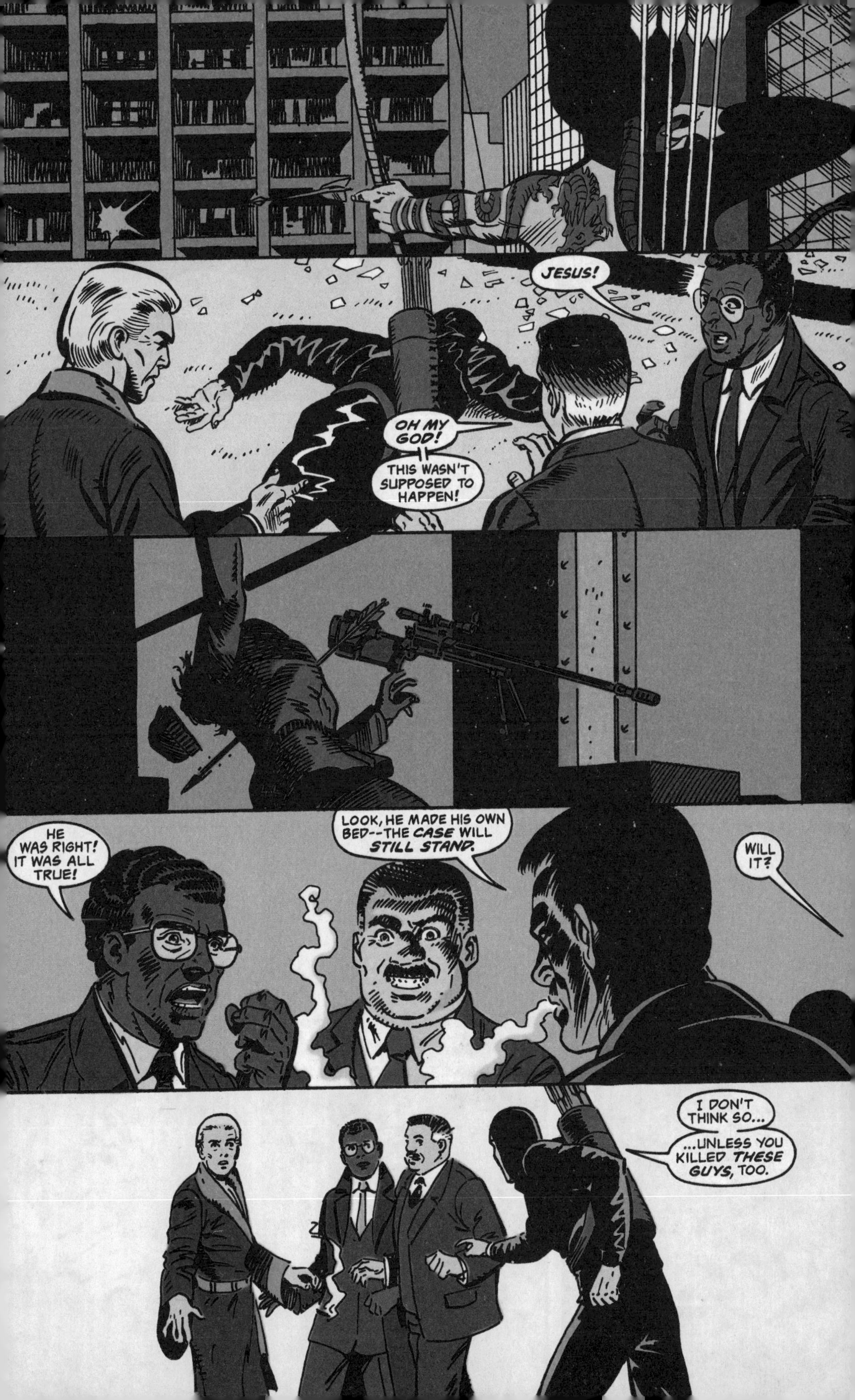
JESUS!
OH MY GOD!
THIS WASN'T SUPPOSED TO HAPPEN!
HE WAS RIGHT! IT WAS ALL TRUE!
LOOK, HE MADE HIS OWN BED--THE *CASE* WILL *STILL STAND.*
WILL IT?
I DON'T THINK SO...
...UNLESS YOU KILLED *THESE GUYS*, TOO.

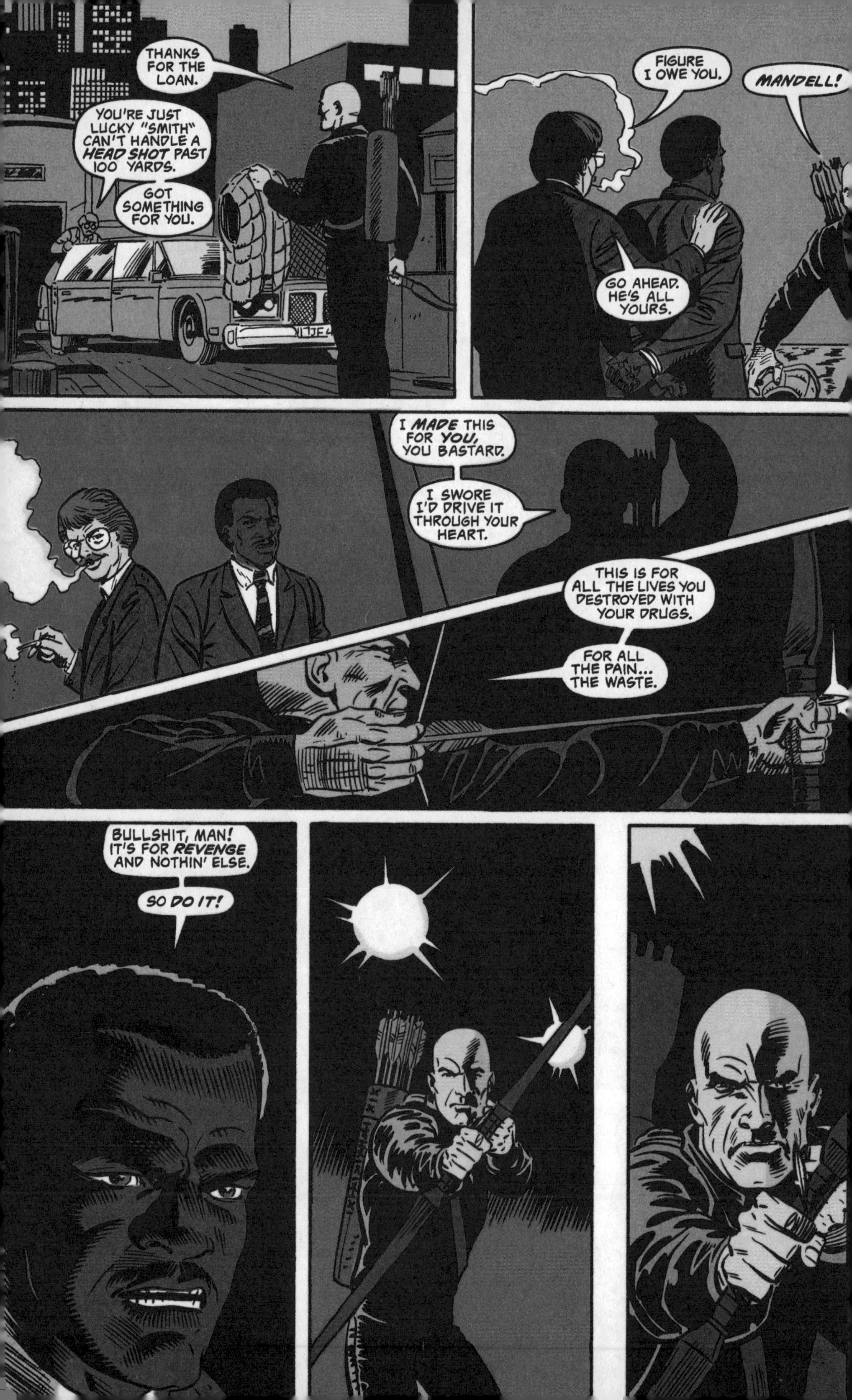
THANKS FOR THE LOAN.
YOU'RE JUST LUCKY "SMITH" CAN'T HANDLE A HEAD SHOT PAST 100 YARDS.
GOT SOMETHING FOR YOU.
FIGURE I OWE YOU.
MANDELL!
GO AHEAD. HE'S ALL YOURS.
I MADE THIS FOR YOU, YOU BASTARD.
I SWORE I'D DRIVE IT THROUGH YOUR HEART.
THIS IS FOR ALL THE LIVES YOU DESTROYED WITH YOUR DRUGS.
FOR ALL THE PAIN... THE WASTE.
BULLSHIT, MAN! IT'S FOR REVENGE AND NOTHIN' ELSE.
SO DO IT!

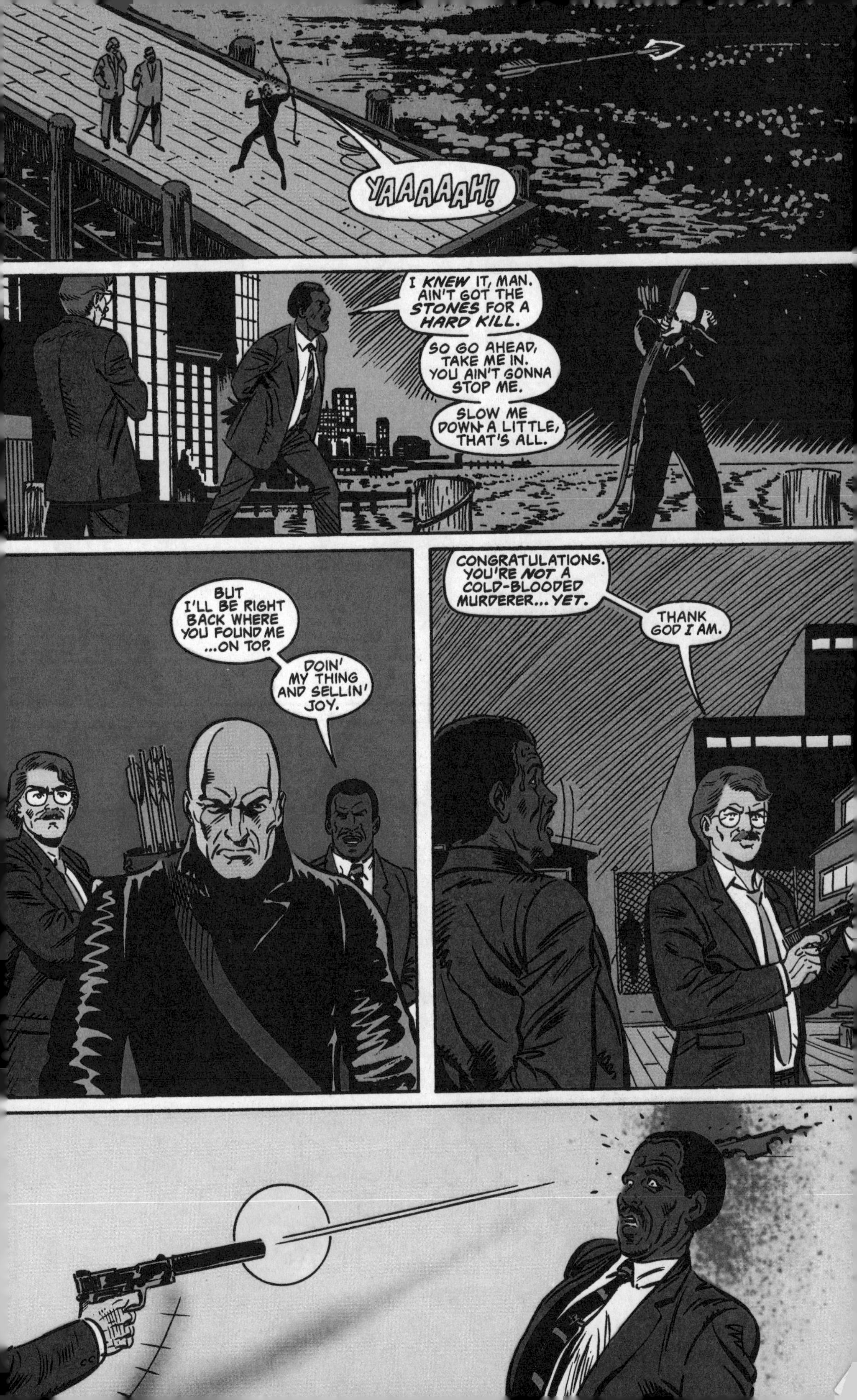
YAAAAAH!
I KNEW IT, MAN. AIN'T GOT THE STONES FOR A HARD KILL.
SO GO AHEAD, TAKE ME IN. YOU AIN'T GONNA STOP ME.
SLOW ME DOWN A LITTLE, THAT'S ALL.
BUT I'LL BE RIGHT BACK WHERE YOU FOUND ME ...ON TOP.
DOIN' MY THING AND SELLIN' JOY.
CONGRATULATIONS. YOU'RE NOT A COLD-BLOODED MURDERER... YET.
THANK GOD I AM.

# EPILOGUE

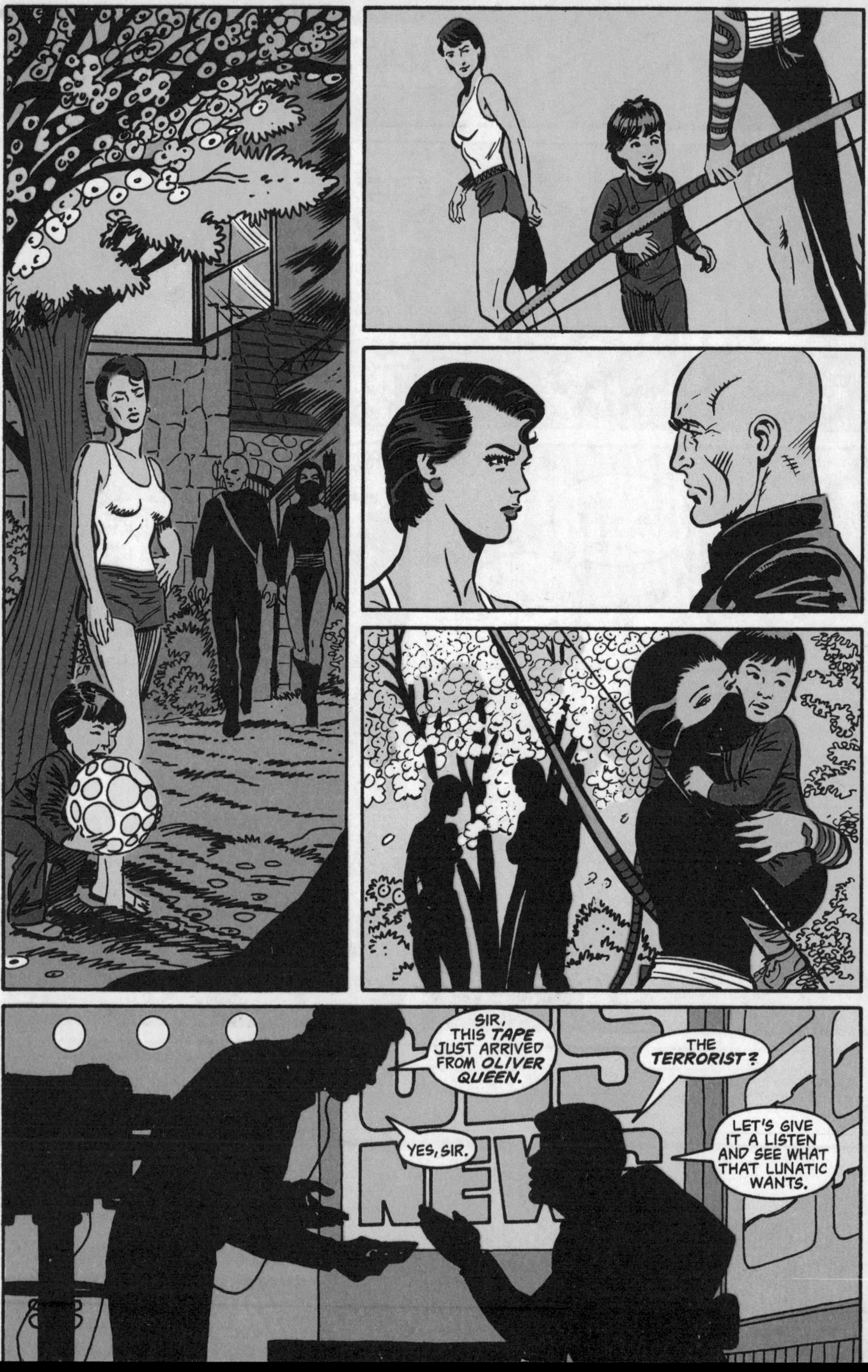

SIR, THIS TAPE JUST ARRIVED FROM OLIVER QUEEN.
THE TERRORIST?
YES, SIR.
LET'S GIVE IT A LISTEN AND SEE WHAT THAT LUNATIC WANTS.

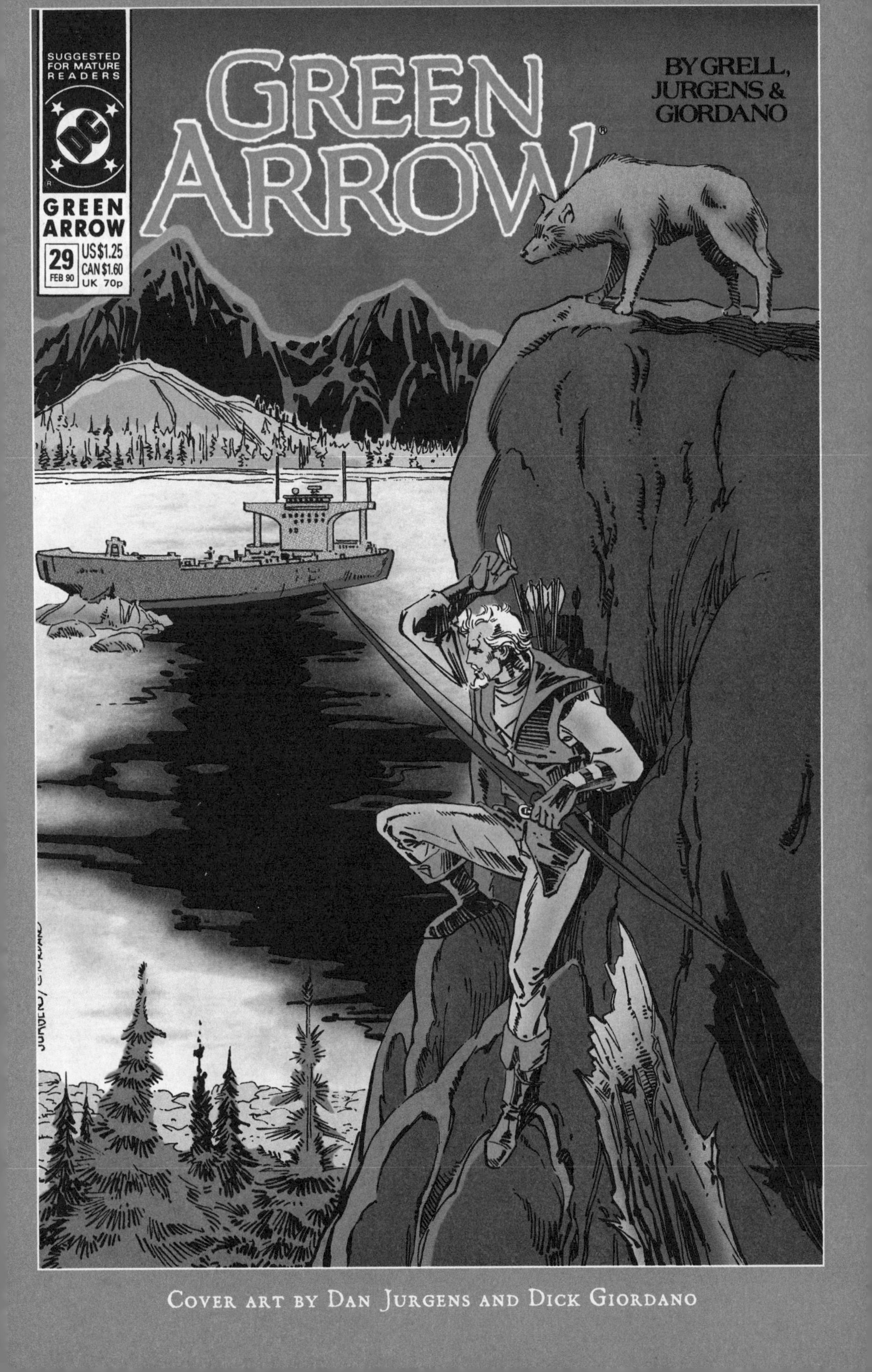
SUGGESTED FOR MATURE READERS
DC
GREEN ARROW
29
FEB 90
US$1.25
CAN$1.60
UK 70p
GREEN ARROW
BY GRELL, JURGENS & GIORDANO
JURGENS/GIORDANO

Cover art by Dan Jurgens and Dick Giordano

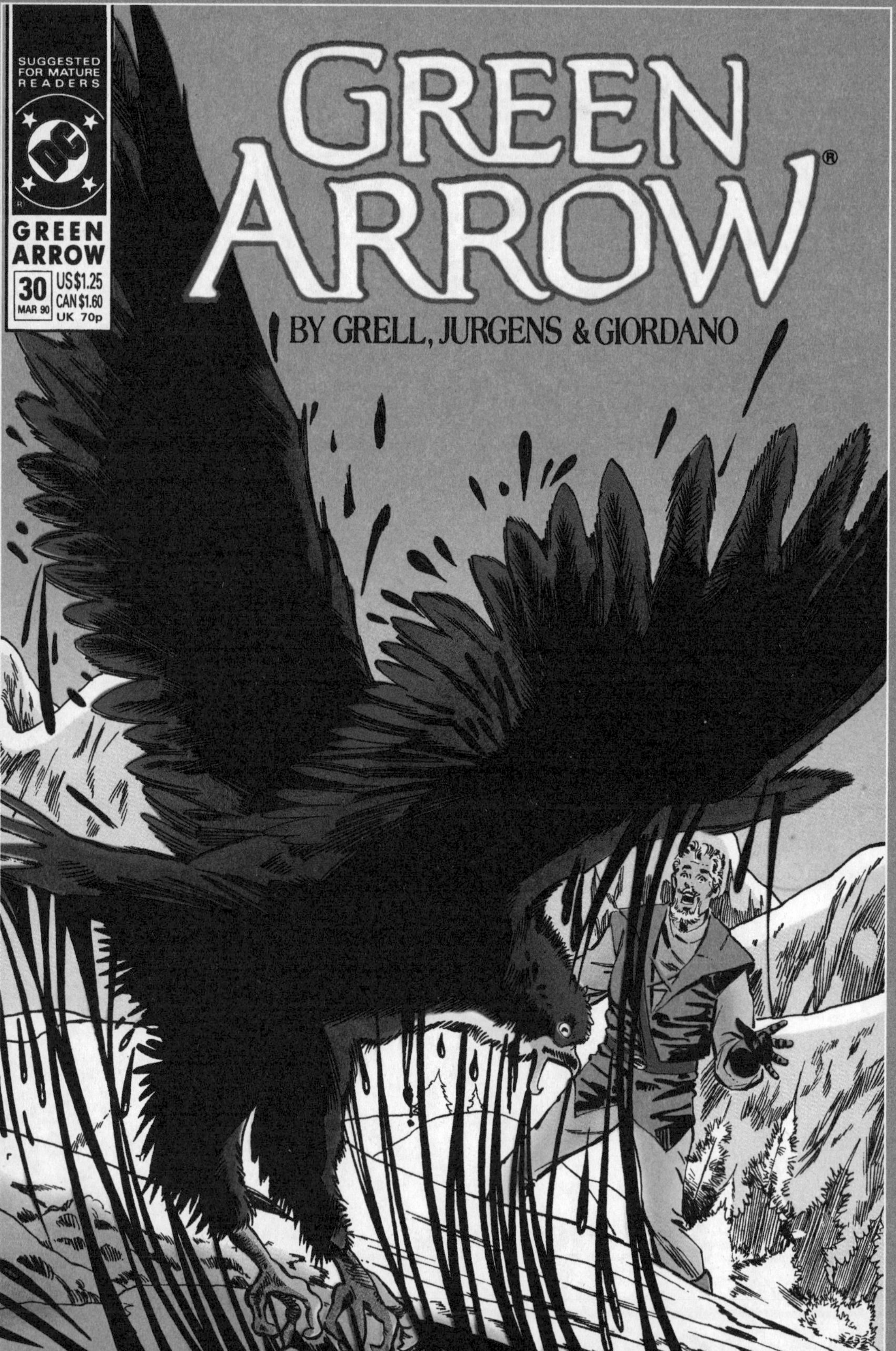
SUGGESTED FOR MATURE READERS
DC
GREEN ARROW
30
MAR 90
US $1.25
CAN $1.60
UK 70p
GREEN ARROW®
BY GRELL, JURGENS & GIORDANO

Cover art by Dan Jurgens and Dick Giordano

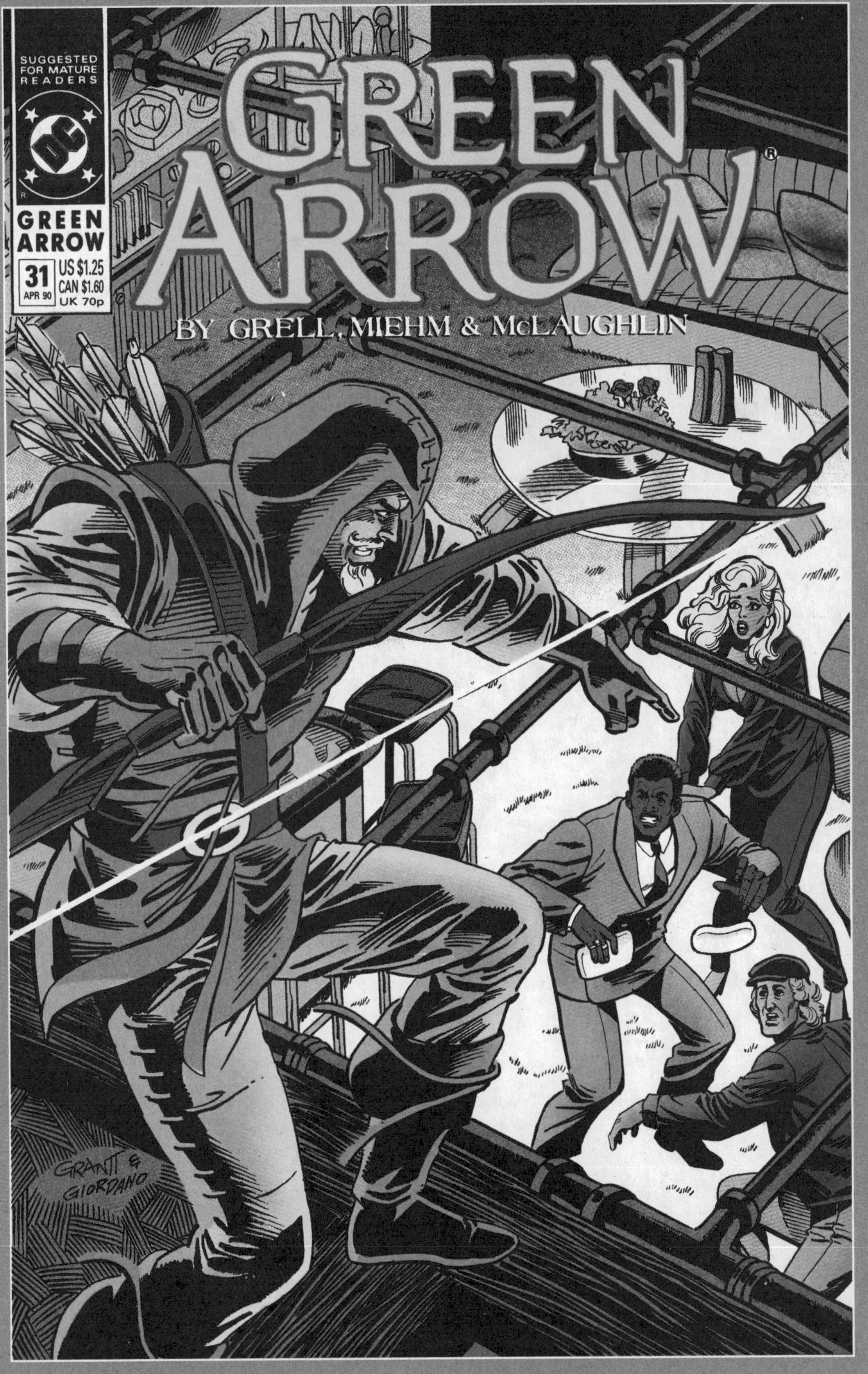
SUGGESTED FOR MATURE READERS
DC
GREEN ARROW
31
APR 90
US $1.25
CAN $1.60
UK 70p
GREEN ARROW
BY GRELL, MIEHM & McLAUGHLIN
GRANT & GIORDANO

Cover art by Grant Miehm and Dick Giordano

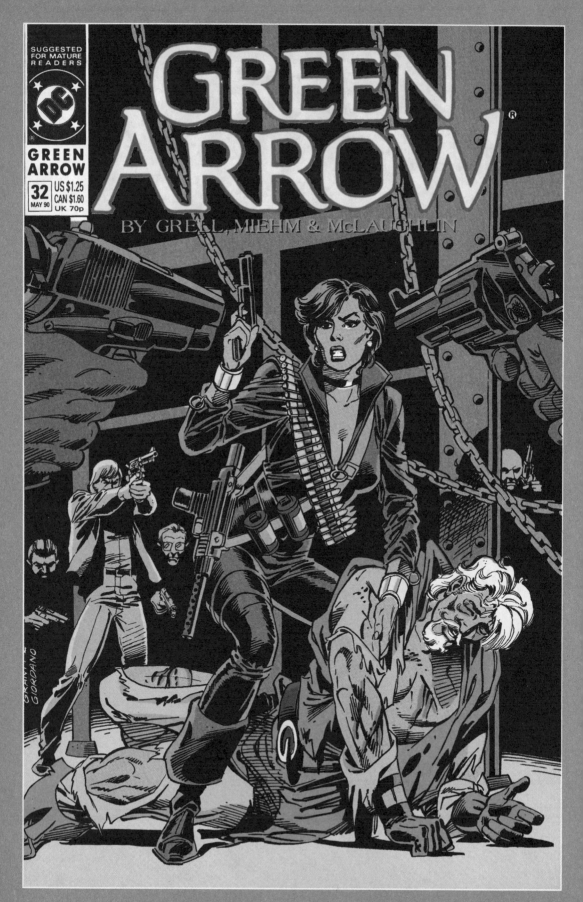

COVER ART BY GRANT MIEHM AND DICK GIORDANO

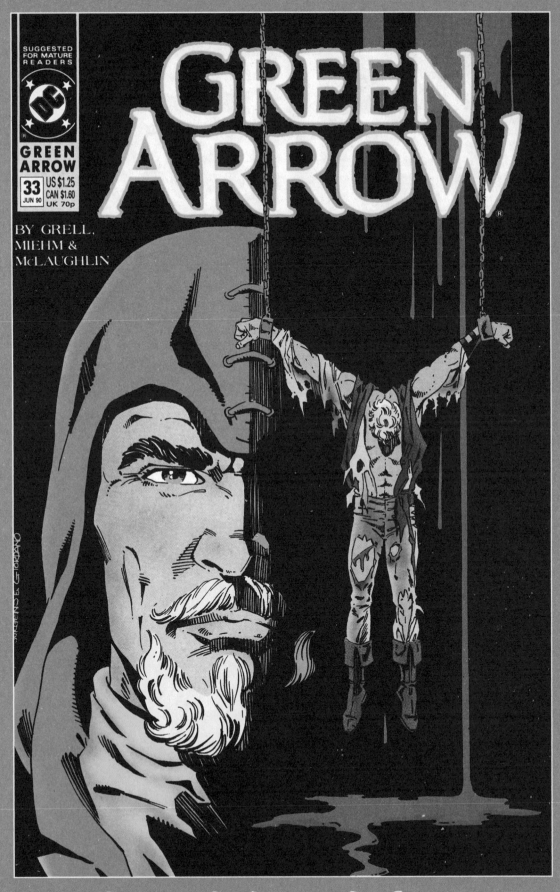

Cover art by Dan Jurgens and Dick Giordano

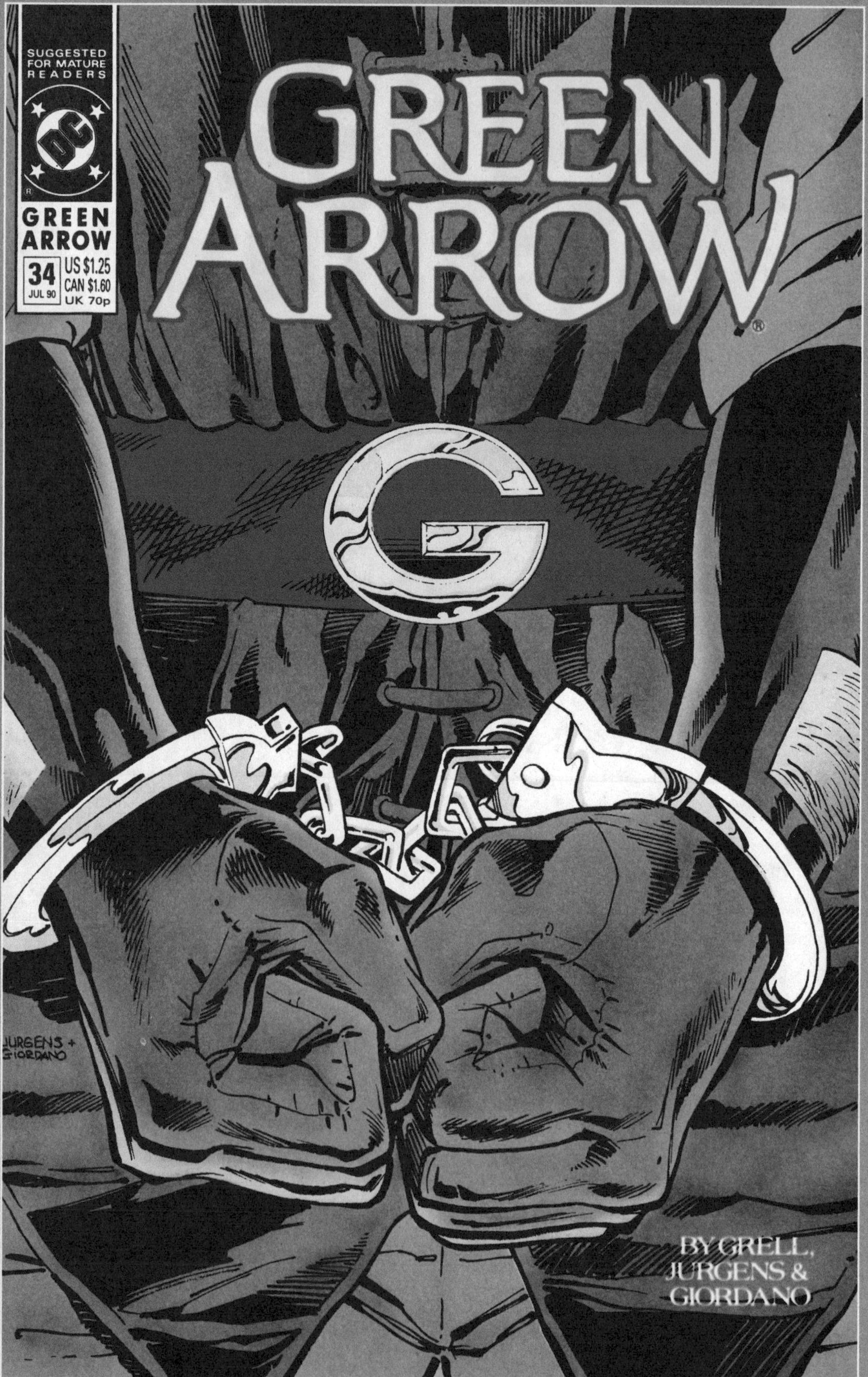
SUGGESTED FOR MATURE READERS
DC
GREEN ARROW
34
JUL 90
US $1.25
CAN $1.60
UK 70p
GREEN ARROW
JURGENS + GIORDANO
BY GRELL, JURGENS & GIORDANO

Cover art by Dan Jurgens and Dick Giordano

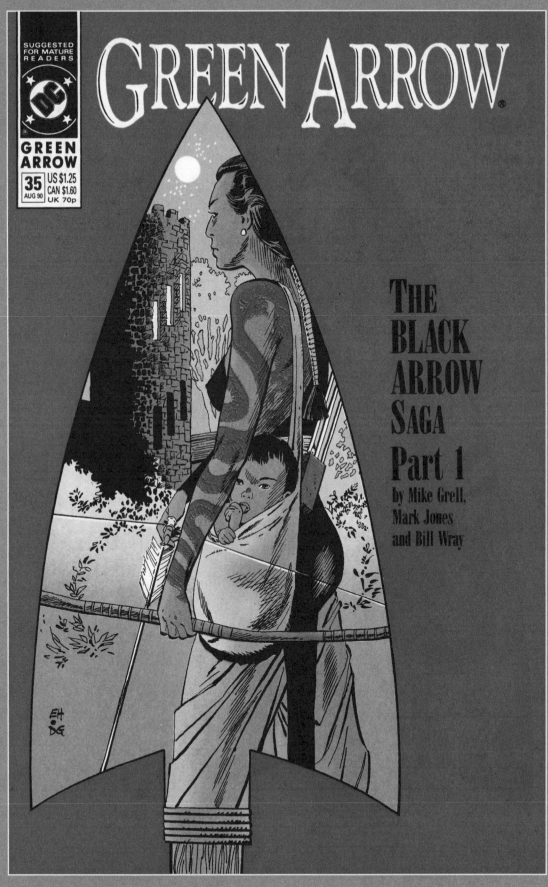

GREEN ARROW

THE BLACK ARROW SAGA Part 1

by Mike Grell, Mark Jones and Bill Wray

SUGGESTED FOR MATURE READERS

GREEN ARROW

35 AUG 90

US $1.25
CAN $1.60
UK 70p

COVER ART BY ED HANNIGAN AND DICK GIORDANO

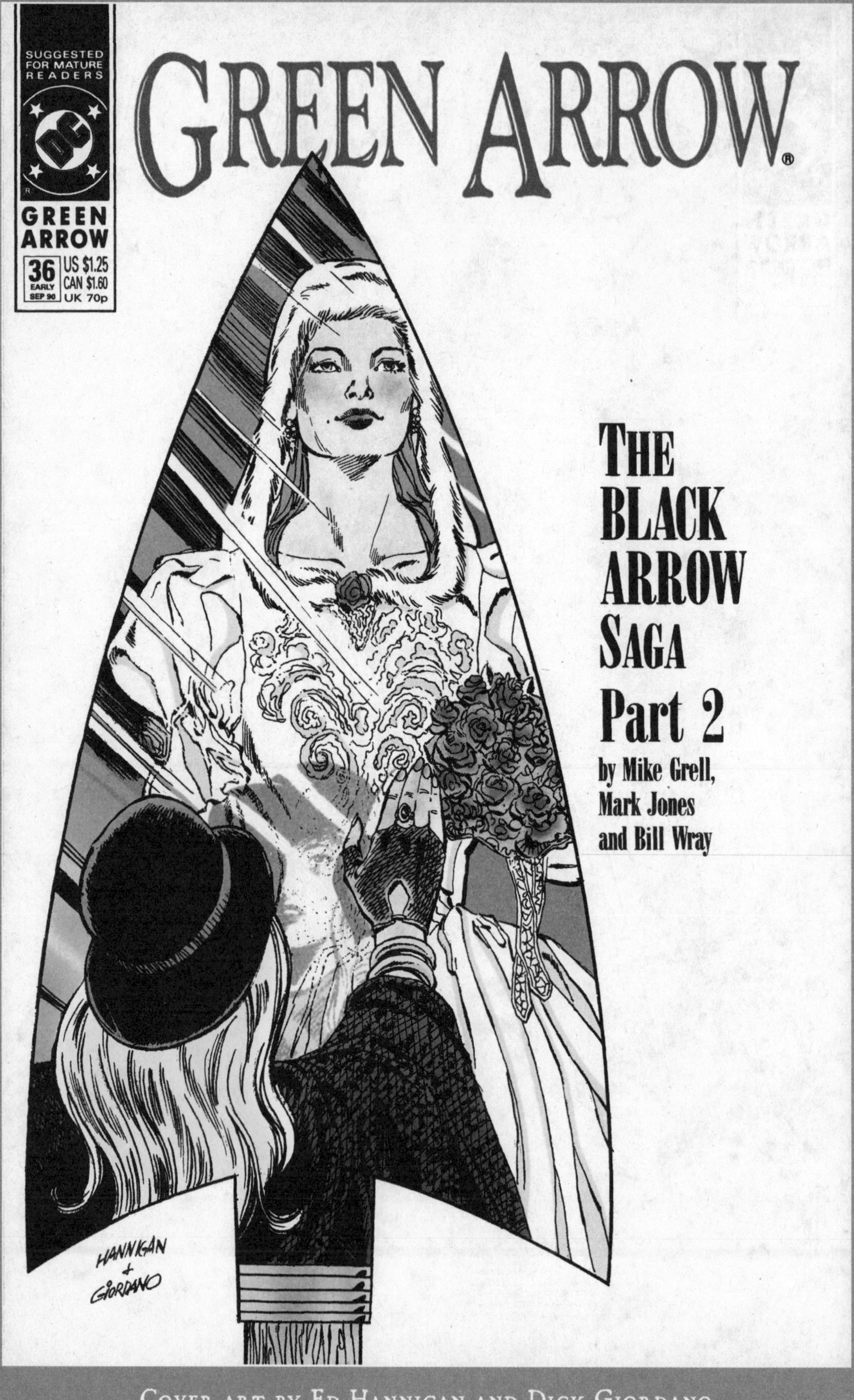
SUGGESTED FOR MATURE READERS
DC
GREEN ARROW
36 EARLY SEP 90 US $1.25 CAN $1.60 UK 70p
GREEN ARROW®
THE BLACK ARROW SAGA Part 2
by Mike Grell, Mark Jones and Bill Wray
HANNIGAN + GIORDANO

Cover art by Ed Hannigan and Dick Giordano

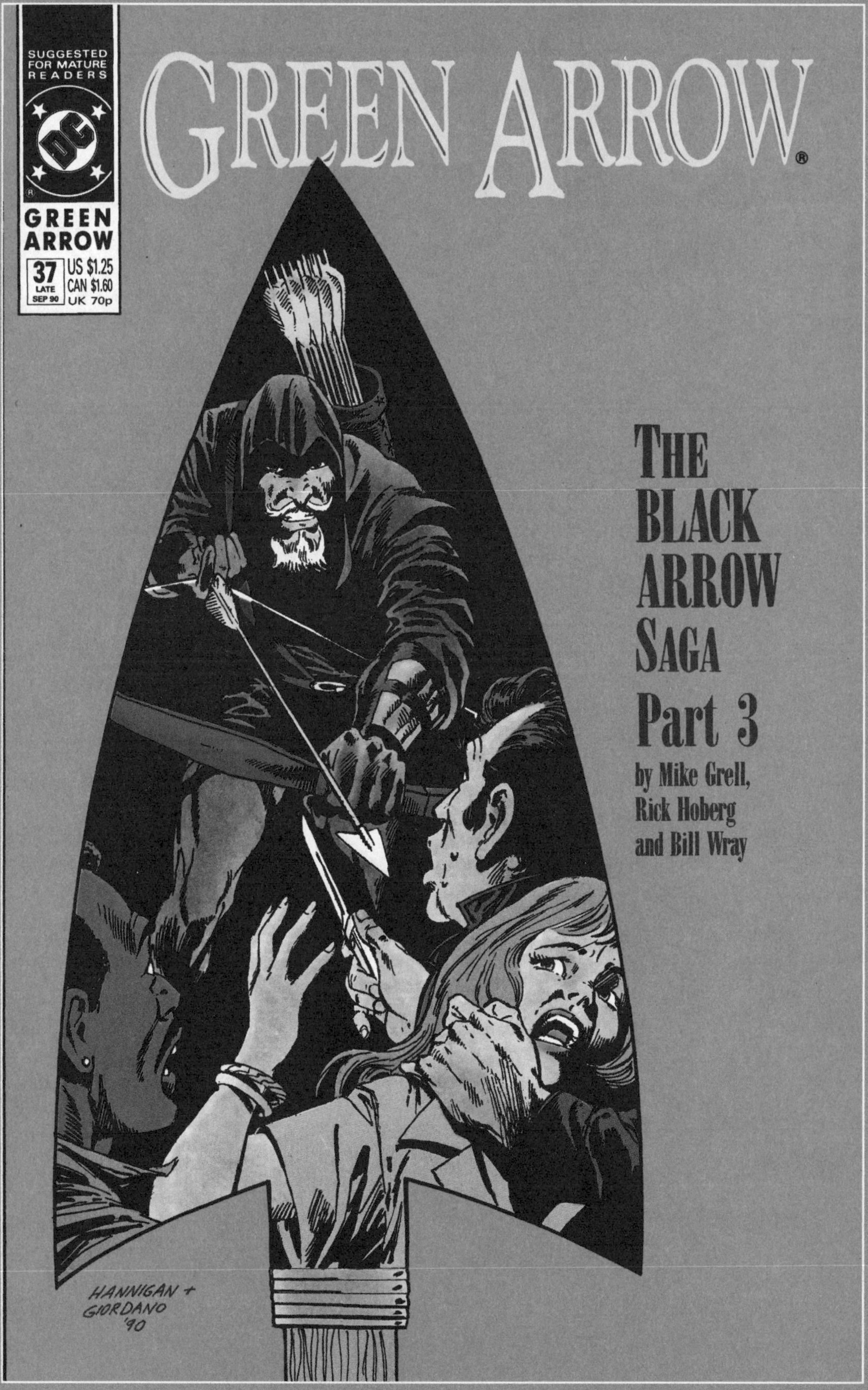
SUGGESTED FOR MATURE READERS
GREEN ARROW
GREEN ARROW
37 LATE SEP 90
US $1.25
CAN $1.60
UK 70p
THE BLACK ARROW SAGA
Part 3
by Mike Grell, Rick Hoberg and Bill Wray
HANNIGAN + GIORDANO '90

Cover art by Ed Hannigan and Dick Giordano

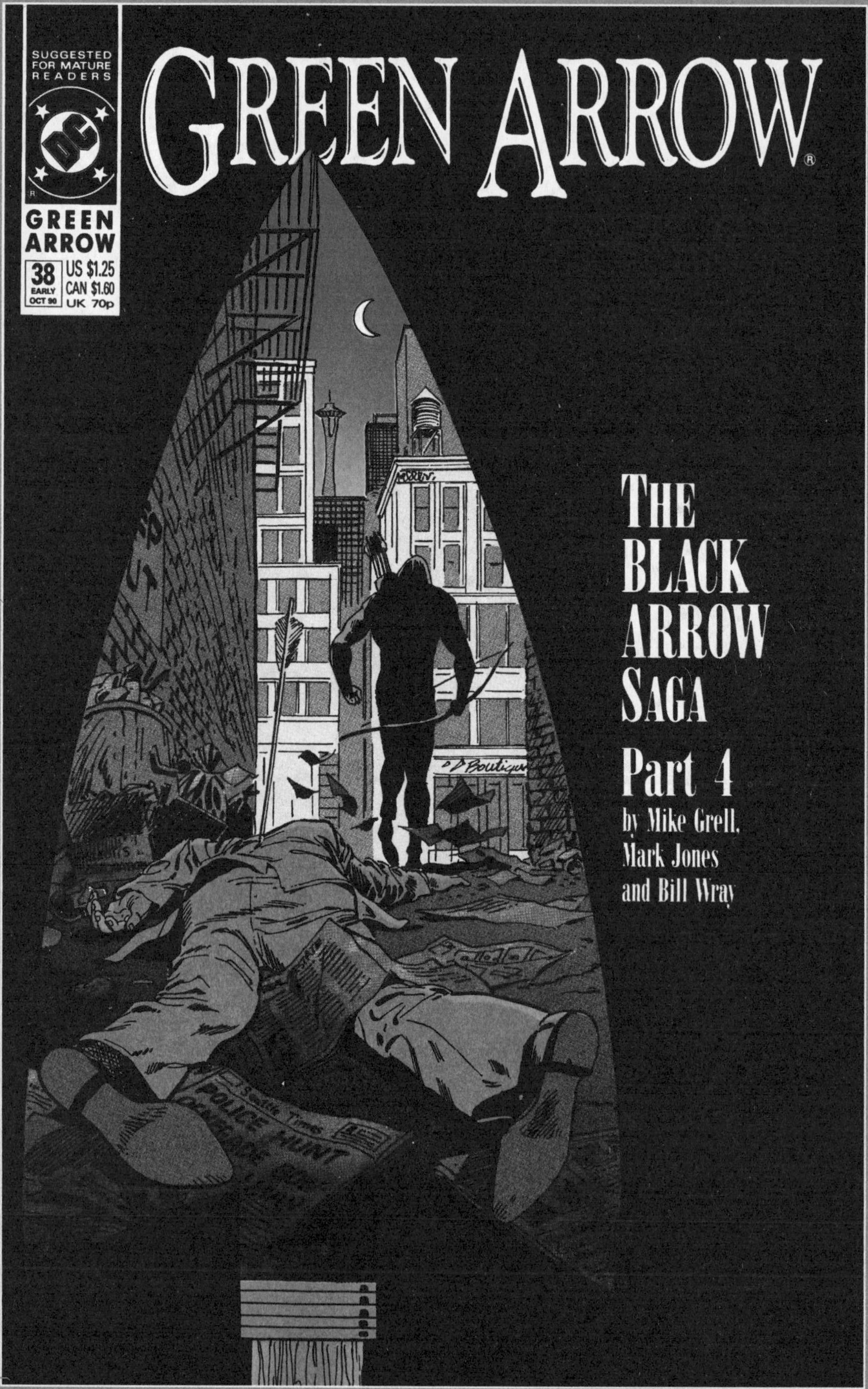
SUGGESTED FOR MATURE READERS
DC
GREEN ARROW
GREEN ARROW
38 EARLY OCT 90
US $1.25
CAN $1.60
UK 70p
THE BLACK ARROW SAGA
Part 4
by Mike Grell, Mark Jones and Bill Wray
POLICE HUNT

Cover art by Ed Hannigan and Dick Giordano

**FROM THE WRITER OF *JUSTICE LEAGUE UNITED* AND *ANIMAL MAN***

# GREEN ARROW
## VOLUME 4: THE KILL MACHINE

GREEN ARROW VOL. 1:
THE MIDAS TOUCH

with KEITH GIFFEN, DAN JURGENS, J.T. KRUL, and GEORGE PÉREZ

GREEN ARROW VOL. 2:
TRIPLE THREAT

with ANN NOCENTI and HARVEY TOLIBAO

GREEN ARROW VOL. 3:
HARROW

with ANN NOCENTI and FREDDIE WILLIAMS III

JEFF **LEMIRE** Andrea **SORRENTINO** Marcelo **MAIOLO**